Child Development
Its Nature and Course

L. Alan Sroufe

University of Minnesota

Robert G. Cooper

Southwest Texas State University

Mary E. Marshall

Advisory Editor
Urie Bronfenbrenner

Cornell University

McGRAW-HILL PUBLISHING COMPANY
New York St. Louis San Francisco Auckland Bogotá
Caracas Hamburg Lisbon London Madrid Mexico Milan
Montreal New Delhi Oklahoma City Paris San Juan
São Paulo Singapore Sydney Tokyo Toronto

Dedication

To Larry—my father and example
To Minnie—my extended family
To June—my collaborator, my partner, my wife
LAS

and

To Bob and Helen—my parents
To Cathy—my wife—and to David—my son
All crucial links in my own development
RGC

First Edition
9 8 7 6 5 4 3

Library of Congress Cataloging-in-Publication Data

Sroufe, L. Alan.
   Child development / by L. Alan Sroufe, Robert G. Cooper, Mary E. Marshall.
      p. cm.
    Bibliography: p.
    Includes index.
    ISBN 0-07-553785-0
    1. Child development. 2. Child psychology. 3. Adolescence.
I. Cooper, Robert G. II. Marshall, Mary E. III. Title.
HQ767.9S725 1987
155.4—dc19
                                              87-26505
                                            CIP

Cover photos: Tom Dunham

Chapter-Opening Photo Credits

Chapter 1: © 1986 Bob Krist/Black Star; Chapter 2: © Bill Binzen/Photo Researchers, Inc.; Chapter 3: © David S. Strickler/Monkmeyer Press; Chapter 4: © Petit Format-Nestle-Science Source/Photo Researchers, Inc.; Chapter 5: © Mimi Cotter/International Stock Photo; Chapter 6: © 1985 Gabe Palmer/The Stock Market; Chapter 7: © Vic Cox/Peter Arnold, Inc.; Chapter 8: © 1985 Cindy McIntire/West Stock; Chapter 9: © Paul Robert Perry/Uniphoto Picture Agency; Chapter 10: © Sonya Jacobs/The Stock Market; Chapter 11: © 1987 Kathleen Brown/West Stock; Chapter 12: © 1985 Viviane Holbrooke/The Stock Market; Chapter 13: © Chris Springmann/The Stock Market; Chapter 14: © 1987 Wayne Easter/The Stock Market; Chapter 15: © Mimi Forsythe/Monkmeyer Press; Chapter 16: © Bob Daemmrich/Uniphoto Picture Agency

Preface

Several years ago at a meeting of the Society for Research in Child Development, the Knopf editors assembled a group of developmental psychologists to discuss the kind of textbook that was needed for the child development course. Despite the diversity of perspectives represented by the group (Urie Bronfenbrenner, Shirley Feldman, Tiffany Field, Marion Gindes, Scott Paris, and Alan Sroufe), there was notable agreement that certain key developmental ideas were not well represented in existing texts. In particular, the systematic and integrated nature of development, the mutual influences of child and context, and the way previous development influenced current development seemed not to be fully conveyed. It was felt that these ideas were well established in the field but had proven difficult to build into a textbook. Facts often are easier to present than principles, and facets of development are easier to convey than the nature of development itself.

Beyond the belief that a child development text organized around coherent principles could and should be written, the working group evolved one provocative, concrete idea—the idea of introducing a set of families to be followed throughout the book. We thought that if done right, such a device could illustrate not only the important role of context (and the systematic interplay between child and environment) but also important developmental principles such as orderliness, continuity, and lawful change. The families could provide a way of showing how various influences come together to determine both normative development and individual development. They could let us bring life to the complex facts and theories about child development.

Each of the authors had previously considered writing a text, but had always decided against it. Busy research agendas and other activities seemed preemptive. But this particular idea would not let go. We were captured by the idea of using family vignettes to create a book that not only presented the latest findings in developmental research but also was organized in a coherent way around a set of recurrent themes, a readable presentation of the complex nature of development.

Our goal was to organize the book around themes and principles of development. The major themes are the role of context, the issue of continuity versus discontinuity, the interplay of social/experiential and cognitive and/or maturational aspects of development, and the contrast between individual and normative development. The developmental principles are order, continuity, and change. These themes and principles provide a framework for the presentation of the facts and theories of developmental psychology and a means of unifying the disparate aspects of development.

FEATURES OF THIS BOOK

This orientation led to a number of features in the book. First we adopted a chronological format. This seemed to be the most suitable way to illustrate the orderly, organic, and integrated nature of development and to underscore our other themes and principles. Like other chronological texts this one has cognitive and social chapters within parts that cover developmental periods. There also are several unique chapters.

In our introductory part, there is a chapter on contexts, which not only brings together information about the various levels of influence on the developing child but sets the stage for considering the interaction of child and environment throughout the text. There is a separate two-chapter part on toddlerhood, which spans the transition from infancy to childhood, and at the end of the book, a chapter on developmental psychopathology, which focuses on abnormal behavior as developmental deviation. Prefacing the chronological parts are the family vignettes, which introduce the basic issues for each developmental period and carry themes forward from section to section. Each part concludes with an integrated part summary in which cognitive and social aspects are interwoven and in which the families and the research are brought together.

Family Vignettes

Our three stories or vignettes begin with the conception of three children, each in a different set of circumstances. One child is born into a working class family where there are two daughters and a son is strongly desired. The second child is born to a teenager, abandoned by her boyfriend and rejected by her own single mother. The third child is an unplanned but welcome addition to an inner city, extended black family. The families were created to represent moderate diversity; for example, none of the children is handicapped and none of the families is from a third world culture. With such a strategy we thought we could illustrate the subtlety as well as the dramatic influence of context and yet keep the stories maximally relevant to students.

The family stories are fictionalized; yet they are drawn from our experience studying hundreds of families longitudinally and conducting research with countless subjects from early infancy through childhood. Our black family was the result of further collaboration with Diana Slaughter and her students at Northwestern University, who created the characters, scenes, and dialogue as part of a graduate seminar entitled "Developmental Tasks of the Black Child in Urban America." In a sense our families are abstractions from real families

grappling with the range of developmental and life issues. At the same time the vignettes were written to be not only engaging but consistent with developmental research. The capacities of the children and the issues they are facing at each age are those reported in the literature. Likewise, the contextual influences on individual lives are based on research; for example, the son in one of our families reacts differently than his sisters to their parents' marital breakup, as suggested by the literature on gender differences in the impact of divorce.

As a teaching device the family vignettes serve several purposes. Reading these engaging stories, students will begin to understand major developmental issues, themes, and achievements for a given period. The stories also help make connections between developmental periods, both in normative terms and in terms of individual children.

Perhaps the major content contribution of the vignettes is to convey a systems perspective to the student. The concept of a system is hard to explain but it can be illustrated. The stories will give students a feel for the direct and indirect influence of context on children, the influences of their particular developmental histories, and the roles of the children in creating their own environments. Child, family, and larger environment adapt to each other in an ongoing process. The text chapters underscore these ideas through the more traditional research and theory presentation, but students will see the workings of systems in the families.

Once students have read the vignettes, the content chapters on research and theory will be both more understandable and more relevant to them. The research questions and methods make sense, and students can see more coherence in the total body of research. The goal is for our questions to be their questions; that is, the presentation of the families should raise the very questions contemporary researchers are pursuing.

Integrative Part Summaries

Themes and critical issues are suggested by the vignettes. Then relevant, contemporary research is organized around these themes in the social and cognitive chapters. Finally, this material is explicitly tied together in the integrative part summaries. Major achievements of the period are summarized across domains, key themes are reviewed, and the research material is applied to the families. Not only does an integrated picture of the child emerge, in a way that students will remember, but cutting edge issues in the field also are made sensible. These themes (e.g., continuity and change, the interplay between child and environment) are introduced one at a time and are reworked throughout the book.

Developmental Psychopathology Chapter and Summary

Time constraints may prohibit some instructors from assigning this chapter, and the text plan permits this. However, the chapter was written to provide a summary and re-integration of the total text. In addition to introducing students to material on childhood disorders, we apply a developmental viewpoint to psychopathology. We refer again to our families to illustrate modern concepts such as buffers, marker variables, and developmental deviation. We discuss why these three children have forged healthy adaptations despite the challenges and issues they faced, and we discuss what might have happened if the circumstances had been different. Such an approach serves to make the complex emerging discipline of developmental psychopathology understandable. It also allows us to restate in a new way all of the major themes of the book.

In the end we hope you will find that this book gives you what you expect from a contemporary child development textbook, but also something more. When you look at theoretical coverage you will find information processing perspectives as well as Piaget; cognitive social learning theory and Bowlby's attachment theory as well as traditional learning and psychoanalytic theories. You will find traditional topics such as gender development and conservation along with newer topics such as social referencing, inner working models, scaffolding, and scripts. You will find very contemporary material on day care, stress, family conflict, and prenatal teratogens such as AIDS and cocaine. But beyond this, we hope

you will find that we have told a coherent story of the unfolding of development.

ACKNOWLEDGMENTS

A number of people helped to make this book happen. At its inception it was a group idea, and numerous people contributed along the way. We would like to see this process continue, and we would be eager to exchange ideas with instructors and to discuss teaching from this book with the aim of improving future editions.

At this time we would like to thank Urie Bronfenbrenner, Advisory Editor, for initiating this project as part of the series on Human Development in Context and for often providing sustaining moral support over the years between conception and reality. We thank Tiffany Field of the University of Miami, Shirley Feldman of Stanford University, Marion Gindes of the Pennsylvania State University, and Scott Paris of the University of Michigan for their participation in the original brainstorming session that led to the concept for this book. We give special thanks to Diana Slaughter (and her students) of Northwestern University, who contributed the first draft of the Williams family and reviewed the entire manuscript. And we thank Dr. Lorraine Cole, Director of the Office of Minority Concerns of the American Speech, Language, and Hearing Association, for reviewing the dialogue in the Williams family story. We also thank Stephen Ceci of Cornell University for his valuable input to the cognitive chapters; Everett and Harriet Waters of the State University of New York, Stony Brook, for their key help and support at all stages of the project; and Sherry Muret-Wagstaff, of the University of Minnesota, for her invaluable assistance with the prenatal and context chapters. Throughout the long writing process a number of reviewers assisted us with their critiques of various chapter drafts. We especially want to thank William Damon of Clark University for his thoughtful and constructive comments, and we thank as well:

Mark Barnett
Kansas State University

Neil Bohannon
Virginia Polytechnic Institute and State University

Marvin Daehler
University of Massachusetts, Amherst

Bernard Gorman
Nassau Community College

Kenneth Kallio
State University of New York, Geneseo

Harriette McAdoo
Howard University

Ardis Peterson
Contra Costa Community College

James Stansbury
Fort Hays State University

Ross Vasta
State University of New York, Brockport

Each of you helped make this book better.

Finally, we would like to thank the production team that has served us so well. First and foremost, we thank Mary Falcon for initiating this project, for not taking "no" for an answer, and for sticking with us no matter what. We thank Judith Kromm and Suzanne Thibodeau who supported early phases of this project, and Elaine Romano who painstakingly worked with our final drafts. We also thank the folks at Visual Education Corporation, especially Susan Ashmore, Lisa Black, Cindy George, Yvonne Gerin, and Sheera Stern, who produced this beautiful book. Although she is acknowledged on the title page, we want to mention here as well our gratitude to Mary Marshall. Her prose made our chapters more readable and the vignettes possible.

LAS
RGC

Advisor's Foreword

This is an unusual developmental text, for it accomplishes that rare, dual feat of translating science into life, and life into science. The achievement is no accident. As the authors note in their preface, their work represents the fulfillment of a dream to produce a new kind of textbook in child development—one that would illuminate contemporary knowledge in developmental science by making it manifest in human lives.

And that is exactly what this book has done. It is first and foremost an excellent textbook— solid in its science, comprehensive in its coverage, and remarkably balanced in its treatment of controversial issues. But the book's most distinctive feature is the way in which these riches are conveyed. For this textbook also tells a story—three stories, in fact. It begins with the anticipated birth of three rather different children in three rather different families, each living in three rather different everyday worlds. The authors then trace the psychological development of the three children, and also their parents, as the families move through time and space.

For those who would follow this developmental journey, an excellent guidebook is provided that describes alternative routes, and the terrain to be traversed, including its history, natural resources, areas of human settlement, the high roads and the low roads that connect them, possible detours, and the dangers and delights to be encountered along the way. It is this comprehensive guidebook, complete with handsome illustrations, that constitutes the main body of the text. It prepares the reader for what lies ahead, and periodically offers a retrospective and integrative view of the ground previously covered.

But, at any point, should we as readers begin to feel overwhelmed by the rich store of information, we need only turn a few pages to find ourselves invisible participants in the life journey itself, accompanying each family as they enter what is for them a new terrain (but for us already familiar ground). We see our three families successively, but not always successfully, coping with new challenges, arising as often from within themselves as from their surroundings. But what the family vignettes communicate most eloquently is perhaps the cardinal lesson emerging from contemporary developmental research; namely that, over time, the balance of forces affecting a child's development generally resolves in favor of psychological growth, and that a major source for this forward movement comes from the child itself—more specifically, from the dynamic nature of the child's evolving capacity to explore and exploit the resources available in its environment. The principal resources in this regard are parents and other persons committed to the child's well-being.

It is this view of development as a process of progressive interaction between an active, growing organism and its environment that constitutes the second hallmark of this somewhat unusual text. And here too, the distinctive feature represents the realization of a conscious goal. When this volume was first conceived, the aim was to produce a textbook that would reflect the significant advances taking place in research on human development. These advances are the result of a convergence in theory and research design that involves a three-fold focus: 1) a view of the child as a dynamic agent that not only responds to but actively interprets, shapes, and even creates its own environment and development; 2) an expansion of the research process beyond the laboratory into the real-life settings, and broader social contexts, in which children live and grow; 3) a conception of development as the progressive reorganization of psychological functioning in which cognitive, emotional, and social processes are treated not as separate domains but as interrelated aspects of a complex living being in an equally complex world.

It is characteristic of the authors' balanced judgment that, in acquainting the reader with the fruits of this new scientific harvest, they do not neglect the established body of theory and knowledge in the field. Rather, what is conveyed is a sense of slow but steady progress in the efforts of human beings to use the methods of science to understand their own development.

The result is a scientific story that matches in its scope and vitality the human story of the three families—a tale that both illumines and is illumined by the authors' coherent and comprehensive exposition of what science has learned about how we evolve as human beings.

Urie Bronfenbrenner

About the Authors

L. Alan Sroufe is professor of child psychology at the Institute of Child Development, University of Minnesota (and professor of psychiatry, University of Minnesota Medical School). He is internationally recognized as an expert on attachment, emotional development, and developmental psychopathology, having published more than 75 articles on these and related topics in major psychology, child development, and psychiatry journals. Sroufe graduated with highest honors from Whittier College in 1963 and received his Ph.D. from the University of Wisconsin in 1967. He completed a clinical psychology internship at the Langley Porter Neuropsychiatric Institute in 1967–68 and has been a visiting professor at the University of Texas and the University of California, Berkeley. In 1984–85, he was a fellow at the Center for Advanced Study in the Behavioral Sciences at Stanford. He has been Consulting Editor or Associate Editor for numerous journals, including *Developmental Psychology, Infant Behavior and Development, Child Development, Developmental Psychopathology,* and *Psychiatry.*

Robert G. Cooper, Jr. is Chairman and Associate Professor of Psychology at Southwest Texas State University. His professional career has focused on the interface between psychology and education. A developmental psychologist, his major research in the area of cognitive development, which has been supported by NIMH and NIE, concerns the development of mathematical concepts. Cooper has published numerous articles and chapters in edited books and, in addition, has contributed chapters for college textbooks. He has been Director of the Graduate Program in Developmental Psychology at the University of Texas, and Director of the Institute for Research and Development in Basic Skills. Cooper graduated with honors from Pomona College in 1968 and received his Ph.D. from the Institute of Child Development at the University of Minnesota in 1973.

Mary E. Marshall, until she became a psychology writer in 1979, was manager of special projects at the college department of Random House. During her ten years in college publishing, she supervised the development of introductory texts such as *Psychology Today, Abnormal Psychology* (2d and 3d eds.), and *Understanding Psychology* (2d and 3d eds.). Marshall is a graduate with distinction of Connecticut College, Phi Beta Kappa and magna cum laude.

Contents

Note to the Student

John and Dolores Williams

"Honey," said John more gently now, "you know we've been over this. We made this baby together, and together we'll see that he gets paid for. It's going to work out. You've got to take things a step at a time. Remember what I told you. Never look back; keep on steppin'. . . ."

Frank and Christine Gordon

Generally, on a week night after a baseball game, Frank would head for the bedroom, leaving Christine to clean up. But tonight he hung around. "You're lookin' good, Chrissie," he said, catching hold of her arm as she passed by. "You could get in trouble lookin' like that."

"I don't know that I want to get in trouble," Christine answered with an uneasy laugh, knowing exactly what Frank had in mind. "You know I'm not so sure about having another baby just yet. . . ."

Karen Polonius

Karen felt numb as she sat in Dr. Rich's office, listening to his sympathetic voice. "As I see it, Karen, you have several choices. You can go through with the pregnancy and give up the baby for adoption. . . ." This can't be happening, Karen thought. It's got to be a mistake. . . .

These extracts are taken from three continuing stories that are presented at the beginning of each part of the book following Chapters 1 and 2. The stories present three family case histories which, while fictionalized, are drawn from the authors' extensive research experience.

In Part One our families are introduced as they consider having a child. Each family lives in different circumstances and each family is unique. Throughout the book, as the three children develop from infancy to adolescence their family situations change as they go through good times and bad. You will see how changing life circumstances influence children and how individual children respond to various life challenges. By getting to know these families, by seeing in a tangible way how individuals unfold within a context, we believe that you will be able to relate your own experiences to the facts and theories of developmental psychology that will be presented in the chapters.

The family stories are used to introduce the major themes and issues that will be the focus of the text chapters in each section. They also are used as examples within the chapters to illustrate the specific points we are making. Then following the chapters, at the end of each part, we have what we call "integrative summaries." Here we specifically tie the content of the chapters to the lives of the children we are following. We think this will not only help you better remember the material you are learning but also serve to give you a more lifelike and holistic picture of the developing child. The facts and theories of child development are indeed interesting. But we think they can be more fascinating when connected to the lives of developing children.

1

The Nature of Development

This book is about child development from conception through adolescence. Like other psychology texts, it tries to explain human behavior. But here behavior is viewed from a particular perspective, the perspective of development. We believe that when behavior is viewed in context it becomes more understandable, and one important aspect of context is development. If you understand the origins of behavior, how it has emerged, and how it will manifest itself in the future, it begins to make more sense. For instance, knowing that a 1-year-old will soon acquire language makes the child's pointing and gesturing much more meaningful. The two behaviors—speaking and gesturing—are linked in the progressive development of communication.

A developmental perspective includes several ways of thinking about children. One way is to recognize that children differ fundamentally from one developmental period to the next. Older children certainly have grown bigger and stronger than younger children and have acquired greater knowledge; but development includes more than this. Three-year-olds, for instance, can communicate with language, know that they exist as separate persons, and experience pride and shame. None of these things are true for 6-month-olds. A developmental perspective also includes the idea that an older child's capacities emerge in an orderly manner from the capacities that child had earlier. For example, what 4-year-olds know about the world and how they behave are natural forerunners of the 6-year-old's knowledge and behavior. One is an outgrowth of the other even though their linkage is sometimes complex.

A third aspect of a developmental perspective is the belief that each individual's development is coherent over time. However different you are now from the person you were in the sixth grade, there are nonetheless many threads of continuity in your behavior. Such continuity is as much a part of human development as is change.

Developmental psychology includes the study of both how general human capacities unfold and why individual differences come about. For instance, developmentalists are interested in the general emotional changes that children undergo from infancy to adolescence, but they are also interested in why one child has different emotional reactions than others. It is our belief that one can better understand a child of any given age by understanding the behavior of younger and older children. Knowing the developmental phases a child has experienced and those the child eventually will enter provides a perspective for viewing where the child is right now. Similarly, understanding a particular child's developmental history makes him or her more understandable at the moment.

In this chapter we begin by exploring the concept of development. As you will learn, development affects a child's thoughts, feelings, and actions in very fundamental ways. Next, we introduce a framework for understanding development. What brings about the remarkable unfolding of human behavior? We consider the interplay of genetic potentials, past development, and current environmental circumstances in the context of evolutionary theory. Finally, we discuss the methods that developmental psychologists use to study children and to collect data that can be used to understand the developmental process. With this information as background, we can then turn in Chapter 2 to some of the major specific theories proposed to explain development.

THE CONCEPT OF DEVELOPMENT

Development and Behavior

The mother of 6-month-old Mikey puts one end of a cloth in her mouth and dangles the other end in front of her baby by shaking her head from side to side, but without making a sound. Mikey grows still and watches the cloth intently. After a period of inspection, he methodically reaches for the cloth and pulls it from his mother's mouth, never changing the sober expression on his face. Soon he is putting a piece of the cloth into his own mouth, as babies this age try to do with everything they grasp.

In the same situation another child, 10-month-old Meryl, behaves quite differently. Meryl watches with rapt attention as her mother dangles the cloth, glancing back and forth between the cloth and her mother's face. Quickly her own face brightens. She smiles, laughs, and *grabs* the cloth away. Then laughing uproariously she tries to stuff the cloth back into her mother's mouth.

What explains the remarkable differences between these two infants? You might suppose that Meryl, perhaps through practicing this game, has acquired skills for playing it that Mikey as yet lacks. This explanation is based on learning. Certainly learning is involved in many actions and plays some role here. However, if you were to try this procedure over and over with a 6-month-old, you would find that repeated practice leads only to boredom, not to uproarious laughter. You would also discover that 6-month-olds already have most of the major skills required for the 10-month-old's reaction: They recognize their mothers as distinct from other people, they frequently laugh in situations such as being tickled, and they have the physical coordination to replace the cloth in their mother's mouth. Yet for some reason their reactions differ sharply from that of a 10-month-old.

Perhaps you think the answer lies in different temperaments. According to this view, Meryl has a sunny disposition and would have laughed at the game at age 6 months, whereas Mikey is a sober child and would not laugh even if older. This explanation is based on individual differences, and when one looks at just two children, it seems plausible. Even infants the same age do differ in how frequently they smile and cry. But if you were to repeat this little experiment with many babies, boys as well as girls of different dispositions, you would find that Mikey and Meryl are typical of their ages. It is virtually impossible to get *any* 6-month-old to laugh with this procedure, and most 10-month-olds at least smile. Neither practice nor individual differences can fully explain this.

A developmental perspective (e.g., Kitchener, 1983) can help make these two behaviors understandable. One can look at the reactions of Meryl and Mikey as part of regularly occurring processes that unfold with age. Six- and 10-month-old infants are *qualitatively different*. Compared with Mikey, Meryl is vastly more capable; she is in a new league. Mikey does not even seem aware of the connection between the cloth and his mother. It is as if his mother recedes into the background as his attention is captured by the cloth. He pulls the cloth out of her mouth just as he would grasp and pull any object. He sees no "game" in this at all. Meryl, in contrast, can keep both the cloth and her mother in mind at once and understand the relation between them. She can remember her mother without the cloth and recognize that mother-with-cloth is out of keeping with what her mother is usually like; that is, mother-with-cloth violates an *expectation* Meryl has. She also knows that she can re-create this incongruity by stuffing the cloth back into her mother's mouth. She laughs because she remembers each previous state and anticipates the outcome of her actions. Far more than Mikey, she has a sense of past and future, as well as present experience. She also has an understanding that people and objects have permanence; they are not really transformed by simple changes in appearance. Mother-without-cloth is still there in mother-with-cloth.

The 6-month-old, of course, is busy acquiring the experiences that, with further maturation, will allow the 10-month-old's capacities to emerge. Links exist between the two ages. A 6-month-old can also "remember" and "anticipate," but these capabilities are primitive compared with those of a 10-month-old. Although both 6-month-olds and 10-month-olds are active learners, 10-month-olds can learn *different things* because of their greater memory capacity and generally greater understanding of the world.

A 10-month-old can enjoy a game of putting a cloth in his mother's mouth because he understands the relation between the cloth and his mother, and he anticipates the outcome of his actions. (D. LaSota.)

The games that infants play reveal a great deal about both their social and mental development. This 7-month-old infant laughs in anticipation of her father's return in peek-a-boo because she remembers that he is behind the balloon and because she anticipates his emergence. Five-month-olds cannot appreciate this game. (*Elizabeth Crews.*)

Developmental psychologists are not only interested in the way children at different ages perceive and learn about the world but also in the process by which the child at one age unfolds through a series of **qualitative changes** or "transformations" to become the child at a later age. As another example, consider the parents who repeatedly explain to their 10-year-old the need to recycle bottles and cans in order to conserve resources. The message at this age seems to fall on deaf ears. But eventually, to the parents' surprise, the same child comes home from school six years later and begins to lecture on the necessity of recycling with all the fervor of an evangelist ("We're running out of landfills; our mineral reserves are quickly being depleted"). This new ability to grasp the significance of an issue is part of a fundamentally new perspective on the world and the future. Compared with 10-year-olds, adolescents have a different sense of the human community and a far greater capacity to project their lives into the future. As a result of this change in understanding, they can learn things that seem beyond 10-year-olds. But 10-year-olds are learning many things about the nature of the observable world that let these later abstract abilities emerge.

Closely related to the concept of qualitative change is the concept of **behavioral reorganization.** Meryl not only has more capacities than 6-month-old Mikey; she also has a new way of *organizing* her thoughts and actions, of using her capacities and fitting them together. It is because she can coordinate her memories, current actions, and anticipation that she laughs at the cloth game. The reorganization of thoughts and actions always results in more complex behavior. At each age the capacities of the younger child prepare the way for the new, more complex patterns to emerge.

The concepts of qualitative change and behavioral reorganization may be understood better by considering an analogy in the business world. Imagine an accounting firm years ago in which the employees did all their work using hand-held calculators. For a while the business grew simply by adding new accountants, each of whom did the same thing (*quantitative* change). But then a computer was installed. This new technology produced dramatic *qualitative* change. Not only was the firm able to handle vastly more accounts, but tasks were performed in very different ways. Specialization occurred. Some staff members worked on designing new computer programs. Some actually worked on inputting information. Some primarily interpreted the output. A more elaborate organizational hierarchy evolved. Granted, knowledge from the old system was used in the new system, but it was now part of a totally *different organization*. So it seems to be with human development.

Qualitative change and behavioral reorganization are evident throughout development. Consider the 3-year-old who picks out a shiny toy truck for his father's birthday present. A 6-year-old suggests a necktie. For both children this is a special occasion, and they want the best for their fathers. But the 3-year-old is not yet able to understand that the truck reflects his own wishes and values. *He* would like a new toy truck so his father must too. He cannot yet think that his father might prefer something different. In contrast, the 6-year-old suggests a gift appropriate for both his father's age and gender. Several developmentalists have argued that as children grow older, they are increasingly able to take into account the feelings, needs, and attitudes of others. At each age children see the world from a broader perspective.

Development during childhood and adolescence refers to certain age-related changes that are orderly, cumulative, and directional (Waters and Sroufe, 1983). By *orderly* we mean that the changes follow a logical sequence, with each one paving the way for future changes and making sense in light of what went before. By *cumulative* we mean that any given phase includes all that went before it as well as something more. When one mixes flour, sugar, eggs, baking powder, and salt and bakes the mixture, one still has those ingredients in the final product. But one also has something more—a cake. And by *directional* we mean that development always moves toward greater complexity.

Development, Growth, and Other Changes

We have been using the term *development* to describe two aspects of the physical and emotional changes that occur as children grow older. Some of these changes might be more accurately called *growth*. For example, children get taller between ages 7 and 9, and as preschoolers interact with peers, they become more skilled at social exchange. Development includes these gradual changes, but it also encompasses more. It also captures the growth spurts and fundamental changes in body shape at adolescence, for example, and the qualitative differences of peer interaction between infants (who play with peers as though they were complex objects) and older children (who have friends).

Not all changes in children are part of either growth or development. Children may behave differently when they are ill or tired, when they

Children not only get taller with age, but fundamental changes in body shape also occur. In other domains, too, children not only add capacities but undergo fundamental changes in the way they perceive the world. *(Gerhard Gscheidle/ Peter Arnold Inc.)*

are rewarded for certain actions, when they are given practice at some skill, or when they have the opportunity to mimic other people. These are important changes in behavior, and they are of interest to developmentalists. But they are not developmental changes. Learning to recognize the word *dog* is not in itself development. But emergence of the understanding that verbal symbols may stand for objects *is* development. The two kinds of changes are related because the child with symbolic capacity is ready to start learning the meaning of words, and learning individual words generally precedes comprehending the more general idea that words have meaning. Mastery of verbal symbols is an orderly, cumulative, and directional change, whereas identifying the word *dog* is a small single step in that process.

Normative and Individual Development

So far we have been discussing **normative development**, the general changes in behavior across ages that virtually all children share. Describing, understanding, and explaining these normative changes are major concerns of developmental psychologists. To many developmentalists, however, individual development is of equal importance.

Individual development actually has two meanings. First, it refers to variations around the average, or normative, course of development of a certain ability. If you were to chart the progress of 100 different children from birth through adolescence, you would find many differences in when and how they reach developmental milestones. This is why we can state only *on average* the ages at which various capacities emerge. For instance, when we say that 22-month-olds recognize their reflections in a mirror, we give that age only as a representative one. Sometimes this capacity emerges later, even in normal healthy infants, while occasionally it can be seen as early as 15 months of age. The point is that there is always a range of variation in human development. Children with the gentic defect that causes Down syndrome do not smile at the cloth-in-mouth game until their second year and do not recognize themselves in a mirror until about age 2½ years (Mans, Cicchetti, and Sroufe, 1978). Still, they progress toward these achievements in the same way as other children, only at a slower pace. Such variation around the norm is one meaning of individual development.

Second, individual development refers to the uniqueness of each individual as a person. Different children evolve different styles, different preferences, different ways of doing things—what are often called different personalities. Many theorists have tried to explain these individual differences, some emphasizing inborn characteristics, others environmental experiences, and still others the interaction of inborn characteristics with environment. All these theorists agree, however, on continuity in the individual over time, continuity that emerges against a backdrop of ongoing developmental change. An exuberant and confident 2-year-old is less likely to end up hesitant and withdrawn three years later than is a 2-year-old with a more negative developmental history (Arend, Gove, and Sroufe, 1979). And even when dramatic changes in individual development do take place, logical reasons for them can still be found. Just as normative development is coherent and predictable, so too is individual development.

A FRAMEWORK FOR UNDERSTANDING DEVELOPMENT

Development is dramatic and predictable. The sequence of fundamental changes in behavior and thought unfolds with amazing consistency and orderliness in child after child. How and why do these profound changes we have been describing come about? In the next chapter we will introduce some specific theories that have been proposed to account for developmental change. But here we raise the more general question: How does development occur at all?

The broadest answer that can be given to this question is that development depends on three factors: (1) a preexisting developmental plan built into the organism, (2) prior development, and (3) supportive environmental conditions. The first two factors may be thought of as existing "in the organism." Every human child carries a set of genes that contains the basic instructions for the unfolding of development (see Chapters 3 and 4). But which genes are "turned on" or in operation depends on the particular point in development a child has reached, that is, on the changes that have gone before. However, the unfolding also depends on current environmental support. Current support includes all of the nutrients, inputs, circumstances, and challenges the developing organism encounters. Somehow, all three influences—genetic potentials, past development, and current environmental circumstances—account for the dramatic process we call development, whereby from just two cells evolves an individual who is capable of reading and understanding this textbook. Understanding how genes, past development, and environment interact to produce ongoing developmental changes is a major task for the field of developmental psychology. Important clues concerning how

Charles Darwin *(Mary Evans Picture Library/Photo Researchers Inc.)*

this process works are found in the evolutionary theory of Charles Darwin.

The Darwinian Revolution

Contemporary theories of human development stress the interaction of heredity and environment largely because of the influence of evolutionary theory. Evolutionary theory is not primarily a theory of child development; rather, it is a more general theory of the development and adaptation of species. As such, it provides a basic biological context for considering development (see Chapter 3).

Charles Darwin, a nineteenth-century naturalist, sought a scientific explanation for the diversity of forms exhibited by the living things on earth and for their ability to exist in all kinds of environments. His careful observations of plants and animals led to one of the most important insights in all of science: the idea that any given species is *designed for* survival in its particular environment. A simple example is coloration that camouflages an animal from enemies. Another example is an animal that has a great many natural predators and so produces a large number of young, some of which always survive. Still other species are designed for survival by drawing on natural resources that competing species ignore. Termites, for instance, feed on wood, which most other animals cannot digest. Darwin noted that each species has its own strategy for living and its own niche in the world. Each is adapted to survive and reproduce in its particular setting.

In addition to observing the adaptations of species, Darwin tried to explain them. Why, for instance, do the lizards on two different islands have colorations that precisely match the local rocks and vegetation? How did this come about? Darwin's answer was **natural selection,** the process by which individuals who are best adapted for survival are more likely to pass on their traits to the next generation. Natural selection is sometimes described as the "survival of the fittest," but we must be careful in how we interpret this phrase. The survival that is important for natural selection is the survival of *genes,* the chemical instructions that determine how a living organism will grow and develop. In evolutionary theory, individuals are merely the temporary carriers of genes from the species' gene pool, the total range of a species' genes that can be transmitted from one generation to the next. For this reason, traits of a particular individual may survive in the gene pool when the individual fails to reproduce if near relatives do reproduce. This is the concept of *inclusive fitness.*

Darwin's theory explains the diversity of living things by arguing that over generations the traits of groups of organisms tend to change in directions better suited to survival in particular environments. Because the earth has so many different environments, this evolutionary process has produced a huge number of species. Plants and animals have adapted to arctic tundras, jungle rain forests, barren deserts, and mountain highlands, as well as to lakes and oceans. And it is not just climates and physical surroundings to which species adapt. Species also adapt to other species, especially those available as food. The long, dexterous arms of an octopus, the powerful claws of a lobster, the thin, tubelike mouthpart of a mosquito are all adaptations to environmental opportunities that other plant or animal species offer.

In recent years controversy has arisen concerning whether evolution is *gradual,* as Darwin theorized, or **punctuated,** a position held by Stephen J. Gould (1977). It seems to be the case that both positions contain some truth. Periods of relative equilibrium and gradual change are occasionally punctuated by periods of rapid change, perhaps brought on by cataclysmic environmental change. Notice that although we are discussing changes in a species over generations, the model of development is the same as we discussed earlier. Development depends on what already exists (the evolutionary history and genetic potentials of the organism) and the current environmental circumstances.

Let's use our example of protective coloration to demonstrate how evolutionary change occurs. Suppose that sea currents carry lizards to a new island. Suppose also that most of them are too dark to blend with the sandy soil found there, and so they are easily spotted by predators. Among the lizards that survive are many slightly lighter in color, who pass the genes for lighter color on to their young. Therefore, in the next

Each animal has its unique adaptive capacities. The cheetah is blessed with great speed. The porcupine has a particular protective device. The anteater has a special capacity for drawing what it needs from the environment. (*G. Ziesler/ Peter Arnold, Inc., Bill Ivy, Miller Services Ltd./Photo Researchers, Inc., Frederick J. Dodd/Peter Arnold, Inc.*)

generation, lighter-colored lizards increase in number, and those with the lightest color have the best chance of reproducing. Over many generations, light coloration is favored because it offers a survival advantage. Alternatively, some of the original lizards might have been dramatically lighter in color due to mutation of their genes for coloration. In this case natural selection would have operated in a rapid, punctuated manner. In any case, the fact that in a few hundred years most of the island's lizards blend perfectly with the sand is itself "proof" of natural selection.

Evolutionary Theory and Child Development

Darwin's theory has important implications for the study of child development. To the question "What develops?" evolutionary theory answers, "survival-enhancing species-specific behavior." Species-specific behavior is behavior that is typical of a certain species, the members of which share a common inheritance as well as a common environment. Virtually all human infants, for example, behave in similar ways: They cry when they are hungry or otherwise distressed; they are drawn to look at other people, particularly at human faces; at an early age they begin to smile and coo when a human face appears before them. These behaviors, in turn, have adaptive value. They serve as signals that elicit care from parents and other adults. Thus, children's innate potentials, along with environmental support, promote their survival. With continued expression of genetic potentials and continued environmental support, the developmental plan unfolds, ultimately resulting in adults capable of producing and caring for offspring.

Another contribution of evolutionary theory to the study of development is the recognition that human adaptations often have parallels in other species that are related to humans. For instance, while human infants smile, coo, and lean against their mothers, baby macaque monkeys cling tightly to the mother's body. Although the specific behaviors vary, infants of both species are showing signs of attachment to the mother. In both species this attachment serves the same function: helping elicit the mother's care and protection of her baby.

Evolutionary theory has made a vital contribution to our understanding of how human development occurs. Evolutionary theory stresses the importance of heredity, the process by which the same human characteristics are passed on from every parent to every child via genes. Evolutionary theory also stresses genetic variation within species. This within-species variation accounts for much of the diversity we see in people. It also provides the building blocks for future evolution. Finally, evolutionary theory stresses the role of environmental support for development.

A key idea to remember is that Darwin's theory assigns an important role to both heredity and environment. One cannot be considered in isolation from the other. Changing environmental demands lead to changing hereditary characteristics, and members of a species evolve to be adapted to *particular environments* having particular qualities. Successful development (reproduction, in evolutionary theory) depends on the fit of organisms and environment. If no one were there to respond to the human infant, it would not matter how the baby cried or signaled the need for care; he or she would surely die. Moreover, a standard for assessing the adequacy of the child's environment becomes clear. The critical factor is the degree to which the environment provides responsiveness to the infant's preadapted and unfolding capacities.

A Viewpoint on Heredity and Environment

In the wake of Darwin's theory, virtually all developmentalists take some stance on the relationship of heredity and environment to development. As we will discuss in the next chapter, current theorists differ considerably on the weight they give to one or the other of these factors. Some researchers emphasize genetic contributions; others emphasize environmental contributions. Although controversy continues, almost all theorists stress some form of interaction between heredity and environment, where both influences are considered simultaneously.

Our own view of heredity and environment is that it makes no sense to say one or the other is more important. Each is essential. Without genetic instructions, there can be no development. But without environmental support, development cannot proceed either. Consider one example from prenatal development, a topic discussed at length in Chapter 4. If at an early stage in the development of a chick embryo, one surgically removes a block of tissue from the base of a bud that will become a leg and places it at the tip of a bud that is going to become a wing, the tissue becomes a normal-looking part of the wing tip. It would have become part of the thigh, but in this new context, or "environment," it becomes part of the wing. If this procedure is performed very late in the development of the embryo, however, the tissue will not be incorporated into the new site. It is too late for the new context to alter the course of development. What if the transplant is done at an intermediate stage? Amazingly, the result is a clawlike structure at the end of the wing! In other words, at this stage the tissue carries instructions to become leg tissue but no final instructions to become thigh. The new context induces the tissue to become a tip—the tip of a leg (see Figure 1.1). A develop-

Figure 1.1
Transplantation of Block of Tissue from Leg Bud to Wing Bud of Chick Embryo
The tissue develops into toes, characteristic of the tip of a hind limb, not of the thigh from which it originated or of the wing tip to which it was transplanted.
Source: Arms and Camp, 1987.

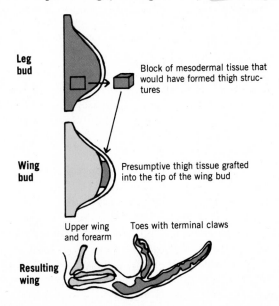

Leg bud

Block of mesodermal tissue that would have formed thigh structures

Wing bud

Presumptive thigh tissue grafted into the tip of the wing bud

Upper wing and forearm

Toes with terminal claws

Resulting wing

mental result thus depends on environment and past development (or developmental stage) as well as on genes. But note that although transplanted leg tissue can become wing tissue, anomalous leg tissue, or a clawlike structure, depending on the stage of growth it had reached when transplanted, in no case can it become a fin even if grafted onto a fish embryo. Its genetic instructions constrain what it can be, regardless of environment. Examples such as this lead us to the position that neither genes nor environment can be considered more important than the other. We will emphasize development in context throughout this book.

We will return to our discussion of the roles of genes and environment and theories of development in subsequent chapters. But next we consider the methods psychologists use to study development, both its normative course and its individual course.

METHODS FOR STUDYING DEVELOPMENT

Several common approaches are taken to study human development. Some, such as the laboratory experiment, are modeled after methods used in the physical sciences. Others, such as observing people in natural settings, are more similar to procedures used in the biological sciences, where description and classification are of major importance. Still others, such as certain methods for interviewing children, are unique to developmental psychology.

Each method for studying development has its strengths and weaknesses. None is more or less "scientific" than the others. A method's power and **validity** (whether it produces meaningful results) depend on how it is used. Basically, the choice of method depends on the question being asked. Some questions are best approached with one procedure, other questions with entirely different techniques. What's more, many issues require a combination of methods before they are fully understood.

The Experiment

Suppose you wanted to answer the question: Do newborn babies have a preference for looking at human faces? You might start by watching some newborns in their homes to find out what they look at. If you kept track of the time they spent looking at faces, you would probably conclude that faces must be attractive to them. But how would you know whether human faces are more attractive than other things to newborns? And just what is it about a face that captures a baby's interest? Is a particular facial feature attracting attention, or is it the face as a whole? Or could it be the sound of a person's voice that makes the baby look at the face from which the sound comes? In the baby's home, separating all these different factors would be difficult. That is why psychologists usually study such issues in a laboratory. There they can use sophisticated equipment to determine precisely where a baby is looking. Also, by systematically controlling the stimuli presented, they can find out what best captures the child's attention.

In the laboratory, researchers can have tight control over what the infant experiences and can also deploy technical apparatus to ensure precise recording. Here an infant's eye movements are being recorded. *(Hank Morgan/Science Source/ Photo Researchers, Inc.)*

Suppose laboratory research showed not only that newborns look at faces, but that they tend to focus their gaze particularly on the hairline (Maurer and Salapatek, 1976). What is it about hairlines that holds infants' interest? One possible answer is the light-dark contrast between the forehead and the hair. To test this possibility, or **hypothesis**, as it is called, researchers could conduct an experiment. An **experiment** is a study in which researchers control conditions so as to rule out all other influences except the one being investigated. In this case, the psychologists would assign a number of babies to one of two groups. This assignment would be made completely at random. Random assignment "shuffles" the subjects, so to speak, thus minimizing the chances that infants with some unusual visual preference inadvertently all get assigned to the same group. The researchers would then show one group of babies a picture of a face with sharp light-dark contrast at the hairline and show the other group of babies exactly the same face with the light-dark contrast removed. If the first group of infants focused longer on the face and on the hairline in particular than did the second group of infants, the researchers would have evidence that light-dark contrasts are indeed appealing to newborns. Note that in a laboratory experiment, researchers can be very systematic in exploring possibilities and ruling out alternatives. They can also be very precise in setting up the conditions for each group of subjects tested. Control and precision are the chief advantages of the laboratory experiment.

Laboratory experiments also have disadvantages, however. For one thing, their results may not always apply to real-life settings. People may behave differently in a laboratory than they do in natural settings, either because the lab is strange and intimidating to them or because they want to "look good" for the experimenter. For example, Daryl Bem and David Funder (1978) found that children's ability to delay gratification in a laboratory (to refrain from touching an attractive toy at the request of the experimenter) did not predict their ability to control impulses at school. Instead, delay of gratification in the lab predicted obedience, lack of curiosity, and submissiveness to adults in real-life situations. Thus, laboratory findings may not always mean what they seem to at first. Psychologists call this the issue of **ecological validity:** Findings inside the laboratory may not generalize to the outside world. And even when laboratory findings do generalize to outside settings, researchers must still be cautious in drawing implications. In other words, if an experiment reveals that a certain situation can cause a certain response, one cannot conclude that this cause and effect are common in the outside world. For example, John Watson (1928) created fear of a rat in a young child by making a loud noise while the rat was nearby. However, many people are afraid of rats without ever having had such an experience.

Another limitation of laboratory experiments is that many questions of interest to developmentalists are not open to experimentation. This is especially true in the area of social development. For instance, because of humanitarian considerations, researchers cannot assign children to abusive conditions just to observe the results. Purposely exposing children to pain and anguish is ethically unthinkable. Nor can researchers create certain everyday events (the birth of a brother or sister, a mother deciding to work outside the home) within the confines of a laboratory. Are socially relevant issues beyond scientific study then? Certainly not. Other research methods can be used.

Observational Methods

An alternative to conducting laboratory experiments is to observe behavior in everyday settings as it occurs naturally. This approach to research has a long history, and in the last century was used by Charles Darwin. In the twentieth century, a field of study called **ethology** has developed; this field seeks to understand animal behavior through careful observation of species in their natural habitats. One example is Jane Goodall's study of chimpanzee social behavior. The information about free-ranging chimps she collected through years of observation in East African forests could never have been obtained by studying chimps in a laboratory.

Much research on human development also uses the technique of **naturalistic observation.** Researchers go to homes, schools, and playgrounds to watch and record the everyday behavior of children and adults. At times they also try to simulate natural settings in their own research rooms. For instance, they might create an attractive playroom, bring in a group of children to play, and observe the children through a one-way window so as not to distract them. Naturalistic observation can also be used to make group comparisons. For example, a researcher could compare the amount of conflict in families with young adolescents versus families with younger children or older adolescents. The families might be observed in their own homes—say, at the dinner table—and the researcher could record the number of disagreements, negative personal comments, and other signs of discord. Sophisticated, automated devices are now available to record such observations (e.g., Sackett, 1978).

In all the various settings where observations are conducted, researchers are precise and systematic in recording what they see. They count the frequencies of particular behaviors, note sequences as they occur, and rate subjects for qualitative factors such as mood or level of enthusiasm. This careful recording of data is what distinguishes the trained psychologist from the casual observer. The psychologist does not just watch and try to remember. He or she is constantly keeping records, usually in quantitative form (e.g., the frequency of aggressive behaviors, the proportion of children who share with others, the number of times a particular child asks an adult for help).

Observation in natural circumstances has the advantage that one can claim with more confidence to be studying the way children or animals usually behave. *(Cliff Haac/Frank Porter Graham Child Development Center.)*

Naturalistic observation has the advantage of describing human behavior in real-life situations, not behavior under laboratory conditions an experimenter sets up and controls. Naturalistic observation is therefore very useful for studying many socially relevant issues. The major disadvantage of the method is its limits in explaining what researchers observe. Suppose you observe greater conflict in families with young teenagers and wonder if the presence of teenagers might be the cause. You have no way of knowing through observation alone whether this hypothesis is correct. Just because two factors are often found together does not necessarily mean that one *causes* the other. For example, a study in England once showed that the number of storks in an area was *positively correlated* with the number of births there—that is, the more storks, the more births. However, this does not mean that storks bring babies. Instead, some third factor, related to both the others, must be at work. As it turns out, that factor is population density. Heavily industrialized urban areas have a large number of big chimneys, where storks like to nest, and these areas also have a high number of births. In the same way, some other factor you are not aware of could be causing conflict in families with teenagers. Using naturalistic observation by itself, you have no way of ruling out all such other factors. One way to overcome this problem partially is to conduct a natural experiment.

THE NATURAL EXPERIMENT

A **natural experiment** is undertaken when it is not possible to assign subjects to groups randomly. For instance, researchers cannot take a large number of families and randomly give a teenager to half and a younger child to half. Instead, they must make do with the families that nature provides. To minimize the chances that some factor other than age of the children is influencing family conflict, the researchers could try to select families that are similar in many ways. For example, they could choose families in which the parents are similar in financial status, in marital satisfaction, in job-related pressures, and so forth. If among these similar parents those with young teenagers still turned out to have the most conflict, the researchers would begin to have some indication that their hypothesis might be right. And if the degree of family conflict were found to increase over time as children moved from childhood into the teen years and decreased again in the same families as the children moved into late adolescence, confidence in the hypothesis would grow (see longitudinal studies below).

Natural experiments are used often in research on child development. To take another example, suppose you observe that most 22-month-olds recognize themselves in a mirror, while most 15-month-olds do not. Is this due to level of cognitive development or simply to more experience with mirrors? You later observe that the few 15-month-olds who *do* show this ability score higher than average on certain tests of cognitive development. This fact is very suggestive. You speculate that cognitive development is the fundamental cause of mirror recognition. But how can you demonstrate this? Cognitive level, after all, is not a factor that can be assigned to people at random. One solution is to take advantage of children who by nature have cognitive levels below the level of their peers. If you find that mirror recognition is much delayed in these mentally retarded children, despite normal exposure to mirrors, the case for your hypothesis is strengthened. And if the degree of delay is closely related to the degree of retardation, as has been found, the case is stronger still (Mans, Cicchetti, and Sroufe, 1978). In natural experiments you take advantage of naturally occurring variations and gradually build a case against alternative hypotheses. Although you can never be absolutely certain of your conclusions, your confidence increases as supporting evidence grows.

OBSERVING CHANGE OVER TIME

Suppose you want to know how children who are placed in full-time day care from their earliest months of life fare in comparison with other children as they grow older. One way is to conduct a longitudinal study. **Longitudinal studies** follow the same group of people over a number of weeks, months, or years. In this case, you would select one group of infants whose parents had placed them in day care by the age of, say, 3 months and another group of infants whose parents planned to raise them entirely at home. Without knowing whether day care had a positive or negative effect, you could not ethically assign or even encourage parents to use or refrain from using day care as part of the research. As best you could, you would try to choose families similar in terms of socioeconomic background, current marital status and satisfaction, general attitudes toward child rearing, and so forth. In this way, day care or home care would be the major difference between the two groups. Periodically you would interview the parents and more directly assess the children's emotional adjustment, social skills, and cognitive growth. Each assessment would allow you to compare how the two groups developed. Of course, if you wanted to follow these children to adolescence, this study would take you at least 12 years.

A way to speed up your investigation would be to conduct a **cross-sectional study**, a study that compares different groups of people at different ages. In this case, you would select a sample of children who ranged in age from 1 to 12 years. Half the children would have been placed in day care by the age of 3 months, while the other half would have been raised entirely at home. Again, you would try to equate the families in terms of other influential factors, such as the parents' socio-economic background and marital satisfaction. Then you would set about assessing and comparing the 1-year-olds, the 2-year-olds, the 3-year-olds, and so forth. In general, this type of research can be used to compare the performance of children at one age with younger or older children as a way of mapping out the course of development. In this particular case you are comparing the progress of children with different day-care experience. If you found systematic differences between the day-care and the home-raised children, you would not have absolute proof that the type of early care was the cause. (Perhaps the two groups of families differed in some other critical way that you had overlooked.) Nevertheless, your findings would certainly be suggestive and might prompt further research.

   Longitudinal and cross-sectional studies are two ways of studying change over time. Each has advantages and disadvantages. Cross-sectional studies can be done more quickly and cheaply, which can be very important when findings have crucial implications for child-rearing practices. Cross-sectional studies, however, are somewhat limited in what they can reveal. Although they can show how children differ at different ages (see Figure 1.2), they are not well suited to showing the process of development, that is, the path from one developmental phase to the next. Also, because cross-sectional findings are statistics about a group examined at a single point in time, they reveal nothing about individual change. The study of physical growth provides a good example. If you were to plot the average height of 1-year-olds, 2-year-olds, 3-year-olds, and so forth, the resulting curve would look smooth and steady. This

Figure 1.2
Comparison of Individual and Averaged Growth Curves
Averaging the changes in height (stature velocities) during early adolescence of several children leaves the impression of smooth growth, though with more rapid growth at around 12 years. However, individual children may not fit this picture at all, and for most, growth changes are quite abrupt.

Source: Adapted from Tanner, 1961, p. 10.

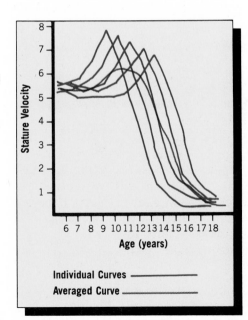

steady-looking curve would be misleading, however. Individual growth is notably uneven, especially in adolescence, when different children experience physical growth spurts at different times. These individual differences can be discovered only by studying the same children over time.

Developmentalists thus rely on a combination of cross-sectional and longitudinal methods, sometimes even in the same study. In what is called an **accelerated longitudinal design,** researchers begin studying several age-groups at the same time and then follow each of them. For example, if you followed groups of 1-, 4-, 7-, and 10-year-olds for four years, you would have covered a developmental span of 14 years in this time. You would also be able to demonstrate that changes observed were developmental changes and not merely changes due to some peculiar factor in your original groups because you could show that your new 4-year-olds (the infants three years later) were comparable to the original 4-year-old group. And you could show that individual performance at each age was predicted by performance at the earlier age.

Developmentalists also combine observational and experimental techniques. Observations often provide the starting point for experiments, as when researchers noted that infants seem to look at faces a great deal. Experiments, on the other hand, are often used to confirm a hypothesis developed through observation, as when research confirmed that light-dark contrasts are especially attractive to newborns. Working back and forth between observations and experiments pervades the study of development. For instance, on the basis of observation, ethologists hypothesized that the tendency for infants to cling to their mothers is a genetically based behavior that helps protect the young, not one that is learned simply because the mother provides food. Psychologist Harry Harlow (Harlow and Harlow, 1966) then conducted an experiment that showed that baby monkeys will cling to a terrycloth ''mother'' even in preference to a wire ''mother'' that dispenses food. Harlow's experiment showed that feeding by a mother is not necessary for a baby's attachment to form; observation showed how infant-mother attachment develops in natural environments. Clearly, research on development requires both these methods.

Chapter Review

1. A developmental perspective is extremely valuable in understanding children's behavior. It includes the idea that children undergo **qualitative change** in their thoughts, feelings, and actions as they grow older. This qualitative change includes the process of **behavioral reorganization**—new, increasingly complex ways of putting capacities together.

2. The age-related changes that make up **development** have certain features in common. First, these changes are *orderly*, meaning that they follow a logical sequence. Second, they are *cumulative*, meaning that each builds on what has gone before. Third, they are *directional*, meaning that they always move toward greater behavioral complexity.

3. Developmentalists are interested in both normative and individual development. **Normative development** refers to the general age-related changes in behavior that virtually all children share. **Individual development** refers to two things. First, it refers to the fact that children progress along the usual, or normative, course of development at their own individual pace. Second, it refers to the unique style of behavior that each person evolves.

4. An important framework for understanding development is Charles Darwin's theory of evolution. According to Darwin, characteristics that a species passes on from one generation to the next are those that produce individuals best adapted for survival. This process is known as **natural selection.** Darwin theorized that traits change gradually over generations to produce offspring better able to survive in particular environments. More recently, Stephen Gould suggested that these periods of gradual change are interrupted, or **punctuated,** by rapid changes in the genetic makeup of a particular species. The demands of the environment often determine which individuals survive and reproduce.

5. A contribution of evolutionary theory to the study of development has been to identify the adaptive significance of human behavior. Humans are designed to adapt to and develop within a social environment. Both the general course of development and the particular requirements for adequate development of children derive from our evolutionary heritage.

6. All researchers agree that both heredity and environment play major roles in development. Current debate concerns how these two influences interact. One view is that one influence is not more or less important than the other; each is equally significant. Genetic influence depends on environmental context, and environmental influence depends on genetic potentialities.

7. Researchers use a number of methods to study human development. In an **experiment** they deliberately control conditions so as to rule out all other influences on behavior except the one being studied. Control in investigating cause and effect is the chief advantage of a laboratory experiment. An alternative to laboratory research is **naturalistic observation,** in which behavior is systematically observed and recorded as it occurs in everyday settings. Another type of observational method is the **natural experiment,** used when a laboratory study is not feasible. In this case researchers compare groups of people whose circumstances differ naturally along the critical dimensions. To observe change over time, developmentalists may use a **longitudinal study,** in which the same group of people is followed over weeks or years. Alternatively, they may conduct a **cross-sectional study,** comparing different groups of subjects at different ages. In an **accelerated longitudinal design** researchers combine both methods by studying several age-groups at the same time and following them across overlapping periods.

2

Theories of Development

To interpret their systematic observations and the information obtained from experiments, developmental psychologists have proposed theories that provide a framework for explaining how children develop. Theories are used to organize information on behavior and developmental change gathered from studies and to guide research. Theories present a cohesive view of our knowledge about child development and also identify areas that require additional study.

In this chapter we introduce some of the theories used to account for the qualitative changes observed as children grow. As we discussed in Chapter 1, all developmental theorists must take some stance on how genetic and environmental influences combine to guide development. Therefore, we start our discussion by examining the historical viewpoints that have influenced modern theorists in determining the roles of heredity and environment in development. We then identify those areas in which modern researchers are in agreement and the areas subject to ongoing debate. Following that, we turn to the role of theory in explaining development and describe how different theories interpret behavioral changes.

Development is characterized by qualitative change as well as continuous or quantitative change. *(Erika Stone/Peter Arnold, Inc.)*

We next consider some of the theories psychologists have offered to explain why development takes the course it does. Are children driven by powerful urges, as Sigmund Freud argued? What makes a baby strive to master a puzzle or acquire a new skill? In this chapter we start providing answers to these and similar questions.

BACKGROUND FOR MODERN THEORIES OF DEVELOPMENT

Historical Viewpoints on Heredity and Environment

As you read in Chapter 1, Darwin's theory of evolution and his hypothesis that natural selection favors transmission of traits that promote survival of a species have had a strong influence on the way many modern theories of development account for the biological basis for behavior. They have also influenced theoretical accounts of the significance of environment, for Darwin viewed environment, too, as critical for development: It provides the context for individual development and also determines which genetic traits are favored for transmission across generations. But even before Darwin's pathbreaking work, there was speculation on the roles of heredity and environment in shaping the development of an individual. These ideas did not focus on the evolution of species but on the basic nature of humans and on how to account for the goodness or badness of individual children. They, too, have had a major impact on modern theories of development.

Historically, there have been two lines of thinking about human development, two ways of viewing the process of change from infancy to adulthood. One stems from an outlook expressed by the seventeenth-century English philosopher John Locke. Locke saw the human infant as a *tabula rasa*, a totally blank slate to be written on by experiences that lie ahead. Children, in Locke's view, are neither good nor bad by nature; they become that way by virtue of their environments. If parents raise their children properly, according to Locke, the children will develop into responsible members of society. Today, traces of Locke's ideas can be seen in social learning theory, which we will examine later in this chapter. Social learning theorists stress the importance of rewards, punishments, and other learning experiences in shaping how children act.

Shortly after Locke died, a French philosopher whose ideas helped establish a different viewpoint was born. This Frenchman, Jean Jacques Rousseau, saw children as individuals from the moment of birth. Rousseau also believed that human development unfolds naturally in very positive ways, as long as society allows it to do so. Parents, Rousseau argued, need not shape their children forcibly; they merely have to let **maturation** take its natural course. In this century, Rousseau's idea of a natural unfolding of development has appealed to those who focus on inherited potentials in children and to those who stress normative developmental patterns. Arnold Gesell, who conducted research at Yale during the 1920s and 1930s on children's physical and motor development, is probably the best known of the modern maturational theorists.

Today, few developmentalists point solely to environment *or* maturation when trying to explain children's behavior. Most take an **interactionist view:** They see a role for both inborn factors *and* environment working together. To an interactionist, asking which factor (environment *or* maturation) is responsible for development is the wrong question to ask. It is like asking which factor (moisture *or* low temperature) is responsible for snow. Clearly, both are necessary. Those who stress the inborn factors still study the way in which environment affects inherited differences (e.g., Scarr and Grajek, 1982). Those who emphasize environmental forces still acknowledge that human biology helps create some of the major developmental issues humans face (e.g., Erikson, 1963). As Robert Plomin (1983) has put it, the issue has become not "how much" do heredity and environment influence development but "how" do they together influence development.

Rousseau believed that "primitive peoples," living in the "natural state," are intrinsically good. It is civilization, he thought, that brings out undesirable characteristics in people. *(Irven De Vore/Anthro-Photo.)*

The Common Core of Contemporary Positions

All modern developmental theories share the Darwinian assumption of a common human heredity and common developmental program. No theorist doubts the role of genetic factors in shaping various aspects of human capacity and the basic developmental timetable. In addition, all recognize that characteristics of individuals are influenced by genetic factors. These include physical characteristics such as hair color and height and apparently also mental characteristics such as intelligence and some forms of depression (see Chapters 12 and 16). In animals, it is also easy to demonstrate genetic influences on behaviors such as activity level, and such variations probably exist for humans as well.

At the same time, developmentalists recognize an important role for environment. Environmental factors influence not only psychological development but basic biological processes as well. Monkeys experiencing loss of a parent undergo biochemical changes in the brain that have been linked to depression (McKinney, 1977). When anorexic adolescent girls starve themselves (see Chapter 16), menstruation ceases. Thus, developmentalists generally share the view that both genes and environment powerfully influence behavior and that biology and experience continually interact. You will see this quite clearly when we discuss prenatal development in Chapter 4.

Another widely shared viewpoint is that human beings from the start are *active organisms*. This has two meanings. First, from birth human infants are active participants in their own experiences (Osofsky, 1979; Stone, Smith, and Murphy, 1973). Virtually no researcher currently sees the newborn as a blank slate waiting to be written upon. Infants are born with many capacities for both stimulating and responding to other people. This view of inborn factors interacting with environment is one you will meet repeatedly as you read about specific theories used in the study of children. Second, individual children are viewed as being active in creating their own environment, including the parenting they receive. Thus, inconsistent parenting may promote difficult behavior in the 2-year-old, but difficult behavior in the 2-year-old may at the same time promote inconsistent parenting. This is referred to as **reciprocal determinism** (Bandura, 1985) or **bidirectional influence** (Bell, 1968).

Continuing Theoretical Diversity

Despite a common core of agreement, developmentalists continue to express a wide range of viewpoints concerning how heredity and environment work together. Researchers differ in the relative role they grant to one influence or the other and in their viewpoints on the nature of the interaction. For example, all may believe that a 2-year-old given to frequent tantrums would be difficult to parent, yet they differ widely in their views of the origins of the 2-year-old's behavior. Some researchers may believe it is due primarily to inborn temperament, whereas others may point to previous parenting. Likewise, one developmentalist may argue that infants are largely responsible for creating their own early environments through the impact of their characteristics on parents (Scarr and McCartney, 1983); another may argue that the quality of care experienced transforms the inborn characteristics of the infant and that only after the first months of life does the child play a major role in creating his or her own environment (Sroufe and Fleeson, 1986). Both positions consider genetics and environment, but the relative emphasis is quite different.

Such disparities are not easily settled at the present time. For example, although differences in 2-year-olds are associated with parenting differences, interpretation of this situation is open: The differences among 2-year-olds may have been created largely through experience, and the parenting differences may have been influenced by the child in the first place. At present little evidence suggests that the characteristics of normal young babies influence the quality of parenting (Blehar, Lieberman, and Ainsworth, 1977; Egeland and Farber, 1984; Jacobvitz and Sroufe, 1987), but perhaps some will be forthcoming.

A major reason for the continuing diversity of opinion concerning the roles of heredity and environment is the difficulty of measuring both environment and important human qualities. Demonstrating the presence of genetic influences has been easy. Identical twins, even when reared apart, tend to be more similar on a number of characteristics, including intelligence, than nonidentical twins (Rowe and Plomin, 1978). Similarly, children who are adopted as infants often show the influence of their biological heritage. But until we can better define and measure environments, it is not possible to say whether genetics or environment has a greater or lesser influence, precisely how much influence each factor has, or most important, how genetics and environment interact. Do some children develop better in one kind of environment, others in another? At the same time many human qualities are themselves quite difficult to measure. A child's amount of movement in a room is relatively easy to measure, distractibility and "impulse control" much harder. Harder still

Identical twins, especially those reared apart from each other, have been used to show that many aspects of individual characteristics are influenced by genetic inheritance. *(Sonya Jacobs/ The Stock Market.)*

Jean Piaget (Anderson/
Monkmeyer Press.)

to measure are more abstract qualities such as creativity, confidence, and self-esteem. The influence of heredity on intelligence test performance is rather conclusive (though even here interaction with the environment is important), but the influence of heredity on more abstract qualities is hard to assess. Thus, there remains plenty of room for disagreement and controversy.

Still, agreement exists on the most basic proposition: Human development is powerfully influenced by both heredity and environment. Those who emphasize genetic or biological factors, such as individual differences in temperament or level of maturation, still see a role for environment in modifying these or in allowing behavior to be expressed. And those who stress the role of experience and quality of care look at these factors in the context of human biology.

We now turn to the way theories are used to explain development and then we will describe the features of some significant modern theories.

THE ROLE OF THEORY

In Chapter 1 we noted that psychologists are interested in describing human development. But more fundamentally they also want to explain the changes they observe. In doing so, they propose theories. A **theory** is an organized set of assumptions about how things operate. It is an attempt to account for current observations and to predict future ones. Observations or isolated facts by themselves do not have much meaning. They take on meaning by being interpreted on the basis of some theory.

Recall our example in Chapter 1 of a 3-year-old's selection of a truck and a 6-year-old's choice of a tie as birthday presents for their fathers. The Swiss developmental psychologist Jean Piaget would have explained this developmental change as a decline in egocentrism, a movement away from viewing the world only from one's own perspective. Piaget theorized that children become less egocentric with age; 6-year-olds are fundamentally less egocentric than 3-year-olds, who in turn are vastly less egocentric than 1-year-olds.

The same observation can take on different meanings when viewed through different theories. For instance, part of Sigmund Freud's psychoanalytic theory holds that beginning at around age 4 children strive to be like, or identify with, the parent of the same sex. This **identification** is an indirect way for children to feel they have power in the world. Viewed through Freudian theory, a 6-year-old boy who picks a tie for his father and a similar tie for himself is doing so partly because of identification with his father. Other theories would bring different interpretations to bear on the boy's actions. For example, some would stress that he has learned cultural stereotypes about gender-appropriate behavior. This is why he selects a tie for his father, not an apron, as he might for his mother.

In addition to providing a framework for interpreting facts and findings, theories also serve to guide scientific research. Researchers could explore an infinite number of questions about human development. Theories help them decide which questions are important to ask and, to some extent, how to ask them. For example, if you held the theory that much of individual behavior is determined by heredity, you might give high priority to contrasting people with similar and dissimilar genetic make-ups (twins versus unrelated individuals, for instance). On the other hand, if you thought that experience is a major determinant of behavior, you would conduct studies contrasting people with different histories. A researcher with an interactionist perspective might well try to examine both genetic and environmental variation in the same study.

Theories are evaluated in several ways. First, they must be sensible, plausible, and consistent. They must not contain propositions that are incompatible with each other or make assumptions known to be fallacious. But more than this, they must organize, integrate, and make coherent the body of research findings on child behavior and development, and they must provide a useful guide to further research. It must be possible to derive statements from the theory that are open to disconfirmation; that is, theories must be specific and testable. However, the validity, or usefulness, of a theory in the behavioral sciences usually cannot be decided by one or two critical facts; rather, an ongoing check of findings and a convergence of results are necessary.

No single theory of child development prevails in the field. The reason is that "facts" often can be interpreted in different ways. For example, 1-year-olds differ in the time they spend crying and fussing. This fact is consistent with (predictable from) a wide number of theories of child development, including those that emphasize inborn differences and those that emphasize learning or other environmental influences. A multiplicity of theories exists because different theorists have sought to explain different aspects of development and, in general, have focused on different questions. Piaget's theory and Freud's theory are very different in part because Piaget was trying to explain the child's changing understanding of the world and Freud was trying to explain the origins of emotional disturbance.

In the next section and throughout this book, we describe some of the most significant theories of development and interpret developmental changes according to those theories. It is not possible to include all of the theories that have been proposed to analyze development; instead we will rely on the work of the major developmental psychologists in the preview that follows and in later chapters to explain the developmental process.

THEORIES USED IN THE STUDY OF CHILDREN

Some theories used in the study of children are explicitly developmental. They emphasize the orderly, cumulative, and directional nature of change in children and their behavior over time. These theories receive special emphasis in this book. But other theories are also important to developmental psychology and guide the work of many researchers. These theories are concerned with the changes in child behavior that result from

Sigmund Freud *(ARCHIV/ Photo Researchers, Inc.)*

environmental events and circumstances and the child's accrued experience in processing information. The focus of these latter theories is on continuous, gradual change rather than qualitative, often abrupt change.

Major Developmental Theories

PSYCHOANALYTIC VIEWS

Psychoanalytic theories of human development originated at the turn of the century with the ideas of Viennese physician Sigmund Freud. Freud was clearly influenced by Darwin's ideas concerning humans' animal heritage. Disordered behavior, he thought, results from inadequate expression of basic drives. Freud specialized in diseases of the nervous system, and in his practice he saw women who had developed strange paralyses. These paralyses did not correspond to what was then known about nerve pathways, so Freud believed they were not the result of nerve damage. What is more, when a patient was put under hypnosis, the paralysis often could be made to disappear. Yet these women were not simply faking. They truly felt no sensation in the affected part of the body. If pricked with a pin, for example, they did not react. The symptoms were "real," but they had no direct neurological basis. Clearly, the cause lay in the patients' minds.

Freud originally suspected that the root of this problem could be traced to a traumatic early childhood event, probably a sexual seduction. He believed that this event caused intense feelings, but because the child was immature he or she could not express them. Instead, the child pushed the traumatic memory into the unconscious, or, as Freud said, **repressed** it. In Freud's view, the symptoms of paralysis could be cured if the early trauma could be uncovered and worked through in a form of therapy called **psychoanalysis.**

Freud's genius lay in recognizing the connection between symptoms and anxiety (Loevinger, 1976). He noted that his patients were often free from anxiety and wondered why. His answer was that their symptoms somehow protected them from feelings of distress. This idea is important because it suggests that even abnormal behavior serves some function.

Ultimately, Freud realized that not all of his patients could have been seduced in childhood. Instead, he thought, many of these early seductions may have been imagined. What the patients repressed was not an actual experience but a forbidden wish or impulse. Freud then argued that anxiety results when these repressed childhood wishes threaten to break through into consciousness. If the anxiety becomes too great, the person may defend against it by developing symptoms, such as paralysis. Often these symptoms take a form that prevents the person from engaging in activities that previously helped to arouse anxiety.

Out of his ideas about the causes of emotional problems Freud developed a general theory of psychological development from infancy to adulthood. He argued that in the beginning the human mind consists only of primitive drives and instincts, what he called the **id.** Over the first few years of life, however, the self, the part of the mind that Freud referred to as the I or **ego,** emerges. The ego's major role, as Freud saw it, is to find safe and appropriate ways for the drives of the id to be expressed. The child, in other words, develops the ability to delay gratification of impulses in order to respond to external demands, particularly the demands of parents. At first it is fear of punishment that encourages this new self-control. But then, beginning in the late preschool years, the child develops a **superego,** or conscience. In other words, the child has internalized the parent's rules and values, has made them part of the self. Now the child feels guilty for misbehavior and tries to be "good" even when adults are not around. Note how Freud's theory describes a developmental process: Fundamental changes are taking place, and these changes are orderly, cumulative, and directional.

In Freud's early theory, only a single motive governs behavior: the desire to satisfy biological needs and thereby discharge tension. This overriding desire is called the **pleasure principle.** Of central importance is the amount of frustration or gratification the child experiences as he or she seeks to discharge tension through different body modes in the course of development. Stages of development—oral, anal, phallic, latency, genital—were defined in terms of the primary body organ used to discharge tension at each particular period. And a particular form of disordered development would occur because of frustration or a failure to experience sufficient drive gratification at the particular stage. Thus, for example, early or harsh weaning would frustrate the infant's oral drive. According to Freud's early theory, such frustration of drive expression could result in **fixation.** The person becomes locked in that particular psychological mode and arena of conflict, forever expressing it in symbolic ways. In the case of oral frustration, serious disturbance could result because the oral stage is the very first or foundation one.

Freud's ideas were constantly changing. In his later writings he went beyond the pleasure principle and introduced what can be called a mastery motive (see White, 1959). Freud observed that children do not always try to avoid painful experiences or to discharge tensions. Often they

Erik Erikson *(Olive R. Pierce © 1970/Black Star.)*

deliberately incorporate conflict into their play. For instance, a little boy who has been terrified by a ferocious dog may reenact the trauma, using a toy animal. Painful experiences are also reenacted in children's dreams, as they are in the dreams of adults. In countless ways we all are drawn to our worries and doubts. Freud saw this confrontation of frightening or painful incidents as a way of trying to cope with and overcome our negative emotions.

Psychoanalysts since Freud have dispensed with his primary focus on the id and its pleasure principle. In their view, people are not just relentlessly driven to satisfy biological urges. Instead, these psychoanalysts consider the ego or self a much more independent force, which allows people to be purposeful and active in mastering their experiences. Freud's idea of conflicts centered around different parts of the body has also been replaced. Later psychoanalysts have thought in terms of broader issues and conflicts faced from infancy through adulthood.

Erik Erikson's writings (1963) are representative of these newer approaches. Like Freud, Erikson, assigns a critical role to feelings and social relationships in a person's development. But unlike Freud, Erikson does not subscribe to a set of developmental stages in which a child may become fixated in the absence of sufficient gratification. Instead, Erikson proposes a series of developmental tasks or issues that all people face and resolve in some way. These developmental issues, along with Freud's psychosexual stages, are summarized in Table 2.1. As you can see, Erikson's issues are much broader than Freud's. For example, while Erikson sees feeding as an important arena for infant-parent interaction, he believes that the quality of care involves much more than feeding alone. Playing, rocking, comforting, changing, and bathing are also opportunities for the baby to learn about the responsiveness and dependability of parents. To Erikson it is the overall quality of care that determines whether the child will develop *trust* or *mistrust*. And whatever the developmental outcome, the child still moves forward to later developmental issues. This emphasis contrasts with Freud's early theory in which a person can become symbolically "stuck" at some developmental stage.

In Erikson's theory you can clearly see how previous developmental outcomes set the stage for current ones. For example, if an infant fails to develop a trusting view of the world, he or she may have trouble developing a sense of autonomy during toddlerhood. In contrast, the child who acquires a trust that his or her needs will be met has the confidence to begin venturing out and exercising independence. At the same time, firm limits set by parents during the toddler stage may further serve to consolidate the child's basic trust. In short, each issue is faced in the context of what went before, and each is reworked in the context of subsequent issues. In this book we trace the course of individual adaptation with respect to the major developmental issues of each period.

PIAGETIAN DEVELOPMENTAL THEORY

The psychologist best known for his **theory of cognitive** (mental) **development** is Jean Piaget. Like Freud, Piaget made a major contribution in pointing to basic aspects of development that need to be explained. But instead of focusing on psychological problems, human emotions, and impulse control, Piaget focused on developmental changes in how chil-

TABLE 2.1 **A Comparison of Freud's Psychosexual Stages with Erikson's Broader Psychosocial Stages**

Age	Freud's Psychosexual Stages	Erikson's Psychosocial Stages	Erikson's Developmental Issues
Birth to 1 year	Oral	Basic trust vs. mistrust	Infants learn to trust others to satisfy their needs and therefore develop feelings of self-worth. Infants receiving inconsistent care may grow to mistrust the people in their world.
1 to 3 years	Anal	Autonomy vs. shame and doubt	Children learn to be self-sufficient by mastering tasks such as feeding and dressing themselves, and they begin to separate from their parents. They also learn to conform to social rules. Children who do not develop autonomy may doubt their abilities and their capacity to act on the world and develop feelings of shame.
3 to 6 years	Phallic	Initiative vs. guilt	Expanding on the autonomy developed in the previous stage, children initiate pretend play with peers and accept responsibilities such as helping with household chores. Sometimes these activities create conflicts with other family members, and these conflicts create guilt. Excessive guilt will inhibit initiative; children can resolve the crisis by learning to balance initiative against the demands of others (e.g., parents).
7 to 11 years	Latency	Industry vs. inferiority	Children must master increasingly difficult skills, particularly social interaction with peers and academic performance. Children whose industry enables them to succeed in these areas develop a sense of mastery and self-assurance. Children who do not experience mastery of particular skills feel inferior and shun new activities.
12 to 18 years	Genital	Identity vs. role confusion	Adolescents build on all earlier experiences to develop a sense of self-identity, particularly in relation to their society. Failure to reach this goal may cause confusion in sexual identity, the choice of an occupation, and the roles they perform as adults.
Young adulthood		Intimacy vs. isolation	Young adults strive to form strong friendships and to achieve love and companionship with another person. Individuals who do not develop a strong identity in adolescence may now have difficulty forming friendships and intimate relationships and experience isolation and loneliness.
Adulthood		Generativity vs. stagnation	Generativity includes responsibilities such as raising and caring for children and productivity in one's work. Adults who cannot perform these tasks become stagnant.
Maturity/ Old age		Ego integrity vs. despair	Older adults achieve ego integrity if they can look back on their lives and view life as productive and satisfying. If they view life as a disappointment, despair results.

dren think about the world, in how they mentally represent and organize reality. Under the influence of the Darwinian biological revolution, he made analogies between the growth of the mind (mental structures) and the physical development of individuals, as well as emphasizing the process of adaptation or fit between child and environment. Also, as a young man studying in Paris in the early 1920s, Piaget took a job assisting researchers who were developing standardized intelligence tests. During this work he made a very interesting discovery. Children of a certain age tended to make the same mistakes when taking intelligence tests. Moreover, children of one age made different types of errors from those of younger and older children. Piaget became convinced that as youngsters mature they do not just acquire more facts. Instead, they think in *qualitatively different ways* than they did earlier.

The revolutionary aspect of Piaget's theory is the idea of **qualitative change** in children's thinking at different periods of development. Young infants, for example, "know" the world only through their own actions. They do not understand a ball as a prop for a game; they know it only in the sense that it can be touched, mouthed, dropped, and rolled. Later, knowledge becomes more conceptual. Children now explicitly recognize the similarities between beach balls and tennis balls, between a ball of clay and a ball-shaped piece of fruit. Ultimately, knowledge becomes even more abstract. Teenagers may be able to understand that a ball is a bundle of matter with potential energy. Piaget's major goal was to describe and explain how these fundamental changes in children's thinking occur.

Piaget's Periods of Development.   Piaget divided cognitive development into three major periods, each characterized by its own cognitive structures. By *cognitive structures* Piaget meant the basic ways of thinking that underlie and organize the child's activities. The first of Piaget's three major periods spans the time from birth to roughly 2 years of age; the second ranges from age 2 through approximately age 11; and the third begins at about age 12 and extends through adulthood. The middle period is often divided into two subperiods. Within these major periods Piaget identified various stages, each with its own accomplishments. He argued that these sequences of development are **invariant:** All children go through the periods and stages in the same order, even though their rates of progress may differ. The reason is that attainments in any current period or stage depend on those achieved in prior ones. Prior achievements, in other words, are never lost to the child. Instead, they are integrated into more complex ways of thinking as development proceeds. Thus, Piaget's depiction of cognitive development is orderly, cumulative, and directional.

Piaget's periods of development are outlined in Table 2.2. The first period, extending roughly from infancy to toddlerhood, is called the **sensorimotor period** because during this period the infant understands or "knows" the world largely through perception and action. Looking at, squeezing, and mouthing an object are ways of knowing about it. Such ways of knowing are more direct and action-oriented than thinking about uses for the object or understanding the cohesion of molecules that make it up. Nonetheless, such ways of knowing lead to better understanding and therefore to cognitive growth. While the entire first two years are called the sensorimotor period, dramatic changes take place within the period. These changes mark stages. For example, after about 8 months of age infants can intentionally carry out an action for the purpose of noting its consequences, as in the case of banging a bottle against the side of the crib to reproduce a sound they accidentally discovered. In the second year the toddler can systematically try a number of different actions, singly or in combination. Such advances allow more rapid discovery of the properties of things even before the development of thought or language. The stages of the sensorimotor period will be discussed in Chapter 6.

TABLE 2.2   Piaget's Periods of Development

Age	Period of Development	Cognitive Structures
Birth to 2 years	Sensorimotor	Infants understand the world through perception and action. Abilities expand throughout this period, so that by age 2 toddlers can purposefully combine their actions.
2 to 11 years 2 to 6 years	Concrete Preoperational subperiod	Children master independently acquired skills. Children are able to form mental representations of objects and imagine actions related to them. Thought is egocentric.
7 to 11 years	Concrete operational subperiod	Children are capable of logical thinking. Their imagination is constrained by reality, and they can perform logical operations on concrete objects.
12 years through adulthood	Formal operational	Children develop the ability to reason abstractly.

The next of Piaget's three major periods is called the **concrete period.** During it, children acquire most of the thinking and reasoning skills commonly used in everyday life. Piaget divided the concrete period into two subperiods. In the first, the **preoperational subperiod,** skills are acquired relatively independently of one another. In the second, the **concrete operational subperiod,** skills are organized into a system of logical thinking that greatly expands the child's cognitive capabilities.

The central achievement that distinguishes the preoperational subperiod from the sensorimotor period of infancy is the ability to form mental representations of things and to imagine actions carried out in relation to them. Infants can act only on real, physically present things. They have no imagination in the adult sense. Preschoolers, in contrast, can act on and manipulate mental images. For example, seeing some cookies on a counter that is too high to reach and spotting some large books nearby, a 4-year-old might consider stacking the books on top of one another to form a platform. Such mental manipulations of images are called representational skills. We will discuss preoperational thought further in Chapters 8 and 10.

The concrete operational subperiod, which follows the preschool years, begins at about age 7 and continues through age 11 or so. During this time children learn to constrain their imaginations in keeping with aspects of reality and to use their representational skills to perform certain logical operations on concrete objects. For example, they become able to classify objects into hierarchical categories (all the brown dogs, all the dogs of any color, all the four-footed animals, and so on) as well as to understand the relationships among these categories. At the same time, children acquire the ability to understand certain basic quantitative concepts applied to concrete objects; for example, that putting liquid in

The adolescent has a concern for abstract concepts such as justice and peace that is far beyond that of the child. *(Marilyn Sanders/ Peter Arnold, Inc.)*

containers of different shapes does not change the total volume. Such abilities will be discussed in Chapter 12.

The ability to reason systematically about hypothetical problems and abstract issues emerges in the third of Piaget's major periods, the **formal operational period** (age 12 years and older). Formal reasoning skills allow adolescents to think about many possible outcomes of a situation that do not now exist and perhaps never will. Imagine, for instance, that you pose the hypothetical situation of a worldwide ban on armies. An adolescent with formal reasoning skills would try to think through the full implication for resolving conflicts if nations had no ultimate recourse to force. This ability to reason systematically about hypothetical issues is the same cognitive skill needed to perform scientific studies. In fact, Piaget sometimes investigated its emergence by presenting children of different ages with "experiments" to perform.

Another hallmark of the formal operational period is the ability to think abstractly about concepts such as justice and freedom. Whereas a school-age child might define justice as "following the rules" and freedom as "doing what you want," an adolescent would typically have much more sophisticated ideas about these concepts. We will discuss the emergence of such abstract thinking in Chapter 14.

Piaget's Explanation of Developmental Change.   At the foundation of Piaget's ideas concerning development is a basic assumption about the nature of the child; namely, the child is an active organism. Piaget postulated a "need to function" or, in other words, an innate tendency to exercise **schemes,** the child's ways of knowing and acting upon the world. Thus babies look at, listen to, mouth, and shake objects around them simply because they can. They are biased to do what they can do. Given this assumption plus physical maturation, development is inevitable. The infant will act on the world by using available means. Inevitably, he or she will encounter a task that is not efficiently mastered (as when an infant already holding an object in each hand tries to pick up a third object). Such failures create a state of **disequilibrium,** which will result in adjustments in behavior to achieve a better fit with the environment and, ultimately, a new developmental level.

Piaget used the term **adaptation** to describe the process by which a child adjusts his or her behavior to meet the demands of the environment. Adaptation occurs through assimilation and accommodation. **Assimilation** is the tendency to try to act on or interpret the world through existing schemes or structures (that is, to make the world conform to previously existing ways of acting or believing). For example, upon confronting a tomato for the first time, a child may try to assimilate it into her scheme for "balls" (round, rolls, and so on). The tendency to alter structures to conform with aspects of the environment is called **accommodation.** For example, observing that a tomato does not bounce when tossed against a wall, a child may alter her "ball" scheme to distinguish objects of varying textures. When the child, through acting in the world, encounters new experiences that are not readily assimilated, she experiences disequilibrium and, ultimately, evolves new and more serviceable structures (and a new state of equilibrium). This process is called **equilibration.**

After the infancy period the child acquires another capacity that promotes growth, a capacity known as reflective abstraction. **Reflective abstraction** is a special kind of generalization whereby the child, by thinking about (reflecting on) behaviors, can see the similarity between two problems or apply the solution of one problem to new problems. This is one example of qualitative change—in this case, between infancy and childhood. Reflective abstraction is also the concept that Piaget used to explain how a more advanced level of thinking can emerge from skills at a lower level.

Criticism and Evaluation of Piaget's Theory.   Like all important theories, Piaget's ideas have been criticized. For instance, some are concerned that Piaget's framework does not sufficiently account for unevenness in cognitive development; that is, children often show more advanced thinking in one area than they do in other areas. Kurt Fischer (1980) has argued that rather than being seen as a nuisance, such variation should be made central to any theory of cognitive development. This is another way of saying that researchers should focus on individual differences in the emergence of cognitive capacities, as well as on normative development. Piaget's critics have also pointed out exceptions to his cognitive stages. Sometimes, under certain conditions, children show some intellectual capacity at an earlier age than Piaget observed (Gelman, 1978).

Today many developmentalists believe that behavior is more influenced by circumstances than Piaget's early work implied (Carey, 1985).

Some researchers have argued that cognitive differences between children at different ages may be due partly to differences in the information they possess and their skills in using that information (Chi and Ceci, 1986). This means that younger children can sometimes be given training that will help them perform at the level of older children.

Robbie Case (1985) has provided an ambitious revision of Piaget's theory that, while maintaining many of the strengths of the former theory, attempts to minimize its weaknesses. Our coverage of Piaget's theory in the cognitive chapters of this book will incorporate some of Case's ideas.

Although Piaget's theory is controversial, it has become a benchmark even for those who disagree with it. His is the theory to which other cognitive developmental researchers tend to compare and contrast their own views. And even though various researchers have objected to many of Piaget's specific claims, his general theory provides one of the dominant frameworks for understanding how children's thinking changes with age (Harris, 1983).

BOWLBY'S ADAPTATIONAL THEORY

As we noted earlier, both Freud and Piaget were influenced by Darwinian ideas. An even more direct descendant of Darwin's theory is the **adaptational theory** of Englishman John Bowlby (1982). Bowlby, a major theorist of our time, has tied together the evolutionary focus on adaptation with Freud's emphasis on the importance of early social relations, along with aspects of several other psychological theories.

Bowlby started out by rejecting the idea that human infants become emotionally attached to parents by associating them with the satisfaction of biological needs, such as being fed. Instead, Bowlby argues, the tendency for babies to become attached to available adults is a built-in part of our evolutionary heritage. The tendency of babies to cling to and remain very close to parents arose in our early ancestors because it served the function of protecting the babies from predators. Because our ancestors were long-haired, the grasping reflex of newborns (see Chapter 5) was adaptive; it permitted them to cling to their mothers' hair and thus avoid separation. The infant-parent attachment still develops today, even though predators are no longer a threat, and infant behaviors such as smiling and cooing are as important as clinging. Human biology destines babies to behave in ways that promote closeness with care givers. If an infant becomes separated from the mother, the infant will cry, call, or crawl after her and will continue this behavior until proximity is achieved. Just as a bird continues building a nest until it is completed, infants will show distress and search behavior until they gain access to their mothers. No special drive needs to be assumed.

Bowlby argues that the tendency to form early attachments is genetic in origin. However, he has retained the psychoanalytic idea that the quality of an infant-adult attachment is heavily influenced by the quality of care the baby experiences. Thus, while the human tendency to form attachments is virtually universal, the **security** of those attachments can vary greatly. Some infants are confident that their care givers will be available and responsive to them. These infants are "secure" in their attachments. Others are less certain about care giver availability. These infants are "anxiously attached."

John Bowlby and Mary Ainsworth, who developed a procedure for investigating his theory, discuss attachment research. *(Erik Hesse.)*

According to Bowlby, the security of attachment is influenced primarily by experience. By the end of the first year, the infant has begun to develop generalized expectations of the care giver as available and responsive (or unresponsive) and, in turn, a complementary view of the self as worthy or unworthy of care. Bowlby refers to these expectations as **internal working models** of self and other. Thus, the infant who is anxiously preoccupied about the accessibility of the care giver probably has experienced inconsistent care. The infant who fails to seek the care giver when threatened probably previously experienced chronic rebuff when needs were directed to that care giver, and such an infant will not expect responsiveness from others now. The social expectations individuals build up are "tolerably accurate reflections" of their actual experiential history.

Bowlby also argues that the security of attachment (the nature of the internal working models) influences personality formation and, in particular, the growth of self-reliance. The infant who has experienced responsive care will internalize a model of others as available and self as potent; that is, from responsive care comes the sense that "I can elicit care" and the more generalized sense that "I can affect the environment." In time, securely attached children believe more generally that they can prevail even in the face of stress or adversity. Anxiously attached children, on the other hand, even those who have been pushed toward "independence" for fear of spoiling, will be notably dependent in childhood. The child who is self-confident has an experiential base for that confidence, namely, a history of reliably responsive care.

While retaining the psychoanalytic emphasis on early experiences within the family, Bowlby's theory is distinctive from Freud's in several ways. Bowlby discards Freud's concepts of drive gratification, infantile sexuality, and fixation or developmental arrest. Regardless of the nature of early care, development proceeds. As in Erikson's theory, each child faces the same series of developmental issues. But development proceeds within the framework of previous patterns of adaptation. New experiences are faced and interpreted within the context of previously formed models of self and other. Early experience is of basic importance because each successive adaptation is a product both of the new situation and of development to that point. From C. H. Waddington (1957), Bowlby drew the model of branching developmental pathways (a tree lying on its side) wherein change is always possible but is constrained by the branching pathways previously chosen (see Figure 2.1).

Finally, Bowlby argues that both of Freud's theories of the relationship between early experience and later problems were wrong. Not all people with problems were literally sexually seduced as children, but neither are their problems due merely to their imagination or wishes. Conflicts are the result of actual experience, but the experience needs to be viewed more broadly than simply as sexual seduction. Quality of care in the broad sense is crucial for the individual's sense of well-being.

As we will discuss in several later chapters, the evidence for Bowlby's general theory and for his two more specific predictions is solid. Security of attachment does seem to depend upon responsive care, and differences in attachment security are related to later differences in self-confidence, peer relationships, and general adjustment. Even studies of change in how well children are developing are in accord with Bowlby's theory because these changes are linked to changing family circumstances (Erickson, Egeland, and Sroufe, 1985).

Other Influential Theories

Some theories do not emphasize behavioral reorganization and qualitative change. Rather, they see change as more continuous than qualitative. Two such theories are social learning theory and information-processing theory. Information-processing theorists, for example, argue that what appear to be qualitative changes are actually due to a more gradual expansion of memory capacity and cognitive skills and that children of one age can, in fact, perform similarly to older children under certain circumstances. Both information-processing theorists and social learning theorists also focus on how environmental factors influence expression

Figure 2.1
Bowlby's Model of Developmental Pathways
Change always remains possible, but "choices" at each point are constrained by directions previously taken. The person following path A and the person following path B may wind up being quite similar in their pattern of adaptation despite different directions taken in early life. The people on paths C and D are quite different and perhaps atypical because of extreme directions continually taken.

of children's capacities or behaviors. For example, a child may be mentally ready to master certain kinds of problems (a developmental change), but the specific problems he or she solves often have to do with particular experiences or circumstances (nondevelopmental factors). Similarly, a child may have the capacity to understand the feelings and needs of playmates, but whether he or she actually shows empathy toward others often depends on particular experiences with teachers, parents, and peers. Because children's behavior is partly the result of what they experience on a day-to-day basis and how they process that experience, social learning theory and information-processing theory are important for an overall understanding of child behavior.

SOCIAL LEARNING THEORY

The origins of **social learning theory** are rooted in a school of thought called **behaviorism,** which stresses the study of observable behavior learned through associations. Early behaviorists studied several different kinds of learning, one of which was **classical conditioning,** a process in which a normally neutral stimulus comes to evoke a response when paired with a stimulus that ordinarily evokes the response. The Russian scientist Ivan Pavlov (1927) first demonstrated classical conditioning in his work with dogs. Ordinarily, the smell and taste of food make dogs salivate, a reaction that occurs automatically when sensory receptors are stimulated. In one of his experiments, Pavlov rang a bell each time he presented the dogs with food. Eventually the dogs associated the bell with the food, and the sound of the bell alone, *without* food following it, was enough to elicit salivation. Pavlov had classically conditioned the salivation response to the ringing of the bell, a stimulus that ordinarily does not elicit salivation. As we noted in Chapter 1, the American behaviorist John B. Watson showed that children can learn to fear things through the very same process (Watson, 1928). While an 11-month-old boy named Albert was watching a laboratory rat, Watson struck an iron bar with a hammer just behind the child's ear. The loud noise so startled Albert that he began to cry. After several pairings of the rat and the loud noise, Albert began to respond with fear to the sight of the rat alone.

Another important behaviorist, B. F. Skinner, developed a procedure called instrumental or operant conditioning. Like classical conditioning, **instrumental conditioning** involves learning an association, but the two processes differ. Whereas classical conditioning involves learning an association between two stimuli (the sound of a bell and food, a loud noise and a rat), instrumental conditioning involves learning an association between a behavior and a consequence. For example, when some behavior routinely produces some positive or rewarding consequence, that behavior is likely to be repeated. The consequent event, which changes the likelihood of a behavior's occurring, is called a reinforcement. Thus, if you give a pigeon a bit of grain for pecking at a button, you increase the chances that the pigeon will peck at the button again. As you can see, instrumental conditioning requires greater activity on the part of the organism than does classical conditioning.

Reinforcement is any event that tends to produce repetition of the behavior that immediately preceded it. If a behavior results in an event that increases the likelihood of the behavior, the reinforcement is **positive.**

A parent hugging a child for performing a particular task is positively reinforcing that behavior. On the other hand, a behavior can be reinforced by removing an unpleasant stimulus; this is called **negative** reinforcement. For example, removing a wet diaper when a baby cries would be considered negative reinforcement if, over time, this practice increased the likelihood of the baby's crying when wet. Finally, **punishment,** presentation of a negative event following some behavior, may also affect a child's behavior.

Skinner has shown that through instrumental conditioning and systematic reinforcement of desired actions, animals can be taught to perform elaborate sequences of behavior. For example, a rat may be taught to press a lever to open a doorway, press another lever to let down a drawbridge, cross the bridge and press a lever to open an elevator door, ride up in the elevator, descend a staircase, and finally press a fourth lever to receive a pellet of food. The rat, of course, must be taught this sequence step by step, with reinforcement given for each response that is closer to what is wanted. Behaviorists say that the animal's behavior is being **shaped** through successive reinforcement. In much the same way, it is argued, children may learn to act as adults wish because they are given praise for "good" behavior. While such behavioral change occurs over time, it is not developmental. It is taught bit by bit, independent of the children's ages, reinforced by the consequences they experience.

Although instrumental theory is not concerned with the process of development, it can help explain why children behave in the specific ways they do. For example, it may not shed light on the emergence of peer relations during the preschool years, that is, on why such relationships become significant at this time. This is a fundamental change in children's behavior that is a prime example of development. However, the theory *can* shed light on why a given child tends to interact in a certain way with a particular playmate, especially in specific circumstances. If Brian shares his toys with Kevin when his mother is looking on, it may be in part because she has reinforced this behavior in the past.

Strict behaviorists like B. F. Skinner have tried to argue that positive and negative reinforcement are sufficient to explain how people act. They contend that we do not need to know how Brian feels when receiving praise from his mother or what he anticipates when he offers Kevin one of his toys. All that is needed to account for his actions, according to Skinner, is a knowledge that in the past Brian's sharing has been reinforced.

Modern social learning theorists disagree with this view. They stress the importance of what goes on in a person's mind during the learning process. For instance, Albert Bandura (1977) has been a pioneer in research on learning through observation and vicarious rewards and punishments. He points out that children often learn new behaviors just by watching others perform them, without ever having tried out those new behaviors themselves. In addition, children often receive encouragement or discouragement for actions when they see others rewarded or punished and think about the implications for themselves.

Bandura has demonstrated these important processes in a classic set of studies in which preschoolers watched an adult model hitting a large inflated doll (Bandura, Ross, and Ross, 1963). Whether the model was

By using reinforcement and shaping techniques, it is possible to train animals such as these polar bears to engage in relatively complex behaviors, even things they would never do in their natural environment. Such behaviors are taught step by step and do not require that the animals have an overall understanding of what they are doing. *(Elizabeth Weiland/Photo Researchers, Inc.)*

rewarded or punished influenced the children's behavior. If the model was rewarded, a child was apt to readily imitate what the model had done. If the model was punished, however, a child was likely to imitate the actions only in a different context. Clearly, cognitive processes are important in explaining these results. How children interpret a situation and what consequences they anticipate will greatly affect their behavior. Social learning theorists, such as Bandura, have a much broader view of behavior, and this includes developmental changes in the child's mental capacities.

Another well-known social learning theorist, Walter Mischel, also stresses cognitive factors. Consider his work on what is called delay of gratification, the ability to postpone getting an immediate reward in order to receive a much bigger reward later (Mischel, 1974). What children think to themselves when trying to delay gratification makes an enormous difference. For instance, if children think of a marshmallow as a puffy white cloud, they can keep from eating it much longer (and get a bigger reward from the experimenter) than if they focus on how good that marshmallow would taste. Mischel has found that young children have trouble delaying gratification in this situation because they keep dwelling on the immediate pleasure of eating the marshmallow. They can, however, be taught to refocus their thoughts, a strategy more commonly used by older children. This cognitive strategy helps even younger children increase their self-control. Such findings show that cognitive processes are an important part of learning.

Increasingly, modern social learning theorists are concerned with a variety of cognitive factors. These include self-reinforcement (giving yourself a mental "pat on the back" for doing something well) and self-concept (the mental image that you have of yourself). Bandura especially has stressed that when you think of yourself as capable and effective, you are more likely to try to overcome problems and so master the challenges you face. This is a long way from Skinner's emphasis on acquiring particular responses in particular circumstances. You will encounter modern social learning theory in many chapters of this book.

INFORMATION-PROCESSING THEORY

Imagine two 8-year-old boys who have just been introduced to a new game involving a seesaw and a set of ten weights ranging from one ounce to ten ounces. The game requires each boy, in turn, to place one of the ten weights somewhere on his side of the seesaw to balance it. For example, suppose that one of the boys places the seven-ounce weight two inches from his end of the seesaw. The other boy may initially attempt to balance the seesaw by trial and error. Perhaps by placing the three-ounce weight five inches from his end of the seesaw, he observes that it tilts toward his partner's side. Each time he places a weight on his side of the seesaw, he watches what happens until finally he becomes quite good at the game. He discovers that he can balance the seesaw either by placing a smaller weight than the one used by his partner closer to his end or by placing a heavier weight than the one used by his partner further away from the end of the seesaw. But the ratio of sizes and distances is governed by a precise formula that children must eventually induce to balance the seesaw perfectly without trial and error. What accounts for the boys' eventual mastery of this calculation?

A social learning theorist would say that the boys' increasing accuracy was reinforced by the satisfaction derived from closer and closer approximations to immediate balance. This perspective is particularly helpful in understanding the two boys' motivation to keep trying to master the seesaw game. It does not, however, tell us how they actually figured out which side of the seesaw will tilt. **Information-processing theory** was developed to provide insights into such solutions. As the name implies, this perspective sees the human being as an information-processing system analogous to a computer but even more complex. Like a computer, a person first *inputs*, or takes in, raw information. (In the above example the two boys intially input data about weights and distances and their effect on the seesaw.) Then the person must engage in *processing* this information by making critical comparisons and adjustments. For ex-

When children play on a seesaw, a smaller child can hold a larger child up, but only by sitting at the very end and with the larger child near the center. With experience, children learn this principle. Information-processing theorists are interested in the steps leading to such discoveries. *(Tom Dunham.)*

ample, to balance the seesaw perfectly, the boys must intuitively arrive at a solution that relies on the physical principle of torque, that is, the greater force of weight at a distance. The side with the greater torque will tilt down, and if the torques are equal, the seesaw will balance. The end result is a rule, or **algorithm,** that yields a final *output* to the problem that was induced from numerous adjustments to the input data. Information-processing theory has attempted to specify the precise steps children take in moving from input to output.

Information processing is a general approach to understanding human intelligence. It has been applied not only to problem solving but to memory, decision making, concept formation, and many other cognitive activities. In terms of the overall subject that information-processing researchers study, their focus is somewhat similar to that of Piaget. However, whereas Piaget sought to identify the *general* modes of thinking that children of different ages use, information-processing psychologists seek to describe in detail each of the various steps involved in performing a mental task.

Researchers who take an information-processing perspective have offered some interesting theories about why children's cognitive performance improves with age. For instance, if you asked a 4-year-old to play with the seesaw, he would *not* be able to master it. Instead, he would simply arrange the weights at random, balancing the seesaw only occasionally, purely by accident. Why this difference in what a 4-year-old and an 8-year-old can accomplish? Robert Siegler (1983), a pioneer in the application of the information-processing view to children's reasoning, has proposed that as children grow older they become able to perform a wider array of operations on the information they input. Chief among the new operations they are able to carry out are procedures called heuristics. **Heuristics** are rule-of-thumb strategies that provide general approaches to solving problems. According to Siegler, the 8-year-old possesses heuristics that the 4-year-old lacks, which is why he succeeds where the younger boy fails.

Other information-processing researchers have explained cognitive development as the gradual removal of limitations on working memory. **Working memory** is what we use to hold the perceptions, images, and concepts we are actively considering at any given moment in consciousness. In people of all ages, the capacity of working memory is limited; we can hold just so much information in consciousness at any one time. This can impose constraints on our ability to solve complex problems in which many things must be held in working memory at once. Robbie Case (1985) has suggested that in very young children the amount of working memory space available to solve problems is much smaller than it is in adults. As children mature, this space increases, allowing more complex thinking and problem solving. An alternative view is that practice and experience play important roles in how efficiently working memory is used. According to this view, as children become more familiar with a task, they learn to group bits of related information into a single "chunk," which is then processed as a whole. As Figure 2.2 illustrates, this chunking reduces the demands on working memory, leaving more room for other data and enabling more complex thought (Case, 1985). We

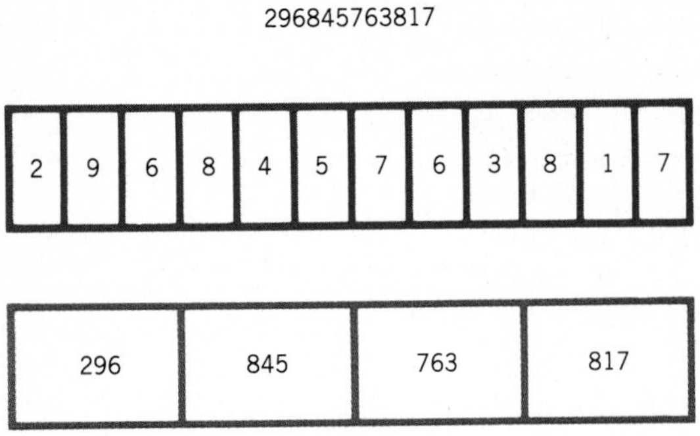

296845763817

2 9 6 8 4 5 7 6 3 8 1 7

296 845 763 817

Figure 2.2
Illustration of Working Memory
If you were to read five of these numbers in rapid succession to a friend, he or she would have little trouble repeating them back to you. Your friend could probably repeat six or seven numbers, although repeating eight becomes much harder. If you read the numbers slowly, one second apart, he or she could repeat eight more easily, and some people could repeat nine or ten numbers. If you gave your friend more time and grouped the numbers in bunches of three, he or she could probably repeat all twelve. These facts illustrate the limits of working memory and the advantage of chunking.

will return to both these views when we discuss cognitive development during infancy in Chapter 6.

A general information-processing model of cognitive development has been proposed by D. Klahr and J. C. Wallace (1976). They argue that the human information-processing system is organized into three subsystems: the *input subsystem*, which consists of perception and attention; the *goal-setting and planning* subsystem; and the *learning subsystem*, which modifies the mental operations a person can perform. The most important subsystem with regard to development is the learning one, for it enables acquisition of new thinking and problem-solving strategies.

The information-processing perspective can be applied to social development as well as to cognitive development. For example, a considerable amount of current research concerns how parental beliefs and attributions (capacities they think children have) influence parenting behavior (Elder and Caspi, 1986; Luster, 1985). The way parents interpret child behavior, researchers suggest, influences how parents will treat children. For example, as children develop, parents interpret their behavior as more purposeful and deliberate and hence have different expectations for them (Dix et al., 1986). Particular interpretations of parents may also be influential. Parents who believe children develop through their own initiative allow their offspring more response options in laboratory teaching tasks and presumably in nonlaboratory settings as well (Skinner, 1985). Finally, adults' preconceptions about children influence their perceptions of behavior; for example, if led to believe the infants they are viewing were born prematurely, adults rate them as less able (Stern and Hildebrandt, 1984). Recently, Urie Bronfenbrenner (1986) has reviewed the scientific literature of the past 30 years and concluded that parental beliefs act to both moderate and mediate children's social-emotional development. More will be said about this later.

Comparing Theories

Danny, a preschooler, is in the living room while a baby, who is just visiting, is sleeping in Danny's bedroom. Suddenly the visiting baby begins to cry. Danny goes into the kitchen, picks up the baby's bottle, and carries it off to the bedroom. Without even taking a sample from the bottle himself, he puts the nipple into the baby's mouth. When the baby moves her head and the nipple slips out, Danny readjusts it. Finally, the baby quiets and begins to suck, but soon the nipple slips again and the bottle falls to the floor. Danny picks up the bottle and puts it in her mouth again. (Adapted from Radke-Yarrow and Zahn-Waxler, 1984.)

What explains Danny's empathy for the hungry baby—his seeming ability to feel and understand the younger child's distress? Let's briefly compare the five major theories we have just described by seeing what each has to say in answer to this question. Theorists from all five positions would agree that empathy is part of the basic human program, but they would differ in their particular explanations of how it emerges.

Classical Freudian theory claims that empathy stems from controlled and redirected sexual and aggressive urges, motivated at first by fear of losing parental love. In learning to inhibit aggressive impulses and to convert sexual desires to caring behaviors toward the parent, a child develops the basic ingredients for empathy. However, contemporary psychoanalytic thinkers put far less stress on primitive urges as motivators of behavior than Freud did. Most would emphasize instead the role of identification in the emergence of empathy. Through experience, Danny is learning to associate discomfort in others with his own pain; he is, in short, learning to identify with others. In showing caring for the distressed child, he is at first giving what he himself would need.

Piaget would take a different approach to explaining Danny's behavior. He would focus on the cognitive capacities that underlie it, particularly role-taking capacity. Role-taking capacity is the ability to take the perspective of another person. To show true empathy Danny must understand that the baby has a perspective different from his own, that the baby can be feeling things that he is not feeling. The baby is hungry and upset even though Danny is not. Danny must also have some understanding of what the baby is experiencing in this particular situation and of what she might need to reduce her distress. Children younger than Danny often show the beginnings of empathy for others, but their thinking is still very self-focused. To a crying baby they might bring *their* teddy bear or *their* mother because these are the things that would comfort *them*. By the preschool years, however, children are much more likely to bring what the *other* person needs.

John Bowlby's adaptational theory also sheds light on empathy, but unlike Piaget's theory it stresses the child's history of relationships with others. Bowlby points out that infants typically are born into a responsive care-giving system: Their cries of distress and other signals elicit comforting responses from parents. While initially infants are mere recipients of responsive care, in time they play an increasingly active role. The infant purposefully signals to the parent and anticipates a response. Through actively participating in such a system, a child develops positive expectations regarding other people, as well as an understanding of responsive personal relationships. The child gains a relational understanding of empathy. Through his responsive relationship with his parents, Danny develops confidence in his ability to elicit care and master his environment. At the same time, he develops an understanding of responsiveness and a disposition to be involved with others. With cognitive

What explains aggressive behavior among young children? Is it related to their limited understanding of alternative ways of resolving problems or their limited understanding of the other's point of view? Is it influenced by the history of care—for example, a history of rejection and hostility? Have the children been reinforced for aggression by getting what they want? Do genetic, temperamental, or hormonal differences play a role? Is it some combination of these? Different theories suggest different answers to the question. *(Marion Faller/ Monkmeyer Press.)*

maturation during the preschool years, he is able to recognize the needs of others and becomes an initiating partner in caring exchanges.

In Bowlby's theory, a child learns responsiveness by being part of a responsive system; he or she learns to care through being cared for. This approach is different from the social learning perspective, which emphasizes more direct and specific teaching of empathy for others. Social learning theorists would argue that Danny's parents have provided him with models of caring behavior. In situations similar to the one Danny experienced, they have probably offered a bottle and comfort to a crying infant. The parents may also have given Danny praise and attention when he did something kind for others. As with Bowlby's theory, social learning theory would also stress that the child has learned that he can be effective and so takes action.

Information-processing psychologists take yet another perspective. They would want to understand the mental steps involved in Danny's decision to help the baby. Some would try to analyze in detail how Danny perceived and attended to the baby's cries, how he interpreted those cries as meaning hunger, how he formulated the plan of getting the baby's bottle, and how he determined the best way to carry out that plan. Other information-processing psychologists would argue that Danny is able to coordinate all these different mental steps because of an increased capacity in his working memory. A younger child, in contrast, probably could not keep in mind all the various thoughts and perceptions needed for Danny's response.

Each of the perspectives reviewed here has value in understanding empathy, but each in its own way also has limitations. Freud can be criticized for stressing negative motivations (fear of losing love) and for relying on difficult concepts such as identification. Piaget can be faulted for focusing on cognitive factors and relatively neglecting emotional ones. Just because a person understands that someone else is in distress, this is no guarantee that the person will offer help. The perspective derived from Bowlby's theory can also be criticized for being too sketchy and not yet fully tested. Social learning theory can be faulted for its relatively narrow focus and because it often gives the impression that each behavior is learned in isolation. Information-processing theory, too, is open to criticism because it tends to downplay human motivations and because some of its concepts have not yet been demonstrated through research. Clearly, none of these theories alone provides the whole answer to Danny's behavior. That is why you should not think of them as either-or propositions. Instead, it is more useful to consider them as complementary viewpoints that together provide a very rich understanding of why children behave as they do.

Chapter Review

1. Historically, there have been two lines of thinking about human development. One is the belief that how a child develops is largely the result of environmental factors and individual experiences. The other is the idea that development is largely the product of a natural unfolding through **maturation.** Today most developmentalists take an **interactionist view:** They see environmental forces and physical maturation influencing each other. Charles Darwin's evolutionary theory is a major influence in this perspective.

2. Observations about children take on meaning by being interpreted on the basis of theories. A **theory** is an organized set of assumptions about how things operate. It is an attempt to account for current observations and to predict future ones. Theories give direction to scientific research.

3. Among the specific developmental theories used in the study of children are **psychoanalytic theories** dating back to Sigmund Freud. Out of his ideas about the causes of emotional problems, Freud developed a general theory of psychological development. He saw the mind as consisting of three parts: the **id** (our primitive drives and instincts), the **ego** (what we

think of as the self), and the **superego** (our conscience). In Freud's early view, a need to satisfy biological urges, called the **pleasure principle,** was the overriding human motive. Freud argued that if requirements imposed by parents unduly thwarted a child's basic strivings, the child could become symbolically locked in that particular psychological conflict, a state Freud called **fixation.** Freud in his later years and psychoanalysts since then have dispensed with his primary focus on the pleasure principle. Instead, they have thought in terms of broader issues and conflicts faced from infancy through adulthood.

4. The psychologist best known for his **theory of cognitive development** is Jean Piaget. Piaget was among the first to argue that qualitative changes occur in children's thinking as they grow older. He proposed that a basic force underlying cognitive development is a process called **equilibration,** in which harmony is restored between some aspect of the world and a child's strategy or **scheme** for dealing with it. When one of a child's current schemes fails to get results, the child must alter his or her behavior to fit the situation. This process of **assimilation** and **accommodation** restores equilibrium and broadens a child's understanding of the world. Assimilation and accommodation allow the child to **adapt** or adjust to the demands of the environment. As children move beyond infancy, they become capable of **reflective abstraction.** This is the ability to see the similarity between two problems or applications of the solution of one problem to new problems.

5. **Adaptational theories** of development can be seen clearly in the ideas of John Bowlby. Bowlby believes that the tendency for babies to become attached to parents is a built-in part of our evolutionary heritage. It is a behavior humans have acquired through natural selection, the process by which capacities that aid in survival are favored in future generations. To this basic biological perspective, however, Bowlby has added ideas from both psychoanalytic and cognitive theories. His approach is a truly integrated one. Bowlby theorizes that self-reliance develops from the **internal working models** of the self and others that an infant builds on the basis of the responsiveness of the care he or she receives in the first years of life.

6. An influential theory that does not emphasize behavioral reorganization and qualitative change is **social learning theory,** which has its roots in the school of thought known as **behaviorism.** Early forms of social learning theory emphasized association learning, either **classical conditioning,** in which individuals can learn to associate two stimuli that were previously unrelated, or **instrumental conditioning,** in which individuals associate stimuli with specific behaviors. **Reinforcement** changes the likelihood of a behavior's occurring and allows behavior to be **shaped.** Contemporary social learning theorists place greater emphasis on the cognitive factors involved in human learning. The child's expectations and inner beliefs influence how he or she performs.

7. A final perspective in the study of children is **information-processing theory.** It seeks to describe in detail the mental steps involved when people solve problems, make decisions, store and retrieve information, and so forth. Proponents of this view compare human cognitive capabilities to the functioning of computers. They have offered ideas about what changes with development to account for the observable changes in children's thinking.

8. The various theories used in the study of children should not be thought of as either-or propositions. It is more useful to view them as complementary perspectives that together can help us understand children's behavior.

Part One

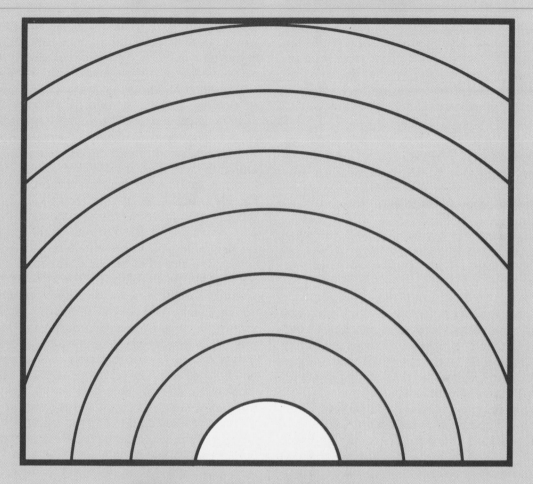

Beginnings

To illustrate the important role played in development by the context surrounding the child we introduce you here to three families, each with different circumstances. We will follow these families throughout the book, to show how changing patterns of family life can influence individual development. While the families are fictionalized, they derive from research in developmental psychology, and they make the theories, methods, and research findings more concrete and more understandable.

Introducing Three Families

John and Dolores Williams

"Three twenty-two, four seventy, sixty-eight cents. . . . Your total is eighty-nine dollars and nineteen cents," the mechanical voice announced.

"Will you listen to this, DeeDee. A talking cash register. What will they think up next? Maybe a substitute for your money. Push a button and money for groceries comes out of thin air. That would be the end of all your worries, baby." John Williams laughed and squeezed his wife, Dolores, affectionately.

"Eighty-one cents is your change. Thank you for shopping at Saver's Mart. Come again soon and have a nice day," spieled the disembodied voice while the check-out girl stared blankly out from strands of lank blond hair.

Dolores Williams was not amused. The way food prices were going up she wondered how they'd be able to feed their family even with her job at the phone company. Of course, 8-year-old Teresa didn't eat much; and Momma Jo and Denise, John's mother and sister, both helped out with the grocery money as best they could. But 11-year-old John, Jr., ate like a horse.

"You're always joking," DeeDee said to her husband as he pushed the cart of groceries toward the car. "I don't see one thing to laugh about. Did you see the price of diapers? We might as well diaper this new baby in dollar bills. I don't know how we're going to manage. What a mistake this whole thing is."

"A mistake?" John asked, stopping to look at DeeDee. "What do you mean a mistake? Were you a mistake? Was I a mistake? My momma had nothin' when my poppa died. She could hardly afford to feed herself let alone two kids. How much do you think black teachers were paid in Mississippi in those days? But she worked hard and she did it. She earned enough to move us here to Chicago and things got better. She always said we could do it if we put our minds to it, and she was right."

DeeDee looked at him doubtfully. She didn't want to struggle like John's mother had. Already she felt tired. Too tired even to try.

"Honey," said John more gently now, "you know we've been over this. We made this baby together, and together we'll see that he gets paid for. It's going to work out. You've got to take things a step at a time. Remember what I told you. Never look back; keep on steppin'. Look for an opening, baby. There's a way to make it."

DeeDee looked at John and started to smile but a squeal of brakes made her quickly turn around. A small crowd was gathering around a young woman who lay on the pavement. She was trying to prop herself up, but her ankle was oddly twisted. Her arms and legs looked frail and thin next to her obviously pregnant belly. "The baby," she said. "My God, the baby."

DeeDee stared. She was struck by the thought of losing a baby, of having a child slip away before you could even see it and hold it. Of course she wanted this baby. It was part of her already, part of both her and John. She wanted it more than anything else in the world.

The driver was bending over the injured woman. "Are you all right? I was just backing up. I was watching, I swear to God I was. But you fell into the car. Are you OK? Someone call a doctor. For God's sake, get an ambulance here!"

DeeDee felt an urge to go to the woman, to try to comfort her. But what would this white woman think of a black woman, a stranger, stepping out of the crowd? DeeDee didn't care. She walked over and knelt beside her. "You'll be OK," she said. "You didn't fall very hard. I think it's just your ankle. Why don't you lie back on my sweater here and try to relax. Someone's gone to call an ambulance."

The woman's head sank into the green of

DeeDee's sweater. "Thank you," she said softly. "It's just . . . It's just . . . This is my first baby."

"I know," said DeeDee. Her voice was almost a whisper. "You don't have to explain to me. I'm pregnant too."

The woman looked at DeeDee and smiled. She reached out her hand and lightly touched DeeDee's wrist. Though DeeDee knew it wasn't possible at such an early stage, she had the sense that she could feel the new life inside her.

Frank and Christine Gordon

"Way to go! Strike that turkey out! What an arm that guy has," exclaimed Frank Gordon as he rose from his chair in front of the TV set to reach for another beer. Dan and Chuck grinned in agreement. Like everyone else in Pawtucket, Rhode Island, they were Red Sox fans.

"Hey, Paula. Game's over. Let's get goin'," Dan shouted to his wife five minutes later.

"Yeah, we're gonna shove off too," Chuck added. "I gotta be on the job early tomorrow."

The three men sauntered into the kitchen, leaving behind them a chaos of pizza cartons, beer cans, and potato chip bags. Their wives were seated around the small kitchen table, laughing and talking over mugs of coffee.

"You'd think you girls never got to see each other the way you go on," Frank commented with a smile, as he tossed Dan and Chuck their jackets. Then Paula and Sarah went into the back bedroom, each to collect a sleeping child.

"See ya soon, Chrissie," they said to their sister, as they picked their way down the dimly lit back steps. As usual, Dan and Chuck were already in their cars, revving the engines.

Generally, on a weeknight after a baseball game, Frank would head for the bedroom, leaving Christine to clean up. But tonight he hung around. "You're lookin' good, Chrissie," he said, catching hold of her arm as she passed by. "You could get in trouble lookin' like that."

"I don't know that I want to get in trouble," Christine answered with an uneasy laugh, knowing exactly what Frank had in mind. "You know I'm not so sure about having another baby just yet."

"What do you mean not so sure? We have two girls; we want a boy. You've said so yourself. It's as simple as that."

"Yeah. Well, I know. But . . . Well, I've been kind of thinking about maybe getting a job at the dress shop where Paula works and. . . ."

"Oh jees, here we go again. Look, Chrissie, I'm not gonna get into another big thing about this. I don't want you workin' and that's that. You belong here at home with the kids. I can support this family just fine."

"That's not really it, Frank," Christine replied. "I was watching this program on TV this morning, you know? And they were talking about how important it is for a woman to have a sense of really doing something, you know? Accomplishing something. . . ."

"So selling dresses to a bunch of broads is accomplishing something and raising your own kids isn't? Is that what you're tryin' to tell me? I swear I can't figure you out. What more do you want for accomplishment? You've got two daughters, a nice apartment, a bunch of fancy gadgets in the kitchen. What's this job of yours gonna get us that we don't already have? Tell me that. I'll tell you what it's *not* gonna get us. It's not gonna get us a son."

"Well, I don't know," Christine answered. "You know, I just think it's something we have to talk about more, kind of work out more."

"So we're talkin' about it now. What more do you want?"

Christine wondered what more she did want. It wasn't something she could put her finger on. Just a vague idea about someday having her own dress shop. Everyone said she had a real flair for clothes. She could make an old dress look terrific with nothing more than a new belt or an inexpensive piece of jewelry. But when she tried to picture getting from her life as it was now to the running of her own business, the whole thing seemed impossible. If I had really wanted to be a businesswoman, Christine thought, I wouldn't have been so quick to marry Frank right after high school.

Christine looked at her wedding picture on top of the TV set. A thin, pretty girl of 19 looked back from beneath a lacy white veil. Beside her was Frank, with an air of self-assurance even at 24. The happiest day of her life, she had thought back then. Frank was so handsome he was the envy of all her friends. Christine's father, Mike, had encouraged the match. He said that Frank was the first "real man" Christine had dated. "He's not like some of those college wimps you've brought home lately," he told her. "You'd be crazy not to hang onto that guy." And hang on Christine did. She built her life around Frank—around his strength, his decisiveness, his self-confidence. He made this once shy girl feel like the most desirable woman on earth. Christine gave up college plans because Frank had told her he wasn't willing to wait. What did she need college for anyway? Nothing but Frank had mattered to her then. It had all seemed so perfect.

"You know what more I want?" Christine asked, staring down at the carpet and slowly looking up. "I want us to feel real close. Remember? Like we used to?"

"Hey. We're married. Seven years. What more close is there?"

"Well, there's having another baby together I guess," Christine answered with a faint smile. "Raising a little all-star for the Red Sox. What more could you accomplish than that, huh?"

"Now you're thinkin' right!" Frank said, failing to notice the lingering touch of doubt in her voice. "That's my babe talkin'."

Karen Polonius

When the bell rang announcing the end of class, 16-year-old Karen Polonius quickly gathered up her books and was the first person out the door. She practically ran down the corridor to her locker. She whirled the combination and tugged open the door, revealing her blue nylon jacket, a jumble of old notebooks, one worn-out pair of tennis shoes, and an impressive array of discarded candy wrappers. Grabbing her jacket, she rushed out the door and managed to jump on the number 6 bus just as it was about to pull away. Karen slid into a window seat, unwrapped a piece of gum, and stared aimlessly at the passing sidewalks. All too soon she reached her stop. Making her way to the rear exit, she got off and walked the two short blocks east. Here she was. There was no more putting it off. Taking a deep breath she stepped inside the building. The sign overhead read: FRESNO FAMILY PLANNING CLINIC.

Karen was no stranger to this place. Six months ago, when she and her boyfriend, Jeff, had first started making love, he had insisted that she begin taking birth-control pills. All the girls at school knew that this was a place a teenager could come without any disapproving remarks or glances. So she had come to the clinic and gone on the pill. But what good had it done her? Forget a few days and she could *still* become pregnant. Well, maybe she wasn't. In a little while she might find out it was just a mistake. Karen began nervously poking through a stack of magazines, waiting to be called. *Newsweek, Redbook, McCall's*—didn't they ever change these things? Ah, here was a new one—*Modern Bride*. Boy, how ironic.

Karen felt numb as she sat in Dr. Rich's office, listening to his sympathetic voice. "As I see it, Karen, you have several choices. You can go through with the pregnancy and give up the baby for adoption. . . ." This can't be happening, Karen thought. It's *got* to be a mistake. Dr. Rich's voice droned on: "At this early stage there would be little risk to you in removing the products of conception, but going this route would of course depend on your personal beliefs. . . ." What did he mean by "the products of conception"? Does he mean the baby? He *must* mean the baby. The trip home was a total blur for Karen. All she could remember clearly was fumbling in her bag for her keys as she stood on the doorstep. Thank God her mother wasn't home from work yet. She could go upstairs and try to get herself together.

Maybe Mom won't even notice anything's the matter, Karen thought to herself as she flopped onto her bed. Mom was always preoccupied these days, trying to sell those dumb houses to those stupid people. Well, maybe she shouldn't knock it. It hadn't been easy for Mom after the divorce. Dad was almost always late with the support payments, and sometimes he didn't even bother to send them at all. "What did I tell you? Men are no damn good. They only think about themselves," Karen's mother would say. "I hope Mom's not right," Karen prayed as she phoned Jeff to tell him that she had to see him that night.

Karen wasn't sure how Jeff would react when she broke the news but she wasn't prepared for what happened. Jeff, usually so cool and easygoing, panicked. Karen's mention of possible marriage only made things worse.

"Married? Are you crazy?" Jeff shouted. "I'm not ready to get married. I don't know about you, but *I'm* going to college. And what about law school, huh? I'm not gonna ruin my life!" They drove in silence. "Let me tell you, Karen," Jeff said as they pulled up in front of her house, "if you keep trying to push this fatherhood thing on me, I'll swear it's not my kid."

So much for Mr. Wonderful, Karen thought bitterly. Mom *was* right. Men are no damn good. All they want is a good time. But what was she going to do? Have an abortion? She didn't think she could. As a little girl she had cried for two days when her mother took the cat to the vet to be spayed. No, abortion was out. She couldn't destroy her own baby. But what then? Adoption? Wouldn't that be like giving away a part of herself? It took Karen two weeks to summon the courage to tell her mother what the problem was. By then she had decided: She was going to keep the baby.

Karen's mother was incredulous. She just stood there with the potato peeler poised in midair, as if she couldn't believe what she was hearing. Then she got angry. "How could you do such a dumb thing? Didn't I tell you to be careful when you went out with that guy? Well, you can't keep the baby."

Karen exploded. She was sick and tired of people telling her she was crazy or ridiculous. "Damn it, Mom! It's *my* body, *my* baby. I have the right. For once in my life I'm going to make a decision without other people telling me what to do. Make love! Get pills! Have an abortion! I've had it with all of you. I'm going to love my baby and my baby is going to love me. And nobody's ever going to hurt my baby the way they've hurt me!" Karen was crying now and nearly hysterical. She ran out the back door, her mother calling, "Karen, come back here!"

Three Children in Context

Three human children will soon be born, each of whom will encounter different circumstances, helping to shape that child's life. John and DeeDee's will face economic struggles and the challenges of being black, growing up in an inner city. This child, however, will also be born into a very supportive family characterized by strong ties of love and commitment. Although at first DeeDee voices reservations about having another child in their economic circumstances, she feels deep down that the baby is a cherished addition to their lives. Christine Gordon is more ambivalent about having another baby. Nevertheless, she finally agrees to become pregnant, largely to give Frank the son he wants. Christine hopes that a son will help provide a feeling of closeness in their marriage. Whether boy or girl, this child will be born into a family-centered environment where traditional sex roles are accepted as the "natural order" of things. Karen Polonius, in contrast, does not even have a chance to try out the traditional role of a wife. The baby she has conceived will be born to a mother who herself is still in many ways a child. Inexperienced at motherhood and lacking emotional support from others, Karen faces a difficult time ahead.

How the course of development is influenced by surrounding circumstances is a major concern of this book. The fictional characters you have just met face different situations, which in turn will affect their children. We have intentionally avoided portraying three families that are radically different. All three families live in urban America, none of them is wealthy, none is bilingual, and none is pursuing an alternative life style, such as communal living. But even with this common ground, enough differences exist among them for each to raise a child in many ways different from the others. Our hope is that by reading about the lives of these three children, you can better appreciate the family's influence on individual development.

We also hope you will discover the two-way interaction between child and environment. While children are affected by the circumstances around them, they also influence those circumstances. Thus, as a child's individual style emerges over time, that style has an impact on those important in the child's world. Lives unfold amid a constant interplay of person and environment. You will witness this process in the lives of our three children.

3

The Contexts of Development

I f you want a seed to develop into a normal, healthy plant, you must provide it with rich soil and appropriate amounts of light and moisture. The quality of its environment will determine how well it matures and flourishes. The development of all living things occurs within a context, and the composition of that context influences the course of development. This is as true of humans as it is of other species. Human development, both physical and psychological, requires an appropriate context for its unfolding. If that context is abnormal, development may be too.

For example, years ago orphaned infants were sometimes raised in very sterile institutions, with almost no physical or social stimulation. The babies were fed and kept clean, but most of the time they were left alone, with little to look at or touch. No one talked to them, played with them, or gave them loving attention. These children soon became apathetic, unresponsive, and withdrawn (Spitz, 1945). In other words, they lacked the physical and social stimulation our species requires. Many even died. Of course, with this kind of uncontrolled observation it is difficult to tell what caused the high death rate. Perhaps the babies were less healthy to begin with or more prone to disease because of crowded conditions. On the other hand, perhaps the absence of a normal environment made these children unusually vulnerable. Recent follow-up studies of children separated from parents before age 4 and reared in institutions show long-term negative outcomes, especially with regard to peer relations and parenting (Rutter, in press).

Other evidence suggesting that infants require an appropriate environment for normal development comes from the occasional discovery of a child who has been isolated from human contact. One such child was Victor, who was captured in a French forest in 1799. Despite intensive efforts at rehabilitation, he remained abnormal in all respects. More contemporary is the case of Genie, who from the age of one was restricted to a small room. There her emotionally unstable father harnessed her in a sitting position during the day and often bound her in a cagelike crib at night. When discovered at the age of 13 she was physically deformed and underdeveloped (from being kept so confined), and she also was seriously retarded in every area of human functioning. In time Genie made some improvements in physical and intellectual development, including modest use of language. However, she remained severely handicapped in establishing social relationships (Curtiss, 1977; Ruch and Shirley, 1985).

It is hard to say at this time whether the results of early environmental deprivation are reversible or irreversible. Victor improved very little, but perhaps he was abandoned because he was seriously abnormal in the first place. Genie improved more, especially in mastery of cognitive skills, but she may have had considerable language stimulation in the first two years. The point is that neither of the studies of these children was an experiment (with normal children assigned to deprivation) and neither used a prospective (forward-going) longitudinal design; that is, measurements were not made before the deprivation began. Therefore, many questions remain. We do not know, for example, whether Genie began acquiring some language because she was mentally more sound than Victor, had more early language experience, or had better teaching. Still, it does seem clear that normal human development depends on environmental support. More recent studies of the effects of early deprivation are presented in Chapter 7.

Even short of such extreme circumstances, the context in which a child grows strongly influences how that child develops. Imagine two children, one born into a traditional Japanese family and one born into a family such as your own. In the traditional Japanese family social roles are strictly demarcated. Women serve their husbands. The oldest male child is prized beyond all others; advanced education is planned for him alone. Family bonds are very tight and relationships are closely dependent. Traditional Japanese mothers *never* part from their young children, even to go shopping (Takahashi, 1986). Infants are quickly comforted if they cry, and when they do cry, the mother feels shame. Respect and agreeableness are highly valued, as are emotional maturity, self-control, and social courtesy (Hess et al., 1980). Conformity to the group rather than individual assertiveness is the principal guide to behavior. The newborn infant is viewed as initially independent (not bound to the

This picture is from a movie about the real-life attempt of Frenchman Jean-Marc Itard to "civilize" a child found living alone in a forest in 1799. At the time of his capture the boy, whom Itard named Victor, was about 12 years old. He scrambled around on all fours, snarled, and bit. Needless to say, he was unable to use language. Even after five years of instruction in human ways, he remained abnormal in all respects. Because no one knows what Victor was like before his life in isolation, we do not know whether lack of human contact *caused* his wild behavior. However, the existence of such children suggests the importance of a normal human environment to normal development. *(Culver Pictures.)*

group), and making the infant dependent and a part of the culture is an urgent task (Caudill and Weinstein, 1969).

How would a person growing up in such a culture differ from you? Obviously, given a common humanity, people raised in different cultures are similar in basic ways. They share intelligence, curiosity, the ability to speak, bonding with kin, and social organization. But people raised in distinctly different cultures vary in attitudes, values, and belief systems, and these differences influence not only individual personality but parent-child relationships and other social relationships as well (Caudill and Weinstein, 1969).

And within the same general culture, living circumstances have an impact on development. The three families we introduced in the opening of Part I differ in economic circumstances, ethnicity, and community. In addition, other factors in their lives are continually changing, such as relationships among family members, and these affect the environment in which their children are raised. Thus, while all three families are influenced by the dominant North American culture, they represent different subcultures and different living situations. Moreover, into each is born an individual infant with a unique set of genes. Development of each child will take place within this matrix of contextual influences, and as you will see, the development of each will be unique. Although the task is enormously complex, developmental psychologists aim to understand how people develop within this matrix.

AN OVERVIEW OF THE CONTEXTS

When we say that human development takes place in context, we are actually referring to many things, many contexts. The contexts for development include human evolutionary history, our biological heritage. Developmental contexts also include the culture in which a child is born, the particular period in history, the subculture and community, the child's family, and the immediate surroundings. All of these influence development—usually in a complex, interlocking way. Many common features of our modern industrial culture, such as the presence of a television set, two working parents, out-of-home care, and formal schooling, do not go together just by coincidence; they are part of the same societal pattern, and their influences supplement one another.

Urie Bronfenbrenner of Cornell University has suggested a way of conceptualizing these many developmental contexts that helps to identify the factors shaping development and to understand their relationship to one another (Bronfenbrenner, 1977, 1979). He proposes a model of concentric rings, with each ring influencing those inside it. As you can see in Figure 3.1, the child lies at the center of the rings, bringing to development his or her biological makeup. Surrounding the child is the first ring, the **immediate environment.** It contains all the settings, the people, and the physical objects with which the child has direct contact. For the North American child, this includes home, family, toys, playgrounds, peers, classrooms, and teachers.

All these settings, people, and objects, however, do not exist in a vacuum. They are embedded in a broader **social and economic context.** For instance, the materials present in a classroom and the curricula teachers teach are shaped by both school boards and economic circumstances. Indirectly, therefore, these other factors influence the child. Similarly, while a child may have no direct contact with a parent's boss, the boss may affect the parent's behavior at home, which in turn affects the child. These broader social and economic factors that often influence the child indirectly make up the second ring in Figure 3.1.

The third ring in Figure 3.1 is the **cultural context.** It consists of all the beliefs, values, and guidelines for behavior that people in a particular society tend to share. For example, most adults in our society believe that the mother should have the major responsibility for raising a young infant, even though the father is expected to help out with the task. This belief is part of our culture and clearly affects how babies are cared for. That most American children are taught to value democracy, independence, and economic success can also be attributed to our culture. Our

Figure 3.1
The Child's Developmental Contexts
Urie Bronfenbrenner has suggested that a child's development is influenced not only by his or her biological heritage but also by the environment in which he or she is brought up.

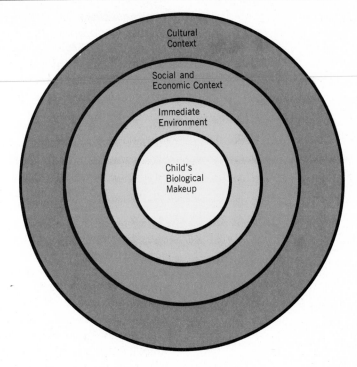

culture, in fact, is the source of most of our ideas about what is "right" and "good."

The rest of this chapter is devoted to looking at each of the major contexts of development. We will examine the impact of these contexts in later chapters as we look at the major periods of child development. As background for these discussions, it helps to have a broad overview of the contexts, and that overview is our goal here. We begin with the child's biological context.

THE BIOLOGICAL CONTEXT

Children do not enter the world as totally blank slates, waiting to be taught a long list of "human" behaviors. Instead, they come equipped with a rich evolutionary heritage, which greatly affects how they act. This heritage consists of certain traits shared by mammals, others shared by primates (the order of animals that includes humans, apes, and monkeys), and still others characteristic of humans alone. For example, human infants, like other primates, have an inherited tendency to seek social stimulation and to form strong attachments to care givers. In addition, human infants have a built-in tendency to detect and attend to human speech sounds, something unique to members of our species. Our evolutionary heritage also includes a rather precise timetable for the emergence of many developmental milestones, from reaching for and grasping a nearby object to showing the emotion of fear. This timetable is followed despite widely different circumstances, suggesting a strong influence of heredity (Suomi, 1977).

Perhaps the most basic of all the biological givens a baby possesses is a strong disposition to act on the environment. From the beginning, human infants are drawn to examine and manipulate their surroundings with any means available to them. This tendency is a hallmark of all mammals, but it is most pronounced in the higher primates with their strong inquisitiveness and inclination to solve problems (Suomi, 1977; White, 1959). For example, monkeys and chimpanzees will work hard to solve a problem, such as unfastening a latch, just for the opportunity to watch other animals through a window (Butler, 1953). Human children, too, solve problems just for the fun of it, as the accompanying photograph shows. The satisfaction we get from discovery has helped our species survive by encouraging exploration and invention (Breger, 1974; Harter, 1980). In exploring and playing with sticks and stones, some early human may have accidentally noticed that a stone could be pried up. Not only was a means invented for getting something from under a rock, but the principle of the lever was also discovered. We may not be blessed with great speed, strength, or toughness, but our innate curiosity is a major force behind our many achievements.

Closely related to our curiosity is our innate propensity for learning. For instance, by the age of three, children around the world can speak their native language quite fluently. Young children, it seems, have a built-in "readiness" to acquire this complex skill (Lenneberg, 1967). Our nearest animal relatives, the chimpanzees, have great difficulty learning even the rudiments of language. Of course, the ease with which we humans learn depends on what we are learning. Researchers at one time were dismayed by the difficulty of "training" newborn babies. However, the trouble they had stemmed largely from the particular behaviors they had chosen to teach. Newborns quickly learn to adjust the strength of their sucking (Sameroff, 1968) or to turn their heads from side to side in a precise sequence (Papoušek, 1969). These behaviors are related to nursing and are vital for survival. Thus, responsiveness to certain kinds of environmental demands is biologically "prepared," or built into the infant. As children mature, what they can readily learn undergoes change. A facility for learning language emerges at about age 18 months; certain abstract concepts are mastered only after adolescence. What we can learn, in other words, depends partly on our level of development. Still, a basic facility for learning is part of our biological inheritance.

As humans we also inherit a predisposition to be social—to interact and form bonds with others of our species. This social predisposition is essential to our survival. Because human children are quite vulnerable for years, forming ties to others helps ensure the care they need. It is therefore not surprising that babies come equipped with behaviors that tend to elicit caring responses from adults. Looking and listening, smiling and cooing, crying, clinging, and following are all innate behaviors that help establish early social relationships. Throughout development the human social predisposition can be seen again and again. The preschooler who seeks out peers to play with, the adolescent who forms a romantic attachment, the adult who marries and raises children are all in part responding to biological tendencies.

This child is working hard to solve this problem. He seems more interested in the problem itself than in the reward the experimenter has provided. For humans, there seems to be something intrinsically rewarding in making discoveries, solving problems, and mastering the environment. *(Dr. Mary J. Ward/Cornell University Medical College.)*

We have been discussing biological influences at the level of the species, that is, as basic features of the human animal. Such features derive from our evolutionary history, as does the particular program of development followed by humans (Gould, 1977). But evolution also requires individual variation within a species. Such variation ensures that the species can meet environmental challenges and survive. It also is the basis for natural selection and evolution itself.

Therefore, each individual (except for identical twins—see Chapter 4) has a somewhat different genetic makeup and a somewhat different biological context for development. Such differences in individual children have both direct and indirect influences on development. Girls and boys, for example, have certain physical differences as a result of their genetic differences. They may have differences in mental abilities as well (see Chapters 12 and 14). Most parents certainly treat them differently, and the effects of this different treatment are part of the indirect influence of genetics. Individual differences also are apparent in the range of children's intellectual potential. Mental retardation, which often is caused by inborn factors, clearly provides a different developmental context than normal intellectual functioning. Finally, some researchers believe that differences in activity level, fearfulness, and other aspects of behavior are strongly influenced by an individual's genetic makeup (Goldsmith, 1983; Plomin and DeFries, 1983; Thomas and Chess, 1977). If this is true, then the biological context takes on additional importance because such features would influence the reactions of others in the child's environment (Scarr and McCartney, 1983).

As we noted in Chapter 1, many developmentalists are interested in how genes and environment interact to produce behavior. A major question concerns the degree to which genes constrain, or put limits on, how much the environment can influence particular capacities. C. H. Waddington (1966) has used the term **canalization** to refer to these genetic constraints. In his view, some behaviors are strongly canalized, or "channeled," from the beginning. For example, babbling appears in all babies at about the same age, regardless of culture or context. Even those who are deaf, and therefore have never heard sound, babble. Thus, even with a great deal of environmental variation this behavior follows its genetically determined course. Other characteristics, such as social competence, are thought to be much more changeable in response to variations in environment.

For some capacities, canalization is strong early in life, and the constraints become more rigid with age. As an analogy, consider what happens when water runs down a sandy hillside (see Figure 3.2). At first, it establishes several broad paths or channels (Part A). If more water continues to pour down, the grooves deepen (Part B). In time, rather massive environmental change is required to reroute the streams thus formed. Some human abilities develop that way. Genes provide the broad outlines, or dispositions, for acting. If the environment supports these dispositions early in life, the tendencies become stronger. Such behavior is susceptible to environmental input at first and becomes difficult to change later on.

For other capacities, strong genetic canalization appears early, but at a later developmental period, there is increased openness to the environment. Robert McCall (1981) has proposed that mental development follows such a course. Until the age of 2, he argues, mental development is strongly canalized by the individual's biological makeup. The range of behavior across children is narrow, and widely differing environments have relatively little impact. After age 2, developmental pathways diverge. Genetically determined tendencies have less of an impact on behavior, and children are more vulnerable to variations in experience.

Biological tendencies, then, are critical factors in human behavior. They influence behavior not only directly but also indirectly by helping to shape other aspects of our developmental context. Through what we seek and respond to, we influence the world around us and to a large extent determine our "effective" environment, the part of the environment that influences us in return. For a child, the effective environment includes the immediate environment, which encompasses objects and people.

THE CHILD'S IMMEDIATE ENVIRONMENT

People are of primary importance to a child's development because they directly interact with the child and are largely responsible for the child's physical surroundings. The people in a child's world generally include parents, peers, and in modern cultures, teachers. Often there are siblings and other relatives as well. In addition to people, the objects a child encounters in the immediate environment help shape development.

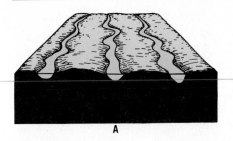 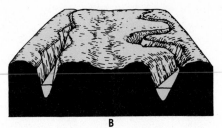

Figure 3.2
Waddington's Landscape of Development
For many behaviors the developmental pathway becomes increasingly well worn over time and more environmental change is required to divert the child to a new path.

The Influence of Objects on Development

While no certain set of toys is required for optimal development, ready availability of objects that are responsive to the child's actions (such as "busy boxes") has been shown to be related to the pace of cognitive development (Elardo, Bradley, and Caldwell, 1975; Yarrow, Rubenstein, and Pederson, 1975). Children learn by doing and are especially attracted to objects that respond to them (Charlesworth, 1969; Watson, 1972).

In recent decades researchers have been interested in the impact of prominent objects in many home environments, such as the television set and now the home computer. Many children view a large amount of television. It is estimated that the average child in the United States will have watched 15,000 hours of television by the time he or she is 18 years old (Lesser, 1974). Even though young children commonly are engaged in other activities in front of the set (Anderson and Smith, 1984), it seems likely that video material influences children. Potential influences on sex roles, racial attitudes, and aggression have all been documented (e.g., Stein and Friedrich, 1975). In general, it might be argued that television has a homogenizing influence, presenting a standard set of values widely held in the culture. While less research has been done on the impact of the home computer, is it clear that by preschool age, children find such devices quite captivating and enjoy working with them with peers (Greenfield, 1984).

The Family Context

The family is a dominant part of a child's immediate environment. Every day family members directly interact with the child, stimulating language development and other cognitive skills (Elardo, Bradley, and Caldwell, 1975, 1977; Wachs, 1976). Family members also provide models for behaviors. Children imitate those around them, especially those they look up to or to whom they are emotionally attached (Bandura, 1965, 1977a; Hetherington, 1965). Chief among such people are parents and older siblings. Family members model not only specific behaviors but roles. Much of a child's understanding of what it is like to be male or female, mother or father, husband or wife comes from the family (Parsons and

While no specific toys are required for optimal development, playthings that respond to a child's actions have been found to be related to the pace of cognitive development. Like most children, the one at the left seems especially attracted to this kind of toy. The child at the right is occupied in an activity that will probably have consumed some 15,000 hours of his life by the time he is 18. *(Left, Sonya Jacobs/The Stock Market; Right, Barbara Kirk/The Stock Market.)*

Bales, 1955; Satir, 1967; Sroufe and Fleeson, 1986). Family members also provide children with the security of nurturing relationships. As you will learn in later chapters, a child's curiosity, problem solving, and interactions with peers are all influenced by the emotional quality of family relationships.

THE FAMILY AS A SYSTEM

For many years researchers who studied the family's influence on children focused almost exclusively on the role of the mother, a practice that now has been criticized (Chess and Thomas, 1982; Parke, 1979). The emphasis arose because mothers have traditionally had the major *direct* impact on infants and young children. The importance of maternal care is also a cornerstone of psychoanalytic theory, which became quite influential earlier in this century. By underscoring the psychological need of children for a warm and emotionally supportive environment, this stress on the mother-child relationship has been beneficial.

However, developmentalists have come to realize that the traditional view of the family must be expanded. Mothers never care for children in a vacuum. The quality of their care giving is influenced by other family members, both directly and indirectly. Today, the developmental influences of fathers and siblings are topics of active study, as is the broader family support system that includes grandparents (Tinsley and Parke, 1984). Also of great interest is the child's own role in shaping family interactions. Modern developmentalists do not see the family as a set of separate relationships existing side by side. Instead, they see the family as an interconnected system (Belsky and Isabella, 1987a; Bugental and Shennum, 1984; Minuchin, 1985; Sroufe and Fleeson, in press).

At the simplest level, the idea of a system implies that all parts are interconnected. A modern heating system is a common example. When the thermostat registers a temperature below a certain level, a connection is made that activates the furnace. Heat is produced and the room temperature rises until the desired level is reached. At this point, the electrical connection is broken and the furnace is switched off. Without the electrical connection, the furnace would not run; without the changes in temperature produced by the furnace, the thermostat would not be functional. Each part depends on the others for its operation, and the role of each is defined by the overall system. Family members are even more complexly interconnected. Each member's behavior depends in part on the behavior of the others. The roles of mother, father, oldest son, youngest daughter, and so forth are defined by the overall family system.

The idea of an interconnected system stresses an important point: The influence between members of the system moves in *two* directions. The furnace and its heat affect the thermostat, but the thermostat and its electrical connection also affect the furnace. So it is in a family. While the behavior of parents helps determine the characteristics of their children, the characteristics of the children in turn influence the parents' behavior. For example, American parents often behave differently toward their sons than their daughters. Toddler girls get hair ribbons; toddler boys get tossed in the air. These different styles of care giving encourage children to act in sex-typed ways; this, in turn, reinforces the parents' beliefs and child-rearing practices. Thus, the behavior of the parents helps shape the children's responses, but the children's responses also encourage the parents' behavior. Developmentalists call this two-way stream of influence a **bidirectional effect** (Bell, 1968) or **reciprocal determinism** (Bandura, 1985).

Arnold Sameroff has introduced a **transactional model** to describe the long-term bidirectional effects of parents and child, taking into account the family's social and economic context as well (Sameroff, 1986; Sameroff and Chandler, 1975). A newborn baby enters the family system with certain innate tendencies. The parents, because of their own circumstances and characteristics, respond to the baby in particular ways. The baby's behavior then gradually changes, partly because of the parents' influences, partly because of maturation. These changes in the baby's behavior in turn elicit new parental responses, which further influence the child, and so on, in an ongoing cycle.

Sameroff's transactional model can help to answer some otherwise puzzling questions, such as why certain moderately premature infants have developmental problems. The answer does not lie solely with the babies, for in general such infants develop quite well. Moreover, those who later encounter developmental problems are physically indistinguishable at birth from those who do not. It seems that the premature babies who have trouble are mainly those in very low income homes (Sameroff and Chandler, 1975).

What is it about living in poverty that puts a moderately premature infant at developmental risk? Sameroff's transactional model can help us understand what goes wrong in these cases. A premature infant requires special care and poses special challenges for parents. These demands can be overtaxing for parents already burdened with the many stresses of poverty. Thus, the baby's condition at birth interacts with the parents' psychological state, which itself is shaped by their economic and social circumstances. The result can be a parent-child relationship not conducive to optimal development.

Note that it is the transaction between *particular* actors in a *particular* context that gives rise to the outcome. In middle-class families, which do not suffer the extra burdens of poverty, moderate prematurity in an infant does *not* predict negative outcomes. In fact, one study of middle-class families found that the mothers of premature babies in general became more "sensitive" care givers than the mothers of full-term infants (Cohen and Beckwith, 1979). **Sensitive care** involves the mother's fitting her own behavior to the infant's wishes and needs. For example, if the baby turns its head away when not ready for more food, the sensitive mother pauses and waits for the baby to turn back. Apparently, premature infants with their special needs tend to elicit sensitive care from mothers who have adequate social support and are not unduly stressed. Although at age 9 months the premature babies in this particular study lagged behind the full-term infants on developmental tests, they had caught up to the full-term infants by the age of 2 years. This positive outcome is much less likely in poor households. There the premature baby often places additional stress on already highly stressed parents. In some cases the parents become less effective care givers, so the baby fails to thrive. The transactional model emphasizes that the total system of individuals, their contexts, and their two-way interactions are all important in explaining developmental outcomes.

The idea of the family as a system means more than that each individual affects the other individuals. It also means that each family member is changed fundamentally by the organization of the whole (Sroufe and Fleeson, in press). Before a child is born, a family system already exists, and the child is fitted into that system more or less smoothly. Consider the Gordon family we introduced earlier. Wanting a son is their primary reason for having a third child. A place in the system is already prepared for the child. If the baby does turn out to be a boy, he immediately has a role of sizable importance: he makes the family "complete." But what if the child turns out to be a girl? Frank may actively show his disappointment toward both the child and his wife. Christine may feel she has failed by not producing a boy. Or if she has a son, she may become angry at Frank if the wished-for closeness with him does not result. The wishes, expectations, and needs of the Gordons will influence how they react to the baby and to each other. People and relationships will be changed by the altered system formed with the child's birth. There are no simple child effects in this view of the family system. Even child effects themselves are partly determined by the larger system.

Family systems are obviously much more complex than a modern heating system. One reason is that they are made up of many subsystems (relationships between siblings, fathers and sons, mother and father, and so forth), all of which are joined together in a coherent, interlocking network. For example, qualities of the siblings' relationships are predictable from qualities of mother-child relationships (Dunn and Kendrick, 1982; Hetherington, in press; Robb and Mangelsdorf, 1987), and one parent's relationship to a child is connected with all other relationships in the family. Thus, if a mother is seductive toward her son, her relationship with her daughter is often characterized by derisiveness (Sroufe et al., 1985) and her relationship with her husband by emotional distance (Sroufe and Fleeson, in press). Rather than saying that the mother-son relationship causes the mother-father distance, or mother-father distance causes seductiveness, we would rather emphasize that the network of relationships within the family is a coherent one. Close, supportive relationships between spouses generally are not found in families where one parent is emotionally overinvolved with the opposite-gender child and vice versa.

The families children grow up in may be the largest single influence on their development. Furthermore, children influence other family members in many important ways. *(Monkmeyer Press.)*

Families are also dynamic, *open systems*, subject to change as well as continuity. Family systems change in obvious ways as members are added and lost. But they also change as circumstances change, as crises are faced, and as members enter new developmental phases (Hill, 1970). Developmentalists are particularly interested in how a child's development influences and is influenced by the overall development of the family. The Gordons' hoped-for boy may initially be given the role of holding the family together, but as he grows older, he may actively seek out this role, particularly if the relationship between his mother and father worsens. As they develop, children become active participants in defining and maintaining the family system. Individual and family development are always closely linked.

Family systems may be described in terms of historical, cyclical influences. For example, marital harmony or discord is related to child personality (Elder, Caspi, and Downey, 1986; Emery, 1982; Patterson and Dishion, in press; Quinton, Rutter, and Liddle, 1984; Rutter, in press). But a child's personality predicts his or her future marital satisfaction and harmony (Cowan et al., 1986; Stolnick, 1981) and even characteristics of spouses chosen (Caspi and Elder, in press). Moreover, in comparison with girls from a more normal family setting, girls from disrupted families more often become pregnant before marriage and select partners with few resources, which leads to troubled marriages (Hetherington, Cox, and Cox, 1978). Thus, it becomes difficult to determine where the cycle of influence begins or ends as patterns are repeated. In one study such cycles of influence were demonstrated across four generations (Elder, Caspi, and Downey, 1986). As you shall see, these cycles may be broken when adequate marital relations are achieved.

FATHERS IN THE FAMILY SYSTEM

The expansion of developmentalists' attention beyond the mother-child relationship has led to new research on fathers' influences on children (Biller and Solomon, 1986; Lamb, 1975; Parke, 1981). In addition to having direct effects, fathers also have indirect effects by influencing the behavior of mother and siblings. In general, *marital harmony* is associated with parental well-being, nurturant parenting, and child adjustment (Belsky, 1984; Easterbrooks and Emde, in press; Hetherington, in press). In particular, it has been found that when a husband provides good emotional support for his wife, her care of their infant is more effective (Belsky and Isabella, 1987; Pederson, Anderson, and Cain, 1977; Rutter, in press; Wallerstein, 1983).

Studies also show that when troubled girls later marry adequately supportive husbands, their child care can be quite adequate (Caspi and Elder, in press). In one such study, Michael Rutter and his colleagues examined the parenting of a group of women who had been reared in institutions most of their childhood (Quinton, Rutter, and Liddle, 1984). In comparison to a control group, many of these women showed parenting problems. However, their parenting was dramatically influenced by the presence of a supportive spouse. Fully half of these mothers provided adequate care, compared to none of those institution-reared mothers without such social support. Interestingly, these supportive marriages were "planned," suggesting again an interaction between personal and relationship factors.

Other researchers have found that mothers and fathers behave differently toward their children when both adults are present. For instance, when a mother and father are together, they tend to show more positive emotion toward children than they do separately (Parke and O'Leary, 1976). This finding suggests that the mere presence of a spouse can affect parent-child interactions.

A great deal of research has been done on father absence, divorce, and related topics. For example, during middle childhood, boys from father-absent homes generally are less oriented to contact sports, less competitive, and more dependent—more so the longer a father has been gone (Hetherington, 1966). This is, of course, another example of an indirect effect. We will discuss this research in detail in Chapters 13 and 15.

A study by Byron Egeland, an educational psychologist, provides a further example of the indirect effects of fathers. Actually, not all the men involved in this study were biological fathers. Some were merely involved on a steady basis with the child's mother, perhaps living with her, perhaps not. All the mothers in the study were on public assistance, meaning their family incomes were low. Egeland assessed the children from birth through school age to see how well they fared over the years. One of his measures of emotional development in infancy was how quickly a child could be comforted after the mother returned from a brief separation. When the children were 2, Egeland examined their persistence, enthusiasm, cooperativeness, and flexibility in solving problems. When the children entered kindergarten, Egeland asked their teachers to rate them regarding a number of possible problems: aggression, distractibility, isolation from others, and so forth.

Egeland identified several different developmental patterns. Some children functioned well at all ages, others poorly at all ages; still others started out functioning poorly but ended up functioning well. Egeland wondered why some children made this positive turnaround. He and his colleagues found one major difference between children whose functioning improved over time and children who showed consistently poor development. The difference was that the mothers of "improving" children were more likely to have formed a stable partnership with a man during the intervening years (Erickson, Egeland, and Sroufe, 1985). Of course, just because these two factors are related does not necessarily mean that one caused the other. A child's improved behavior could have been due to other changes in the mother's situation that just happened

Fathers commonly are quite involved with their toddlers and especially engage them in playful activities. *(Index Stock International.)*

to coincide with the forming of a stable relationship. On the other hand, the new "stepfather" could have had a direct and positive influence on the child. Another possibility is that the mother's partner had an indirect effect on her parenting. This third possibility is the one that Egeland thinks is most likely.

Developmentalists have also studied the *direct* effects of fathers. Many have found that children are involved with their fathers and emotionally attached to them even in infancy (Clarke-Stewart, 1978a; Cohen and Campos, 1974; Lamb, 1981). Such involvement intensifies during the toddler period, especially with boys. In later chapters you will read about the influences of fathers on sex-role learning, cognitive development, achievement motivation, and personality development. All are active areas of research.

SIBLINGS IN THE FAMILY SYSTEM

Within the family system siblings, too, have both direct and indirect effects on younger children. Their direct effects include serving as companions, teachers, and models. In one study that compared girls with and without older siblings, those with older brothers were found to be more competitive, while those with older sisters were more "feminine" (Clarke-Stewart, 1977). This finding suggests that when an older sibling is present, a younger child may directly learn from that sibling's behavior. At the same time, siblings indirectly influence each other's development through their arrival and through the impact they have on their parents' behavior (Dunn and Kendrick, 1982). Consider research by Sandra Scarr and Richard Weinberg (Scarr, 1982). They have found that siblings differ more in personality than one would expect given that, on average, they

Birth order may affect the social development of children within the same family. *(Catherine Nooren/Photo Researchers, Inc.)*

have 50 percent of their genes in common. In fact, siblings are often more different from one another than unrelated children are. This odd finding may be due in part to the parents' responses when another child is born. In the process of differentiating their children, parents may exaggerate whatever differences exist and perhaps create other differences through expectations and role assignments (the "smart" one, the "boy" of the family, and so forth). In this way the siblings influence each other indirectly through the effects they have on the parents.

Some researchers believe that sibling influences are responsible for what are called **birth order effects:** systematic differences in children's behavior depending on whether they are first-born, second-born, third-born, and so on (Zajonc and Markus, 1975). For example, second-born children tend to be less motivated by achievement than first-borns, but they are also more sociable and outgoing (Clarke-Stewart, 1977). Many factors may contribute to these differences, but all arise from direct or indirect influences of siblings. For instance, parents' attention necessarily becomes more divided when a second child is born, so the second-born may get less stimulation and less encouragement for reaching goals. The parents also may adopt a more relaxed attitude toward a second child. In addition, the second-born, from the start, has a live-in peer to interact with, which could promote a more sociable nature.

More insight into how the birth of another child influences the family system will come from future research. One study on this topic is underway at the Max Planck Institute in Berlin. Kurt Kreppner and his colleagues are conducting a longitudinal study of families that have a second child when the first child is between 2 and 3½ (Schütze, Kreppner, and Paulsen, 1982). This study is of special importance because of its systems emphasis. The researchers want to know the extent to which the functioning of the three-member family forecasts the functioning of the four-member family, especially the emergence of two subsystems (parents on the one hand, siblings on the other). This study also has a developmental focus in that it examines changing pressures on the family as the second-born becomes a toddler and begins to infringe on the prerogatives and property of the first-born. Recent research by Judith Dunn shows some of these forces at work (e.g., Dunn, in press; Dunn and Kendrick, 1982). Dunn reports that the quality of the mother's relationship with the first-born affects the quality of the siblings' interaction. The degree to which mothers discuss the new baby as a person with wants, feelings, and needs also influences their relationship. In addition, developmental changes in both first-born and second-born influence the degree of harmony between them.

You will learn about other sibling influences as you read this book. The important point for now is that many of these factors, and the reasons for them, could never be discovered if researchers failed to view the family as a system. Sibling relations clearly affect a child's development. Parental treatment of siblings influences sibling relationships, and the quality of sibling interactions has an impact on the parents, with each relationship touching every other (Hetherington, in press).

THE SOCIAL AND ECONOMIC CONTEXT

While the family is a crucial context for child development, the family itself is embedded in a broader social and economic context (the second ring in Figure 3.1). This social and economic context can directly affect children, as when youngsters in city slums experience unsafe housing, poor health care, high crime rates, and general overcrowding. At the same time, the social and economic context indirectly affects children by influencing their parents' behavior. If parents are stressed by the hardships of poverty or the uncertainty of losing a job, the quality of their child care may diminish. If parents receive aid and support from relatives, friends, and social institutions, their interactions with their children may improve. The ledger of hardships and challenges on the one hand balanced by social support on the other seems to be important in understanding individual development (Belsky, 1984; Rutter, in press). This will become apparent in the stories of our three children.

Family Changes Caused by Social and Economic Factors

A popular TV show of the 1950s always began with the businessman father arriving at his house in the suburbs after a hard day's work. "Margaret, I'm home!" he would call out, as he swung open the front door. In the kitchen his homemaker wife, who had spent the day tending the house and children, was making dinner. Wiping her hands on her clean apron, she would rush to the door to greet the family breadwinner.

Few contemporary American families fit this traditional domestic pattern. The reasons have to do with social and economic forces that have changed the way most families live. For example, changing values and aspirations among women have led many to pursue careers outside the home. At the same time, economic circumstances have created new financial pressures, further contributing to the entry of married women into the paid labor force. As Figure 3.3 shows, in the years between 1947 and 1985, the proportion of working mothers grew from 20 to 60 percent (Newberger, Melnicoe, and Newberger, 1986; Norton and Glick, 1986). Partly because of greater financial demands, women with school-age children are even more likely to work than married women who as yet have no children. Of course, many contemporary women also work because

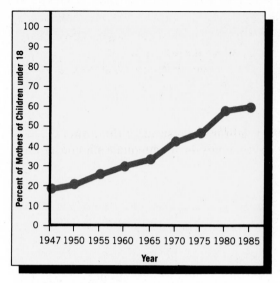

Figure 3.3
Employed Mothers of Children Under 18 Years, 1947–1985
The proportion of mothers in the work force who are also raising children has tripled in less than 40 years—an economic fact of great significance for child development.

Source: Data from Norton and Glick. 1986; Kamerman and Hayes, 1982. Adapted from Newberger, Melnicoe, and Newberger, 1986.

they want to, because their jobs have meaning for them (Rubin, 1979). Fully 75 percent of employed women have said they would go on working even if financial need was not a consideration (Veroff, Dorwan, and Kukla, 1981).

New norms and values have led to other changes in American families. One that has had a significant effect on child development has been the increase in the number of single-parent homes. As of 1982, 22 percent of U.S. children lived with only one parent (Newberger, Melnicoe, and Newberger, 1986). It is estimated that 50 percent of children in our society will spend at least some of their time in a single-parent household (Norton and Glick, 1986). The rise of single-parent families is due to both an increasing divorce rate and an increased tendency for unmarried mothers to keep their babies. Many of these single mothers are quite young (see Figure 3.4), and many live in poverty.

In summary, as Figure 3.5 makes clear, a large percentage of today's children will experience living with only one parent. Very often the mother will work outside the home, even in two-parent households. Add to this the increasing tendency for adults to marry later, bear children later, and have fewer children, and you can see that the U.S. family has changed dramatically over the past few decades. What are the consequences of these dramatic changes for contemporary children? Let's begin by looking at single-parent families—first those created by teenage pregnancy, then those created by divorce.

SINGLE PARENTING AND ITS EFFECTS

Researchers have found that children of unmarried teenage mothers often encounter developmental problems. However, since the mothers frequently have very low incomes, the stresses of being poor (not single parenting as such) may be largely responsible for the troubles the children experience. One way to assess the contribution of poverty in these cases is to compare the children of low-income *single* mothers with the children of low-income *two*-parent families. Such comparisons reveal no obvious differences between the two groups, at least not in the early years (Egeland and Brunnquell, 1979). Apparently, poverty is a negative factor for children no matter what the parents' marital status. Also, the effects of single parenting are partly indirect: Having children alone can bring financial problems, which in turn can cause stresses and child-rearing difficulties.

Single parenting also can influence children indirectly through an absence of social support. When adults have support from others, such as relatives and friends, the result tends to be adequate parenting and adequate child development (Belsky, 1984; Crockenberg, 1981; Egeland and Farber, 1984; Gottlieb, 1980; Salzinger, Kaplan, and Artemyeff, 1983). A stable marriage or partnership is often a major source of social support, so it is not surprising that single parenting can be difficult. If Karen Polonius, the head of one of our three families, must raise her baby without social support, her child will have a greater chance of experiencing some developmental problems.

But what if a single mother has adequate social support and is not overwhelmed by the stresses of poverty? Does her single status still have notable consequences for her children? This question turns out to be a difficult one to answer. Some partial insights come from the study by Byron Egeland we mentioned earlier. He and his colleagues compared three groups of mothers: (1) those without a male partner, (2) those with a stable "living-together" relationship, and (3) those with an ongoing heterosexual relationship but not living together. Interestingly, it was women in the last group, not the first, whose children tended to have the most developmental problems. Why this is so is still unclear. Perhaps an uncommitted relationship is stressful for a mother, or perhaps women who have difficulties with adult relationships also have difficulties with parenting. Regardless, Egeland's findings suggest a complexity of influences on child development. A mother's marital status cannot be looked at in isolation.

Developmentalists are concerned not only with the consequences of being raised by an unmarried mother. They also are interested in the

Figure 3.4
Adolescent Birth Rates, 1970–1982
While the number of births to adolescents in general is currently fairly stable, births to unmarried adolescents continue to rise.

Source: Reducing Poverty Among Children (Washington, D.C.: Congressional Budget Office, 1985). Adapted from Newberger, Melnicoe, and Newberger, 1986.

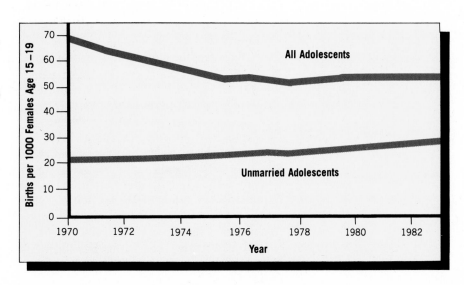

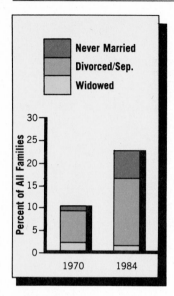

**Figure 3.5
Mother-Headed Households,
1970 and 1984**
Mother-headed households
continue to increase. The
average income level in
such households is dramatically lower than in father-
headed or two-parent families.

Source: Data from Norton and Glick.
1986. Adapted from Newberger et
al., 1986.

consequences of being raised by divorced parents. Children may experience certain negative effects after divorce. School-age boys, for instance,
show a decline in school achievement and become more demanding and
less obedient of their custodial parent (Hetherington, in press). Researchers have tried to determine whether these consequences result from divorce itself or from the parents' conflict (Block, Block, and Gjerde, 1986).
They have found that divorce that ends parental conflict seems better for
children than a conflict-ridden marriage, but divorce in which the parents' animosities continue appears worse for children than a marriage
with conflict (Hetherington and Parke, 1979). This finding suggests that
both conflict and separation from one parent (more often the father) can
contribute to problems in children. As you might expect, ongoing contact
with the noncustodial parent, in the absence of serious conflict between
the parents, generally reduces the negative consequences of divorce
(Hetherington, in press).

Thus, present evidence suggests that divorce need not be devastating
to children. It is, however, a major life change, so we would expect some
consequences. These consequences depend not only on the parents' level
of conflict and the degree to which the children maintain contact with
both parents; they also depend in part on the age and gender of the
children, as well as on the recency of the divorce and whether the
custodial parent remarries (Hetherington, in press). In general, short-term
consequences appear to be more serious for boys, but after two years the
most obvious effects seem to fade. However, effects on gender behavior
and social relationships may persist in subtle ways. Divorce can also have
a continuing impact on children if the custodial parent experiences the
stresses of a sharp decline in income. This, unfortunately, is very often
the case. While the median income for married couples with two children
was almost $30,000 in 1983, the median income for a woman raising two
children alone was less than $10,000 in that year (Norton and Glick,
1986). Being a single parent often means loss of not only social support
but economic support as well. Divorce will be discussed further in Chapters 13 and 15.

MATERNAL EMPLOYMENT AND ITS EFFECTS

Like the influences of divorce, the influences of a working mother are
complicated. The consequences depend on a host of factors, including
the child's age, the amount of time the mother spends at work, the quality
of shared time remaining (are both parents exhausted when they get
home?), the quality of substitute care, the strength of the parent-child
relationship, and, perhaps most significant, the meaning of the woman's
employment to both her and her husband (Hoffman, 1984; Newberger,
Melnicoe, and Newberger, 1986). Investigating this last factor, Marion
Yarrow found that child development is affected by the mother's satisfaction with her employment status, *whether working or not.* Mothers
who are unhappy with their situation, especially dissatisfied *nonworking*
mothers, have more problems with child rearing than those who are
satisfied. These women enjoy their children less, are less confident as
parents, and have more difficulty controlling their children (Yarrow et
al., 1962). Yarrow's basic idea has been supported by a recent study by

Rita Benn (1986). She found that the quality of attachment between infants and their working mothers was mediated by the mothers' feelings about their situation. Of course, a satisfied working mother does not guarantee an absence of developmental problems. For instance, other studies have shown that a father may have more negative feelings toward his children when he is displeased about his wife's working. In some families the mother's working is linked to the father's feeling lower status, especially, he thinks, in the eyes of his sons (Hoffman, 1979). Thus, when considering the effects of a woman's employment we must take into account her own, her husband's, and her children's feelings about her job.

The consequences of a mother's working also seem to depend on her child's gender. Some evidence suggests that sons of working women perform somewhat more poorly in school than other boys (Brown, 1970; Gold and Andres, 1978). This is not true of daughters of working mothers. Not only is their school achievement undiminished, but they also tend to have more positive images of women and are more self-sufficient and less dependent than other girls (Baruch, 1972; Douvan, 1963). Developmental researchers are actively pursuing all these possible consequences of a mother's employment.

Social Class, Poverty, Stress, and the Family

In addition to changing the American family, by encouraging an increase in both one-parent households and in mothers who work outside the home, social and economic factors affect the family in another way. They determine what is called social class. In the past, developmentalists have been interested in how social class affects child rearing. It seems reasonable that living conditions and life opportunities might influence a person's values, attitudes, and expectations regarding children. Researchers have in fact reported many differences in child-rearing practices between working-class and middle-class parents. For example, working-class parents in general use more physical means of discipline, whereas middle-class parents are more likely to "reason" with their children (Hoffman, 1963; Kohn, 1963, 1979).

It is easy to slip into making value judgments about these differences, but doing so can be misleading. Both styles of parenting have potential drawbacks. "Reasoning," when carried to extreme, can induce much guilt in children, just as physical discipline, when excessive, can become physical abuse. Excellent and poor-quality child care cut across class lines (Egeland and Sroufe, 1981). Moreover, poor-quality care is not caused by social class in itself any more than it is caused by the simple fact that a mother works. In the Egeland study we mentioned before, mothers who had adequate social support and stable life situations did quite well with their children *despite* very low incomes.

Our concern about an inappropriate social class stereotype is not to underplay the consequences of poverty. Various factors that accompany poverty can have serious consequences for child development. More than 12 million children in this country are being raised in families below the poverty level, with more than half of these living in female-headed households (Select Committee Report, 1984). It is important to know just what effects being poor may have on these children.

First, children of poor families, compared with middle-class ones, are much more likely to suffer prenatal problems, poor physical health at birth, and death during infancy (Egeland and Brunnquell, 1979; Newberger, Melnicoe, and Newberger, 1986). In addition, youngsters living in poverty receive generally poorer medical care and poorer nutrition throughout childhood. These are the health costs of poverty (National Council, 1976; Riessman, 1962; Select Committee Report, 1984).

Second, poverty households usually experience much more life stress than do middle-class families. This increased stress is due to crowded conditions, financial uncertainty, and general instability in life circumstances (Egeland, Breitenbucher, and Rosenberg, 1980; National Council, 1976). Numerous studies have shown that stress can affect parenting and child development adversely (Belsky, 1984; Hoffman, 1960; Patterson and Dishion, in press; Vaughn et al., 1979). In particular, mothers who live in poverty have been found to exhibit notably more anger and punitiveness toward their children than do middle-class mothers (Radke-Yarrow, Richters, and Wilson, in press). When stress is coupled with the social isolation often associated with being poor, it can take an even higher toll on the quality of child care (Egeland and Brunnquell, 1979; Gottlieb, 1980; Rutter, in press; Salzinger, Kaplan, and Artemyeff, 1983).

Third, the stresses of poverty are related to negative community conditions, such as interpersonal violence and drug addiction (Select Committee Report, 1984). While these social problems have complex origins, researchers have shown repeatedly that they are linked to poverty. For example, studies during economic recessions reveal that job loss and its hardships are associated with conflict and violence in the family, including child abuse (Belsky, 1980; Garbarino, 1981; Margolis, 1982).

Finally, the effects of poverty can be seen in the average level of adjustment among children of the poor. They are more likely than middle-class children to have behavioral and emotional problems. They are more apt to drop out of school, to be labeled learning disabled, and to spend time in a correctional institution as adolescents (National Council, 1976; Riessman, 1962). Being raised in poverty is also associated with serious mental disorders, such as schizophrenia (Wolkind and Rutter, 1985).

Drawing upon a natural experiment, Glen Elder and his colleagues (e.g., Elder, Caspi, and Burton, 1987) examined the consequences of paternal unemployment and loss of income during the Great Depression. Material available before and after this striking family stress showed changes in family relationships (with mothers assuming more responsibility), increased irritability and conflict between parents, and less consistent discipline of children.

For many families poverty is a self-perpetuating trap. The isolation and instability associated with poverty put children at an extreme educational disadvantage. Because of school failure, dropping out, and frequent trouble with the law, people's job opportunities are limited. Lack of adequate employment, in turn, ensures poverty, and the cycle repeats itself. Stress negatively influences parenting, and children inadequately nurtured grow up less able to cope with stress (Patterson and Dishion, in

TABLE 3.1 **Child-Care Arrangements for Children Under Age 5 Years in 1982***

	Mother's Employment Status	
	Full Time (%)	Part Time (%)
Care in own home	25.7	39.3
By father	10.3	20.3
Other	15.4	19.3
Care in another home	43.8	34.0
Relative	19.7	15.6
Nonrelative	24.1	18.4
Group care center	18.1	7.5
Other arrangements	11.7	19.2

* Figures expressed as percent distribution of type of child-care arrangements for preschool children who have employed mothers.
Source: Data from U.S. Bureau of the Census. In Newberger, Melnicoe, and Newberger, 1986, p. 699.

press). Anyone concerned about the development of healthy children must also be concerned about the developmental problems caused by poverty.

Social Settings Outside the Family

As children grow older, they increasingly find themselves in settings outside the family. Aspects of the child's neighborhood or community, especially the social support available, have a definite influence on development (Bryant, 1985). In addition, three settings that have a major role in development are day care, the peer group, and the school. We will be saying much more about the influences of these settings in later chapters of this book. Here we simply provide an introduction and raise some of the questions that researchers have tried to answer.

THE DAY-CARE SETTING

As the proportion of single parents steadily rises and as more and more married women seek work outside the home, the use of day care is increasing. By 1985, 10 million American children were receiving care from someone other than a parent for a sizable block of time each week, and that number continues to climb (Abernathy, 1987; Gamble and Zigler, 1986). Fifty-five percent of these children are infants, toddlers, and pre-schoolers, while the rest are older youngsters in need of supervision during nonschool hours. Contrary to common belief, most of these children are not enrolled in formal day-care centers (see Table 3.1). More than 80 percent of all families requiring child-care services use a more informal arrangement. About half use **family day care,** which consists of several children being cared for in someone else's home. Another large percentage use individual baby-sitters, usually in the child's own home. This leaves only a little less than 20 percent who use organized day-care centers (Newberger, Melnicoe, and Newberger, 1986).

Ten million children under the age of six now spend some time being cared for by someone other than their parents. Most of these children are in informal day-care arrangements in homes, as shown here. Currently, only 7 percent of major U.S. companies provide day-care arrangements at the workplace (Abernathy, 1987). *(Elizabeth Crews.)*

Since the use of day care in America is so widespread and is growing so rapidly, developmentalists are greatly concerned about its impact. Many important questions still require answers. The effects on cognitive growth appear to be minimal (Gamble and Zigler, 1986). But, what are the short-term and long-term effects of the various kinds of day care on children's social and emotional growth, and how does day care affect parent-child relationships, especially in infancy? Does the developmental impact differ depending on the age at which day care begins? Does it differ depending on the social class from which a child comes? What constitutes quality day care, and how many facilities meet the standards? Are the day-care arrangements currently available to most American families adequately meeting the parents' needs as well? If not, what additional stress is day care placing on family life? These are some of the issues we will be raising in subsequent chapters, particularly in the unit on infancy.

THE PEER GROUP

The child's peer group as a setting for human development ranks second in importance only to the family (Hartup, 1983). And the peer group's influence increases at each developmental period. By adolescence, peers exert a heavy influence on dress, tastes, and activities (Brittain, 1963). Later, in adulthood, the nature of a person's relationship with parents changes dramatically. Now friends and spouses play many of the roles that parents previously did.

The growing importance of peers can be seen in the increasing time that children spend with them as they grow older. By age 11, peers occupy about as much of the average child's time as do adults (Barker and Wright, 1955; Wright, 1967). Teenagers spend seemingly endless hours with their special friends and often find activities with parents an intrusion. What are children learning in all these hours spent with peers? What skills, values, and expectations do peers convey to one another?

One thing the peer group teaches is how to interact in equal-status, or *symmetrical*, relationships. Relationships between children and adults are inherently unequal. However warm and caring the interactions may be, the adult always retains the power to *tell* the child what to do. This is not so within the peer group. Here no child holds any formal authority over the others. As a result, the peer group is a critical setting for practicing and understanding concepts such as fairness, reciprocity, and cooperation. It is also a major setting in which children learn to manage interpersonal aggression (Hartup, 1983).

Another powerful learning experience within the peer group is frequent reinforcement of cultural norms and values. Take the example of sex roles. Although parents initially convey what is expected of girls and boys, peers are the most dogmatic enforcers of these standards. This is particularly true within male peer groups, where a preference for "feminine" toys or pastimes meets with derision even among preschoolers (Langlois and Downs, 1980). It may be that young children are such cultural "hard liners" partly because they are still trying to get important norms and values firmly established in their own minds (Maccoby, 1980). Exaggerating norms and values may help to clarify them, just as carefully enunciating a new word makes its sounds clearer. Whatever the reason, much of the process of learning to follow society's rules takes place within the peer group.

We will first examine the peer group in the unit on early childhood; then in later chapters we will follow its influence into the elementary and high school years. In the process we will answer some important questions. Why do some children find it easy to get along with peers while others are socially isolated or actively rejected by them? When do true friendships between children emerge, and what underlies this development? When do children begin to think of their peer groups as having boundaries—of their own friends as "we" and other children as "they"? What promotes this sense of peer solidarity? How conforming are children to their peer groups, and why does conformity seem to intensify during middle childhood and early adolescence (Costanzo, 1970)? To what extent do the norms and values of adolescent peer groups conflict with those of parents and other adults? Research findings regarding these questions are of great interest to many who study child development.

THE SCHOOL

The school is often thought of as the child's workplace. Here, by age 6 or 7, children spend six hours daily, five days a week. School activities vary with a child's age. Nursery schools are often flexibly structured with an emphasis on social activities. More formal instruction usually begins in the early elementary school years, and some research supports the child's cognitive readiness at this time (White, 1965). Generally, though, not until middle school do children begin to have different teachers for different subjects. The earlier practice of having one central teacher each year rests on the belief that such a relationship is important for preadolescents, who are more emotionally dependent than older children.

The fact that American children spend so much time in the classroom, as well as in extracurricular activities, makes the school a potentially powerful influence on their development. American children learn much more at school than the information in their textbooks. Like the peer group, the school is also a great instructor in cultural norms and values. For example, studies show that elementary school teachers respond to their students in ways that reinforce traditional sex roles (Block, 1979; Frey, 1979). Schools are also strong conveyors of mainstream American values such as neatness, discipline, punctuality, competition, hard work, and material success. Because the running of a public school must please the majority of people in a community, schools tend to be staffed by those who hold the same ideas about good and bad that most Americans do.

What about the impact of schools on cognitive, social, and emotional development? Do American schools have positive effects in these important areas? There is some evidence that how a school is run and how teachers interact with students can make a difference in the extent to which the school experience is positive for children (Frey and Ruble, 1985; Rutter et al., 1979). Unfortunately, however, this is a topic about which we as yet have few definitive answers (Minuchin and Shapiro, 1983).

The school does more than teach basic skills. It also supports mainstream cultural values. *(S. Anderson/ Magnum Photos, Inc.)*

Culture has a dramatic influence on the behavior of children. *(Bruno J. Zehnder/Peter Arnold, Inc.; John Zoiner/Peter Arnold, Inc.)*

THE CULTURAL CONTEXT

In a nursery school in Beijing, China, a teacher is showing a group of 3-year-olds a mechanical Ping-Pong game. The toy consists of a miniature table with net and two players who stiffly swing their paddles. The teacher explains how the new toy works and then places it on the ground so the children can observe it in action. A sea of little bodies, dressed in padded jackets and trousers, quickly surrounds the toy. Thirty pairs of eyes intently watch the performance, but not a single hand moves. Those in the front do not even stretch out an arm to hold or finger the toy. The children squat quietly in a tightly packed circle, staring in delighted fascination. At the back of the circle a teacher is holding a Western child, the son of a diplomat stationed in Beijing. She lets the boy down, and without hesitation he breaks through the ranks and lunges for the toy. The teacher quickly scoops him up, while the Chinese children look on (Kessen, 1975).

These differences in behavior between Chinese youngsters and a Western child are largely a reflection of two different cultures—two different sets of values and guidelines for behavior that people in a particular society tend to share. The cultural context is represented by the third ring in Figure 3.1. Families, peer groups, schools, and communities always exist within a culture and are greatly influenced by it. These influences, in turn, affect the developing child.

Cultural Influences

One way in which a culture exerts its influence is by shaping the structure of the various settings in which children find themselves. To Western eyes, for example, a Chinese nursery school might seem relatively spartan because there are few toys and little play equipment. As opposed to allowing free play, Chinese teachers are responsible for initiating and organizing most of the daily activities, a practice that teaches and reinforces the value of group cooperation. As we discussed earlier, television, a cultural invention, exercises notable influence on children in the United States.

Even one particular family structure is not a cultural universal. For example, some societies have no concept of a nuclear family, a husband and wife with their young children living together as an independent group. Instead, parents, grandparents, aunts, and uncles live in the same household, and all the adults have equal authority over all the children. If an uncle gives a directive, a child is obliged to obey just as if the directive came from the father (Whiting and Whiting, 1975). How different this is from our own society, where a nuclear family arrangement is considered "natural." Virtually every setting in which human development takes place is structured to a great extent by a society's culture.

Culture also shapes the values that people in a society hold. For example, Chinese and Americans value different behavior patterns, even for very young children. Whereas the Chinese expect self-control and group cooperation, Americans tend to consider self-expression and individuality important. And adults encourage behaviors that match their cultural values. So Western visitors to China who see disciplined nursery school children might assume that these youngsters are innately different from their more boisterous American peers. However, these differences probably are not caused by genetics. Studies have shown that Chinese American children, in families that have adopted Western life styles, behave similarly to other Americans (Li-Repac, 1982). It is far more likely that adults, influenced by their culture, are promoting the behaviors they think children *ought* to have.

As another example, Lebanese parents believe that prayer and family relations are of great importance, but they place little emphasis during early childhood on either relations with peers (except cousins) or on verbal inquisitiveness (encouraging questions about the world). Not surprisingly, when such children are enrolled in Western schools and expected to perform according to different cultural standards, difficulties arise (Goodnow et al., 1984).

Laboratory studies also illustrate the impact of culture. Some years ago, for example, Millard Madsen at UCLA developed a series of two-person games that could be used to study children's inclinations to cooperate or compete (Kagan and Madsen, 1972; Madsen, 1971). In one game, four hands were needed to open a box. Only if the two players worked together, pushing all four latches at the same time, would either of them get a prize. In another game, the players moved toward a goal by putting marks in circles. Sometimes the first child to reach the goal won a prize. Other times both children received a prize when either reached the goal. In another variation, one of the players was prohibited from

When children are given tasks important for community survival, responsible behavior is promoted. *(Lippman/UNICEF.)*

winning a prize, but he could still make the other player lose his. Madsen found dramatic differences in behavior between urban Anglo-American and rural Mexican children. The Anglo-Americans were far more competitive, especially older ones. They even clung to a competitive strategy when it had no benefit for them. The rural Mexican children, in contrast, avoided competition at all costs, even when a competitive strategy would have benefited *both* players. Madsen does not argue that one playing style is better than the other. His point is that different cultural values lead to distinctly different behaviors. Moreover, these different behavioral styles were not viewed as genetic because *urban* Mexican children were much more competitive at Madsen's games than their rural counterparts.

Why do different cultures have such different values? Why do adults in one society encourage children to be cooperative, while adults in another society encourage competitiveness? Anthropologists who specialize in the study of cultural diversity believe that these differences are generally *adaptive*. By adaptive, they mean that the values adults instill tend to produce the kinds of children best able to perform the activities required in their particular society. Beatrice and John Whiting (1975) demonstrated this in a study of six different cultures: North America, India, Africa, Mexico, Okinawa, and the Philippines. Children in the nonindustrialized cultures were given tasks important to the well-being of their families, such as caring for younger siblings and tending the goat while mothers worked in the fields. These children showed nurturant and responsible behavior, traits suited to the roles they performed. If they failed to tend the goat, there was no milk. In contrast, children in industrialized cultures were more egoistic and self-centered. Apparently, the economic efficiency of industrialized societies reduces the need for children to contribute to their family's survival, so a self-centered orientation can be tolerated in them (Munroe and Munroe, 1975). In fact, some would argue that egoism is actually an asset in societies that depend on a desire for personal profit to motivate economic growth.

Kissing and Playing with Babies

Kissing

The kissing of an infant on the mouth should never be permitted, under any circumstances, by either adult or child. Diphtheria, tuberculosis and syphilis have often been communicated in this manner, for even healthy adults often have the germs of these diseases, and although they may never suffer from them, they can communicate them to a baby. Children suffering from contagious diseases in their earliest stages often transmit the disease by kissing.

Infants ought never to be kissed by any one, except on the forehead, and even that should very seldom be permitted.

Playing with Babies

To play with, or amuse an infant under the age of six months is actually injurious, and may be the means of making him nervous and irritable. Even such slight amusements as swaying a baby, or rocking him, all tend to stimulate the rapidly growing brain, and are harmful for this reason.

Even after the age of six months, it is wiser to let an infant amuse himself, *as he will soon learn to do, if left alone.* When constant efforts are made to amuse a child, he is apt to become nervous and fretful, to sleep badly, and to suffer from indigestion. He should never be played with immediately before bedtime at any age.

The practice of allowing young babies and children to be present at any celebration can not be too strongly condemned. The gratification of showing off the baby and seeing him admired is not worth having at the expense of his nerves and health.

Figure 3.6
Excerpts from a Child-Rearing Guide of 1916
These admonitions were actually given in a 1916 guide for mothers. Developmental psychologists today would certainly disagree with such ideas.
Source: Tweddell, 1916.

Cultural Change and Child Development

A certain culture once maintained that the most important goal in raising children was to establish strong parental control. Training the child to be obedient was to begin in the first year. To avoid "spoiling" a baby, only the infant's physical needs were to be met. Babies who merely wanted attention were strongly discouraged, and sentimental treatment was avoided. Infants were never picked up when they cried and were punished for touching themselves. They also were fed on a strict schedule, not when they wanted to be fed.

Where in the world did such harsh practices exist? This is not a description of some remote culture but of our own society a mere 50 years ago (Newsom and Newsom, 1974; Truby-King, 1937; Watson, 1928)! Figure 3.6 describes some other practices recommended early in this century. Up until quite recently, children in Western cultures were viewed as miniature adults and pressured toward adult responsibility as soon as possible. People did not recognize the specialness of childhood or the need for an extended period of nurturant care giving. This outlook prevailed for many centuries. Perhaps it was due to the harshness of life in earlier times. Even as late as the eighteenth century, death at birth or during childhood was common, and many infants of poor families were abandoned because their parents could not support them. In Paris at that time, one out of every three babies was abandoned (Piers, 1978). Children admitted to foundling homes usually died. Out of 10,272 babies admitted to one Dublin institution, only 45 survived (Kessen, 1965). These harsh conditions have gradually changed as technological progress has steadily raised both the average standard of living and our ability to combat disease. This change may be the reason why modern-day parents can afford the luxury of devoting themselves to their children's emotional welfare.

Undoubtedly, broad cultural changes will continue to affect parenting and child development. In some societies these cultural changes are happening very rapidly. For instance, far-reaching change is taking place in China, where a family-centered culture is being totally transformed into a state-centered one. Imagine the consequences of establishing universal preschool education in a society where young children have always been cared for in the home. Imagine the effects of a one-child-per-family policy in a culture that previously considered large families a blessing. The results of this major cultural "experiment" are just now being revealed to Westerners. Even in our own society cultural change is evident from generation to generation. American children today are being raised in a world far more technologically advanced than the world their parents knew as children. American children today are also more aware of the threat of nuclear war. Developmentalists are concerned about the impacts of these important cultural changes. As yet, little is known about how children may be shaped by them.

Subcultures

We have talked about societies as if all their members share a single culture. However, especially in complex, industrialized societies, this is seldom the case. Many societies have a number of **subcultures,** that is, particular groups whose members adhere to norms and values that differ in some ways from those of the dominant culture. In the United States, the Eastern Europeans, Chicanos, Japanese Americans, and so forth who practice their traditional ways are members of subcultural groups.

The norms and values of a subculture may influence the way children are raised. You will see this in our story of the Williams family. As black Americans living in an urban center, they are influenced by certain subcultural norms and values. Their lives provide a good example of how subcultural influences continually interact with broader cultural forces.

DEVELOPMENT AS CONTEXT

No discussion of developmental contexts would be complete without mention of development itself as a context for further development. Development provides a context in several ways. First, it gives each person a developmental history, which influences the course of his or her future development. This idea is central to Erik Erikson's theory, discussed in Chapter 2. According to Erikson, the way a child negotiates the issues of a particular developmental period depends in part on development during earlier periods. Consider, for example, a toddler who is faced with

Each culture and subculture has its unique features. *(Bill Anderson/Monkmeyer Press.)*

the emergence of a sense of autonomy and a capacity for self-assertion. That toddler's tendency to comply with parents' demands and limits is forecast by the nature of the *infant*-parent relationship (Ainsworth, Bell, and Stayton, 1974; Londerville and Main, 1981; Matas, Arend, and Sroufe, 1978). In other words, part of the context for development in the toddler period is development in the preceding infancy period. Similarly, children enter preschool with different orientations toward their peers and teachers and with different expectations about their own capacities to master new situations. These different orientations and expectations, based in each child's developmental history, become part of the context for development in the preschool period.

Development also provides a context for future development by changing children both physically and intellectually through the process of maturation. The transformations in physical and cognitive capacities that occur with maturation have a dramatic influence on how children interact with their environments. Consider once again the toddler. Because of maturation the toddler is much more mobile than the infant, much more able to "get into things." This new mobility encourages parents to impose new demands, and the child's world consequently changes. At the same time, the toddler begins to understand and use language as a result of cognitive maturation. This opens up a whole new avenue of parental influence, which greatly affects future development. Maturation as a context for future development can be seen in other periods, such as adolescence. The physical and cognitive changes at puberty lead to profound changes in teenagers' self-concepts, in their communications with parents, and in their orientations toward peers, including an emerging interest in sexual relationships and strong loyalty to same-sex friends. A key context for all these developmental changes is prior development through maturation.

CONTEXTS IN INTERACTION

This chapter's central message has been that human development always occurs within a set of contexts: the biological context, the child's immediate environment, social and economic spheres, the cultural environment, and even the child's history of development. None of these contexts exists in isolation. None exerts its influence apart from the others. All are constantly interacting, helping to shape the child's development.

One important point to remember in thinking about developmental contexts is that certain environmental factors tend to go together. Economic advantage, job satisfaction, adequate food and housing, a stable home life, and social support often accompany one another. Thus, when you find an infant living in physical neglect (unbathed, without toys, without a proper place to sleep), it is also common to find an overstressed and isolated parent with limited education and little chance of finding satisfying work. The out-of-home care available to such babies is typically haphazard and of poor quality (Vaughn, Gove, and Egeland, 1980). This is not to say that these environmental factors *always* go together. Sometimes parents with very limited economic resources still have excellent social support systems, stable relationships, well-organized households, and a remarkable tolerance for stress. In general, however, very negative life situations tend to diminish how well people cope, including their ability to cope with the raising of children.

Another point to remember when thinking about developmental contexts is that all the environmental influences we have discussed in this chapter are funneled to some extent through the family. For instance, children are not *directly* affected by their parents' job stress or social isolation. Instead, these factors have an indirect influence by affecting the quality of care the children experience at home. Even the influences of day care, the school, and the peer group are not removed from the family. It is parents who arrange for out-of-home care, select schools for their children, and promote or fail to promote peer relationships (Lieberman, 1977). In short, the significance that various developmental contexts have for a child is always affected by decisions and interactions within the child's family. Biological, socioeconomic, and cultural factors provide both the challenges parents face and the resources they may draw on for the task of child rearing.

We will return to developmental contexts again and again in this book. Our view is that these contexts dramatically influence how children develop. In the next chapter we will focus on important aspects of a child's biological context, namely, how the genetic instructions contained in two tiny cells combine to produce the human infant. As you will see, this early development involves an intricate interplay of genes and environment.

Chapter Review

1. Optimal development greatly depends on a good developmental context. The contexts of human development include a child's biological inheritance. Babies come equipped with many built-in tendencies, including a strong disposition to explore and master the environment, an innate propensity for learning, and a predisposition to become social. All these are part of our evolutionary heritage.

2. Another important developmental context is a child's **immediate environment.** It contains all the physical objects, the people, and the settings that touch the child's life. The family is a dominant part of a child's immediate environment. Family members stimulate cognitive development, model various roles and behaviors, provide nurturing relationships, and filter other developmental influences. Contemporary researchers think of the family as an interconnected system in which each member's behavior and each relationship depend in part on the behaviors of the others. Arnold Sameroff's **transactional model** focuses on **reciprocal determinism,** or the **bidirectional effects** parents and children have on each other, taking into account the family's overall social and economic context.

3. All parts of a child's immediate environment are embedded in a broader **social and economic context** and are greatly influenced by it. For instance, the general social and economic climate in modern-day America has encouraged some dramatic changes in the average family setting. Compared with families 30 years ago, contemporary families are much more likely to include just one parent. This trend is due both to more divorce and to more children born outside of marriage. Contemporary families are also more likely than families of the 1950s to include a mother who works outside the home. Developmentalists have found that these modern family trends have complex impacts that are very dependent on individual circumstances.

4. The social and economic context has an especially important influence for children living in poverty. Poor nutrition and medical care are likely to cause them health problems both before and after birth. Poverty households are also apt to experience high levels of stress due to overcrowding, financial uncertainty, and generally unstable life circumstances. This stress, coupled with isolation and lack of social support, can adversely affect parenting and child development.

5. As children grow older, they increasingly find themselves in settings outside the family. One such setting is day care, which a growing number of American children are experiencing. About half of these children are in **family day care,** in which several children are cared for in someone else's home. Another setting is the peer group, a child's circle of same-age companions. In peer groups children learn about such concepts as fairness, reciprocity, and cooperation, as well as about society's norms and values. Schools are also conveyors of social norms and values. Because American children spend so much time in classrooms, school, like the peer group, can have a powerful influence on their development.

6. A child's **cultural context** consists of all the many beliefs, values, and guidelines for behavior that people in that particular society tend to share. You can see the effects of culture in the different ways that social groups and institutions are structured. Its effects can also be seen in the different traits that children around the world possess. These cultural traits tend to be adaptive, meaning that they are suited to the kinds of activities people in a given society must perform. Since cultures are always changing, researchers are concerned about how such changes may affect future child development. Researchers are also interested in the effects of **subcultures,** groups whose norms and values differ in significant ways from those of a society's dominant culture.

7. Even development itself provides a context for future development. It gives each person a developmental history, which in turn affects how that person deals with new demands and challenges. Development also entails the process of maturation, which changes children both physically and intellectually. These changes then have a dramatic influence on how children interact with their environments and continue to develop.

8. All the many contexts of development interact with one another. Two aspects of this interaction are especially important to remember. First, certain environmental factors (economic advantage, adequate food and housing, a stable home life, a network of supportive friends and relatives) often go together. Second, many of the environmental factors that children experience are funneled to some extent through the family.

4

Heredity and Prenatal Development

I f you stand outside a maternity-ward nursery, you are apt to find adults searching for family resemblances in their newborns. "Those big eyes are just like her mother's," someone might observe, or "He has his father's dimple in the chin." Many such family resemblances are the product of genes, the chemical blueprints for development that each of us inherits from our parents. In this chapter you will learn how genes express themselves and how their effects interact with those of the environment. A major theme of this chapter is that genes are only one part of a complex developmental system. Genes help to guide development, but they can function only with appropriate environmental support. We stress the role of context and the importance of a systems or transactional view throughout this book. That viewpoint is especially apparent during the period prior to birth, which is called the **prenatal period.**

Another important theme of this chapter is that development follows the process of *differentiation,* proceeding from the general to the refined and specific. For example, every human begins life as a single cell, which divides to produce cells that are similar to one another. Soon, however, as more new cells are created, they begin to take on specialized forms and functions (Beck, Moffat, and Lloyd, 1973; Parker and Bavosi, 1979). Bone cells differ from blood cells, muscle cells from fat cells, nerve cells from skin cells. Just as the one-celled creatures that first appeared on this planet differentiated into many species over millions of generations, so the initial cell that begins a human life differentiates in successive generations of cell division to produce all the parts of the body.

But human development encompasses more than differentiation alone. As cells differentiate, they also undergo *reorganization.* Cells migrate and form tissues, each different from the other. Then, influenced by contact with one another, the cells of these tissues reorganize further, building organs with intricate structures. At the various steps in this complex process, the developing organism undergoes *qualitative change.* The embryo at five weeks is fundamentally different than it was at two weeks; at eight weeks it is fundamentally different than it was at five weeks (Parker and Bavosi, 1979). By fundamentally different we do not mean simply that new parts have been added, but that the developing human has achieved new levels of organization and functioning.

A final theme of this chapter is that during prenatal development new structures and capacities emerge in an *orderly* manner from those that existed before. When you look at the pictures in this chapter of human embryos, you will see that each stage is a logical outgrowth of the previous one. Like all human development, prenatal development is orderly, cumulative, and directional (Parker and Bavosi, 1979).

In this chapter we will trace the development of a human being from conception through birth. In order to understand an individual's biological makeup—that is, the genes he or she inherits—we begin with a look at human heredity within the framework of evolution. What are genes made of? How do they affect growth and development? And how can each individual receive a set of genetic instructions that no one else has ever possessed? We then turn to the moment of conception, the joining of egg and sperm, which sets the long process of human development in motion. From there we examine prenatal development all the way to birth, with special attention to qualitative changes in development that are the product of the interaction between genes and environment.

GENES, HEREDITY, AND EVOLUTION

Living things exhibit enormous diversity. Their tremendous range of forms permits plants, animals, and microorganisms to survive in all kinds of environments. As you will recall from Chapter 1, Charles Darwin's evolutionary theory explains the diversity of living things by arguing that, over generations, the traits of groups of organisms tend to change in directions better suited to survival in particular environments. Evolution has established the particular limitations and potentials of the human species. We don't have four legs for speed, claws for fighting, or wings for flying. But we do have large brains for conceptual intelligence and flexible problem solving, and hands with opposable thumbs for fine manual dexterity. The result is that we can build race cars, weapons, and spacecraft, allowing us to travel rapidly, subjugate other species, and explore the heavens. We also have evolved to be a group-living species with the potential for cooperation and conflict.

Evolutionary theory explains not only the diversity among species but also the diversity *within* them. The members of any higher-animal species are never exactly alike. Each member has its own variations on the basic species patterns, a phenomenon known as **polymorphism.** For example, humans have four blood types (which will be discussed shortly). You may wonder why, over millions of years, one "best" example of each species hasn't evolved. The answer is that diversity within species offers adaptive advantages. Such diversity means that when the environment changes in some significant way (such as the appearance of a new disease-causing virus) some members of the species usually are able to survive. In addition, for social animals diversity makes different individuals better able to perform different tasks. In our own society, for instance, some people are endowed with small hands that can manipulate delicate instruments, whereas others have large, strong hands more suited to heavy work. Such diversity also is the basis for slow or gradual evolutionary change, as populations with different characteristics become isolated and genetically drift apart.

Mutations add to the genetic diversity that underlies these physical variations. **Mutations** are naturally occurring changes in genes that alter the instructions they give. Most mutations are not adaptive; in humans and other mammals they often lead to miscarriages and stillbirths. However, mutations sometimes arise that are beneficial to an individual's survival. They may then enter the species' gene pool, be acted upon by natural selection, and become widespread. For generations, plant and animal breeders have taken advantage of mutations to develop new strains of stock. Recently scientists have acquired the ability to induce mutations by actually inserting new genes into simple organisms, a process called **genetic engineering.** Such work has been important in developing new cures for diseases.

The Mechanisms of Heredity

Every organism is made up of cells, fundamental units that carry out all the various functions essential to life. The heart of a living cell, its command center, is the cell nucleus, a membrane-bound structure that contains a copy of the organism's genetic material. In human cells, this consists of 46 **chromosomes** arranged in 23 pairs. Each chromosome is composed of threadlike molecules known as **DNA (deoxyribonucleic acid).** A DNA molecule consists of two strands that curl around each other in a pattern resembling the banisters of two spiral staircases (see Figure 4.1, part A). **Genes** are segments of DNA. As many as 20,000 genes

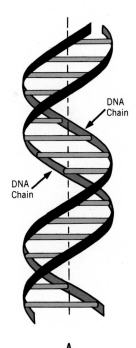

DNA Chain

DNA Chain

A

Figure 4.1 (A)
DNA, the Double Helix
DNA consists of two long strands of molecules (like the railings of two spiral staircases) connected by several short strands (resembling steps).

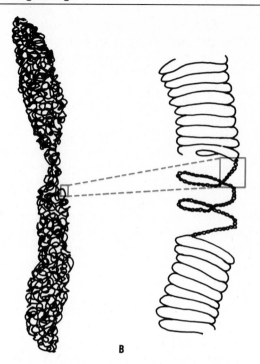

Figure 4.1 (B)
Genes and Chromosomes
Genes are segments of the long threadlike DNA molecules that make up a chromosome. The chromosome is the tangled mass of threads shown on the left, and a single gene is represented in the colored portion on the right.

Source: Part (B) is adapted from Fisher and Lazerson, 1984, p. 83.

B

may be positioned along a single chromosome (see Figure 4.1, part B). Genes that regulate the same aspects of development are always located on the same chromosome. This is known because visible damage to a specific chromosome has predictable consequences. The two chromosomes in each pair are said to be **homologous,** meaning that their corresponding genes affect the same aspects of development.

In order for genetic information to be transmitted from parents to offspring, special reproductive cells (sperm and egg) containing half the number of chromosomes must fuse. This means that one member of each chromosome pair came from the person's mother, while the other member came from the person's father. We will now take a closer look at this process.

MITOSIS, MEIOSIS, AND THE RANDOM ASSORTMENT OF GENES

Human life begins with one cell—a fertilized egg containing one set of 46 chromosomes. Over the next nine months, billions of new cells will be formed through cellular division, with each cell containing a copy of the original chromosomes (Parker and Bavosi, 1979). This duplication of chromosomes is essential if the cells are to do their work, for the genes on each chromosome carry the instructions for all of a cell's activities. This type of cell division, in which a single cell forms two virtually identical daughter cells, is called **mitosis.** During mitosis, chromosomes duplicate themselves. Then each original chromosome links up with its newly formed duplicate and aligns along the cell's center. The duplicates then move toward opposite ends of the cell as the cell begins to elongate. Eventually the cell splits down the middle forming two new cells, each with the 23 pairs of chromosomes (see Figure 4.2). Such cell division is needed not only for the developing fertilized egg but also for human growth and maintenance after birth. For example, mitosis is responsible for rapid bone growth in children and replacement of skin cells in adults. Differentiation, the process by which the cells of the fertilized egg form specialized organs and tissues, occurs following mitotic cell division.

To produce offspring, however, a special form of cell division is required (Hogarth, 1978). If the mother's egg cells and the father's sperm cells contained 46 chromosomes like all other cells, the fertilized egg would contain 92 chromosomes, double the correct number. There must be a way for the chromosomes in egg and sperm cells to reduce their number to only 23 each, so that a fertilized egg has only 46 chromosomes. This "reduction division" occurs in a process called **meiosis** (see Figure 4.3). During meiosis, each chromosome in the parent's reproductive cell duplicates itself. The original chromosomes attached to their copies align themselves in the center of the cell. After this occurs, the cell divides to produce two cells, each having 23 pairs of chromosomes. Then a second division takes place producing **gametes** (either sperm or egg cells) with only 23 chromosomes in each cell.

Figure 4.2
Mitosis
Mitosis is the process of cell duplication that produces two identical daughter cells. The basic mechanism for growth and maintenance of body tissues, it begins with each chromosome in the cell duplicating itself and is followed by cell division. In this way each of the new cells contains all of the genetic information of the previous cell.

Source: Adapted from Shaeffer, 1985, p. 84.

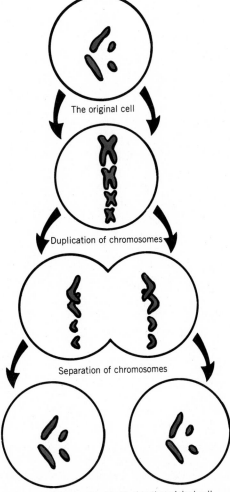

The original cell

Duplication of chromosomes

Separation of chromosomes

Each new cell is identical to the original cell

The random movement of chromosomes during meiosis causes an enormous variety of gene combinations in the resulting gametes. In addition to random alignment prior to the first meiotic division, the non-duplicate chromosomes in each set can join at several points along their length during the alignment process. When this occurs, some of the genes on one chromosome switch places with genes on the other. This process is called **crossing over** (see Figure 4.4). Crossing over randomly shuffles the genes in homologous chromosomes, mixing those from an individual's mother with those from that person's father. Then, during the first meiotic cell division, homologous chromosomes separate without regard to their original sources. In one pair of homologues, the chromosome originally from the person's father may move to the left, while the one derived from the mother moves to the right. In another pair, the movements may be exactly the reverse. The side to which a particular chromosome travels is determined purely by chance; the only requirement is

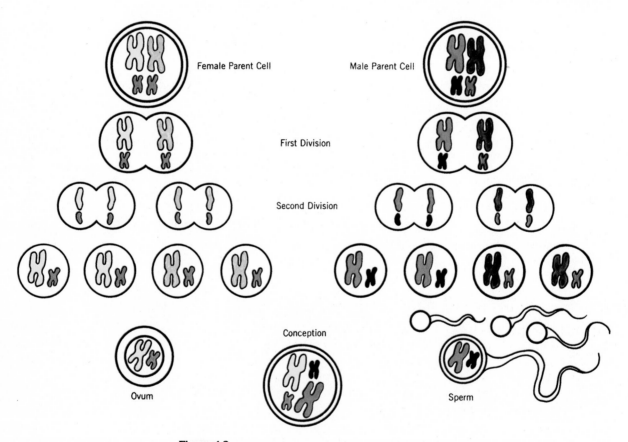

Figure 4.3
Meiosis
Meiosis is a special form of cell division unique to reproductive cells. In the process the cells produced have the number of chromosomes reduced by half, so that when a sperm cell combines with an egg cell there will be only the normal complement of 46 chromosomes. Meiosis also allows for the great diversity in human offspring because each produced cell has different combinations of chromosomes.

Source: Adapted from Hall, Perlmutter, and Lamb, 1982, p. 81.

Figure 4.4
Crossing Over
Variety in human offspring is greatly increased because during meiotic cell division chromosomes cross over, exchanging genetic material.
Source: Adapted from Shaeffer, 1985, p. 81.

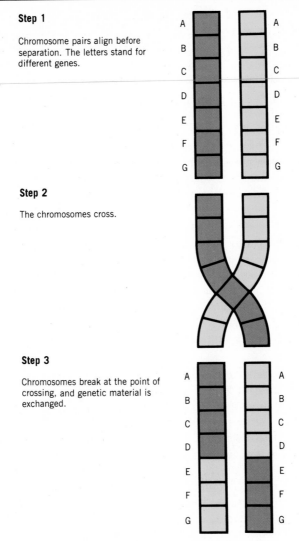

Step 1

Chromosome pairs align before separation. The letters stand for different genes.

Step 2

The chromosomes cross.

Step 3

Chromosomes break at the point of crossing, and genetic material is exchanged.

that homologous chromosomes from each pair go in *opposite* directions. The end result is that every sperm or egg cell receives a random member from each of the 23 pairs of chromosomes that a person possesses.

Let's look at the variability produced by meiosis from a different angle. Even without the process of crossing over, the random assortment of chromosomes during meiosis allows production of about *8 million* different chromosome combinations. Now consider a husband and wife, each with the potential for creating 8 million different sperm or egg cells. The chances that they will both produce the same genetic combination twice and give birth to identical siblings is 1 in 64 *trillion*. (Because of crossing over, the actual probability is even less.) This is why, except for twins who develop from a single fertilized egg that splits into two separate units, children of the same parents look different from one another. These differences vary depending on the amount of genetic material the siblings share.

HOW DO GENES INFLUENCE DEVELOPMENT?

How genes influence development is not yet fully understood. Scientists have just begun to solve the mystery of this highly complex process. The key is to understand that particular genes are not always "turned on." We then need to discover how it is that different genes are turned on in different cells (Beck, Moffat, and Lloyd, 1973). One thing we do know is that it makes no sense to talk of genes as if they acted independently. Genes are always embedded in an environmental context, which both enables them to be expressed and shapes developmental outcomes. Just as a child's behavior is influenced by the family environment and other aspects of the surrounding context (see Chapter 3), so too are genes influenced by the environmental context.

The environment of genes is ultimately the cells of the body, which in turn can be affected by a host of outside factors (from nutrients to drugs to viruses that enter the organism's bloodstream). In addition, the genetic environment is influenced by the organism's own developmental history, the cumulative effects of all the changes that have taken place so far. Consequently, it is best to think of genes as only one part of an intricate developmental system that includes both heredity *and* environment. One clear example of this dual system at work is the development of a person's gender.

Interaction of Genes and Environment: The Case of Gender Development. The development of human gender begins at the moment of conception, when sperm fuses with egg. The fertilized egg's gender is determined by just one of its 23 pairs of chromosomes, the pair that scientists conventionally label number 23. If the twenty-third pair consists of two long chromosomes, called **X chromosomes,** the stage has been set for the development of a female. If the twenty-third pair consists of one X chromosome plus another much shorter **Y chromosome,** the stage has been set for the development of a male. Note that in males, with their XY pattern, not all the chromosome pairs are completely homologous. The X and Y chromosomes in the twenty-third pair are homologous only along a small portion of their lengths.

A little deductive reasoning will tell you that a baby's sex must be determined by the father's sperm. Women, with their two XX chromosomes, can produce only egg cells containing X chromosomes. Men, in contrast, with their XY chromosome pattern, produce both X-carrying and Y-carrying sperm. Whichever type of sperm fertilizes the egg sets in motion the beginnings of gender development.

You may think that a person's gender is fully determined at the moment of conception, when sperm penetrates egg. As we said earlier, however, this is only the beginning. The 23rd chromosome pattern created upon fertilization simply determines whether an embryo will develop testes or ovaries. This developmental event, moreover, does not occur right away. Sexual differentiation is one example of how the action of genes is sometimes delayed until a critical period in development is reached (Hogarth, 1978). For the first six weeks after conception, the primitive gonad (or sex gland) tissues look exactly the same in males as in females. It is not until precisely the seventh week that the presence of

Some traits have long been known to be due to genes located on the Y chromosome. These traits, such as baldness and hemophilia, are referred to as "sex-linked" because they appear only in males. *(Freda Leinwand/Monkmeyer Press.)*

a Y chromosome will trigger part of this primitive gonad tissue to begin differentiating into testes, the male sex glands. If no Y is present, in another week or so the gonad tissues instead start differentiating into ovaries, or female sex glands. At this point the sex chromosomes have done their work. From here on, **hormones,** glandular secretions that are a part of the embryo's internal environment, influence gender development. Let's see what these hormones do.

Once the testes are partially formed in a Y-carrying embryo, they begin to secrete male sex hormones, called **androgens.** Androgens cause certain primitive structures to differentiate into the male reproductive tract, and they also induce formation of a penis. At the same time, the testes secrete a second hormone that causes atrophy of structures with the potential to become parts of the female reproductive system. Interestingly, in XX embryos, it is not necessary for female sex hormones to be present in order for female sex organs to develop. All that is needed is the absence of male hormones (Hogarth, 1978).

How do researchers know that the presence or absence of androgens is the key factor causing these aspects of gender development? Some evidence comes from studies in which scientists have manipulated prenatal hormones in animals. By the withholding of androgens at the critical point in development, genetically male embryos will proceed to develop female organs. Conversely, by the administration of large doses of androgens to XX embryos, these genetic females will develop male-looking organs (Bennett, 1982). Similar evidence comes from the study of humans whose prenatal exposure to androgens accidentally went wrong. For instance, baby girls are sometimes exposed to abnormally high levels of androgens during the embryo stage, either because their mothers receive hormone treatments without knowing they are pregnant or because their mothers' adrenal glands secrete excessive amounts of androgens. These girls often develop masculine-looking genitals. Conversely, genetically male embryos sometimes develop female-looking genitals because the cells of their bodies for some reason are insensitive to androgens (Money and Ehrhardt, 1972).

The development of secondary sexual characteristics, such as facial hair, when a child reaches puberty is also governed by hormones. In this case, however, the absence of androgens is no longer enough to complete a girl's sexual development. Whereas in adolescent boys a stepped-up secretion of androgens causes the development of facial hair, a deeper voice, broader shoulders, and so forth, in adolescent girls it is the increased secretion of female hormones called **estrogens** that triggers sexual maturation, by influencing yet other genes to become active at this time. More will be said about this in Chapter 14.

The most important point that our discussion of sexual development makes is the extent to which genes and environment interact to guide development. Genes have their effects as part of a developmental system that also includes the environmental context. Thus, if you ask whether the genes in a fertilized egg are sufficient to produce a male or a female, the answer would have to be no. Genes contain information with the potential for guiding development, but how that information is actually used depends on the environment in which the genes operate. For instance, the presence of a Y chromosome in certain cells of the embryo's body causes those cells to develop into glands that produce androgens. But note the great importance of the *location* of the genes. Not all the embryo's cells differentiate into testes, even though all of them contain a Y chromosome. The critical factor is the particular environment in which the Y chromosome operates. In short, the overall system—genes *and* environment—is what produces development. Similarly, an embryo may develop testes, which in turn produce androgens; but if the critical cells of the body are insensitive to those hormones, the child will not develop normal-looking genitals. Again, it is the overall developmental *system* that matters, not genes or hormones alone.

How Genes Affect One Another.   To add even more complexity to the developmental system, genes interact not only with the environment but also with one another. A simple example can be seen in the development of blood type. We mentioned earlier that there are four human blood types. How are they produced genetically? Each person inherits two genes, one from each parent, which code for blood type. Because these genes code for the same trait, they are located at the same point on homologous chromosomes. There are three possible blood-type genes a person can have: one that codes for type A blood, one that codes for type B, and one that codes for type O. Alternate forms of genes for the same trait are called **alleles.** In this case, the alleles are A, B, and O.

What effects do various allele combinations have? If a person inherits the same allele from both parents, that is, AA, BB, or OO, that person is said to be **homozygous** for this trait, because the genes inherited are the same. A homozygous person will always display whatever characteristic the two identical genes code for. A different outcome occurs in people who are **heterozygous,** that is, who carry two alternate genes (alleles) at a certain point on homologous chromosomes. Sometimes one allele dominates the other; other times the two share dominance. For instance, people who inherit one allele for type A blood and one for type O will turn out to have blood type A because the A allele is **dominant.** The same is true of people with a B and O combination: They will have type B blood because the B allele dominates the O. The only way for the **recessive** O allele to be expressed is if a person is homozygous for it. On the other hand, if a person inherits one A allele and one B, *both* blood types will be expressed, and the person will have blood type AB. Neither allele A nor allele B overrides the other; the two are **co-dominant.**

The example of blood type shows that you cannot always tell people's **genotypes** (the genes they possess) simply by looking at their **phenotypes** (their observable physical traits). The reason is that the presence of recessive alleles is sometimes masked by dominant ones. In the case of blood types, there are actually six genotypes (AA, AO, BB, BO, AB, OO), but only four phenotypes (A, B, AB, and O). The recessive O gene can be masked by a dominant A or B.

Recessive genes can make it hard to predict what traits children are likely to have simply by looking at their parents. If both parents show a recessive trait (type O blood, for instance), the task is easy, because both must carry only the recessive allele and so can produce only children with the same genotype. But if both parents show a dominant trait, the task is much more difficult. Without testing the blood, we have no way of telling if the parents are homozygous or heterozygous for that dominant gene. If both are homozygous, they will produce only children with the same genetic pattern. However, if both are heterozygous, their offspring could have any one of several genotypes. Suppose, for example, that a man and woman both have one A blood-type gene and one O. A child they produce would have an equal chance of receiving any one of the following four patterns: an A gene from both parents, an A from the father and an O from the mother, an A from the mother and an O from the father, or an O from both parents. In the first three cases the child would have type A blood; in the last case, type O. In other words, such a child has a 75 percent chance of having the same blood type as the parents. But we cannot tell with certainty what the chances are unless we know the parents' genotypes.

The interaction of genes in human development is even more complex than our simple blood-type examples show. Many human characteristics are influenced not just by a single pair of genes but rather by numerous gene pairs, often on different chromosomes. Such characteristics are called **polygenic.** Examples include height, weight, skin color, and intelligence. In fact, any trait for which people show a large range of variation (rather than a few "either/or" types) is probably polygenic. We will explore two important polygenic characteristics later when we discuss the development of intelligence and the mental disorder schizophrenia.

Finally, there are some genes that do not influence traits directly. Instead, these so-called **modifier genes** influence the way other genes operate. For example, phenylketonuria (PKU) is a genetic disorder caused by a pair of recessive genes, but its severity depends on modifier genes (Rosenblith and Sims-Knight, 1985). Babies afflicted with PKU lack an enzyme that converts phenylalanine (a chemical common in many foods)

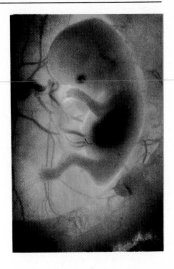

The interaction of genes with each other and with the environment helps to determine the course of fetal development. *(Petit Format/ Nestle/Science Source/Photo Researchers, Inc.)*

into other substances. Phenylalanine and its by-products therefore build up within the child's body, causing permanent brain damage and mental retardation. However, the amount of phenylalanine that accumulates is influenced by genes other than those that originally caused the condition. In short, these other genes modify the extent to which the two recessive genes are expressed in the child's phenotype.

Fortunately, once doctors understood the PKU problem they were able to devise a treatment for it. Children can be tested for PKU at birth and put on a special diet if they are found to have the disorder. If, starting in their first 6 months, they do not eat foods containing phenylalanine, such as dairy products, the recessive genes have little harmful effect (Rosenblith and Sims-Knight, 1985). This is a clear example of both the critical-period concept and how genes interact with environment to produce developmental outcomes. Starting the special diet before 7 months of age resulted largely in children who later displayed the normal range of intelligence (IQs of 70–100), whereas starting between 7 and 18 months yielded children with IQs below 70. Thus, by changing a person's environment (in this case diet) we can often change how genes are expressed. One complexity is that the required diet is very restrictive; some phenylalanine is required for normal development, so monitoring of these children must be done carefully.

CONCEPTION

For thousands of years, people have understood the link between intercourse and **conception,** when development within the fertilized egg begins. But it is only quite recently that we have come to understand exactly what takes place during conception. Up until the eighteenth century, the doctrine of preformation prevailed. It held that inside either the egg or the sperm was a miniature person, called a *homunculus,* already fully formed. All that was needed was to trigger growth of this tiny person. In one version of the theory, the sperm was said to trigger growth of a homunculus inside the egg. Our modern view of conception, of course, is very different. We know that instead of a homunculus, sperm and egg contain genes that help guide the complex developmental process, resulting in a new human being. In this section we will explore the joining of sperm and egg that initiates this process.

Events Leading Up to Conception

Like many other aspects of development, conception depends on appropriate timing of a chain of events. This chain is influenced indirectly by the genetic make-ups of the man and woman involved. Their genes control hormone secretions, which in turn affect the woman's menstrual cycle and the man's production of sperm. As we will see in discussing infertility, conception is also influenced by a variety of environmental factors.

In most women an egg cell, or **ovum,** ripens in one of her ovaries about every 28 days. When ready for fertilization (penetration by a sperm

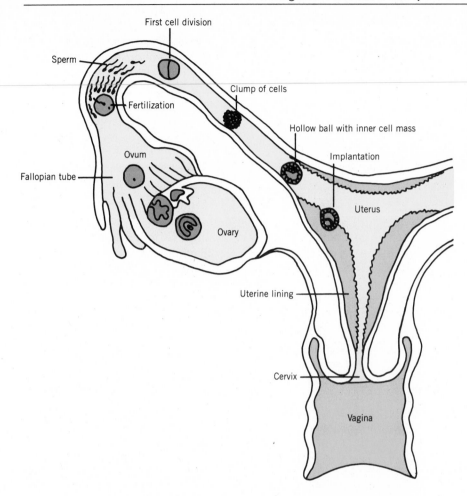

First cell division

Sperm

Fertilization

Ovum

Fallopian tube

Ovary

Clump of cells

Hollow ball with inner cell mass

Implantation

Uterus

Uterine lining

Cervix

Vagina

Figure 4.5
Fertilization
Fertilization normally occurs at the upper end of the Fallopian tube. The fertilized egg begins the process of cell division even while it travels to the uterus. In normal pregnancies this clump of cells will then become implanted in the uterine wall.

Source: Adapted from Hall, Perlmutter, and Lamb, 1982, p. 80.

cell), the ovum is released into one of the Fallopian tubes, passages that lead to the uterus. The journey down the Fallopian tube, as shown in Figure 4.5, takes the ovum several days. If it is not fertilized by a sperm within the first 24 hours, it disintegrates upon reaching the uterus. However, if sexual intercourse has occurred at the appropriate time, the ovum will meet thousands of sperm, sometimes as many as a million. These sperm are just part of several hundred million released during ejaculation. The sperm swim randomly, and some find their way into the Fallopian tubes. If one of these sperm penetrates the ovum's outer membrane, a tiny organism called a **zygote** is produced. Once an ovum has been penetrated, a biochemical change occurs that prevents other sperm from penetrating (Sutton, 1975).

We have outlined the usual steps leading to conception, but sometimes there is an important difference: Occasionally a woman's ovaries will release more than one ovum at a time. In fact, with the use of modern fertility drugs, this is becoming increasingly common. If two ova are fertilized by two different sperm the result is **dizygotic twins** ("two zygotes"), also called fraternal twins. Since different ova and sperm produce dizygotic twins, they are no more similar genetically than any other pair of siblings.

For so-called identical twins to form, a single fertilized egg must split into two separate units during its early cell divisions. Since twins produced in this manner are the product of only one ovum and sperm, they are called **monozygotic twins** ("mono" meaning one). Monozygotic twins by definition are genetically identical. They are thus of great interest to researchers studying the interaction of genes and environment. We will discuss various studies of monozygotic twins in later chapters.

Infertility

Approximately one married couple in ten remains childless after trying to have a baby for a year or longer, and another one in ten would like to have more children but is unable to (Menning, 1977). Such couples are **infertile,** that is, unable to conceive a child. Couples cannot be easily classified as fertile or infertile. About 25 percent of women trying to become pregnant will succeed in one month, 60 percent in six months, and 80 percent in 12 months. Others require years to conceive, and some never conceive at all. Thus fertility can best be thought of as a spectrum along which people vary. Because conceiving a child requires two people, high fertility in one may compensate for low fertility in the other.

Although anxiety may be responsible in about 5 percent of cases involving couples who have trouble conceiving, most such problems result from physical causes. Male infertility is most frequently caused by reduced numbers of sperm per ejaculation; less often it is caused by sperm with low activity and a low survival rate. The reason for infertility in a woman is harder to diagnose. Most often it results from failure to ovulate or to release an egg cell from the ovaries. Another common cause of female infertility is blockage of the Fallopian tubes. A third cause is cervical mucus that is hostile to sperm, either killing the sperm or preventing them from entering the uterus. A recent rise in female infertility is a result of women postponing their attempts to become pregnant until after age 30.

Surgical techniques, hormone treatments, and drug therapies often can combat infertility and allow couples to conceive through normal intercourse. Sometimes, however, other procedures are needed. For instance, **artificial insemination** enables a husband with a low sperm count to pool together the sperm from several ejaculations, which then are inserted into the uterus at once. If the husband is completely sterile, artificial insemination with sperm from a donor can be employed. When the wife is sterile, her husband's sperm can be used to artificially inseminate another woman (called a **surrogate mother**) who has agreed to carry the fetus through birth. Finally, if neither husband nor wife is sterile but they still cannot conceive, they can try the latest technique: **extra-utero fertilization,** or fertilization outside the uterus. Doctors extract one or more mature egg cells from the woman's ovaries and collect sperm from her husband. Each ovum is then fertilized in the laboratory; if cell division begins, the growing mass of cells is placed in the woman's uterus, which has been readied by hormone treatments. Extra-utero fertilization allows some women who lack normal ovulations to become pregnant.

The study of infertility highlights the complexity of the first crucial steps in creating a new human being. Conceiving a child requires the perfect timing of interconnected systems. Problems or obstacles at any one point can lead to infertility. But as complex as human conception is, the next nine months of prenatal development are even more so. Transforming a single fertilized egg into a human being is such an intricate process, it seems truly miraculous every time it occurs successfully.

PRENATAL DEVELOPMENT AND BIRTH

The prenatal period, from conception to birth, is a time of not only rapid growth but also tremendous differentiation. Starting with just a single fertilized egg, cells divide, migrate, and interact with one another to take on specialized functions. Out of all this cellular activity emerges a human fetus and its life-support system. As you read the following sections, notice how increasingly complex structures develop out of initially limited resources. This is characteristic of all human development: The simpler capacities present at one stage pave the way for fundamental reorganizations and the emergence of new, more complex patterns.

Within 36 hours of fertilization the first cell division occurs. Then cell divisions continue at shorter intervals until, by the end of the first week, more than a hundred cells have formed in a cluster. This hollow, ball-like structure is called the blastocyst. *(Petit Format/Nestle/ Science Source/Photo Researchers, Inc.)*

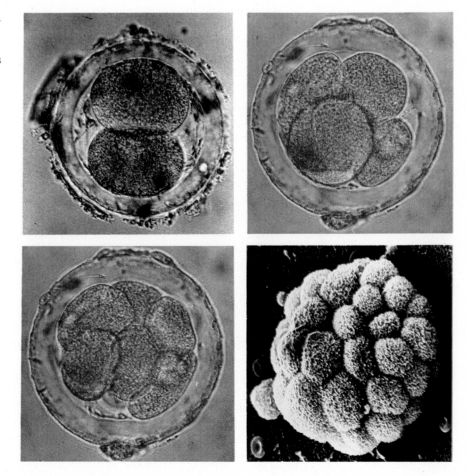

The Stages of Prenatal Development

Prenatal development consists of three major periods: the germinal, the embryonic, and the fetal. Although the boundaries separating these periods may be somewhat fuzzy, the developing organism is qualitatively different in each one. By qualitatively different we mean not only distinct in structure and organization but also in function. During the germinal period a tiny, self-contained cluster of cells becomes established in the mother's uterus. During the embryonic period, the major organs and body parts develop, the heart beats, and blood flows through microscopic vessels. During the fetal period, not only does the organism greatly increase in size, but it becomes a moving, sleeping, waking, "breathing" baby. As you read about prenatal development in the following pages, notice how it follows a predetermined schedule, with different structures and capabilities emerging at specific times. In this way prenatal development provides a model for later development in which qualitative changes in children unfold according to relatively predictable timetables.

THE GERMINAL PERIOD: CONCEPTION TO WEEK TWO

During the **germinal period,** the newly formed zygote becomes deeply implanted in the lining of the uterus and begins to form the life-support system that allows it to feed off the mother. About 30 hours after fertilization, the first mitotic cell division occurs, and after another 30 hours these two cells divide to make four. At first, all of these cells are structurally similar. They are not identical, because the cytoplasmic material (the environment surrounding the nucleus) that accompanies each daughter cell following division is not identical. Cell divisions continue at shorter intervals, until by the end of a week there are more than a hundred cells clustered together in a hollow, ball-like structure called a **blastocyst** (Parker and Bavosi, 1979). By this time an amazing process has already started: Cells in the blastocyst have begun to differentiate, to take on specialized forms and functions. A group of cells at one end of the blastocyst will develop into the embryo, while the rest of the blastocyst (known as the **trophoblast**) will become the life-support system without which the embryo could not survive. This process illustrates a remarkable feature of development, namely, qualitative change. The zygote is now a fundamentally different organism than it was just a week ago. We will return later to the problem of how it is possible that cells with the same genetic information, which had simply been reproducing themselves, now begin differentiating sharply, ultimately to become parts of complex organs and structures of the fetus.

While the cells of the blastocyst are dividing and differentiating, another essential process is taking place. About the sixth day after fertilization, the blastocyst makes contact with the lining of the mother's uterus. Hormone secretions have stimulated this lining to become engorged with blood so it can provide nutritional support to the new organism. The trophoblast rapidly grows tendril-like extensions that burrow into the uterine wall. If all goes well, by the end of the second week, the organism is firmly attached to the uterus, drawing nutrients and oxygen from its blood vessels.

TABLE 4.1   Developmental Milestones of the Embryo

Time After Conception	*Physical Changes*
12–13 days	Implantation complete.
14 days	Mature placenta begins to develop.
3 weeks (15–20 days)	Development of three-layered (trilaminar) disc. Neural tube begins to form. Disc becomes attached to wall by short, thick umbilical cord. Placenta develops rapidly.
4 weeks (21–28 days)	Eyes begin to form. Heart starts beating. Crown-rump length 5 mm (less than ¼ in.); growth rate about 1 mm per day. Neural tube closes (otherwise spina bifida). Vascular system (blood vessels) develops. Placenta maternal-infant circulation begins to function.
5 weeks	Arm and leg buds form.
7 weeks	Facial structures fuse (otherwise facial defects).
8 weeks	Crown-rump length 3 cm (slightly more than 1 in.); weight 1 g (about 1/30 oz). Major development of organs completed. Most external features recognizable at birth are present.

Source: Rosenblith and Sims-Knight, 1985, p. 24.

This implantation process, however, does carry some risk. Only about half of all blastocysts become successfully implanted (Roberts and Lowe, 1975). Those that fail are probably defective in some critical way or they attempt to implant in an inappropriate area. Two errors of implantation are *ectopic pregnancies,* in which the blastocyst embeds in one of the Fallopian tubes, and *placenta previa,* in which implantation occurs near the cervix. Both are very serious problems that can even threaten the mother's life.

THE EMBRYONIC PERIOD: WEEKS TWO THROUGH EIGHT

By the end of the germinal period, if it is successful, the blastocyst is firmly implanted and is thereafter called an **embryo.** It is during the **embryonic period,** from the end of the second week to the end of the eighth, that rapid differentiation of cells begins. **Organogenesis** takes place: All the vital organs form, as do other major parts of the body (Parker and Bavosi, 1979). Table 4.1 lists some of the major developmental landmarks during the embryonic period, and Figure 4.6 shows how quickly these dramatic changes take place. Let's look more closely at what occurs during these important prenatal weeks, beginning with further development of the embryo's life-support system.

The support system for the developing embryo consists of three major parts: the placenta, umbilical cord, and fluid-filled amniotic sac. The

placenta is a mass of tissue that forms partly from cells of the uterine lining and partly from cells that make up the trophoblast. The placenta supplies oxygen and nutrients to the embryo and carries away waste products. Blood vessels lead to and from it on both the embryo's side of the organ (via the **umbilical cord**) and the mother's side. But the blood cells of the embryo and the mother are too large to pass through the placenta and mix. Only smaller molecules, such as oxygen, carbon dioxide, nutrients, and hormones, are able to diffuse across the cell membranes. Thus, the placenta effectively filters out some substances that could be harmful to the embryo. Most bacteria, for instance, are kept out because they are too large. The placenta does not entirely protect the embryo, however. Some viruses, alcohol, and many other drugs are able to pass through it, with effects you will see later in this chapter.

Another major part of the embryo's life-support system is the fluid-filled **amniotic sac.** It provides a closed, protective environment within which the embryo develops. Because of the amniotic sac, foreign substances cannot come in contact with the embryo except by way of the placenta and the umbilical cord. The amniotic fluid also insulates the embryo from any bumps and jostling. Recall the minor parking lot accident that DeeDee Williams witnessed in the story at the beginning of this part. Because of the protection of the amniotic fluid, the pregnant woman's fetus was probably unharmed. At the same time, amniotic fluid helps to minimize temperature changes as the mother experiences warm and cold environments.

While the placenta, umbilical cord, and amniotic sac are developing, the embryo itself is also undergoing much change. During the third week of pregnancy (the first week of the embryonic period), the new organism becomes oval in shape and then indented. This indentation is the beginning of what will become the mouth and digestive tract (Nash, 1978). Cells on the surface of the embryo migrate to this indentation and then move inward to form a central layer between the two outer ones. By the end of the week, three layers of differentiated tissues are formed: the endoderm, the mesoderm, and the ectoderm. Endoderm cells will develop into internal organs such as the stomach, liver, and lungs; mesoderm cells will become the muscles, skeleton, and blood; and ectoderm cells will form the central nervous system, sensory organs, and skin (Beck, Moffat, and Lloyd, 1973; Parker and Bavosi, 1979).

The movements of cells that give rise to these three differentiated layers set the stage for important interactions among tissues, interactions that eventually shape the various parts of the body. These critical tissue interactions, which trigger developmental changes, are called **embryonic inductions.** Scientists believe they are caused by chemical substances that spread from one tissue to the other. Embryonic inductions provide another example of how the environmental context (in this case, the placement of cells) plays an indispensable role in carrying out an organism's genetic potential.

The first embryonic induction occurs when cells of the mesoderm induce overlying ectoderm tissue to begin further differentiation into a brain and spinal cord. The cells of the mesoderm are actually causing different genes in the overlying ectoderm to be "turned on" or "turned off." Significantly, if some of the tissue that will form the mesoderm is

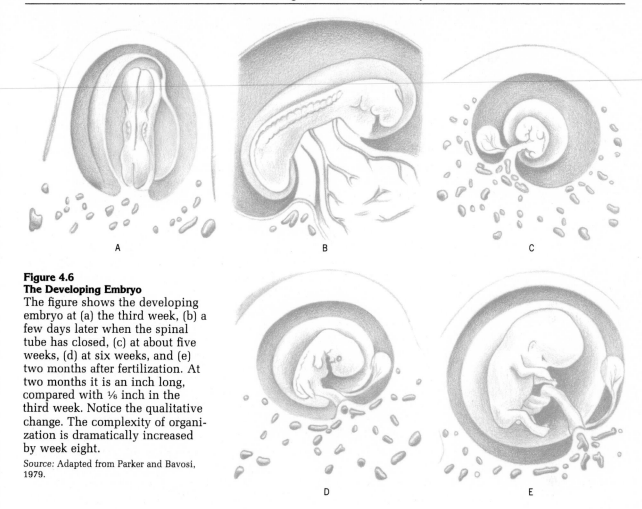

A   B   C

D   E

Figure 4.6
The Developing Embryo
The figure shows the developing embryo at (a) the third week, (b) a few days later when the spinal tube has closed, (c) at about five weeks, (d) at six weeks, and (e) two months after fertilization. At two months it is an inch long, compared with ⅙ inch in the third week. Notice the qualitative change. The complexity of organization is dramatically increased by week eight.

Source: Adapted from Parker and Bavosi, 1979.

transplanted to another embryo at the same stage of development, that transplanted tissue will trigger formation of a second brain and spinal cord on the host. Another of the many embryonic inductions that scientists have studied controls the formation of the eye's lens. The lens develops wherever a certain outgrowth of the forebrain comes in contact with the outer surface of the embryo. Animal studies show that if this outgrowth is transplanted so it contacts, say, the embryo's back instead of the front of its face, a lens will proceed to form in this odd location (Beck, Moffat, and Lloyd, 1973). Once again we see that genes alone do not create a human being. Genes are part of a developmental system that also includes the cellular environment. Genes acting together provide instructions. But which genes are operating—and what instructions are given—depends on context, including the embryo's point in development.

Timing often determines the many gene-environment interactions that take place during the embryonic period. Suppose the outgrowth of the forebrain that induces formation of an eye lens is transplanted from the head of a younger embryo to the back of an older one. The older embryo is well beyond the stage at which the lenses of the eyes normally form. Will this older embryo go on to acquire yet another lens? As you may suspect, the answer is no. The cells on the surface of the older embryo's back are now *committed* to being skin, and induction of a new lens is no longer possible. The time preceding this cellular commitment is one illustration of a critical period. A **critical period** is a limited time during which some part of a developing organism is susceptible to influences that can bring about specific and permanent changes. In this case, the critical period is the time during which an embryo's ectoderm tissue can be induced to develop in one of several directions.

Figure 4.7 shows the critical periods for the emergence of some of the body parts in a human embryo (and in the fetus as well). As you can see, embryonic developments occur in a very predictable order, according to a strict timetable. By the end of the third week of pregnancy, the central nervous system has started to form, and the beginnings of the eyes can be seen. By the fourth week, the heart (and, though not shown, the digestive system) is appearing; by the fifth week, limb buds that will become arms and legs are visible. Finally, in the sixth through the eighth weeks, fingers and toes start to emerge and the bones begin to harden. This sequence reveals two principles of prenatal growth. First, rapid development of the embryo proceeds from the head downward, called the **cephalocaudal pattern.** Second, parts at the center of the body develop earlier than those at the extremities, called the **proximodistal pattern.**

Pediatricians use the highly predictable sequence and timing of embryonic development when examining an infant at birth. For example, they look carefully at the newborn's outer ear, not because the outer ear has particular importance in its own right, but because it develops at the same time as the kidneys do (Beck, Moffat, and Lloyd, 1973). If disruptions in prenatal development caused the outer ear to malform, it is very likely that the same disruptions caused some defect in the kidneys, and this could be life threatening to the baby. Note that if something goes wrong during a critical period and an organ does malform, that defect cannot be corrected later, except through surgery. At a later stage the tissues involved have completed their differentiation. The embryo, in short, is now a qualitatively different organism than it was previously.

Interestingly, the embryonic period, during which so much crucial development occurs, is a time when the mother may not yet be aware that she is pregnant; consequently she may neglect to take precautions concerning medications and other chemical substances. Some fatigue, nausea, and swelling of the breasts are common early symptoms of pregnancy, but a woman who does not expect to become pregnant may misinterpret them. Of course, cessation of the menstrual cycle accompanies all pregnancies, but about 20 percent of pregnant women experience some early bleeding, which could be interpreted as menstruation.

THE FETAL PERIOD: WEEK NINE TO BIRTH

From the ninth week until the thirty-eighth, when birth usually occurs, the developing organism is called a **fetus.** The **fetal period** differs from the embryonic period in several fundamental ways. For one thing, while the embryonic period is the time when most of the major body parts are

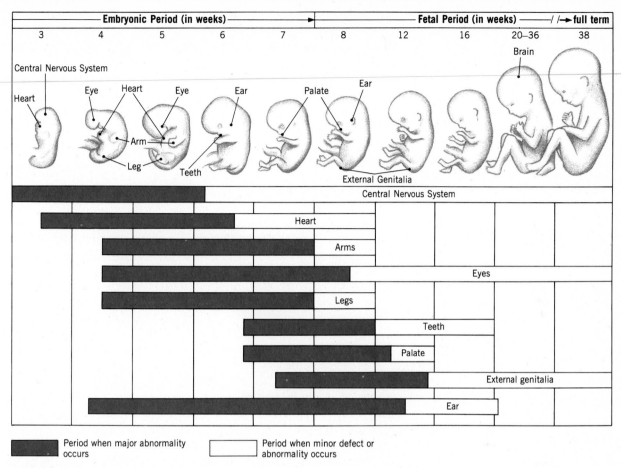

Figure 4.7
Critical Periods in the Development of Various Organs, Systems, and Body Parts
Each organ, system, and part has its own critical timetable and, as we shall see, is most susceptible to disruption during that time.
Source: Adapted from Moore, 1974, p. 96.

formed, the fetal period is the time when those parts grow rapidly and become refined in structure. Table 4.2 shows that growth in length reaches its maximum rate early in the fetal period and then tapers off, whereas weight gains are greatest as the time of delivery approaches. Refinements in body parts occur throughout the fetal period, with each change taking place on a predictable schedule. For example, in the fourth month the pads on the fingers and toes form; in the fifth month eyebrows and eyelashes grow; and in the seventh month the male testes usually descend into the scrotum. Note that although these and other refinements are very important, they differ from the laying down of basic structures that occurred during the embryonic period.

Another major difference between the embryonic and fetal periods is the responsiveness of the fetus. During the embryonic period, the developing organism merely floats in the amniotic fluid, moored by its umbil-

TABLE 4.2   **Length and Weight Gains During Prenatal Development**

Week	Length	Weight
8	1 in.	⅔ oz.
12	3 in.	1 oz.
16	6 in.	4 oz.
20	10 in.	1 lb.
24	12 in.	2 lb.
28	15 in.	3 lb.
32	17 in.	4½ lb.
36	18 in.	7½ lb.

ical cord. By the tenth week of pregnancy, however, another qualitative change occurs. The nervous system is now mature enough so that the fetus will flex its entire trunk if any part of its body is touched. Such a global reaction occurs even if the stimulation is directed to a specific body part. Gradually, fetal movements become less global and more specialized. By the twelfth week the fetus spontaneously moves its arms and legs, swallows, and "breathes" (inhales and exhales amniotic fluid). Still later, as the nervous system becomes increasingly refined, more precise limb and finger movements are possible. When various parts of the fetus's body are now touched, the reactions are very specific. For example, touching the sole of the foot produces a leg withdrawal, not movement of the entire body as occurred before. Again the fetus has achieved a fundamentally more advanced way of responding. Notice, too, how these qualitative changes in behavior are directly linked to qualitative changes in the organism's structure, especially its nervous system. Development, as you will see throughout this book, always involves a change in structure *and* in function (Gottlieb, 1976).

Not only is the fetus far more responsive than the embryo, but its behaviors also become increasingly regular and integrated (Beck, Moffat, and Lloyd, 1973). The initially weak and irregular heartbeat that is hard to detect in the embryo becomes regular in the fourth month and strong enough in the fifth to be heard with a stethoscope. The fetus also develops a relatively regular sleep-wake cycle, usually adopting the same position for sleep. If the mother moves into a position that causes the fetus discomfort, it will move until it finds a more comfortable position. At 7 months some fetuses regularly suck their thumbs or hands while they are sleeping. Their eyelids, which previously were fused shut, now separate and allow them to open and close their eyes. By the eighth month, fetuses are responsive to moderate-level sounds; they can hear and react to some of what goes on in the world outside the womb. All these changes again show that an initially passive organism is gradually being transformed into an active, adapting baby.

The first half of the fetal period is often the most enjoyable part of pregnancy for the mother. In obstetrics this time is called the second **trimester,** the whole of pregnancy being divided into three trimesters, or three-month periods. The trimester concept (with the first trimester beginning at the time of the woman's last menstruation) makes sense if you are looking at pregnancy from the mother's point of view. If the mother experienced fatigue and nausea during the first trimester, these symptoms usually disappear as the second trimester begins. By the middle of the second trimester, at around 4½ months of pregnancy, the fetus is big enough for the mother to begin to feel its movements. At first these seem like only faint stirrings, but they give the mother new awareness of what is going on inside her. Although the mother's condition is now apparent to all but the most oblivious, she is not yet so large as to feel awkward and burdened. In the last trimester, her size becomes more of a problem, as the fetus and placenta put pressure on her internal organs. Fetal kicking, initially a source of joy, can now extend for long periods, sometimes causing sleeplessness or discomfort. By the ninth month of pregnancy, most women are eager to deliver.

Environmental Effects on Prenatal Development

Given the enormous complexity of creating a human being, most people are amazed that the process can take place without error. In delivery rooms parents commonly count the fingers and toes on their newborn to make sure everything is there. Abnormalities present at birth can come from two sources: a defect in the infant's genes or an aberration in the prenatal environment. We have already discussed genetic disorders that result from parents transmitting recessive alleles to offspring, as in the case of PKU. Other genetic defects arise if errors in meiosis produce sperm or egg cells with incorrect numbers of chromosomes or damaged chromosomes. Some of these will be discussed in the section on detecting fetal disorders. Environmental agents that can cause abnormalities are called **teratogens,** and the study of their effects is called **teratology.** Teratology reveals very clearly what a critical role environment, in addition to genetic normality, plays in healthy development.

Teratogens usually cause detrimental effects by preventing or modifying normal cell division and differentiation. As a result, the potential danger of teratogens generally is greatest during the embryonic period, when the major body parts are forming. Later development, as we have said, consists primarily of refinements on existing structures, so teratogens can generally do less damage then. This is not to say that the older fetus is immune to environmental hazards. All of prenatal development is important, so teratogens should be avoided throughout pregnancy. In the following sections we'll take a look at some of the most common teratogens.

DRUGS

Most people realize that illegal drugs, such as heroin and cocaine, are harmful to the embryo and fetus. Fewer, however, are wary of legal drugs, such as alcohol and tobacco, and fewer still of common over-the-counter medications, such as aspirin and antihistamines. Yet all these substances have been implicated as teratogens. Space does not permit mention of all the drugs that adversely affect prenatal development; instead, we will discuss just a few of the most widely studied. Because there are so many

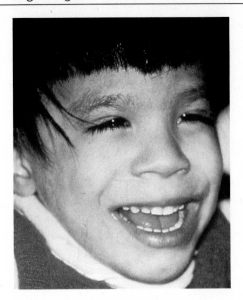

A flattened nose, an under-developed upper lip, and widely spaced eyes are three common physical symptoms of fetal alcohol syndrome. Mental retardation and behavioral abnormalities also result. *(National Clearinghouse for Alcohol Information.)*

drugs whose effects are not yet known, pregnant women are often cautioned to avoid all drugs except those proven safe.

Alcohol.   It is often difficult to convince women about the dangers of drinking during pregnancy, because most know cases in which the expectant mother drank and her child was born perfectly normal. Nonetheless, the odds of having a healthy baby are greatly reduced if the mother consumes alcohol during pregnancy. Heavy drinkers are thought to have a 1 in 6 chance of a stillbirth and a 1 in 2 chance of delivering a child with some birth defect (Larsson, Bohlin, and Tunell, 1985; Rosenblith and Sims-Knight, 1985).

The many problems caused by heavy alcohol consumption during pregnancy are collectively called the **fetal alcohol syndrome.** They include retardation in growth and intellectual development, as well as defects in facial features, limbs, the brain, and internal organs. In addition, children with fetal alcohol syndrome may exhibit behavioral disorders such as irritability and short attention span (Jones et al., 1973; Streissguth, 1977). In the United States fetal alcohol syndrome occurs in at least one in every 1,000 births (Centers for Disease Control, 1984). The symptoms, including retarded growth, cannot be overcome by adequate diet after the baby is born. This example points to the potentially lasting effects of teratogens. Even children whose mothers drank only moderately during pregnancy have a higher than average chance of behavioral disorders at 4 years of age (Landesman-Dwyer, Ragozin, and Little, 1981; Streissguth et al., 1984). How much alcohol is safe for a pregnant woman to drink? Since there is no clear answer to this question, many doctors are now recommending that women abstain completely from alcohol during pregnancy.

Tobacco.   The harmful effects of smoking on a fetus have been under investigation for the last 30 years. Expectant mothers who smoke are more apt to deliver prematurely, and the more they smoke the greater the risk (Butler and Goldstein, 1973; Ferreira, 1969). In addition, babies of women who smoke are more likely to have low birthweights (Frazier et al., 1961; Niswander and Gordon, 1972). A low birthweight is cause for considerable concern. The likelihood of death is higher in low birthweight babies, particularly those under three pounds, and extremely low birthweight infants are more apt to have impairments in cognitive, sensory, and motor capabilities (Institute of Medicine, 1985; Kavale and Karge, 1986; Kopp and Parmelee, 1979).

Do the correlations between tobacco smoking, prematurity, and low birthweight mean that smoking directly causes these negative outcomes? The answer is not yet certain. In one study, women who did not begin smoking until *after* delivery of their babies still had low birthweight infants. Perhaps some third factor that both encourages smoking and causes poor weight gain in a fetus is operative (Kavale and Karge, 1986; Verushalmy, 1972). At the same time, smoking does have certain effects on the body that could be the direct cause of prenatal problems. For instance, smoking raises carbon monoxide levels in the blood, which decreases the amount of life-sustaining oxygen the blood can carry to the fetus. Cigarette smoke also contains nicotine, a stimulant that causes constriction of tiny blood vessels, including those in the placenta. This constriction again reduces oxygen to the fetus. Not surprisingly, a rise in fetal heart rate (resulting from low oxygen levels in the blood) can be observed after a pregnant woman has smoked two cigarettes in ten minutes (Quigley et al., 1979).

Researchers are still trying to determine if smoking during pregnancy is related to any longer-term problems other than prematurity and low birthweight. Some studies have shown a link between mothers who smoke and retarded physical growth, attention problems, and learning disabilities in their children (Streissguth et al., 1984; U.S. Department of Health, Education, and Welfare, 1979). However, a study that carefully matched subjects to control for other possible influences found that smoking in pregnancy had no effect on a child's physical or intellectual development (Lefkowitz, 1981). The long-term consequences of smoking during pregnancy are therefore still uncertain. But the short-term consequences are negative enough to strongly advise against it.

Thalidomide.   In the 1960s a mild sedative called thalidomide was sold over-the-counter in Europe and Canada as a remedy for morning sickness, a common symptom of early pregnancy. The drug was kept off the market in the United States because Frances Kelsey, a physician at the Food and Drug Administration, wanted more evidence of its safety than the animal studies that had been conducted. As it turned out, what was safe for developing rats was not at all safe for humans. Women who took thalidomide during the first two months of pregnancy gave birth to children with a variety of severe malformations. The particular defect depended on exactly when the drug was taken. For example, if it was taken about three weeks after conception, the baby was apt to be born without ears. If the drug was administered about four weeks after conception, the child was apt to have deformed legs, or even no legs at all. If first taken beyond the eighth week, however, once the major body parts had formed, no birth defects were likely (Apgar and Beck, 1974; Newman, 1986).

Several lessons can be learned from the thalidomide case. First, drugs that are safe for some animals may not be safe for humans. Second, repeated use of a drug is not required for it to have a negative effect on development. Some women who used thalidomide for only one or two days gave birth to children with deformities (Taussig, 1962). This could happen because developmental change occurs so rapidly in the embryonic period, and once tissues have differentiated incorrectly there is no turning back to a former state in which their structure and function are yet to be determined. Third, the thalidomide tragedy shows how precise the timetable for prenatal development is. Dramatically different but predictable abnormalities occurred in each of the early weeks of pregnancy. Finally, the thalidomide tragedy underscores the fact that teratogens are particularly hazardous during the critical embryonic period, when all the basic body parts are forming. The developing embryo, in short, is fundamentally different from and more vulnerable than the fetus. The tremendous amount of organ and tissue differentiation going on within it is highly sensitive to chemical changes in the cellular environment (Newman, 1986).

Heroin and Methadone.   Narcotic drugs such as heroin are carried in the blood of a pregnant user and pass through the placenta to her embryo or fetus. Children of chronic users of heroin or methadone (used to wean addicts from heroin) are born addicted and commonly have suffered growth retardation in the uterus (Brackbill, 1979). After birth these babies go through withdrawal, experiencing breathing difficulties, tremors, and other symptoms (Ferreira, 1969; Kron et al., 1977). Addicted newborns are usually put on maintenance doses of narcotics and then withdrawn slowly to minimize the negative effects. Narcotic use during pregnancy is related to behavioral problems in later childhood. These include hyperactivity, short attention span, and retarded mental and motor development (Householder et al., 1982; Ostrea and Chavez, 1979). However, since mothers who use narcotics often provide poor environments for their children, it is not clear whether prenatal exposure to the drugs is the sole cause of these problems.

Cocaine.   The dramatic increase in cocaine use in the last decade has focused attention on possible negative effects for the fetus. One early study showed that maternal cocaine abuse significantly increases the risk of low birthweight, stillbirth due to premature separation of the placenta, and a variety of congenital malformations despite normal chromosome patterns (Bingol et al., 1987). The cardiovascular effects of the drug are thought to interrupt the blood supply to various fetal tissues. The type and extent of damage depend on the stage of development of the embryo or fetus.

Hormones.   As medical science has progressed, we have learned to use hormones to help control a number of biological processes. Birth-control pills, fertility drugs, and drugs to prevent miscarriages all contain hormones. But because hormones are also important in controlling prenatal development, they must be used with caution during pregnancy. For example, if a woman who does not know she is pregnant continues to use birth-control pills, her infant faces a higher risk of heart defects and circulatory disorders (Heinonen, Slone, and Shapiro, 1977).

The most widespread problem caused by hormone treatments resulted from the drug diethylstilbestrol (DES). From the 1940s through the 1960s, DES was often prescribed to prevent miscarriages. Since millions of normal-looking babies were born to women who took DES, it appeared to be perfectly safe. However, when these children became adults problems began to appear, such as a high rate of genital-tract cancers in women and more frequent abnormalities of the testes in men. Such incidents show that teratogens can sometimes have effects that do not become apparent for years.

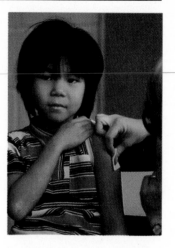

Immunization can prevent some diseases from harming the development of future offspring. *(Guy Gillette/ Photo Researchers, Inc.)*

DISEASE

Many viruses can pass through the placenta and affect the developing embryo or fetus. Children whose mothers had **rubella** (German measles) early in pregnancy have a high incidence of blindness, deafness, mental retardation, and heart defects. If maternal rubella occurs during week three or four, the probability of birth defects is 50 percent. That rate drops to 20 percent in the second month and to 7 percent in month three (Michaels and Mellin, 1960). Again we see evidence of a strict timetable for development and of greater vulnerability during the period when the embryo's basic structures are forming.

Rubella causes some of the same birth defects that thalidomide did. Often quite different teratogens have identical effects when present at the same critical time in development. This makes sense when you consider that a certain set of changes is occurring in the embryo at any given point, so anything that disrupts those changes is apt to cause similar abnormalities. By the same token, if two women are exposed to the same teratogen but at different times in pregnancy, the effects will probably differ because the developments taking place in the two embryos differ. Thus the various defects that rubella causes depend upon exactly when the mother gets the virus. Birth defects from congenital rubella syndrome have declined dramatically since approval of the rubella vaccine in 1969. However, an estimated 10 to 20 percent of women in their childbearing years today lack effective immunization (Centers for Disease Control, 1986).

Acquired Immune Deficiency Syndrome (AIDS) is a rapidly spreading viral illness with severe consequences for babies born to mothers with the disease. Affected newborns often show marked growth failure with small heads and facial deformities. Within months, many acquire repeated infections and show developmental delays. No cure is known, and more than half the children diagnosed with AIDS have died (Rubinstein, 1986).

Many other diseases are known to have harmful effects on prenatal development. Among these are syphilis, gonorrhea, chlamydia, herpes, influenza A, mumps, pneumonia, and tuberculosis. Syphilis, unlike many of the others, takes its toll later in pregnancy by attacking organs that have already formed. Fortunately, syphilis can be detected in the mother's blood and effectively treated. But for those infected women who do not receive appropriate medical treatment, syphilis can have disastrous effects, sometimes even killing the fetus or newborn.

EMOTIONAL STRESS

Because emotional stress is so subjective, it is hard to study its effects on prenatal development. How can we even measure the amount of stress a person is experiencing? Some researchers have used negative life events (such as divorce or loss of a job) to estimate levels of stress, while others have used more direct measures of a person's physiological state. Studies using both these yardsticks suggest that stress during pregnancy may contribute to such conditions as newborn irritability and later behavioral problems (Davids, Holden, and Gray, 1963; Institute of Medicine, 1985; Molitor et al., 1984). It is difficult to rule out all other possible explanations for these findings. However, studies do suggest a relationship between heightened levels of stress and difficulties during pregnancy (Nuckolls, Cassel, and Kaplan, 1972).

How might stress in a pregnant woman adversely affect her baby? For one thing, stress stimulates production of the hormone adrenaline, which alters blood flow. Long-term stress, therefore, may reduce the supplies of oxygen and nutrients to a fetus. In addition, stress may cause general changes in the mother's body chemistry, producing substances that can cross the placenta. But periodic stress by no means causes frequent prenatal harm. If it did, far more children would be born with developmental problems, for occasional stress is very hard to avoid. Thus, mild, periodic stress is of little concern to developmental researchers.

MATERNAL NUTRITION

Good nutrition both before and during pregnancy is important to producing a healthy baby. As with other influences on prenatal development, the presence or absence of particular nutrients may have different effects at different times. A study of babies conceived and born during the Dutch famine toward the end of World War II offered proof of this. The famine greatly reduced the population's fertility rate and increased infant mortality. Moreover, if a woman was malnourished during her last three months of pregnancy, the time when the fetus normally gains the most weight, her baby was apt to be born small and thin (Stein et al., 1975). Apparently, even good nutrition in the first six months of development cannot compensate for shortages at the end of pregnancy.

Researchers still debate whether poor nutrition in the last few months of pregnancy (particularly protein deficiency) irreversibly lowers the number of brain cells a person is born with (Winick, 1975). Several studies of children born to malnourished mothers seem to support this contention, but all these studies have flaws. The clearest evidence comes from studies of rats raised in controlled conditions. Those that experienced significant prenatal malnutrition did have fewer brain cells and also had learning disabilities (Winick, 1975). However, generalizing from rats to people may be unwise. Some psychologists remain unconvinced that nutrition directly affects nerve-cell development in humans (Fischer and Lazerson, 1984). In the Dutch study mentioned earlier, no IQ differences were found among children born during the wartime famine and children born afterward. But it could be that the fetuses who managed to survive the famine would normally have been even more robust and intelligent than their peers. This problem is common in interpreting natural experiments: Alternative explanations are often difficult to rule out. We believe that prenatal nutrition does directly affect neural development. Neural development is complex, involving growth and migration of neurons, differentiation of neuron parts (axons and dendrites), development of the neuron sheath (a structure necessary for nerve impulses to be conducted through the body), and so forth (Cowan, 1979). Such complicated processes often are sensitive to disruption. However, because nutrition also affects other factors, including survival rate, this link is hard to demonstrate.

Maternal nutrition is an example of an environmental factor that can have an effect on development. *(Tom Dunham.)*

The need for specific vitamins and minerals during pregnancy is another widely researched topic. Calcium, for instance, is essential to the production of bones and teeth. If the mother's diet is deficient in calcium, some of it will be drawn from her own bones to partially meet the fetus's needs. In general, however, the fetus cannot take nutritional stores from the mother's body to compensate for deficiencies in her diet. Consequently, doctors often recommend vitamin and mineral supplements for pregnant women. But excessive vitamin intake, particularly of fat-soluble vitamins that the body can store, is also a danger. Either deficiencies or excesses of some vitamins can cause birth defects. Therefore, expectant mothers should let a doctor prescribe their nutritional supplements.

MATERNAL AGE

If we examine the rates of stillbirths and infant deaths as a function of maternal age, an interesting pattern emerges: The rates are highest for teen-agers and for women over 35. The optimum age for a woman to bear children appears to be around her mid-twenties.

Why would teen-agers have generally less successful pregnancies than 25-year-olds? One possibility is that the teen-agers' reproductive organs are not yet fully mature and so are more apt to have trouble supporting the fetus. A second possibility is that teen-age mothers, because they are often single and poor, are less likely to receive good prenatal care and nutrition.

Older-than-average mothers have problems for different reasons. After age 30, the weight of the uterus begins to decline, and it becomes less susceptible to implantation of a fertilized egg. In addition, since all of a woman's ova are present (in immature form) from the time she is born, the older woman's egg cells have been exposed over more years to drugs, diseases, and radiation. Such exposure may make many eggs defective, unable to produce a viable fetus.

The number of previous pregnancies a woman has had, called **parity**, is often related to age and can influence the success of childbearing. First pregnancies are more likely than subsequent ones to end in miscarriage, low birthweight, or malformations. On the other hand, after four pregnancies the incidence of problems again rises (Institute of Medicine, 1985). Reproductive fatigue may be the cause: Women who have had more than four pregnancies are apt to have had them in rapid succession, without enough recovery time in between.

Environmental causes are known to account for about 10 percent of

Almond-shaped eyes, a flattened broad face, and poor muscle tone are prominent features of Down syndrome. The children are variously retarded, with a small subset approaching normal intelligence. *(Elizabeth Crews.)*

all human malformations, and most of these are related to maternal disease. Genetic causes account for about 25 percent, while the reason for 65 percent of malformations is unknown (Beckman and Brent, 1986).

Detection and Treatment of Fetal Disorders

Many disorders can now be detected early in pregnancy. **Ultrasound,** a technique that produces a computer image of the fetus by bouncing sound waves off it, allows physicians to detect structural abnormalities as small as a cleft lip. Ultrasound, in combination with other tests, has made it possible to diagnose more than 20 types of heart defects and rhythm disturbances before birth (Chervenak, Isaacson, and Mahoney, 1986). Ultrasound can also be used to guide instruments safely to obtain samples of amniotic fluid, fetal blood, and the like for further diagnostic analysis.

In **amniocentesis,** a needle is inserted through the mother's abdomen at about the fifteenth or sixteenth week of pregnancy to withdraw a sample of the fluid that surrounds the developing fetus. Cells that the fetus has shed into the fluid can then be analyzed for over 70 chromosomal anomalies (Chervenak, Isaacson, and Mahoney, 1986). One of the first to be detected was **Down syndrome.** Down syndrome involves an error in the chromosomes labeled number 21. The most common error is the presence of three twenty-first chromosomes, rather than the normal two. This can happen if the twenty-first pair of chromosomes fails to separate during meiosis when egg or sperm is formed. The result is one cell with two twenty-first chromosomes and another with none. If the egg or sperm with two twenty-first chromosomes joins with another reproductive cell, the new individual will have three twenty-first chromosomes and will develop Down syndrome. Down syndrome fetuses are rather unusual in their ability to survive. Most chromosome errors are lethal, since so much genetic material is faulty. In fact, 90 percent of all conceptions that involve chromosome errors spontaneously abort; such errors are found in only about 3-5 percent of live births (Rosenblith and Sims-Knight, 1985).

The physical development of Down syndrome children is abnormal in a number of ways. They are usually short, with stubby fingers, a broad face, and rather flat facial features which gave rise to the old name for this disorder, mongolism. Many also have heart defects and die by early adulthood (Smith and Wilson, 1973). Down syndrome children are often severely retarded, although in some the degree of retardation is much less marked (Kopp and Parmelee, 1979). Despite their retardation and delayed language development, Down syndrome children show the same sequences of development as normal children, only delayed (Beeghly and Cicchetti, in press). With supportive environments they tend to achieve more normal functioning, and designed programs are particularly helpful during infancy (Cicchetti and Beeghly, in press; Cicchetti and Sroufe, 1978; Stedman and Eichorn, 1964). But there is no reason to expect that environmental intervention will be as effective for Down syndrome as it has been for PKU. The complexity of the problem is very much greater in Down syndrome.

Fortunately, Down syndrome is relatively rare, affecting about 1 in every 600 births. Its frequency, however, increases with the age of the mother (and perhaps the age of the father too). For women under 30 the rate is one in 1,500 births, whereas for women over 45 the rate is one in 65 (Kopp and Parmelee, 1979). Scientists believe that this higher incidence in older women is caused by damage to egg cells over time. We know that meiosis can be adversely affected by viruses, x-rays, and a variety of chemicals (Hirschhorn, 1973). Such factors may be involved in the chromosome error that leads to Down syndrome.

Neural tube defects, such as absence of part of the brain or skull or failure of the spine to close, also can be detected through amniocentesis, because **alpha-fetoprotein** is leaked from the fetus into the surrounding fluid. This fetal serum protein can also be measured in the mother's blood, allowing simple screening for such defects. Low concentrations of the protein indicate the need to test further for Down syndrome.

In a new technique called **chorionic villus sampling,** cells can be suctioned from the developing placenta via a small tube passed through the vagina and cervix. These cells then can be analyzed to determine the fetus's genetic make-up. Because it can be performed early, in weeks eight to 12, and safely, it is an important alternative to amniocentesis (Chervenak, Isaacson, and Mahoney, 1986).

The burgeoning field of fetal diagnosis has opened the way for transfusion, drug therapy, and surgery for the compromised fetus. It also has created difficult moral and emotional dilemmas. What should prospective parents do if they discover their fetus is seriously malformed or diseased? The diagnostic procedures are not risk free, and they are generally undertaken only to test for abnormalities that could be treated medically.

Birth and Birth Complications

After nine months of gestation, human infants are ready to be delivered. In most cases the process is routine, as it has been for thousands of years. The fetus prepares for birth by moving into a head-down position, and the mother's body responds with contractions, which help move the baby through the birth canal.

Not all pregnancies and deliveries are routine. One major concern in birthing is the maintenance of a steady supply of oxygen to the infant. A lengthy disruption in the oxygen supplied, referred to as **anoxia,** can cause damage to the infant's brain. Anoxia can result in two basic ways. First, the umbilical cord may become pinched during delivery, cutting off the oxygen supply from the mother. This is most common when, instead of being born head-first, an infant is delivered in a bottom- or feet-first position. Such **breech births** often take longer to complete, and in the final stages of delivery the cord may become tangled or pinched. Second, the infant may be deprived of oxygen if he or she fails to begin breathing after birth.

Late or **postterm** babies may become too large to be delivered easily. They also may suffer from poor oxygenation since the placenta fatigues during the last weeks. Generally, however, when babies are overdue, physicians induce labor by giving mothers **oxytocin,** a hormone that stimulates contractions.

To determine the effects of any birth complications, a standard set of medical tests and procedures is performed on the infant immediately and five minutes after birth, including the Apgar scale shown in Table 4.3. The baby's score on this test is the sum of the ratings for heart rate, respiration, reflexes, muscle tone, and skin color. A score below five is cause for concern and immediate medical treatment.

TABLE 4.3   The Apgar Scale

Sign	Criterion*	Score
Heart rate (beats/minute)	100 or more	2
	Less than 100	1
	Not detectable	0
Respiratory effort	Lusty crying and breathing	2
	Any shallowness, irregularity	1
	Not breathing	0
Reflex irritability	Vigorous response to stimulation (e.g., sneezing or coughing to stimulation of nostrils), urination, defecation	2
	Weak response	1
	No response	0
Muscle tone	Resilient, limbs spontaneously flexed and resistant to applied force	2
	Limpness, lack of resistance	1
	Complete flaccidity	0
Skin color	Pink all over	2
	Partially pink	1
	Bluish or yellowish	0

* Observations made at 60 seconds after birth.
Source: Apgar et al., 1958.

LOW BIRTHWEIGHT AND PREMATURITY

The question of how old a fetus must be before it is able to survive outside of the womb cannot be answered precisely. Babies as young as 22 weeks or as small as 1½ pounds have managed to survive, but this is very unusual. Even with our rapidly improving medical technology, babies smaller than 2½ pounds have less than a 50-50 chance of survival, and this weight is not achieved until about the twenty-seventh week. Up to the average full-term birthweight of 7½ pounds, the heavier a fetus is, the greater its chances of survival. Since rapid weight gain occurs late in prenatal development (when it reaches a peak of over 2 ounces a day), staying in the womb for the full 38 weeks is highly advantageous.

Babies who are born too small face increased risk of neurodevelopmental handicaps, congenital anomalies, and lung problems compared with babies of ideal weight. In fact, the 6 percent of babies in the United States born at weights below 5½ pounds suffer twice the neonatal mortality rate of larger newborns. Most infants weighing less than 2 pounds do not survive. While neonatal intensive care units have made dramatic strides in keeping low-birthweight babies alive and enhancing their developmental outcomes, we have done little in the past two decades to reduce the proportion of babies born too small.

Small birth size can be due to premature delivery, retarded growth and development in the uterus, or both. Premature babies born after seven months of normal gestation may suffer no ill effects (Beckwith and Parmelee, 1983). However, babies born small compared with others of the same gestational age remain at risk for later difficulties.

Low birthweight is strongly associated with poverty and low maternal educational status. Promising efforts to optimize the quality and length of gestation include programs to make early prenatal care accessible to all, improve nutrition, avoid pregnancy at the extremes of the reproductive age span, and alert women to the hazards of smoking and alcohol use in pregnancy (Institute of Medicine, 1985).

TRENDS IN CHILDBIRTH

Providing hospital birthing centers with a homelike atmosphere, using nurse midwives, and permitting mothers to room in with the newborn are all childbirth trends in the United States. Another trend has been toward natural childbirth, the most popular approach being the **Lamaze method.** Lamaze involves several approaches to lessening fear and pain and making birth a more positive experience. These include prior knowledge of the birth process, participation of both parents in the pregnancy and delivery, and breathing techniques during labor.

A major advantage of natural childbirth methods such as Lamaze is a decreased reliance on pain-killing drugs during labor. Drugs commonly used during birth include anesthetics (which either block sensory signals or induce complete unconsciousness), analgesics (which reduce pain), and sedatives (which reduce anxiety). In this country about 95 percent of deliveries are accompanied by some anesthetic (Brackbill, 1979). Anesthetics and analgesics can affect the baby in two ways. First, they tend to lower the mother's blood pressure and the oxygen content of her blood, which in turn lowers the amount of oxygen supplied to the child. This is of particular concern because birth is a time when the baby is already at some risk for damage due to lack of oxygen. Second, most anesthetics and analgesics rapidly cross the placenta and directly affect the infant both during and after birth. These effects include reduced responsiveness to stimuli, poorer motor control, and a diminished attention span. Since a newborn's capacity to eliminate drugs from the body is not well developed, these negative effects may linger for a year or more (Brackbill, 1979). The current trend, therefore, is to limit the amount of pain-killers given during labor.

Another innovation in modern-day deliveries is the **Leboyer method,** which focuses on the baby's experience of birth. The delivery room is softly lighted, warm, and quiet. At birth, the newborn is placed on the mother's stomach and is softly stroked. The umbilical cord is left intact for several minutes. The child also is given a warm bath. The aim is to make the transition from the uterus to the outside world as gradual and gentle as possible. Although this method has strong advocates, it is not widely practiced, and studies do not detect any measurable advantages for babies who experience it (Nelson et al., 1980).

Modern-day obstetrics has also seen an increase in deliveries by **Caesarean section,** that is, by surgical incision in the abdomen and uterus. Caesarean deliveries are used when fetal heart-rate monitors indicate fetal distress, when normal delivery is otherwise not going well, and when the mother's pelvis is very small and the baby's head is very large. The frequency of Caesarean delivery is currently high in this country, more than 15 percent (National Institutes of Health, 1981).

PRENATAL DEVELOPMENT IN CONTEXT

A major theme of this book is that development can be fully understood only by examining the context in which it occurs. That theme is very apparent in this chapter. Prenatal development unfolds partly in a hereditary context: a set of genes that each individual inherits from his or her parents. Those genes include blueprints for constructing a new human being—a person in many ways like all human beings, in other ways unique. Prenatal development also unfolds in an environmental context: a set of hormones, nutrients, and other substances that help shape the way the individual forms. Sometimes these substances are a product of the developing organism itself. Other times they come from outside the womb via the placenta and the mother's bloodstream. Moreover, it is not just present events that create the current environmental context. That context is also a product of past developmental changes. For instance, when an embryo develops masculine genitals under the influence of male hormones, that embryo's current environment is being influenced by a critical past event—either the formation of androgen-producing glands or an influx of androgens from some other source. Past development, in other words, is part of the context for present development.

Genes and environment always interact. The enormous importance of the environmental context in prenatal development can be seen by considering a paradox. At the moment of fertilization the new organism

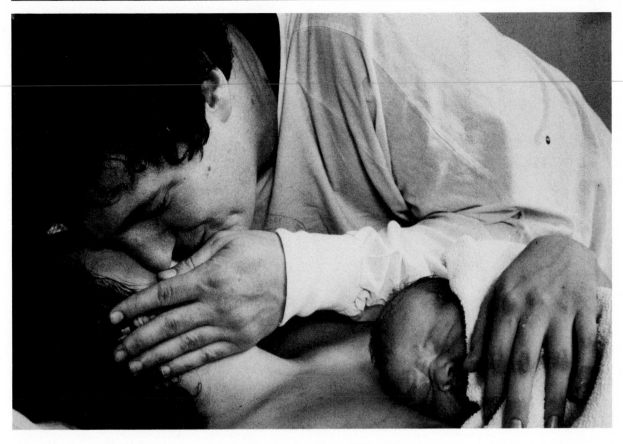

Often, the birth of an infant is an unparalleled joy for parents. *(Mimi Cotter/ International Stock Photo.)*

receives all the genetic material it will ever have. Each cell contains the same genetic information. As development proceeds, these genes are duplicated millions of times, and each new cell receives an identical set. Thus it would seem that the genetic information in the initial fertilized egg must be sufficient to guide all of development. After all, in those rare cases where the initial fertilized cell forms two separate units after duplication, identical twins result, not two half-children. Yet, if this information is truly sufficient, how could we explain the remarkable differentiation of cells that occurs? How can one cell "know" to use some of its genes to function as a blood cell, while another cell "knows" to use other genes to function as part of a muscle or nerve? The answer is that genes alone are not enough. For development to occur, cells must also be influenced by environment, including interactions with other cells. Recall from Chapter 1 (Figure 1.1) that the same tissue from a young chick embryo could become part of a thigh or a wing tip, depending on its location. This same process of influence by surrounding cells is what leads some cells on the surface of the new embryo to migrate into the core to become the human nervous system and so forth. You have seen the importance of this genetic/environmental system throughout the chapter, and you will see it again in all later sections of this book.

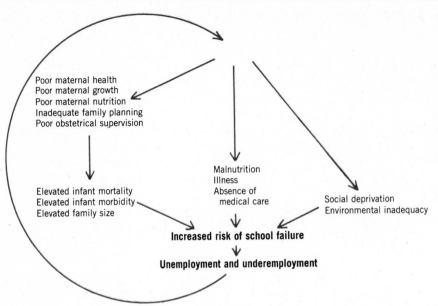

Poor maternal health
Poor maternal growth
Poor maternal nutrition
Inadequate family planning
Poor obstetrical supervision

Elevated infant mortality
Elevated infant morbidity
Elevated family size

Malnutrition
Illness
Absence of
  medical care

Social deprivation
Environmental inadequacy

Increased risk of school failure

Unemployment and underemployment

Figure 4.8
The Cycle of Poverty
Poverty is a self-perpetuating cycle. Economic and educational disadvantage leads to poorer health for mother and infant and increased risk for school failure and unemployment, which contribute again to poor prenatal and postnatal development.

Source: Adapted from Birch and Gussow, 1970.

Development is never simply the product of some initial genetic blueprint. Previous development and current circumstances always influence it too (Bowlby, 1973). This is the hallmark of all development, whether cell, embryo, fetus, newborn, or child.

In assessing the environmental aspects of the developmental system, we cannot stop by looking just at the organism itself. In the prenatal period, for example, the mother's body is also of great importance. But the environmental context of prenatal development does not stop there. The mother herself is embedded in an environment that can greatly affect the pregnancy. Expectant mothers living in deprived environments are much more likely to encounter poor nutrition, poor health, inadequate medical care, and high levels of stress, all of which can have an impact on the developing fetus.

Figure 4.8 illustrates the self-perpetuation of these negative influences. Children who experienced deprived prenatal environments are much more apt to have developmental problems, to do poorly in school, to have trouble finding work when they become adults, and to raise their own children in the same impoverished conditions. This **cycle of poverty** tends to continue generation after generation, with the poverty of grandparents predictive of developmental problems in grandchildren (Newberger, Melnicoe, and Newberger, 1986).

As disheartening as it is to see the cycle of poverty perpetuated, you should not conclude that prenatal development forever determines a child's fate. The environmental context of development is important throughout life, and major changes in that context can dramatically alter outcomes. Keep in mind that no one experience destines a child to an irreversible course of development. As you will discover in many parts of this book, significant change in the quality of development is always possible.

Chapter Review

1. Prenatal development includes several important processes that occur in other developmental periods too. One is an interaction of genes and environment in shaping the characteristics a person shows. Another is the process of differentiation, in this case the differentiation of cells and tissues in the body. As cells differentiate, they also undergo reorganization, giving rise to qualitative change.

2. **Genes** are segments of long, threadlike molecules of DNA located on structures called **chromosomes.** Every cell in the human body, except reproductive cells, contains 23 *pairs* of chromosomes, or 46 in all. The two chromosomes in a pair are said to be **homologous,** meaning that their genes affect the same aspects of development.

3. A special kind of cell division, known as **meiosis,** occurs in reproductive cells. During meiosis, reproductive cells divide so that the sperm or egg that is formed contains only 23 *single* chromosomes. Later, upon fertilization, two sets of single chromosomes unite to form a **zygote** having the normal 23 pairs. Meiosis creates a great variety of gene combinations, partly because of **crossing over,** a process in which homologous chromosomes exchange some genes, and partly because the chromosomes in each homologous pair are randomly "shuffled" when they separate to form daughter cells.

4. Gender development is a good example of how genes and environment interact as part of a complex developmental system. The presence of one **Y chromosome** results in primitive gonad tissue differentiating into testes, whereas the presence of two **X chromosomes** causes the same tissue to differentiate into ovaries. Subsequently, hormones—a part of the embryo's internal environment—influence further gender development. Genes cannot operate without an appropriate environmental context.

5. In addition to interacting with the environment, genes also interact with one another. Alternate forms of a gene for the same trait are called **alleles.** Sometimes one allele is **domi-** **nant** over the others, which may be **recessive.** In other cases, no single allele dominates, and **co-dominant** alleles determine how a characteristic is expressed. Many human characteristics are influenced not just by a single pair of genes, but rather by several gene pairs, often on different chromosomes. These are called **polygenic characteristics.** In addition, many genes do not influence a person's characteristics directly. Instead, these **modifier genes** influence how other genes operate.

6. The 38 weeks of prenatal development can be divided into three major periods. During the **germinal period** (from conception to week two) the new organism becomes implanted in the uterine lining and begins to form the life-support system that allows it to feed off the mother. During the **embryonic period** (from week two through week eight) that life-support system develops fully, and the embryo itself acquires all its major body parts according to a strict timetable. Finally, during the **fetal period** (from week nine to birth), the fetus grows rapidly in size and weight, its structures become refined, and it becomes increasingly active and responsive to its environment.

7. The developmental changes that occur within an embryo are often triggered by interactions among tissues. These interactions, called **embryonic inductions,** are another example of the vital role the cellular environment plays in the overall developmental system. Apparently, a cell's location exposes it to substances from neighboring cells, which in turn activate certain genes, causing the cell to take on a specific structure and function.

8. The developing organism is qualitatively different in each of the three periods of prenatal development. By this we do not mean simply that the organism acquires new structures. Qualitative differences involve whole new levels of organization and functioning. One example can be seen in prenatal behavioral changes. In the embryonic period the nervous system is not yet connected to the muscles, so the organism is motionless. Then, early in the fetal period, nerves and muscles develop

enough for the organism to flex its entire body if it is touched anywhere. Still later more specific reactions become possible, such as moving a leg when it is stimulated. At each stage a fundamentally more advanced way of responding emerges. These qualitatively different ways of functioning go hand-in-hand with the structural changes taking place.

9. Qualitative changes during prenatal development also explain why teratogens generally do more harm to embryos than to fetuses. A **teratogen** is any environmental factor that can cause developmental abnormalities. Common teratogens include many drugs, hormones, and viruses. Teratogens usually have their detrimental effects by preventing or modifying normal cell division and differentiation. Since a great amount of cellular differentiation goes on during the embryonic period, embryos are especially sensitive to teratogens.

10. After conception, fetuses at risk for genetic defects can be screened by using **ultrasound** in combination with **amniocentesis** or **chorionic villus sampling.** These procedures are used chiefly to detect chromosome defects, such as **Down syndrome.**

11. The environmental context in which a woman lives can greatly affect what she is exposed to during pregnancy and how her child fares. Those living in deprived environments are much more likely to encounter adverse conditions negatively affecting prenatal development. These detrimental conditions tend to repeat themselves generation after generation, in what is called the **cycle of poverty.**

Part Two

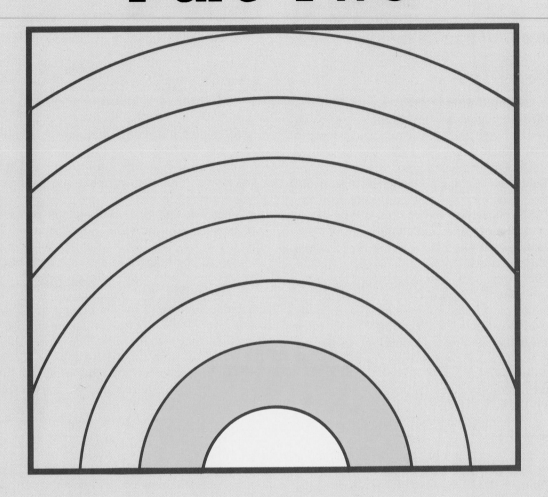

Infancy

Three Children as Infants

Malcolm Williams

"Let me hold him first, Momma," Teresa pleaded the moment her mother and father walked through the apartment door. "I get to hold him first 'cause I'm a girl, so I'm next in line to be a momma."

"What about me, girl?" laughed 19-year-old Denise, as she and the other members of the Williams household crowded around DeeDee and the tiny baby she cradled in her arms. "Are you sayin' that this boy's aunt is never gonna find herself a man?"

"My Lord. Look at that red hair!" Momma Jo exclaimed. "Where'd he get that from? Where on earth? And his eyes are already wide open like he can see everything. I never have seen a brand new baby looking 'round like he does. Hi, sugar. Hi. I'm your gran'ma. Can I give you a kiss?" Momma Jo moved the pale blue blanket aside for a better look. As she bent closer, the baby's face puckered and he began to cry with the same piercing wails that had announced his birth two days earlier. "That cry is just gran'," Momma Jo declared, clasping her hands together. "Just gran'!"

"Sounds like I better keep my earphones handy," laughed 12-year-old John, Jr. Eight-year-old Teresa watched in fascination as the baby wriggled forcefully and turned a glowing shade of dark auburn.

"So what will we name him?" DeeDee asked. "Is it going to be Muhammad, the great Ali, or Malcolm, the great protestor? What do you think, Momma Jo?"

"Well, I sure don't like some pagan name like Muhammad. I prefer Malachi from the Old Testament. The prophet who foresaw the judgment day."

"Oh, Momma. No one's named Malachi anymore. Other kids would tease him."

"Then name him Malcolm if that's your pleasure."

"What do the rest of you think?" asked DeeDee.

"Malcolm, 'cause he's red, like Malcolm X was," John, Jr., said with a grin.

"Yeah. Malcolm, okay," added Teresa thoughtfully.

"John, what's your pleasure?" DeeDee asked, passing the baby to him.

"My pleasure is Malcolm Muhammad Williams. The kid's a class-A fighter and he needs a name to cover him right."

"Then Malcolm M. Williams it is," said DeeDee smiling, and the others nodded in agreement.

"You're one helluva kid, man," John whispered proudly into little Malcolm's ear.

In the weeks that followed, DeeDee was amazed at Malcolm's energy and alertness. He seemed to fix his large brown eyes on everything that came into his view. The family began to respond to those inquisitive eyes as if Malcolm was much older. John began to tell him about all the little hearts that he would soon be breaking. Momma Jo reminded him, while he nestled in her arms, that he would someday become a great scholar. And Teresa brought toy after toy for his inspection, enthusiastically demonstrating how each one worked. Mealtime was one of Malcolm's most sociable periods. He would eat at the table with the rest of the family, passed from person to person as he sucked hungrily at his bottle. Even awkward positions in the arms of Teresa never seemed to disturb him. He intently studied every face that smiled and talked above his.

By the middle of his fourth month, Malcolm's weight gain was above the 98th percentile on the pediatrician's chart. Although his fiery coloring had subdued into a rich, clear brown, his activity level remained as high as ever. As he lay on his back on a blanket spread on the living room floor, his little arms would cycle around and around, and his feet would kick vigorously. He could turn himself from back to stomach in an instant. On his belly he pushed and pulled his legs so hard that he looked like a frog swimming.

"Motor Man I'm gonna call you," John, Jr., said one evening, catching hold of Malcolm's furiously kicking feet. "How's the little Motor Man?" Malcolm froze for an instant, then brought a fist up to his mouth. He began to suck on all five fingers so intently that the whole family laughed. Malcolm gurgled with pleasure and started kicking again.

The next week a freezing rain enveloped Chicago for days. Although it seemed that spring would never come as ice covered the windows, DeeDee knew that Friday would be the first of March. Her four-month maternity leave was almost over. When she was still pregnant, she had thought this time would go by slowly, but life with Malcolm was like a bobsled ride. He made her feel younger and more energetic than she had felt in years. The idea of going back to her job at the phone company seemed very dull in comparison. But the family needed the money. There was no question she had to work.

"When people call in tomorrow complainin' about their phone service, I'm gonna tell them just what I really think," DeeDee told the family at the dinner table Sunday night. "Honey, I'm gonna say, of *course* we're slow in gettin' your bill corrected. This is the *phone* company you're talkin' to, darlin'. What did you expect? Now if you want to see *fast* you should come 'round to my house and see my son Malcolm in action. . . ." At that moment Malcolm screeched in glee and beat the air with his fists. Everyone roared with laughter.

The following morning DeeDee's spirits were far less buoyant. Momma Jo carried Malcolm down to the front steps of the apartment so that she could wave his little hand goodbye as DeeDee left for work.

"Come on now, baby," John said to her gently, as she looked out the window of the car. "It's nothin' to cry about. He knows you're his momma. He's not gonna love you any less."

"I know," DeeDee answered. "I never thought that for a minute. It's just that I miss him so already. Can you believe that? And I guess, too, I see that boy pushin' and shovin' his way into the future so fast that I'm afraid I'm gonna miss it all if I'm gone too much. Do you know what I mean?"

"I know exactly what you mean," John said, covering her hand with his.

Mikey Gordon

Christine Gordon woke to a faint thud coming from the direction of Mikey's room. The orange numerals on the digital clock-radio read 5:45 A.M. Maybe it's my imagination, she thought hopefully. Maybe he'll give me 15 minutes more sleep. But no. She could hear him jabbering away distinctly now, his monologue of nonsense syllables interspersed with happy, high-pitched squeals. "See what he's up to, will ya," Frank muttered, without lifting his head from the pillow. Christine climbed out of bed and shuffled toward the door, stumbling over the family dog still asleep on the floor. Down the hall she went to Mikey's room and pushed open the door. There he was at the foot of his crib, flinging his toys over the side. Christine turned on the lamp just as Mikey hurled his tattered blue dog toward the rocking chair. As usual, the crib was a shambles. Mikey had pulled the blanket and sheet completely off the mattress, dumping them haphazardly in one corner. "Yi," he said turning to Christine and giving her his warmest eight-toothed smile. Her 13-month-old son, Michael Francis Gordon, was ready to start a new day.

Frank had been ecstatic when Mikey was born. He hung a king-sized bed sheet on the front of the house and wrote on it in huge blue letters: IT'S A BOY!!! The next day a reporter from News-Watch 10 stopped by to interview him. "I just want everyone to know," Frank explained, beaming into the TV camera after a few beers. "A new starting pitcher for the Red Sox has just been born. You should see the hands on him already! What a kid!"

Now 13 months later, on a warm August morning, Christine picked up the little baseball-star-apparent to change his soggy diaper. This task completed, the two of them went down to the kitchen to get breakfast going. As Christine began to measure coffee into the percolator, Mikey stood tugging at her nightgown, chanting, "joos, joos."

Through the kitchen wall Christine could hear the toilet flushing in the bathroom They'd have to do something about that plumbing. Noisiest plumbing she'd ever heard. Oh well. She shouldn't complain. At least they had a house of their own now, which was what Frank always wanted. Those nights last winter back in the old apartment had been the final straw. Mikey had been sleeping in their room because there was just no space with the girls. His presence began to put a real cramp in their sex life.

"Do you think he can hear us?" Christine would whisper when they started making love.

"For Christ's sake, what does it matter? He's only five months old! How the hell will he know what we're doing?"

"That's just it. He may think something terrible is going on. I read that. . . ."

"Nuts to what you read! I'm not going to let some Sigfried Freud crap turn me into a monk. If it bothers you so much why don't you let him sleep in the living room?"

"Keep your voice down! You'll wake him. There, now you've done it!" And by the time Christine had nursed Mikey a little and rocked him back to sleep, Frank had also drifted off—with an angry scowl creased into his face.

So a bigger place was a must or they'd end up in divorce court. They had a bank account of $10,500, scrimped and saved over eight years of marriage, and they borrowed an additional $3,000 from Christine's father. That gave them just enough for a downpayment on a $68,000 house. And $68,000 didn't buy you very much these days. The kind of place that real estate agents describe as "needing a little work." In reality that meant bad plumbing, poor heating and insulation, and just about everything else starting to rust, peel, or fall apart. But at least it was their own home. At least it was a start. And with three bedrooms and a fenced-in backyard, it was better for their growing family.

By 6:30, with sunlight streaming through the window, the Gordon family had assembled at the kitchen table. Mikey sat loftily in his highchair, banging his feet against the footrest and pressing little nuggets of Cocoa Puffs into his mouth. The sugar-coated cereal stuck to his wet fingers, making the job of feeding himself easier. "Remember it's Wednesday," Christine said to Frank as she passed a spoonful of scrambled eggs in Mikey's direction. "I need the car to make a delivery to the dress shop."

"I know, I know," Frank answered irritably. He hated to be reminded that Christine now had "a job of sorts," as he called it. It was such an odd kind of job that he didn't really have much reason to object to it at first. It all started the Christmas Christine was pregnant with Mikey. She had made a pair of matching dresses for Janie and Becky. They were red, hand-smocked, with green appliqué Christmas trees on a wide white collar. Everyone had oohed and aahed over them Christmas day. Christine's sister, Paula, had taken lots of pictures and showed them to her boss at the dress shop. That had started everything rolling. The woman wanted Christine to make some girls' dresses to sell on consignment at the store. It seemed harmless enough to Frank at the time. Something to keep Christine busy until the new baby was born. How was he to know that the things she made would become such a hit? Within a few months, the store had turned a large storage closet into a special area to display Christine's clothes. Frank felt as if he had somehow been tricked into going along with something he never wanted. If it wasn't for the extra money and the fact that Christine did all the sewing at home, he would *make* her quit. He looked at her with growing annoyance across the kitchen table. As if on cue to break the tension, Mikey strained forward pointing at Christine's toast and demanding "beh, beh."

"Hey! I think he said bread," Frank said excitedly, momentarily forgetting his annoyance. For the next five minutes he kept pointing to the toast that Christine had placed in Mikey's fingers, repeating "bread," over and over. Mikey grinned and slapped the tray of his highchair in unrestrained delight.

That evening Christine sat at her sewing machine in a corner of the living room, with Janie and Becky sprawled on the floor beside her, collecting leftover pieces of fabric for future doll clothes. "That blue one's mine," Becky said, pulling a large turquoise scrap out of Janie's pile. "No it's not. Mommy gave it to *me*. Mommy, make her give it back!"

"Quiet, you two," Frank demanded. "Chrissie, will ya quiet things down over there. I'm tryin' to watch this program. Us men can't get any peace around here, can we Mikey?" Frank added, addressing the little boy beside him. "Jees. Now we've got another damn commercial!"

In response, Mikey crawled onto his father's lap and sat facing him. "Dee!" he said, looking up with bright, eager eyes. "Wanna bounce, huh?" Frank said, smiling, his irritation fading. Soon father and son were engrossed in a game they had invented several months earlier. Frank would hold Mikey on his lap and bounce him vigorously. Then he would suddenly spread his knees apart and let Mikey drop between them, still supporting him by the arms. As Mikey squealed with laughter, Frank would hoist him back up and start all over again.

Now's as good a time as any, Christine thought as she walked over to the living-room sofa. "Something happened at the store today," she started, trying to sound casual. "The owner, you know, Helen? She'd like to expand the kids' clothes a bit, in addition to my stuff, you know. And she asked me to go on a buying trip to Boston with her. Help her pick things out. Just for a day. What do you think?"

"I think it's a rotten idea! What do ya need to do that for? You got plenty to keep you busy here. And who's gonna take care of the kids? Tell me that."

"That's no problem," Christine answered quickly. "I'd have my mom come over for the day. And Helen's going to pay me, you know. A hundred dollars! Can you believe it? I nearly fainted."

"A hundred bucks, huh?" Frank muttered with grudging interest. "When does she want ya to go?"

"Next Thursday. She's got the schedule all set up. What do you say? Okay?"

"I'll never hear the end of it if I say no," Frank grumbled. "Yeah. Go ahead. A hundred bucks. Why not?"

Meryl Polonius

"We'll be back with our third game of the day right after this!" the host of the TV quiz show announced with a huge artificial smile. I really should rinse out those sheets Meryl threw up on, Karen thought with a sigh, as she sat slumped in the worn tweed armchair. Then after Meryl's nap I can take them down to the Laundromat.

In an effort to shake herself out of her lethargy, Karen slid down to the floor beside her daughter, Meryl. The baby was busily stacking brightly colored rings onto a plastic post. She performed this task slowly and soberly, as if diligently trying to master it. It's easy to love her at times like this when she's not fussing or screaming, Karen thought. Watching the child's tiny fingers clumsily handling a small red ring, Karen felt a warm glow.

Bored with the rings, Meryl looked around and eyed the laundry basket. Soon she was crawling toward it. "Oh no you don't," Karen warned as she scooped her off the floor. "You'll tip it over and I'll have to pick everything up." Meryl immediately began to cry and wriggled to escape from Karen's arms. "Someone's tired," Karen declared. "It's time for your nap." Meryl cried even louder as they headed toward the bedroom. "Let's go look for teddy," Karen said, trying to soothe her daughter. "I'll bet teddy's already asleep. Shhh. You don't want to wake him, do you?" Meryl's cries turned into piercing screams. "Hey, come on," Karen pleaded, as she put Meryl into her crib. "Be good and go to sleep, and when you wake up I'll give you a cookie." Meryl's face was now a deep crimson as she screamed and pulled at the crib rail.

"Tough," muttered Karen, closing the bedroom door behind her. "You're just going to have to cry it out." Meryl's screams grated on Karen as she sat back down in front of the TV. But at least things were a lot better than they had been a year ago. Those first few months of Meryl's life had been really terrible. A small baby at birth, weighing just six pounds, Meryl was a fitful sleeper and a poor eater from the start. Often she would take only an ounce or so of formula and then spit it up. Karen had tried breast feeding at the urging of Meryl's pediatrician, but nursing was difficult for her, and the baby still remained colicky. Finally Karen found a formula that Meryl could tolerate. This was a definite improvement. Nevertheless, Meryl continued to cry often and for long periods of time.

The strain got to Karen and to her mother. It seemed to Karen that her mother was constantly harping at her, telling her what she was doing wrong. One day at the Fresno Teen Mother Project, while waiting to talk with her counselor, Karen began pouring out her gripes to a girl named Kay. "Hey, that's really tough," Kay had said sympathetically. "But you don't have to take that crap from your mother. I'm lookin' for someone to share my apartment. Why don't you and Meryl move in with me and Ashley?"

"Yeah, what'll I do for money?" Karen asked, with a curt laugh. "I've got *nothing*."

"You can collect from welfare, dummy," Kay answered. "That's what I do."

So Karen had moved into Kay's apartment above a shoe-repair shop. Her mother had been furious. "You're going to live *where?*" she asked Karen. "On West End Avenue near the freeway? That neighborhood's terrible! And going on welfare to boot. I can't *believe* it. You're doing this just to spite me!" When the counselor at the Teen Mother Project tactfully suggested that living apart might help mother and daughter bridge the gap between them, Karen's mother threw up her hands in a gesture of total futility and walked out of the room. The next day, Karen moved clothes, toys, crib, and highchair into her new home. She felt apprehensive as she climbed the steep stairs leading up from the alley, but Kay's enthusiasm put her at ease. "Here," Kay smiled, "let me take that." And she dragged Karen's heavy suitcase into the shabby bedroom that Karen and Meryl would share.

Karen soon discovered that life with Kay and her daughter, Ashley, was far from ideal. About a week after Karen was settled, Kay's brother arrived, asking if he could stay for a day or two. That day or two dragged on into weeks, and soon the apartment was overrun with his friends. As if Meryl wasn't fitful enough, all the disruption was making her unbearable. Karen began thinking about going back to her mother's. Then one night Kay got a call. It was Eric, Kay's on-again-off-again boy-friend, also the father of Ashley. He was in Texas, working on construction, making all kinds of money, so he said. He wanted Kay and Ashley to come for a visit. "Maybe this time we can work things out," he had told Kay over the phone. Two days later, when she got the busfare from Eric, Kay was off to Dallas. The same day Kay's brother moved to his new girl-friend's apartment, leaving Karen and Meryl alone.

Karen was determined to make things better for Meryl. She took the few dollars she had saved from her monthly check and bought Meryl a new toy. It was Oscar the Grouch from Sesame Street in his battered garbage can. When you pressed a bulb attached to the side, the scowling Oscar would pop up like a jack-in-the-box. Karen couldn't wait to unwrap the toy when she got it home. She placed it in front of Meryl, who began to inspect it quietly. Then Karen pressed the bulb and Oscar jumped up, the lid of the garbage can perched on top of his head. Meryl startled, her lower lip protruded, and she began to cry. "Come on, honey. It's Oscar the Grouch," Karen said. "I got this nice new toy just for you." Meryl turned her head away as Karen pushed the toy toward her. "Don't you *like* it?" Karen asked, moving around to stay in front of Meryl's averted face. In exasperation she made the monster pop up one more time. Meryl wailed louder.

As the weeks rolled by and Kay did not return, the loneliness began to get to Karen. Some afternoons, when Meryl just wouldn't stop crying at nap time, Karen would have a sudden urge to walk out the door. She could picture herself walking down the street, the sun warm and inviting, with the cries of her baby growing fainter and fainter behind her. Karen was horrified at these fantasies. She loved Meryl; she knew she did. But sometimes it all just seemed too much. Karen often wished that she could talk to her mother the way daughters were supposed to be able to. But whenever she tried, they always seemed to end up fighting. Even Karen's old friends from high school seemed to have deserted her. The few who hadn't gone off to college were busy working and having fun. Sitting around in a dumpy apartment with a cranky baby wasn't their idea of a good time. If it wasn't for the counselor at the Teen Mother Project, Karen didn't know what she would do.

That night as Karen sat in the living room, listening to the traffic in the street below, tears welled up in her eyes. "Damn you, Jeff," she whispered. "Damn you!" And pressing Meryl's teddy bear to her face, she cried as if her heart would break.

5

First Adaptations

Karen Polonius watched as Dr. Bryant, a pediatrician, prepared to give newborn Meryl her first physical exam. "She may be small, Karen," Dr. Bryant said, "but she's very alert."

"She is?" Karen answered doubtfully. To her, Meryl looked totally helpless and unaware of the world.

"Sure," said Dr. Bryant, smiling. "Watch." And he began to talk to Meryl in gentle, soothing tones. "Hi there, little one. Hi, sweetie. Going to show your mommy how smart you are, hmmm?" Meryl immediately quieted and looked up.

"She hears you," said Karen.

Then Dr. Bryant slowly moved a bright orange ball across Meryl's field of vision. Meryl's eyes followed it.

"She sees it!" Karen exclaimed.

"Now you try," said Dr. Bryant, encouraging Karen to move her head slowly back and forth while she talked to the baby.

"She sees me!" Karen smiled, looking up at the doctor. "Does she know I'm a person? Does she know I'm her mother?"

"Not yet," Dr. Bryant answered kindly, "but she will. In a few months she'll have learned a great deal about people, and she'll know you from all others."

New parents with their first child are frequently uncertain about what an infant can see or feel or learn. *(Eve Arnold/Magnum Photos Inc.)*

Meryl faces developmental tasks similar to those we all face: She must meet her essential physiological needs, learn about the world, and engage in significant social relationships. But newborns like Meryl confront these challenges at a distinct disadvantage. While adults can draw upon extensive past experience, newborns cannot. Meryl must learn from scratch that objects exist, that different objects have different properties (which sometimes change), and that actions on objects have consequences. In addition, she must learn that people are very special objects—ones that possess their own wishes and feelings and that engage in actions independent of hers. In the process, Meryl must come to the realization that she, too, is a person.

How do newborns make these discoveries with no prior knowledge of the world? How will Meryl come to know about objects and people? How will she come to grasp the relationship between herself and an orange ball she sees, between herself and her mother? Fortunately, Meryl, like all other newborns, comes equipped with certain built-in capacities that will help her tackle these tasks. These capacities include reflexes, perceptual abilities, motor skills, and learning abilities. All will enable Meryl to make her first adaptations—her first efforts to adjust to and understand the world.

As you read about infants' earliest capacities and how they change in the first year, think about how these skills allow babies to interact with parents and other people from the very moment of birth. At the same time, think about how the limitations on infants' abilities restrict what they are able to perceive and learn. For example, as you read about the limitations on early visual capacities, imagine how hard it would be for a newborn like Meryl to actually *see* the difference between her mother and some other woman.

While young infants, of course, have many limitations in what they can do and what they can learn, a major theme of this chapter is that babies are born with, or develop during their first year of life, an impressive array of competencies. These early competencies, which are the building blocks of more complex behaviors, have one or more of the following characteristics:

1. The infant's competencies often meet a direct *survival need*: the sucking reflex to get nourishment, the gagging reflex to prevent choking, and the crying reflex to elicit care, for example.
2. From the very beginning the infant's competencies involve *organization of behavior*. Behavior is organized if the response to a stimulus is a sequence of motor acts that serves some function for the infant. Although organized sequences are simple in newborns, they become more elaborate with further development. A good example is turning the head in the direction of a sound, as Meryl did when Dr. Bryant spoke to her. The behaviors in this response are highly organized, requiring close coordination between hearing and head movement. Later, when Meryl is some months older, she will conduct more elaborate and intentional searches to locate the source of a sound.
3. The infant *selectively responds* to the environment. For instance, young infants do not look with equal attention at everything around them. Instead, they tend to look at things that are fairly large and have

high contrast, such as a pair of eyes or the border between a person's hair and forehead. This early example of selective looking is an automatic action and does not involve a conscious or intentional focusing of attention. Nevertheless, this automatic selective response provides the infant with opportunities to learn about the distinguishing features of the human face.

4. The infant is able to detect the *relationship between actions and their consequences.* For example, a newborn may explore the connection between where the thumb is put and the feelings generated. (A thumb in the eye does not feel good, whereas a thumb in the mouth does.) Such connections between an action and its consequences are called **contingencies.**

This chapter focuses on the capacities that infants possess for interacting with the world, on what infants do, and on their skills for obtaining information about their environment. In the next chapter, the infant's developing *knowledge* about the world will be examined.

First we describe the sleeping, waking, and crying episodes in the life of a newborn, or **neonate,** and how they change during infancy. The pattern of these **states** provides the framework within which an infant experiences the world. Next, we examine some of the capacities present at birth, called reflexes, which sometimes serve as building blocks for more elaborate behaviors. Reflexes are actions that occur when a stimulus from the environment is detected and the body reacts automatically. In the third section we discuss early sensory capacities and developmental changes in perceptual abilities, with particular emphasis on vision and hearing. Then we examine infant motor abilities. Finally, we look at the infant's learning capabilities, which provide one means by which changes in behavior take place. Throughout the chapter we will be concerned with the way in which the infant's engagement of the world is organized, the "rules" that govern its behavior.

INFANT STATES

Parents sometimes describe their newborn infant's behavior as consisting of only three things: eating, sleeping, and crying. This sort of distinction is similar to the one developmentalists make among the different states that constitute the basic rest-activity cycle of infants. Infants' states have been categorized in a number of ways. One frequently used system consists of the following six states: quiet sleep, active sleep, awake and quiet, awake and active, fussing, and crying (Brazelton, 1973; Prechtl and Beintema, 1964). These states correspond to two kinds of sleeping, two kinds of wakefulness, and two kinds of crying.

States and transitions between states are important to those studying the capabilities of infants because infants respond to the environment very differently depending on their current state. For example, a bell sounded to the right of where a newborn is currently looking may elicit an eye movement or head turn in the direction of the sound if the baby is in an awake and active state, but not if the baby is in an active sleep or fussing state. As we describe the developmental changes in the state patterns of infants during their first few months of life, you will see why it is easier to study older infants than neonates.

Average newborns spend more than 16 hours sleeping each day (Berg and Berg, 1979). Time spent sleeping decreases rapidly during infancy and childhood, and then more gradually, until it declines to a little more than six hours in old age (Roffwarg, Muzio, and Dement, 1966). Newborns distribute their sleeping and waking time equally between day and night, which creates difficulties for parents, who usually have their sleep-wake cycle organized in the traditional way. Although it will be many months and sometimes years before an infant sleeps through the night consistently, Figure 5.1 shows that by eight weeks infants begin to exhibit signs of the traditional day-night pattern (Sostek and Anders, 1981). In the first two months, the time spent sleeping decreases during the afternoon hours and increases in the time period between 10 P.M. and 2 A.M. Conversely, the amount of time spent fussing and crying increases in the afternoon and decreases at night.

The pattern of sleep also changes with development. Adults spend about 20 percent of their sleeping time in rapid eye movement, or REM, sleep. Active sleep in newborns has some of the properties of REM sleep in adults; neonates spend 50 percent of their sleeping time in this state (Roffwarg, Muzio, and Dement, 1966). When newborns are sleeping, their active and quiet sleep are intermixed irregularly, including the time during the onset of sleep. This pattern is unlike that of adults, for whom REM sleep usually occurs after 90 minutes of non-REM sleep and then repeats at approximately 90-minute intervals (Kalat, 1984). In addition, the brain-wave patterns that occur during the different stages of sleep in adults are not apparent in newborns (Spitz, Emde, and Metcalf, 1970). These differences between newborns and adults can be attributed to the newborn's immature brain development. Substantial changes are apparent by 3 months, when non-REM onset of sleep is the rule and the brain-wave patterns seen with adult sleep can be detected.

Much research has been done on the crying state, which occupies less than 10 percent of most infants' time. Three distinct crying patterns have been reported for infants: hungry cries, which start with a whimper and become louder and more sustained; upset cries, which are louder and often show a more rapid onset; and pain cries, which begin with a high-pitched and high-intensity wail followed by loud crying. Peter Wolfe (1969) has reported that even inexperienced mothers respond more rapidly to the pain cry than to either of the other two. Mothers are better at distinguishing among the types of cries of their own infants than of infants they do not know (Wiesenfeld, Malatesta, and DeLoach, 1981). Similarly, experienced nurses who work in hospital nurseries are better able to discriminate among different types of cries than are those with less experience (Wasz-Hockert et al., 1968).

Crying infants may soothe themselves or they may be soothed by a care giver. Although the transitions between the states are a normal component of infant behavior that seems biologically determined, the capacity to be soothed is also biologically provided. When infants soothe themselves, sucking is often part of the process. Allowing infants to suck on a pacifier is one effective soothing technique (Field and Goldson,

Figure 5.1
Changes in Infants' Sleep/ Wake Cycle

At 2 weeks of age infants do not follow the conventional sleep/wake cycle of sleeping more at night and being awake more during the day. Although they still do not sleep through the night, 8-week-olds sleep more between 10 P.M. and 2 A.M., and are awake more between 2 P.M. and 6 P.M., than during other time periods.

Source: Sostek and Anders, 1981.

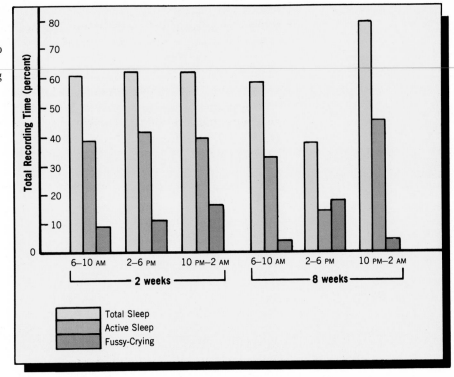

1984). Others include voice stimulation, rocking, embracing, and swaddling. Not all techniques are effective with all babies, and babies display stable individual differences in the ease with which they can be soothed (Bates, 1980).

In early infancy, when state changes are frequent, the process of changing states (going to sleep, waking up, starting to cry, being soothed from crying) requires much parental involvement. By 5 months, when the states are more stable and the transitions more predictable, parental involvement focuses much more on behavior within the awake and active state. Thus biologically predetermined state characteristics of infants are part of the context within which development occurs.

REFLEXES IN THE NEWBORN

Newborns display many reflexes, some of which disappear as the baby grows older. A **reflex** is an automatic or "built-in" reaction elicited by particular stimuli. Blinking your eye when an object is poked at it is one example of a reflex. Other examples are given in Table 5.1.

What do reflexes do for newborns? Why do they have them at all? One way of thinking about reflexes is as a set of behaviors enabling infants to have organized, adaptive responses to their environments before they have had a chance to learn. For example, newborns automatically suck when an object is placed in the mouth, a reflex that allows them to obtain nourishment before they learn to associate a nipple with food. Certain other reflexes found in newborns have less obvious functions. Some seem to provide initial responses, which learning later modifies, thus allowing rapid acquisition of important new behaviors. Examples of these include the grasping and stepping reflexes. Still other reflexes may be a legacy of our evolutionary past. For instance, when a newborn's head or body is allowed to drop backward, the arms fling out and then come back toward the body's midline, with the hands curling in as if to grasp something. This is called the **Moro reflex.** Might it be the response of an animal trying to grasp its mother or the limb of a tree to keep from falling? If so, the Moro reflex was once crucial to our early ancestors' survival.

Survival Reflexes

Some of the reflexes present at birth—such as blinking, sneezing, gagging, and breathing—clearly serve critical functions. The breathing reflex is absolutely essential to survival, and the others help an infant deal with various threats to the body. But because these reflexes remain stable throughout a person's life, they are not of great interest to developmentalists, who are more concerned with those survival reflexes present at birth that disappear as the infant acquires more advanced skills.

TABLE 5.1   Examples of Infant Reflexes

Reflex	Description	Developmental Pattern
Blink	To a flash of light or a puff of air, an infant closes both eyes.	Permanent.
Babinski	When the side of an infant's foot is stroked from the heel toward the toes, the toes fan out and the foot twists inward.	Disappears around 1 year.
Babkin	When an infant is lying on his back, pressure applied to the palms of both hands causes the head to turn straight ahead, the mouth to open, and the eyes to close.	Disappears around 3 months.
Grasping	Pressure on an infant's palms produced by an object like a parent's finger causes the fingers to curl with a strong enough grasp to support the infant's own weight.	Weakens after 3 months and disappears by 1 year.
Moro	This reflex pattern, which involves extending the arms and then bringing them rapidly toward the midline while closing the fingers in a grasping action, can be triggered by several kinds of startling stimuli, such as a sudden loud noise or holding the infant horizontally face-up and then rapidly lowering the baby about six inches.	Disappears around 5 months.
Rooting	When an infant's cheek is stroked lightly, he turns his head in the direction of the stroked cheek and opens his mouth to suck the object that stroked the cheek.	Disappears around 4 months.
Stepping	When an infant is held above a surface and then lowered until the feet touch the surface, the infant will make stepping movements like walking.	Disappears around 3 months.
Sucking	When an object such as a nipple or a finger is inserted into an infant's mouth, rhythmic sucking occurs.	Changes into voluntary sucking by 2 months.
Tonic Neck	An infant placed on his back tends to turn his head to one side and extend the arm and leg on that side while flexing the limbs on the other side (like a fencing position).	Disappears around 4 months.

Rooting and sucking are examples of reflexes present at birth that later disappear. The **rooting reflex** can be elicited by stroking a newborn's cheek or touching a corner of the child's mouth. The baby responds by turning the head toward the side that was touched, in an apparent attempt to find something to suck. When the mouth captures something, the **sucking reflex** is activated. These reflexes, and their organization together, have obvious survival value to newborn mammals, who must find and suck the mother's teat to get food.

Both the rooting and sucking reflexes disappear at around three to four months of age and are replaced by voluntary eating behaviors. Note how important it is for the sucking reflex to disappear if the baby is to begin eating solid foods. If an infant continued to suck automatically every time food entered the mouth, the child would never learn to chew.

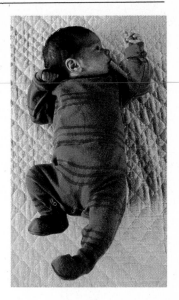

Tonic Neck Reflex.
When young infants are placed on their back, they turn their head to one side and extend their arm and leg on that side. The arm and leg on the opposite side are flexed. *(Elizabeth Crews.)*

Other Reflexes

Some reflexes that are present at birth and disappear as the baby grows older have no apparent survival value. However, the basic behavior patterns displayed in these reflexes later become part of more sophisticated voluntary actions. Examples are the grasping and stepping reflexes.

The **grasping reflex** is elicited by stimulating the palm of a newborn's hand. The baby responds by automatically curling the fingers inward. If an adult uses his index fingers to stimulate a newborn's palms, the infant will grasp each finger so firmly that the adult can lift the baby up. Since a newborn's grasp is reflexive, the child cannot voluntarily let go, although fatigue will eventually set in and weaken the firmness of the grip. The inability to let go clearly makes the grasping reflex unsuitable for elaborate interactions with the world. By the end of the third month, the grasping reflex declines, and the baby begins to show a more voluntary grasp, usually elicited by visual stimuli (Bower, 1977). For instance, when Meryl is 4 or 5 months old, the sight of a bright orange ball will probably cause her to reach out and try to grasp it. This voluntary grasp, which becomes more adept with age, is a very important capability. It allows older infants to secure and manipulate objects they wish to explore.

Another example of a reflex that gives way to voluntary actions is the **stepping reflex.** The pediatrician who examined Meryl could have elicited this reflex by holding her upright and then lowering her toward a table until her feet touched the surface. Meryl would have responded by reflexively moving her feet in a rhythmic stepping motion that resembles walking. If this reflex is not exercised regularly, it disappears when an infant is 1 to 4 months old. As long as the leg movements in the stepping reflex are automatic responses to stimulation on the bottoms of the feet, they are not useful in learning to walk. However, the same movements *are* part of walking when exercised under voluntary control.

Stepping Reflex.
Newborns appear to be able to walk when supported, but the behavior is purely a reflex that disappears before true walking occurs. *(Ida Wyman/International Stock Photo.)*

Developmentalists have been fascinated by reflexes such as these, the movements of which are eventually incorporated into more complex, voluntary actions. Some have suggested that early in development the grasping and stepping reflexes are probably controlled by lower brain centers. As the baby grows older, however, higher brain centers take control and allow the reflexes to be stopped. This voluntary control then enables the formerly reflexive actions to be integrated into more complex sequences of behavior.

SENSING AND PERCEIVING THE WORLD

When John and DeeDee Williams brought Malcolm home from the hospital, all the members of the family, talking and smiling, clustered around to see him. How did newborn Malcolm perceive all of this commotion? Could he see distinct faces peering into his? Could he hear different voices and distinguish speech from laughter? Could he smell the scent of soap on Momma Jo's hands as she gently touched his cheek?

For years people have wondered how newborns like Malcolm experience the world. Since they respond reflexively to a variety of stimuli, their sensory systems must be working to some extent. But exactly what do babies experience when they see, hear, taste, smell, and touch things around them? And what causes them to direct their senses to one thing or another?

Sensory Systems in the Newborn

VISION

What do babies see when they look at faces? The pictures on page 147 illustrate how a mother's face may look to an infant of 1, 2, and 3 months of age. These pictures are created by computer and are based on estimates of the average baby's visual acuity. **Acuity** refers to the fineness of detail a person can see. If very small black dots or lines are placed closely together on a white background, the overall impression is of uniform grayness, because the acuity of the human visual system is not great enough to see the individual black and white areas. You can observe this limitation in acuity yourself by examining one of the black-and-white photographs in this text with a magnifying glass. Adults possessing normal vision have greater acuity than young infants do and hence can see more fine detail. How do researchers determine an infant's visual acuity since babies cannot *say* how clearly they see? Answering this question is a good way to start exploring the baby's visual world.

Determining How Clearly Babies See. One method of determining an infant's acuity takes advantage of a visual reflex. When vertical stripes are moved horizontally in front of a baby, the child's eyes automatically follow them for a while and then jump back to the starting point in a jerky movement called a **saccade.** Obviously, this visual reflex (known as *optokinetic nystagmus*) can occur only if the stripes are large enough for the baby to see. If the stripes are very thin and close together, they will be seen as a solid gray. To determine visual acuity, then, a researcher finds the minimum size and spacing that reliably elicits the optokinetic nystagmus reflex. Robert Fantz and his colleagues gathered these data for infants ranging in age from 4 days to 6 months (Fantz, Ordy, and Udelf,

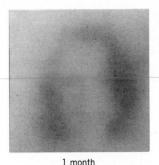
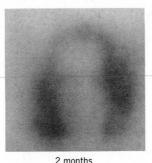

1 month   2 months   3 months   Adult

Infants of different ages receive different visual information when looking at a person from a distance of about 6 inches. Poor acuity in younger infants can be partly overcome by allowing them to view from a closer distance.

(From Sensation and Perception, 2nd edition by E. Bruce Goldstein. © 1984 by Wadsworth Inc. Used by permission of the publisher.)

1962). Later, other researchers translated those findings into the familiar ratios used to describe adult acuity (Banks and Salapatek, 1983). Apparently, at 2 weeks of age, a baby's acuity is about 20/300: The child sees at 20 feet what an adult with normal vision can see at 300 feet. Five months later, a baby's visual acuity usually has improved to about 20/100.

A second method of measuring infants' acuity takes advantage of a baby's motivation to try to look at things. Thus, if you place two cards side by side—one solid gray, the other with broad black and white stripes—even a newborn is motivated to look longer at the striped card with its contrasting features. This preferential looking enables researchers to tell when a baby can see the difference between two stimuli. By adjusting the width and closeness of the lines on the striped card, the researchers can determine at what point preferential looking disappears. Presumably, this point is reached when the baby begins to see the stripes as a uniform gray. Results from a study using this procedure to estimate acuity in babies from 2 weeks to 6 months old (Allen, 1978) were very close to those obtained using the other method we described, as is illustrated in Figure 5.2. Because we are making judgments about the abilities of infants who cannot talk, the similarity of results is reassuring and gives us confidence that our interpretation of the studies is accurate.

The specific reasons for young infants' limited acuity are not yet well understood. The optical quality of an infant's eyes is quite good and allows a sharp image to be focused on the retina at the back of the eye. The limitation probably lies somewhere in the system that changes this image into neural signals, transmits them to the brain, and then analyzes the information; but the contribution of each component of the system is not known (Banks and Salapatek, 1983).

The findings about visual acuity in the first few months of life tell us that young babies have trouble discerning the fine details of objects. Researchers once thought that this limitation partly resulted from newborns' inability to **accommodate**—that is, the lenses of their eyes did not adjust their focus in response to an object's distance. More recent studies show, however, that infants' eyes *do* focus in response to the distance of an object, even though this accommodation does not reach an adult level

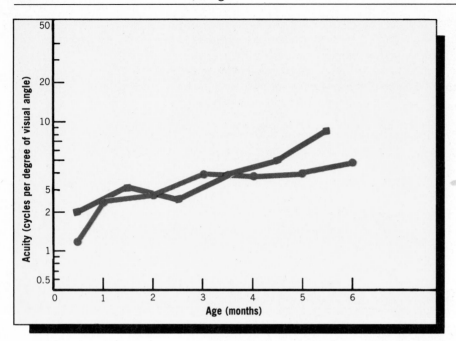

Figure 5.2
Development of Acuity During the First Six Months
This graph illustrates the improvement in visual acuity during the first six months, as measured by two different techniques. The squares are from a study using optokinetic nystagmus (Funty et al., 1962) and the circles are from one using preferential looking (Allen, 1978).

Source: Banks and Salapatek, 1983.

until 4 months of age (Banks, 1980; Brookman, 1980). Interestingly, for the younger baby the limitations on visual acuity probably limit accommodation, not the other way around (Banks and Salapatek, 1983). Low acuity, with its general lack of sharp detail, reduces the ability to detect when accommodation is needed. Thus, if you want a young baby to see something clearly, you should hold the object relatively close to his or her face so that the limited acuity can be overcome by making the details of an object larger.

Research shows that babies are sensitive to blur and motivated to see objects clearly. For instance, Ilze Kalnins and Jerome Bruner (1973) showed a series of slides to babies 1 to 3 months old, allowing the infants to control the focus of the projector. The researchers cleverly did this by taking advantage of the sucking reflex. Although the reflex is automatic—that is, an infant will suck on any object placed in the mouth—the rate of sucking is subject to voluntary control. To monitor the babies' reactions, Kalnins and Bruner connected the focusing mechanism of the projector to a device that measured the babies' rate of sucking on a pacifier. When the babies sucked rapidly, the picture came into focus; when their sucking slowed, the picture blurred. The infants quickly adjusted their rate of sucking and "worked hard" to keep the slides clear. In addition to showing that babies are motivated to see things clearly, this study also demonstrates **contingency** learning. These infants detected a contingency between their own rate of sucking and the clarity of the slides. This kind of learning, called **instrumental conditioning,** was described briefly in Chapter 2 and will be discussed in the last section of this chapter.

Can Infants See Colors? Determining whether young infants perceive color has been difficult because of the need to distinguish between color (determined by the wavelength of light) and brightness (determined by the light's intensity). When you see the difference between a red car and a blue one on a color television set, you are doing so on the basis of color. When you see a difference between the same two cars on a black-and-white set, you are doing so on the basis of brightness. Thus, when you show two different colors to a baby and the child looks longer at one than the other, you have to make sure that this visual preference is based on color, not relative brightness.

By carefully controlling the intensity of stimuli, researchers have been able to show that infants as young as two months can discriminate on the basis of color alone (Bornstein, 1978, 1981; Oster, 1975; Schaller, 1975). Mark Bornstein has argued that a 3- to 4-month-old baby's color vision is similar to an adult's. The potential limitations on an infant's color vision are much like those for acuity: The limitations arise in the receptors that change the colored light into neural signals, in the system that transmits this information to the brain, and in the interpretation within the brain itself. Because color vision in adults is relatively well understood, new information on the development of color vision during the first six months of life will allow greater understanding of the development of the sensory component of the nervous system.

HEARING

It has long been known that pregnant women report feeling the fetus move seconds after there is a loud noise (Forbes and Forbes, 1927). More controlled studies have revealed that this movement can be elicited by making a loud noise near the abdomen of a woman who is carrying a fetus at least 31 weeks old—that is, seven weeks before delivery (Sontag and Wallace, 1935). As you would expect, infants who are born prematurely but are otherwise normal have the ability to hear (Aslin, Pisoni, and Jusczyk, 1983), as do all normal babies. But modern researchers still want to know how sensitive a newborn's hearing is and how that sensitivity increases over time.

How do researchers determine a baby's hearing sensitivity? They can do so by monitoring eye blinks, changes in heart rate, and changes in the brain's electrical activity as sounds are presented. Using such measures, researchers have found that in order for infants to hear a noise it must be 10 to 20 decibels louder than for adults to hear it (Hecox, 1975; Schulman-Galambos and Galambos, 1979). To give you some idea of how much 10 to 20 decibels is, Table 5.2 lists the approximate level in decibels of some familiar sounds. Adults can just detect a 1 decibel sound in otherwise quiet conditions. For a sound to be just detectable by a baby (especially a low-pitched sound), it must be substantially louder (e.g., Sinnott, Pisoni, and Aslin, 1983). Of course, a child's sensitivity to sound gradually improves with age, but it may take 12 to 13 years to be equal to an adult's (Eagles et al., cited in Pick and Pick, 1970).

We know that babies can hear sounds of an appropriate loudness, but can they differentiate one sound from another? And just how different must two sounds be for babies to notice the difference? One of the most popular ways of answering these questions depends on the infant's tendency to get accustomed to stimuli. When something new is perceived in the environment, attention tends to be focused on it. If it is repeated over and over, it loses its ability to draw attention. This phenomenon,

TABLE 5.2	Some Common Sound Levels in Decibels

Sound	dB
Barely audible sound (threshold)	0
Leaves rustling	20
Quiet residential community	40
Average speaking voice	60
Loud voices	80
Subway	100
Rock band	120
Jet engine at takeoff	140

called habituation, has provided the basis for a very powerful research technique used to study infants. In hearing studies, researchers repeatedly present one sound until the baby apparently loses interest in it. Then they change the sound. If the baby responds with renewed attention, they conclude that the child has detected the change. Using this method investigators have found that 6-month-olds can distinguish between sounds that differ in loudness by as little as 10 decibels, and perhaps even less (Aslin, Pisoni, and Jusczyk, 1983; Moffitt, 1973). By the time they are 5 to 8 months old, babies are also quite good at detecting small changes in pitch (Olsho et al., 1982). It turns out that infants are sensitive to a broad range of pitches and hear higher frequencies than adults do. This may be one reason that adults learn to talk high-pitched "baby talk" to infants.

Interestingly, young infants are especially good at discriminating among various speech sounds, even better than they are at discriminating pitch. This ability may well be tied to the importance of language in human adaptation. Researchers have discovered this capacity by employing techniques such as the high-amplitude sucking procedure, which is similar to the method that gives babies control over the focus of a slide projector. The infant is given a pacifier, and forceful sucking triggers presentation of a speech sound (for example, "mad"). Since infants seem to be motivated to listen to stimuli, they suck hard to hear these sounds. However, when the same sound has been presented over and over, the child habituates and sucks less actively. Now the researchers change the speech sound (for example, to "dad"). If the baby can hear the difference between the two sounds, he or she will suck forcefully again.

Using the high-amplitude sucking procedure, Peter Eimas and his colleagues (Eimas, Siqueland, and Jusczyk, 1971) found that even babies 1 month old could discriminate the syllables /ba/ and /pa/, which are the same except for the beginning consonant. Further, Eimas demonstrated that babies' discrimination of speech sounds is like adults' discrimination. Eimas used speech sounds generated by a computer, which made it possible to produce a continuum of speech sounds between a normal /ba/ and /pa/ sound. When these sounds are presented to adults, they do not hear them as sounds between /ba/ and /pa/. Rather, those closer to the /ba/ sound all sound like /ba/, and those closer to the /pa/ sound all sound like /pa/. This phenomenon of perceiving stimuli that vary along a continuum as belonging to an unchanging category is called *categorical* perception (Liberman et al., 1957). Infants' discrimination exhibited the same pattern. For a range of sounds, infants showed no discrimination. Then at the same point in the sound continuum that adults make the distinction between /ba/ and /pa/, infants were able to discriminate. Other research has demonstrated the same categorical perception phenomenon in infants when other speech sounds are used (Eimas, 1985). Thus, although speech perception does change with development and depends partly on experience, the basic sensory system needed to learn language appears to be genetically given (Eimas, 1985).

SMELL AND TASTE

Young infants are very sensitive to odors. When various odors are placed on cotton swabs and held beneath a baby's nose, the child's facial expressions and body movements indicate reactions similar to those of adults. For instance, infants respond positively to the odor of a banana, somewhat negatively to fishy odors, and very negatively to the odor of rotten eggs (Steiner, 1977). Very fine discriminations may be shown when babies are habituated to one smell and then are presented with another to see if they detect the difference (e.g., Alberts, 1981; Engen and Lipsitt, 1965). In one such study, 5-day-old infants could actually discriminate the breast pads of their mothers from those of other women on the basis of odor (MacFarlane, 1975). Perhaps smell plays a role in the developing bond between mother and infant.

If babies can discriminate odors, can they also discriminate tastes? By studying the tongues of premature and full-term babies, researchers know that taste buds are present throughout the mouth prior to birth. Taste buds then become more localized on the tongue around the normal time of delivery. Investigators have determined that newborns can discriminate the sweet taste of a fairly weak sugar solution from the taste of plain water (e.g., Engen, Lipsitt, and Peck, 1974). This ability to detect sweetness and the sweetness of mother's milk help explain the early development of a preference for sweetness. Researchers also have found that young infants can discriminate sweet from the remaining three basic tastes. However, whether they can differentiate among bitter, sour, and salty is still in dispute (Crook, 1978). Newborns have the taste buds to

When babies begin eating solid food, parents quickly learn about their infants' taste preferences, which are based on both taste and smell. *(Ida Wyman/ International Stock Photo.)*

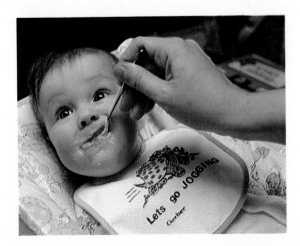

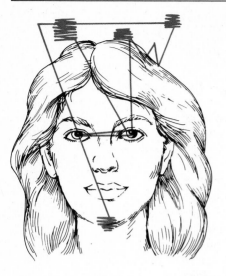

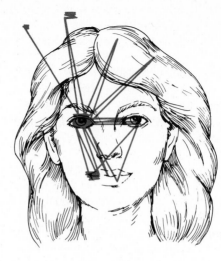

Figure 5.3
Development of Infant Scanning Patterns
One-month-olds do not look at faces as much as 2-month-olds do. When they do look, they tend to concentrate on the outside edges of the face. Two-month-olds look more at the internal features, particularly the eyes.

Source: Maurer and Salapatek, 1976.

1-Month-Old   2-Month-Old

detect bitter, sour, and salty, but the part of the nervous system that interprets signals from these receptors may not yet be fully developed.

The Organization of Infant Sensory Behavior

The young infant has an impressive array of sensory capacities. Moreover, the newborn uses these capacities in an organized way. Not only do newborns look at and listen to particular things, but their processing of the environment appears to be guided by certain "rules" (Haith, 1980). When awake and alert, babies will visually scan the environment rather than simply stare straight ahead. In an active and quiet state, they will direct their gaze toward the source of sound. If not attracted by sound, they will scan until they find an edge (a border of light/dark contrast). Having found an edge, they will scan the zone of the edge for some time, passing back and forth over it (see Figure 5.3, scanning of the hairline). While in time, with development, their pattern of visual scanning will change (looking at internal features of a stimulus rather than its borders, for example), what does not change is the organized nature of behavior. It is so in infancy, and it is so throughout development. This organized pattern of sensing the world guarantees that infants will attend to and learn a great deal about people, who are initially seen as patterns of light and dark and who talk to newborns, attracting their attention.

Development of Perceptual Abilities

Just because Malcolm can see lines and colors does not mean that he interprets these sensations as we do. For instance, when Malcolm looks at the faces of his family clustered around him, can he tell that some are closer and others farther away? Or when DeeDee turns around and faces in the opposite direction, does Malcolm know he is still viewing the same head as before, but from a different angle? These questions focus on visual **perception**—the process by which the brain interprets information from the senses, giving it order and meaning.

DEPTH AND DISTANCE PERCEPTION

When can a baby estimate how far away an object is? Eleanor Gibson and Richard Walk (1960) provided a partial answer through a very clever experiment. The apparatus they used is shown in Figure 5.4. It consists of a large sheet of thick glass, one side of which has a checkerboard surface directly underneath it (the "shallow" side), while the other side has a similar surface several feet below (the "deep" side). As you can see, the side with the checkerboard surface some distance below the glass gives the illusion that there is a "cliff." Gibson and Walk observed whether babies old enough to crawl would venture over this visual cliff. They found that the babies preferred the shallow side, a preference that increased with age. These findings suggest that babies 6 or 7 months and older (when crawling usually begins) must be able to perceive depth.

Joseph Campos and his colleagues tested even younger babies for depth perception, using Gibson and Walk's visual cliff (Campos et al., 1978). Placing infants face-down on the deep side and the shallow side and measuring their physiological responses, they showed that babies only two months old could distinguish a difference between the two sides. However, *fear* of the deep side did not emerge until a child could crawl. It appears that direct experience with edges, drops, and distances

Figure 5.4
Visual Cliff Experiment
By the time infants can crawl, they are reluctant to cross to the deep side of this apparatus.

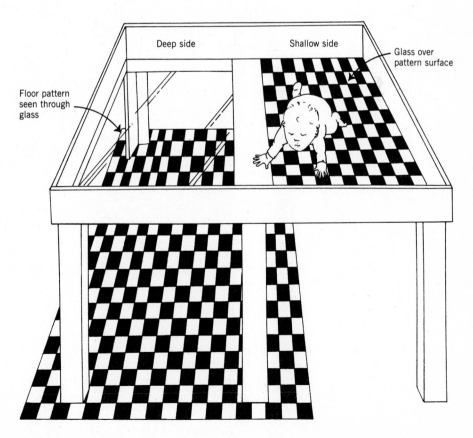

contributes to a fear of heights in humans (Campos, Bertenthal, and Caplovitz, 1982).

Psychologists have long been interested in how people see depth, since the images projected onto the eye are in two dimensions only. Apparently cues about depth and distance give us a sense of seeing a three-dimensional world. Developmentalists want to know when children begin to use each of these various cues and ultimately organize them to obtain adultlike depth perception.

Some cues about depth and distance result from the fact that visual information reaches the brain from two eyes rather than one. These are called **binocular depth cues.** One binocular depth cue is **convergence.** This occurs when the eyes turn inward to focus on a near object. Figure 5.5(A) shows two eyes "pointing" toward a distant object. Notice that the center of each eye is facing almost straight ahead. Now look at Figure 5.5(B), which shows two eyes focused on a nearer object. You can see that each eye must point inward to accomplish this. The closer an object is, the more the eyes must angle inward if both are to see "front-on." Your brain uses the degree of convergence to help estimate distance.

Richard Aslin (1977) measured infants' degree of convergence as they watched objects that were moved closer and farther away. He found that 1-month-old babies converged and diverged their eyes in the appropriate directions, but they were not good at locating the correct angle for a given distance. In contrast, 2- to 3-month-old babies were fairly accurate in the angles at which they converged their eyes. By age 5 months, infants have been shown to use convergence as an effective cue to determining distance when they reach for something (Von Hofsten, 1977).

Another binocular depth cue, called **retinal disparity,** also seems to become effective at about 5 months of age (e.g., Gordon and Yonas, 1976; Yonas, Oberg, and Norcia, 1978). Retinal disparity arises because the eyes are set apart from one another and view the world from slightly different angles. Since the degree of retinal disparity is affected by changes in the distance between the eyes, children must have to "recalibrate" this depth cue as they grow older and larger (Banks, 1987).

A critical period exists during which environmental factors can influence the ability to use binocular depth cues. Evidence comes from study-

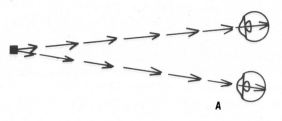
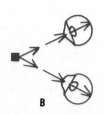

Figure 5.5
Convergence Angle as Information About Distance
(A) When viewing a more distant object, the eyes look almost straight ahead; (B) when viewing a closer object, the eyes rotate toward the nose.

Figure 5.6
Sensitive Period for Developing Binocular Vision
The three lines in this graph are from three different studies that assessed the role of binocular experience in developing binocular vision. Notice
that the period from 6 months to 4 years is the
most important.
Source: Aslin and Banks, 1978.

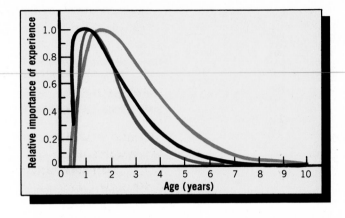

ing children who were born with their eyes misaligned. These children
are often called cross-eyed or wall-eyed, but the medical term for their
condition is strabismus. Children with strabismus get little practice coordinating their eyes in a normal manner. Fortunately, surgeons can correct
the condition by readjusting the length of the eye muscles. Richard Aslin
and Martin Banks (1978) wondered if the timing of this operation would
affect the later quality of binocular depth perception. Figure 5.6 shows
their findings. Notice that people who had been born without strabismus
were not significantly different from those who had had the problem
corrected during early infancy. However, when the surgery was performed
after one year of age, binocular depth perception declined substantially.
And when the surgery was performed after four years of age, the amount
of binocular depth perception was usually very small. From these data,
it appears that the critical period for the development of binocular vision
occurs during the first year of life.

People who lack binocular vision still have some ability to judge
depth. Indeed, some have managed to pilot airplanes and play professional baseball. Obviously depth cues must be available through each eye
independently, so-called **monocular depth cues.**

One monocular depth cue is **linear perspective**—the seeming convergence of parallel lines as they extend away from the viewer, thus giving
the impression of increasing distance. Figure 5.7 shows how a trapezoidal
window looks when viewed with two eyes. However, if this same window
is viewed with one eye only, it appears to be rectangular and slanting
away from you (Ames, 1951). This depth effect occurs because you interpret what you see using linear perspective. Albert Yonas and his colleagues fitted babies with a patch over one eye and allowed them to look
at a trapezoidal window (Yonas, Cleaves, and Pettersen, 1978). They
found that 5-month-olds reached equally often toward each side of the
window, but 7-month-olds reached more often toward the "closer" side.
The finding suggests that infants begin to use linear perspective as a cue
to distance sometime between 5 and 7 months of age.

Another monocular depth cue is **interposition**—the partial overlap of
objects that makes the ones being partly covered appear farther away. For
instance, when interpreting Figure 5.8 most adults assume that the left-

hand square is the nearer. When do babies make a similar interpretation? Granrud and Yonas (1984) showed that 5-month-olds with a patch over one eye reached equally often for the left and the right squares, but that 7-month-olds reached more often for the "nearer" one. The latter is the same age that babies start to use linear perspective. The simultaneous development of many depth cues suggests that neural maturation plays a significant role in determining the timing of these developments.

SIZE AND SHAPE CONSTANCY

As Christine Gordon walks toward Mikey to lift him out of his crib, her image on Mikey's retina (the light-sensitive inner surface of the eye) grows larger and larger. Does Mikey therefore think his mother is growing in size? When Christine hands Mikey a bottle and he tips it up to drink, does he think that the bottle changes shape as he views it from a different angle? At his present age of 13 months, Mikey makes neither of these mistakes. He possesses perceptual skills called size and shape constancy.

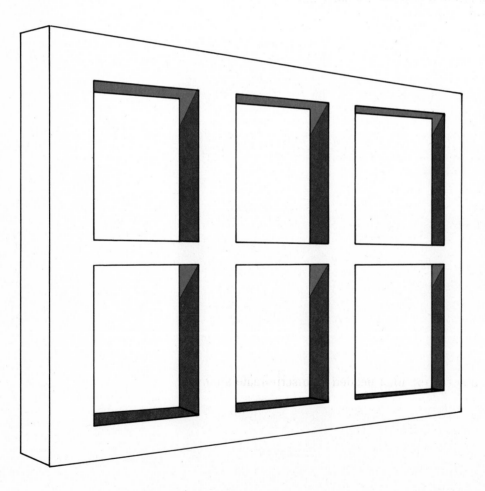

Figure 5.7
Trapezoidal Window Illusion
When viewed binocularly (with both eyes open), the figure clearly appears as a trapezoid. When viewed monocularly (with one eye closed), it appears rectangular and slanted because of linear perspective. Infants become sensitive to linear perspective at around 6 months.

Size constancy is the perceptual process of seeing the size of an object as constant, even though the size of the retinal image is changing—if those changes result from changes in distance. **Shape constancy,** similarly, is the perceptual process of seeing the shape of an object as constant. Both these processes are crucial to perceiving the world as relatively stable. When do infants first develop them?

A study by Albert Caron, Rose Caron, and V. R. Carlson (1979) illustrates one method used to answer this question. These researchers repeatedly showed one group of babies a square displayed at different angles but never directly perpendicular to the child's line of sight. As a result, the image on the retina was always trapezoidal, not truly square. After the infants habituated and lost interest in this stimulus, the researchers presented them with a real trapezoid displayed head-on. Infants as young as 4 months showed a preference for looking at this new stimulus, meaning that they could distinguish it from a square held at an angle. In other words, they exhibited shape constancy.

The most recent evidence leads most developmentalists to conclude that shape constancy emerges around 3 months (Banks and Salapatek, 1983). Thus very young babies perceive objects around them as relatively stable, unchanging things, which is an important step in organizing their physical world. Understanding that there are *particular* objects and people begins with perception of constancy.

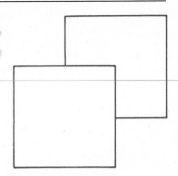

**Figure 5.8
Interposition Information for Distance**
Most adults perceive the square on the left to be in front of the square on the right. By 7 months most infants make use of interposition information in this way.

PERCEPTION OF FACES

When does an infant recognize its mother's face? Recognition of faces requires discriminating one object from another and treating different views or versions of an object as the same. Infants can discriminate simple shapes in the first month of life, but they do not discriminate a square with a circle in it from one with a triangle in it (Bushnell, 1979; Milewski, 1978), which suggests that they do not make use of information other than outline shape in perceiving objects (see Figure 5.9). To perceive the differences among faces, an infant must pay attention to internal features on the face, such as eyes, shape of the nose, and shape of the mouth.

Where infants look on a face tells us something about the information they are taking in. As we discussed earlier and illustrated in Figure 5.3, when 1-month-olds look at faces, they scan only a small portion of the face and tend to look at the outer edges, whereas 2-month-olds scan within the face and spend time looking at internal features (Maurer and Salapatek, 1976). Between 1 month and 3 months, infants increase the time spent looking at faces and their internal features (Haith, Bergman, and Moore, 1977). By 3 months an infant can recognize photographs of his or her mother and prefers to look at her rather than a stranger (Barrera and Maurer, 1981). By 5 months infants can remember and distinguish between the faces of strangers (Olson and Sherman, 1983). Thus, by 5 months infants make subtle distinctions needed to discriminate among faces. Even as adults, we have trouble discriminating the faces of members of racial and ethnic groups with whom we have had little or no experience. This phenomenon illustrates that at least part of infants' improving skills for perceiving faces must be a consequence of the experience of looking at faces.

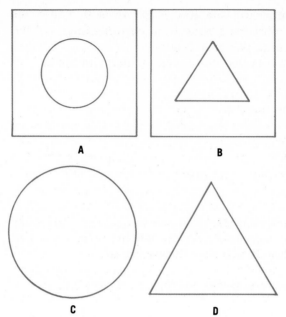

Figure 5.9
Form Discrimination by 1-Month-Olds
One-month-olds do not discriminate (A) from (B) because they pay attention solely to the outer shapes, both of which are squares. However, they do discriminate (C) from (D), which indicates that they can tell the difference between a circle and triangle.

INFANT MOTOR SKILLS

When Mikey was born, Christine knew from past experience that it was necessary to keep his fingernails well trimmed. If his nails were allowed to grow too long, he could easily cut his face as he moved his arms and hands around in the poorly coordinated manner of newborns. By the time Mikey was 1 year old, his motor skills had improved dramatically and were much better organized. Now he could sit unsupported, crawl rapidly wherever he wished, pull himself up into a standing position, and take a few tentative steps while hanging onto furniture. In addition, the random flailing of his arms seen when he was born had been replaced by much more deliberate and coordinated movements. Guided by sight, he could reach for and grasp an object, pick it up for inspection, and move it from hand to hand. Figure 5.10 summarizes some of the major milestones in motor development during a child's first two years, giving the average age at which each occurs.

Many areas of motor development illustrate the developmental principle of differentiation—movements that at first are global and poorly defined developing into a set of precise movements, each adapted to a specific function. Charlotte Buhler (1929) provided an early description of differentiation with her observations of infants' reactions when the mouth and nose are covered by an observer's hand. The newborn reflexively reacts with the total body; arms and legs go into random motion, the body twists, the infant wails. Such a global reaction may, of course, result in removing the obstacle and is, therefore, adaptive. Some weeks later, arm movements are more prominent and are directed toward the center of the baby's body. The baby thus increases the chances of inadvertently batting away the observer's hand. But not until halfway through the first year does the infant precisely push the hand away using a directed swipe, perhaps with only one arm. A month or two later, the infant may even block the observer's hand from covering the nose and mouth by using a specific anticipatory movement.

Other researchers have described two general patterns in the unfolding of infant motor skills. (These patterns mirror those of physical growth during the prenatal period.) One is the tendency for control over motor movements to progress from head to toe. This is called **cephalocaudal development.** For example, refined motor skills emerge first with regard to sucking and eye movements and last with regard to walking. The second, related pattern is for control over motor movements to progress from the center of the body out to the extremities. This is called **proximodistal development.** For example, a baby shows refined control of head movements before arm movements, and of arm movements before hand movements. These patterns seem to be caused by differences in the rates at which the muscles involved develop and the brain areas that control those muscles mature. Rather than discussing all the motor skills that emerge during infancy, we will focus on a few representative ones: controlled eye movements, reaching and grasping, and walking.

Eye Movements

Your eye movements are so automatic that you probably don't think of them as a motor skill. However, controlled eye movements are one of the earliest motor skills to develop. Without them, Mikey could look only at what happened to be in his line of sight. He could not study the different parts of an object one after another, follow people visually as they moved about, or keep his eyes fixed on something despite movements of his own head and body. If infants lacked control over their eye movements, their ability to learn about the world would be severely limited.

Even newborns show some controlled eye movements. Without a stimulus to look at, they move their eyes more often and farther than normal as if searching for something to see (Salapatek and Kessen, 1966). As the weeks pass, babies become more effective at controlling where they look. For instance, when 1-month-old infants look at a person's face, they tend to focus on border areas of high contrast. If a new stimulus appears off to one side, the baby may move the eyes to look at the new object. This tendency is more pronounced, and the eye shifts are more

The development of motor skills like crawling and walking greatly expands the range of experiences for infants. *(George Ancona/ International Stock Photo.)*

Figure 5.10
Milestones in Motor Development

Source: Adapted from Shirley (1933).

accurate, by the time the child is 2 months old (Aslin and Salapatek, 1975). Obviously, it is important for this system to be well organized early in order to allow infants to explore the world visually. But improvement of controlled eye movements continues until at least 7 years of age (Zaporozhets, 1965).

Shifting your gaze to a new object involves **saccadic eye movements—** rapid, jerky movements of the eyes. When an object suddenly starts to move, your eyes move saccadically to catch up. Then you follow the object using smooth, continuous motions called **pursuit eye movements.** When are babies able to "track" a moving object with pursuit eye movements?

If a newborn is presented with a moving object, the child's eyes tend to move in the appropriate direction, but neither accurately nor smoothly. Two months later, however, smooth pursuit eye movements are common (Dayton and Jones, 1964). The eye movements that emerge at about 8 weeks are typically only for slow-moving stimuli. The ability to follow more rapidly moving objects develops over the next two months (Aslin, 1981). The young infant's organization of visual tracking behavior probably accounts for why care givers tend to move their heads slowly from side to side when talking to babies, rather than quickly or up and down.

Reaching and Grasping

For more than half a century developmentalists have known that infants are capable of directed, visually guided reaching by the age of 5 months (Halverson, 1931). This skill then gradually improves, and at 15 months smooth and accurate reaches are common. By 6 months of age, the grasping reflex has declined enough for the baby voluntarily to pick up and let go of objects. The child still uses a whole-hand grasp, however, making it hard to pick up things that don't fit in the hand. By 9 months the infant is able to use the thumb in opposition to the fingers, but the fingers still act primarily in unison. It is not until around 2 years of age that a child is finally able to oppose the thumb and forefinger in a manner that mimics a proper lady or gentleman drinking a cup of tea. Figure 5.11 illustrates some important developments in grasping during the first year.

Recent discussions of reaching, and to some extent grasping, have focused on the early appearance of these skills, followed by their disappearance, and then by their reappearance in more advanced forms (see Bower, 1974). T. G. R. Bower claims that "all the components of reaching and grasping can be elicited in fetuses at a conceptual age of 14 to 16 weeks" (1974, pp. 149–150). He reports that reaching can be elicited from infants in the first month of life relatively easily, but only with great difficulty from infants who are 4 to 20 weeks old. T. Humphrey (1969) has offered an explanation for the early presence, intermediate disappearance, and later reemergence of reaching based on change in neural control of reaching. He has argued that motor control systems for reaching are genetically "wired into" the human nervous system. But since infants given continual practice with reaching do not show the usual decline from 4 to 20 weeks, neural maturation cannot be a complete explanation (Bower, 1974).

We would argue that at birth babies lack control over these systems, which therefore operate automatically as reflexes. To bring the systems under voluntary control, the infant must first acquire the ability to stop them. As this ability develops, the early forms of the behaviors gradually disappear. Then the child is ready to learn to put the actions back together in a purposeful way.

Walking

By 7 months of age Malcolm Williams had learned to slide along the floor on his stomach, propelled by his legs. His family was suddenly faced with all the challenges posed by a baby who could go wherever he wanted. Nothing was safe any longer. Infants this age often acquire different styles of locomotion. Some push themselves by their legs; others pull their bodies along with their arms; still others sit upright and scoot across the floor on their bottoms. Later, many babies learn to creep on their hands and knees. Before their first birthday they can usually hoist themselves into a standing position and "cruise"—that is, walk along while holding onto things. Most babies take their first "solo" steps shortly after the age of 1, although the onset of walking varies greatly among individuals. Malcolm walked early; Mikey at an average age; Meryl somewhat late. The age at which a baby starts walking and the pattern of

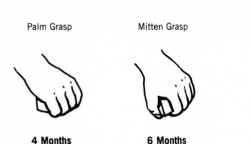
Palm Grasp

4 Months

Mitten Grasp

6 Months

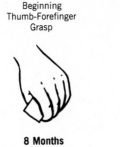
Beginning
Thumb-Forefinger
Grasp

8 Months

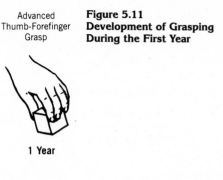
Advanced
Thumb-Forefinger
Grasp

1 Year

Figure 5.11
Development of Grasping
During the First Year

development of prior abilities, such as crawling, are unrelated to later intelligence. Thus, parents should not be concerned about early walkers who never crawled or about late walkers unless the delay is extreme.

As with reaching, developmentalists have sought to understand how walking emerges from early reflexive behavior. Esther Thelen (1981) has illustrated the role of early rhythmic, repetitive movements in this transition. As infants develop, their initial random and often jerky movements change into smoother, more controlled ones. For example, all normal infants show stereotypic leg movements, such as kicking like a frog, shown in the photos on page 163. These movements, mentioned in our story about Malcolm Williams, begin to appear around 1 month of age and peak at 5 to 6 months. After this, they decline. Stereotypic leg movements are not reflexes, since a wide variety of stimuli can elicit them. Often, infants lying on their backs reach a certain level of excitation and then begin to kick repetitively. Evolution may have provided these coordinated motor patterns to help prepare the infant to practice what will be voluntary and useful movements later. No other reason for this behavior is apparent; infants simply do it as part of being excited. Interestingly, infants do not learn to control their leg movements until after the rhythmic, repetitive patterns have appeared (Rovee-Collier and Gekoski, 1979). Thus, these rhythmic patterns seem to be an important way station between reflexes and learned motor behaviors.

What determines when a baby finally starts to walk? Although we don't yet have the full answer to this question, we know that the onset of walking depends partly on maturation of the muscles and nervous system, and partly on practice. The motor movements of walking are apparent in the stepping reflex, which is present at birth and then declines around 2 months of age. As in the case of reaching, some developmentalists have argued that inhibitory connections must develop to bring the reflexive activity under useful control. Thelen (1986) has presented data showing that the reflex can continue to be elicited in 7-month-olds if they are supported over a treadmill. Such responses show that what is occurring is not just the development of inhibition. Thelen argues that walking depends on many systems that must be integrated. Studies of balance in infants show that even 5-month-olds begin to make appropriate motor movements to remain upright when sitting, although not always successfully (Woollacott, in press). While not yet sufficiently refined for walking, this balance system is necessary for later walking.

To investigate the role of practice, researchers have studied babies who differ in their opportunities to walk. For instance, many years ago

Wayne Dennis and M. C. Dennis (1940) studied Hopi Indian babies who spent much of their first year bound to cradle boards. The babies were unbound to have their clothes changed, but otherwise they had little chance to move their legs. Toward the end of the first year, the Hopi infants were given the same freedom of movement that babies in a control group had enjoyed since birth. Surprisingly, children in *both* groups learned to walk at about the same age. Physical maturation thus may exert a greater influence over the onset of walking than does a child's total amount of practice moving the legs. Other studies, using different methods, have led to the same conclusion (e.g., McGraw, 1935, 1940).

With enough of the right kind of practice, however, the onset of walking *can* be speeded up. In one experiment, researchers regularly exercised the stepping reflex in a group of young infants (André-Thomas and Dargassies, 1952). This practice had two effects: First, the stepping reflex did not decline as rapidly in these babies as it usually does. Second, these babies walked somewhat sooner than control infants who did not have their stepping reflex exercised. Both findings are consistent with the theory that reflexes are the raw materials out of which more advanced skills are built. But note that even with all their early practice the experimental babies did not walk a great deal sooner than others. Maturation still plays the major role in the onset of walking. We do not recommend that parents exercise the stepping reflex in their infants. The time spent in this effort could be better used interacting with the baby in other ways.

Photos (a) through (f) break down the movements of a single kick cycle in a 6-month-old infant. In (a) the infant begins the cycle with the leg extended. In (b) the baby starts to bend the leg and ankle. This movement continues until the hip, knee, and ankle are fully bent (c). The infant then begins to extend the leg (d). The leg is completely extended in (e) and returns to a more relaxed position with the heel supported on the underlying surface and the ankle still slightly bent (f). (*Behavioral and Neural Biology*, volume 32 (1981), pp. 45-53.)

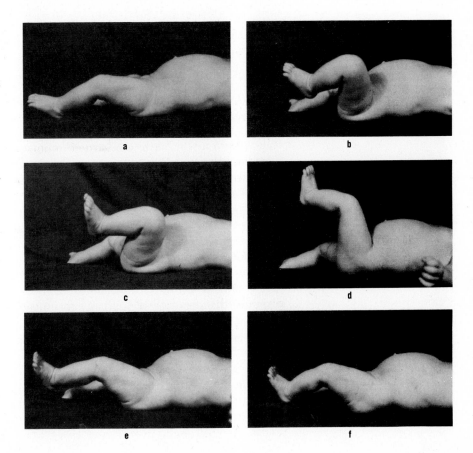

Though restrained as infants in cradle boards, Hopi Indian children learned to walk at about the same time as infants who were not so confined. *(John Running/Black Star.)*

INFANT LEARNING

After Malcolm Williams was born, the members of his family took charge of most of what happened to him. Where he lay, what he saw, what he heard, and what he felt were largely controlled by other people. But within six months this situation had changed substantially. Malcolm was now able to do many things for himself. He could turn over, sit up, grasp objects and put them in his mouth; he was even starting to crawl. By the time he was 1, he had acquired many other skills, including taking his first steps and saying a few single words. What accounts for these dramatic changes in Malcolm's behavior?

Modern developmental psychologists view changes in behavior as the joint outcome of genetic control and of learning. By this they mean that the changes are based on a biological unfolding as well as on experience. Some changes are more dependent on learning, others more dependent on genetic control. But both factors are needed to produce the dramatic transformations that occur in a baby's first year.

In examining the interaction of learning and genetic control, developmentalists ask questions such as: When do infants start learning? What limitations are there on the things they can learn? Does the way infants learn and unlearn, remember and forget, change as they grow older? The answers to these questions are not just of scientific interest; they are also of very practical interest to parents. Does reading to a baby improve the child's later reading skills? What kind of toys are best for babies? Will a baby remember an injury, illness, or other trauma that happened early in life? Research into infants' learning capabilities can help shed light on such concerns. In the following sections we'll look at several different kinds of learning, beginning with a very basic process called habituation.

Habituation

Habituation is one of the first signs that even newborns are able to retain information about their environments. As described earlier, **habituation** is essentially a decrease in attention that occurs when the same stimulus is presented repeatedly. For example, when the pediatrician first spoke to Meryl, she ceased her other behaviors and attended to his voice. This is called an **orienting response.** An orienting response includes certain physiological changes that casual observers wouldn't notice, such as a change in heart rate and a slight dilation of the pupils. Researchers, however, have measured these changes in the laboratory and have found that when the same stimulus is presented over and over, the orienting response disappears and the baby resumes other activities. The novelty of the stimulus has apparently worn off. Such a decline in responding is due to learning and not merely fatigue, because presentation of a new stimulus again elicits the orienting response.

The same processes of orientation and gradual habituation also occur in adults. Imagine that you are lying in bed alone in a strange house. As the wind begins to blow, a tree outside the window makes a groaning noise. Initially you are startled and attend carefully to the sound. But soon you become used to it and simply ignore it. Then a door somewhere in the house begins to creak. You find yourself orienting again to this new sound. The return of the orienting response is an indication that you have noticed a change. Infants, too, must notice a change when they orient to one stimulus, habituate to it, and then orient again to a different stimulus. Noticing such a change requires two things: First, the person must learn enough about the first stimulus to realize it is the same from one presentation to another. Second, the person must make some kind of comparison between the first and second stimulus, recognizing the second one as new.

In our discussions of infant sensory systems, we saw how habituation enables researchers to study infants' perceptions of the world. Research relying on habituation provides insight into what kinds of stimuli babies can distinguish, how many repetitions are required for a memory to form, and how long a memory will endure once it has been formed.

Associative Learning

Psychologists have spent a great deal of time studying **associative learning**—how infants learn that certain events tend to go together or to be associated. Researchers have wondered at what stage infants are able to learn associations. One kind of associative learning they have explored extensively is classical conditioning.

CLASSICAL CONDITIONING

Classical conditioning is the kind of learning that Ivan Pavlov demonstrated in his work with dogs (see Chapter 2). Pavlov was able to produce the salivation reflex in dogs by ringing a bell each time he gave them food. Eventually, the sound of the bell alone caused the dogs to salivate. Pavlov classically conditioned the dogs' salivation response to a stimulus that normally does not elicit it.

Classical conditioning is a learning process in which a new stimulus becomes capable of eliciting an established reflex response. In Pavlov's experiment, the dogs' initial salivation was the reflex response, caused by the sensation of taste. Food in the mouth is called the **unconditioned stimulus (UCS),** and salivation is the **unconditioned response (UCR).** *Unconditioned* means that the connection between the two does not have to be learned. In contrast to food in the mouth, the sound of the bell initially had no effect on salivation. But after repeatedly being paired with food, the bell came to elicit salivation. The bell is therefore called the **conditioned stimulus (CS),** and the dogs' salivation to it is called the **conditioned response (CR).** *Conditioned* means that this new stimulus-response connection must be learned. In Pavlov's experiment, dogs learned to associate the bell with food.

Are newborn infants capable of being classically conditioned? Researchers have tried to find out. In 1940 Delos Wickens and Carol Wickens used classical conditioning procedures to get 12 young infants to learn to withdraw a foot at the sound of a buzzer. The unconditioned stimulus they paired with the buzzer was a mild electric shock to the sole of the foot, which causes reflexive foot withdrawal. The babies received 12

A new object in the environment will elicit a response from an infant, especially the first time it is presented. *(Eva Demjen/ Stock, Boston.)*

pairings of the buzzer and the shock on three successive days. On the fourth day, nine of the 12 infants showed clear withdrawal of a foot when the buzzer was sounded alone.

This result seems to suggest that classical conditioning had occurred. However, consider the behavior of infants in two control groups. The 12 babies in one control group were pretested for response to the buzzer alone, but they were never exposed to the shock. On the fourth day, only one of these babies retracted a foot in response to the buzzer alone. This low response rate is just what you would expect. A surprise came with the second control group, however. The 12 babies in this group were exposed to the shock but not to the buzzer. Given these circumstances, none of the infants in this group should have learned to retract a foot when the buzzer sounded. Yet on the fourth day, 11 of the 12 withdrew a foot in response to the buzzer alone. Psychologists have interpreted this outcome in a number of ways: For example, the shocks may have sensitized the infants by lowering their thresholds for arousal. The buzzer then aroused the infants, and foot withdrawal was a reflexive response to the arousal (see Stevenson, 1972, pp. 12–13). Our main point is that Wickens and Wickens could not claim they had demonstrated classical conditioning, for these control infants were also showing foot withdrawal in response to the buzzer alone. This experiment was just one of many from the 1930s through the 1950s that failed to unequivocally demonstrate classical conditioning in newborns. Still, many of these studies did demonstrate changes in behavior produced by experience, and thus learning of some kind.

More recent studies of classical conditioning in newborns have met with greater success, although some are still being criticized for not ruling out all alternative explanations (Sostek, Sameroff, and Sostek, 1972). In one of the studies least open to criticism, Lewis Lipsitt and his colleagues (Lipsitt, Kaye, and Bosack, 1966) conditioned a strong sucking response to a stimulus (a small rubber tube) that ordinarily doesn't elicit one. The tube was their conditioned stimulus. For the unconditioned stimulus, they delivered a sugar solution through the tube, to which newborns automatically respond with vigorous sucking. After several pairings of the tube and the sugar solution, the tube alone elicited strong sucking. Next the researchers repeatedly presented the tube on its own, without the sugar following. The babies began to suck less and less vigorously on it. This gradual decline in a conditioned response is called **extinction.** As is true of classical conditioning in general, the conditioned response could be reestablished by once again pairing the tube with the sugar solution.

Classical conditioning by itself cannot explain the emergence of any *new* behavior. The response to be conditioned must always be one that the person already performs when the unconditioned stimulus is present. Classical conditioning simply causes an old response to be elicited in a new situation. You saw a good example of this in Chapter 2 when we discussed how John B. Watson conditioned an infant named Albert to fear a white rat (the conditioned stimulus) by pairing the rat with a sudden loud noise (the unconditioned stimulus). Note, however, that Albert already possessed the fear reaction. All Watson did was to make the initially neutral rat into an effective elicitor of fear. Thus, classical conditioning may play a role in certain aspects of emotional development, especially during infancy, but it cannot account for the crucial emergence of new behaviors and skills.

INSTRUMENTAL CONDITIONING

When Mikey Gordon uttered "beh" while pointing at a piece of bread, his father immediately showered him with praise and encouragement for saying a new word. From our discussion of B. F. Skinner's work on reinforcement in Chapter 2, you probably can identify Frank's positive reaction to Mikey's efforts at speech as a form of reinforcement, because it increases the likelihood that Mikey will say "beh" again in a similar situation.

Positive and negative reinforcement are important to the type of learning called **operant** or **instrumental conditioning,** in which behaviors are influenced by the consequences they seem to have. If those consequences include a pleasant stimulation, such as a hug from a parent, the child is said to be positively reinforced (or rewarded) and is likely to do the same thing again. Similarly, when a behavior—crying, for example—is followed by the removal of an unpleasant stimulus, such as a wet diaper, that behavior is said to be negatively reinforced and is more likely to occur again. Both positive and negative reinforcement increase the likelihood of a particular behavior. Punishment, the presentation of a negative stimulus following a behavior, is different from negative reinforcement.

In older children and adults, behaviors that are instrumentally conditioned are generally ones over which the person exerts strictly voluntary control. In newborns, however, researchers usually choose to condition behaviors with an underlying reflexive component, such as sucking on a nipple (related to the sucking reflex) or turning the head from side to side (related to the rooting reflex.).

Sucking rates of 3-day-old infants have been instrumentally conditioned. Newborns automatically suck in a "burst-pause" pattern: a succession of rapid sucks followed by a period during which little sucking occurs. Andrew DeCasper and William Fifer (1980) measured the average interval of time between a baby's bursts of sucking on a nipple to establish what is called the **base rate.** Then the researchers reinforced half the babies every time the interval between their sucking bursts was *longer* than average, and the other half every time this interval was *shorter* than average. The reinforcement they used was simply the sound of the child's mother speaking. As expected, the sucking rate of the first group of babies decreased, while that of the second group increased. This experiment not only demonstrates instrumental conditioning, but it also shows that a human voice can be reinforcing for an infant only 3 days old.

Instrumental conditioning is of particular interest to psychologists because it provides one possible means of acquiring new behaviors. Consider again Mikey Gordon learning to say "bread." When he utters something that just vaguely resembles this word, his father provides reinforcement in the form of smiles and attention. Mikey may respond by saying "beh" again. Over time, Frank may become more selective in his reinforcement. He may require that Mikey say something closer to the real word before giving him praise. The requirement of gradually closer approximations to some target behavior is an example of **shaping.** If Mikey, for instance, were to utter the sound "breh," his father might grin and exclaim, "That a boy!" In time, Mikey may say the word "bread."

Systematic shaping can sometimes result in quite remarkable feats. For example, Hanus Papousek (1967b) has produced complex sequences of behavior in babies only a few weeks old. When the infants turned their heads in one direction, they were rewarded with a taste of sugar solution. Soon they were turning their heads repeatedly in that direction. Next the babies were rewarded for two head turns, and again they learned the pattern. Eventually they were required to perform even longer chains of responses, such as two head turns to the right, then two to the left!

It is apparently much easier to instrumentally condition newborns than to classically condition them. In fact, the classical conditioning results obtained with the rubber tube and sugar solution mentioned earlier may be partly due to instrumental effects. As the infants sucked on the tube, sweetness followed. The difficulty of classically conditioning newborns and the relative ease by 3 months probably reflect the newborn's immature brain status. The ease of instrumental conditioning suggests that human infants come preadapted to respond to contingencies, a point to which we will return.

Imitative Learning

Earlier we suggested that Mikey Gordon's acquisition of language might be helped along somewhat by shaping. But imagine how difficult learning to talk would be if shaping were the only learning technique available to him. Mikey's parents would have to wait until he happened to make some sounds that remotely resembled an English word. Then they would have to reinforce him immediately and continue offering reinforcement every time he came closer to the correct pattern. This laborious process would have to be repeated for every word Mikey learned. This is the only way totally deaf children can learn to use spoken language. However, children with normal hearing face a far easier task. Such children are motivated to attend to and imitate speech sounds, even when they don't understand what those sounds mean. This **imitative learning** helps explain why Mikey will acquire speech so rapidly in his early years.

Psychologists have proposed that imitation is a powerful mechanism for learning (e.g., Bandura, 1977). Compared with shaping, it is a much faster way of acquiring new skills. But in order to imitate a new behavior a child must be able to do two things. If Mikey is to imitate a word his father says, he must first be able to translate the sounds he hears into a set of movements of his own lips and tongue. Second, Mikey must also be able to form some memory of these movements for future use. Both these abilities are needed for the imitation to be successful.

Jean Piaget (1952) has argued that these abilities develop gradually during a child's first two years. In a set of studies on the development of imitation, Ina Uzgiris has observed a four-step sequence in general agreement with Piaget's view (Uzgiris, 1972; Uzgiris and Hunt, 1975).

During the first step, in the first six months of life, infants are able to match behaviors of others or reproduce their own behaviors based on similarity of perceptual consequences. For example, if a young infant makes a cooing sound and an adult imitates it, then the infant will often make the sound again. In the next chapter you will discover that Piaget referred to this kind of sequence as a circular reaction. During the second step, which begins at around 6 months, babies try to imitate behaviors they see or hear that they have never done before. Frequently they only manage a partial imitation or they fail altogether. For example, during the second half of the first year babies begin to imitate some of the characteristics of the language they hear, so their babbling begins to sound more like normal speech, but it is not yet composed of words that are understandable. During the third step, which begins at around 12 months, babies become much better at imitating unfamiliar behaviors. Their imitation of language leads to some intelligible words. A 15-month-old may watch a preschooler stacking blocks and then try to produce a similar tower. Such imitations are often coupled with frequent checking of the other child's behavior to assure that the imitation is right. During the final step, at around 18 months, children's imitations, even of novel behaviors, become very accurate and require little checking to monitor success. They become adept at imitating actions when they cannot directly monitor the success of their own imitations, such as imitating the facial expressions of others (see Abravanel and Gingold, 1985).

Although psychologists still hotly debate what underlies the development of imitation, most agree that these basic steps occur. Most also would acknowledge that imitation is an extremely powerful and long-lasting form of learning.

Many issues about the development of imitation are still unsettled. One is explaining exactly how the baby's early imitative abilities change into the much more elaborate ones of later infancy and toddlerhood. Piaget argued that the answer is in the development of the child's underlying cognitive capacities. According to Piaget, young infants possess very limited capacities for thought. Over the first two years, however, their cognitive capacities systematically develop. This, in turn, affects many behaviors, including imitation. In the next chapter you will read about the cognitive changes that Piaget thought occur during infancy.

Jerome Bruner agrees with Piaget's basic viewpoint that infant cognitive development involves a gradual removal of earlier limitations. But unlike Piaget, Bruner conceptualizes the emergence of imitation as the development and organization of skills (Bruner, 1970, 1981). Thus, Bruner would attribute a child's early imitative failures to limits in organization—that is, limits on skills for putting together past behaviors into a pattern we would call imitation. Piaget, in contrast, would attribute the same early failures to the inability to remember the behavior of a model or to mentally translate such a memory into a required set of actions.

Regardless of their differences, Piaget and Bruner shared the view that imitation develops gradually. The ability to imitate facial expressions, for example, is generally thought to emerge quite late in the process (the fourth step in our earlier description). Such imitation requires children to "match" an expression when they aren't able to see their own face. Piaget would have argued that very young babies are not cognitively ready for this. On this point, a study by Andrew Meltzoff and M. Keith Moore (1977) has become controversial. These researchers had adults display facial gestures to infants only 12 to 21 days old. The gestures included sticking out the tongue and opening the mouth wide. The babies often seemed to imitate the adults. Some researchers have replicated this finding; others have been unable to do so (see Harris, 1983; Olson and Sherman, 1983). It seems that newborn "imitation" is another reflexive behavior that gives way later to more purposive voluntary behavior.

One criticism of the Meltzoff and Moore study is that the behavior they observed may not have been true imitation. Some activities you might try with a young infant are suggested in a paper by Sandra W. Jacobson (1979). Suppose that rather than sticking your tongue out, you made a circle with your thumb and fingers and pushed a pencil through it in the baby's direction. Don't be surprised if the baby again responds by sticking out the tongue. Many things may elicit this reflexive response. As another little experiment, try interlocking your fingers in front of the baby's face. The child will not be able to duplicate this gesture, because the behaviors that you can elicit from young infants are limited to ones they already do spontaneously. Imitation as a means of learning *new* behaviors must await further development. In fact, more than a year must pass before the baby will be able to imitate new behaviors quickly and without error. This speed and accuracy are what give imitation its special importance as a learning mechanism.

The Concept of Preparedness

The example of trying to get a baby to imitate interlocking fingers stresses something important about infant learning. Some things are relatively easy for young infants to learn; some things are difficult. Notice how many of the learning studies we have discussed rely on behaviors such as mouth movements and head turning. For example, Arnold Sameroff (1968) showed that even newborns can rapidly learn to adjust the two components of sucking (squeezing and drawing) to obtain a sweet liquid. Likewise, Meltzoff and Moore used mouth opening and tongue protrusion in their efforts to show early imitation, and Papousek used head turning in his instrumental conditioning studies. These popular behaviors have two things in common: They may be elicited reflexively and they have obvious survival value. For the newborn, being able to turn the head toward the nipple and to suck appropriately are matters of vital importance. On the other hand, behaviors that babies do not spontaneously engage in are usually very difficult to instill. Thus, the answer to the question of whether newborns can learn is more complicated than yes or no. It depends partly on what is to be learned and how. Heredity seems to have endowed infants with a predisposition to acquire some behaviors but not others. The genetic predisposition to learn certain things is called **preparedness** (Seligman, 1970).

Many developmentalists argue that some of a baby's early social behaviors are prepared responses. Examples are smiling back when an adult smiles, or cooing when an adult speaks. These responses are easy for young babies; they seem biologically inclined to learn them. Other easily learned behaviors emerge in later infancy. For example, in the second half-year a baby readily babbles the sounds of the language spoken in the home. Think how complex a process it is to distinguish and reproduce speech sounds. Evolution must have prepared human babies to acquire this skill quite early. Thus, one way of thinking about the limitations on

Adults in everyday life sometimes try to elicit imitation from infants, and sometimes they are successful. *(Jean-Claude Lejeune/ Stock, Boston.)*

infant learning is through the concept of preparedness. Babies learn most easily those behaviors they are prepared to learn; they learn other behaviors more slowly or not at all.

Part of prepared learning is a predisposition to analyze the connection between certain behaviors and their consequences. For example, humans (as well as other animals) are prepared to analyze the connection between the taste and smell of what they eat and any subsequent feelings of nausea (Garcia and Koelling, 1966). For this reason you readily develop an aversion to the food you ate just before you got sick. Note that you don't acquire a similar aversion to the people you ate with or the color shirt you wore. Your brain is programmed to focus on the food-nausea connection, not the other ones. Babies, too, are prepared to learn certain contingencies between their own actions and the consequences produced. Instrumentally conditioning infants is often very easy when the association to be learned is one they're *prepared* to discover.

The idea of contingency analysis adds an important dimension to our understanding of infant learning. During the first year of life, a major task babies face is learning how to control their environment (Watson and Ramey, 1972). By learning the connections between their own behaviors and subsequent reinforcements, infants gradually discover the things they can do to get what they want. In the process the helpless newborn who merely responds reflexively to stimuli is transformed into an agent who quite actively controls many aspects of the world.

THE PREADAPTED INFANT

We discussed earlier that, in addition to having a variety of sensory capacities, the infant deploys its attention in a systematic way. Infants are biased, or **preadapted,** to select and attend to certain kinds of features. Because of these biases, they are attracted to the sound of human voices, they follow horizontal movements of the care giver's face, and they scan the face—first the features of greatest light-dark contrast, and then, by 2 to 3 months, the details of internal features as well. As we will discuss in Chapter 7, expressive behaviors such as smiling and cooing likewise are organized to ensure social exchange.

Infants are preadapted to detect contingencies—consequences of their actions as revealed in environmental changes. Such a capacity will serve them well as they explore the properties of objects and deepen their understanding of the physical world (see Chapter 6). It also represents an important foundation for developing social relationships. Other people, and care givers in particular, are the most complex, contingently responsive objects in the infant's world. Infants are biased to attend to and direct behavior to others, who likewise are disposed to respond to infantile behavior, thus setting up a primary contingency relationship that further motivates the infant's engagement. Such is the process of forming relationships in infancy, which we will discuss in Chapter 7.

Chapter Review

1. Newborn infants come equipped with certain built-in capacities that help them to adapt to their new environments. These capacities include reflexes, perceptual abilities, motor skills, and learning abilities.

2. Developmentalists divide the infant's rest-activity cycle into several states. One system for categorizing this cycle divides it into six periods: quiet sleep, active sleep, awake and quiet, awake and active, fussing, and crying. The state an infant is in determines how the environment is perceived and acted upon.

3. A **reflex** is an automatic, or "built-in," reaction elicited by particular stimuli. The reflexes found in newborns enable them to respond adaptively to their environments before they have a chance to learn. Examples of newborn reflexes with clear survival value are the **rooting reflex** (whereby the baby automatically turns the head toward the side of the face that has just been stroked) and the **sucking reflex** (whereby the baby automatically sucks on an object placed in the mouth). Examples of reflex actions that are later incorporated into more complex voluntary behaviors are the **grasping reflex** (whereby stimulation of the palm causes the fingers to curl inward) and the **stepping reflex** (whereby stimulation on the soles of the feet when the baby is held upright results in a "walking" motion).

4. Newborns also come equipped to sense the world around them. For example, research shows that babies' visual **acuity** (the amount of detail seen) is not as good as normal adults',

but they do see and do visually inspect their surroundings. Their acuity gradually improves in the first year. They are attracted in particular to objects that have light-dark contrasts, such as the human face, and they are quite good at following slowly moving objects. Babies also can hear sounds and can discriminate one from another, especially human speech sounds, and they will turn toward the source. Likewise, newborns discriminate a variety of odors and at least some of the four basic tastes. Thus newborns have a range of sensory capabilities and they are biased to detect certain kinds of stimulation. Initially, sensory capabilities are integrated with motor responses to form **reflexes.** During the first year reflexes become part of more complex and differentiated organizations of behavior.

5. Developmentalists have also studied **perception** in infants—the process by which the baby's brain interprets information from the senses, giving it order and meaning. Children only 2 months old have some ability to see the world in three dimensions (that is, to perceive depth), even though the images the eyes receive are in two dimensions only. Adultlike depth perception appears to emerge gradually as a baby becomes increasingly effective at using various depth cues. Important **binocular depth cues** are **convergence** and **retinal disparity. Monocular depth cues** include **linear perspective** and **interposition,** which most babies begin to use between 5 and 7 months of age. As the infant begins to crawl, having good depth perception has obvious protective advantage.

Around 3 months infants are also showing **size and shape constancy,** enabling them to ignore moment-to-moment alterations in the size or shape of visual images if those alterations are caused by changes in either distance or viewing angle. The ability to perceive objects and people as constant clearly is essential for learning about them.

6. During their first two years children show remarkable development of motor skills. Control over motor movements tends to progress from head to toe (**cephalocaudal development**) and from the center of the body out to the extremities (**proximodistal development**). Motor development follows the principle of **differentiation,** whereby global actions become more refined and specific, and the principle of **integration,** whereby previously available reflexes are integrated into more elaborate behavior. One of the earliest skills that emerges is control over eye movements, both the **saccadic movements** used to locate objects and the **pursuit movements** used to follow them. By the middle of the first year, babies intentionally reach for and grasp objects, and soon after the age of 1 most start to walk. Psychologists believe that an important part of motor development during the first year is the inhibition of early reflex systems, followed by increasingly refined voluntary control over movements.

7. One of the first signs that infants are capable of learning is a process called **habituation.** Habituation is a decrease in attention when a person is repeatedly presented with the same stimulus. At first the person shows an **orienting response** and becomes alert, but interest gradually drops as the stimulus becomes familiar. Habituation shows that infants are able to retain information about their environments: They are able to remember enough about a stimulus to recognize it as being the same from one presentation to another.

8. Psychologists have spent a great deal of time studying **associative learning**—learning that certain events in the world tend to go together or be associated. One kind of associative learning is **classical conditioning,** a process whereby a new stimulus, through association

with an old one, becomes able to elicit an established reflex response. Some studies suggest that newborns can be classically conditioned, especially if the association is one that human infants have a predisposition to learn. However, classical conditioning, by itself, cannot explain the emergence of any *new* behaviors.

9. Another form of associative learning is **instrumental conditioning,** whereby a person's behaviors are influenced by the consequences they have. When those consequences are pleasant, the behavior is said to be **positively reinforced** (or rewarded) and the person is likely to perform the same behavior again. Likewise, **negative reinforcement** can encourage specific behaviors if unpleasant stimuli are removed. Research has shown that even newborns can be instrumentally conditioned. Moreover, systematic reinforcement can be used to gradually **shape** a sequence of responses that an infant has never before displayed.

10. **Imitative learning** is a very rapid way of acquiring new behaviors. The ability to imitate others quickly and without error develops gradually over the first year and a half of life. Psychologists still debate what underlies this important advancement.

11. Heredity seems to have endowed babies with a predisposition to acquire certain behaviors. This genetic predisposition is called **preparedness.** Part of prepared learning is a predisposition to notice **contingencies**—especially the relationship between one's own behaviors and the consequences they seem to have. Contingency learning helps babies gain control over their environments.

12. More noteworthy even than the impressive capacities of the newborn is the way these capacities are organized in the service of development. The alert newborn is motivated to scan the environment, to seek out certain kinds of stimulation, and to process that stimulation. The result of infants' particular biases, or **preadaptations,** is that they will pay attention to and learn about important features of their environment, including people. Such a disposition encourages responsiveness from others, which further promotes infant engagement.

6

Infant Cognitive Development

One day when Mikey Gordon was 7 months old he crawled over to a stack of pictures his sister Becky had drawn. Reaching out his hand he grasped the top one, wrinkling the corner as he brought it toward himself. The thick paper made a pleasant rustling sound. Mikey dropped the first picture and reached for another, wrinkling it with two hands and then shaking it. The paper rustled and flapped. Mikey smiled and reached for a third. Intently he grasped the sheet in both hands and pulled his hands apart. The paper responded by ripping down the middle with a wonderful crackling noise. Mikey dropped one half and put the other in his mouth, feeling it grow soft and moist as he stroked it with his tongue. Just as he was reaching for a brightly colored drawing of a little girl jumping rope, Becky walked

During infancy, behavior changes from reflexive single acts to organized sequences of goal-directed behaviors. *(G. W. Piccolo, Elizabeth Crews/Stock, Boston.)*

into the room. "Mikey, no!" she screamed, as she ran to rescue her artwork. "Look what you've done to my drawings. You're bad! I'm gonna tell Mommy!"

Why did Mikey destroy Becky's pictures? Was he really being bad? In this chapter you will discover that Becky's explanation is highly unlikely. The mind of a 7-month-old does not grasp the concepts of "my drawings" or even "bad." Mikey cannot yet understand language; nor can he imagine how Becky must feel about what he has done. This example makes a very important point about development: How children perceive and interpret what they experience depends on their level of cognitive development. Mikey is incapable of feeling shame and remorse because his understanding of the world is as yet too limited. But he may be able to grasp the distressed tone of Becky's voice, something that six months ago he would not have been able to do.

In this chapter we will examine how a baby's understanding of the world develops. We might say that we are going to explore the changing intelligence of infants. In psychology, however, the term *intelligence* usually is used to talk about *individual differences* in thinking. This chapter is concerned with changes in thinking skills that are common to all normal infants. We refer to these general skills as **cognitive abilities.**

As you read this chapter, you will encounter several major themes. The first theme is the *orderly nature of cognitive development.* In part this orderliness arises from previous capacities paving the way for newly emerging ones. Inborn reflexes are building blocks for early voluntary actions, and these early actions provide the foundation for later capacities. The orderliness also seems to result from maturation of certain general capacities that are important for all areas of development, such as the ability to coordinate actions and the capacity to store and retrieve information from memory more efficiently.

A second theme is that infants are *active participants* in their own development. Infants engage the environment with every means they have available, practicing the skills they have and thereby encountering problems beyond their capacities. On the basis of feedback from these encounters and continuing neural maturation, infants evolve more advanced and serviceable abilities. While at first these capacities seem to be applied automatically, in time infants become *intentional planners*, deliberately trying out actions and investigating their consequences, moving their understanding forward at an ever-increasing pace.

At birth Mikey Gordon did not possess any sense of purpose; his behaviors were either reflexive or undirected. By 7 months, however, he was deliberately reaching for and investigating interesting objects, such as Becky's drawings. By 13 months, as we saw in our earlier story, he remembered a game that he enjoyed and encouraged his father to play it. These changes reflect an important developmental trend: the emergence of greater and greater purposefulness in infants.

A final theme is that infant cognitive development is marked by both *advancements and continuing limitations*. Several major achievements occur in infancy. First infants develop a basic understanding of *causality*, especially the idea that their own actions can produce particular effects. In accord with the active participant theme, when infants note some consequence of an action, they repeat the sequence over and over, apparently for the simple joy of mastery. Second, an important advance occurs in *understanding means and ends*. Before the end of the first year infants understand that sometimes doing one thing will enable them to do another (such as removing an obstacle to get to a toy). A third achievement of profound significance is development of an *understanding of object permanence*. During the end of this period, infants learn not only that objects exist outside their perceptual experience but that objects may change their location in space even if the change is not seen. Such knowledge reflects a fourth major advance in infancy: the ability to store and recall information from memory.

Even though each new level of understanding represents an advance over prior levels, infants do have limitations. Infants know the world primarily through action. In fact, infancy may be defined as the period prior to the development of symbolic thought, the capacity to let one thing stand for, or *represent*, another. With the emergence of symbolic thought, young children can understand many things that infants cannot, no matter how much experience parents provide. Yet infants make great strides in their first two years, as you will see as we describe the skills they master as reflexes become intentional actions.

In this chapter we begin our exploration of infant cognitive development with an overview of the stages in the sensorimotor period as described by Piaget and other theorists. With this pattern of cognitive development as background, we turn to two important advances during the first two years: an understanding of object permanence and an improved memory capacity. Although Piaget's work gives us a framework for understanding how cognitive development progresses, we will also consider other more recent theoretical viewpoints. Most of these theories are derived from the work of Piaget or set themselves up in contrast to Piaget. As you will learn, the field of cognitive development currently is charged with theoretical controversy.

THE COURSE OF INFANT COGNITIVE DEVELOPMENT

Cognitive development during the period of infancy has been described in a variety of ways. Piaget, for example, called infancy the **sensorimotor period,** and he subdivided this major period into six sensorimotor stages. Table 6.1 compares Piaget's stages with those proposed by Robbie Case (1985) as part of his own theory of cognitive development and those presented by Kurt Fischer (Fischer and Lazerson 1984) as a summary of a number of theories including his own. Although details of the theories may differ, the general description of the course of cognitive development in infancy is similar.

Piaget's initial description of these stages was drawn from observing his own three children as infants (Piaget, 1952/1963). Although some of his ideas have since been modified because of findings from later experiments, Piaget's book on infancy, *The Origins of Intelligence,* still demonstrates how much one can learn from careful observation of individual children. In providing a general description of infant cognitive development, we will use the age norms and labels from Piaget's six-stage system, but information from the other researchers will be included. Refer to Table 6.1 to determine the labels that Case and Fischer would use.

As you read about these stages, remember two things. First, these theorists are describing the most advanced level of performance that can be seen at each stage. Early in a stage a baby is only beginning to attain these accomplishments. Second, the age ranges given are approximate:

TABLE 6.1   Comparison of the Stages of Infant Development Proposed by Jean Piaget, Robbie Case, and Kurt Fischer

Piaget	Case	Fischer
0–1 month Stage 1: Reflexes		0–2 months Level 0

1–4 months
Stage 2: Primary
    Circular Reactions
	1–4 months
	Substage 0: Operational
	    Consolidation
		2–7 months
		Level 1: Single Actions

4–8 months
Stage 3: Secondary
    Circular Reactions
	4–8 months
	Substage 1: Operational
	    Coordination
		6–12 months
		Level 2: Relations of
		    Actions

8–12 months
Stage 4: Coordination
    of Schemes
	8–12 months
	Substage 2: Bifocal
	    Coordination	

12–18 months
Stage 5: Tertiary
    Circular Reactions
	12–20 months
	Substage 3: Elaborated
	    Coordination
		10–20 months
		Level 3: Systems of
		    Actions

18–24 months
Stage 6: Beginnings of
    Representational
    Thought
		18–36 months
		Level 4: Single
		    Representations

Babies enter and complete each stage at different paces. What is important in stage theories is the *sequence*, not the precise timing, of the stages.

Stage 1: Reflexes (Birth to 1 Month)

Piaget and Fischer have proposed that in the first month of life a baby's capabilities are limited to genetically programmed reflexes. Development in the first month consists of minor refinements of these reflexes; no truly new behaviors emerge. Piaget used the term *reflexes* in a much broader sense than most American psychologists. To him a **reflex** is any built-in behavior pattern. For instance, the active looking that Malcolm engaged in when he came home from the hospital would be considered a reflex because these eye movements are a built-in response to visual stimuli. In addition to eye movements, other behaviors that are refined during the first month include sucking, grasping, and larger movements of the arms and hands. Piaget was particularly interested in these early reflexes because they provide the building blocks for later development.

Stage 2: Simple Actions (Primary Circular Reactions, 1 to 4 Months)

One evening when John Williams was putting 2-month-old Malcolm to bed, he took a minute to sit and watch the baby as he lay on his back in the crib. Malcolm was moving his arms in a seemingly random but rhythmic up-and-down pattern. As his semiclenched right hand brushed against his face, he turned his head to the right and his arm movements became smaller. The next time the hand brushed against his face, he opened his mouth and captured his hand. After sucking for a while he released the hand, moved it up and down again, and then recaptured it with his mouth. Over and over Malcolm repeated this sequence. John Williams was observing what might be called a simple action, or what Piaget called a primary circular reaction.

A **circular reaction** is a behavior producing an event that leads to the behavior's being repeated. The reaction is circular in the sense that the end of one sequence triggers the start of another. A **primary circular reaction** like Malcolm's is one that involves only a person's own body, no external objects or events. You are engaging in a primary circular reaction when you accidentally discover that putting a cool hand to your sunburned face makes the burn feel better and so you repeat this behavior.

Thumb sucking frequently is learned as a primary circular reaction, just as Malcolm learned to suck his whole hand. As a young baby's hands and arms move randomly, a thumb often comes in contact with the mouth. This stimulation may then trigger the sucking reflex. You might think that once the thumb is inside the mouth, the child would go on sucking until he or she grew tired. Often, however, this is not what happens. Piaget noticed that infants frequently pull the thumb out and attempt to repeat the actions that led to their sucking on it. The babies seem to be trying to gain control over behaviors that originally occurred by accident.

Inborn behaviors are the foundation of the primary circular reactions that develop during stage 2. For one thing, innate reflexes (such as moving the arms and sucking) determine the kinds of events likely to happen by accident. In addition, when something happens that produces an inter-

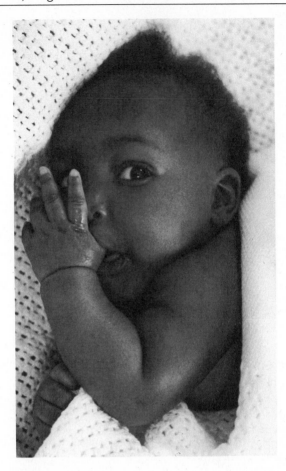

Moving the hand to and from the mouth so a thumb, fingers, or fist can be sucked is a common example of a circular reaction. *(Suzanne Szasz/Photo Researchers, Inc.)*

esting sensory result, the baby is intrinsically motivated to try to repeat the behavior. Malcolm does not consciously think about the connection between capturing the fist in his mouth and the pleasant sensation of sucking on it. For him, repeating this behavior is automatic, not intentional. As we noted in Chapter 5, in the discussion of contingency analysis, it is simply the nature of babies to try to repeat an action that causes an interesting sensory consequence. Piaget's stage 2 marks the emergence of new behaviors as a result of this intrinsic motivation.

Case (1985) also emphasizes the refinement of inborn behaviors. He suggests that this period is a time of consolidating such behaviors, as is apparent from studies of the visual tracking behavior of infants. By the end of this stage, infants can move their eyes smoothly to follow an object traveling along any trajectory. Additionally, Case feels that infants at this stage master behaviors that permit them to repeat a sensory experience, just as in Piaget's circular reaction. Fischer (1980) emphasizes control over the action, be it an eye movement or the grasping of an object. In addition, he believes that this control occurs only for single actions; young infants can grasp and move objects or move their eyes to look at objects, but at 3 months such infants cannot move an object in front of their eyes to look at it (except by accident). Thus, all three theorists emphasize simple actions of the infants during this period, actions which involve primarily their own bodies.

Stage 3: Actions on Objects (Secondary Circular Reactions, 4 to 8 Months)

At breakfast one day 6-month-old Meryl accidentally knocked a spoon off her highchair tray. The spoon clattered to the floor, and Karen picked it up, putting it back on the tray. Moments later Meryl knocked it to the floor again. This was not an attempt by Meryl to make Karen angry; rather, it was an example of what Piaget called a **secondary circular reaction.** In such a reaction, infants actively investigate the effects their behaviors have on *external* objects. As with a primary circular reaction, the interesting sensory consequence is at first produced by accident. But the baby then repeats the behavior, causing the consequence again.

An experiment that Piaget conducted on his infant son, Laurent, shows both the skills and limitations of babies at this stage. Piaget tied a string from Laurent's wrist to a rattle suspended above his crib. If Laurent moved his arm vigorously enough, the rattle would make a noise. Just by randomly moving his limbs, Laurent soon caused the toy to rattle. At this point he stopped, listened, and then moved his whole body so the sound occurred again. Repeating this secondary circular reaction, Laurent gradually adapted his movements until he moved only the appropriate arm. The next day Piaget again tied the string from Laurent's wrist to the rattle, but Laurent did not spontaneously start to move the arm. Only when his father first shook the rattle for him did Laurent revive the previous day's circular reaction. On the third day Piaget tied the string to Laurent's *other* wrist. Again he had to reinstate the circular reaction by first shaking the rattle himself. Only then did Laurent begin moving his arm, and he moved the one that *didn't* have the string. When no sound resulted, Laurent moved his body more extensively until the toy finally rattled. As Laurent repeated the circular reaction, his movements again adapted until he eventually shook only the arm connected to the rattle.

We can say that Laurent acquired a rudimentary understanding of the connection between moving his arm and the resulting sound. This understanding, however, was quite limited. Even when the wrist to which the string was tied was in clear view, Laurent moved the *wrong* arm. He in no way grasped that the arm pulled the string, which in turn shook the rattle. Instead, he merely learned a connection between a particular motor behavior and a particular sensory consequence.

According to Piaget, it is these kinds of sensorimotor pairings that a child learns in the first year of life. Another example of them can be seen in the early form of imitation that emerges during stage 3. When 6-month-old Malcolm coos, for instance, DeeDee may coo back, causing the baby to coo in return. Here Malcolm is learning a connection between making a certain sound and having his mother repeat it. The baby is not yet consciously mimicking the parent. According to Piaget, such circular reactions are limited to behaviors Malcolm can already perform and that he can actually hear or see himself produce.

Case emphasizes the active exploration that characterizes infants. Although infants in the previous stage can initiate voluntary actions, they are unable to coordinate them to produce exploratory sequences, such as observing an object and grasping it. From Case's perspective, secondary circular reactions are but one example of infants' new ability to initiate behaviors that allow them to learn about their world. The crucial characteristic of this stage is the appearance of behaviors that are assembled out of two previously present behaviors, such as visual tracking and hand reaching.

Fischer also notes the advance that comes when two actions can be coordinated. In the stage he labels *relations of actions,* he includes the simple coordination described above and the means-end coordination that both Piaget and Case reserve for the next level of development. Hence, Fischer combines two levels that Piaget and Case believe are distinct. That they are conceptually distinct is clear; whether they are developmentally distinct is still open to question.

Stage 4: Coordination of Actions (Coordination of Secondary Schemes, 8 to 12 Months)

When Meryl was 7 months old, she would become very frustrated if she wanted a toy and some other object was blocking the way. Karen thought it was strange that Meryl should cry. Why make such a fuss when she could grasp the unwanted object and put it to one side? Karen decided the reason must be Meryl's "cranky" nature. Then one day when Meryl was 9 months old, she started crawling over to inspect the television plug. Karen quickly placed a large toy dog directly in front of the socket. To her surprise, this tactic failed completely. With a sweep of her arm, Meryl knocked the dog out of the way and reached for the cord. This kind of action—in which a baby performs a behavior in order to do something else—clearly indicates Piaget's stage 4 thinking.

In stage 4, infants begin to put actions together into **goal-directed chains** of behavior. In other words, they sometimes do a thing not for its own sake but as a means of accomplishing something else. Piaget called this the "coordination of secondary schemes" because the baby is coordinating schemes applied to external objects to achieve some goal. Meryl, for instance, knocks the dog out of the way *in order* to get to the electrical cord. Notice that this action requires her to first anticipate the results of hitting the dog. The ability to anticipate future consequences is a major cognitive leap forward, even though it is still limited to well-learned motor actions. Piaget claimed that this kind of behavior is the first clear sign of purposefulness in infants, although Fischer would claim that this kind of coordination occurs earlier and both Case and Fischer would claim that purposeful behavior occurs earlier. Regardless of when it begins, clearly Meryl purposely *intends* to grasp the plug, and she knows that if she hits the dog it will no longer be in the way. Thus, by coordinating her hitting, reaching, and grasping schemes, she gets what she wants.

The term that Case chose for this stage, *bifocal coordination,* emphasizes the "two views" that constitute the new type of coordination that appears around age 8 months. Actions involving two objects or two events must be integrated to produce a desired outcome. For example, a baby at this stage can learn to use a spoon to transport food to the mouth for eating (Brazelton, 1969). Case describes the new capability as involving the integration of two sensorimotor routines, whereas Piaget emphasized the planning involved in doing one thing in order to do another.

Use of a spoon for eating illustrates the infant's growing sophistication in organizing behaviors to accomplish some goal. *(Gene Jeffers/Alpha.)*

Piaget also argued that infants at stage 4 understand their own behavior well enough to imitate actions they seldom perform spontaneously. For instance, Piaget's 9-month-old daughter Jacqueline gradually learned how to imitate her father as he bent and straightened his index finger, something that the baby rarely did on her own (Piaget, 1952/1963b). At this stage, infants are quite able to imitate unusual actions they can't see themselves performing, such as moving their lips in unusual ways.

Stage 5: Exploration by Variations of Actions (Tertiary Circular Reactions, 12 to 18 Months)

Thirteen-month-old Mikey is standing at the top of the stairs, his way blocked by a wooden gate. As he peers over the gate with a rubber ball in one hand, the ball accidentally drops and bounces all the way down. Mikey watches intently as the ball rolls on and hits the front door. He then picks up his blue stuffed dog and drops it over the gate, watching to see what happens. The dog lands on the top step, somersaults down another, and stops when it hits the third, nose draped over the edge. Christine comes out of the bedroom just as Mikey is forcefully hurling a shoe over the gate. Mikey's behavior illustrates what Piaget called a tertiary circular reaction. As with primary and secondary circular reactions, a **tertiary** (or third-order) **circular reaction** begins when some action accidentally leads to an interesting sensory consequence. But rather than just repeating the same behavior again, the infant at this stage "experiments." In Mikey's case, he tries dropping other objects over the gate and launching them in a variety of ways. These purposeful, trial-and-error variations allow him to discover new cause-and-effect relationships rapidly. His understanding of the world and schemes for acting on it greatly expand as a result.

As you would expect, infants at stage 5 get into everything. They actively explore each new object they encounter, trying to discover its potential for responding. This exploration affords many opportunities to learn new means of reaching goals. The active exploration of stage 5 babies may also explain why children around 18 months of age rapidly begin to acquire simple tool-using skills (Flavell, 1985). Children at a little over a year and a half may, for instance, spontaneously begin using a stick to "help dig" the flower garden. According to Piaget, the active trial-and-error approach of stage 5 infants enables them to learn readily to imitate behaviors they have never before performed.

Case emphasizes the growing flexibility of infants after 1 year of age in figuring out the relationship between actions and outcomes (*means-ends* relationships). For example, in trying to get a toy that is out of reach, an infant at this stage is more likely than previously to recognize that this can be done by pulling a blanket underneath the toy. Fischer theorizes that simple coordination of actions and means-ends relationships become part of systems of actions. Pulling on the blanket is just one of many means-ends relationships that might be appropriate in this example. The systems of actions arise as the child learns many such relations among actions in the previous stage, permitting infants to be more effectively planful in their behavior.

Stage 6: Beginnings of Representational Thought (18 to 24 Months)

> Jacqueline had a visit from a little boy of 18 months whom she used to see from time to time, and who, in the course of the afternoon, got into a terrible temper. He screamed as he tried to get out of a playpen and pushed it backward, stamping his feet. Jacqueline stood watching him in amazement, never having witnessed such a scene before. The next day, she herself screamed in her playpen and tried to move it, stamping her foot lightly several times in succession. (Piaget, 1952/1963b, p. 63)

This example of **deferred** (or delayed) **imitation** illustrates one of the new capabilities that mark stage 6 intelligence. Piaget's daughter, herself about 1½, watched another toddler throw a temper tantrum. A day later, without ever having tried out these tantrum behaviors beforehand, she performed a good imitation of them. Apparently, she stored in memory a representation of screaming, pushing, and stamping that she used the next day in a sensorimotor scheme. The ability to form mental representations like this one is a very important cognitive advance.

Piaget described stage 6 as the start of the transition from sensorimotor to *symbolic* or **representational thought,** the term Piaget used to describe the ability to make one thing stand for something else. In this case, Jacqueline created a mental image of a tantrum that stood for or repre-

Pretending calls upon a child's capacity for representational thought, in which mental images represent real objects and actions. *(Bruce Roberts/Rapho/ Photo Researchers, Inc.)*

sented the actual behaviors. Stage 6 children also start to solve problems "in their heads," without having to go through the physical actions involved. Their symbolic thought is still quite limited, however, in that it is confined to sensorimotor schemes that the child *could* act out. Nevertheless, the ability to have actions "in mind" without performing them is a great cognitive leap forward.

For both Case and Fischer the behaviors of children in the second half of the second year of life also mark the transition from a sensorimotor to a representational approach to the world. Fischer considers the beginning of pretend play, as in pretending that a block is a truck, to be an early example of the emergence of representational skills. It marks the transition from the world of real objects and actions to the world of the mind.

DEVELOPING THE CONCEPT OF OBJECTS

The development of the concept of objects is a major task of infancy. When you look around, you do not simply see patterns of light. You see books, chairs, pencils, and other objects. You know that these objects have a durability that goes beyond their color or the shadow they cast, both of which disappear in the absence of light, and beyond your perception in general, which depends on your presence. Such a realization is central to your whole understanding of the world, including your knowledge that you are distinct from other people.

Some of Piaget's most fascinating ideas concerned the concept of objects. He argued that newborns have no such concept. This concept, like other knowledge, is "actively constructed." Furthermore, for young infants, there is at first no **object permanence:** When an object disappears from sight, to the young infant it ceases to exist. While much controversy swirls around the details of Piaget's argument, researchers agree that certainly by the end of the second year all normal children have an advanced understanding of objects. Let's examine the emergence of this fundamental capacity.

Development Through the Six Sensorimotor Stages

STAGES 1 AND 2

In stages 1 and 2 of the sensorimotor period, infants become able to track moving objects with their eyes and to reach for such objects if they are close enough. However, if an object the baby is watching moves behind something else, the child loses interest in it and gazes off in another direction as if it has ceased to exist. In addition, babies this young respond in an interesting way when an object is partially covered. For example, suppose a stage 2 infant is hungry and looking at a bottle. Then, while the infant is looking, you cover the nipple end with a cloth so the infant can see only the bottom end. Frequently such a young infant will quickly lose interest and begin looking at other objects. It is as if the baby cannot imagine the "missing" part and no longer perceives the object as familiar.

STAGE 3

In the third sensorimotor stage infants are not deterred from reaching when an object is partially covered. A partial view of the object is enough to elicit a concept of the whole. Yet if an object is totally covered while the infant is watching, the child won't try to reach for it (see Figure 6.1). Apparently, babies at this age need at least some perceptual cues to remind them that an object still exists. You saw a similar cognitive limitation in Piaget's son, Laurent, at stage 3. The day after playing with the rattle connected to his wrist by a string, Laurent at first did not remember how to make the interesting sound. However, once his father shook the rattle, that minimal cue revived the whole secondary circular reaction. In order to understand objects young infants depend on current percep-

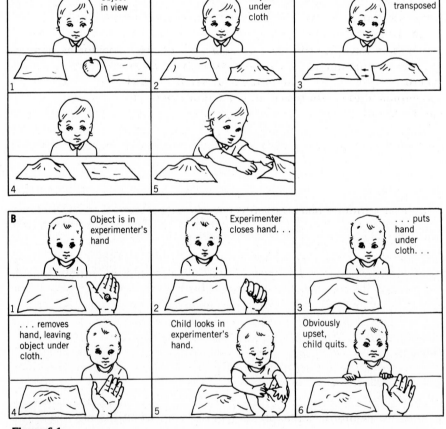

Figure 6.1
Assessment of Object Permanence
In the top sequence (A), an object is repeatedly hidden under the cloth on the infant's left. The infant immediately searches under the cloth and finds the object. When the cloths are transposed so that the object is hidden under the cloth on the right, the Stage 4 infant still searches on the left. In the bottom sequence (B), the Stage 5 infant searches wherever the object is hidden, but when the object is transported in the adult's closed hand to the cloth, the infant still searches in the adult's closed hand.

tual information to "remember," though the whole object need not be in view.

STAGE 4

In the fourth stage infants search for hidden objects. If you cover a toy with a pillow, for instance, the child will remove it to get the toy. This behavior is an example of the stage 4 baby's ability to combine sensori-motor schemes into goal-directed actions. It also indicates that the baby understands that an object can be recovered after searching.

One might conclude that infants now possess an adultlike concept of object permanence. Studies show, however, that this is not true (e.g., Gratch, 1975). The child's understanding of objects is still "flawed." For example, suppose you repeatedly hide a rattle under a yellow pillow, each time letting the child retrieve the toy. This game is so interesting for an 8- to 10-month-old baby that he or she will play it for a long time. Now, while the infant is still watching, you put the rattle beneath a blue pillow. Surprisingly, the infant will continue to look for the toy underneath the *yellow* pillow, where it has always been before. Failing to find the rattle there, the baby will search randomly, perhaps finally discovering it under the blue pillow where he or she *saw* you put it. Many researchers have interpreted the continued search behavior as demonstrating that the infant knows the object is permanent and must be somewhere (Siegler, 1986). But looking under the yellow pillow shows an incomplete understanding of the constraints that govern where an object can be found. Piaget's view was that infants in stage 4 still connect the reappearance of the object to their own motor activities. For them the object does not yet have a permanence independent of their own activity.

STAGE 5

In the fifth stage infants no longer make the stage 4 error. Instead, they search for a hidden object wherever it last disappeared from sight. Once again it may seem that the baby has attained an adultlike understanding, but the following demonstration reveals otherwise. In this demonstration, you show the baby a small toy until the child's attention is captured; then you close your hand around it and place your hand under a yellow pillow. You do not leave the toy under this pillow, however. Instead, you withdraw your hand, still concealing the toy, and place it under a nearby blue pillow. Here you leave the toy. All these movements of your hand, although not the toy itself, are in full view of the baby. Where do you think the child will search when you show that your hand is now empty? At this stage the infant looks first under the yellow pillow and then, when the object isn't there, begins searching at random. The child may or may not move the blue pillow and find the toy. Apparently, children of this age cannot *imagine* an object's moving when the moving object itself is hidden from view.

STAGE 6

In the sixth and final sensorimotor stage children at last acquire a mature object concept. They can now imagine movements of an object that they do not actually see. As a result, if you perform the stage 5 experiment with them, they will search under the blue pillow after failing to find the

The concept of object permanence develops through a series of stages until children finally acquire a mature understanding. *Doug Goodman/Monkmeyer Press.)*

toy under the yellow one. This ability to imagine an object's moving is another example of early representational thought. Just as Jacqueline could form a mental image of a temper tantrum, stage 6 babies can also form mental representations of movements and actions.

Ongoing Research on Infants' Understanding of Objects

Researchers have continued to be very interested in how and when infants develop an understanding of objects. The object concept is, after all, central to a general understanding of the world. Some investigators have approached this subject by attempting to replicate Piaget's original studies. They have found that infants do pass through the sequences of behavior that Piaget recorded, even though many reach the various developmental milestones at somewhat earlier ages (e.g., Corman and Escalona, 1969; Kramer, Hill, and Cohen, 1975; Uzgiris and Hunt, 1975).

But some researchers have questioned Piaget's *interpretation* of his basic findings. They contend that babies younger than Piaget's stage 4 may understand that objects are permanent. However, younger babies may lack the skills either to determine where an object is or to carry out an effective search (Bower, 1977; Harris, 1974, 1983). If so, they would "know" more about objects than they appear to in Piaget's experiments. Researchers have therefore devised other tests of the object concept that do not require the baby to search for and locate something.

For instance, T. G. R. Bower (1967) has presented young babies with disappearing objects while recording their rates of sucking on a pacifier. Bower contends that if an infant believes objects are permanent, he or she should be surprised if something suddenly disappears as if by magic. This surprise would cause an interruption in the child's normally steady rate of sucking. In contrast, if an object simply moves out of sight behind a screen, this should not surprise a baby with a basic understanding of objects. The results of Bower's experiments suggest that babies only 2 months old can distinguish between "usual" and "unusual" forms of disappearance. At present, however, we cannot conclude that this finding means babies this young understand that objects are permanent. Perhaps just the novelty or suddenness of a "magically" disappearing object startles the infants so that they temporarily stop sucking.

René Baillargeon (Baillargeon, 1986, in press; Baillargeon, Spelke, and Wasserman, 1985) has conducted a series of experiments that suggest babies 5 to 7 months old understand that one object can block the movement of another, even if the blocking object is not visible. In one study, a screen was pivoted forward and backward 180 degrees while a baby watched. Then a block was placed so that it interfered with the backward movement of the screen. On "trick" trials, when the screen was moved through the space that should have been occupied by the block, infants looked at the event longer, suggesting that they detected something unusual. Baillargeon has argued that this behavior demonstrates that the infants know the block is there even when they cannot see it.

Other tests of the object concept that do not require babies to search manually for something often confirm Piaget's contention that an understanding of the continued existence of objects is a stage 4 development.

For example, William Charlesworth (1966) showed babies an object, covered it up, removed it without the babies seeing, and then lifted the cover and showed them that the object had disappeared. The facial expressions of 8-month-olds showed that they were startled or puzzled by this event, but no such reaction occurred in younger infants, suggesting that the younger babies didn't understand that an object cannot just temporarily vanish. In another study, researchers moved an object horizontally across a baby's field of vision, in which there were also two screens with a gap between them (Moore, Borton, and Darby, 1978). Most of the time, the object could be seen disappearing behind one screen and then emerging from it before it went behind the second screen and ultimately appeared at the other end. On some trials, however, the researchers made the object disappear behind the first screen and then emerge from behind the second without ever being visible in the gap. This "impossible" sight disrupted the looking behavior of 9-month-olds but not of 5-month-olds. Such findings strongly indicate that the limitations Piaget observed in very young infants did not occur merely because these babies lacked skills for conducting searches. Instead, they suggest that the concept of object permanence does not emerge until some time between 5 and 8 months of age.

But even though Piaget was fairly accurate about when the concept of object permanence first emerges, some of his ideas about why infants make various object-related errors have not proved correct. For instance, Piaget speculated that the stage 4 infant mistakenly looks for a hidden object in its *previous* location because the child connects the act of searching in that place with the object's reappearance. Looking under the yellow pillow brought the object back before—why not another time? Research shows, however, that this explanation cannot be entirely right. For one thing, stage 4 babies do not always search in the previous location when a hiding place has been changed; they do so only about 50 percent of the time (Butterworth, 1974, 1975, 1977). More important, if you let stage 4 infants search *immediately* after an object is hidden rather than delaying them a bit, they go to the right location 100 percent of the time (Gratch et al., 1974). Why would this be if the babies thought that searching in the old hiding place was what made the object reappear?

To explain the common "stage 4 error," try to put yourself in the baby's place. Where would you search for an object if you didn't know where it was? A logical answer is in the place where you had previously found it. Perhaps stage 4 babies are doing precisely that when they search in the old place. If so, we need to know why the infants so quickly forget seeing the object disappear in the new location. This question is about the limitations of babies' memories, which we will explore next.

MEMORY DEVELOPMENT DURING INFANCY

Several years ago, while on a vacation, one of the authors of this book and his family were involved in an automobile accident. The author's son, then less than a year old, was taken to a hospital by ambulance to have minor injuries treated. Two years later the family was driving through the same town where the accident occurred. The little boy, now 3 years old, looked around and spontaneously asked: "Are we going to see the ambulance now?" Did he remember the accident from two years earlier when he knew the meaning of only a few words (*ambulance* certainly not among them)? And if babies *can* form lasting memories of things that happen to them, why do most of us recall almost nothing about our infancies?

All cognitive development theorists are interested in memory development. Some view memory as one of many significant features that undergo development during infancy. Others consider the development of memory as the key to understanding cognitive development. We will examine both of these views in the next section when we compare theories. Here, we will consider memory in infants as just another way to describe how babies come to know about the world. It is an important component of infant cognitive development, regardless of the particular theoretical orientation you endorse.

As a component of an infant's developing cognitive system, the features of memory that are most important are changes in the length of time that information can be remembered and changes in what is remembered. For an infant to build a stable picture of the world from learned information, the learned information must be either stored in memory for extended periods of time or reencountered frequently so that it is relearned before it is forgotten. If what can be remembered changes, then the information out of which an infant is building a model of the world will change. Thus the focus of this section is on retention intervals and on the content of the information remembered; in subsequent chapters other features of older children's memory systems will be discussed.

Memory in the First Six Months of Life

You already learned in Chapter 5 that infants have some kind of memory as soon as they are born. Newborns readily habituate to novel sights and sounds, indicating that they must remember enough about a stimulus to recognize it as familiar (Kiselevsky and Muir, 1984; Slatter, Morison, and Rose, 1984). The concept of preparedness also gave you insight into the nature of memory during infancy. Young babies learn most easily those things they are *prepared* to learn. In other words, the brain of an infant is predisposed to retain certain kinds of information—often information related to survival and mastering the environment.

Although learning has been demonstrated in newborns, attempts to show that information is remembered over a 24-hour period have failed (Rosenblith and Sims-Knight, 1985). However, researchers have concluded that memories lasting more than 24 hours are possible for infants only a few weeks of age. For instance, experiments in which infants less than 1 month old were conditioned to turn their heads upon hearing a certain sound suggest that this kind of learning is retained for more than a day (Papousek, 1959, 1967a). Another study demonstrated memory for a word repeated 60 times a day for 13 days (Ungerer, Brody, and Zelazo, 1978). The extensive training needed to demonstrate memory over a 24-

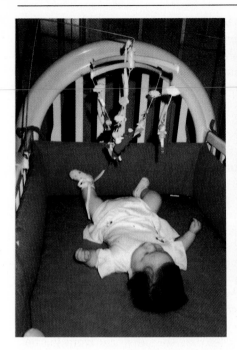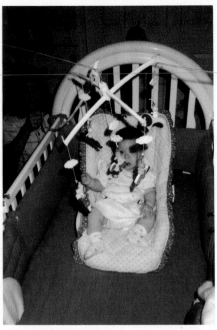

Left, a 3-month-old infant during a reinforcement phase with the ankle ribbon attached to the stand supporting the mobile. The other stand, clamped to the opposite crib rail, will hold the ribbon during periods of nonreinforcement. *Right,* the same infant during a reactivation treatment. The mobile and ribbon are attached to the stand supporting the mobile, but the ribbon is drawn and released by the experimenter, concealed from the infant's view at the side of the crib. *(Carolyn Rovee-Collier/Rutgers University.)*

hour period in very young infants makes it seem unlikely that they retain information about their experiences in the first month of life.

We know more about the memory capabilities of slightly older infants. In an interesting set of studies Carolyn Rovee-Collier and her colleagues explored the long-term memories of 2- to 4-month-olds. The babies learned to kick their legs to make a mobile move, the amount of movement depending on how hard they kicked. Six to eight days later, these infants showed they remembered what they had previously learned by starting to kick when they were placed in the experimental setting. They did not spontaneously start to kick after a two-week interval, however (Sullivan, Rovee-Collier, and Tynes, 1979). Does this mean that after 14 days the memory had totally faded?

A second study suggests otherwise. In this experiment the researchers found that memory of the connection between kicking and moving the mobile could be "reactivated" if the babies were shown the mobile the day before testing (Rovee-Collier, 1979; Rovee-Collier et al., 1980). This finding differs somewhat from Piaget's observations since just seeing the rattle above his crib was not enough to get Laurent to start moving his arm again. Piaget had to actually shake the rattle for Laurent to remember this connection. What is interesting is that in both these experiments the babies' memories had to be triggered by some perceptual reminder. The implication is that although young babies do form long-term memories, they may have trouble retrieving them without clear-cut cues.

Clear-cut retrieval cues always are provided in **recognition tests** of memory. In these tests an infant is shown some previously seen stimulus while the researchers look for signs that the child recognizes it, a form of remembering. In many recognition tests the researchers use the amount of time the baby looks at an object as an indication of whether the child considers it novel or familiar. A study of this type showed that 5-month-olds can recognize previously seen faces even after an interval of two weeks (Fagan, 1973). This study is one of several that illustrate increasing memory between 3 and 6 months for characteristics of people. Before that age, there is little evidence that information is organized and stored as concepts of particular people (Olson and Sherman, 1983). By 6 months, though, infants know about behaviors that are characteristic both of people in general and of specific people (Olson, 1981).

Several researchers have used simple visual stimuli to study the limitations of memory in the first six months of life. Both Marcelle Schwartz and R. H. Day (1979) and Leslie Cohen and Barbara Younger (1984) have studied infants' memories for the angles between two line segments and the orientation of these angles (see Figure 6.2). The two studies agree that at 4 months infants can remember angles, but they disagree on the limitations of younger infants. Cohen and Younger interpret their results as showing that young infants remember only single features, such as lines, whereas 4-month-old infants can remember the relations among simple features, such as the angle formed by two lines. You may feel that knowledge about infants' memories for angles is not crucial to understanding the progress of their development. However, studies using very simple stimuli provide the information that helps us understand why very young infants might have difficulty remembering more relevant stimuli. If they remember each feature independently rather than the relation among features, then such infants cannot remember complex patterns such as faces.

Notice that all the tests of memory we have talked about so far are variations of a recognition test. These are the only memory tests that researchers have been able to devise for children who are not yet able to use language. If you accept Piaget's view that young infants cannot yet form any kind of mental representation, recognition tests would seem essential for exploring a baby's earliest memories. The limits of sensorimotor thinking would require a young infant to actually perceive or interact with an object again to retrieve a memory of it.

Memory in the Second Half-Year

In the second half-year, babies obviously retain long-term memories. For example, at this time children begin to display strong emotional bonds toward their parents. As you will see in Chapter 7, they smile, gurgle, and coo when their mother or father approaches and cry when that person departs. Clearly, they must have formed a set of long-term memories about the important adults in their lives. By the end of the first year, most babies also start to say their first words. Being able to use a word correctly from day to day and week to week again shows long-term memory.

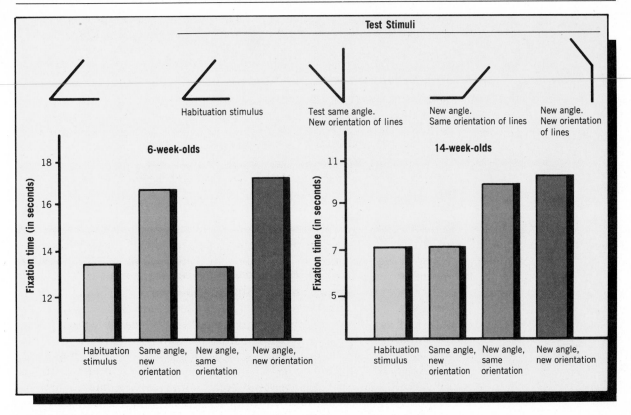

Figure 6.2
Infant Memory for Angles
Cohen and Younger habituated very young infants and 4-month-olds to angled stimuli like that on the left. After habituation, a variety of test stimuli were presented to the infants to see which ones they thought were different, as indicated by longer looking times.
Source: Adapted from Cohen and Younger, 1984.

Recognition tests can be used to determine the kinds of things that older babies notice and remember. Suppose one day an infant is fed from a bottle with a pale, translucent nipple rather than the light brown nipple the child has used before. Will he or she notice this difference? Probably not. To most babies, this "new" bottle will not seem novel at all. The reason is that in identifying a bottle, the child tends to ignore the nipple's color because it is not significant. This example illustrates an important facet of human memory. People do not store precisely detailed memories of everything they see. Instead, they filter what they see through general categories they have formed and remember things partly as instances of those categories. Researchers wonder when infants begin to categorize the world. When do they start to remember two or more distinguishable objects as broadly similar?

In one experiment designed to help answer this question, Joseph Fagan (1979) habituated one group of 7-month-olds to pictures of different male faces and a second group to a picture of only one male face. Later, babies in the first group showed renewed interest when a *female* face, but not a new male one, was presented. Apparently, they had learned the

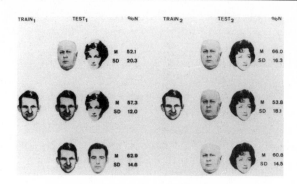

Joseph Fagan used pictures of male and female faces to study infants' ability to perceive and remember categories. *(Dr. Joseph Fagan.)*

category male faces and had grown tired of seeing repeated examples of it. In contrast, babies in the second group showed renewed interest for either of the new pictures, female or male. This experiment shows that for infants to perceive and remember a category such as male faces, they must be presented with more than one instance of it.

Leslie Cohen and his colleagues (e.g., Cohen and Strauss, 1979; Husaim and Cohen, 1982; Younger and Cohen, 1986) have performed extensive studies of the categories infants use to store information about artificially constructed animals. For example, in one study they used pictures of animals that varied in type of body, type of tail, and type of feet. When 4-, 7-, and 10-month-olds were presented with several different pictures of animals, the 4-month-olds did not learn that certain features such as type of feet went with certain other features such as type of body; that is, they did not learn categories of different types of animals. The 10-month-olds did learn such categories. The 7-month-olds were only able to use categories when the three types of features were perfectly correlated with one another, that is, when no variation existed within a category. Thus, the use of categories to store information in memory seems to develop in the second half of the first year of life.

In addition to studying when babies start to remember things in categories, researchers have also been intrigued by when infants start to process numerical information into memory. The ability to notice how many objects are present is called the perception of numerosity. Prentice Starkey and Robert Cooper (1980) tested 6- to 8-month-olds for their perception of numerosity by using habituation. They showed one group of infants drawings with three dots each, the arrangement of the dots varying from picture to picture. They showed the three other groups of babies varying arrangements of two, four, or six dots (see Figure 6.3). After the babies' interest declined, the researchers changed the number of dots. Infants who had habituated to sets of three dots showed renewed attention when presented with two dots, whereas those who had habituated to two dots showed renewed attention to three. Apparently, these babies could perceive and remember small numerosities, a skill that may emerge before 2 months of age (Antell and Keating, 1983).

When an infant perceives that a picture has three dots, exactly what does the child store in memory—a visual image of the particular group or a more abstract notion of how many things are present? It may surprise you to learn just how abstract the baby's perception is. In one recent study researchers presented 6- to 8-month-olds with two arrays of objects side by side, one array containing two objects, the other three. When the babies heard two drumbeats, they tended to look at the two-object set; when they heard three drumbeats, they tended to look at the set of three (Starkey, Spelke, and Gelman, in press). This finding suggests that what babies remember and match in such studies is a concept of how many, not physical characteristics of the stimuli.

But although babies perceive and remember small numerosities, larger ones present more of a problem. In Starkey and Cooper's study, switching from four dots to six dots or from six dots to four did *not* prompt renewed attention even in 8-month-olds. Emergence of this more sophisticated skill must await further cognitive advances. The gradual development of infants' abilities to perceive and remember numerical relations as well as categories is currently the focus of much research (e.g., Cooper, 1984; Strauss and Curtis, 1984; Younger and Cohen, 1985). Although many questions still remain unanswered, we know that these abilities start to emerge early and that they change during the first year of life.

EXPLANATIONS OF COGNITIVE DEVELOPMENT

Piaget's Theory

Having described the general course of cognitive development, we will now examine theoretical explanations of this development. Piaget's theory was the first comprehensive one. The sensorimotor period he described is part of his larger theory of development, which, as we noted in Chapter 2, includes two additional major periods: concrete operations and formal operations. As you will recall, the period of concrete operations has two major subperiods: preoperations and concrete operations. The major periods differ from one another in the kinds of logical operations that the child uses to understand the world. The view that cognitive development proceeds as the child constructs a system for understanding the world and is not a simple consequence of the acquisition of new facts is one of Piaget's enduring contributions to developmental psychology.

THE GENERAL NATURE OF DEVELOPMENT IN INFANCY

During the first two years of life, Piaget contended, a child's knowledge of the world is limited to what he or she knows through perceptual awareness and motor acts (hence the term *sensorimotor period*). Piaget believed that the interaction between perceptual and motor skills provides the opportunities for cognitive growth at this age. Mikey Gordon, for instance, learns about the world by perceiving the effects of his motor actions. He grasps a sheet of paper and watches it wrinkle, thus learning that this object is flexible. He shakes the sheet and hears it rustle, thus learning that paper makes a faint, pleasant sound. Mikey's knowledge is growing through the interplay of action and perception. His thinking does not include language or abstract concepts. What Mikey knows and remembers is directly tied to what he can see, hear, feel, taste, and do.

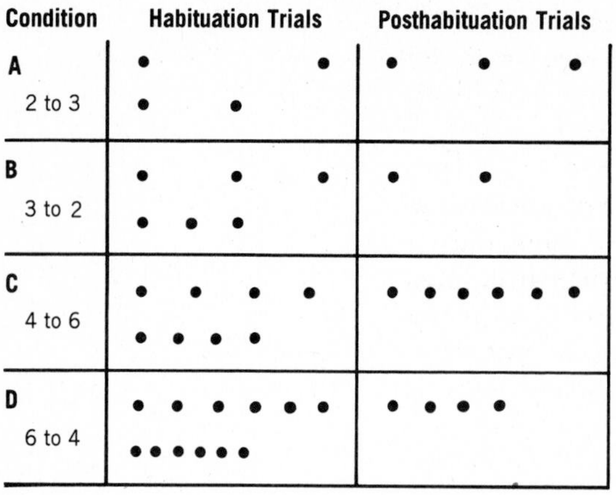

Condition	Habituation Trials	Posthabituation Trials
A 2 to 3	• • / • •	• • •
B 3 to 2	• • • / • • •	• •
C 4 to 6	• • • • / • • • •	• • • • • •
D 6 to 4	• • • • • • / • • • • • •	• • • •

Figure 6.3
Infant Memory for Numerical Information
In Starkey and Cooper's experiment, 6 to 8-month-olds increased their looking times on posthabituation trials in conditions A and B but not in conditions C and D. They could discriminate numerosities less than four but not greater.
Source: Starkey and Cooper, 1980.

Although not all developmentalists agree with Piaget's explanation of cognitive skills during the first two years of life, they do agree on the general character of the limitations during this period of development. For example, learning theorists characterize early development as associations between sensory input and motor responses (Kendler and Kendler, 1962). Similarly Fischer (1980), from a neo-Piagetian perspective (*neo* meaning "new"), and Case (1985), from more of an information-processing perspective, describe development during the first 18 months of life as limited by sensory and motor levels of knowledge. However much the infants' understanding of the world has progressed, it is still based largely on action, not reflection.

But even though a baby's knowledge is limited in this manner, a great deal of cognitive development occurs in the first two years. At birth Mikey had only his inborn reflexes. When the side of his face was gently stroked, for example, he automatically turned his head. Specific perceptions, in other words, triggered specific responses with no conscious intention on Mikey's part. When we see Mikey seven months later, the contrast is dramatic. He is purposefully reaching for and inspecting Becky's drawings, trying out various motor actions and observing the results. This is a good example of Piaget's view that infants are busy, active learners, trying to understand their world. At first, of course, the discoveries babies make occur by accident as they look around, move their limbs, manipulate parts of their bodies, and suck on what they can put into their mouths. Later discoveries become more intentional. Older infants deliberately try out actions and investigate their consequences. At all stages, however, children are active participants in the processes that lead to more mature cognitive skills.

When Piaget said that infants are active participants in their own cognitive development, he used the term *active* in two senses. First, the baby's participation is active in that it involves motor activity. Infants do not wait for things to happen to them. They do whatever they are capable of doing and perceive the results. Second, the baby's participation in cognitive development is also active because the infant must mentally construct an understanding of the world. Infants do not just passively absorb bits of information. Instead, they actively put together a rudimentary interpretation of how things in the world work.

What infants can learn from any particular experience depends on their current level of cognitive development. Similarly, Piaget proposed that older children are limited by their current level of cognitive development. Each major period and each stage within these periods can be characterized by the operations or logical structures that are available for understanding the world. Thus, Piaget considered development gradual and incremental because the logical structures used for understanding the world emerge over time. Piaget's belief that general logical structures limit understanding at each level of development is not shared by many other developmentalists. However, his view of infants and older children as active learners in the two senses described above is part of Piaget's theory that most developmentalists do share.

PROCESSES OF CHANGE

When Meryl had just turned 6 months old, Karen tried giving her a sip of milk from a cup. As the rim touched her lips, Meryl started sucking to draw the milk out. The liquid spilled down both sides of her chin. With practice, however, Meryl soon learned how to use her lips and tongue to drink successfully from a cup. In time she much preferred drinking from a cup than a bottle. Piaget would have said that Meryl's responses show two key mechanisms of development: adaptation and equilibration. The two account for developmental changes at every age.

To Piaget, **adaptation** is the process by which a person changes in order to function more effectively in a certain situation. This process is analogous to evolutionary adaptation, which we discussed in Chapters 1 and 4. In evolutionary adaptation, the traits of a species change in ways that improve its members' chances of survival. Piaget, of course, was talking about *individual* change, not change in an entire species. But like the evolutionists, he was interested in how behavior can be modified to better meet the challenges a person faces. You saw an example of Piaget's concept of adaptation when Meryl altered her style of drinking to get milk from a cup. Without this change in her behavior, she would continue to function poorly in this situation.

Meryl adapts not only in her actions but in her underlying thinking. For example, during her first year Meryl will acquire object permanence. Without this knowledge, her search for objects will be very inefficient; with it she will function much better in her environment. Piaget would have said that Meryl's thinking is adapting to the demands and realities of the world in which she lives.

But just because a skill or concept is useful does not mean it will be acquired through adaptation. Adaptation involves modifying some capability a person *already has* to make it more effective. Thus, Meryl adapts her sucking behaviors in learning to drink from a cup, and she adapts her new-found understanding that objects are permanent to include a sense of where to look if something suddenly "disappears." Because prerequisite capacities must be present if more advanced skills are to emerge, infants cannot learn many things. For instance, Mikey cannot yet learn to draw pictures like Becky's. He simply does not possess the prerequisite skills for this task. Just as evolution can occur only through change in existing genes, adaptation in a child can take place only by modifying what the youngster already knows and can do.

When sucking a new object, a baby has to adapt his or her sucking behaviors. The more different the objects that have been sucked, the more differentiated the baby's sucking skill becomes, and the less the baby has to adapt when new objects are sucked. *(Barbara Alper/ Stock, Boston.)*

We can more fully understand how adaptation works by considering its two subprocesses: assimilation and accommodation. As you learned in Chapter 2, **assimilation** is the process of applying an existing capability to various situations. For instance, when Meryl was first born, a nipple placed in her mouth was assimilated to her sucking reflex: She applied this innate, automatic response and obtained nourishment. Later when Meryl was presented with different kinds of objects (fingers, hands, toys, and so on), she learned that her sucking strategy had to be modified to suit different sizes and shapes. **Accommodation** is the process of making these modifications in order to continue dealing successfully with the world. Through accommodation Meryl gradually refined her genetically given reflex into different sucking patterns appropriate to different objects. Still later, when confronted with the challenge of learning to drink from a cup, Meryl had to accommodate again, modifying the movements of her lips and tongue so the liquid wouldn't spill. This skill now acquired, she is adapted for drinking from any cup.

As these examples of Meryl show, adaptation is always the joint product of assimilation and accommodation; They always occur together. During the first two years of life, assimilation and accommodation operate together to modify genetically given capabilities into a variety of sensory and motor skills that the baby applies to many situations. Thus, developmental change occurs at the level of mental structures that coordinate sensory and motor information. In later periods of development the same processes are at work, enlarging and refining the child's understanding of ideas and concepts, so development occurs at the level of mental structures that coordinate representations.

You have seen that adaptation results in a child's acquiring more and more sophisticated skills and complex understandings. What ensures that cognitive development moves in this forward direction? To Piaget, the answer is a mechanism called equilibration. **Equilibration** is a self-regulatory process that leads the child toward increasingly effective adaptations. For example, when Meryl sucked on the rim of a cup and the milk ran down her chin, her behavior was out of sync with the challenge she faced; she was in *disequilibrium*. As a result, she adjusted the movements of her tongue and lips to keep the milk from spilling. Gradually, through trial and error, she came closer and closer to the correct responses. When she finally succeeded, she had restored equilibrium between this aspect of the world and her strategy for dealing with it. Just as the test of a genetic adaptation is whether the species can better survive, so the test of a child's adaptation is whether he or she functions more effectively. Ideally, each change that is part of the process of equilibration decreases the size of any subsequent changes needed.

Equilibration is a mechanism that helps children effectively adapt the concepts and strategies they apply to *specific* situations. In addition, however, Piaget believed that children periodically undergo more fundamental changes in the structure of their thinking. With enough experience operating at a given cognitive level and with further maturation of the brain, children experience qualitatively new ways of thinking, ways that are more complex in organization than anything experienced before. **Reflective abstraction** is the mechanism in Piaget's theory that allows a more advanced level of thinking to emerge from skills at an earlier level. An example can be seen in Mikey's understanding of how to find his way around the house. At 7 months he begins crawling toward whatever captures his attention. Gradually he learns how to navigate from one place to another. However, the process of representing this knowledge in the form of a mental map of the house is a major step that Mikey has not yet taken. In this step Mikey must transform his sensorimotor understanding (in which he knows only by doing) into a representational understanding (in which his knowledge consists of a mental image). Piaget described this major step as requiring a reflective abstraction. Just like adaptation, reflective abstraction is a response to disequilibrium and is controlled by equilibration.

The processes for producing and controlling change are only one part of Piaget's theory. The other is the structures that are produced and changed. In infancy, these structures are called **schemes,** the mental structures that underlie and organize patterns of behavior. For example, there are sucking schemes, grasping schemes, and looking schemes. Schemes are an important component of Piaget's theory throughout development, although in later periods, Piaget frequently used the term *operations* rather than *schemes*. Schemes develop from the very primitive and limited behaviors known as reflexes. As infants interact with their environment, the schemes become more adapted to various situations. In stage 4 the infant becomes able to combine schemes to create even more elaborate organizations of behavior. Development through the six sensorimotor stages occurs as more complex and adapted schemes develop, with each successive stage representing a different and more advanced level in this development.

As Piaget developed his theory during his long professional life, certain characteristics of the theory changed. In his early work he believed that the structures that were produced during cognitive development were very general. For example, an infant who developed a new organization of looking, reaching, and then grasping could use this scheme in various circumstances. In addition, the structure required to integrate looking, reaching, and grasping into an effective sequence could organize other schemes like these three into similarly effective sequences. Because these abilities were very general, Piaget thought it reasonable to describe an infant as being at a particular stage of sensorimotor development. When evidence began to accumulate that an infant or child could be at different stages for different skills or abilities, Piaget at first elaborated his theory to accommodate such evidence while maintaining the general nature of cognitive structures. In the last ten years of his life, Piaget retreated somewhat from this position, although he never offered an explicit alternative. We shall see shortly that this is one area where the work of neo-Piagetians and information-processing theorists has gone further than Piaget's.

The schemes of the sensorimotor period are important in Piaget's theory in part because they make up the cognitive skills of infancy but also because they provide the basis for the skills in the later periods of development. Just as reflexes provide a starting point for the sensorimotor period, sensorimotor schemes provide the basis for the beginnings of representations that initiate the next major period.

Alternatives to Piaget's Theory

REASSESSING THE CONCEPT OF STAGES

Critics of Piaget's theory focus in part on his concept of developmental stages. For each of the six sensorimotor stages Piaget proposed, he offered detailed descriptions of how infants function when confronted by various tasks. Understanding the nature of objects is just one of these tasks. In addition, Piaget investigated the tasks of imitating others, of understanding cause and effect, of grasping spatial relationships, and so forth. He argued that if an infant is in a particular stage with respect to understanding objects, that baby should be in the same stage regarding other major tasks. Piaget reasoned that certain general cognitive advances characterize each stage and these general advances enable simultaneous progress in a number of different areas. Was Piaget correct in this assumption?

When Ina Uzgiris and J. McVicker Hunt (1975) tested a large number of infants at different stages of sensorimotor development, they found a great deal of inconsistency in what each baby had achieved. For instance, an infant might be at stage 4 regarding an understanding of objects but at stage 3 or 5 regarding other cognitive tasks. And no single ability seemed to develop in all infants first. One baby might be most advanced in imitative skills, another in understanding cause and effect, a third in grasping the concept of object permanence. Some researchers view this inconsistency as a major problem in Piaget's theory (Fischer, 1980; Gelman and Baillargeon, 1983). If it is a problem, it is one that Piaget was aware of. He called the phenomenon *decalage*, a French word that describes the unevenness in different areas of development. But he never adequately explained it and so has been subject to criticism.

The phenomenon of *decalage* has led many researchers to see cognitive development as partly the acquisition of *separate* skills and understandings. This view is especially characteristic of neo-Piagetians, who subscribe to Piaget's general approach but disagree with some specific aspects of his theory. Fischer (1980) argues that children do encounter *general* cognitive advances and constraints, like those Piaget described, but also advances and constraints related to *specific* areas. As a result, an infant's progress in mastering any particular cognitive task is partially independent of the child's progress in other tasks. A baby's understanding of objects, for instance, may be a stage or two ahead of that child's grasp of cause and effect. According to Fischer, however, these two cognitive developments are not *entirely* independent. Consequently, their developmental pace will never be more than a stage or two apart.

Theories differ as to the sequence in which infants will exhibit specific behaviors, such as reaching and grasping, and the developments that enable a child to move on to more complex behaviors. *(George Ancona/ International Stock Photo.)*

Robert McCall and his colleagues have studied interrelations among skills during infancy, and their findings support Fischer's view (McCall, 1979). McCall uses the word *skill* because he analyzes infant development in terms of what infants can accomplish with their behaviors. In the first two months of life, a set of skills controlled by the baby's state can be observed. For example, when infants are in either awake state (awake and active or awake and quiet), they will reflexively look at high-contrast stimuli, will visually track slow-moving objects, and will become more alert if a new sound is heard. In the period from 2 to 7 months of age, infants acquire skills that produce direct perceptual consequences—for example, shaking a rattle to hear the sound. During the period from 7 to 13 months, goal-oriented skills, such as picking up a blanket to retrieve an object underneath it, emerge. Finally, in the period after 13 months, representational skills, such as linking a name with an object, develop. McCall found that at the beginning of each period, not all the skills expected to emerge do so immediately. Instead, particular skills take time to develop, and babies differ as to which skills they acquire first (McCall, Eichorn, and Hogarty, 1977). According to McCall, development from one stage to the next occurs when some important new capacity is acquired. The new capacity allows infants to overcome previous obstacles or constraints in the development of skills, but specific experience is still required for the development of particular skills.

COGNITIVE CONSTRAINTS IN INFANCY: FISCHER AND CASE

What kind of constraint could control the acquisition of various cognitive skills? Several developmentalists have suggested that limitations in the information-processing capacity of infants and children could produce limits on the sequence and rate of their cognitive development. As early as 1894, James Mark Baldwin proposed the concept of **attention span,** a limit on the number of mental elements that could be considered at any one time (Case, 1985). The neo-Piagetian Juan Pascual-Leone (1970, 1976) proposed a related concept, **mental power,** often called "M-power" or "M-space." He analyzed some of the skills that Piaget had studied in terms of the amount of mental power they required. In this book we will refer to this limited information-processing capacity as **working memory** to separate it from the claims of any specific theory. To find a hidden toy, imitate an action, or apply a familiar strategy to a new situation, an infant must use this working memory to remember objects and to initiate and control behaviors. If a baby's working memory becomes temporarily "filled" before a task is finished, the child faces a kind of information overload that stymies further progress.

Both Baldwin and Pascual-Leone believed that working memory increases with age and maturation of the cortex of the brain. According to this view, as the size of working memory gradually increases, the child is able to master more complex skills. Alternatively, with repeated practice, a child may start to perform a new skill as one large "chunk" of behavior rather than as a series of related but separate tasks. As a result, performing that skill no longer exceeds the capacity of working memory, and the child readily masters it (Case, 1985; Shatz, 1978). The skill then becomes a building block for acquiring other abilities because the child can use it and still have room left over in working memory.

To better understand how limitations on working memory might account for stages of cognitive development, consider Fischer's description of development (Fischer and Lazerson, 1984). At the first of his four levels of cognitive development, the baby is restricted to performing single actions. At his second level, the infant can carry out related actions. This, in turn, is followed by the ability to coordinate several actions into a more complex system, with each cognitive level providing the building blocks for the next. At first, you'll recall, Meryl can only reach her hand toward the TV plug, not reach *and* grasp it. Later she can coordinate reaching *and* grasping, and still later she coordinates knocking away the dog with both reaching and grasping, performing an integrated system of behaviors. Finally, Meryl, like all other children, reaches the stage of forming single mental representations. She can create a mental image of the TV plug even when it is not in view. When Meryl initially reaches a new level, she remains there for some time. Perhaps this is because performing a new ability requires the entire capacity of her working memory. As working memory grows or as the ability becomes more practiced and automatic and its cognitive demands decrease, the freed space in working memory allows for further advances.

Case (1985) presents an important new working memory theory. His term for working memory is **executive processing space.** Some consider Case's theory an information-processing theory of development (Siegler, 1986), although Case presents himself as a neo-Piagetian in many ways. The theories of Piaget and Case are similar in that they characterize development as a set of increasingly sophisticated mental structures, they examine development across a broad number of tasks, and they view infancy as a sequence of stages. However, for Piaget, development consists of acquiring logical operations that are relatively independent of specific tasks, whereas for Case development is acquiring specific skills for operating in particular contexts.

Case recognizes the problems inherent in his theory that cognitive development consists of the acquisition and integration of a set of specific capabilities. If development consists of the acquisition of specific skills that build on one another, what limits the rate of development so that almost all individuals fall in the same general pattern over an 18-year period? If the prerequisite skills have been learned, why aren't the skills that depend on them immediately acquired? A second related problem is the frequently found ineffectiveness of instruction to speed development substantially. Finally, the parallel development of different specific skills poses problems. If development consists of the acquisition of specific, separate, and unrelated skills be

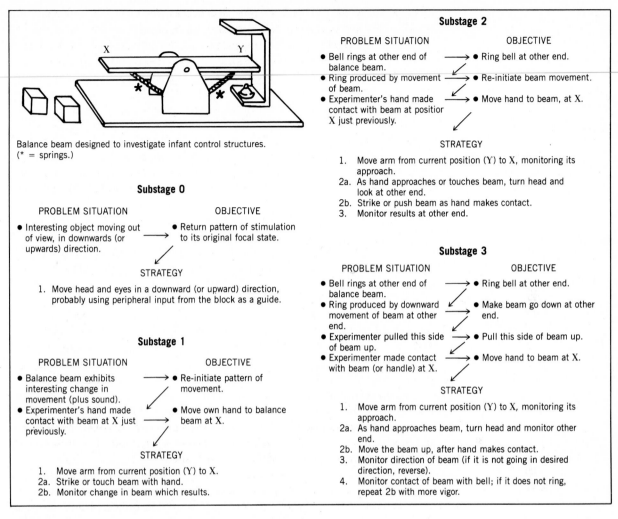

Balance beam designed to investigate infant control structures.
(* = springs.)

Substage 0

PROBLEM SITUATION	OBJECTIVE
• Interesting object moving out of view, in downwards (or upwards) direction.	⟶ • Return pattern of stimulation to its original focal state.

STRATEGY

1. Move head and eyes in a downward (or upward) direction, probably using peripheral input from the block as a guide.

Substage 1

PROBLEM SITUATION	OBJECTIVE
• Balance beam exhibits interesting change in movement (plus sound).	⟶ • Re-initiate pattern of movement.
• Experimenter's hand made contact with beam at X just previously.	⟶ • Move own hand to balance beam at X.

STRATEGY

1. Move arm from current position (Y) to X.
2a. Strike or touch beam with hand.
2b. Monitor change in beam which results.

Substage 2

PROBLEM SITUATION	OBJECTIVE
• Bell rings at other end of balance beam.	⟶ • Ring bell at other end.
• Ring produced by movement of beam.	⟶ • Re-initiate beam movement.
• Experimenter's hand made contact with beam at position X just previously.	⟶ • Move hand to beam, at X.

STRATEGY

1. Move arm from current position (Y) to X, monitoring its approach.
2a. As hand approaches or touches beam, turn head and look at other end.
2b. Strike or push beam as hand makes contact.
3. Monitor results at other end.

Substage 3

PROBLEM SITUATION	OBJECTIVE
• Bell rings at other end of balance beam.	⟶ • Ring bell at other end.
• Ring produced by downward movement of beam at other end.	⟶ • Make beam go down at other end.
• Experimenter pulled this side of beam up.	⟶ • Pull this side of beam up.
• Experimenter made contact with beam (or handle) at X.	⟶ • Move hand to beam at X.

STRATEGY

1. Move arm from current position (Y) to X, monitoring its approach.
2a. As hand approaches beam, turn head and monitor other end.
2b. Move the beam up, after hand makes contact.
3. Monitor direction of beam (if it is not going in desired direction, reverse).
4. Monitor contact of beam with bell; if it does not ring, repeat 2b with more vigor.

Figure 6.4
Case's Four Stages in Infant Response to a Balance Beam
In substage 0, infants visually track a block moving up and down on the balance beam. In substage 1, they imitate an adult's action that makes the balance beam move. In substage 2, they move the balance beam in order to make a bell ring, thus showing purposeful means-end behavior. In substage 3, they show that they understand the relationship that when one end goes down, the other goes up.
Source: Case, 1985.

acquired at approximately the same time by most individuals? To explain these findings, Case proposes that growth in processing capacity is a consequence of both biological and experiential factors. Our common biological heritage as a species is the reason that normal individuals develop according to the same general time table; but individual developmental variations, such as the early ability to perform a specific skill, can be altered by experiential factors. Both biological and experiential factors influence the efficiency with which the executive processing space can be used but do not influence its total capacity.

The four stages of infant cognitive development that Case proposes are illustrated in Figure 6.4. This figure shows infants' responses to the balance beam at the top of the figure and Case's analysis of these responses. In each of the four situations, an adult performed an action on the balance beam and then the infant was allowed to respond. The purpose of this figure is to show the increasingly complex cognitive processing that occurs within infancy and to illustrate Case's system of analyzing infants' cognitive activities.

Working memory theories of constraints on cognitive development seem plausible, but they have not been widely accepted. One reason is that researchers have not in general been able to measure either the capacity of working memory in infants or infants' ability to "chunk" pieces of information. Instead, supporters are simply *hypothesizing* changes in the size or use of working memory to account for the diminishing cognitive limitations observed as babies grow older. More experimental results are needed to test whether infant working memory capacity does increase. Without compelling evidence to support working memory theories, researchers continue to pursue other approaches.

THE APPROACH OF JEROME BRUNER

One approach that has had a substantial impact on our understanding of cognitive development over the last 20 years is that of cognitive psychologist Jerome Bruner. Bruner (Bruner, Olver, and Greenfield, 1966) has offered a general model of cognitive development through childhood. In contrast to Piaget's focus on the development of increasingly mature cognitive structures (ways of thinking that organize the child's behaviors), Bruner focuses on how children's representations of the world change. Infants are limited to the first mode of representation that Bruner proposes, the **enactive mode.** Enactive representations of objects and events are associated with motor acts. Thus, like Piaget, Bruner emphasizes the role of motor activity in cognitive development in infancy. However, unlike Piaget, Bruner thinks even newborns have a rudimentary way of representing their environment.

Bruner's studies of infant development have focused on the acquisition of specific skills. To Bruner, a skill is any goal-oriented activity consisting of sequentially organized actions (Bruner, 1970, 1973, 1983). Note that Bruner attributes rudimentary *intentions* to infants right from the start, whereas Piaget contended that intentions do not develop until a baby is about 8 months of age. In Bruner's theory, infants also come equipped with an innate set of action patterns (looking, grasping, sucking, and so forth). These action patterns are the building blocks out of which skills are constructed. Infants must learn to assemble these action patterns in appropriate ways so that they may interact with their environment skillfully. For example, young infants frequently close their hand when reaching for an object before they are in contract with the object. They must learn to reach first and then grasp.

Bruner believes that infants are motivated to engage in **mastery play.** They shake, bang, and suck on objects to discover their properties; they take things apart and try to put them back together, all in an effort to learn how to master the environment. According to Bruner, this mastery play provides critical feedback that enables babies to acquire skills.

In contrast to Piaget, then, Bruner endows the young infant with representations, goals, and intentions that Piaget contended develop during the course of the sensorimotor period, and he does not propose an invariant stage theory of infant development. But like Piaget, Bruner stresses the role of action in infants' cognitive advancements and the role of intrinsic motivation in infants' learning about their environment.

ADVANCES AND LIMITATIONS: AN OVERVIEW

In this chapter you have learned that as infants grow older their cognitive capacities change dramatically. From initially being limited to a set of inborn responses, babies develop an increasingly refined understanding of the world they live in and an ever greater purposefulness to their behavior. These developmental trends are very important both in their own right and as preparation for the verbal world of the toddler.

You have also learned that infants take an active role in influencing their own development. Through their efforts at mastery and the "mistakes" they make in the process, they learn to adapt their actions to better suit environmental demands. What babies learn also is influenced by the concepts they form to help make sense of their experiences. These concepts, in turn, are products of children's daily interactions with objects and other people.

But though children acquire many abilities during infancy, this is also a time of significant limitations. Babies cannot learn many of the things that older children can, no matter how much training adults give them. Developmentalists may dispute the reasons for these constraints on an infant's cognitive attainments, but none deny that they exist. Discovering how cognitive constraints affect a baby's view of the world remains a challenging task for developmentalists.

Chapter Review

1. Developmentalists are in general agreement concerning the broad course of cognitive development in infancy. But descriptions of the number of stages and criteria used in defining them may vary. Piaget identified six stages in what he called the **sensorimotor period.** He argued that these stages are invariant: All children go through them in the same order, even though their rates of progress may differ. In stage 1 (birth to 1 month), cognitive development is limited to minor refinements of the baby's inborn reflexes. In stage 2 (1 to 4 months), primary circular reactions emerge. A **circular reaction** involves a behavior that produces an observable event that leads to the behavior's being repeated. A **primary circular reaction** is one that involves only a person's own body. In stage 3 (4 to 8 months), **secondary circular reactions emerge.** Now infants investigate the effects their actions have on external objects. In stage 4 (8 to 12 months), babies begin to coordinate their actions into **goal-directed chains** of behavior. This is the first clear sign of purposefulness in infants. In stage 5 (12 to 18 months), **tertiary circular reactions** appear. Babies intentionally *vary* a behavior that produces an interesting consequence so as to further explore the cause-and-effect connections.

Finally, in stage 6 (18 to 24 months), representational thought begins to emerge. Children are now able to have in mind mental images that stand for actual behaviors.

2. One focus of studies of early cognitive development has been on how babies come to understand that objects still exist even though they disappear from sight. This is called the concept of **object permanence.** Piaget argued that this concept emerges in stage 4, when babies begin to search for things that become hidden from view. Such searching indicates they know the objects still exist somewhere. However, not until stage 6 do infants have a mature understanding of objects. At this stage they can imagine an object moving even though they do not see it move. Contemporary research suggests that while Piaget was correct in his description of the general pattern of development of the object concept, he may have been wrong in some of his ideas about why babies make certain "mistakes" with regard to objects.

3. The study of early cognitive development has also focused on memory development. We know that even newborns must have some kind of memory judging from their ability to habituate to stimuli. Still not clear is how long their memories last. Studies suggest that when babies forget things previously learned, the problem sometimes lies in lack of appropriate cues to help retrieve those memories. By the second half-year, many signs indicate that babies are forming quite permanent long-term memories. At this stage they also start to remember things in categories, and they begin to perceive and remember small numerosities. These are both important advances toward a more mature understanding of the world.

4. Explaining cognitive development has proved more difficult than describing it. The central problems are explaining how and why movement from one level to the next occurs and why various capacities tend to move forward together.

5. In Piaget's view, cognitive development both within and between periods occurs because of two key processes: adaptation and equilibration. **Adaptation** is the process by which a person changes an existing way of thinking or behaving in order to function more effectively in a given situation. Adaptation involves two subprocesses: **assimilation** and **accommodation.** When children assimilate, they apply an existing capability in various circumstances. When children accommodate, they modify a strategy so as to continue dealing successfully with the world. **Equilibration** is the overall self-regulatory process that leads toward increasingly effective adaptations.

6. Critics of Piaget agree with his view of the infant as an active learner and with his emphasis on the role of action. Disagreements center on his concept of developmental stages, especially on his assumption that general cognitive advances at each stage allow simultaneous progress in a number of different areas. There is inconsistency as to when various cognitive skills emerge in relation to others. Many contemporary researchers have therefore argued that cognitive development is partly the acquisition of *separate* skills and understandings.

7. Important alternatives to Piaget's view are the cognitive developmental theories of Kurt Fischer, Robbie Case, and Jerome Bruner. Instead of focusing on the emergence of increasingly mature cognitive structures as Piaget did, Fischer emphasizes advances and constraints in *specific* areas of cognitive development, and Case stresses the role of **executive processing space** as underlying cognitive limitations. Bruner focuses on how children's representations of the world change. In recent years Bruner has become especially interested in how infants acquire specific skills or goal-oriented behaviors. According to him, infants are motivated to engage in **mastery play,** which provides critical feedback-enabling skills to emerge.

8. Despite notable advances in all spheres of cognitive development in infancy, infants have limitations. Infants' knowledge of the world is limited to what they can directly perceive and do. They are not yet able to manipulate mental images as preschool children can. By the end of infancy they can begin to let one thing stand for or *represent* another, which is the beginning of symbolic thought.

9. In summarizing cognitive development in the first two years of life, three general themes stand out. First, a baby's present abilities pave the way for future accomplishments. The reflexive skills of the newborn, for instance, provide the building blocks for later, more advanced abilities. Second, all infants are active participants in their own development. By seeking out new experiences and trying to master their environment, they give themselves opportunities to grow cognitively. During infancy children gradually become increasingly purposeful. From the newborn who has no conscious intentions emerges the older baby who deliberately tries to produce consequences. Third, infant cognitive development is marked by both advances and limitations. Although children acquire numerous abilities during their first two years, many things remain beyond their understanding.

7

Infant Social Development

One day when Mikey Gordon was 4 months old, he woke up early from his morning nap. Cooing contentedly to himself, he began kicking his legs. The toys on his crib gym jangled, and he kicked some more. Then he waved his arms and batted a bright red ring, gurgling happily as it bobbed in response. Christine arrived and stood by the crib, smiling down at the baby. Mikey's face brightened. He broke into a broad grin and kicked his feet harder. "That's right!" Christine said. "Here's your mommy to get you! Yes I am. I'm gonna get you." Then leaning slowly toward him with her index fingers extended she repeated the words in a drawn out fashion: "Iiiiii'm goooonna getchu!" tickling Mikey's ribs on the last syllable. He chortled in glee. Anyone watching would have no doubt of the special relationship developing between them.

This chapter is about the emergence of a child's first social relationships, particularly the close partnerships that form with the principal care givers. Such partnerships are the culmination of all social and emotional development in the first year of life. To become a social partner a baby must first achieve a certain amount of internal regulation—organized patterns of sleeping and eating and increased periods of alert wakefulness

Six-month-old infants will laugh in response to vigorous stimulation. *(Jean-Claude Lejeune/Stock, Boston.)*

during which the child is open to stimulation. The baby must also be attracted to social encounters; human faces and voices must engage the child's interest. With development, the infant must learn to sustain attention, to follow complex changes in a person's voice and face. In addition, the infant must learn to tolerate the excitement caused by social stimulation. Soon the baby begins to go beyond reacting to others; the coordinated turn-taking of true social interaction emerges. Mikey smiles and kicks his feet, and his mother talks and touches in return. Mikey chortles and kicks again, and his mother smiles and touches him some more.

For a true attachment to form to the care giver, as distinct from other people, the baby must learn to differentiate persons. Mikey, for instance, must do more than simply recognize his mother; he must understand that she is a specific, "constant" person. This understanding is related to the concept of object permanence we discussed in Chapter 6, a concept that emerges in the second half-year. By the time Mikey is 8 or 10 months old he will show his understanding that Christine is a constant, differentiated person by becoming distressed when she temporarily leaves him with someone else. He will know that his mother still exists even when out of sight, and he will want her *specifically*. As you learned in Chapter 6, the second half year is also the time babies develop both expectations and purposefulness. The 8-month-old is surprised when an object "magically" vanishes, angry when an intended action is thwarted, and joyous when a goal is achieved. Events and feelings are now intimately connected; perception, cognition, and emotion are all integrated (Sroufe, 1979a). Experiences are categorized partly by the emotions associated with them. A 10-month-old, for example, may react negatively to a physician *immediately* upon sight, evaluating that doctor in terms of the feelings he generated in the past.

The attachment between infant and care giver develops in the context of this differentiating emotional and social world. By the end of the first year, infants feel secure in the presence of their care givers, turn to them purposefully when distressed, and organize play and exploration around them. The care givers take center-stage in the child's world and provide the basis for many of the baby's expectations about the environment.

In this chapter we will trace the infant's emerging capacity for social relations from the very first weeks of life. How does a newborn, with only primitive reflexes, develop into an active social partner who can anticipate another's actions, respond to social overtures, and even purposefully direct social give-and-take? The answer lies in a developmental process that we will explore in our first major section. In our second major section we will consider social development in the second half-year. How does the infant acquire a specific attachment to the principal care giver, and what influences the quality of this important early relationship? Finally, in our third major section, we turn to the overall importance of quality care. What problems are associated with inadequate care during infancy, and what environmental factors tend to promote these problems? Equally important, how resilient are children in overcoming any negative effects of poor-quality care giving?

DEVELOPMENT IN THE FIRST HALF-YEAR

In the last two decades researchers have been probing the competencies of the newborn. This subject has produced two extreme viewpoints: one historical, the other recent. The historical view is closely associated with the nineteenth-century psychologist William James. James believed that human babies are born with no perceptual or social skills whatsoever. Their world is meaningless and chaotic, a "blooming, buzzing confusion." Directly opposing this outlook is the more recent view that newborns are socially quite advanced, able to imitate complex behaviors, to infer another person's perspective, and to feel disappointment when social expectations aren't met (Meltzoff and Moore, 1977; Trevarthan, 1977; Tronick et al., 1978). This view, in short, sees even very young infants as possessing desires, expectations, purpose, and even will.

From a developmental perspective neither of these views is satisfactory. The first raises the problem of how to get something from nothing, and it is at odds with much contemporary research. The second view, while a useful antidote to the first, also runs counter to some important current findings. For instance, the cortex of a baby's brain, which is used for thinking and reasoning, is not fully functional at birth. Interconnections among cortical neurons are not well established, making it hard to imagine how a baby could possess expectations and purpose (Ellingson, 1967; Salapatek and Banks, 1967; Spitz, Emde, and Metcalf, 1970). Moreover, we need not assume that newborns are socially competent in order to account for some of the things they soon become able to do. All we need to assume is that their simpler capacities prepare or "preadapt" them to become part of a social system under normal care-giving circumstances.

The care giver's response to the newborn's cry begins a pattern of communication that will be refined over time. *(Don Mason/West Stock.)*

The Newborn as Preadapted

In the modern developmental perspective, newborns are seen as coming equipped with certain predispositions that enable them to participate in early social exchanges, provided they are part of a responsive care-giving system (Ainsworth and Bell, 1974; Sander, 1975). These predispositions are what we mean when we say that the newborn is *preadapted* to becoming social. But note that a certain developmental context is needed for this social potential to unfold, much as the turning on of genes in certain cells depended on surrounding cells during prenatal development (see Chapter 4). If care givers provide the baby with appropriate stimulation and are responsive to the child's inborn reactions, then, and only then, will coordinated social exchanges be possible, exchanges that will ultimately lead to genuine social partnerships.

What are the newborn's predispositions that make these developments possible? One is a built-in ability to "signal" psychological and physiological needs in ways that adults can interpret and are likely to respond to. These early signals take the form of the newborn's lusty cries. Babies cry whenever their nervous systems are overly excited, whether that overexcitement is due to hunger, cold, pain, or simply too much stimulation (a loud noise, for example, or even excessive touching and patting). Note that the newborn's cries are purely reflexive, much as you shiver when you are cold. Young babies do not cry to be defiant or to "get their way." They are not capable of formulating any particular goal. An infant's cry is involuntary, not intentional. Nevertheless, it becomes the precursor of a true social signal when caring adults respond by administering to the baby's needs. This is a subtle but important point: A newborn's behaviors serve the function of social communication only to the extent that others think of those behaviors in that way (Newson, 1974).

In addition to the predisposition to draw attention to their own needs, newborns also have a built-in inclination to be attracted to social stimuli. For instance, as discussed in Chapter 5, the newborn's visual system is designed in such a way that the baby is naturally attentive to light/dark contrasts and to movement (Haith, 1966; Salapatek and Banks, 1967). Since adult faces have several light/dark contrasts and adults tend to smile and nod when looking at a baby, a newborn is innately drawn to faces. This attraction does not occur because the baby recognizes the social significance of faces, but simply because the child's visual system is especially sensitive to the kind of stimulation that faces provide. The newborn's inspection of faces is further encouraged by the fact that care givers tend to hold their heads about eight inches away from a baby's when interacting face-to-face. As you learned in Chapter 5, this distance is completely congruent with a newborn's visual acuity (Haynes, White, and Held, 1965).

In a strikingly parallel way, newborns are also predisposed to respond to human speech. Not only can babies discriminate among different speech sounds at a very early age, but they can also hear quite well in the pitch range of human voices, including the squeaky baby-talk voice used by many mothers (Eisenberg et al., 1964; Moffitt, 1971). Newborns also have built-in coordination between their hearing and their head movements. This causes them to turn automatically in the direction of a voice and look at the face of the person who is speaking to them.

Another predisposition that helps the newborn become part of a social system is the baby's tendency to "fall in step" with the care giver's behavior. As an illustration, consider a study in which babies soon to be given up for adoption were cared for 24 hours a day by one of two nurses, Nurse A or Nurse B (Sander et al., 1972). Compared with Nurse B, Nurse A did not respond as quickly to her babies' cries of distress, but when she did respond her caretaking was less hurried and less perfunctory. Within ten days, the infants in her charge were more regular in their sleeping and eating patterns than those cared for by Nurse B. The behavior of Nurse A's babies, in other words, seemed to mirror her own easygoing style. Even more striking, when the infants were suddenly switched from one nurse to the other, they showed marked disruptions in sleeping and eating. Apparently, babies have a built-in inclination to adapt to the kind of care they receive.

Louis Sander (1975) and others who have conducted such studies argue that this adaptation is an early form of learning, which involves a contingency between the babies' distress and the care giver's intervention. On a very rudimentary level, the infants are detecting a connection between their cries and the results that follow (see Chapter 6). This sensitivity to relationships between their own behavior and effects in the environment preadapts infants to become part of a social system. Again we see a predisposition of great importance to social development, even though that predisposition is not in itself social.

What we observe in a newborn baby, then, is a range of tendencies and abilities that prepare the child to enter rapidly the social world. Yet if you ask whether the newborn is innately social, the answer would have to be no—not in the sense of organized, intentional interaction with others. The newborn, however, is exquisitely attuned to *becoming* social, provided that responsive social partners are available. How this true social give-and-take develops is the subject we turn to next.

The Origins of Reciprocity

Over the first few months of life, developmental changes take place that set the stage for the emergence of true social interactions involving mutual exchanges, or *reciprocity*, between the partners. One of the developmental changes underlying reciprocity is the baby's ability to stay alert for increasingly longer periods, during which he or she actively engages the environment. At the same time, the infant becomes able to control attention, coordinate looking and reaching, and turn toward or away from stimulation *voluntarily*. Coupled with this is the baby's ability to punctuate attentive looking with smiles, coos, and motor actions. Parents take advantage of these newfound capacities to build longer and more complex chains of interactions with their infants. Consider this example of Christine Gordon interacting with Mikey when he is 5 months old:

> Hi there, little guy. Whatcha lookin' at? Can you look at me? That's right. Hey! Momma's gonna get ya. Yes she is. (Brief pause.) Momma's gonna get ya and

By 6 months of age, infants can coordinate their looking and reaching, making interaction with their care givers possible. *(Elizabeth Crews/Stock, Boston.)*

gobble ya right up. What do you think of that? Come on. Come on, you little dickens. Let me see those gums. Hmmm? (Pause.) Yeah, that's right . . . that's right. (Mikey smiles broadly and bobs his head. His mother responds in kind.) Well, now, are ya gonna say somethin'? Are ya? (Another pause during which Christine nods her head and widens her eyes.) Come on! (She pauses again, and Mikey starts cycling his arms and kicking his feet.) Come oooon! (Longer pause. Then Mikey gurgles happily.) Yeah, that's right! (Christine's smile broadens and she laughs.)

Notice how Christine stages or "frames" this interaction. First she waits for a time when Mikey seems receptive. Then she creates a proper climate for him to respond by beginning with gentle vocal and visual stimulation. Next she builds Mikey's interest by varying the stimulation and gradually increasing its intensity. She takes cues from Mikey about the timing of her words and actions. Equally important, she pauses often and waits for Mikey's responses, thus creating opportunities for him to take his turn in the shared "dialogue." Berry Brazelton, who has studied such mother-infant dialogues extensively, sees the mother as providing a "holding" framework for the baby. She holds the infant with her hands, her eyes, her voice, her smile, and with changes from one form of stimulation to another. "All these holding experiences are opportunities for the infant to learn how to contain himself, how to control motor responses, how to attend for longer and longer periods. They amount to a kind of learning about organization of behavior in order to attend" (Brazelton, Kowslowski, and Main, 1974).

The mutual joy at the end of exchanges between care givers and infants appears to be the goal toward which the sequence is organized (Stern, 1974). Infants can play their part and share in the joyful outcome only if care givers appropriately guide the interaction (Hayes, 1984; Kaye,

1982). In our example, Christine must allow the level of tension to rise and fall in its natural course until the joy spills over. She cannot *force* interactions on Mikey when he is unreceptive. If Mikey temporarily looks away to slow the pace of the stimulation, Christine cannot pursue him or else he is likely to cry. She must wait for him to indicate his readiness to continue. Only if the pair stays in synchrony is the joyful outcome possible.

Christine's role in such interactions is clearly quite complex. She must call forth and enhance Mikey's attention and involvement, pacing and modifying the stimulation in coordination with signs from him. Daniel Stern (1977) and Mary Ainsworth call this process "attunement." It is part of a more general style of behavior known as **sensitive care** (Ainsworth et al., 1978). Sensitive care involves being aware of a baby's feelings and needs and responding to them promptly and effectively. Sensitive care is something that can be learned in the natural course of tending to a baby. Through hours of interaction most parents become able to read the moods and signals of their infant and modify their own behavior accordingly. At its best, this coordinated interaction has the grace of a dance in which each partner's movements influence the other's.

How long does it take to develop this intricate, coordinated interaction? Surprisingly, the beginnings can be seen in the first few weeks. Consider the feeding of a newborn, for instance. As we mentioned in Chapter 5, the newborn's sucking is organized into a "burst-pause" pattern: a succession of rapid sucks followed by a period during which little or no sucking occurs. Lower brain regions control this pattern; the baby does not intentionally produce it. Yet mothers often interpret the pause as a cue to respond by stroking, cuddling, or talking to the infant (Kaye and Wells, 1980). In this way, a kind of turn-taking emerges: The baby sucks, then pauses; next the mother talks and moves; then the baby starts sucking again. The mother is behaving as if the baby's pauses were intended to elicit some response. In fact, this is only a "pseudo-dialogue" (Schaffer, 1979). The mother is single-handedly orchestrating the pattern by timing her own behavior to the baby's sucking reflex. In the process, however, she is initiating her child into the turn-taking characteristic of human communication.

Soon the baby's involvement in social encounters becomes more complex. By age 3 or 4 months infants have acquired many behaviors that can be used in interactions—everything from smiles and other facial expressions to a rich range of coos, gurgles, and sounds. Even more important, babies this age have very mature control over their head movements, thus giving them substantial influence over the type of stimulation they pay attention to and its pacing (Stern, 1977). When social overtures are dull and repetitive and the child's arousal level falls too low, he or she typically will search for something more interesting to look at. On the other hand, when social overtures become too arousing, a baby typically will turn away as if to reduce the stimulation temporarily, or perhaps to process it. Ideally, the care giver is sensitive to such cues from the infant for more or less stimulation, or for stimulation of a different kind. The baby, in short, has a "voice" in how the interaction unfolds.

But despite this greater participation on the infant's part, the turn-taking is still orchestrated by the care giver, as you saw in the earlier

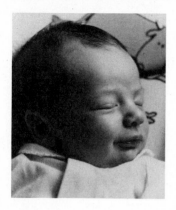

Infant sleep smile. *(T. Hop-mann.)*

dialogue between Christine and Mikey. It will take several more months for Mikey to anticipate Christine's actions, and more time still for him to deliberately seek out certain responses. True reciprocity is learned gradually, with each advancement setting the stage for another one. The process is analogous to teaching Ping-Pong to a child (Sroufe and Ward, 1984). First you simply hit the ball right to the child's paddle so that it can be "hit" back without much active involvement by the child. The child's shots may go anywhere, and you must adjust and recenter. At this stage, it is your job alone to keep the ball moving and to maintain the appearance of a game. Next you encourage the child to start to swing the paddle and gradually to learn how to aim the ball. In time the youngster is a full participant in the give-and-take. So it goes with the development of reciprocity. Over the first year of life the infant gradually becomes a true partner in social interactions.

Becoming an Active Participant: The Example of Social Smiling

The emergence of reciprocity that we have been describing is typical of how social skills emerge in a baby's earliest months. In the beginning an infant does not consciously seek out social interaction. The child is merely attracted to certain patterns of stimulation. A picture of a scrambled face draws no more or less attention than one of a normal face (Salapatek and Banks, 1967). To a newborn only the lines and contrasts are of interest; the picture itself has no meaning. From these rudimentary beginnings how does the child develop into a purposeful, social being? Part of the answer lies in the care giver's responses to the baby. What the newborn pays attention to and how the child behaves normally prompt adults to provide stimulation that leads the infant toward more focused and organized interaction. Since this interaction is pleasurable, it tends to be repeated. Gradually, the care giver provides richer stimulation and encourages more of the baby's participation. Ultimately, in a spiraling fashion, a genuine social partnership develops.

An excellent example of this developmental process can be seen in the emergence of a baby's social smiling. Imagine Christine in the hospital soon after Mikey is born. She has just finished nursing him, and as he drifts off to sleep the corners of his mouth twist up in a tiny smile. Christine is elated. She is sure that Mikey is "telling her" that he is warm, full, and content. Like Christine, many parents attribute to very young infants emotions such as joy, anger, fear, and surprise (Emde, 1985).

Technically Christine's interpretation is not correct. Newborn smiles do not really indicate pleasure; they are due merely to spontaneous discharge in lower brain regions. How do researchers know this? One clue is that newborns smile almost solely during sleep (Emde and Koenig, 1969). If their smiles were a sign of pleasure, why don't they occur when infants are wide awake as well? Other evidence comes from the study of premature infants and of those born without a cerebral cortex (the part of the brain that controls higher mental activities). The typical newborn smile is more common in these babies than it is in normal youngsters (Emde, Gaensbauer, and Harmon, 1976). This observation suggests the involvement of lower brain regions, as does the fact that in normal babies

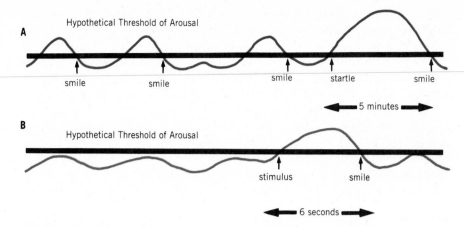

Figure 7.1
Hypothetical Threshold of Arousal
The newborn's smiles during sleep are due to fluctuations in central nervous system arousal or excitation. These may occur spontaneously, as is shown in part (A), when the infant's depth of sleep changes. Notice that following a startle reaction, it is some time before the excitation falls below the arousal threshold and the smile recurs. Sleep smiles may also occur following stimulation, as shown in part (B). Here a rattle is shaken, and six seconds later a smile occurs.

the newborn sleep smile disappears as the cortex matures (Spitz et al., 1970).

You may wonder what happens in lower brain regions during sleep to cause the newborn smile. The answer seems to be a temporary rise above, followed by a drop below, some critical threshold of arousal, thus causing the facial muscles to relax into a little smile (see Figure 7.1). In keeping with this theory, a newborn who is sleeping lightly will tend to smile some five to eight seconds after you gently shake a rattle. It takes time for the newborn's arousal level to rise slightly and then fall, bringing on the smile. Also, if you gently shake the sleeping baby toward wakefulness, you will get a series of these little smiles. Finally, if you startle a sleeping newborn, causing the arousal level to shoot up, no sleep smiles occur for quite some time. All this suggests that arousal fluctuations around some low threshold are what cause the newborn's smiles (Sroufe and Waters, 1976).

Even though Christine is mistaken in the meaning she gives to Mikey's first smiles, these winsome little expressions strike a chord within her, drawing her closer to the baby. Over the next few weeks Mikey will begin to smile when he is awake, as Christine talks to him, nuzzles him, and gently claps his hands together. She will spend quite a bit of time engaged with him, partly because his smiling and cooing is so rewarding to her (Stern, 1974). As most parents do, she will interpret her baby's behavior as more advanced and "intelligent" than it really is. For instance, at 5 weeks when Mikey grins and coos as Christine chirps at him, she assumes it is because he has a special "liking" for her voice. In fact, any gentle stimulation (music boxes, bells tingling on his crib) can produce the proper degree of excitation to elicit a smile (Emde and Koenig, 1969; Wolff, 1963). But soon her voice will be special to him.

This 7-week-old shows a broad, active smile in response to stimulation by a care giver. *(Tom Sheridan/ Monkmeyer Press.)*

At 8 to 10 weeks Mikey begins to smile when Christine's face appears above his, looking down into his crib. Is he smiling because he "knows" her, as Christine thinks? A closer look at his behavior suggests not. At this age Mikey's smiles are not reserved for his mother. He smiles when the kicking of his feet makes his mobile turn, when his sister repeatedly presents him with the same clown doll, and when *any* face appears before him (Shultz and Zigler, 1970; Watson, 1972). These smiles are due to a form of mastery called **recognitory assimilation** (Piaget, 1952; Zelazo, 1972). With effort, Mikey is making sense of some familiar object; he is recognizing it as something seen before. In Piaget's terms he is assimilating an event to an established scheme. This effort causes tension, which is broken by recognition, and the smile follows. Again you see fluctuations in arousal leading to a smile, but here those fluctuations are due to cognitive effort and assimilation. Turning mobiles, dangling clowns, and human faces can all be assimilated with effort at age 10 weeks, so all produce smiles. Since these smiles are related to the meaning of the events for Mikey, we can say that he is now smiling in "pleasure." The mastery of recognition, in other words, is an enjoyable experience for him.

Does it matter that Christine misinterprets the reason why 10-week-old Mikey smiles at her? Not in the least. Her feeling of being special to him only serves to encourage further interactions. As you read in Chapter 5, by age 3 months, infants can discriminate familiar from unfamiliar faces and prefer to look at familiar faces. By age 4 or 5 months, Mikey will not only discriminate Christine's face from other people's, but he will react specifically to her face. At this point he will stop smiling at strangers (Sroufe and Waters, 1976). Now his mother really is special in this sense. Christine's responses to this specialness, stimulated by Mikey's truly social smiles, help promote his ongoing development.

In summary, Mikey's social development is a product of the interplay between him and his parents. Partly on the basis of Mikey's responses when she talks to and plays with him, Christine experiences meaning in their interactions. That meaning prompts her to continue her attentions toward Mikey and to elaborate the stimulation she provides him. In time Mikey comes to share in the meaning of their social exchanges. By 10 weeks he feels pleasure in interacting with her; by 4 or 5 months he recognizes her as distinct from others. Gradually he comes to participate actively in the games they play, even initiate them. Thus, what were at first merely built-in reactions to the stimulation Christine provided have led to truly social behavior by the end of Mikey's first 6 months. A similar development would be seen between Mikey and Frank as they play together in the evenings.

DEVELOPMENT IN THE SECOND HALF-YEAR

As extraordinary as development is in the first 6 months, it is equally rapid and far-reaching in the second 6. Cognitively, the second half year is a period during which the baby is increasingly able to differentiate among persons. More and more the child is recognizing people as separate, independent entities who act and can be acted upon. At the same time, the baby is developing a rudimentary sense of self. These advancements have important implications for the emergence of many sophisticated emotions, such as anger, fear, sadness, and joy. Also in the second half year of life, the baby's social behavior becomes increasingly organized around the principal care giver, with a purposefulness not seen in earlier months. Ten-month-old Mikey greets his mother joyously and he intentionally seeks her out when distressed. These behaviors indicate that he has formed a specific attachment to her, a special closeness and sense of security in her presence. This specific attachment is one of the major developmental landmarks of infancy.

Developments in the second half-year are so dramatic that they can be considered qualitative, not just quantitative. Remember from Chapter 1 the enormous difference that exists between the 6-month-old and the 10-month-old confronted with the sight of mother with a cloth in her mouth. The older baby is a fundamentally different child from the younger one. This difference was demonstrated in a classic study on the effects of hospitalization during infancy (Schaffer and Callender, 1959). Babies older than 7 months protested being hospitalized, were negative toward the hospital staff, and needed a period of readjustment after returning home, during which they showed much insecurity centered on the mother. Apparently, disruption in the relationship with the mother formed the core of the problem. Babies younger than 7 months, in contrast, had none of these adverse reactions. They had not yet undergone the critical emotional changes that occur during the second half year. In the section that follows we'll take a look at some of these changes.

Emotional Development

If we define **emotions** as states of feeling that arise when we psychologically process certain kinds of external stimuli, by age 3 months infants certainly experience emotion. We saw emotion when 10-week-old Mikey smiled after effortful recognition of a human face. No longer does Mikey smile merely because of physical stimulation, such as being jostled. Now he smiles because of his success at imposing a primitive form of meaning

Surprise, like fear and anger, is one of many emotional reactions that emerge in the second half year. This is an example of the classic surprise expression, first seen at this time. *(Erika Stone/Peter Arnold, Inc.)*

on the world. The accompanying state of feeling is the genuine emotion of pleasure.

In the second half year, Mikey's emotional capacity will become much more advanced. Because he is increasingly purposeful in his actions, he can experience both the joy of intentional mastery and the anger of a blocked goal (Sroufe, 1979; Stenberg, Campos, and Emde, 1983). During this time he becomes able to anticipate the behavior of others, and this also influences emotional expression. Ten-month-olds who laugh when pulling the cloth from their mother's mouth and stuffing it back in do so partly because they anticipate the outcome of their actions. All of this is congruent with what you learned in Chapter 6 about the fourth stage in Piaget's sensorimotor period.

The ability to anticipate also allows mistaken expectations and the emotion of surprise. William Charlesworth (1969), by using a highchair with a trap door in the tray, demonstrated that surprise occurs in 10-month-old babies. He showed the infants a toy, covered it with his hand, and then dropped it through the trap door, which he operated with a foot pedal. The babies would first move his hand and discover that the toy had vanished. Then they would stare at the empty tray and back at the researcher's hand, actively searching for the object. Their heart rates slowed (a sign of attention), and their widened eyes and slightly opened mouths showed parts of the classic expression of surprise. Other researchers have likewise observed expressions of surprise in babies of this age (Hiatt, Emde, and Campos, 1979; Vaughn and Sroufe, 1979). Five- or 6-month-old infants, in contrast, do not show this reaction.

Figure 7.2
The Onset of Stranger Distress
Several studies have demonstrated a notable increase in wariness toward strangers in the second half year. This developmental trend is illustrated here in both filmed reactions of infants and maternal reports from interviews.

Source: Data from Emde, Gaensbauer, and Harmon, 1976.

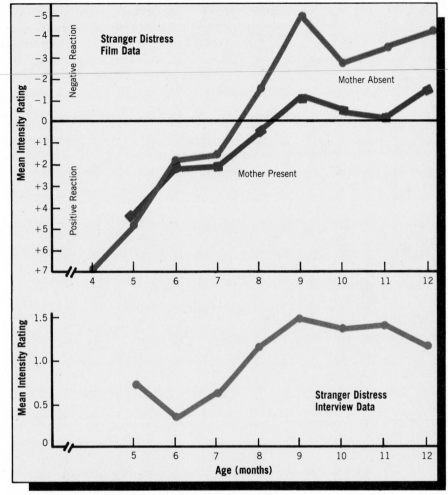

STRANGER DISTRESS

Other increasingly mature emotions appear during a baby's second half-year. One widely studied emotion is wariness of strangers. While at 3 months of age babies smile at all faces rather indiscriminately, by 5 months they begin to smile preferentially at care givers. If a stranger locks 5-month-olds in a fixed stare, they often peruse the stranger soberly and start crying after 30 seconds or so (Bronson and Pankey, 1977). A few months later (in our culture between ages 7 and 10 months), babies begin to react negatively to strangers even without prolonged inspection of them (see Figure 7.2). This **stranger distress** usually continues for 2 or 3 months, sometimes extending into the second year (Emde, Gaensbauer, and Harmon, 1976; Waters, Matas, and Sroufe, 1975). The degree of stranger distress varies greatly from baby to baby. At its most intense it has all the earmarks of real fear, with wary looks, followed by turning away, pulling away, and occasional whimpering and crying. Significantly, at this same age infants first show fear in other situations, such as high places, impending collisions, or being approached by people wearing masks (Hruska and Yonas, 1971; Scarr and Salapatek, 1970; Schwartz, Campos, and Baisel, 1973).

Why this distress reaction toward strangers? Is it just that the child is responding with wariness toward unfamiliar things in general? Research shows that this cannot be the reason. For instance, a 10-month-old's mother can do something highly novel (like cover her face with a mask in the infant's presence and then approach the child), and the result will usually be squeals of delight. Yet if a stranger dons a mask and approaches, the baby typically gets upset; and if after this, the mother approaches with the *same* mask, the infant also becomes distressed (Sroufe et al., 1974). Clearly, the context of the situation matters. An infant reacts differently depending on how a stranger behaves. Babies may smile at a stranger who is merely standing across the room but become alarmed if the stranger walks over and tries to pick them up (Water, Matas, and Sroufe, 1975). In fact, the more rapidly a stranger approaches and the more intrusively he or she behaves, the more apt the baby is to become distressed. Interestingly, too, familiar surroundings can substantially reduce stranger distress. Babies show less fear of strangers in the home than in a laboratory, and less when the mother is close by. Stranger distress is even reduced when the newcomer uses familiar formats to interact with the infant, such as playing with a favorite toy in the same way mother does (Gunnar, 1980; Skarin, 1977; Sroufe, 1977).

Why would the baby's degree of wariness vary depending on the situation? One interpretation is that by age 10 months infants are capable of making a rudimentary **evaluation** of a stranger, a kind of appraisal of the threat posed. This evaluation depends on the stranger's behavior and the context in which it occurs (Sroufe, 1977). Particularly important aspects of the context are the child's sense of security (is mother present?) and the options left open to the baby (can the child still crawl or turn away?). On the basis of such factors and previous experience with strangers, the infant categorizes the present event as liked or disliked. This explains why a baby who is wary on the first approach of a stranger becomes upset even more quickly on the person's second approach: The child can now rapidly evaluate this particular interaction as unpleasant. If novelty were the cause, the infant should be less frightened the second time the stranger approaches. Of course, such an appraisal requires quite sophisticated cognitive abilities, which not all psychologists believe 10-month-olds possess. Yet all the findings concerning infants' reactions to strangers suggest that something this complex is indeed occurring.

EMOTIONS RELATING TO CARE GIVERS

At about the same age that infants begin to show stranger distress, they also begin to show distress when the principal care giver temporarily leaves them. When Mikey was 9 months old, for instance, and Christine left him one evening in the care of her mother, Mikey tried to follow and cried when she closed the front door. Christine had apparently become a source of security for him, so her leaving caused distress. The onset of this **separation anxiety** varies somewhat across cultures. In societies where mothers remain in constant contact with their infants, it tends to appear a little earlier (Ainsworth, 1967). As Figure 7.3 shows, though, the reaction is apparent virtually everywhere by the age of about 9 months (Kagan, Kearsley, and Zelazo, 1978; Schaffer and Emerson, 1964).

Like stranger distress, separation anxiety is closely related to cognitive

Figure 7.3
The Developmental Course of Separation Anxiety
Across a variety of cultures, separation anxiety emerges in the second half-year. Unlike wariness of strangers, separation distress continues to increase until the early toddler period, after which it declines.

Source: Kagan, Kearsley, and Zelazo, 1978.

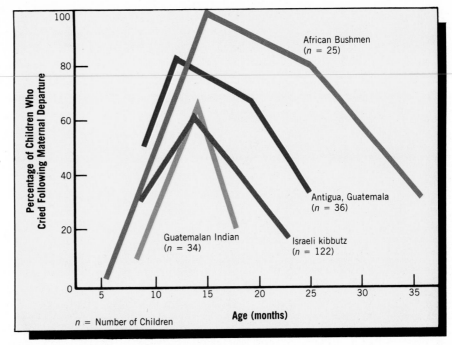

development. We know this because its onset is substantially delayed in retarded babies (Cicchetti and Sroufe, 1978). But exactly what cognitive advances are needed for separation anxiety to emerge? For one thing, the child must be able to discriminate the care giver from other people. For another, the child must know that the care giver still exists even when out of sight. The appearance of separation anxiety also suggests that the infant is developing the beginnings of a conscious will (Brazelton, 1969). The baby cries when the mother leaves against the child's wishes, *not* when the infant voluntarily crawls away from the mother. A sense of self is thus emerging; and separation anxiety, with its feeling of aloneness, probably helps to elaborate that sense (Brody and Axelrod, 1970).

If Mikey cries when Christine temporarily leaves him, you should not be surprised that he also shows joy when she returns. Between 7 and 9 months of age, babies begin to greet their care givers in ways that have clear emotional overtones. As soon as Christine appears in the doorway, Mikey smiles, squeals, bounces up and down, and stretches out his arms (Vaughn, 1978). He does not look, ponder his mother, and wait for some social signal. The joyous response is immediate. Apparently Christine has become linked in Mikey's mind with special, very positive feelings. Things in the baby's world are acquiring emotional significance, just as they do for adults. That Mikey gives his lavish greeting solely to Christine, Frank, his sisters, and grandmother testifies to the fact that he is differentiating among people. He is singling out his parents and others close to him as focal points for much of his attention and activity.

THE BEGINNINGS OF COPING

The infant's capacity to cope with emotionally arousing situations also expands dramatically in the second half year. Newborns have built-in

This infant's exuberant greeting of his arriving father reveals important mental and emotional development. *(Jeffrey W. Myers/Stock, Boston.)*

coping mechanisms, such as sleeping deeply following surgery or falling asleep in the face of repeated noxious stimulation (Tennes et al., 1972). But such global reactions are involuntary and remove the infant entirely from interaction with the environment. By 4 or 5 months infants have somewhat expanded coping techniques. They can, for example, turn away from the source of stimulation. But again, such a response is fairly global and not well controlled by the infant; for example as discussed above, they have difficulty turning away from a staring stranger. Instead they are drawn back to the stranger's face, and become locked in, ultimately crying. Crying is another coping technique, for it may elicit help, but again it terminates contact with the environment.

By 10 months, however, the infant is capable of more subtle, flexible, and serviceable techniques. A remarkable example can be seen in the stranger approach procedure (Waters, Matas, and Sroufe, 1975). As the stranger approaches, many infants show a pattern of brief glances down and away from the stranger, followed by looking again. As shown in Figure 7.4, these gaze aversions are precisely coordinated with heart rate acceleration, an index of emotional arousal. The heart rate accelerates, the infant glances away, the heart rate slows again, the infant again looks at the stranger, and so forth. Infants who show this pattern typically do not cry and are more accepting of the stranger on a second approach. Infants who cry or turn completely away typically are more upset on a second approach.

Another important coping technique that emerges during the second half-year is purposeful signaling to the care giver (calling, gesturing, distress signals) or moving to the care giver when threatened. Unlike crying, these techniques help the infant maintain organized behavior and stay in contact with the environment. They also pave the way for the toddler's signaling and ''referencing'' at a distance, topics we will discuss in Chapter 9. This use of the care giver as a way of coping with novelty or threat is a hallmark of attachment.

The Development of Attachment

Attachment may be defined as an enduring emotional bond between infant and care giver (Bowlby, 1969/1982). This relationship has special emotional qualities, as is evident not only in separation distress and joyous greeting on being reunited but also in the security the child seems to derive just from being in the care giver's presence. By age 12 months, babies want to be picked up by the care giver *specifically*, they will seek the care giver out when they are distressed, and they are happier exploring new surroundings when the care giver is nearby (Ainsworth et al., 1978; Tracy, Lamb, and Ainsworth, 1976). This emotional bond develops over the first year and continues to evolve during toddlerhood and beyond. It is the product of countless hours of interaction during which the care giver and infant learn to coordinate their behavior. Attachment is distinct from *bonding*, which refers to the mother's tie to the infant, which some argue forms in the first hours of life (Klaus and Kennell, 1976).

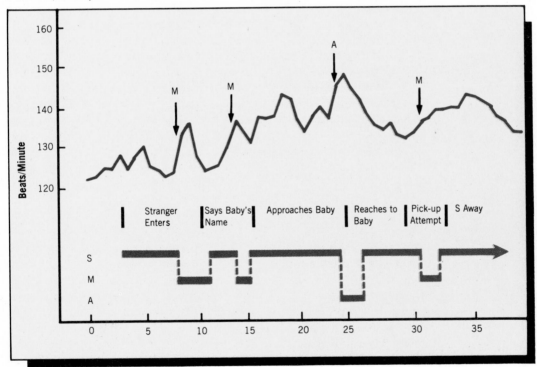

Figure 7.4
Heart Rate and Visual Regard
Visual-regard behavior and continuous heart rate (2-beat averages) for a 10-month-old male rated ''wary'' at reach and pick-up. A denotes looks away, and M denotes looks to mother. Arrows above indicate onset and direction of looks away from the stranger.
Source: Waters, Matas, and Sroufe, 1975.

Since attachment is the product of repeated interaction, it is not surprising that adopted or premature infants separated from their biological mothers at birth also become attached to care givers (Rode et al., 1981) or that infants can become attached to more than one person. For instance, Israeli kibbutzim infants, who are largely tended by communal nurses but who spend time each evening with their mothers, become attached to *both* these care givers (Fox, 1977). Similarly, in the Gusii, an East African community, infants become attached to siblings as well as the mother, because siblings are also involved in their care (Kermoian and Liederman, 1982). In our own society babies become attached to fathers and mothers, though generally they tend to seek out the mother during times of threat (Cohen and Campos, 1974). This preference is probably due to the greater involvement that North American mothers usually have with infants. If someone other than the mother is the principal care giver, in terms not only of time but also of emotional commitment, that person is likely to become the child's main attachment figure. (There will be an extended discussion of the role of fathers in early development in Chapter 9.)

Infants may even develop a primary attachment to other infants if caring adults are unavailable. Researchers have documented one such case of children whose parents had died in Nazi gas chambers; these children were together in concentration camps and institutions since the age of 1. When observed in an orphanage after the war, they showed strong and very exclusive attachments to one another. They protested separations, defended one another fiercely, and were highly solicitous toward any member of the group who became distressed. Toward outsiders, in contrast, they were aloof and even hostile (Freud and Dann, 1951). But while these children clearly gave strength and security to one another, their attachments probably were not fully adequate from a developmental point of view. It took them quite some time to accept other people, and their attachment to one another had a desperate, anxious quality. These traits are similar to those seen in baby monkeys raised solely with peers. Such monkeys are more fearful, less curious, and tend to spend a great deal of time clasping one another (Suomi, 1977).

EXPLAINING ATTACHMENT

Since babies apparently will develop a specific attachment to whoever is emotionally available to them, the inclination to form such bonds must be very strong. John Bowlby (1969/1982) has proposed that this strong inclination is a product of the environment in which the human species evolved. In a world filled with predators, the infant who tended to stay near adults (especially in times of threat) had a survival advantage. Thus, through natural selection a strong predisposition evolved for the human child to focus attention on adult care givers, to feel secure in their presence, and to organize most activities around them—in short, to become attached. According to Bowlby, this predisposition is built into our human biology. All that is needed to bring it out is the chance for interaction with others. That is why all infants, however they are treated, form attachments to their care givers. The development of attachment is biologically guaranteed. Others, in elaborating on Bowlby's position, stress the function of attachment relationships as providing a source of security

Clinging to the attachment figure when distressed is strongly built into the primate infant. *(G. Goodwin/ Monkmeyer Press.)*

for the infant and, therefore, promoting exploration and discovery (Bischof, 1975; Sroufe and Waters, 1977).

A now-classic set of studies by Harry Harlow and his colleagues at the University of Wisconsin illustrates the strength of this built-in tendency to form attachments (e.g., Arling and Harlow, 1967; Harlow and Harlow, 1966). Harlow separated baby rhesus monkeys from their mothers and raised them instead with various kinds of surrogate (substitute) mothers. In one study, each baby was raised with two surrogate mothers, one made of stiff bare wire, the other covered with soft terry cloth. Only the wire mother was equipped with a bottle for feeding. From a position based on classical conditioning, infants might have been expected to become attached to the wire mother. After all, this surrogate would have been associated with food. But the babies clearly preferred the terry-cloth mother. They spent more time with the cloth mother and quickly ran to it when distressed. Apparently, for the development of an attachment, the ability to cling to the terry-cloth mother and derive security from it was more important than feeding. Human infants, too, do not become attached to their parents simply because the parents feed them. Human attachment is closely linked to the baby's need for a secure base from which to learn about the world.

THE QUALITY OF ATTACHMENT

Though all babies form attachments of some kind due to a strong biological predisposition, the quality of those attachments varies. After some of Harlow's surrogate-raised monkeys were made pregnant as adults, they proved to be rejecting and punitive parents. Still, their infants were clearly attached to them. The attachments had an anxious quality, however, with the infants constantly trying to cling to their mothers. Human infants often react similarly if mistreated (Egeland and Sroufe, 1981).

Mary Ainsworth, a psychologist at the University of Virginia, has pioneered in the study of qualitative differences in attachment. On the basis of observations in both the home and the laboratory, she has identified a pattern of attachment that she calls *secure* and patterns that she calls *anxious* (see Table 7.1).

Most infants (around 70 percent) are **securely attached.** These children show a good balance between play and exploration on the one hand, and seeking proximity to the care giver on the other. In Ainsworth's laboratory experiments, they separated readily from the mother to explore a novel playroom. When a minor source of stress was introduced (the appearance of a stranger), they were usually not unduly wary. But when distinctly threatened and upset (following a brief separation from the

---

TABLE 7.1   Patterns of Attachment

Secure Attachment
  A. Care giver is a secure base for exploration
      1. readily separate to explore toys
      2. affective sharing of play
      3. affiliative to stranger in mother's presence
      4. readily comforted when distressed (promoting a return to play)
  B. Active in seeking contact or interaction upon reunion
      1. if distressed
          a) immediately seek and maintain contact
          b) contact is effective in terminating distress
      2. if not distressed
          a) active greeting behavior (happy to see care giver)
          b) strong initiation of interaction

Anxious/Resistant Attachment
  A. Poverty of exploration
      1. difficulty separating to explore, may need contact even prior to separation
      2. wary of novel situations and people
  B. Difficulty settling upon reunion
      1. may mix contact seeking with contact resistance (hitting, kicking, squirming, rejecting toys)
      2. may simply continue to cry and fuss
      3. may show striking passivity

Anxious/Avoidant Attachment
  A. Independent exploration
      1. readily separate to explore during preseparation
      2. little affective sharing
      3. affiliative to stranger, when care giver absent (little preference)
  B. Active avoidance upon reunion
      1. turning away, looking away, moving away, ignoring
      2. may mix avoidance with proximity
      3. avoidance more extreme on second reunion
      4. no avoidance of stranger

Source: Adapted from Ainsworth, Blehar, Waters, and Wall, 1978.

mother), they quickly and effectively sought the mother out and remained with her until reassured. Usually this comforting was smooth and rapid; before long the child was crawling or toddling off contentedly to explore the world again. Throughout, the child's responses to the mother were emotionally positive, not tinged with anger. In play, the securely attached infant smiled at the mother often and shared discoveries and delights with her.

In contrast, **anxiously attached** infants are unable to use the care giver as a secure base for exploration. The reasons for this problem vary. One pattern is **anxious resistant** attachment. Children who exhibit this pattern readily seek contact with the care giver. In fact, in Ainsworth's novel playroom situation, they were reluctant to separate from the mother despite an array of attractive toys. And when they finally did venture forth on their own, even a minor stress often sent them scurrying back to mother. Typically, they were quite upset if the care giver temporarily left them. Yet ironically, they couldn't be readily comforted by her when she returned. Many just continued crying and fussing despite the mother's efforts to reduce their distress. Most important, they tended to mix bids for physical closeness with *resistance* to such contact. One moment they were raising their arms and asking to be picked up, the next moment they were twisting and squirming, pushing away, or kicking their feet in anger. Their approach to the mother was clearly ambivalent, which greatly interfered with their ability to settle down and begin exploring the environment again.

Equally negative in its impact on the motivation to explore is the **anxious avoidant** pattern of attachment. Children who exhibited this pattern readily separated from the mother in Ainsworth's experimental playroom and began examining the toys. Typically they were not wary upon the arrival of a stranger, nor did they usually cry when mother first left the room. Yet what was striking about these children was their response when the mother returned. They actively *avoided* her, turning away, increasing their distance, or scrupulously ignoring her. Normal infants display this pattern following separation from the care giver for several weeks (Heinecke and Westheimer, 1966).

Significantly, this avoidance of the mother was even more pronounced following a second separation, during which many of the babies clearly became upset. Yet when the mother returned, they still didn't seek her out, nor did they respond to contact with her. It seems the greater their distress, the more they avoided interaction with the mother. Again, such a pattern tends to inhibit exploration and mastery of the environment, for the more the child needs contact in order to feel secure, the less apt he or she is to seek it. As a result, play and exploration remain superficial.

Individual differences in attachment are thought to be important because of their implications for later development. The crux of Bowlby's theory is that different patterns of attachment behavior reflect differences in the infants' expectations or "models" concerning the social world. An infant who has experienced reliable, responsive care, and who is secure in his or her attachment, has begun to develop a model of the care giver as available and, at the same time, of the self as worthy of care and as effective in obtaining care. In Bowlby's own words:

When distressed, securely attached infants actively seek contact with their mothers. *(Terry Evans/ Magnum Photos.)*

In the working model of the world that anyone builds, a key feature is his notion of who his attachment figures are . . . and how they may be expected to respond. Similarly, in the working model of the self that anyone builds a key feature is how acceptable or unacceptable he himself is in the eyes of his attachment figure. . . . [T]he model of the attachment figure and the model of the self are likely to develop so as to be complementary and mutually confirming. Thus an unwanted child is likely not only to feel unwanted by his parents but to believe that he is essentially unwantable. . . . (1973, pp. 203–204)

Bowlby refers to these models as **inner working models**—inner because they are attitudes and representations that are carried forward, and working because they are subject to change. His position is that these models influence later experience, coloring the child's perceptions and interpretations of events, as well as influencing experiences that are sought out or avoided.

Attachment classifications in infancy have been shown to be related to attachment behavior in the home (Ainsworth et al., 1978), to be stable in typical samples, (Waters, 1978), and to be predictive of how well children will function later. Mastery of skills, curiosity, enthusiasm in solving problems, high self-esteem, and positive relations with teachers and peers have all been found to be strongly linked to the quality of early attachments, as we will discuss in Chapters 9 and 11.

EARLY DAY CARE AND ATTACHMENT

If secure attachment to parents is so important in a child's life, is there any reason to fear that early day care could hurt the quality of the parent-child relationship? This question is particularly important in our society, where more and more women are entering the paid labor force. Today over half of all mothers work outside the home, and that proportion is expected to rise to three-quarters by the end of this decade. Especially significant, the fastest growing subgroup of working mothers is the group of women with children under the age of 2 (Gamble and Zigler, 1986; Zigler and Gordon, 1982).

When the use of day care first began to increase rapidly, concern was expressed that it might actually prevent attachment to the mother by reducing the opportunity for mother-child interaction. This concern, however, has proved to be groundless. Children in day care still become attached to their mothers, and in general these attachments remain more important than those that form to the substitute care givers (Belsky and Steinberg, 1978; Rutter, 1982). As long as the mother is the child's primary care giver outside of working hours, she will become the child's central attachment figure.

But does day care affect the *quality* of attachment to the parents? This issue is an important one that researchers are still investigating. Encouragingly, most of the studies conducted to date indicate that day care per se does not make parent-child attachments anxious. Most children in day care have secure attachments to the mother. The question is therefore: Under what conditions might children attending day care face a higher risk of developing attachment-related problems?

Logic suggests that important factors to explore are *amount* and *timing* of the child's entry into day care. If a baby is placed in *full-time* day care earlier than 12 months, when attachment to the parents is still forming, might not this have a disruptive effect on the parent-child relationship? Recent research is suggestive (Farber and Egeland, 1982; Barglow, Vaughn, and Molitor, in press; Belsky and Rovine, in press; Schwartz, 1983; Vaughn, Gove, and Egeland, 1980). Brian Vaughn, Byron Egeland, and their colleagues analyzed three groups of babies from economically disadvantaged homes: those starting full-time day care early (before 12 months of age), those starting it later (between 12 and 18 months), and those not placed in day care at all. These children were then followed over time. When the quality of attachment was assessed at age 12 months, 47 percent of those already in day care were classified as anxiously attached. Of these, *all* displayed the anxious avoidant pattern, which tends to be associated with a mother who is physically or emotionally inaccessible. In contrast, 28 percent and 18 percent, respectively, of children in the other two groups were classified as anxiously avoidant. Careful assessment of the children and their mothers at the very beginning of the study convinced the researchers that *preexisting* differences among the groups didn't account for these results. Instead, early out-of-home care seems to have increased the proportion of avoidant attachments.

Yet early day care by itself doesn't necessarily cause anxious avoidant attachment. Even in this study, the majority of early day-care children (53 percent) were classified as securely attached. After extensive comparisons of mothers and infants within the early day-care group, researchers felt that the *type* of early out-of-home care may be the crucial factor. In this sample of low-income families, the day care available was often haphazard and of poor quality. Others also have found quality of day care to be an important influence (McCartney et al., 1985). Thus, it may be early *and* low-quality out-of-home care that produce a negative effect. Or it may be a combination of early, poor-quality day care and high family stress (such as in poverty households) that leads to negative outcomes

Children receiving early day care out of the home experience varying effects depending upon the amount and probably the quality of day care and the availability of care givers during time spent at home. *(Cliff Haac/ Frank Porter Graham Child Development Center.)*

(Gamble and Zigler, 1986). However, recent studies with middle-class samples also have found an increase in anxious attachment among infants experiencing early day care, suggesting that early full-time day care itself may have negative influences (Barglow, Vaughn, and Molitor, in press; Belsky and Rovine, in press). It is important to discover whether these influences persist.

Since the quality of early day care seems so important, it becomes crucial to define exactly what constitutes high-quality care. Two factors often mentioned are consistency in substitute care givers (as opposed to rapid turnover in day-care personnel) and the opportunity for sensitive interaction between infant and day-care worker (Belsky, Steinberg, and Walker, 1982; Gamble and Zigler, 1986; Rutter, 1982). These conditions presumably allow formation of a secure secondary attachment to the substitute care giver, which in turn may enhance development by giving the child additional experience with a caring adult (Sroufe and Ward, 1984).

Not yet clear are the consequences, if any, when these conditions are not met. Certainly, serious attachment problems can result when insensitivity or rapid turnover in day-care workers is coupled with inadequate care giving at home. Such children have to cope not only with unresponsive parents but also with the daily intrusion of other unsatisfactory care givers. But what about children who receive good at-home parenting coupled with poor day care? Will they suffer, and if so, under what particular circumstances? Unfortunately, we do not yet have the answers (Rutter, 1982).

In summary, research suggests that good-quality day care, especially if started after 12 months, does not have harmful effects on development. In fact, studies of older children in day care have often reported some positive influences, presumably because of enriching experiences with the staff and peers (Belsky, Steinberg, and Walker, 1982). However, we need to know more about particular types of day care. Most of the research so far has been conducted in top-quality, university day-care centers with carefully designed programs. Because this kind of day care is unavailable to most families, important questions remain about the effects of average- and below-average-quality care (Gamble and Zigler, 1986).

THE IMPORTANCE OF QUALITY CARE

Problems of Inadequate Care

So far in this chapter we have placed great importance on the quality of care an infant receives, both inside and outside the home. Developmentalists are concerned about this issue because they have seen the serious consequences that poor care giving can have. What are some of the problems associated with inadequate care? The most severe arise in infants raised under conditions of extreme deprivation.

EXTREME DEPRIVATION

Studies show that depriving a baby animal of all sensory stimulation causes markedly abnormal development, including abnormalities in the nervous system (Hubel and Wiesel, 1964; Rosenzweig, 1966). But what about depriving an infant of only social contact? Will that also cause adverse effects? In a series of studies with baby monkeys, Harry Harlow and his colleagues found that the longer the isolation, the more severe the consequences. "Whereas 6-month isolates are social misfits," these researchers concluded, "monkeys isolated for the first year of life seem to be little more than semi-animated vegetables" (Suomi and Harlow, 1971, pp. 506–507). Moreover, isolation in the first 6 months has more profound effects than isolation in the second 6, suggesting that the infant's first experiences with the world are particularly important (Sacket, 1968). A monkey that has been isolated for its first 6 months of life is later very inept with peers and sexually incompetent (Novak and Harlow, 1975). Only with special efforts to rehabilitate them can formerly isolated monkeys manage to overcome their social handicaps. And many that live their entire first year in isolation never become socially normal (Suomi, Harlow, and McKinney, 1972).

Not only is early contact with other members of one's species important, but infants must also have a certain amount of "mothering" in order to develop normally. As we mentioned earlier, baby monkeys raised only with peers show some abnormalities, including excessive clinging to one another, sucking on their own hands and toes, and general fearfulness (Suomi, 1977a). These monkeys are intensely afraid of a novel stimulus at an age when mother-reared infants can use the parent as a secure base from which to explore unfamiliar things.

All the evidence suggests that humans, too, are adversely affected by inadequate mothering in infancy. In fact, because of the greater complexity of their social and emotional development, human children may be even more vulnerable to early deprivation. For instance, you saw in Chapter 3 the profound effects on babies when they are raised in near-total isolation by an emotionally unhealthy parent (e.g., Ruch and Shirley, 1985). You also learned that infants raised in sterile institutions show marked abnormalities in social development. Separated from others except for routine physical care, they tend to become very indifferent and lethargic (Casler, 1967; Yarrow, 1964). Recent studies that followed up early institutionalized children found that as adolescents they had difficulty establishing close contact with peers and later encountered problems in parenting (Quinton, Rutter, and Liddle, 1984; Roy, 1983, cited in Rutter, in press). The earlier and longer the institutionalization, the more profound the effects (Rutter, in press).

While some of these effects are due to lack of sensory stimulation, the lack of responsive social interaction also plays a part, as a classic study by Harriet Rheingold showed. Rheingold (1956) provided eight institutionalized 6-month-olds with responsive social interaction, while a control group received only the routine (physically adequate) institutional care. After 8 weeks of treatment, the experimental group was much more socially responsive. These babies smiled and vocalized more in interactions with adults than the control infants did. Many psychologists now believe that the *quality* of social stimulation, not just the quantity, is important to a child's social development. By quality they especially mean how responsive other people are to the infant (Ainsworth and Bell, 1974; Clarke-Stewart, 1973; Lewis and Goldberg, 1969; Watson, 1972).

NONORGANIC FAILURE TO THRIVE

Even infants raised at home can suffer notable developmental problems. Some are said to have what is called **nonorganic failure to thrive syndrome.** The term "failure to thrive" refers to a lack of normal growth. Either these babies show an actual decline in growth or their growth is below the 3rd percentile on standard age charts. Many also have delays in motor development, as well as skin disorders such as rashes and impetigo (Barbero and Shaheen, 1967; Evans, Reinhart, and Succop, 1972). Often they smile and vocalize little, tending to avoid eye contact (Deitrich, Starr, and Weisfeld, 1983; Shapiro, Fraiberg, and Adelson, 1976; Steele, 1986). In general these infants are withdrawn and apathetic, tending to prefer distance in interaction rather than closeness (Barbero and Shaheen, 1967; Rosenn, Loeb, and Jura, 1980). Failure to thrive is called "nonorganic" when no physical cause can be found for these disturbing symptoms.

Research has revealed problems in the general quality of care received by infants with nonorganic failure to thrive (English, 1978). Often difficulties surround feeding, with the mother misperceiving the baby's calorie needs and being inconsistent in meeting them (Shapiro et al., 1976). Such problems, however, are part of a more general pattern of inadequate care. The mothers of these children tend to be indifferent and neglectful, sometimes even showing anger and hostility toward the baby (Evans et al., 1972; Shapiro et al., 1976). Often a cycle develops, where an anxious or depressed mother produces a child who feeds poorly. The feeding difficulty is then misinterpreted by the mother, who terminates feedings prematurely, leaving the infant hungry and angry (Skuse, 1985).

What factors contribute to this serious problem? Research shows the cause is not just the personality of the mother (Robert and Maddux, 1982). Many factors seem to play a part, including the mother's history, her current levels of stress and depression, and the degree of social support she receives (Leonard, Rhymes, and Solnit, 1966; Pollit, Eichler, and Chan, 1975). Studies repeatedly show that women who were rejected or unloved themselves as children are at risk for producing failure to thrive syndrome in their infants. These women tend to be consumed by their own emotional or social problems, so interaction with the baby suffers. As you will see later, to change this troubled relationship and get the infant thriving emotionally again requires some effort.

INSENSITIVE CARE

Not surprisingly, children who are persistently neglected or abused by their parents have developmental problems, including failure to thrive (Egeland and Sroufe, 1981; Gaensbauer et al., 1984; Gordon and Jameson, 1979). But what about parents who simply have trouble "reading" their infants' signals? Do their children also face developmental risks? This style of care giving is often called **insensitive care** because it is out of synchrony with the baby's needs. Research suggests that insensitive care is common among the roughly 30 percent of infants who develop anxious attachments. Let's look more closely at what insensitive care involves.

Figure 7.5 shows interactions between two different mothers and their babies (Brazelton, Koslowski, and Main, 1974). These interactions were

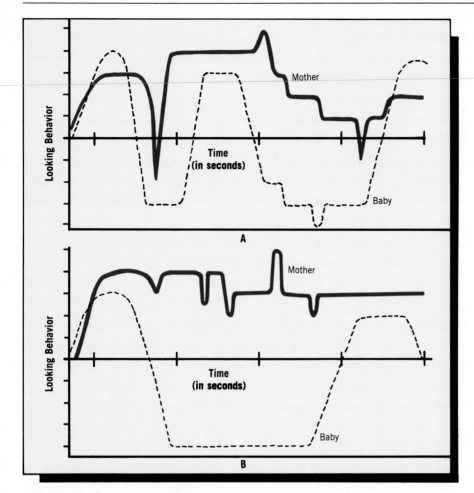

Figure 7.5
Sensitive and Insensitive Interactions
These figures show the reactions of two different mothers to their babies' efforts to pace the interaction by turning away. The dashed line shows the babies' looking behavior. When the babies look away from mother, the dashed line is shown below the center line. The other line shows the mothers' behaviors (talking, touching, making faces, etc.). The mother in part (A) reduces her stimulation when the baby looks away; he soon looks back to her, and she stimulates again. The mother in part (B) keeps stimulating her baby, which seems to drive him away.
Source: Adapted from Brazelton, Koslowski, and Main, 1974.

originally filmed and then summarized in the graphic form that you see here. Note in graph (A) how the mother is in tune with her child's need. for periodic withdrawal. She rapidly deescalates her visual, auditory, and tactile stimulation when the baby turns away. She even looks away herself. Then she starts to build stimulation by smiling and gently talking. Almost immediately this recaptures the child's involvement.

In contrast, the mother in graph (B) is out of synchrony with her baby. She continues to bombard the baby with social stimulation when the child tries to withdraw. Her actions serve only to keep the baby looking away from her. If these interactions were typical, the mother could be said to be **overcontrolling** (Stern, 1977). When the baby averts his or her gaze, such mothers sometimes move their face and body back into the child's view. Not surprisingly, interaction between the pair is likely to be tense and dissatisfying because the infant is denied any role in how the dialogue proceeds. It is as though the care giver is responding to her own needs for interaction and imposes this on the baby regardless of his or her needs. As you saw in our earlier stories of the three children we are following, a relationship having some of this quality seems to be developing between Karen and Meryl.

At the opposite end of the spectrum are mothers who tend to be **undercontrolling** in social interactions with their infants (Stern, 1977). When the baby looks away, the mother takes it as a sign of rejection. Hurt and upset, she abandons her overtures, and the baby, quite naturally, seeks stimulation elsewhere. This only confirms the mother's fears that her baby doesn't love her; it also increases the likelihood that, instead of initiating future interactions, the mother will wait for the baby to "come to her." But since the mother is dejected, her routine care giving is unlikely to involve behaviors that elicit much social responsiveness from the infant. As a result, a vicious circle unwittingly sets in.

Mary Ainsworth has devised procedures for recording the degree of sensitivity care givers display to their infants' signals. Insensitive care givers tend to do one of three things: They may pay little attention to the baby's signals; they may misread those signals (assuming, for example, that the baby is hungry when actually the child is wet); or they may fail to respond promptly or appropriately to the infant's needs. Insensitive care givers tend to do things *to* the baby in terms of their own needs rather than *with* the baby in cooperation with the child's needs.

Five separate studies have found that insensitive care is associated with anxious attachment (Ainsworth et al., 1978; Bates, Maslin, and Frankel, 1985; Belsky and Isabella, 1987b; Egeland and Farber, 1984; Grossman et al., 1985). In those studies, researchers observed mother-child interactions in the home for several days when the baby was 6 months old (and sometimes at other ages too). On the basis of these observations they rated the mother's degree of sensitivity as a care giver. Later, when the infant was 1 year old, the researchers assessed the quality of the child's attachment to the mother. Problems appeared largely in those infants who had experienced insensitive care of various types. In particular, anxious avoidant attachment tended to be associated with a mother who was either indifferent and emotionally unavailable or who actively rejected her baby when the child sought physical closeness. Anxious resistant attachment, on the other hand, tended to be associated with a mother whose care was inconsistent (Sroufe, 1985).

In summary, insensitive care givers are not inclined to answer the baby's signals effectively. When the child cries, they may ignore it, respond inappropriately, or give comfort in a perfunctory way. The sensitive care giver, in contrast, answers the baby's cries promptly and tries to alleviate the problem fully. You might think that the sensitive care giver is encouraging the baby to cry often by "rewarding" crying with attention and comforting. This, however, turns out not to be the case. When mothers promptly and effectively respond to their infant's cries, these babies actually cry *less* by the end of the first year and are generally securely attached (Ainsworth and Bell, 1974). These children have not learned to be "crybabies" through reinforcement. Instead, a broader learning seems to occur. Infants who have sensitive care givers apparently learn that their signals will receive quick and appropriate responses, that adults can be counted on to help. By age 12 months they are confident enough of prompt responses that they don't need to signal alarm at the least little thing. They know that if ever serious distress arises, comfort will be quickly provided.

The Context of Care

We have been stressing the importance of quality care for infant development. Does this mean that care givers are to blame when development goes poorly? To blame the parents is to fail to view parenting in its broader social and psychological context. Many factors greatly influence parents' success at caring for a baby. Among these are the life stresses that the parents face, the social support available to them, and the particular characteristics of their baby.

LIFE STRESS AND SOCIAL SUPPORT

Both the amount of stress parents experience and the social support they get have been linked to the quality of the infant-parent attachment and to other aspects of development (Belsky, 1984; Crockenberg, 1984; Egeland, Breitenbucher, and Rosenberg, 1980; Furstenberg, 1980; Furstenberg and Crawford, 1978; Tinsley and Parke, 1984; Vaughn et al., 1979). Life stress and social support are closely interrelated. Apparently, people have an easier time coping with stressful problems when friends and family members offer them help and reassurance. This applies to the stresses of parenting as well. Research shows that even teenage mothers, as inexperienced as they are, can raise a child relatively free of developmental problems as long as the young mothers have adequate support from their families (Furstenberg, 1978, 1980). In the absence of such social support, developmental difficulties are more likely, including anxious patterns of attachment. It should come as little surprise, therefore, that Karen Polonius would have such a hard time raising her daughter, Meryl. We will return to this topic in Chapter 9.

INFANT CHARACTERISTICS

Many psychologists have argued that an infant's temperament affects the way the parent-infant relationship develops (Kagan, 1984; Thomas and Chess, 1977). By **temperament** they mean the general style of responding to the world that the baby displays. Even very young infants have differing styles of responding (Korner, 1972; Osofsky and Connors, 1979). Some, for example, are highly active. They tend to kick their legs and flail their arms much of the time. Others are much more passive. When placed in a basin, crib, or infant seat, they tend to remain quite still. Some infants are described as "cuddly," because they seem to like being held closely and even adjust their body posture to conform to the care giver's arms. Other babies, in contrast, are considered "non-cuddly," because they often squirm and fuss when they are held (Schaffer and Emerson, 1964). Babies also differ in their levels of irritability. Some are

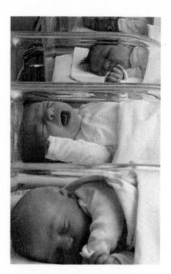

Do differences in crankiness or irritability lead to caregiving problems? *(Burt Glinn/Magnum Photos, Inc.)*

TABLE 7.2   Infant Temperament Characteristics

Characteristic	*Description*
1. Activity	General degree of mobility as reflected in the frequency and tempo of movement, locomotion, and other activity; from highly active to inactive.
2. Rhythmicity	Extent to which sleeping, resting, eating, elimination, and other body functioning is regular and predictable; from regular to irregular.
3. Approach-Withdrawal	Type of first reaction a child has when encountering a new situation such as a different person, place, toy, and so on; from approach to withdrawal.
4. Adaptability	Extent to which initial withdrawal response to a new situation becomes modified over time; from adaptable to nonadaptable.
5. Intensity	Typical intensity of the child's reaction to internal states or environmental situations; from intense to mild.
6. Threshold	Strength of the stimulus needed to cause the child to respond; from high threshold to low threshold.
7. Mood	Typical behavior patterns related to a general quality of mood; from pleasant to unpleasant.
8. Distractibility	Difficulty or ease with which the child's ongoing activities can be interrupted; from high to low.
9. Persistence of Attention	Extent to which the child remains engaged in an activity and/or returns to the activity after interruption; from high to low.

---

easily upset, while others take minor disturbances in stride. Table 7.2 lists some other ways in which infants' temperaments vary.

Some researchers see these behavioral differences as largely inherent in the newborn, although they can be influenced by environment (e.g., Loehlin, Willerman, and Horn, 1982; Thomas and Chess, 1977). According to this view, the child's temperament is well established by 2 to 3 months of age (Thomas and Chess, 1977). The baby, therefore, can exert a strong influence on the kinds of interactions that develop with the parents. For instance, might not the mother of a highly irritable baby, one who cries at the least little thing, be less likely to respond to the baby promptly and effectively? Could this be part of Karen's problem in responding effectively to Meryl? At its most extreme, this view could be used to argue that inconsistent or harsh care is simply a reaction to the child's inherent nature (Segal and Yahraes, 1978).

The role of a baby's temperament in social relationships has been difficult to demonstrate, however. It does seem true that seriously ill, premature infants (as opposed to physically healthy ones) pose problems for parenting and socioemotional development (Plunkett et al., 1986). But no studies have yet shown any link between measurements of normal variations of temperament in the earliest months of life and failure to thrive, anxious attachment, or other developmental problems (Belsky and

Isabella, 1987; Sroufe, 1985). This is not surprising when you consider that a newborn's behavioral tendencies are quite unstable (Blehar, Lieberman, and Ainsworth, 1977; Sameroff, 1978). A newborn who is irritable at one assessment may not be irritable at the next. Which occasion reflects the child's true temperament? Much more predictive of later developmental problems, even in the earliest weeks of life, is how responsive the parents are to the needs of their particular infant (Belsky and Isabella, 1987b; Blehar, Lieberman, and Ainsworth, 1977).

Jay Belsky (Belsky and Pensky, in press) has argued that temperament and quality of care may operate at different levels. He found that measures of sensitive care predict whether infants are securely or anxiously attached to their mothers, whereas measures of temperament predict behavioral differences among securely attached infants or among anxiously attached ones. For example, temperament was found to be related to whether securely attached children expressed their security through active contact seeking or active greetings and other behaviors at a distance.

As a child grows older, however, behavioral tendencies do become fairly stable, and certain kinds of temperaments may be related to developmental problems (Thomas and Chess, 1977; Lee and Bates, 1985). These temperaments, though, are not necessarily inherited. They may instead be caused by prenatal experience or early care, or they may reflect parental expectations and preceptions. Studies have shown, for example, that difficulties in the newborn period are predicted by maternal anxiety during pregnancy (Davids, Holden, and Gray, 1963; Molitor et al., 1984). Also, research has shown that when mothers *expect* their newborns to be difficult, the babies do indeed become difficult. In another study, Chris Heinecke (Heinecke et al., 1983) at U.C.L.A. found that characteristics such as the woman's confidence in visualizing herself as a mother were predictive of persistence and other aspects of child behavior at 12 months. Finally, temperament is often assessed by using parent questionnaires, and these descriptions may at least in part represent parental perceptions that only imperfectly reflect infant behavior (Bates, 1980). Recently, Charlie Zeenah, Tom Anders, and colleagues gave such questionnaires to women during pregnancy, in some studies before fetal movements would have begun, and again after birth. Remarkable consistency was apparent in their "descriptions" across time, even though the early descriptions clearly were based on imagination (Zeenah et al., in press). Other research has shown that parents' descriptions of their infant are influenced by social support, including marital satisfaction (Belsky and Isabella, 1987b; Easterbrooks and Emde, in press; Engfer, in press).

Temperament remains a useful concept, and it is likely that inborn differences in activity levels, attention spans, adaptability to new situations, intensity of reactions, and other aspects of temperament influence both parenting and child development. But demonstrating this remains difficult, as we will discuss further in Chapter 9.

THE INTERACTION OF FACTORS

One promising avenue of research is to investigate how the infant's behavioral tendencies (whatever their cause) interact with environment to influence the course of development. In one such study, 100 week-old infants from economically disadvantaged homes were assessed along certain behaviorial dimensions (Waters, Vaughn, and Egeland, 1980). The researchers found that the newborns who would later develop an anxious resistant attachment to their mothers were generally less alert and responsive during this early exam, relatively weak and uncoordinated, and more inclined to emit spontaneous startle responses. How can we explain the connection between these seemingly unimportant newborn traits and the emergence some months later of an anxious attachment? Perhaps these babies were more difficult for an adult to interact with, so their early social relations got off to a poor start. If so, the fact that the infants' behavioral tendencies later changed significantly, as they often do, may not have mattered. After only a few weeks the patterns of interacting may have become so firmly established that they tended to persist over time (Osofsky and Conners, 1979).

Were the infants in this case largely responsible for the development of insecure attachments? Studies show that the answer is a definite no. Other factors also enter into this complex developmental process, many of which have to do with the environmental context in which the mother and infant live. For example, when mothers of generally irritable babies receive a high degree of social support from family, friends, or professionals, they are much more likely to provide sensitive care and to raise securely attached children. Similarly, mothers who otherwise have little stress in their lives are also apt to cope successfully with an irritable infant. Thus, newborn irritability is *not* predictive of anxious attachment in middle-class families, where stress is generally low and social support relatively high (Belsky and Isabella, 1987b; Crockenberg, 1981). But when a person without adequate psychological resources is left alone to cope with the stresses of both financial insecurity *and* a difficult baby, problems in parenting are more likely to occur. Such a situation was described for Karen Polonius and Meryl.

Thus, in order to fully understand why differences in the quality of attachment develop, we must look to the family's total environment. Infants, parents, and parenting contexts are all part of the picture, and each of these factors may affect the influences of the others. For instance, if Karen is ambivalent about being a mother, and Meryl is cranky as a newborn, interaction between the two will tend to intensify these traits. As long as Karen's situation does not improve, Meryl is apt to become a truly difficult child, even though her initial irritability could have been only temporary in different circumstances (Egeland and Sroufe, 1981; Oates and Yu, 1971). This is the transactional model in operation: The various parts of the system all affect one another (see Chapter 3).

Intervention and Resiliency

Much is still unknown about how lasting an impact poor care in infancy has. Intellectual development does seem to rebound if the poor care is eliminated. For example, babies initially raised in very deprived settings improve toward normal intellectual functioning when placed in favorable surroundings (Clarke and Clarke, 1976; Skeels, 1966). Whether social and emotional development is as resilient is more doubtful. Children who spend their early years in institutions often show problems in adoles-

When one is unprepared to have a baby and has little social and emotional support, anxious attachments are likely to develop. Many intervention programs are now being developed to provide the necessary support and assistance for young mothers. *(Carrie Boretz/Archive Pictures Inc.)*

cence and adulthood (Quinton et al., 1984; Roy, 1983, cited in Rutter, in press). One child raised in near total isolation stayed socially abnormal despite years of therapy, but this was an extreme case (Ruch and Shirley, 1985). A significant obstacle to studying this issue in less severe cases is that patterns of child care often tend to persist. A child who experiences inadequate care during infancy frequently faces continuing inadequacies during later years (Vaughn, 1980). Moreover, children themselves in part create their own later environments by isolating themselves, alienating others, and so forth (Sroufe, 1979b, 1983). Thus, it would not be strictly correct to suggest that early deprivation *causes* later problems.

Psychologists suspect that the earlier an intervention program begins, the more readily developmental problems can be reversed. However, we can be optimistic about reversing problems even in later childhood: Longitudinal studies suggest that children with poor social and emotional development during infancy often do rebound when their family circumstances change (e.g., Erickson, Egeland, and Sroufe, 1985; Vaughn et al., 1979). Such findings encourage efforts to help those parents who are apt to have special problems raising an infant (teenage mothers, for instance, or families with a premature baby), as well as those parents who already face serious developmental disorders, such as failure to thrive syndrome (Bromwich, 1976; Cohen and Beckwith, 1979).

Several successful programs for parents with an infant who is failing to thrive have been reported (Evans et al., 1972; Fraiberg et al., 1976; Mira and Cairns, 1981; Ramey et al., 1975). Not surprisingly, the more serious the relationship problem that exists, the more difficult the case is to treat. For instance, Sue Evans and her colleagues (1972) were successful in treating 13 of 14 cases in which the problem stemmed from a recent loss the mother had experienced, causing her to become unable to respond to her baby. But these same researchers were much less successful in treating cases in which the mother had a bizarre personal history and was extremely hostile toward the child.

What exactly do programs for failure to thrive involve? In general, they try to improve the quality of parent-child interaction, rather than just get the mother to feed the baby adequately, for example. In a study by Craig Ramey and his colleagues (1975), infants with failure to thrive syndrome were all given nutritional rehabilitation. Those parents in the experimental group, however, were also given a one-hour tutoring session each day by a specialist in child development. Among other things, the specialist trained the parents to respond positively when the baby was able to perform various behaviors. At the end of the study all of the infants showed adequate weight gain, but only those in the experimental group also vocalized more and were better able to master new tasks. Ramey's approach, with its stress on response-contingent stimulation, derives from the social learning tradition.

In contrast, Selma Fraiberg and her colleagues (1976) have designed a program based on the psychoanalytic approach. They view the problem of failure to thrive as one of "ghosts in the nursery"—that is, repressed memories parents have about their own childhoods, which are partially revived by the birth of a baby. These researchers have tried to help such parents gain access to those memories and to understand the causes of related fear and conflicts. Ideally, the parents will then strive to protect their children against repetition of their own pasts. This approach was quite successful in treating one intensively studied case of failure to thrive.

Without interventions like the ones we've just discussed, many troubled infant-parent relationships simply persist. In one study, for instance, a high percentage of failure to thrive infants who were left untreated went on to develop anxious attachments to their care givers (Gordon and Jameson, 1979). Parents who have serious problems interacting with their babies seem to need special help to break the negative patterns that have developed. Given the promising results of intervention programs to date, future research in this area should be very productive.

Chapter Review

1. Newborn infants are equipped with certain predispositions that enable them to become participants in early social exchanges, provided they are embedded in a responsive care-giving system. These predispositions include the ability to "signal" their needs to adults, the tendency to be attracted to and actively seek social stimuli (especially human faces and voices), and the inclination to "fall in step" with the care giver's behavior. In these ways the newborn is preadapted to becoming social.

2. Reciprocity in social interaction, involving truly mutual exchanges, is something that is learned gradually. At first the care giver must orchestrate social dialogues. He or she must call forth and enhance the baby's attention and involvement, pacing and modifying the stimulation in coordination with signs from the child. This process, called *attunement*, is part of a more general style of behavior known as **sensitive care.** Sensitive care involves being aware of a baby's needs and feelings and responding to them promptly and effectively. In time the baby's involvement in social encounters becomes more complex. By age 3 or 4 months, infants can smile broadly and make a wide range of sounds that can be used in interactions. They also have good control over their head movements, allowing them to influence the stimulation they pay attention to and its pacing. Still later, in the second half year, infants become able to anticipate others' actions and deliberately seek them out. They are now full partners in social give-and-take.

3. Developments in the second half year of life are so dramatic that they can be considered qualitative, not just quantitative. Among these developments is the emergence of quite complex **emotions,** such as the joy of intentional mastery, the anger of a blocked goal, the excitement of anticipation, and surprise when an expectation is not met. Another reaction appearing at this age is **stranger distress.** Some psychologists believe it involves making a rudimentary evaluation of the stranger, which in turn depends on the stranger's behavior and the context in which it occurs. Babies in the second half year also show **separation anxiety** when the principal care giver temporarily leaves them, as well as joyous greetings when the care giver returns. These emotional reactions indicate that the care giver has become linked to special, very positive feelings.

4. **Attachment** is an enduring emotional bond between infant and care giver, which develops out of many hours of interaction. Babies ap-

parently form an attachment to whoever is consistently available to them. John Bowlby has proposed that a strong inclination to become attached evolved in our early ancestors because infants who displayed such a tendency had a survival advantage. According to Bowlby, this inclination is built right into our human biology. All that is needed to bring it out is a chance to interact with others.

5. Depending on how responsive the care giver is, a baby's attachment may be secure or anxious. **Securely attached** infants are able to use the care giver as a secure base from which to explore the world. When upset they quickly seek out the care giver and are easily comforted. **Anxiously attached** infants, in contrast, do not show these characteristics. Those with an **anxious resistant** pattern of attachment tend to mix bids for physical closeness with resistance to such contact even though they need comforting. Those with an **anxious avoidant** pattern of attachment actively avoid interaction with the care giver in stressful situations. Anxious resistant attachment is linked to inconsistent care, while anxious avoidant attachment is related to a care giver who is rejecting, indifferent, and/or emotionally unavailable. Currently, debate continues about the effects of infant day care on attachment. The issues are complex. By itself, day care for young children probably does not cause anxiety. But the risk of attachment problems may increase when a baby receives full-time day care beginning in the first year and this occurs in the context of high family stress.

6. Poor care giving can clearly have very negative consequences for infants. Lacking others who are responsive to them, babies display serious symptoms such as **nonorganic failure to thrive.** Infants with failure to thrive show stunted growth, social withdrawal, and general apathy with no physical cause. Usually their mothers are indifferent and neglectful, sometimes even showing hostility toward the baby. Less severe in its effects, but also quite negative, is **insensitive care,** in which the parent is simply out of synchrony with the baby's needs. Insensitive care is a common experience among the roughly 30 percent of infants who develop anxious attachments.

7. Social and emotional development occurs within a context, which greatly influences its outcomes. Parental success at caring for a baby is affected by a variety of external factors, including the amount of stress the parents face and the social support available to them. Some researchers have argued that a baby's **temperament** also affects the way the parent-child relationship develops, but temperament itself may be to some extent a product of the child's environment. The most promising avenue of research is to investigate how the infant's behavioral tendencies (whatever their cause) interact with environmental factors to influence development.

8. Much is still unknown about how lasting the effects of poor-quality care in infancy are. Psychologists suspect that the earlier an intervention program begins, the more readily developmental problems can be reversed. We can remain optimistic, however, about reversing problems even in later childhood.

Infancy

In all respects development during the first year of life is rapid and dramatic. Physically the newborn is weak and uncoordinated, interacting with the world largely by means of preprogrammed reflexes. But 12 months later the same child is voluntarily reaching for, manipulating, and inspecting objects, while at the same time skillfully navigating by creeping or even walking. Cognitively, too, the child has made remarkable progress. The infant now has a good grasp of object permanence and can recognize and even categorize many things. These categorization skills are directly related to the infant's improving memory abilities. The 12-month-old also has expectations and intentions regarding the environment, plus a growing understanding of contingency relationships. In addition, he or she shows many quite complex emotions, such as joy of mastery, surprise when something unexpected happens, and anger if a goal is blocked. Socially the child is now able to engage in true give-and-take exchanges and has formed the close relationships to care givers known as attachments.

All these advancements are closely interconnected (see table on page 246). For example, the beginning of social relationships is intimately tied to the cognitive ability to detect contingencies (such as the link between the child's own crying and a parent's responses). At the same time, interactions with care givers provide a wealth of new opportunities to learn about contingencies. To take another example, consider attachment. Although it is viewed as an aspect of social and emotional development, it is based on the cognitive abilities to distinguish among people, to form expectations based upon past interactions, and to understand that a care giver continues to exist even when out of sight. Concurrently, social exchanges with the care giver provide the infant with many chances to develop and practice these important cognitive skills. These examples point to the integrated nature of development. Cognitive, social, and emotional growth all proceed together.

Three Infants

You have witnessed three infants begin a developmental journey—a journey toward becoming both unique individuals and members of a common human community. In many ways these children started life with the very same endowments. Each had essentially the same biological equipment—the same inborn sensory and motor capabilities, the same innate inclination to seek and respond to social stimuli. None was retarded, seriously ill, or otherwise significantly impaired. All presented their parents with the normal challenges of raising a healthy baby. Over the course of their first year, each went through the same set of developmental sequences, though at somewhat different rates. Each came to recognize the basic properties of objects and to form attachments around which their social, emotional, and cognitive worlds became organized. Each experienced good enough care so as not to suffer failure to thrive syndrome or some other severe developmental problem.

Yet despite these shared characteristics and

Stages (in months) of Cognitive Development and Related Changes in the Affective and Social Domains.

Cognitive Development (Piaget)	Affective Development (Sroufe)	Social Development (Sander)
0-1 Use of Reflexes minimal generalization/accommodation of inborn behaviors	**0-1 Absolute Stimulus Barrier** built-in protection	**0-3 Initial Regulation** sleeping, feeding, quieting, arousal beginning preferential responsiveness to care giver
1-4 Primary Circular Reaction first acquired adaptations (centered on body) anticipation based on visual cues beginning coordination of schemes	**1-3 Turning Toward** orientation to external world relative vulnerability to stimulation exogenous (social) smile	
4-6 Secondary Circular Reaction behavior directed toward external world (sensorimotor "classes" and recognition) beginning goal orientation (procedures for making interesting sights last, deferred circular reactions)	**3-6 Positive Affect** content-mediated affect (pleasurable assimilation, failure to assimilate, disappointment, frustration) pleasure as an excitatory process (laughter, social responsivity) active stimulus barrier (investment and divestment of affect)	**4-6 Reciprocal Exchange** mother and child coordinate feeding, caretaking activities affective, vocal, and motor play
	7-9 Active Participation joy at being a cause (mastery, initiation of social games) failure of intended acts (experience of interruption) differentiation of emotional reactions (initial hesitancy, positive and negative social responses, and categories)	**7-9 Initiative** early directed activity (infant initiates social exchange, preferred activities) experience of success or interference in achieving goals
8-12 Coordination of Secondary Schemes and Application to New Situations objectification of the world (interest in object qualities and relations, search for hidden objects) true intentionality (means-ends differentiation, tool-using) imitation of novel responses beginning appreciation of causal relations (others seen as agents, anticipation of consequences)	**9-12 Attachment** affectively toned schemes (specific affective bond, categorical reactions) integration and coordination of emotional reactions (context-mediated responses, including evaluation and beginning coping functions)	**10-13 Focalization** mother's availability and responsivity tested (demands focused on mother) exploration from secure base reciprocity dependent on contextual information
12-18 Tertiary Circular Reaction pursuit of novelty (active experimentation to provoke new effects) trial and error problem solving (invention of new means) physical causality spatialized and detached from child's actions	**12-18 Practicing** mother the secure base for exploration elation in mastery affect as part of context (moods, stored or delayed feelings) control of emotional expression	**14-20 Self-Assertion** broadened initiative success and gratification achieved apart from mother
18-24 Invention of New Means Through Mental Combination symbolic representation (language, deferred imitation, symbolic play) problem-solving without overt action (novel combinations of schemes)	**18-36 Emergence of Self-Concept** sense of self as actor (active coping, positive self-evaluation, shame) sense of separateness (affection, ambivalence, conflict of wills, defiance)	

experiences, we also see in these three children the beginnings of three distinct individuals. Malcolm, for instance, is ahead of the others in physical maturation. He is a strong, robust baby who starts to "do for himself" earlier than Mikey or Meryl. This characteristic poses special challenges and pleasures for his family. Malcolm, Meryl, and Mikey also differ in what is called temperament, although the origins of these differences remain unclear. Meryl is a rather cranky, difficult baby, easily irritated. Mikey and Malcolm, in contrast, are good-natured and exuberant, rarely showing distress. Mikey and Malcolm would both fit Thomas and Chess's (1977) description of an "easy" baby. Such differences in children's habitual styles of responding can best be understood by returning to the concept of adaptation, the process whereby the child and the social environment constantly adjust to each other. Let's look at our three children's care-giving environments and then examine how child and environment interact and mutually adapt.

Three Care-Giving Environments

Just as our three children have basic biological traits in common, so their parents also face the same basic care-giving tasks. All the parents must meet their babies' physical needs while providing an environment with enough regularity so that the children's cycles of feeding, sleeping, and interacting with the world can become reasonably organized and stable. The parents must also provide appropriate social stimulation and be adequately responsive to their infants. To a large extent, they must shape their own behavior to that of the babies, so the children's capacity to adapt is not overtaxed. In the process the children will learn that it is possible to have an impact on the environment.

Although all the parents in our stories face these common tasks, how they perform them is greatly influenced by the contexts in which they live. John and DeeDee Williams, for example, are embedded in a network of caring relationships among the many members of their household. In raising Malcolm they are supported by their two other children as well as by John's sister, Denise, and his mother,

Momma Jo. Malcolm's early development is, therefore, taking place in a system of social, psychological, and economic support that is difficult for a parent operating alone to match. In facing the challenges of urban minority-group life, Malcolm is surrounded by a buffering circle of warmth, love, and nurturance.

Mikey's situation has some of these same elements. Both parents are clearly very attached to him. Frank prizes the "all boy" he so wanted, and Christine is a competent, responsive mother who offers Mikey a rich social environment. Christine, too, has some emotional support from her mother and sisters in raising the new baby. Moreover, Mikey's own sisters, who have been well nurtured themselves, occasionally help their mother care for their brother. But one important difference separates Mikey's home from that of Malcolm Williams: In the Gordon household the seeds of serious conflict exist between husband and wife. Frank is intolerant of Christine's desire to have a life beyond that of wife and mother. Christine, although still generally accepting of Frank's wishes, is beginning to realize that her talents are appreciated outside the home. She is vulnerable to feeling that her goals are being unfairly blocked by Frank. Some signs point to Mikey becoming a buffer between his parents, as when his demands at the breakfast table ("beh! beh!") distract Frank from an argument with Christine. Despite these undercurrents of tension, however, Mikey is developing quite nicely as an infant.

Meryl's situation contrasts sharply with those of Malcolm and Mikey. An unplanned child, she is born to a mother who is not well prepared to respond to a baby's needs. Karen is not only young and financially dependent but also socially isolated—cut off from Meryl's father and her former high-school friends and alienated from her mother, who might have been her one reliable resource. Kay, who is Karen's one new friend, turns out to have a chaotic household and to lead an unpredictable life. When she leaves for Dallas, Karen is completely alone except for weekly counseling at the Teen Mother Project. Because of her own unmet needs for care and nurturance, Karen, not surprisingly, has trouble adequately nurturing Meryl. Karen is torn between her strong desire to be a good mother and her feelings of being totally overwhelmed by the task. She clings to the dream that Meryl will fulfill her fantasies of a happy "storybook" life, thus making it hard to understand Meryl as a separate human being with her own individual needs and ways of acting.

The Interplay Between Child and Environment

Child and environment constantly interact, each adapting to the other to achieve a temporary fit. The adjustments that are made then serve as a starting point for a new round of interactions and adaptations. A good example can be seen in Frank Gordon's early interactions with Mikey. Frank responds to his normal, healthy son as if he were the most robust, athletic infant ever born. In so doing he draws Mikey's behavior toward more and more exuberance and a greater tolerance for rough stimulation. As Mikey increasingly shows these "masculine" qualities, Frank's expectations about the child are confirmed and he is further encouraged to treat the baby like a "real boy." In this way father and son interact to create the active child Frank so much desires.

Similar interactions and adaptations are taking place in our other two households. Malcolm, for instance, enters the world as a loud and lively infant. Rather than being viewed as irritants, these characteristics are cherished in his family. Upon hearing Malcolm's lusty wails, Momma Jo calls them "just grand!" and John Williams tells his son he is "one helluva kid." In this context Malcolm becomes a sociable, good-natured, "easy" baby, which further promotes positive responses from the members of his family. Not all infants with Malcolm's characteristics would develop this way, however. Karen Polonius probably could not have coped well with such an active, expressive baby. Without the easygoing acceptance found in Malcolm's household, what became sociability and exuberance could instead have become hyperactivity and a demanding nature.

Meryl and Karen provide a final example of the transaction between infant and care-giving environment. Meryl was a fitful, colicky newborn who cried a great deal. Did these characteristics cause Karen's insecurity in her role as a mother or did Karen's insecurities, including her stress and anxiety during pregnancy, give rise to the psychological problems Meryl displayed? Clearly it is difficult to answer this question, to specify cause and effect, because each side of the process feeds on the other. Meryl's difficulties lower the confidence of an already insecure mother, and Karen's doubts and anxieties perpetuate and worsen Meryl's fussiness. Mother and child are locked in a negative care-giving cycle that is unlikely to cure itself easily. Meryl is a prime candidate to become anxiously attached. Most likely she would show the anxious resistant pattern of attachment associated with inconsistent care.

These, then, are the initial adaptations of our three children and their care-giving environments. These adaptations will be carried forward to become part of the developmental context during the toddler period. Meryl, Mikey, and Malcolm now have individual styles of behavior that will affect how others respond to them. Likewise, the expectations of those close to these children have increasingly crystalized, which in turn will further influence the kind of care family members provide.

Many questions remain, however. Is Meryl destined to be a difficult and troubled preschooler? Under what circumstances might she evolve a more positive adaptation? If circumstances dramatically improve for Meryl, will she still be vulnerable in certain ways? Might Mikey, too, have certain vulnerabilities, and how could they manifest themselves in later periods of development? How will the very active Malcolm fare when he enters school, where strict demands for orderliness and quiet will be imposed upon him? What special challenges will he face as a black child in a densely populated urban setting? We will address these and other questions in the following units of this book.

Part Three

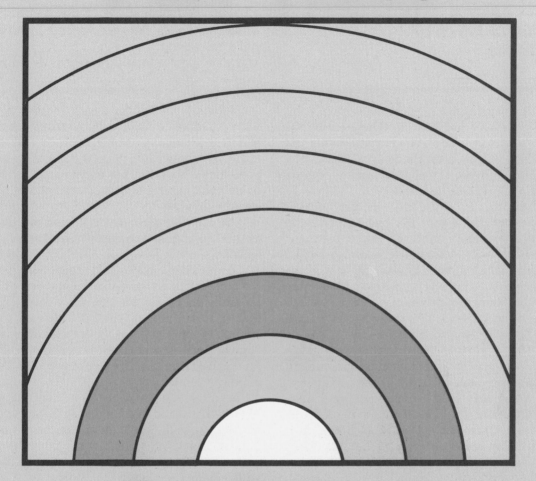

Toddlerhood

Three Children as Toddlers

Malcolm Williams

A breeze rippled the water in the wading pool, sending a large leaf floating slowly across the surface. The little boy leaned over the edge and stretched out his arm. He could almost touch the leaf with his fingers. He reached a little farther, then a little farther.

"Malcolm M. Williams, you get yourself away from that water this instant or you're gonna be one sorry chil'!"

Two-year-old Malcolm turned and looked in Momma Jo's direction. Glancing back at the water he started to reach for the leaf one more time but then stopped himself. Momma Jo's tone meant business. He knew better than to defy her when she sounded like that.

"That boy's just like his father was at his age," Momma Jo commented to an elderly woman she often sat with in the park. "You turn your back for just one second and there he's gone and got himself into a pile of mischief. Yes," she laughed softly, "a pile of mischief!" She gazed lovingly at her grandson, who was now intent upon catching a small gray poodle with a rhinestone collar.

"Doggie, doggie, doggie, doggie," Malcolm crowed gleefully as he ran back and forth, his arms outstretched.

Momma Jo stood up and buttoned her coat against the growing chill. "Well, we best be goin'," she told her friend reluctantly. "It's gettin' dark so early these days. Winter's almost on us, that's for sure. Malcolm, honey, we're leavin' now. You let that dog be 'til tomorrow." And taking Malcolm firmly by the hand, Momma Jo started toward the park exit.

"Happy to you! Happy to you!" Malcolm sang to himself as they walked along.

"It's not your birthday anymore, honey," Momma Jo explained to Malcolm with a smile. "That was last week. Now you have to wait a whole year more for another birthday. Then you'll be three."

"Malcky two!" the little boy said proudly with an energetic hop-skip as they stopped at the curb.

"I don't know why you want to grow up so fast," Momma Jo answered, reaching for the button to change the traffic light. At that moment, the doors of the nearby fire station flew open and a large red fire engine sped out, its lights flashing and siren screaming. Malcolm stared entranced.

"Do 'gin, MomJo," he exclaimed excitedly, as the engine disappeared from sight. "Do 'gin!"

"You think *I* made that engine roar out?" Momma Jo asked in amazement. "How? By pressing the traffic button? Silly chil'! Why that's . . . Well, now maybe I did after all," she smiled, looking at Malcolm's crestfallen face. "Maybe I just did after all. But come on now, honey. We've gotta hurry. We're real late. Your momma's gonna worry."

At the corner of First Street and Delany, Momma Jo had to make a decision. She could go down past the excavation site for the new post office and cut a few blocks off her normal route. But Delany Street was deserted and filled with boarded up buildings. It was not a safe place after dark. What could anyone want with an old woman and a baby, Momma Jo thought to herself as she decided to risk the short walk down Delany after all. "We'll be home quicker this way," she said to Malcolm, reaching down to make sure the hood of his coat was securely tied beneath his chin.

"Who that?" Malcolm asked, pointing a mittened hand at four teenage boys leaning against the construction site fence.

"No one we know, honey," Momma Jo answered. "Come on now Malcolm, we're gonna walk on the other side of the street." But the four boys crossed with them, two in front and two behind. Quickly they made a circle around Momma Jo and Malcolm.

"Where ya hurryin' to, Momma?" one of the four asked.

"Just let us by," Momma Jo said. "We don't want any trouble."

"No trouble, Momma," the ringleader answered. "We just wanna know what you got in that bag of yours."

"Take the bag and just let us be," Momma Jo pleaded, the tension mounting in her voice.

Malcolm looked up at Momma Jo and then at the four strangers. "Go 'way," he said quietly at first; then louder, "Go *'way.*"

The four boys looked at Malcolm and started laughing. "You heard what the man said," the ringleader hooted. "He said, 'Go 'way!' " The other three laughed louder. "Are we gonna go 'way like the little man said?"

Momma Jo put an arm protectively around Malcolm, but his attention was drawn elsewhere. "Look!" he said in his soft, babyish voice, and his mittened hand shot up. Everyone turned to see a police car cruising slowly down the street. The four boys scattered.

"Everything all right here?" the police officer asked as he stopped beside Momma Jo and Malcolm.

"It is now," Momma Jo answered. "But we sure would appreciate an escort to the corner in case those hoodlums decide to come back."

"I'll do better than that," the officer said. "Hop in and I'll drive you home."

"I still can't believe you were walkin' there!" John Williams said to his mother after dinner that night. "You read about things happenin' there all the time. Where was your head, Momma?"

"They're safe now," said DeeDee, as she cleared the dishes off the table. "That's all that matters. So let's just forget it."

"If I'd been there, I would've showed them," 14-year-old JJ remarked, punching the air with his fists. "I ain't afraid of no gang turkeys."

"That's enough of that talk," his father snapped back. "Those dudes are nothin' to mess with, you hear me? You could get yourself hurt good, boy. Hurt real good."

"Hurt. Band-Aid. Kiss it better," Malcolm added knowledgeably. And despite himself John Williams smiled.

Later that night, as DeeDee was getting Malcolm into his pajamas, she stopped and held him by the shoulders. "I know it may be hard for you to understand," she said, "but I want you to know I'm real proud of you for stickin' up for your grandma today."

"Malcky MomJo go p'lice car!" Malcolm answered, still brimming over with excitement.

"I know, baby, I know," DeeDee said and hugged the little boy closely.

Mikey Gordon

"Where's my little all-star?" Frank Gordon called out as he swung open the back door and stepped into the kitchen. Twenty-five-month-old Mikey, grinning from ear to ear, ran to greet his father and be scooped up into his arms. "There's my tough guy," Frank said, grinning back at Mikey as he held him at arm's length above his head. Mikey laughed and crowed gleefully: "Daddy home!"

"How was your day?" Christine asked as she washed vegetables at the kitchen sink. But Frank was too involved to answer. Mikey had run off to the living room and Frank ran after him, imitating Mikey's clumsy toddler gait. "Here I come!" yelled Frank, and when he caught Mikey, he picked him up and tossed him in the air. Mikey squealed with delight.

"Be careful now," Christine called from the kitchen. "You don't want him to bump his mouth again."

"Women!" Christine could hear Frank saying to Mikey. "They don't understand us men, do they Tiger?"

"No!" said Mikey emphatically with a shake of his head, even though he had no idea what he was agreeing to.

"So, anything good happen today?" Frank asked Christine as he came back into the kitchen to get himself a beer. From long experience Christine knew exactly what this question meant. Frank wanted to know if anything special had happened with Mikey that day.

"Well, when I was cleaning up in the living room this morning," Christine began, "Mikey accidentally knocked over that half full can of beer you left on the coffee table. And so he looked up at me, you know, with those big eyes and said: 'Uh-oh, rain beer!' " Frank chuckled and shook his head. "What a kid," he said.

Later that night, when she had washed and dried the dishes, Christine tried to lead Mikey upstairs to bed. "No!" said Mikey, pulling his hand away and holding it tightly against his chest.

"Maybe he's not tired," Frank remarked from his seat in front of the TV.

"Frank, he's exhausted," Christine shot back. "But you get him so worked up in the evening he can't get to sleep."

"Yeah, yeah, it's always *my* fault," Frank answered irritably.

By now Christine had Mikey in her arms and at the foot of the stairs. "No!" he said squirming to get down. "I do it!"

"OK, sweetie," Christine answered. "Let's see you do it yourself." And she watched with amusement as Mikey determinedly climbed the stairs alone, cautioning himself as he gripped the balusters: "Careful. Hold on."

"Well, he's all settled in," Christine announced to Frank as she came back downstairs after reading Mikey a story. She flopped down beside Frank on the sofa, slid off her shoes, and put her feet up on the table. "The girls are ready for bed, too," she added. "I told them they could play one more record and then lights out."

"Quiet," said Frank. "This is a good program."

"You know," said Christine, "I wouldn't mind if just once in a while we could talk at night instead of you shushing me up all the time so you could watch the damn TV."

"I talked before and what'd it get me? A lousy put-down, that's what," Frank answered belligerently.

"All I said was that Mikey was tired," Christine protested. "And he was."

"It's the *way* you said it," Frank answered, and he got up and punched the off button on the TV. "OK. What is it? I know you got somethin' to say. So just say it. Let's get it over with so I can get some peace around here."

"That's right. Break the TV while you're at it," Christine answered, standing up and looking angrily at her husband. "Yeah, I've got something to tell you," she said, her voice rising. "I've been thinking about this a long time now, wondering if I should. But tonight you make me mad enough to be really sure. Helen's opening a new shop just for kids' clothes, and she wants *me* to be manager. And I'm gonna say yes whether you like it or not! What do you think of that?"

"Oh great! What is this? The new independence? The modern woman crap? It's those damn buying trips I've let you go on. Give you an inch and you want a mile!"

"I *know* I can do it," Christine answered defiantly. "I've got it all figured out. Five mornings a week in the shop, and the rest of the time at home where I can still do my sewing. I've even looked into day care for Mikey."

"Dump Mikey in day care?" Frank shouted, the veins in his neck standing out. "Now you've gone too far, Chrissie! What the hell kind of mother are you?"

"I'm a good mother!" Christine answered. "This isn't just any old day-care center. It's run by experts on kids. People who teach at Brown."

"Screw experts!" Frank screamed in a fury. "I don't want any eggheads messin' with my kid. They'll turn him into a pansy just like themselves!"

"Oh, Frank!" Christine said. "Anyway, I figure I could bring in nearly $15,000 a year between this new job and my sewing. And we could really use the money around here the way you've been doing lately."

As soon as the words were out of her mouth, Christine was sorry. It was true that Frank's hours had been cut back at work. But that wasn't his fault. The construction business was slow all over the state. Her remark had been so unfair, she thought, she'd have to ask his forgiveness. As she looked up to form the words, she felt her head snap sideways. With his large, powerful hand Frank had struck her across the face. Christine was stunned. It was not so much the pain, which was bad enough, but the shock paralyzed her. Frank had never in his life even so much as raised a finger to her.

"Chrissie," Frank said. "God, I didn't mean to. It just happened. When you said that . . . Look, we'll work this out; OK, Chrissie?"

Mikey came down to breakfast full of smiles as usual. Although at first he had protested being left at day care in the mornings, he now looked forward to going. As he had for the last week and a half he carried with him an old Raggedy Ann doll that once belonged to Becky. Mikey was oblivious to the doll's shabby condition. He loved it passionately, perhaps because of the little red heart on its chest. Mikey parked the doll beside his bowl of cereal and began to eat noisily. His father seethed across the table. Finally, he reached out and picked up the toy.

"Mikey," Frank said, "you're a big boy now, and big boys don't play with dolls. Only girls and sissies do. You don't want to be a sissy, do you?" Mikey didn't understand what his father was talking about. All he knew was that his favorite toy had just been taken from him. He let out a loud wail.

"Frank," Christine protested, "it's just a phase."

"Stay out of this, Chrissie," Frank snapped back. "It's that damn day-care center, and I'm not gonna let it happen." Then more gently he said to Mikey: "Don't cry, Mikey. We'll go to the store and get you a brand new red tanker truck. Would you like that?"

Mikey stopped crying and wiped his face. For a few days he asked his mother where "Rang-ety" had gone. But soon he forgot all about the doll with the little red heart on its chest.

Meryl Polonius

A barrage of large raindrops spattered against the windows. Water overflowed from the gutters and gushed noisily onto the back steps. Sitting warm and dry on the kitchen floor, 15-month-old Meryl Polonius was oblivious to the rain that beat upon the house. For what seemed to her mother like the hundredth time, she was carefully inspecting the contents of the kitchen cabinets. Whenever she took a pot or other utensil, she would hold it up and exclaim: "Eh! Eh!" Besides something that sounded like "muh" (used to refer to her mother as well as her grandmother), "eh" was Meryl's only other word. But she used it very expressively. "Eh?" she asked while pointing to some new-found object, obviously wanting to know what this wonderful strange thing was. "Eh!" she de-

manded while holding up a set of sticky fingers, clearly wanting someone to hurry and clean off the mess.

Karen sat at the kitchen table, aimlessly twirling a lock of hair around her index finger. She pored over the Sunday want ads, a red felt-tip pen in her hand. "Let's see. 'ASSEMBLY LINE—light packaging, full-time days.' Forget that. 'CLERICAL—word processing and data entry.' Computers? Are you kidding? 'DELIVERY PERSON—must have own truck or van.' Fat chance. 'RECEPTIONIST—good typing skills essential.' Ha! I can't even type my name without a mistake."

In the midst of this dreary round of pessimism, the kitchen door opened and Karen's mother, Margaret, burst in. "What weather!" she said to Karen, pushing the wet hair back from her face.

"Did you sell the house?" asked Karen, looking up from the paper.

"No. The snooty woman didn't like the color of the tile in the bathroom. And her husband saw that the chimney was leaking a little. What doesn't leak in monsoons like this I tried to tell him. But his mind was made up."

"Tough luck," said Karen and turned back to her job search.

Karen had moved back in with her mother about a month ago, right before Christmas. Living alone had become unbearable for her. The counselor at the Teen Mother Project had helped to get Karen and her mother back together. At the second of three sessions they had together, Margaret Polonius poured out her feelings of guilt over Karen's pregnancy. "I feel I failed you as a mother," she told Karen with tears in her eyes. "I wasn't much older than you when I got pregnant and had to marry your father. I of all people should have been able to guide you better. I'm sorry, honey, if I let you down." Karen had cried out of sheer relief that someone in the world really cared about her. She and her mother still disagreed on many subjects, but at least they could talk to each other now without the old defenses taking over.

"See any interesting prospects?" Karen's mother asked, bending over her daughter's shoulder to see what she had circled in the paper. "Look at all these listings. There's got to be something here, Karen. It doesn't have to be the greatest job to start with, you know. Just something to get you out of the house a little and meeting new people!''

"I'm not being fussy!" Karen snapped. "It's just that I'm not qualified for anything. What do I know except housework and babies. Ha! That's it. I'll get a part-time job as a nurse-maid!''

"What about these waitress jobs?" Margaret Polonius pressed on. "Here. 'WAITRESSES—immediate openings, full- or part-time, apply in person, The Green Door.' That's a nice place. What's wrong with that?''

"But I'm not *experienced*, Mom. That's what's wrong. They want only experienced people.''

"How do you know that if you don't try? You're bright and attractive. If I had a restaurant, you'd be just the kind of girl I'd want to hire.''

Karen rolled her eyes in exasperation. "Mom. Look. It says *immediate*. I'm not ready immediately. I don't have a sitter lined up for Meryl. And she's so cranky and difficult sometimes it's gonna be hard to find anyone who wants the job.''

"Well, I've been looking into that," Karen's mother said, cutting off her daughter's last excuse. "Arlene Springer down at the office told me about this wonderful woman on Cragmont Street who takes care of children in her home. She's raised five children of her own, and one of them's a doctor. How much more qualified could she be? Just do me a favor, Karen, and apply at The Green Door. I think it could be perfect for you.''

The following January was another rainy month in Fresno. Continual rain and local flooding kept traffic moving slowly. It was almost 5:00 when Karen finally arrived at Mrs. Jaspers' house to pick up Meryl. Usually she arrived by 4:30, right after her 11–4 shift at the restaurant. But today she had had to stop at the store, and the lines at the check-out counters had been long. Meryl was sitting on the floor in front of the television set when Mrs. Jaspers opened the door and let Karen in.

"Ready to go home?" Karen asked Meryl, picking up the child's little yellow raincoat and hat.

"No!" said Meryl, who kept staring at the television.

At first Mrs. Jaspers had been hesitant about accepting Meryl into her family day care. With Meryl's long list of allergies and shyness with other children, Mrs. Jaspers thought that the child might be too much of a problem. In the beginning Meryl *was* a problem. All day she would follow Mrs. Jaspers about, whining and pouting when urged to play with the other children. At home Meryl's tantrums, which were bad enough already, became even worse. Her behavior toward Karen was oddly ambivalent. Sometimes she would show a great deal of anger; at other times she would cling and demand to sit on Karen's lap.

In time, however, Meryl settled down at Mrs. Jaspers' house and became more interested in playing with the toys. Recently, she had begun to play a make-believe game in which a family of stuffed bears acted out everyday activities. "Bye-bye. Go work now. Don't cry, baby. Mommy be back." Most of her other favorite pastimes were quiet, solitary activities, such as stringing large wooden beads. When she was finished, she would take her creation to Mrs. Jaspers, requesting "Tie pwease," and then wear it around her neck for the rest of the day. Outdoors Meryl's behavior was equally reserved. When Mrs. Jaspers installed a seesaw, Meryl was the only child who refused to try it out, although she quietly watched the other children from a safe distance. When Mrs. Jaspers tried to coax her on, Meryl retreated to the sandbox, where she took up the more secure activity of spooning sand into little plastic cups. But despite this reserve, Meryl had adapted to day care. She no longer gave Mrs. Jaspers any trouble to speak of. Her whining and uncooperativeness tended to surface only when it was time to go home.

"No?" asked Karen of Meryl as she stood holding out one arm of the yellow raincoat. "You don't want to come home with me? Don't you want to have your dinner? I know I'm a little late, but I got held up at the store. What if we have ice cream for dessert. Then will you come home with me?''

"No, I don't!" answered Meryl.

Karen glanced over at Mrs. Jaspers, who was busily picking up toys. Meryl didn't say no to her as often as she did to Karen. A few weeks ago Karen had asked Mrs. Jaspers why she thought that was. Mrs. Jaspers had smiled that motherly smile and put her arm around Karen's shoulders. "Children need to mind, dear," she said kindly. "They know when you don't mean it. You just love her and mean what you say, and Meryl will be just fine." It sounded so simple. But for Karen it didn't come easily.

"Please, Meryl, come on," Karen tried again, doing her best to sound firm. "We can have ice cream."

"Chocowat?" Meryl finally asked after considering the offer for several seconds. And when her mother nodded assent, she stood up so Karen could put on her coat. At least this time there wasn't a tantrum.

8

Toddler Language and Thinking

Meryl was 16 months old before she finally said her first recognizable word. When Karen went into Meryl's room to wake her from her nap, Meryl announced with a serious look: "mama." Karen was elated. "Mama! Yes, mama! I'm your mama!" she told Meryl, picking her up and giving her a hug that made the little girl squirm. Minutes later Karen was on the phone sharing the news with her mother at work.

To parents, a child's first words are one of the most exciting developments. Language opens up new, much more efficient means of communication. The parents can now hear some of what the child is thinking; they can ask a question or give an instruction and get a verbal response.

In addition, emerging language is one example of the more general capacity for **representation,** having ideas or images that stand in place of objects and events. This capacity marks a major transition from infancy to childhood. The toddler period, as this transition is called (because it

Language vastly expands a child's ability to communicate. *(Rhoda Sidney/Monkmeyer Press.)*

is also when the child first walks effectively), extends from roughly 12 to 30 months of age.

Because language is such an important human function, it will be the primary focus of this chapter. Language is a complex communication system that employs arbitrary symbols, which can be combined in countless ways to convey information. Language is not simply synonymous with speech. People who are totally deaf and unable to speak but who can use sign language possess a genuine language. Their hand signs are symbols that allow them to express any idea they wish. Conversely, a parrot that can mimic the words of its trainer is not displaying true language. To the parrot, words are just sounds to be imitated; they do not symbolize anything.

The emergence of language reinforces major themes seen throughout this book. One theme is that of intrinsic motivation. Just as infants actively explore and master objects, so toddlers are intrinsically motivated to learn language and to communicate with others. This can be seen in very young toddlers, as the following "conversation" shows:

Adult: What's that?
Child: Ah.
Adult: Would you like to turn the page of the book?
Child: Ah.
Adult: Why don't you talk to Mummy on the telephone?
Child: (picking up toy telephone) Ah, ah, ah.
(Romaine, 1985, pp. 160–161)

In one sense this child has nothing to say, but note how he seems motivated to keep the dialogue going. This ability is characteristic of normal youngsters. Not long after they start to talk, toddlers develop general strategies to initiate and maintain conversations, strategies such as asking the questions "What that?" and "Know what?" (Corsaro, 1977). At the same time, children this age are motivated to convey meaning, as is evident in the great frustration they can show when they are not understood (Clark, 1983).

A second theme of this book is the biological basis for development. Toddlers are genetically prepared to learn language, just as in infancy they were genetically prepared to learn about contingent relationships between actions and outcomes. Toddlers acquire language remarkably fast, given the complexity of the task. In a few months they learn the names of many actions, objects, and descriptive features, such as *big* and *red*. Once they begin to string words together, their grasp of language structure grows rapidly. Such remarkable advancements would seem hardly possible if a child's brain were not in some way biologically prepared to make them.

A third theme of this book is the qualitative changes in behavior that accompany development. Language learning is another instance of such change. The infant does not know that things have names, whereas the toddler knows the names of many things. Moreover, a 2-year-old does not simply have a larger vocabulary than a 12-month-old. The 2-year-old can put words together in meaningful combinations, and slightly older children can master the grammar of their language.

This chapter begins with a general look at early language: What do children typically say when they first start to talk, and how do they begin to put words together into longer utterances? We then explore the components of human language: What sounds, combinations of sounds, and rules must a child learn to become a competent communicator? Next we consider the various steps in early language learning, including mastery of sound patterns, the meaning of words, and rules for combining them into sentences. Following this, we take up three different perspectives on how toddlers acquire language. Since each perspective sheds light on a different aspect of this complex process, an empirically adequate account of language development must include elements from all three. We therefore assess the strengths and weaknesses of each of these perspectives. Finally, before presenting an overview of the toddler period, we discuss the relationship between language and thought.

THE NATURE OF EARLY LANGUAGE

First Words

When children first start saying recognizable words, they use only one word at a time. To an adult, a single word is usually just a label for a single object, action, or quality. To a toddler, however, a single word often is an attempt to communicate much more. For example, when Meryl says the word "mama," is she merely labeling Karen, or is she trying to convey a more complex idea? Your interpretation of Meryl's meaning would probably depend on the context in which she says the word. If she says "mama" when Karen enters the room, she might be trying to communicate "Here is mama." If she says "mama" upon seeing Karen leave the house, she might be trying to tell someone "I want my mama." Or if she says "mama" while holding up Karen's purse, she might be trying to express the idea "This belongs to mama." This usage of single words to convey different thoughts constitutes a true language. Although toddlers do use single words (e.g., *mama*) simply as a label (Flavell, 1985), more often they use them to convey what an adult would express with a phrase

Toddlers' first words often are names of familiar objects or persons. The naming of the object frequently is accompanied by pointing, an earlier and much less differentiated form of communication. *(Ernesto Bazan/Archive Pictures.)*

or sentence (de Villiers and de Villiers, 1978). A word that is used to convey such broader meanings is called a **holophrase.** Although researchers currently disagree about the extensiveness of holophrastic speech (Flavell, 1985), apparently some toddlers begin to use holophrases soon after they acquire their first words. To interpret a holophrase the listener has to consider the context, pay attention to the child's gestures, and occasionally resort to a crystal ball.

What do children talk about during the single-word phase? In general, children's first words *refer* to familiar persons ("mama"), body parts ("nose," "feet"), animals ("doggie"), clothing or footwear ("shoe"), and appliances ("TV," "toaster"). In addition, their first words *express* affect ("naughty") and movement ("allgone," "bye-bye"), as well as social commands that are units in themselves and not easily disassembled into their component words ("I don't want to"). For example, as Meryl watches a car disappear down the street, she might comment "bye" or "allgone." Notice that although "allgone" is two words for adults, many young toddlers treat it as one. Another common topic of speech during the single-word phase is expression of the concept no. Young toddlers often develop several versions of negation. In addition to the traditional "no," they might say "me" or "myself," meaning, we suspect, "No, that's for *me*" or "No, I'll do it *myself.*"

From diary accounts, we now know that children 50 years ago used the same types of words when they began to speak (Clark, 1983). It has been found that children differ in the relative amounts of words they use to "refer" to objects and events (nouns, some verbs, and adjectives) and to "express" social routines (pronouns, formulas such as "stop it"); such differences are related to other aspects of their social and cognitive development (Nelson, 1981). For example, "expressive" children tend to be second-born and from less educated families than "referential" children are. Referential children initially tend to acquire words faster than expressive children do, though the two groups speak equally grammatically (Clark, 1983). As we learn more about expressive and referential children, additional details may emerge about their cognitive abilities.

First Sentences

Usually at around 18 to 24 months of age, toddlers start to put two words together. At the beginning of this phase, they may not really be saying two-word sentences. Often they appear to be expressing two *separate* ideas, one after the other. For example, psychologist Katherine Bloom's daughter Allison said both "daddy, car" and "car, daddy" when her father would leave in the car (Bloom, 1973). The little girl paused between one word and the other, as if she were conveying two related, but separate thoughts ("Away goes *daddy*. Daddy's in the *car*."). Such a pause is not characteristic of true sentences. And since Allison spoke these two words in no particular order, the word order was unimportant to what she wanted to convey. In true English sentences, in contrast, word order *is* significant. Thus, the words that toddlers initially speak in close succession may not be genuine sentences. Instead, they may be a kind of transitional step from earlier one-word statements.

When toddlers start to produce true two-word sentences, the sentences usually are composed of nouns, verbs, and adjectives. No articles, conjunctions, or prepositions, such as *the*, *and*, or *of*, appear, even though these words are common in adult speech. Nor do toddlers inflect words with suffixes or prefixes to alter their meanings (adding *s* to make a noun plural, or *ed* to make a verb past tense). They also ignore most auxiliary verbs, such as *can*, *may*, or *would*. When 22-month-old Meryl wants to express the idea "I can see the truck," she says simply: "See truck." The child in this phase seems to be eliminating all but the words that are essential to conveying the central meaning. This style of talking is called **telegraphic speech** because it sounds somewhat like the terse wording of a telegram. Interestingly, young toddlers use telegraphic speech even when adults specifically model longer sentences for them. When Karen repeatedly encouraged Meryl to say "I love my grandma," Meryl's words came out simply "Love gra'ma." It is as if saying more than two words to express a single idea exceeds her current cognitive capacities.

Although a child's earliest sentences are telegraphic, they are not just arbitrary groupings of words. Instead, toddlers seem to be conforming to rudimentary grammars, implicit sets of rules concerning how words should be ordered. Developmentalists are searching for an appropriate way to characterize the rules that govern early two-word combinations. Table 8.1 lists a number of toddlers' two-word sentences and what they may try to convey. When you consider the number of different ideas expressed here with just two words, you can begin to see how hard it is to specify the grammars that these young speakers are following.

THE COMPONENTS OF LANGUAGE

At the heart of human language are agreed-upon conventions for combining sounds into meaningful words, and words into meaningful sentences. Toddlers must master these conventions when they first learn to speak. At the same time, children must also master the rules that govern how language is used in everyday conversation, rules that sometimes vary

TABLE 8.1   Categories of Meanings Expressed in the Two-Word Stage

Category of Meaning	*Description*
Identification	Utterances such as "See doggy" and "That car" are elaborations on pointing, which emerged in the preverbal stage, and naming, which began in the one-word stage.
Location	In addition to pointing, children may use words such as *here* and *there* to signal location—as in "Doggy here" or "Teddy down." To say that something is in, on, or under something else, children juxtapose words, omitting the preposition—as in "Ball [under] chair" or "Lady [at] home."
Recurrence	One of the first things that children do with words is call attention to, and request, repetition—as in "More cookie" or "Tickle again."
Nonexistence	Children who pay attention to the repetition of experiences also notice when an activity ceases or an object disappears. Utterances such as "Ball allgone" and "Nomore milk" are common at this stage.
Negation	At about age 2, children discover that they can use words to contradict adults (pointing to a picture of a cow and saying, "Not horsie") and to reject adults' plans (saying, "No milk" when offered milk to drink).
Possession	In the one-word stage children may point to an object and name the owner; in the two-word stage they can signal possession by juxtaposing words—as in "Baby chair" or "Daddy coat."
Agent, object, action	Two-word sentences indicate that children know that agents act on objects. But children at this stage cannot express three-term relationships. Thus, "Daddy throw ball" may be expressed as "Daddy throw" (agent-action), "Throw ball" (action-object), or "Daddy ball" (agent-object). Children may also talk of the recipient of an action by using similar constructions—saying, "Cookie me" or simply "Give me" instead of "Give me a cookie."
Attribution	Children begin to modify nouns by stating their attributes as in "Red ball" or "Little dog." Some two-word sentences indicate that children know the functions as well as the attributes of some objects—for example, "Go car."
Question	Children can turn types of sentences described here into questions by speaking them with a rising intonation. They may also know question words, such as *where,* to combine with others—as in "Where kitty?" or "What that?"

Source: Adapted from Brown, 1973. From Wortman/Loftus, 1988.

depending on the social situation. Let's look more closely at these various components of language to better understand the task the toddler faces.

Sounds, Structure, and Meaning

The study of language is often divided into four major parts: phonology, morphology, syntax, and semantics. **Phonology** is the study of the sounds of a language. When you speak, you are producing a series of sounds that are part of the English language. These sounds, known as **phonemes,** are the smallest units that can change the meaning of a word. The sound of the /d/ in *dog* is a different phoneme from the sound of the /l/ in *log* which is why you immediately recognize these two words as different. Not all languages use the same phonemes that English does, as anyone who has struggled to pronounce foreign vowels and consonants knows. In English, in addition to the sounds represented by the letters of the alphabet, phonemes represent such sounds as the /ch/ in *church,* the /sh/

The child's ability to communicate becomes much more flexible and precise with the emergence of language. While some interpretation often is required to make sense of the toddler's early language, deciphering the meaning of the infant's cry is a much more difficult task. *(Linda Benedict-Jones/ The Picture Cube, Elizabeth Hathon/The Stock Market.)*

in *ship,* and the soft /g/ in *generous.* When Meryl, Malcolm, and Mikey were beginning to babble (consonant-vowel or vowel-consonant repetitions), they not only made sounds corresponding to some of the 41 English phonemes but also used some sounds that are phonemic only in other languages, not in English. As toddlers, however, they no longer produce many of these foreign phonemes without explicit instruction. A related feat can be observed in deaf 6-month-olds; they vocalize most of these phonemes too. This ability of infants to vocalize sounds that are not part of their acoustic environment suggests that this phase of early phonemic development is largely insensitive to input from the environment. Such input becomes very important after the first 6 months.

While phonemes were defined as the smallest units of sound that change the meaning of a unit or word, **morphemes** are the smallest units of meaning. **Morphology** is the study of these smallest meaningful units. Many words are single morphemes, such as *child, language,* and *speak.* Other words consist of several morphemes strung together. The word *unspeakable,* for example, has three morphemes: the prefix *un-* (meaning not), the root word *speak,* and the suffix *-able* (meaning capable of being done). Because each of these is a meaningful unit, it is considered a separate morpheme.

Syntax is the study of the rules that govern how words are organized into sentences. In English, following the rules of syntax allows you to convey the meaning you intend. The sentence "The boy kissed the girl" and the sentence "The girl kissed the boy" mean very different things because of a single change in word order. But in Latin or Japanese, for instance, you could tell who did the kissing by the endings of the words.

Semantics is the study of the meaning that language conveys. A sentence might be perfectly correct according to the rules of syntax but nevertheless be confusing because it breaks semantic rules. For instance, if a preschooler told you "My daddy is having a baby," you would ask for clarification, even though the child's grammar is flawless. Psychologists interested in how people put their ideas into words and how they understand what others say are concerned mainly with the meaning of sentences. However, those who are interested in the early development of these skills are also concerned with the meaning of single words.

Conversational Rules

In addition to mastering the rules of phonology, morphology, syntax, and semantics, children must learn about the rules that govern conversations. Studying the various understandings people have and conventions they follow when they talk to one another is called **discourse analysis.** For instance, if you asked another person "Can you open a window?" you would not expect him simply to answer "Yes, I know how to do that." Speakers of English implicitly know that this question is really a request. Somewhere in the process of learning language, children must acquire this implicit knowledge.

One area of discourse analysis is called **pragmatics,** the study of rules governing how language is used in different social contexts. How you talk to your best friends and how you talk to your professors differ substantially even when you are conveying the same basic information. Words directed to a professor are much more formal and deferential than those directed to a friend. Similarly, if you were explaining how to play a game to a 5-year-old, your choice of words would be quite different from those you would use in speaking to an adult. In each case your language is guided by different pragmatic rules. Such rules about appropriate and effective use of language in different situations are learned throughout development as new social contexts are encountered. Sometimes children learn them through trial and error. Other times they are specifically taught. Most parents have probably at some time said to their children something like this: "Now, when we go to grandma's house don't say _____, and don't tell her I told you not to say it." These children are receiving instructions in the rules of pragmatics.

Research suggests that young children already possess considerable pragmatic knowledge. When asked to describe the rules of a game to a child younger than themselves, 5-year-olds reduce the complexity of their sentences, speak slower, and repeat more often than when they describe the rules to an adult (Shatz and Gelman, 1973). Toddlers seem to have learned that while other toddlers may understand what they say, infants and cats don't. Thus, without ever being told to do so, these children have discovered that the communication abilities of younger children are limited (Tomasello and Mannle, 1985).

Another aspect of discourse analysis is **sociolinguistics,** the study of differences in people's use of language as a result of belonging to different social groups or social categories. For instance, Malcolm and Mikey will develop different styles of language by virtue of the different ethnic groups to which they belong (Labov, 1970). Language also differs as a result of social class and age differences among people. All these slightly varying styles of speaking a single language influence what children acquire when they learn to talk.

Productive and Receptive Skills

Another way to look at what children must master when they learn their native language is in terms of the mental skills required. Actually, two sets of mental skills are needed to communicate effectively—one set, **productive skills,** for putting ideas into words, and a second set, **receptive**

Subcultures may have not only unique word usages but unique grammatical forms as well. Interestingly, such variations tend to follow similar rules. For example, any language has a certain amount of redundancy, as in the plural s in the sentence, "The man bought four books." (Since there are four, we already know *books* is plural.) The black dialect sentence, "The man he bought four book" has the same amount of redundancy, though in a different place (Labov, 1970). *(Chester Higgins, Jr./Photo Researchers, Inc.)*

skills, for understanding what other people say. Children must acquire both skills to carry on conversations.

Many parents feel that their children can grasp much of what they are told *before* being able to talk. Although parents tend to overestimate this ability in children, they are basically correct that receptive skills emerge sooner than productive ones (Huttenlocker, 1974). This can be seen in every aspect of language development. Consider Meryl, who as a toddler cannot pronounce the phoneme /l/. Her *l*'s come out sounding like *w*'s. One day Karen teasingly said to Meryl, "Wet's go!" Meryl responded "No. Not wet's. Say *wet's*." Although she still mispronounced the sound of /l/, she could hear the difference between a correct and an incorrect pronunciation by someone else. Her receptive phonology was more advanced than her productive phonology. In a similar manner, young children understand sentences that are much longer and more complex than the ones they speak. Again we see receptive skills leading to productive skills.

MAJOR TASKS IN EARLY LANGUAGE LEARNING

What progress is made in each of the areas outlined above during the toddler period and the stage immediately following it (the preschooler period)? This is the topic that we turn to next. In this section, we will concentrate first on how toddlers master the sound patterns of their native language and how they learn the meaning of individual words, and second on how they will later develop a set of morphological and syntactic rules for recombining units of meaning into words and for transforming words into sentences.

Learning the Sound Patterns of a Language

One of the more difficult aspects of learning a language is mastering its sound patterns. Think about when you first heard a foreign language. The

The toddler's receptive language commonly progresses in advance of his or her expressive language. Parents understand this. *(Elizabeth Crews.)*

sounds seemed strung together with no pauses between them. Where did one word end and the next begin, you wondered to yourself. How could anyone decipher such rapid-fire speech? Now imagine the task confronting children who do not even know that words exist. Somehow, just by hearing others talk, they must learn the various phonemes of the language and begin to produce those phonemes themselves. Ultimately they must group sounds together into recognizable words. What steps lead children to these accomplishments?

In the first year of life, dramatic changes in babies' vocalizations take place, changes that indicate they are becoming able to produce speech sounds. This early period can be divided into four stages. In the first, the baby is capable only of **crying.** To understand the meaning of these cries, care givers use context. Young infants cry whenever they are overly aroused, and the reason for this overarousal (hunger, pain, wetness, and so forth) makes little difference in the cry itself. Care givers can, however, discriminate pain cries from other types of cries. In the second stage, the baby begins to make additional sounds, mostly vowel-like ones. This behavior is called **cooing,** probably because the sound of /u/ is produced so frequently. The third stage, known as **babbling,** is reached by the middle of the first year, as children begin to put together consonant-vowel and vowel-consonant combinations such as "mamamama." Now the child's vocalizations begin to sound more speechlike. At the start, however, children are not yet imitating the particular phonemes of their native language. As we noted above, infants around the world babble similar sounds, despite being exposed to very different languages. Not until the fourth stage, that of **patterned speech,** do children begin to tune in on the speech sounds around them and produce a range of sounds like the phonemes of their native language. Fifteen-month-old Meryl's "eh" and "muh," for instance, are produced strictly from English speech sounds. She no longer rolls Spanish r's or forms gutteral German *ch*'s. It is from a limited set of speech sounds, all appropriate to their native language, that children construct their first real words.

This developmental sequence suggests that two things are needed to prepare children to begin speaking. First, children must gain control over the speech apparatus—the mouth, lips, tongue, and vocal cords—to be able to produce speech sounds intentionally. Second, children must learn the phonemes of their particular native language. They must pay close attention to the speech sounds they hear around them and begin to imitate those sounds. Only when they can recognize and produce at least a small repertoire of appropriate speech sounds are they ready to start learning the meaning of words and combining sounds to make words.

Learning Words and Their Meanings

Toddlers' vocabularies grow quite quickly after they begin to speak, although the exact rate of growth is not certain. An early study suggests that the average *productive* vocabulary of a 3½-year-old is 1,222 words and of a 6-year-old, 2,526 words (Smith, 1926). More recent work suggests that from the moment children utter their first word at around the age of 12 months, they add, on average, five to eight words a day to their productive vocabularies—between 8,000 and 14,000 words within the brief span of 5 years (Carey, 1977; de Villiers and de Villiers, 1978). Despite the differences in the absolute rate of development, all studies show the same general pattern. The rate of new word acquisition is slower than average during early toddlerhood, but it increases dramatically between 2½ and 3½ years of age, as is indicated in Figure 8.1.

Children's receptive vocabularies are considerably larger than their productive vocabularies, indicating a truly remarkable growth of word knowledge and use during this 5-year period between the ages of 1 and 6. One estimate is that by the time children reach the age of 6, the rate of new additions to their receptive vocabulary is a remarkable 22 words a day (Miller, 1981)! This learning task seems all the greater when you consider that, at first, the child doesn't even know that words exist. A milestone in language development comes when the child finally discovers that everything has a name. This discovery speeds vocabulary building as the toddler begins to ask incessantly, "What that?"

Interestingly, however, toddlers start to say words even *before* they begin to grasp the concept of words or names. We can only speculate about what lies behind this very early language learning. One possible explanation involves the fact that young children tend to imitate what they hear. This tendency helps them learn the phonemes of their language and is probably also instrumental in producing first words.

Another possible explanation centers on the attempts all normal pre-speech children make to communicate through gestures and sounds. We illustrated this in our story of 15-month-old Meryl as she sat on the kitchen floor, holding things aloft and "commenting" in her own way. Even younger babies will point at a bottle or toy they cannot reach and begin to whimper for it. Although they do not as yet have real language, their gestures and sounds serve a similar communicative function. The linguist Michael Halliday (1979) has referred to these types of prelingual sound patterns that are uttered by the child in conjunction with speech-like intonation contours as **protolanguage.** Malcolm's mother was sure that he was using such a sound pattern to refer to JJ whenever Malcolm saw one of his brother's possessions, even though his utterance was unintelligible. Momma Jo began jokingly to imitate Malcolm's utterance whenever she addressed JJ in Malcolm's presence. This motivation to communicate, coupled with the tendency to imitate others, could prompt a child to begin saying what sounds like words.

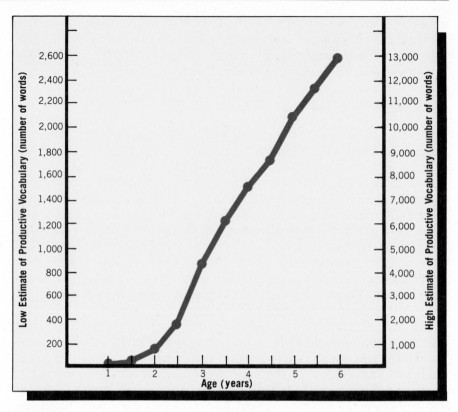

Figure 8.1
Estimates of Vocabulary Growth as a Function of Age
This figure illustrates the slow initial growth of productive vocabulary, followed by very rapid growth starting around 3 years of age. In addition, the two scales indicate the uncertainty about the size of toddlers' and preschoolers' vocabularies.

Source: Based on Carey, 1977; Miller, 1981; and Smith, 1926.

A third possible reason why toddlers say words before grasping the concept of language has to do with adult feedback. For instance, when 1-year-old Mikey first said "baw" in the presence of a bright red beach ball, Christine responded "Yes, that's a *ball!*" and got the toy for him. Mikey soon discovered that saying "baw" elicited both attention and an attractive object. Here he is using what adults call a word without his understanding the concept of language. All he knows is that a certain vocal behavior leads to interesting and desirable consequences.

THE CHALLENGE OF MASTERING WORDS

How does Mikey make the all-important next step: learning that a certain combination of sounds refers to a particular object, action, or quality? Suppose Christine points to the red beach ball and says the word "ball." How is Mikey to figure out that "ball" is the name of the thing itself, not one of its qualities (red, round, large), or even one of the actions being applied to it (look, point)? The child's ability to master language seems even more impressive when you consider learning the meaning of more abstract words such as *to, and, of, the, some, never.* Not surprisingly, such words are learned relatively late in the process of language acquisition. To add even more complexity to the task children face, consider that many of the words they learn are not often spoken in isolation. Sometimes they must discern the critical grouping of sounds from a larger string of sounds the adult is making. When Christine says to Mikey "Look at the ball *roll*," Mikey must extract the new word "roll" from his mother's flow of speech. Yet all normal toddlers manage to do this. They sort out key words in the sentences they hear and, given cues and context, assign meanings to those words (Carey, 1977).

What kinds of errors could toddlers make in this difficult process? You might think that they would assign the wrong meaning to a word. Mikey, for example, might decide that "red" means any round object that bounces, and so scream "Red!" when his father comes home with a new soccer ball. Although toddlers sometimes do make these kinds of errors, they are not very frequent, at least not in the words toddlers speak. Such errors may be more frequent in the meanings young children assign to words they hear others say. If an adult says a word the toddler doesn't know, the child will be forced to guess at its meaning, and that guess may be off the mark. When it comes to actually using a word, however, toddlers do not seem to guess very often. They appear to understand the difference between guessing and *knowing* the meaning of a word.

The kinds of errors toddlers are much more likely to make are errors of under- and overextension. **Errors of underextension** occur when a word is used correctly but in too restricted a way. Suppose Mikey is given a toy dump truck and told that this is a "truck." He then starts to use the word to refer to toy trucks only, not to full-sized trucks he sees on the road. Mikey would be said to have an *underextended* concept of truck. The meaning he attaches to the word does not extend to all instances of trucks. In **errors of overextension,** toddlers make the opposite mistake: Because they do not have a sufficiently restricted definition of a certain word, they sometimes use the word when it doesn't really fit. Suppose Mikey was shown the truck Frank drives at work, and afterward said "truck" whenever he saw any wheeled vehicle. Cars, trains, even wagons would all be trucks to Mikey. Here Mikey is using the term *truck* too broadly; he is *overextending* its meaning. As you will learn, most of these are smart mistakes, however. There is a logic to them. The child might say "truck" when he sees a car, but he probably would say "car" in the same circumstance, if it were in his vocabulary.

THEORIES OF WORD LEARNING

In developing theories of how children learn language, researchers pay close attention to the errors toddlers make. Errors can provide clues to the *process* of language acquisition—the way in which the child perceives things in the world and applies labels to them. Suppose Mikey starts to learn the meaning of the word *ball* by associating it with all or most of the features possessed by the first ball Christine showed him. To him a ball would therefore be a large, round, red object that rolls across the floor. Later when Frank uses the word *ball* to refer to a stationary soccer ball, Mikey would have to revise his thinking and eliminate color and movement from his definition. Still later, when he hears his sister Becky say "ball" when pointing to a yellow tennis ball, largeness would also

How will the child discover that the first and third objects are named ball, but the second is not? *(Tom Dunham.)*

have to be considered irrelevant to this concept. Eventually Mikey would zero in on shape and function as the primary defining features. If toddlers did customarily learn the meaning of words in this way, errors of *under-extension* would be common. During the initial stages of acquiring a new word, they would tend to use the word in too restricted a manner.

Are errors of underextension in fact frequent among toddlers? It is not easy to say just by listening to different toddlers speak, for underextensions simply mean that a child will not use a word where it *could* have been used. By carefully observing individual toddlers over time, however, we can see that they do sometimes underextend word meanings. For instance, one little boy at age 8 months responded to the word *shoes* by crawling to the shoes in a *particular* closet (Reich, 1976). Gradually he generalized the meaning of this word to shoes in another closet, then to shoes left outside closets, and finally to shoes on people's feet. A similar pattern can be seen in Bloom's daughter, Allison, who at first applied the word *car* only to cars moving on the street outside her living-room window (Bloom, 1973). Six months passed before she extended the meaning to encompass cars in other situations. Such early underextensions suggest that young children do sometimes restrict the meanings of new words, only later broadening their definitions to match those of adults. However, researchers no longer consider this an adequate *general* description of how children learn word meanings.

Most current models of how the meanings of words are learned propose that children usually acquire *part* of the definition before they acquire the whole. Let's return to Mikey's learning the meaning of *ball*. Researcher Katherine Nelson (1974) suggests that he would first pay attention to how the object functions or how it moves. In this case Mikey might conclude that a ball is something that rolls. He would, therefore, overextend the meaning of this word to any rolling object, such as an egg that is rolling across the kitchen counter. When told "No, that's not a ball; that's an egg," Mikey would have to focus on additional features that distinguish these two objects. Eventually, he would arrive at the correct meaning of each word.

A popular version of this gradual learning process is called the **semantic feature hypothesis** (Clark, 1973). This model views words in terms of their semantic features, or defining characteristics. For example, the meaning of the word *truck* might consist of these features: vehicle, engine-driven, four or more wheels, carries cargo. If a child at first focuses on only *some* of the features (say, on the wheels, as Mikey did in an earlier example), the result will be overextensions of the word's meaning.

Researchers working within the semantic feature framework are particularly interested in explaining the order in which children learn a word's defining characteristics. This interest has prompted a number of theories. One recent example is the **lexical contrast theory** (*lexical* meaning pertaining to words). Eve Clark (1983, 1987), who proposed this model, believes that a child's communication needs and current state of knowledge are what promote attention to particular features, encourage new words to be acquired, and cause further restrictions of still overextended meanings. According to Clark, toddlers actively search for new words when they become aware of gaps in their vocabularies. They want to talk about a particular kind of object, action, or quality, but lack the word for doing so. Mikey, for instance, wants to call the color of the beach ball to Christine's attention, but he has no word for this feature. Later when he hears "red" spoken in reference to this toy, he assumes that it must contrast in meaning with the word *ball*, which he already knows. He therefore explores features for which he does not yet have labels as possible meanings for *red*. When he hears *red* also applied to his toy fire truck, as well as to his overalls and new pair of shoes, he deduces that *red* must be the name for this particular color.

If the semantic feature perspective is accurate, we would expect over-extensions to be very common among toddlers. This is in fact the case. The word *ball*, for example, is frequently applied to most relatively small, round objects, just as Mikey used it to label an egg. Most overextensions, like this one, refer to objects broadly similar in appearance, especially to those similar in shape (Clarke, 1983). Less frequently toddlers overextend verbs and other parts of speech by applying them to broadly similar actions. One toddler, for instance, initially used the word *out* to refer to opening or closing a door. Later the child generalized the meaning of *out* to peeling fruit, shelling peas, and undoing shoelaces (Clark, 1973, 1983).

One study of language development in six children found that the rate of overextensions was very high in the initial stages of building a vocabulary. Then, as the toddlers learned more words, the rate of over-extensions dropped dramatically. This pattern makes a great deal of sense. The more words children know, the higher the likelihood they will know the particular word to use in a given context. Put yourself in the position of Mikey, who wants to call attention to a bus that just went by. If he knows the word *truck* but not the word *bus*, he is apt to use *truck* in this situation.

Notice the problem of interpretation that this example raises. Does Mikey really think that *truck* is the right term to use? Or is he merely using the word in his vocabulary that has the closest meaning to what he wants to say? If the first of these two explanations is correct, Mikey seems to be learning word meanings according to the semantic feature hypothesis: His initial understanding of the word *truck* takes into account

Suppose a 22-month-old child has the words cheese, truck, toast, mama, cookie, kitty, dada, blankie, go, and milk in his or her vocabulary. How will he or she label the objects shown here? Quite likely the child will call the first truck, the second toast or cookie, and the third cheese. While such labels are wrong, they represent smart mistakes. The child has chosen the best word available. None of these objects would be labeled kitty or blankie. *(Tom Dunham.)*

only *some* of a truck's defining features. If, however, the second explanation is correct, this particular overextension does *not* provide support for the initial semantic feature model. Nevertheless, it is consistent with Clark's later lexical contrast theory. Mikey has become aware of a gap in his vocabulary and is searching for a word to fill it.

Is there any way we can estimate the extent to which one or the other of these two explanations is right? One way is to study overextensions not regarding what children say, but regarding what they understand *others* to be saying. When researchers take this approach, they find that the incidence of overextensions is much lower. For example, even though Mikey may label a bus as a "truck," if he were shown several objects, including a truck and a bus, he would have little difficulty choosing the correct object corresponding to each label (Clark, 1983). This suggests that he has the concept of *bus* even though the label for it may be less well learned than the label for *truck*, which he knows overlaps with the bus concept. Many of the overextensions toddlers produce thus are the result of saying the closest word available when the correct word is not known. Toddlers, in short, may know more about the true meanings of words than their own speech implies.

To summarize, some evidence suggests that, when words are first learned, they tend to be used only in the specific contexts in which they were first encountered (e.g., Bowerman, 1981; Carey, 1978). This very early period of language acquisition is one of underextensions. Later the child begins to explore the limits of word meanings. Does *ball* mean all roundish objects? Does *truck* mean anything with wheels? Overextensions occur in this stage. At the same time, toddlers often knowingly overgeneralize a word because it is the closest one available in their vocabularies. In these cases children can be thought of as searching for the right word, and, not surprisingly, they are very responsive to corrective feedback from adults ("No, that's not a truck; that's a *bus*"). Receiving feedback following errors of overextension is probably one of the most effective ways that children learn new words.

Learning Morphological Rules

The words that children first learn are usually single morphemes: Mommy, Daddy, milk, doggie, go, more, cookie, sock. Each is a unit of language that represents a single object, action, or quality. Then, during the preschool years, new kinds of morphemes emerge—grammatical ones. **Grammatical morphemes** include prefixes, suffixes, and auxiliary verbs that change the meaning of words. For instance, the sound of /s/ added to the end of a noun such as *sock* changes its meaning from singular to plural. The suffix *s*, therefore, is a grammatical morpheme.

Roger Brown (1973) studied the learning of grammatical morphemes in three children: Eve, Adam, and Sarah. He found that they acquired these morphemes in a consistent order, the same order revealed in a cross-sectional study of a large number of children (de Villiers and de Villiers, 1978). First, children master grammatical morphemes indicating plural nouns, along with the suffix *ing* to form the present participle of a verb (as in *going* or *running*). Somewhat later, children acquire the suffix *ed* to form the past tense of verbs (as in *jumped*), as well as the suffix s to form the third person singular (as in "she sits"). Among the last grammatical morphemes to be mastered are those that form contractions of the verb "to be" (the 's in "it's big," for example, or the 're in "they're playing").

Why are grammatical morphemes learned in this particular order? Roger Brown (1973) has offered two hypotheses. First, forms that are *grammatically* simplest might be learned first. By grammatically simple Brown means close to the active, declarative form of a verb (as *going* is close to *go*) or close to the base morpheme of a noun (as *socks* is close to *sock*). Second, *semantic* complexity may govern the order of learning. By this Brown means the complexity of the ideas that the grammatical morpheme adds. The *ing* that forms the present participle, for instance, adds to the verb the quite simple idea of ongoing action. In contrast, appending an *s* to a verb to form the third person singular adds several ideas: (1) that we are talking about someone else, (2) that only one person or object is referred to (he, she, or it, not they), and (3) that the action takes place in the present ("she sits"). Since grammatical complexity and semantic complexity are highly correlated, it is hard to determine which exerts more of an influence on the order in which preschoolers learn grammatical morphemes. Perhaps both are influential.

Probably also affecting the order of this learning are the general strategies children adopt in trying to master language. Dan Slobin (1973) has proposed that one such strategy (for learners of English) is paying attention to the endings of words. This strategy could explain why English-speaking children learn suffixes earlier than prefixes. Since strategies for learning language vary depending upon the structure of the particular language, such strategies can also explain why children learning different languages acquire grammatical morphemes in different orders.

Acquiring grammatical morphemes is of particular interest to developmentalists because it shows that language learning involves discerning rules. For instance, children do not learn the plural forms of nouns word by word, as if each one is an entirely new entity. Instead they learn a general rule about forming plurals: Add the suffix *s* or *es* and the noun becomes "more than one." In an interesting study, Jean Berko (1958) showed how children apply morphological rules even to words they have never heard before. For example, she taught children that the name of an unusual birdlike creature was a *wug*. Then she showed them a picture of two of these creatures and said "Here are two _____." The children's task was to fill in the blank. Those who had acquired the rule of adding *s* to form the plural readily answered "wugs." Berko's study shows the great *productivity* of language—the fact that it allows almost unlimited output. Because language combines morphemes according to general rules, we can take even an unfamiliar word and modify its meaning in ways that others will understand.

The large number of exceptions to morphological rules presents one potential stumbling block in mastering them. Most nouns can be made plural by adding *s* or *es*, but in some cases this rule does not apply (mouse/mice, for example, or foot/feet). Similarly, although the usual way to form the past tense of a verb is to add the suffix *ed*, irregular verbs don't follow this convention (go/went, come/came). You might think that children would learn the regular forms first and only afterward tackle the

This is a wug.

Now there is another one.
There are two of them.
There are two _____.

Figure 8.2
Berko's Study of
Morphological Rule Formation
The ability of young children to make the noun *wug* into the plural form *wugs* indicates that they have learned the morphological rule for forming plurals.
Source: Berko, 1958.

By listening to spoken language children learn grammatical rules that they then apply in forming new sentence combinations. *(Elizabeth Crews.)*

exceptions. This, however, is not the pattern researchers have observed. Instead, the correct irregular past tenses and plurals often appear early in a child's speech, with the child correctly saying "came," "did," "mice," "feet," and so forth (Dale, 1976). Shortly thereafter an odd thing happens. The child starts to impose regular forms on irregular nouns and verbs so that "mice" becomes "mouses," or "feet" becomes "foots," "came" becomes "comed," and "did" becomes "doed." These errors are referred to as **overregularizations.** Significantly, overregularizations appear about the same time as a dramatic increase in the child's use of regular past tenses and plurals. It is as if the youngster has suddenly deduced the *ed* and *s* rules and so begins to apply them universally. Finally, as the child grows a little older, the correct irregular forms reappear in his or her speech. By early school age the youngster is using correct forms almost 100 percent of the time (Cazden, 1968).

This interesting pattern provides important insights into the cognitive processes that underlie language learning. When learning something complex such as a language, children seem to search automatically for regularities and rules. To find these regularities, however, they must first learn a number of examples from which the rules can be drawn. At this early stage they learn both regular and irregular forms, each one as a separate entity. From this pool of known examples they then filter out the irregular ones and zero in on the grammatical morpheme used in the majority of cases. With this rule figured out, they then begin to apply it in other cases (including those with irregular nouns and verbs). For example, Mikey, having learned the meaning of the suffix *ful* from words like *beautiful, forgetful,* and *thoughtful,* might describe a woman with long hair as "hairful." Gradually, children become aware of their overgeneralizations and begin using the correct irregular forms once again.

This learning process is clearly very complex, as anyone knows who has ever tried to master the irregular words in a second language. Yet preschoolers seem to accomplish it with little effort just from hearing language being spoken. Long before adulthood the rules and most exceptions to them seem second nature to us, even though we may still be caught off guard when asked what the plural of *moose* is or whether the past tense of *fly* is ever *flied.* (It is, in the sentence "The batter flied out.") Our hesitation in answering such questions reminds us what a difficult achievement young children are making when they master rules about morphology. From the toddler's early acquisition of the present progressive (*ing,* as in *walking*), each grammatical morpheme must be learned from a set of specific examples.

Developments in Syntax

Syntax is a language's rules for ordering words into sentences. A standard word order in English is subject, verb, object as in the sentence "John kissed Mary." We interpret the sentence "Mary kissed John" to have a different meaning, because we automatically assume it follows the rule for forming an English sentence in the active voice. We therefore identify Mary as the subject and John as the object of her affections. As young children become more skilled at language, they must master this and many other rules of syntax, gradually forming and understanding longer, more complex sentences.

Any system of syntax has two especially important characteristics. First, syntactic rules apply to abstract elements of speech: subjects, verbs, objects, modifiers, connective words, and so forth. These rules limit the ways in which such elements can be put together. Thus, when learning syntax, children cannot extract the rules directly from the words they hear spoken. Instead, they must first understand those words as examples of elements that perform certain roles within sentences. From a grasp of these elements, children can then deduce the rules that govern word placement.

A second important feature of syntactic rules is their productivity. Just as morphological rules allow for tremendous output in the way words can be used to express ideas, so syntactic rules allow for countless possible sentences just by placing different words in the various roles. Once children know the rules of syntax, their ability to create new and meaningful sentences becomes virtually unlimited.

In exploring how young children acquire syntax, we will focus on two areas that have been studied quite extensively. These areas are an understanding of the passive voice and an understanding of how to construct various kinds of questions. Research on both these topics nicely illustrates children's step-by-step mastery of the syntax of their language.

UNDERSTANDING THE PASSIVE VOICE

The verb in a sentence frequently can be expressed in either the active or the passive voice. In an active-voice construction, the subject of the sentence performs the verb's action. In a passive-voice construction, the subject merely receives that action passively. Whether children correctly interpret passive-voice constructions depends on both their developmental level and the particular sentence.

Tom Bever (1970) demonstrated this in an interesting study of children ages 2 through 5. He presented various sentences and asked the children to act out the meanings by using toys and other objects. Virtually all the subjects correctly acted out sentences in the active voice, such as "The girl picked the flower" or "The car hit the truck." When it came to sentences in the passive voice, however, a curious pattern emerged. The 3-year-olds correctly interpreted a passive rearrangement of the first example ("The flower was picked by the girl") but not of the second ("The truck was hit by the car"). The 5-year-olds correctly interpreted *both* these passive constructions, but the 4-year-olds, oddly enough, correctly interpreted *neither*.

Why did the 4-year-olds make more mistakes than the 3-year-olds? Bever argued that the answer lies in the strategies used to interpret the sentences. Three-year-olds seem to approach a sentence with a *semantic* strategy: They interpret the meaning so that the sentence makes sense. A girl can pick a flower but a flower can't pick a girl. Three-year-olds, therefore, correctly identify the girl as the actor even in the passive-voice construction. This kind of sentence is called *nonreversible* because if you try to switch the actor with the thing acted on the sentence becomes nonsensical. Note that a semantic strategy doesn't work for *reversible* sentences like "The truck was hit by the car." Either the truck or the car can do the hitting or receive the hit. Because of this potential reversibility, 3-year-olds interpreted in terms of the most common word order in English: actor, action, object.

Four-year-olds, in contrast, have reached the point of having a *syntactic* strategy for interpreting sentences, but that strategy is still too simple. Four-year-olds seem to assume that the first noun in a sentence is always the actor. This strategy works fine for sentences in the active voice, but it leads to mistakes regarding passive-voice sentences, both reversible *and* nonreversible. Thus, superficially they seem to regress because they start misinterpreting sentences that earlier they correctly understood. Developmentalists do not consider this kind of error a regression, however. Instead, they regard it as a **growth error** because it is caused by the emergence of a more advanced way of thinking. Notice that this is the same kind of error children make in gradually mastering morphological rules: They overregularize irregular plurals and past tenses. But though they are making more mistakes and seem to be losing ground, in fact they are making progress toward understanding the organizational rules of their language.

Failure to interpret passive-voice sentences correctly disappears as children begin to acquire more advanced syntactic strategies. By age 5, children have apparently learned to discriminate between the active and passive voice. If the verb is active, they consider the first noun the actor; if the verb is passive they assign the second noun this role. They then refine their earlier knowledge of syntax, broadening their ability to use and understand language.

CONSTRUCTING QUESTIONS

All languages have two types of questions. **Yes/no questions** can always be answered with a simple yes or no ("Did you do that?" "May I have a copy?"), while **wh questions** always begin with an interrogative word (what, where, when, why, who, how), almost all of which in English begin with *wh*. Children learn to form the various types of questions step-by-step, which often involves complex combinations of rules. We base our discussion of this process on the research of Ursula Bellugi and her colleagues, who have extensively studied the acquisition of grammar in preschoolers (Brown, Cazden, and Bellugi, 1969). Let's begin with the learning of yes/no questions.

Yes/no questions change a declarative sentence into a question that asks whether the declarative statement is true. For example, "Can Sally read?" turns the declarative statement "Sally can read" into a yes/no question. In a sentence like this one the question is formed by moving the auxiliary verb (*can*) in front of the subject. Other declarative sentences have no auxiliary verb, so one must be mentally added before the question can be formed. For instance, the sentence "Sally read the book" is first given an auxiliary verb ("Sally *did* read the book"), and then that auxiliary verb is moved in front of the subject ("Did Sally read the book?"). If the declarative sentence happens to be negative ("Sally cannot read"), another rule comes into play. The auxiliary verb and the negative are first contracted and then moved to the front of the sentence ("Can't Sally read?"). Finally, yes/no questions also can be formed by adding a tag with an auxiliary-negative contraction in it onto the declarative sentence as in "Sally can read, can't she?"

Two-year-olds have not yet learned any of these rules for forming questions. To ask a yes/no question, they simply raise their intonation at the end of a sentence, as in "Mommy go?" or "I play?" At around 3 years of age, children speak in longer sentences and use auxiliary verbs. At this age they begin to move the auxiliary verb to form a question and they also add auxiliary verbs when needed ("Can I play?" "Did Mommy go?"). In addition, they correctly construct negative yes/no questions, as in "Can't I play?" or "Didn't Mommy go?" Only the yes/no question with a tag ending is still absent from the child's speech. This is not surprising when you consider that this construction deviates quite a bit from the other ones. After creating a contraction of an auxiliary verb and *not*, the child must move it to the *end* of the sentence (not the beginning) and remember to accompany it by the appropriate personal pronoun ("Mommy went, didn't she?"). Because the combination of rules required to form tag questions is so complex, they do not emerge until about age 4.

Wh questions are even harder to form than yes/no ones, which is why young children make many errors in constructing them. To form such a question, the speaker usually must move an auxiliary verb in front of the subject ("Where did he go?"). However, when the verb "to be" is the main verb in the sentence, its various forms are what get moved ("What is his name?" "Why am I here?"). In addition, the correct interrogative word (*where, what, why,* and so forth) must be appended, generally at the very beginning of the sentence, although sometimes at the end ("You went where?"). Keeping track of all these elements provides more opportunities for mistakes.

Only at the very end of the toddler period are *wh* questions appearing, and they take the following form: "What Mommy doing?" "Where you go?" Notice that all the child has done is put the appropriate interrogative word at the beginning of a simple declarative sentence. Even at age 3½, when children are correctly moving the auxiliary verb to form yes/no questions, they are still saying things like "What I did yesterday?" and "How he can be a doctor?" It is as if it is too complicated to identify and move an auxiliary verb while keeping track of all the other aspects of asking *wh* questions.

By about age 4½, children are correctly posing questions such as "Why are you thirsty?" The negative forms of these questions, however, remain a problem for them ("Why you aren't thirsty?" the child may ask). Again, the cognitive demands of combining several syntactic rules (forming a negative contraction, moving it in front of the subject, and adding an interrogative word) seem to overload the child's capacities. Not until children are approximately 5 years old do they being constructing negative *wh* questions properly.

Several major points should be stressed in summing up the development of syntax during early childhood. First, language changes dramatically from the very limited creation of two- and three-word sentences to the use of a highly complex and productive communication system. Second, much of what accounts for this dramatic transformation is the learning of syntactic rules. It is not enough to learn these rules as separate

Some experiences are marvelously filled with novelty, giving the 3-year-old ample opportunity for questions. *(Peter B. Kaplan/Photo Researchers, Inc.)*

entities. Children must also acquire the ability to use various rules in combination. This learning task is enormously complex, so that the strides young children make in mastering syntax are truly amazing.

A Closer Look at the Language Environment

The environment in which language develops strongly influences how children learn to speak. The more a mother talks to an infant in the first year, the larger the child's vocabulary is likely to be at 17 months of age (Clarke-Stewart, 1973). Greater exposure to language, in short, speeds language learning. But what about the *type* of speech to which young children are exposed? Can it, too, facilitate language acquisition?

Several researchers argue that adults modify their speech with toddlers in ways that make it easier for the children to learn language (e.g., Ferguson, 1964; Slobin, 1975; Snow, 1972; Tomasello, Mannle, and Kruger, 1986). These speech modifications are known as **child directed speech (CDS),** or **motherese,** even though many fathers make them as well (Gleason, 1975). If you are wondering exactly what motherese entails, listen to this mother who is sitting with her 19-month-old daughter ready to draw a picture:

> *Mother:* What should I draw first?
> *Child:* Bi goggie.
> *Mother:* A big doggie. All right. Is that big?
> *Child:* Oggie bi. Bi gog.
> *Mother:* What's this? What's this part of the doggie? Is that a big enough doggie?
> *Child:* Bi goggie.
> *Mother:* Well, I did make a big doggie. Look.
> *Child:* Bi goggie.
> *Mother:* You make a big doggie. Make a kitty.
> *Child:* Kiki.
> (Genishi and Dyson, 1984, p. 45)

How does CDS differ from normal adult speech? The answer lies partly in how the sentences are structured. CDS is grammatically simpler than normal speech and has fewer grammatical errors (Molfese, Molfese, and Carrell, 1982). CDS is also spoken in a higher than normal pitch, its intonations are more exaggerated, and it has fewer lapses in fluency (Garnica, 1974). The content of CDS tends to focus on objects and events discussed in the present tense, using concrete nouns. The adult frequently comments on what the child is doing or on what is going on around the child. CDS also tends to be quite redundant. The mother above, for instance, finds many different ways to repeat the words *big* and *doggie* (Molfese, Molfese, and Carrell, 1982). Notice, too, how this mother often asks her daughter questions about their joint project: "What should I draw? Is this a big enough doggie? What part of the doggie is this?" Such frequent questioning about objects and events is typical of CDS (Snow, 1977).

Fathers speaking motherese differ from mothers in that they more often ask for labels and explanations ("What's this?" "What does it do?")

Adults often change their speech when talking to young children. *(Larry Voigt/Photo Researchers, Inc.)*

and for repetitions and clarifications (Masur and Gleason, 1980). Thus fathers are not simply secondary mothers, but they make a genuine contribution to the child's linguistic environment by readying him or her for the social world in which clarity is important (Smolak, 1986).

Interestingly, adults are only partially successful in talking CDS when young children are not around (Snow, 1972). What's more, they are not fully able to produce the speech pattern until children are old enough to respond verbally to them (Phillips, 1973). These findings suggest that something about toddlers and their responses to speech elicits CDS from adults.

Does CDS really facilitate language learning as some researchers have proposed? Although in general a relationship seems to exist between the use of CDS and the rate of language acquisition, this relationship is not particularly strong (Newport, Gleitman, and Gleitman, 1977; Molfese, Molfese, and Carrell, 1982). Perhaps the reason is that CDS is most effective when tailored to the individual needs of a child. Toni Cross (1977) found that adults tend to adjust certain aspects of CDS to the child's particular skill level, aspects such as the length of their utterances and the number of ideas per utterance. Apparently, the most important adjustments to make are ones that enable the child to participate actively in the conversation.

The age of the child also is a significant factor in the influence of CDS. One recent study found a stronger relationship between CDS and level of language development in children age 19 months than in children 25 months of age (Gleitman, Newport, and Gleitman, 1984). This finding makes sense when you consider that more language modifications are needed to make speech comprehensible to a younger toddler. In general, a responsive language environment, one that is sensitive to the child's level of understanding, seems to be an important factor in early language development.

Some recent evidence suggests individual characteristics of mothers are related to the way they speak to their children. Barbara Bettes (1986) studied women who had given birth to a first child within the past year. She tape recorded the mother-infant dyad and subjected the recordings to several types of analyses, including an acoustic analysis of the mothers' voice contours, pitch, and exaggeration. She discovered that mothers who were mildly depressed used less intonation in their CDS, as well as lower pitch, and took longer to respond to their children's vocalizations. These depressed mothers also were more variable in responding to vocalizations, sometimes taking only a fraction of a second, other times taking up to 10 seconds to respond. Future research will determine whether such differences in CDS and other aspects of emotional expressions are important in determining the cognitive and social problems found in children of depressed mothers (see Chapter 16).

GENERAL PERSPECTIVES ON THE BEGINNINGS OF LANGUAGE

In this chapter you have already encountered several theories designed to explain relatively small aspects of language development, such as how children learn word meanings. Such small-scale theories with a specialized focus are products of larger, more general perspectives on language acquisition. The three major perspectives in this field are the behaviorist, the nativist, and the cognitive (Maratsos, 1983). Each tries to identify the most important general factors enabling toddlers to learn a language. The behaviorist perspective argues that learning language is no different from learning anything else. Children's early nonword utterances initially are reinforced by adults around them and as a result are repeated. Adult attention later is withheld until the utterance more closely resembles adult speech. The nativist perspective on language acquisition argues that human beings come to the task of learning a language equipped with a special talent. And finally, the cognitive perspective argues that a few powerful cognitive processes influence language learning. For example, all over the world language can be classified according to the same semantic relations (agent, action, object), and this similarity is taken as evidence that language and cognition develop in synchrony. More will be said about each of these perspectives below.

The Behaviorist Perspective

The **behaviorist view** on language acquisition is closely associated with psychologist B. F. Skinner. In his book *Verbal Behavior* (1957), Skinner argued that parents and others instrumentally condition children to talk. When the baby begins to babble, the parents smile, pay attention, and talk to the child in response. Their attention reinforces the infant for babbling, and so babbling becomes more frequent. The increased frequency of babbling raises the probability that the baby will, just by chance, says things that sound like words. When the parents hear these wordlike sounds, they reinforce them in preference to nonword sounds. The child responds by repeating what sounds to the parents like words, and so "words" enter the baby's repertoire of verbal behaviors. Skinner has argued that the meaning of words also is acquired through such reinforcement, as is the grammar of a language. Parents reinforce grammatically correct statements and reject or show confusion over incorrect ones. As a result, the child learns proper grammar. As can be seen, Skinner considered language no different from anything else that is learned; he argued that the child brings nothing special to the language-learning task.

Researchers have tested Skinner's view on language acquisition by examining how parents respond to their young children's speech (Brown, Cazden, and Bellugi, 1969). They have found that parents are much more likely to correct a statement when it is untrue than when it is grammatically incorrect. For instance, when Malcolm says "Me sit doggie chair," while parking a new toy elephant on top of the sofa, DeeDee ignores his rough-edged grammar but tells him gently, "That's an elephant, honey, not a doggie." This response is typical of most parents, who sometimes make their own grammatical errors and therefore do not provide perfect models of language (Brown and Hanlon, 1970). The central point is that it is the truthfulness of Malcolm's remark, not its grammatical form, that prompts a correction from DeeDee. Yet despite this pattern of reinforcement, most children learn to use correct grammar, even though they don't always use it to tell the truth. How could children learn grammar if reinforcement is as central to language learning as Skinner proposed?

A related problem with the behaviorist perspective comes from observations of the way language is acquired in other parts of the world. Bambi Schiefflin and Elinor Ochs (1983) studied the Kaluli people of southern New Guinea. Kaluli mothers do not believe their infants are able to communicate or comprehend what is said in their presence, even in a rudimentary manner. So, they avoid looking at their faces and carry them facing away. When these mothers talk about their babies, as all

Sign language can be taught to chimpanzees and gorillas. If they teach it to their offspring, and the latter to their offspring, the theory that humans are uniquely and innately adapted to learning language will have to be modified. In this photograph, the chimpanzee is responding to a question about a woollen cap with the American Sign Language sign, "hat." *(R. A. and B. T. Gardner.)*

mothers do, their statements are unrelated to the infants' behavior. Despite these differences from the way American mothers interact with their babies, Kaluli babies develop language normally, according to a timetable comparable to that of American babies. This finding would seem to call into question the predominant role that behaviorists assign to environment in shaping the child's language behavior.

Even more damaging to Skinner's position was a review of his book by the well-known linguist Noam Chomsky (1957). Chomsky argued that Skinner's view of how children acquire language was totally inadequate. You could not pack into an entire lifetime all the reinforcement episodes needed to learn language through instrumental conditioning, Chomsky contended. Children speak an extraordinarily large number of sentences, and each of these could not have been learned separately through reinforcement. Even if you add imitation as a learning mechanism, you can still explain only how children learn to repeat the things they have heard. But children do not simply repeat other people's sentences. One of the most important features of language, Chomsky pointed out, is that words can be combined to say things that we have never heard anyone else say.

So compelling was Chomsky's critique of Skinner's book that most developmentalists strongly agreed with his reasoning. Still, of course, most developmentalists do *not* believe that reinforcement and imitation are irrelevant to language learning. Reinforcement and imitation have a place in acquiring language, as when we described Frank shaping Mikey to say "bread" in Chapter 5. The behaviorist perspective is particularly useful for explaining some of the details of language learning (Akiyami, 1984; Hirsh-Patek, Treiman, and Schneiderman, 1984; Whitehurst, 1982). However, it is not sufficient to fully explain language acquisition.

The Nativist Perspective

As an alternative to Skinner's reinforcement approach, Chomsky (1957) offered a **nativist view,** which focuses on the child's innate (unlearned) capacities. Chomsky argued that all languages share certain structural characteristics. These shared features show that languages and the human mind evolved together. Our early ancestors fashioned language as they did because of certain innate capacities of the brain that led them to perceive and understand their world in quite specific ways (e.g., in terms of agents, actions, and objects of actions, as well as past, present, and future). The same innate capacities allow very young children to extract the rules of any language that they hear spoken, especially the language's syntax. Chomsky called these innate capacities the **language acquisition device,** or **LAD** for short. He maintained that part of the brain is specially adapted for language learning. When a toddler is merely exposed to language, the LAD automatically focuses on the rules that govern it.

Research on the specialized functions of specific areas of the brain has been used to support the concept of innate, or "prewired," neural mechanisms for language learning. One region of the brain is responsible for understanding and producing language, among other things. Damage to specific sites in this region can destroy speech (Broca's area) and comprehension (Wernicke's area), as the family members of some cardiovascular-stroke victims can sadly attest. According to some preliminary evidence, even the brains of newborns are specialized for language. Electroencephalographic studies of the newborn's brain show that the phonemes /b/ and /p/ produce different patterns of electrical activation in different regions of the brain (Molfese and Molfese, 1979). This is impressive evidence for some sort of prewiring.

Related to this biological argument is the finding that there appears to be a critical period during which language can be learned with relative ease. Eric Lenneberg (1967) was the first to provide empirical evidence in support of this hypothesis, but a number of others have done likewise (e.g., Asher and Garcia, 1969; Oyama, 1973). Puberty is thought to mark the end of the critical period for acquiring the phonological system. Hence, some speakers of English who have lived in the United States for many years still speak with an "accent" because they did not learn English until after the onset of puberty (Labov, 1970). If learning a language is similar to other forms of learning, as the behaviorists maintain, why would the laws governing the learning of phonology become less effective after puberty?

Just as there are behaviorist approaches other than Skinner's, so there are nativist approaches other than Chomsky's. Chomsky focused on the mastery of grammatical rules. In contrast, certain other nativist perspectives have focused on mastering the concepts that underlie words and their meanings. But regardless of their particular slants, all nativist approaches have several things in common. They all seem to be motivated by the same observations about language acquisition. One is the remarkable speed with which children learn language, without anyone's "teaching" them to talk. How could this ease of language learning be explained if the capacity for it were not innate? Then there is the observation that language acquisition proceeds in essentially the same way regardless of differences in the languages being learned. Dan Slobin (1972) has documented the similarities that exist in the language acquisition of 20 different linguistic communities around the world. What could account for this striking similarity if not an innate program within the human brain? Nativist perspectives also have in common a stress on the interaction of heredity and environment. Although all nativist theories for language propose innate machinery that guides and constrains language development, they acknowledge that experience influences the particulars of what children learn. The interaction of heredity and environment is the aspect of nativist perspectives that most interests developmentalists.

Children throughout the world learn grammatical language in the first few years of life, and they do so with apparent ease. How to explain this remains controversial, but the basic fact of its universal occurrence is accepted. *(Nicole Toutounji/ UNICEF.)*

The Cognitive Perspective

A third major approach to understanding language acquisition is the **cognitive view,** which differs from the behaviorist view by proposing much more complex mechanisms of learning. It is similar to the nativist perspective in assuming an innate disposition for certain kinds of learning. However, these innate mechanisms are *not* seen as specially evolved for mastering language. In the cognitive perspective, language is just one of many complex skills children acquire using the general cognitive capacities they are developing (Bates and MacWhinney, 1982; Maratsos, 1983; Piaget, 1969).

Cognitive theorists question the nativist hypothesis of a special mechanism for language acquisition for several reasons. First, they point out the relative recency of human language—it is between 10,000 and 100,000 years old (Swadesh, 1971). This length of time is probably not sufficient to have evolved a language-specific neural mechanism, since it took more than 2 million years for advanced cognitive functioning to have evolved (Miller, 1981). Second, children around the world differ much more in the way they acquire language than scientists had previously thought, which calls into question the universality of language acquisition and, by implication, some of its prewired nature (Akiyami, 1984). The only real universal to language learning seems to be that children acquire the purely linguistic (syntactic) features of their language much later than the semantic and phonological aspects (Slobin, 1973). This similarity would be predicted if the development of conceptual understanding is central to the process of language development.

Michael Maratsos (1983), a cognitive theorist, has described two important assumptions of the cognitive perspective. First, children are *active* agents in learning language. As their cognitive capacities develop, they begin to grasp the meaning of concepts and they wish to express those meanings clearly to others. This need to communicate motivates them to acquire words and, later, the rules of grammar. Parents do not have to coax their children to learn about language. Children actively seek to master this skill. Second, what children understand about concepts and categories of meaning helps them to analyze the grammar of the language they hear. For instance, toddlers' developing understanding of the concept of agent, action, and thing being acted on prepares them to begin to construct sentences. Once these concepts are known, it is a logical step to understanding the related linguistic categories of subject, verb, and object.

Still another assumption made by all cognitive theorists is that because language is acquired as a result of a set of general cognitive strategies not specifically evolved for language learning, then language acquisition should be linked to the development of other cognitive skills, such as symbolic play, memory development, and block building. Cecilia Shore (1986) recently examined a group of 2-year-olds on a battery of tasks to determine whether their performance on one task (language) could be predicted from their performance on others (memory and symbolic maturity). In general, she found evidence supportive of the cognitive perspective. The children's language development *was* related to their block-building, memory, and symbolic-play ability. The increase in efficiency with which children between the ages of 1 and 3 can remember a sequence of things seems to be linked to their ability to put together a string of several words into a well-formed sentence. This result is counter to the nativist hypothesis, which posits that the first sentences must await the emergence of grammatical ordering rules unique to language (Bloom, 1973).

Despite similarities in their overall perspective, cognitive theories of language development do differ from one another. Each describes a somewhat different general mechanism of development which can be applied to language learning. These various cognitive theories are treated throughout this book.

Block building has been identified as a cognitive skill that seems to be related to the development of language. *(Elizabeth Crews.)*

THE RELATIONSHIP BETWEEN LANGUAGE AND THOUGHT

The beginning of language is a dramatic hallmark of the toddler period. As we noted earlier, it reveals the toddler's emerging capacity for representation. One example of representational thought was provided in Chapter 6, when we discussed how, by the end of the second year, children can imagine the invisible movements of an object. This ability is especially obvious in the toddler's play. Several investigators have separately demonstrated a lawful sequence in the development of symbolic play during the toddler period (Belsky and Most, 1981; Nicolich, 1977; Motti, Cicchetti, and Sroufe, 1983). Initially, symbolic representation is seen in behaviors directed to the self. A 16-month-old may, for example, pretend to drink from a toy cup. Later, toddlers will direct such acts to others (as in pretending to feed a doll). Before the end of the second year, they can combine a series of such acts around a theme (e.g., building a "fence" with blocks around pretend animals). In these examples, toddlers are showing that they are no longer restricted to understanding the world solely through direct perception and action.

The emergence of representation and language in the toddler period raises questions about the relationship between thought and language. How do they influence each other? Does acquiring language mark an important developmental shift in the thinking of young children? Might children who learn to speak different languages end up thinking differently? Could you even learn to speak if you did not already have some underlying concepts to communicate?

To answer such questions it is essential to distinguish language from thought. Language is defined as a system for communication with others. **Thought** consists of all the concepts, representations, and active manipulations of information that go on within a person's mind.

Much of the research on the relationship between language and thought has been conducted with children older than toddlers (see Furth, 1966). What is the relationship between a toddler's general cognitive representations and the older child's use of language? For example, which comes first: words or the conceptual meanings to which words refer? In previous sections we talked about learning word meanings as if toddlers already had the world mentally organized into concepts and their task was simply to learn the names they should attach to those concepts. But some developmentalists think that early language also has a marked influence on how toddlers think about and organize the world in their minds. Others think that the early development of language is basically independent from thought, that the two do not influence one another until a child is about 2 years old. Let's look more closely at these various viewpoints.

Piaget's View

Jean Piaget believed that cognitive development is primary; language development is just one manifestation of more general cognitive changes. At least until a child reaches the period of formal operations (adolescence), cognitive development is relatively unaffected by language, according to Piaget.

The principal cognitive development of toddlerhood in Piaget's view is the emergence of symbolic capability—that is, the ability to let one thing stand for another that is not physically present. Symbols can be purely mental representations, or they can be words, objects, or actions. When Mikey forms a mental image of a piece of candy, he is using a symbol to represent an object that he wants. When Malcolm tells his grandmother, "Daddy go work," he is using words as symbols for something that has already happened. When Meryl takes a paper plate and pretends it's the steering wheel of a car, she is using the plate and her actions as symbols for the real act of driving.

Implicit in Piaget's notion of symbols is the ability to manipulate them intentionally, thus creating new ideas and thoughts. In the case of linguistic symbols, the child becomes able to combine words together. This deliberate manipulation of symbols enables the child to say anything imaginable. In Piaget's view, a toddler's first words are not really symbols, because they refer only to objects or events in the here and now. Not until a child begins to talk about things that are not currently present does he or she use language symbolically as Piaget defined the term. This point in language development usually occurs between 18 and 24 months of age. Recall from Chapter 6 that this age range marks the last of Piaget's six sensorimotor stages.

According to Piaget, the general symbolic abilities that emerge in middle toddlerhood are a developmental outgrowth of sensorimotor activities. In particular, Piaget emphasized the role of imitation in the development of a toddler's use of symbols. Consider the following observation he made of his daughter Jacqueline:

> At 15 months Jacqueline was playing with a clown with long feet and happened to catch the feet in the low neck of her dress. She had difficulty in getting them out, but as soon as she had done so she tried to put them back in the same position. . . . As she did not succeed she put her hand in front of her, bent her forefinger at a right angle to reproduce the shape of the clown's feet, described exactly the same trajectory as the clown, and thus succeeded in putting her finger into the neck of her dress. She looked at the motionless finger for a moment, then pulled at her dress, without of course being able to see what she was doing. Then satisfied, she removed her finger and went on to something else. (Piaget, 1952, p. 65)

Notice how Jacqueline is imitating with the action of her finger the previous action of the clown's feet. This is not yet true symbolic representation, but it is the forerunner and helps to show the origins of this important new ability. By the end of the sensorimotor period, Piaget contended, the child's imitations become more abbreviated. For example, rather than going through the whole process of imitating the clown's feet getting caught in her dress, Jacqueline at 20 months might simply flex her finger slightly to stand for the shape of the feet. Notice how the child is now able to employ a rudimentary symbol that bears a much less obvious relationship to the thing being symbolized. Still later she will use words ("feet caught") to represent the incident with purely verbal symbols. Piaget maintained that the meaning of any symbol lies in the child's current schemes for interacting with the thing symbolized. Symbols, in other words, do not represent things in themselves; instead, they represent the child's present understanding of things.

In Piaget's view the child's general symbolic capacity logically occurs prior to the acquisition of words. In fact, the ability to represent things mentally *without* words can be thought of as an impetus for building a vocabulary to communicate those representations to others. In this respect, Piaget's view is compatible with Eve Clark's lexical contrast theory. Clark proposes that children sometimes look for a word that will allow them to express a concept for which they currently have no word. Here the child has mentally represented a concept *before* acquiring a word to express it. Clark also argues then when children first hear a word, they will search in the conceptual "spaces" among the words they already know. To do this the child must again have mental representations of concepts that as yet have no labels. Thus, to both Clark and Piaget a toddler's conceptual world cannot be fully understood just by analyzing that child's knowledge of language.

Language continues to be of major importance to development throughout childhood. *(Richard Hutchings/ Photo Researchers, Inc.)*

Bruner's View

For Jerome Bruner (1964), language is a crucial part of the child's symbolic representation system, not just one of many manifestations of it. In fact, for Bruner language seems to be the initial source of all symbolic thought, which he distinguishes from two other forms of representation— action (enactive mode) and image (ikonic mode). As language develops, so too do other forms of symbolic representation.

The semantic feature hypothesis about how word meanings are learned is most compatible with Bruner's approach. According to this view an understanding of a word's meaning develops at the same time and by the same process as an understanding of the underlying concept to which the word refers. Malcolm, for instance, initially learns the word *in* with reference to putting toys inside a shoe box. He is later heard to generalize the term to similar situations: "Milk *in* cup." "Candy *in* hand." "Daddy *in* car." Then one day he places a cracker he has been eating underneath a spoon and announces to his mother: "Cracker *in* spoon." DeeDee smiles and corrects him: "It's *under*, honey. The cracker's *under* the spoon." Feedback like this forces Malcolm to narrow the original meaning he attached to *in* and to draw a new conceptual distinction between *in* and *under*. Thus, with the help of language development, Malcolm is acquiring a more advanced understanding of the relationships among objects. Notice how in Bruner's view language is a crucial part of cognitive development. Language is not just something that reflects cognitive development, as it does in Piaget's theory.

Vygotsky's View

Another perspective on the relationship between language and cognitive development comes from the Russian psychologist Lev Vygotsky (1934/ 1962). According to Vygotsky, language and thought at first develop separately. At around 2 years of age, the two lines of development begin to

As young children carry out activities, they often talk to themselves about the task. Such self-instruction seems to help them stay on track and carry out complex sequences of behavior. _(Elizabeth Crews.)_

merge: Toddlers' thought processes begin to determine more of what they say, and language starts to facilitate thought and help integrate their ideas. One example can be seen in Mikey's comments as he climbed the stairs in our earlier story. He remembered his mother's prior cautions about stair climbing, and these recollections determined what he said: "Careful. Hold on." At the same time, Mikey's words helped to facilitate his thoughts about this activity and to integrate those thoughts with his own behavior (climbing slowly while gripping the banister). In much younger toddlers words and thoughts do not interact in this fashion. The idea that language is the mechanism for internalizing rules for controlling behavior is central to the work of a Russian psychologist, A. R. Luria (see Chapter 11).

Vygotsky's position differs from Piaget's in that it sees language as initially separate from cognitive development, rather than one of many manifestations of it. Vygotsky's position also differs from Bruner's by arguing that, at first, language and thought do not significantly influence each other. Vygotsky contends that as language develops further it differentiates into two kinds of speech: inner speech and social speech. Inner speech is an abbreviated, internalized form of language that is not vocalized at all. Its purpose is to facilitate thinking. For example, when Mikey is much older and is learning to tie his own shoes, he may say to himself as he makes the bow "Loop—around—through—pull" as a way of helping himself to get the procedure right. Social speech, in contrast, develops for the purpose of communicating with others. Sociolinguistic and pragmatic concerns play an important role in its development.

The Learning/Mediational View

A fourth position on the relationship between language and thought is the **learning/mediational view.** Proponents believe that at first words are merely verbal responses learned to particular stimuli, just as any other response might be learned to a stimulus. Mikey sees a round, rolling object and responds by saying "ball." Meryl sees her mother and responds by saying "mama." Spoken words themselves can serve as stimuli to which other responses may be learned, including other verbal responses. You can see such a connection between a verbal stimulus and response in our story of Malcolm. When Malcolm hears his father say the word "hurt," he automatically responds by saying "Band-Aid. Kiss it better." Here the word "hurt" seems to be serving as a stimulus that triggers a verbal response from Malcolm.

So far there is nothing special about language according to this perspective. Learning to say certain words in response to certain stimuli is no different from learning to go to the door when the door bell rings. What makes language special in the service of developing thought is the child's growing ability to abbreviate and internalize it. In more formal terms, language provides **verbal mediators** between stimuli and responses. Verbal mediators serve to connect a stimulus to an ultimate overt response by setting up a chain of internal, covert responses. For instance, one day when Malcolm is a little older he sees a bag of candy kisses that DeeDee is putting in the cupboard and he says to himself "candy." Through a number of internal chains of association, the word *candy* is linked in Malcolm's mind to the idea that "good boys" get candy. Thus, just seeing the candy kisses leads Malcolm to be good, even though he has never before received this particular candy as a reward. The stimulus-response connection is started by using the verbal mediator *candy* to classify the objects that he sees.

Evaluating Different Approaches

Undoubtedly, changes in a toddler's thinking skills occur at the same time as the child acquires language. Still unclear, though, is the extent to which language is the cause of some of these early cognitive changes, as Bruner and the mediational theorists would have us believe. Alternatively, language and cognitive development may initially be independent of each other, as Vygotsky proposes; or language development may depend on cognitive advances, per Piaget's claim. We will return to the interrelationship of language and cognitive development in later chapters of this book. There you will see more reciprocal or back-and-forth influences than in any of the theories we have so far discussed. It may be that one or another of these theories is basically correct in how it describes the connection between language and thought very early in childhood. However, as children grow older a combination of several theories seems to be needed to adequately account for the developments taking place.

THE TODDLER PERIOD: AN OVERVIEW

In this chapter we have looked at the representational skills that begin emerging in toddlerhood and have focused on language development. The infant who knew the world through physical actions has grown into the toddler who is capable of mental actions or manipulations. Such representational abilities will allow dramatically greater flexibility and planfulness in behavior. Despite these advances, the toddler's thinking is still limited by a lack of logic in using these mental skills. Advances in logic will take place in the preschool period.

The infant actively explored the world of objects by grasping them, manipulating them, combining them. Likewise, the toddler actively manipulates symbolic elements, such as words, thereby learning both about the rules that interrelate them and about the entities themselves.

The symbolic thinking skills that begin emerging during toddlerhood provide the foundation for more elaborate social interactions, for pretend play, for dreams and nightmares, and for new kinds of problem solving. These skills enable children to think about the world in new, more complex ways. Consider, for example, a form of fantasy play that Mikey Gordon invented when he was about 2½. He pretended that the living-room couch was his boat, the rug was the ocean, the coffee table was an island, and an umbrella was his fishing pole. Once when his sister Janie walked through the room, he complained to her crossly: "No walk water!" The ability to engage in make-believe play grows dramatically between ages 1 and 3 (Flavell, 1985).

Developmental psychologist John Flavell believes that make-believe play marks the beginnings of the child's awareness of a distinction between appearance and reality. The distinction between what is real and what is not, which is critical to the child's cognitive progress, will expand rapidly during the preschool years.

Chapter Review

1. Toddlerhood is the period from roughly 12 to 30 months of age. Its major developmental changes include learning to talk and to use symbols to think about and interact with the world. Learning to communicate through language is an excellent example of how children are intrinsically motivated to gain competence. Language learning also is an excellent illustration of qualitative change. Older and younger children express ideas in fundamentally different ways.

2. First words are used singly, often to convey what an adult would say with a phrase or sentence. A word used to express such broader meaning is called a **holophrase.** Around 18 to 24 months of age toddlers start to construct two-word sentences. Because such sentences are composed mainly of nouns, verbs, and adjectives, they are called **telegraphic speech.** Telegraphic speech is not just random word combinations. It conforms to rudimentary grammars, or rules of organization.

3. The components of language include **phonemes,** the sounds of a language; **morphemes,** the meaningful units of speech; **syntax,** the rules that govern how words are organized into sentences; and **semantics,** the meanings that language conveys. In addition, children must learn the various rules of conversation. **Pragmatics** concerns the rules governing how language is used in different social contexts, while **sociolinguistics** concerns how language varies among different social groups. Children must also develop two sets of skills to use language: One set, **productive skills,** is for putting ideas into words; the other set, **receptive skills,** is for understanding what other people say. In general, toddlers' receptive skills emerge in advance of their productive skills.

4. Several developmental changes in the first year of life indicate that children are becoming able to both produce and imitate phonemes. At first babies are capable only of **crying,** but soon they also start to **coo** vowel-like sounds. This phase is followed by **babbling,** in which infants' vocalizations become more speechlike. Finally, children reach the stage of **patterned speech,** in which they tune in on the phonemes they hear around them and start narrowing down their range of sounds to those of their native language.

5. One theory of word learning holds that children initially associate a word with all of the features possessed by the first object to which that word is applied. Then later, when they hear the same word applied to somewhat different objects, they eliminate part of their original definition and gradually focus on the relevant features. If this theory were right, we would expect children to make many **errors of underextension.** Although toddlers do make mistakes of this type very early in language learning, they also go through a period of many **errors of overextension.** Thus, in a large number of cases children acquire only *part* of a definition first. Then in the process of exploring the limits of a word's meaning, they focus on additional features until their definition is correct. A popular version of this theory is called the **semantic feature hypothesis.**

Another view that sheds light on how children learn word meanings is the **lexical contrast theory.** It argues that children search for new words when they become aware of gaps in their vocabularies. When they hear an unfamiliar word, they assume it must contrast in meaning with words they already know, so they search for possible meanings among concepts for which they do not yet have labels.

6. Children's first words usually are single morphemes, but as language develops in the toddler period, they add grammatical morphemes. **Grammatical morphemes** include prefixes, suffixes, and auxiliary verbs that change the meaning of words. Studies suggest that children learn the grammatically simplest or semantically simplest forms first (adding *ing* to verbs and *s* to nouns), and master more complex grammatical morphemes and exceptions somewhat later. Acquiring grammatical morphemes demonstrates that children are learning rules. In mastering **syntax**, children must learn to understand how words function within sentences. As children learn to use the passive voice and to form questions, they demonstrate their ability to understand syntax, which requires the ability to employ syntactical rules in combination.

7. Adults tend to modify their speech toward toddlers in ways that may make it easier for the children to learn language. These speech modifications, including simple sentence structure, repetition of key words, and a focus on present objects and events, are known as **motherese,** or **child-directed speech** (CDS). Research suggests that this kind of sensitivity to a child's level of understanding is an important factor in early language development.

8. Theories of how toddlers learn word meanings are products of larger, more general perspectives on language acquisition. One of these larger perspectives is the **behaviorist view.** It holds that adults reinforce children for the use of both meaningful words and proper grammar. But the behaviorist view has been criticized partly for its failure to explain how children do more than simply learn to repeat others' speech. One alternative to it is the **nativist view.** Nativists contend that a specialized, innate capacity of the human brain enables children to extract the rules of any language they hear. This innate capacity allows very rapid language learning as long as an appropriate language environment exists. According to a third major perspective, the **cognitive view,** children learn language by using general cognitive capacities, not ones specially evolved for language.

9. Many developmentalists have offered theories about the relationship between language and thought. In the Piaget view, changes in thinking skills are central; language development is merely a manifestation of these more general changes. During toddlerhood the principal cognitive development is the emergence of symbolic capacity—the ability to let one thing stand for another that is not physically present. Words are just one kind of symbol that toddlers come to use. In contrast to Piaget's view, Bruner believes that language is a crucial part of a child's symbolic representation system. For Bruner language seems to be the initial source of all symbolic thought. In the view of Vygotsky, language and thought at first develop separately. Not until a child is about 2 years old does thought begin to determine more of what is spoken, while language starts to facilitate and help integrate thought.

Another theory on this subject is the **learning/mediational view,** which sees early language as nothing more than a set of learned responses to stimuli. As children grow older, however, they become able to abbreviate and internalize speech. Language is thus able to provide verbal mediators between stimuli and overt responses.

10. Developmentalists do not yet agree on which of these theories is more accurate. We do know, however, that the newly emerging symbolic capacities of toddlerhood pave the way for more complex social interactions, for make-believe play, and for new kinds of problem solving.

9

Toddler Social Development

Twelve-month-old Mikey sits playing with toys a few feet away from his mother. As he examines various objects on the floor around him, his attention is suddenly captured by a large wooden piece of a puzzle. It is a bright orange carrot with a cluster of emerald green leaves. Mikey grasps the wooden carrot with widened eyes. Then in a smooth motion, as though automatically, he turns and extends the piece toward Christine. "Ya-ka!" he says with a broad smile. "Yes sweetie, that's a carrot," his mother answers, smiling in return. "Do you like carrots?" "Ya-ka!" Mikey repeats happily.

A little more than a year later Mikey is with his mother at the Brown University child study laboratory. Mikey has been presented with a series of problems to solve. The final problem is difficult. It requires him to weight down a long board in order to lift candy through a hole in a Plexiglas box. Mikey attacks the problem eagerly, but it is beyond his cognitive abilities. He promptly calls upon Christine for help. She gives him clues and leads him step-by-step to see that he must weight down the board with a large wooden block. Mikey cooperates with her suggestions and is ecstatic when he gets the candy. "I take it out!" he exclaims proudly.

Mikey has undergone dazzling development in just a little more than a year. At age 2, he is not only able to talk and solve quite challenging problems, but he is also able to interact with others on a much more mature level. Mikey's new social capacities and the changes that underlie them are a major subject of this chapter. In this chapter we will also explore how the quality of the parent-child relationship that formed during infancy paves the way for the kinds of adaptations the child makes during toddlerhood.

Developmentalists have increasingly recognized the importance of the toddler period as a transition from infancy to childhood. This importance stems from the major cognitive changes that occur then, especially the emergence of language and other forms of symbolic thought. But it is also due to dramatic changes in the parent-child relationship. During toddlerhood, children move from almost complete dependence on their parents toward greater self-reliance. As toddlers become motivated to exert their own will, parents must learn to impose control when needed while still fostering independence and growth. Since this is also the period when children first develop a rudimentary sense of self, the way in which parents handle the issue of autonomy at this time can greatly influence children's self-esteem and ultimately their capacity for flexible self-control.

In addition to moving toward greater self-reliance, toddlers also start to acquire the rules, standards, and values of their society. This important process is often called **socialization** (Sears, Maccoby, and Levin, 1957). At first socialization simply involves responding to the expectations that parents and others in authority hold. In time, however, the child begins to *internalize* these standards—to incorporate them into the self. This second phase in the socialization process does not take place until the preschool years and beyond. In this chapter we focus on the first phase, the one in which the child comes to recognize and conform to limits set by parents. This early phase of socialization is a major task of toddlerhood in Western societies. As children become more mobile, especially when they start to walk, and as their learning of language opens up new means of communication, most parents in our culture greatly increase the demands they impose. Children can now "get into things" and can understand the word *no* and so parents start establishing some rules. At the same time, weaning from the breast or bottle is accomplished, and not long thereafter toilet training begins. In other words, during the toddler period, parents begin to expect a fair degree of compliance to social norms.

To summarize, toddlers in our culture face two important tasks: (1) to move from near total dependence on their parents toward greater self-reliance and (2) to begin complying with social rules and values. Although children around the world must confront these same two tasks, cultures vary in how the tasks are presented and in how rapidly they are carried out (Whiting and Whiting, 1975). In our own society the demands parents make regarding independence and compliance change rather gradually. Nevertheless, by the age of about 5, children are expected to do many things for themselves, to be able to exert considerable control over their own impulses, and to have a sense of appropriate and inappropriate behavior that they are expected to act on even when adults are not present.

In this chapter you will learn more about how toddlers acquire greater self-reliance and what is involved in learning to comply with parental rules. We begin with a closer look at socialization, exploring how this important process can best be described. We then examine some major accomplishments of toddlers to give you a better idea of what children this age are like. Here you will see that the general trend toward greater independence goes hand in hand with a number of other social, emotional, and cognitive changes. Next we turn to parent-child relations during toddlerhood, focusing on the role the parent plays in encouraging the youngster's development. This leads us to a discussion of individual adaptations, the roots of personality in toddlers. What causes one toddler to be eager and cooperative, while another is persistently prone to tantrums? As you will see, a major answer lies in the parent-child relationship. Finally, we take up the issue of parental neglect and abuse of toddlers. Although abuse can be directed to children of any age, toddlers are particularly vulnerable to it.

The inventive toddler can get into things. *(Elizabeth Crews.)*

TWO VIEWS OF SOCIALIZATION

Traditionally, socialization has been thought of as a process in which rules and values are imposed on an unwilling child by parents and other adults. This imposing of appropriate behavior can be thought of as "socialization from the outside." In their early forms both psychoanalytic and social learning theories adopted such a view. More recently, however, many contemporary developmentalists have argued in favor of a perspective that might be called "socialization from the inside." According to this view, children naturally want to learn social rules and values and to comply with parents' requests. Let's look more closely at the origins of these two different perspectives.

Socialization from the Outside

In his early thinking, Freud considered the infant a seething mass of biological drives and impulses. Society's job was to curb these innate impulses and channel them in acceptable directions. If parents blocked the expression of biological drives to a moderate degree, the child would learn to redirect this energy toward more socially desirable goals. The end result would be compliance with the parents' wishes in order to maintain their love and nurturance. Freud called this blocking and redirecting of biological drives **sublimation.** As long as the child was not excessively thwarted and overwhelmed by anxiety or anger, sublimation in Freud's view was a positive process.

Early social learning theory had in common with Freud's view the idea that as children grow older social rules and values are actively imposed on them. Some early social learning theorists suggested that children comply with these standards to maintain closeness with the

Children learn to comply with adult standards in many ways. Here a child imitates the parent's behavior. *(Elizabeth Crews.)*

parents, who have been associated with gratifying hunger and other basic needs. The most common theme in the traditional social learning view, however, has been the direct teaching of acceptable behavior. Children, this perspective argues, are rewarded when they act "good" and punished when they act "bad." As a result, they come to behave properly.

Contemporary social learning theorists put less emphasis on the direct teaching of appropriate behavior than their predecessors did (Bandura, 1977; Mischel and Mischel, 1983). Instead, they underscore the importance of imitation and vicarious rewards and punishments (those the child sees *others* experiencing). In this view, children come to behave appropriately just by being exposed to desirable behavior in others whom they love or respect and by seeing those people socially rewarded for complying with norms and values. Mikey, for instance, may observe his mother comforting a neighbor's child who has fallen and hurt himself. When the child's mother appears on the scene, she thanks Christine profusely. From these observations Mikey learns a set of actions that can be used with others in distress. He also learns that kindness is the "right" response here and that being kind may result in gratitude and praise. Note how modern social learning theorists emphasize the various cognitions Mikey acquires. They believe that once Mikey understands the behaviors considered appropriate in this situation he will naturally tend to adopt those behaviors. Mikey, like all children, wants to be socially effective, and learning society's rules is one way of acquiring such competence. Here you can see how modern social learning theory is leaning increasingly toward the view of socialization from within.

Socialization from the Inside

Mary Ainsworth has argued persuasively that socialization emanates from inside of children. She believes that in the natural course of events, children *want* to comply with their parents' requests and expectations. This desire on the child's part stems from our evolution as a group-living species. It is also encouraged by the social context in which children are embedded from birth. Take Mikey, for example. Early in life he became a participant in a smoothly operating relationship with his mother. His behavior became organized around Christine, who represented a base of security for him. Upon entering toddlerhood Mikey would naturally want to maintain this close and harmonious relationship. There is no reason to assume that Mikey would inherently resist his mother or that Christine would have to force his compliance through punishment or threat of withholding love. Mikey *enjoys* pleasing his mother and participating in their partnership. Christine has been reliable and responsive toward him. Why wouldn't he want to be responsive in return? Ainsworth's research shows that most children do behave in this manner. Children whose care givers have been consistently responsive have been found to be more compliant as early as 12 months of age, and to be secure in their attachment (Ainsworth, Bell and Stayton, 1984). Such a tendency also is seen at age 2 years (Londerville and Main, 1981; Matas, Arend, and Sroufe, 1978). Only the 30 percent or so of infants who are anxiously attached seem to resist the care giver persistently.

Most toddlers are of course negativistic at times. Even those who have secure relationships with their parents will periodically oppose parental wishes and demand their own way, at times with great intensity. For this reason the toddler period is often called the "terrible twos." Some negativism is a natural and inevitable outcome of the toddler's expanding capabilities coupled with the movement toward greater self-reliance. When Mikey refuses to let Christine help him up the stairs, he is showing a normal desire to exercise his new-found skills and autonomy, Ainsworth's point is simply that a motivation toward cooperation and compliance is as natural in toddlers as the thrust toward independence. Negativism, in short, normally is not entrenched or endless (Matas, Arend, and Sroufe, 1978; Rheingold, 1983). When a toddler seems dedicated to thwarting the parents, when he or she consistently opposes or ignores most parental requests, this suggests a problem in the parent-child relationship, not something inherent in the toddler's nature. Later in this chapter you will read about several studies that demonstrate this point. But first you should get a better picture of what a toddler is like by looking at the major social developments of this important period. As you read, notice how these accomplishments are closely tied to the general trend toward autonomy and how they would fundamentally change the nature of the child's social relationships.

Toddlers will tolerate notable distance from care givers when it is they who initiate the separation. *(Tom Dunham.)*

MAJOR DEVELOPMENTS IN THE TODDLER PERIOD

Moving Out

One of the most obvious developmental changes in the toddler period is a decline in physical closeness to and contact with the care giver. The mobile toddler readily separates from the care giver to play and to explore. The distance toddlers venture from the parent can be quite substantial when they are the ones who initiate the separation (Rheingold and Eckerman, 1971). Occasionally, in the course of other activities, the toddler will return to the care giver before going off again. But more often the child will merely show a toy or vocalize across a distance, as in our opening example of Mikey at 1 year of age. Whereas Mikey as a young infant needed *physical* contact with his mother to support his explorations, he is now moving instead toward *psychological* contact (Bischof, 1975; Bretherton and Ainsworth, 1974). This psychological contact can be maintained by interactions that do not involve any physical touching, interactions such as exchanges of words, smiles, and looks. Note that as both an infant and a toddler, Mikey's secure attachment to Christine supports his mastery of the environment. As a toddler, however, he is now able to draw support from cues across a distance, which in turn enables him to be more independent.

Several studies have illustrated this important development. In one, researchers placed a screen between mothers and their toddlers as the children played in a room full of toys (Carr, Dabbs, and Carr, 1975). These children tended to play less than toddlers who were not blocked from viewing their mothers. It was as if in losing visual contact with the mother they had lost a significant support for their explorations. The same children tended to compensate for the screen by chattering away to their mothers vocally. Interestingly, when the screen was not present, the toddlers did not actually look at their mothers very often. The mere possibility of visual contact was sufficient support at this age. The critical factor is that the toddler knows that the mother is available *if needed*. Another study demonstrated this point. Mothers were instructed to read a magazine and pay no attention to their toddlers while the children played (Sorce and Emde, 1981). These toddlers played less than ones whose mothers did not ignore them. Apparently, toddlers require little actual contact with the care giver to support their explorations in normal circumstances, but they do need to know that the care giver is potentially accessible to them.

In addition to tolerating more physical distance from the care giver, toddlers also show decreased distress when the care giver temporarily leaves them (Clarke-Stewart, 1973; Marvin, 1977). When left alone for a short while in a laboratory setting, 12-month-olds often need considerable contact with the mother when she returns. In contrast, most 18-month-olds require only brief contact before they settle down and are off again to play (Sroufe and Waters, 1977). Apparently, by age 18 months, most children have acquired the expectation that contact with the care giver will alleviate distress, and so they are comforted quickly. Again you see a developmental change that serves to bolster the toddler's growing autonomy.

Sharing of Emotional Experiences

One of the ubiquitous behaviors of toddlers is their constant communication about objects they discover. Toddlers persistently point at things, talk about them, and bring them to others for inspection (Rheingold, Hay, and West, 1976). Such behavior is important for two reasons. First, it illustrates the general sociability of the toddler, a subject we will return to shortly. Second, it reveals that the child is becoming able, in a rudimentary way, to take the perspective of another person. When Malcolm deliberately seeks out Momma Jo to show her some new-found treasure, he must understand that in order for her to see and appreciate the object, her attention must first be directed to it. Simply because *he* sees it does not mean Momma Jo does too.

Related to this frequent sharing of discoveries is the toddler's sharing of emotions, called **affective sharing** (Waters, Wippman, and Sroufe, 1979). When Mikey turns, smiles exuberantly, and extends the wooden puzzle piece toward his mother, exclaiming happily "Ya-ka!" he is doing more than merely calling attention to an object. Mikey is also sharing his pleasure. While toddlers point at and show things to a variety of people, automatic displays accompanied by happy smiles and vocalizations are directed almost exclusively to attachment figures. Mikey shares his joys with Christine in particular, as he would also with Frank. When positive feelings well up inside him, he turns toward her as a matter of course and shares those feelings with her. In doing so he is showing emotional and social advances as well as cognitive ones. Mikey can now initiate exchanges and coordinate his thoughts, feelings, and actions; he also has a well-developed sense of what Christine's reaction is likely to be.

Social Referencing

Another development seen in toddlers is the ability to use the care giver's facial expression or tone of voice as a cue for how to deal with a novel situation. This "reading" of another person to guide one's own behavior is called **social referencing** (e.g., Lamb and Campos, 1982). In one study that demonstrated social referencing, 12-month-olds were enticed across a low table to the edge of a thick sheet of glass raised a foot above the floor (Sorce, Emde, and Klinnert, 1981). As a child peered over the edge of this variation of the "visual cliff" (see Chapter 5), the mother was instructed either to smile broadly at the child or to show exaggerated fear. Whereas most of the children whose mothers smiled crossed over the glass, none of the children whose mothers showed fear were willing to take this risk. The youngsters apparently took their cues as to the safety of the glass from the mother's face. In a similar study, 15-month-olds interacted more positively with a female stranger if they had previously seen their mothers engage in a friendly exchange with her (Feiring, Lewis, and Starr, 1984).

Research shows that the toddler looks to the care giver as a social reference largely in ambiguous situations where the right response is not clear. In one experiment, for example, Megan Gunnar showed children ages 12 to 13 months a pleasant, an ambiguous, or a frightening toy. She asked each child's mother either to smile (suggesting the situation was positive) or to adopt a neutral face. As expected, a mother's smile encouraged play with the ambiguous toy, but it had no effect on behavior toward the other two playthings. The children consistently avoided the frightening toy regardless of a smile from the mother, and they generally approached the pleasant toy even if the mother looked neutral (Gunnar and Stone, 1985). You can see the role of ambiguity in social referencing in our story of Malcolm. When first accosted by the group of boys, Malcolm doesn't know what to make of the situation. He therefore takes his cues from Momma Jo's face and voice to interpret the encounter as a negative one. This responsiveness to care givers' emotional signals increases rapidly between the ages of 1 and 2 years (Cummings, Zahn-Waxler, and Radke-Yarrow, 1981).

Active Experimentation

Recall the incident from Chapter 6 in which 13-month-old Mikey is exploring the effects of throwing objects over a gate and down the stairs. We pointed out how Mikey is not just repeating an action; he is actively experimenting with cause and effect. Through active experimentation Mikey is learning more than simply how to do things (Garvey, 1977; Hutt, 1966). He is also learning to integrate his various capabilities in new and purposeful ways. He is learning that it is fun to explore and manipulate objects and that the possibilities for exploration are unending. Mikey's motivation to discover is fed by these experiences. Perhaps most important of all, he is learning that "I" can do things, that "I" can be in charge. Charles Wenar (1976) calls this **executive competence.** As toddlers like Mikey begin to understand that they can use things for their own ends,

Sharing of affect is one way that toddlers continue to feel close to care givers even when at a distance. *(Elizabeth Crews.)*

they start to develop a sense of personal agency, of knowing that they are autonomous forces in the world. This rudimentary sense of personal agency coupled with an attraction toward objects helps promote toddlers' movement toward greater independence.

Growth of Sociability

We mentioned earlier when discussing affective sharing that toddlers are generally more sociable than infants. One indication of this is a decline in wariness of strangers during a child's second year (Emde, Gaensbauer, and Harmon, 1976). Another sign is a marked increase in social behavior directed toward peers. Whereas 12-month-olds will spend more time in solitary play than in play with peers, 24-month-olds will spend more time playing with peers if given the opportunity. Twenty-four-month-olds will also spend more time playing with peers than playing with their mothers when all are together in a playroom (Eckerman, Whatley, and Kutz, 1975). Most of these peer interactions are positive in tone. Children typically smile as they vocalize to each other and give and take objects. They display relatively little aggression or negative emotion (Bronson, 1981; Brownell and Brown, 1985; Ross and Goldman, 1977). At times the children even seem to take turns, with one child performing an action, then waiting for the other to respond in some way (Mueller and Lucas, 1975).

This increased sociability with peers should probably not be called peer *relations*. That term implies true personal interactions, which are seldom seen between two toddlers. Instead, the play between toddlers is largely object centered. In one study, 88 percent of the contacts observed between toddlers involved some object of mutual interest (Mueller and Lucas, 1975). Toddlers do things together mainly because of this common interest in exploring tangible things. This makes their interactions much less socially mature than those of older children. Moreover, the ability of toddlers to coordinate their behavior, while improving notably in the second year, is still quite primitive compared with that of preschoolers. Toddlers, however, are clearly attracted to their peers, and in "doing together" they are laying the groundwork for later "being together."

The toddler is quite interested in other young children. *(Erika Stone/Peter Arnold, Inc.)*

Awareness of Self

Although a person's self-concept and sense of identity evolve throughout life, knowledge of one's own existence as a separate individual begins in the toddler period. Children at this time become aware that their own behaviors and intentions are distinct from those of others. In this sense, we can say that the self first emerges during toddlerhood.

Several lines of research suggest the existence of self-awareness in toddlers. First, self-awareness can be inferred from what we know about cognitive development. If toddlers can form mental representations of objects, they should be able to mentally represent themselves as people and actors. A good deal of evidence suggests that representational skills unfold rapidly during a child's second and third years (e.g., Nicolich, 1977; Ungerer et al., 1981). Observations of children at play show that by age 24 months toddlers clearly know that self and other are independent agents (Watson and Fischer, 1977).

Self-awareness in toddlers is also revealed by studies of children's reactions to their image in a mirror. Using a procedure first introduced by Gordon Gallup in his work with chimpanzees, children of different ages were presented with a mirror to look in (Amsterdam, 1972). Then, unobtrusively, a dab of rouge was placed on each child's face and the child was shown the mirror again. If the child reached directly to the spot of rouge, not in the reflection but on his or her own face, the child was assumed to know he or she was the person in the mirror. This reaction was common by about 20 months of age and sometimes appeared by 18 months or even a little earlier. Subsequent researchers have confirmed these findings. In one study, three-quarters of the children between the ages of 21 and 24 months touched their rouge-marked noses when looking into a mirror, thus showing self-recognition. In contrast, only one-quarter of the children ages 15 to 18 months and none of the children ages 9 to 12 months responded in this way (Lewis and Brooks, 1978). Self-recognition seems to be closely tied to general cognitive development. The age at which a child with Down syndrome starts touching his or her rouge-marked nose when it is revealed in a mirror is directly related to the child's degree of mental retardation. The more severe the retardation, the more delayed the youngster is in showing this sign of self-awareness (Mans, Cicchetti, and Sroufe, 1978).

The final indication of self-awareness in toddlers is the addition of "I" to the vocabulary (as in "I do it!") coupled with clear examples of self-assertion and will (e.g., Breger, 1974). Here is how child psychiatrist Louis Sander (1975) describes this change:

> In the 14–20 month period there emerges a new capacity of the child to organize his world actively, to assert himself, and to widen his initiative to determine and select his own direction of activity. The child's aim at this time often seems to be to possess the initiative for its own sake. During the toddler period the child has a heightened awareness of his own intentions. . . . Spitz associates this process with the emergence of the "I" experience. (p. 140)

Parents of toddlers will know immediately what Sander is referring to. Most can remember times when their child intensely opposed one of their requests or insisted on doing things "by myself," as we illustrated in our stories of Meryl and Mikey. Putting pajamas on a steadfastly unwilling toddler can be a very trying experience. However, when such behavior is viewed as a sign of the child's emerging self, it takes on a different complexion. Toddlers sometimes resist their parents' wishes not because they are stubborn or obstinate. They do so to exercise their new-found sense of separateness, the sense of being an individual with ideas and desires of their own.

Understanding of Others

Closely related to the emergence of a sense of self is a changing understanding of others. In fact, theorists such as George Herbert Mead (1934) and James Mark Baldwin (1897) have argued convincingly that the concepts of self and other develop together, each encouraging the other. Understanding yourself as being an independent agent carries with it an understanding that others are also agents separate from you.

Dennie Wolf (1982) has suggested three major steps in toddlers' developing concept of others. In the first step, when children are about age 1, they recognize that others can do things they cannot, but they do not yet grasp that others are agents in their own right. Wolf gives the example of a mother initiating a game of peek-a-boo by covering her face with her hands, and her 1-year-old son responding by covering his own face similarly. When he later lifts his hands away, he is surprised to find that his mother's face is still covered. It is as if he has blurred the distinction between the two sets of hands and the two faces.

As the second year of life proceeds children reach step two. Now they are able to understand the boundaries between their own actions and

This child knows it is she in the mirror, and she touches her garment in response to the image. *(Mariette Pathy Allen/Peter Arnold, Inc.)*

"Do it myself." (Elizabeth Crews.)

those of other people. This allows them to engage in genuine turn-taking. To some extent, however, toddlers' grasp of the concept "other" is still limited. Consider this exchange:

Child: Picks up a lid and hides his face behind it.
Father: Noticing, says "Where's J?"
Child: Peeks out, then darts the lid back in front of his face.
Father: "Where is J?"
Child: Peeks out again, then crosses the room, holds out the lid to father and says, "Dada."
Father: Takes the lid, covers his face, and peeks out.
Child: Pulls the lid away, laughing.
(Wolf, 1982, p. 312)

Notice how the child now knows that to reveal his father's face his *father's* hands must be lowered, not his own hands. This is a clear advancement over earlier thinking. The toddler now seems to understand that two equivalent human actors participate in this game. However, the little boy does not say, "Where Dada?" and wait for his father to reveal his face by himself. Instead, *he* assumes the father's role and takes the lid away. It seems as if the child does not yet have an adultlike grasp of the two independent roles involved.

By the end of the second year there emerges a genuine understanding that people are independent agents. In this third step children come to grasp the fact that each actor in a social exchange is playing a role separate from the others. Now toddlers can finally play a real game of hide-and-seek. At a younger age children are likely to jump out of hiding before you find them, as if the distinction between hider and seeker is blurred in their minds. By age 2, waiting to be found may still be difficult for them, but at least they run in the opposite direction when the seeker comes near. Their action implies they recognize the separateness of people's roles, intentions, and aims. This new recognition underlies the battles of will that tend to arise during toddlerhood. It also underlies the compromises found when parents set limits. Mikey goes to bed when his mother tells him, but he climbs the stairs "by myself." Here he understands that his mother and he have independent wishes. As a result, their social interactions become more sophisticated.

Ongoing cognitive advances also influence toddlers' interactions with peers. For example, during the second year, toddlers came to understand the "possession" rule, the idea that if someone else already is engaged with an object they have some claim on it. Thus, 24-month-olds try less often to take an object from a peer than do 18-month-olds and they engage in negotiation concerning the object more often (Brownell and Brown, 1985). And 24-month-olds were more likely to relinquish the object when a partner, who had played with it earlier, tried to take it away. Such changes in interaction follow from a growing sense of self and other; they also further promote this understanding.

PARENT-TODDLER RELATIONS

All the developmental changes we have just outlined dramatically influence the parent-child relationship. On the one hand, they offer parents new sources of pleasure and new avenues for communication. On the other hand, they create new demands and challenges for care givers. In this section, we look at the parents' role in the parent-toddler relationship. This sets the stage for our subsequent discussion of how a child's personality and self-concept evolve in the toddler period.

The Parents' Task

The parents' task during the toddler period is to adjust their own behavior in keeping with the child's current capacities and limitations. Parents can do this by participating in the toddler's strivings to communicate with language as well as in the youngster's affective sharing of newly discovered objects. Christine does this automatically in her interactions with Mikey. She responds even to his nonsense words as if they conveyed real meaning; she expresses delight when Mikey shows her the simplest of objects. At the same time, Christine allows Mikey to try things on his own and push his capacities to the limit, always being available to help if his resources are exceeded. You can see this tendency in how she handles the stair-climbing incident, and later the situation in which Mikey is involved at the child study lab. The parents' task is to create an arena in which the child has space and support to develop. Such a concept has been referred to by Jerome Bruner as "scaffolding" and by Lev Vygotsky as the "zone of proximal development" (see Chapter 10). In a variety of ways Christine promotes Mikey's growth and autonomy while still setting limits when they are needed (Brazelton, 1977; Erikson,

1963; Sroufe and Ward, 1984). As you might expect, parents tend to be consistent over time in the extent to which they support their children's autonomy while maintaining limits (Pianta, Egeland, and Sroufe, in press; Ward, 1983). Christine, for instance, probably behaved with much the same consistency toward her daughters when they were toddlers as she does toward Mikey.

Why do modern developmentalists stress limits as much as they do? Why would limits be as important to a child's progress as opportunities for growth and self-reliance? The reasoning is this: If children can be confident that their parents will impose limits when they are needed, the youngsters may then explore their capacities freely, testing how far they will reach. Notice that what is important in this view is the parents' *general* approach toward the child, not specific child-rearing practices. Research supports this belief. For instance, there is no evidence that the specific age of weaning or toilet training a child has a major impact on the child's development (Hetherington and Brackbill, 1963; Sears, Maccoby, and Levin, 1957). However, there is evidence that the general quality of care parents provide does make a difference in how well a child fares (Clarke-Stewart, 1973; Erikson, Egeland, and Stroufe, 1985; Matas, Arend, and Sroufe, 1978; White and Watts, 1973).

Fathers and Toddlers

Research suggests that fathers as well as mothers play a direct role in promoting a toddler's development. For many fathers this direct impact marks somewhat of a change from their role when the child was an infant. While some fathers are actively involved in the care of a baby, others are involved very little. One study found that on the average fathers spent only *37 seconds per day* directly interacting with the baby during the child's first three months. (Rebelsky and Hanks, 1971). Granted, this study was conducted some time ago; more recent research with older infants does not reveal such an extreme picture. Nevertheless, even today mothers tend to spend vastly more time with infants than fathers do (Clarke-Stewart, 1978; Kotelchuck, 1976; Lamb, et al., 1982).

When fathers do interact with infants, their behavior is often quite different from that of mothers. Fathers are less often involved in the care and nurturance of a baby and more often involved in playful exchanges (Parke and O'Leary, 1976). This pattern was found even in families in Sweden, where fathers were given paid leave and spent some part of the child's first year at home with the baby (Lamb et al., 1982). When the researchers came to observe in the evenings, they found that the mothers did most of the nurturing while the fathers largely engaged the child in play. This father-child style of interaction continues into the toddler period. We illustrated this with our description of Frank's interaction with his son, Mikey.

The amount of time a father typically spends with his child increases during toddlerhood, especially if the child is a boy (Clarke-Stewart, 1980; Lamb, 1981). This behavior can be found in both Western and non-Western cultures as well as among nonhuman primates such as monkeys (Barry, Bacon, and Child, 1957; Suomi, 1979). The father's playful style is well suited to the child's general orientation at this age. Since a major

By the end of the toddler period the child knows enough about different roles that he or she can play more complicated games. *(Robert A. Isaacs/Photo Researchers, Inc.)*

task for the toddler is to evolve new ways of relating to parents, ways that are more in keeping with growing independence, the father's input may be very helpful now. At the same time, the father's increased involvement with and emotional support of the toddler may ease the beginnings of psychological separation from the mother. Thus, having two care givers with somewhat different styles of interaction may not be disadvantageous for a young child.

INDIVIDUAL ADAPTATIONS: THE ROOTS OF PERSONALITY

A toddler's new-found self-awareness has broad implications. It includes particular attitudes and expectations about the self that influence how the child responds to other people and to opportunities and challenges in the environment. As George Herbert Mead and James Mark Baldwin have argued, social interactions help to shape self-concept, but self-concept in turn affects the child's individual style of responding to others. This individual style of responding, or **pattern of adaptation,** forms the roots of personality.

Becoming a Separate Person

Margaret Mahler has described in detail the development of a sense of self, a process she calls **separation-individuation** (Mahler, Pine, and Bergman, 1975). This term refers to the child's psychological separation from the care giver coupled with a growing awareness of being an individual. Along with René Spitz and other developmentalists, Mahler argues that in the first few months of life a child has no sense of self. Newborns are aware of various sensations, such as warmth, pain, and hunger, but they can't distinguish those arising from within the body from those arising outside it. Since the newborn has no coherent understanding of objects, he or she can have no understanding of the self as an object and an actor. Psychologically, the infant is still unborn.

The first step toward development of the self is formation of a close bond with the care giver. This process starts after the age of about 3 to 4 months, when infants begin to recognize their care givers, to distinguish them from other people. Then, in the second half-year of life, infants become increasingly able to anticipate the care giver's reactions, to intentionally signal their own needs, and to coordinate their own behavior with that of the care giver. These abilities enable the attachment relationship to form. Mahler calls this the **symbiotic period** because of the closeness of the infant/care giver bond. She argues that although the infant now distinguishes between "in here" and "out there," the "in here" includes the care giver. A sense of true separateness has not yet emerged.

Further self-development is related to conceiving of the care giver as an object. A baby has countless experiences seeing, hearing, feeling, and otherwise sensing the care giver. By late in the first half-year the child begins coordinating these various sensations. He or she becomes aware that the mother's face, voice, touch, and scent go together. In the second half-year the child recognizes the mother as a seeable, hearable, touchable object independent from the child's direct control. From this awareness of the mother as she who looks, talks, touches, and so forth comes the realization that "I" am the one who is looked at, talked to, and touched.

The compelling thing about Mahler's analysis is how these early phases of development inevitably lead to a further unfolding of the self. The infant's closeness with the care giver supports venturing forth into the surrounding world, which in turn brings with it an inevitable sense of separateness. As children move away from the care giver and experience doing things on their own, they increasingly realize that they are independent, that their actions are apart from the care giver's. How the bond with the care giver supports this progress toward greater autonomy and a sense of self is beautifully described by the philosopher Sören Kierkegaard (1938, p. 85):

> The loving mother teaches her child to walk alone. She is far enough from him so that she cannot actually support him but she holds out her arms to him. She imitates his movements, and if he totters, she swiftly bends as if to seize him, so that the child might believe that he is not walking alone. . . . Her face beckons like a reward, an encouragement. Thus, the child walks alone with his eyes fixed on his mother's face, not on the difficulties in his way. He supports himself by the arms that do not hold him and constantly strives toward the refuge in his mother's embrace, little suspecting that at the very same moment he is emphasizing his need of her, he is proving that he can do without her, because he is walking alone.

The Challenge of the Second Year

As toddlers become more aware of their own separateness and autonomy, they may grow anxious about leaving behind the former closeness with the care giver. The security of the symbiotic relationship, after all, is a great deal to leave behind. But at the same time, toddlers are inherently drawn toward exploring and mastering the surrounding world. They naturally want to maintain and expand their new-found sense of initiative. Herein lies a major developmental crisis in Mahler's view. How can the toddler reconcile a need for closeness and security with a striving toward independence?

Louis Sander (1975) has described a solution to this challenge. He points out that toddlers do not exclusively try to achieve self-reliance. Instead, their strivings toward autonomy are balanced by bids for a continuing emotional partnership with the care giver. The success of these bids has important psychological consequences. If toddlers know they can reclaim the former closeness with the care giver—if they have confidence that the attachment relationship is secure—they will feel free to explore their capacities to the fullest. Such confidence is a product of each child's history of interactions with the care giver. The parents' reliability during infancy breeds a basic trust, which then enables initiatives toward independence in toddlerhood. As Erik Erikson notes, trust supports autonomy during this period of development. At the same time, how the care giver responds to the child's bids for autonomy is also important. According to Erikson (1963), the care giver's role is to accept and encourage the child's initiatives but also to impose limits when needed.

Walking opens a world of new adventures for the toddler. *(Phoebe Dunn/D.P.I.)*

You have seen this developmental process going well with both Mikey and Malcolm. These toddlers have been able to become more autonomous while still maintaining psychological contact with their care givers. Even when Mikey does things against his mother's wishes and temporarily annoys her, he remains confident that the closeness between them can be reclaimed. Mikey's bids for independence do not threaten his strong emotional bond with Christine. Since the early attachment relationship has been so secure, Christine is able to accept her son's growing autonomy. Mikey, for his part, is sure of Christine's continued availability, readily reassured by her in times of stress, and accepting the limits she sets. Like other toddlers who have had these positive experiences, Mikey and Malcolm are confident, eager, resourceful, and secure.

A more negative outcome is illustrated in our story of Meryl and can be seen in other toddlers who have experienced less secure relationships with their care givers. When children are unduly anxious about the care giver's availability, when autonomy is forced upon them too early, or when their bids for independence are viewed with suspicion, self-reliance is compromised (Matas, Arend, and Sroufe, 1978; Sroufe, Fox and Pancake, 1983; Yarrow, 1972). This compromising of self-reliance can take many forms, including timidity and continued preoccupation with the care giver, unremitting power struggles, persistent angry interactions, lack of emotional interest in mastery, and general emotional detachment. We have described some of these reactions in Meryl.

Research on the Influence of Attachment History

A number of studies support the view of toddler social and emotional development that we have just described (Clarke-Stewart, 1973; Londerville and Main, 1981; Matas, Arend, and Sroufe, 1978). These studies show a clear link between the quality of the infant/care giver relationship and how well the child later functions as a toddler. In one research program Leah Matas and her colleagues studied 2-year-olds who at ages 12 and 18 months had been assessed for the quality of their attachment to the mother. The researchers presented the children with a series of problems that required the use of simple tools to solve. The first two problems were relatively easy, such as using a long stick to push a lure from inside a tube. The final two problems were more difficult. The last and hardest was the one that we described Mikey solving at the beginning of this chapter: weighting down the end of a board with a large wooden block in order to raise candy through a hole in the top of a box. This problem is beyond the capacity of almost all 2-year-olds, but in this study each child's mother was there as a potential resource. The researchers looked at the quality of each toddler's problem solving, including his or her emotional responses, enthusiasm, and ability to face challenges without quickly becoming frustrated. They also looked at the child's persistence and flexibility regarding the task, as well as the ability to accept the mother's help when needed. At the same time, the researchers examined the timing and clarity of the mother's clues and the degree of emotional support she provided.

The findings in this study were striking. Two-year-olds who had been securely attached as infants (confident in their care giver's availability) were more enthusiastic in approaching the problems, showed more positive emotions and less frustration, were more persistent and flexible, and cooperated more with their mother to reach a solution. In contrast, the children who had experienced an insecure attachment during infancy showed a variety of maladaptive responses. Some were intermittently clingy and dependent or whiny and prone to tantrums, quickly becoming frustrated or embroiled in conflict with their mother, the problem to solve fading into the background. This reaction was most common in children like Meryl with a history of anxious-resistant attachment. Other anxiously attached toddlers showed no enthusiasm or pleasure and little involvement in the problems. They either ignored or refused to act on their mother's suggestions, or they expressed rejection of her indirectly. (For instance, when a mother said "Get the block," the child did get it but put it on the floor instead of on the board.) Such reactions were most common in children with a history of anxious-avoidant attachment.

The quality of the early attachment was also closely tied to the mother's behavior in this study. Mothers of toddlers who had been securely attached as infants were rated higher on the quality of their help and emotional support. Laboratory assessments of attachment thus capture the quality of the mother-child *relationship* and can therefore predict the behavior of either partner later. You can easily imagine the secure relationship between Mikey and his mother promoting positive responses in Christine as she watches her son tackling the board and box problem. Christine encourages Mikey's efforts, gives him appropriate hints, and offers reassurance if he starts to falter. Mothers like Christine who were responsive to their children as infants tend to support the children's autonomy during the toddler period (Pianta, Egeland, and Sroufe, in press). One study has found that a secure relationship with a first-born even predicted emotional support of second-born toddlers (Ward, 1983).

Toddlers enjoy working
hard to solve a problem. *(B.
Vaughn.)*

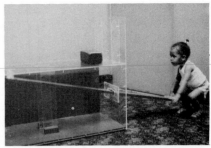

Other researchers have further examined the behavior of mothers whose toddlers were securely attached in infancy. These mothers seem to adjust their behavior depending on the particular demands of the situation and the child's needs (Gove, 1983). In the problem-solving situation we just described, Christine allows Mikey to proceed on his own until he approaches the limits of his own resources. She provides him with little help on the easy problems, but as the problems become more difficult, she increases the number of clues she offers and even gives direct assistance when Mikey signals he needs it. In this way Christine anticipates possible frustration and takes steps to avoid it. She also stays calm and is increasingly supportive of Mikey. In sharp contrast to this pattern, mothers of children with a history of anxious-avoidant attachment fail to increase the amount of help they offer. Most remain rather uninvolved throughout the child's efforts, even in the face of increasingly difficult problems. Mothers of children with a history of anxious-resistant attachment show yet another pattern. Although they increase the amount of help they give, that help becomes less and less appropriate and clear. Both mother and child become more disorganized as the pressure of the situation mounts. This failure to set clear guidelines is very different from the actions of mothers whose toddlers were securely attached as infants. These mothers tend to be very clear in establishing limits for their children, and they are also firm in maintaining those limits once they are set.

How can we summarize the developmental sequences that all this research suggests? Apparently, from a history of secure attachment during infancy a child develops confidence in mastering the environment and a firm conviction that the care giver will be there to help should the child's own efforts fail. A toddler with this developmental history need not be concerned about maintaining constant contact with the care giver. He or she can venture forth, having an "internal representation" of the relationship with the care giver as secure (Bretherton, 1985; Main, Kaplan, and Cassidy, 1985). Because the care giver has repeatedly demonstrated reliability in the past, the child has little reason to question the limits the care giver now sets. The toddler who is far more likely to oppose parental wishes and limits persistently is one with a history of anxious attachment. Much more than most children, such a youngster needs clear, firm, and consistent support from adults. Support, however, is the very thing that the child's care giver has had trouble providing. A child without adequate support shows a variety of maladaptive behaviors that are not conducive to achieving optimal self-reliance.

In addition to being linked to the degree of self-reliance and joy in mastery a toddler shows, the security of the early attachment relationship also seems to be tied to the amount of self-control that develops during toddlerhood. Mary Main (personal communication) has considered this in her study of toddlers' responses after the mother has prohibited some action. Children with a history of secure attachment may later begin to perform the forbidden act but then stop *themselves*. Other researchers have likewise seen early signs of self-control in some toddlers (Emde, Johnson, and Easterbrooks, 1985). We illustrated such signs in Malcolm when he stopped himself from reaching for the leaf that floated on the wading pool in the park. Such behavior will increase dramatically as Malcolm grows older. But even a rudimentary capacity for self-control reduces sources of tension between children and their care givers. Now it is the children who sometimes say no to themselves, rather than the parents always assuming this role.

Other Factors Influencing Toddler Adaptations

You have seen that toddlers' individual adaptations are strongly affected by the quality of earlier attachment relationships. Whether a toddler is eager, persistent, and resourceful or timid, clingy, and easily upset depends greatly on secure or insecure foundations developed in infancy. What other factors are important? Specifically, to what extent are individual differences in behavior a product of inherent differences in temperament? And to what extent must we look to the broader social context of a family in order to explain the patterns of child care that develop within it? Researchers have explored these two important questions.

WHAT ROLE DOES TEMPERAMENT PLAY?

We said in Chapter 7 that early in infancy it is difficult to demonstrate stable, individual differences in behavior. A newborn who is irritable one day may be placid the next, making it hard to say that the baby has a certain "temperament." By the end of the first year, however, both parents and unbiased observers begin to describe a given infant's patterns of behavior in much the same way, suggesting that certain characteristic responses are emerging (Wilson and Matheny, 1983). Some evidence demonstrates that these early patterns of response tend to stabilize over the toddler period and beyond (Matheny, Wilson, and Nuss, 1984). For instance, Jerome Kagan and his colleagues (Reznick, Kagan, and Snidman, 1986) have found that a small number of children classified as either very timid or very bold at 2 years of age are still classified the same way 2

Some toddlers are quite hesitant in the face of novel situations, whereas other toddlers embrace them. Researchers actively debate the origins of such differences. *(Dorothea Mooshake/ Peter Arnold, Inc.)*

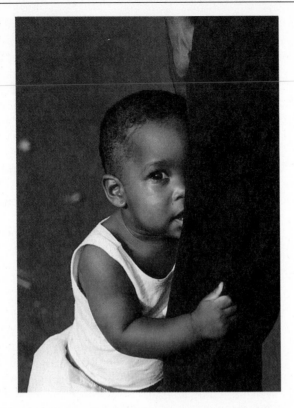

years later. But such findings do not tell us what causes these behavioral patterns. They may be the product of inherent differences in temperament, or they may arise because of the type of care the child has experienced. Nonetheless, temperamental classifications do tend to become stable and the characteristics they are based on influence the behavior of parents and others. Kagan and his colleagues, who favor temperament as an explanation, are conducting research to help answer these questions.

Inborn temperament and care-giving history may influence toddler development in different ways. Temperamental factors may operate on a different level than care-giving influences. Temperament may affect the pacing or strength of a child's reactions, while interactions with care givers may affect the overall quality of the child's adaptation. For instance, Malcolm's high activity level may be largely a product of his temperament, but his enthusiasm and cooperativeness toward members of his family may stem from the positive experiences he has had with them. Children with rapid tempos like Malcolm may be curious and socially competent, or they may be anxious and hostile, and so forth (Sroufe, 1983). Placid children may be pleasant, easygoing, and persistent, or they may be emotionless, withdrawn, and asocial. The overall *quality* of adaptation in a toddler probably is best viewed as arising from the history of child/care giver relations, while some particular characteristics may be due to factors in the child.

Beyond the question of where behavioral differences in toddlers come from is the question of what significances those differences have, not just for the child but for the child/care giver relationship as well. If we view the family as a social system, then the child is a part of that system and influences all other parts. By the toddler period, the child is strongly affecting the parents' responses and thereby the care that he or she receives. Thus, the child whom parents perceive as "difficult" receives more negative responses from them (Lee and Bates, 1985). We have illustrated this in our description of the relationship between Karen and Meryl. Meryl resists her mother's wishes, throwing tantrums when Karen tries to insist. So Karen often backs down and lets Meryl have her way, just to keep peace. Here Meryl's behavior is clearly affecting her mother's, but the reverse is also true. By vacillating and failing to set firm limits, Karen is helping to promote Meryl's difficult behavior. This is what is meant by bidirectional effects or the transactional model we introduced in Chapter 3 (Bell, 1968; Sameroff and Chandler, 1975). The child is influencing the parent at the same time the parent is influencing the child.

A LOOK AT THE FAMILY CONTEXT

The concept of bidirectional effects helps to show that a parent is not solely responsible for the relationship that evolves with a child. Once a parent has started to respond to an infant in a certain manner, the child's reactions often work to maintain the parent's style of care giving. But another reason why a parent should not be blamed for developmental problems is that parent and child do not operate in a vacuum. They are surrounded by a larger social environment that includes other adults and children in the family, as well as people and institutions with which the family comes in contact. This larger social environment can impose pressures and challenges or offer various kinds of support. Developmentalists increasingly stress the need to view child/care giver interactions as partly a product of this broader social context (e.g., Belsky, 1981).

Developmentalists are becoming especially interested in how the quality of adult relationships, the amount of stress a family experiences, and the various forms of social support available to parents influence the quality of care children receive. These factors interact with one another, often aggravating or lessening one another's effects. For instance, the loss of a job or a serious illness may produce enough stress to tax a parent's capacity to emotionally support a child. However, if the parent has supportive relationships with other adults, that stress may be easier to cope with and its negative effects greatly reduced. Particularly important is the quality of the mother-father relationship. Research shows that when the father is supportive of the mother, she is more affectionate and responsive toward their child (Belsky and Isabella, 1987b; Easterbrooks and Emde, in press; Lewis and Feiring, 1981). Without such psychological backing, a person tends to take less pleasure in parenting and is more susceptible to its stresses.

The importance of stress as a potential influence on the quality of child care is illustrated in a study of toddler development conducted by Byron Egeland and his colleagues (Vaughn et al., 1979). These researchers found that the quality of a child's attachment to the mother sometimes changes during the toddler period. A relationship classified as anxious when the child is 12 months of age might be classified as secure 6 months later and vice versa. Significantly, a switch from an insecure to a secure

The broad social environment has a tremendous impact on the development of a child. A supportive family atmosphere can help parents and children to cope well within their environment. *(Erika Stone/Peter Arnold, Inc.)*

attachment was linked to a reduction in disruptive life changes and stress the mother was experiencing. Since the finding is merely a correlation, we cannot say for certain that one factor caused the other. Nevertheless, it suggests that when parents have greater stability in their lives they are better able to provide for the emotional needs of a child.

But immediate pressures are not the only factor that can impair the quality of parent-child interactions. Also important are problems encountered in the parent's own developmental history. David Morris (1983) examined the life histories of 18 mothers whose children were thriving in their second year and 18 mothers whose toddlers were showing poor adaptation. He found that the mothers whose children were having developmental problems had more chaotic early lives than the other mothers did. In particular, the need of these women for love and security when they were children had usually not been met; nor did they have positive images of their own mothers as nurturing figures. Other researchers have made similar findings (Cox et al., 1987; Main, Kaplan, and Cassidy, 1985; Ricks, 1985). In general, a woman's own reported experiences as a child are quite good predictors of how well her children will fare. Mary Main, following Bowlby's theory, interprets this in terms of the mother's "representation" of her own early attachment. Thus, having no images of parent-child nurturance and feeling unworthy of care herself, such a woman has no foundation for nurturing her own children.

A troubled childhood, however, does not predestine a woman to have difficulty with parenting. As you might expect, past developmental history interacts with present circumstances. In a further study of some of the women David Morris had interviewed, researchers compared those who came from abusive backgrounds but whose children were doing well with similarly maltreated mothers whose children were showing problems (Egeland, Jacobvitz, and Sroufe, in press). Three key differences emerged: (1) many of the mothers who had turned things around had formed a stable, supportive relationship with some adult during childhood; (2) many of these women had undergone extensive psychotherapy; and (3) all of them currently enjoyed a stable partnership. The implication is that a woman's past, however troubled, may not impair her present functioning if she has had a chance to experience positive relationships and if her current social support is adequate. Inner working models can be changed. Rather than blaming parents for children's problems, we should commit ourselves to their support. Cycles of poor child care and development *can* be altered. We will return to this issue in the next section, which deals with child abuse.

PARENTAL ABUSE AND NEGLECT OF TODDLERS

Although parents may abuse or neglect their children at any age, abused children are more likely to be under 3 years of age (Garbarino and Gilliam, 1980). Toddlers can be very challenging, which may partly account for this fact. An adult might easily misinterpret their behavior as contrary, naughty, or even malicious. At the same time, toddlers have not yet

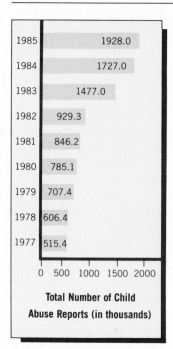

Figure 9.1
Increase of Reported Child Abuse
Despite the dramatic increase in reported abuse from 1977 to 1985, these figures still underrepresent the actual amount of abuse and neglect in the US.

(American Humane Association, 1987)

learned how to avoid parental mistreatment, making them particularly vulnerable to abuse.

The consequences toddlers suffer when they are abused or neglected vary, depending on the particular form of mistreatment (Egeland and Sroufe, 1981). Physical neglect (not meeting the child's basic needs for food, warmth, cleanliness, and so forth) tends to produce a lack of competence in dealing with the world of objects. Physical abuse and emotional unavailability often promote behavioral and emotional problems, including avoidant attachment relationships (Egeland and Sroufe, 1981; Schneider-Rosen and Cicchetti, 1984), aggressiveness with toddler peers (George and Main, 1979), and blunted emotions (Schneider-Rosen and Cicchetti, 1984). Emotional unavailability, which is often tied to depression in the parent, is particularly devastating (Garbarino, Guttman, and Seeley, 1986). Over time the child shows a marked decline in functioning, eventually becoming apathetic, lacking in joy or pleasure, and easily frustrated and upset (Egeland and Sroufe, 1981).

The incidence of child abuse and neglect is difficult to establish, partly because of differences in definitions and reporting procedures. However, the fact that reports skyrocketed after all 50 states adopted mandatory reporting laws suggests that the problem is widespread. Each year hundreds of child deaths are attributed to maltreatment, and many thousands of other cases of serious abuse occur (Kempe and Kempe, 1978). Psychologists want to know what would lead parents to physically abuse or seriously neglect their own child.

Searching for Causes

While abuse seems to be generally associated with poverty, lack of education, and young parents who are unprepared for raising a child, it certainly is not confined to these groups (Brunnquell, Crichton, and Egeland, 1981). The problem crosses all ethnic, social class, age, and religious lines. Surprisingly, many abusing parents appear to outsiders to be devoted mothers or fathers. Most want to do well by their children but are unable to. The question is why.

CHILD CHARACTERISTICS

In the past some researchers have proposed that abused children may have certain inherent characteristics that elicit mistreatment from adults (Segal and Yahres, 1978). Prematurity, physical defects, and infant irritability and fussiness have all been suggested as *causes* of abuse (e.g., Frodi, 1984). However, these suggestions were based on investigations made *after* cases of child abuse were reported. In such studies people's perceptions and memories might easily become distorted in order to help explain the known outcome. Much more reliable are the findings of prospective studies, those in which assessments of the children are made *before* abuse occurs. Such studies have failed to find any association between prematurity or early irritability in a baby and later child abuse. Moreover, only a very modest relationship exists between complications of pregnancy or birth and a woman's subsequent mistreatment of the child (Brunnquell, Crichton, and Egeland, 1981). This modest relation-ship may not be one of cause and effect. Abusive mothers generally receive less adequate prenatal care, thus raising the risk of childbearing complications. And some of the same factors that could prompt a woman to neglect her health during pregnancy could easily encourage her to later neglect the baby.

Sometimes only one child in a family is singled out for abuse, and that child may later go on to be abused by foster parents as well. It has been suggested that the children involved in such cases seem to be the fundamental cause of their own mistreatment. This reasoning, however, is weak on several counts. First, a pattern of abuse directed exclusively toward one child probably is not very common. Second, even when it occurs the child may have been singled out for mistreatment for a variety of reasons. Perhaps the child, as part of an abusive system, has learned behaviors that elicit hostile reactions from the parents. As we will discuss later in Chapter 11, mistreated children do later elicit rejection from their preschool teachers (Motti, 1986). But this is not the same as saying that those behavior patterns were part of the child's inherent nature.

To date, then, the evidence is scant that inherent characteristics of certain children are major causes of child abuse. In some cases an infant who is ill and difficult to care for may add to the pressures on an already overstressed parent and the end result is mistreatment. But here we are talking about the cumulative effects of stress on parents, not the child's nature, as the specific cause of their reactions. Of course, an abused toddler will probably become a difficult child, thus adding to the cycle of abuse (George and Main, 1979). But the child's contribution in this case is a learned set of behaviors, the product of a past history of mis-treatment.

PARENT CHARACTERISTICS

If child abuse cannot be explained by inherent characteristics of the children involved, perhaps it can be explained by mental disturbance in the parents. Although this line of inquiry seems reasonable, it turns out not to be very productive. Most instances of child abuse do not involve parents with severe mental disorders. Estimates are that only one in ten abusing parents is seriously disturbed (Kempe and Kempe, 1978). Nor does child abuse seem to stem from a particular set of personality traits in parents (Brunnquell, Crichton, and Egeland, 1981; Parke and Colmer, 1975). No clear evidence points to abusing parents scoring higher on such general traits as impulsiveness or hostility. Does this mean no character-istics can help predict which parents are likely to become abusers? No, it simply means that instead of looking at the parents' general personality makeup, we must look instead at their specific thoughts and feelings about the child and child rearing.

In one large-scale study, researchers interviewed women before they gave birth to their first baby as well as during the child's infancy (Brunn-quell, Crichton, and Egeland, 1981; Egeland and Brunnquell, 1979). They found that those who later became abusers differed from nonabusers in two ways. First, they were less able to cope effectively with the ambiv-alent and stressful emotions inherent in a first pregnancy; and second, they had significantly less understanding of what is involved in caring for an infant. Here is how the researchers described these women:

> It appears that the mother at risk for abuse or neglect is characterized during pregnancy by a lack of understanding and knowledge concerning parent-child relationships and a negative reaction to pregnancy. After the baby arrives, her anxiety and fear increase in response to the difficulty presented by the child. She is unable to understand the ambivalence she experiences and responds to her anxiety and fear by becoming more hostile and suspicious. Her increased hostility and suspiciousness interfere further with her ability to relate to the baby and cope with the demands of the situation. (Brunnquell, Crichton, and Egeland, 1981, p. 689)

Thus, the stage is set for this unprepared parent to spiral downward into a pattern of child abuse.

Tragically, parents' own past experiences may provide them with models of hostile and neglectful ways to deal with the stress they are feeling and may have left them with generally low self-esteem as well. Although many abusing parents were not abused themselves, a strong link exists between being abused as a child and later abusing one's own children (Parke and Collmer, 1975; Egeland, Jacobvitz, and Papatola, in press). Apparently, abusing parents often learn at an early age maladaptive responses to the pressures of child rearing. Some researchers think that the violence in our culture also contributes to our child abuse problem (Gelles, 1978). In a culture like Japan's, which places great stress on harmony and personal restraint, the physical abuse of children has been virtually unknown.

THE ENVIRONMENTAL CONTEXT

To sum up, the majority of child abusers are not inherently "sick" or mentally disturbed. They are better described as the victims of unusual stresses coupled with a lack of opportunity to learn effective coping strategies. Child abuse, in other words, is influenced by context (Belsky, 1980). Poverty, isolation, and lack of education all set the stage for it. Within low-income families, the greater the stress experienced (frequent moving, loss of jobs, serious illness, and so forth), the greater the chances that the parents will mistreat their children (Egeland, Breitenbucher, and Rosenberg, 1980).

Just as unusual pressures can encourage child abuse, a high degree of social support can help prevent it. Consequently, although child abuse is generally associated with poverty, poor neighborhoods differ greatly in their incidence of the problem. Factors differentiating low-abuse from high-abuse neighborhoods include interaction among families and social institutions, the presence of parents in the home when children return from school, cohesiveness within the family, and community pride and involvement (Garbarino and Sherman, 1980). On a personal level, support for the principal care giver is extremely important. In the large-scale study we mentioned earlier, less than half of the mothers who mistreated their children had adequate support as opposed to virtually all of the mothers providing adequate care (Egeland and Brunnquell, 1979). Even mothers who themselves were mistreated as children are unlikely to abuse their own children if they have adequate social support (Crockenberg, 1986; Egeland, Jacobvitz, and Sroufe, in press). Susan Crockenberg (1986), for example, found that mothers mistreated as children were not angry and punitive toward their 2-year-old children if they had high levels of support from their spouse or other significant persons. And it is not just the presence of another adult in the home that makes for adequate social support. While abusive parents are more than twice as likely to be single as nonabusers, having an unsupportive partner is apparently more of a liability than having no partner at all (Kempe and Kempe, 1978).

Prevention and Intervention

With our current understanding of the causes of child abuse and neglect, we are able to identify parents who are likely to develop these problems. Those who are young, poorly educated, low in income, single, and socially isolated are more at risk than others. In addition, a woman's attitudes toward her pregnancy and forthcoming child turn out to be quite good predictors of her later care of the baby. Similar factors likely would apply to fathers. In the Egeland and Brunnquell (1979) study we have cited, mothers who subsequently abused their children had this early profile: Only 17 percent planned the pregnancy (compared with 48 percent of control women matched for income level and social class); only 30 percent attended childbirth classes (compared with 100 percent of controls); only 29 percent prepared living quarters for the baby by arranging a place for the child to sleep and so forth (compared with 88 percent of controls); and only 18 percent were judged to have realistic expectations about raising an infant (compared with 90 percent of controls). Egeland and Brunnquell conclude that a woman who is young, with little understanding of infants and the task of caring for them, and who reacts negatively to her pregnancy and the prospects of having a baby should be considered at risk for child abuse or neglect. Factors promoting abuse by fathers are currently less well understood, but certainly understanding of the child, life stress, and developmental history play prominent roles.

The ability to identify parents at risk for child abuse or neglect is especially important because early intervention has been shown to have a significant impact (Kempe and Kempe, 1978). Intervention programs work by providing parents at risk with the educational and emotional support they need to cope with raising a child in stressful circumstances. Parent anonymous groups have also had considerable success by providing parents with similar support networks.

But though intervention programs are a positive step, they cannot eliminate the causes of child abuse entirely. Child abuse is a very complex problem, not reducible to a single cause. The parents' social and economic circumstances, their attitudes about child rearing, and their own life histories and experiences within the family all contribute to the way in which they understand and cope with the complex feelings the child evokes (Belsky, 1980). Abuse is not an isolated event but an overall pattern of care and needs to be viewed as such. Researchers must continue

The presence of other supportive adults can help parents to deal with their children in a positive way. *(Junebug Clark/Photo Researchers, Inc.)*

to meet the urgent need for documenting the consequences of various forms of child mistreatment, ultimately discovering how those consequences unfold.

Chapter Review

1. Dramatic social and emotional development occurs during the toddler period. Compared with infants who require physical contact in order to feel closeness, 12- to 15-month-old children are able to maintain a psychological closeness with the care giver. This psychological closeness involves interactions across a distance, including exchanges of looks, words, smiles, and positive emotions, and is called **affective sharing.** Toddlers are thus freed for more active exploration of their physical and social worlds. Through this exploration emerge the beginnings of a sense of self, accompanied by a growing understanding of people as independent agents.

2. Although early in toddlerhood the child remains rather centered on the principal care giver, by the end of the second year the child has developed into a much more autonomous person. Now the toddler is likely to want to do things without assistance, tackling even very difficult challenges "by myself." This further encourages the sense of being an independent force in the world. Hand in hand with the toddler's psychological separation from the care giver comes an increase in sociability toward others, especially toward peers. Children this age are very attracted to doing things with other toddlers, particularly giving and taking objects. These early peer interactions set the stage for later peer relationships.

3. The role of the care giver at this time is to support the child's movements toward independence while still being available to step in when the youngster's capacities are exceeded. Parents of toddlers must set and maintain reasonable limits to their children's behavior. Such limits help to give toddlers a sense of security in acting on their new-found independence.

4. In general, toddlerhood is a time when parents begin to set rules and limits of many different kinds. The process of learning what parents and other authority figures consider appropriate behavior is often called **socialization.** Although socialization has traditionally been thought of as a process by which rules and values are imposed on an unwilling child, psychologists increasingly see the child as actively seeking to comply with the parents' requests as well as with his or her own understandings of proper behavior.

5. As toddlers become aware of their own separateness and autonomy, they may grow anxious about leaving the former closeness with the care giver. How can they reconcile this need for closeness and security with a striving toward independence? One answer that some psychologists have proposed focuses on the security of the child/care giver relationship. If toddlers know they can reclaim the former closeness with the care giver, if they have confidence that the attachment relationship is secure, they will feel free to explore their capacities to the fullest. If, on the other hand, children are anxious about the care giver's availability, their self-reliance is likely to be compromised. A number of studies support this view of toddler development. The early relationship with the care giver affects the child's view of the world and ways of responding to it, which in turn establish the roots of personality.

6. The child/care giver relationship is itself a product of the surrounding context. Developmentalists are becoming especially interested in how factors within the family context affect the quality of child care. Chief among these factors are the amount of stress a family experiences, the quality of adult relationships in the home, and the various forms of social support available to parents.

7. One example of the importance of the developmental context can be seen in explaining child abuse. Prospective studies discredit the idea that some children by nature draw forth abuse from otherwise nurturant parents. There is also no support for the idea that the majority of abusive parents are mentally disturbed or simply hostile and impulsive people. Instead, child abuse is better viewed as an overall pattern of care that develops when parents who are subject to unusual stress, including the stress of child rearing, lack knowledge and social support needed to cope effectively with it. Poverty, isolation, lack of education, lack of experience with parenting, and a history of abuse all contribute to the problem.

PART THREE SUMMARY

Toddlerhood

In Part II you learned that babies are largely bound by their immediate experiences. Granted, toward the end of the first year of life, advances in memory enable infants to remember past experiences and anticipate future outcomes. For example, when 10-month-old Mikey spotted a jar of sea shells his sister Becky had collected, he recalled the interesting sound he had recently made by shaking this object. So he grasped and shook the jar again, anticipating the result. Note, however, that an immediate situation was required in order for this memory and anticipated outcome to be triggered. Mikey had to actually *see* the jar in order to think about it. He was not yet able to *imagine* the jar if it was not physically present. As you know, the ability to imagine—to represent things mentally—is an extremely important development that emerges in the toddler period. Let's review this milestone as well as some of the other major developmental changes that occur during toddlerhood.

Milestones in Toddler Development

You have seen examples of toddlers' emerging representational skills and symbolic thinking, especially in Chapter 8. Children are now able to *infer* things they do not actually experience with their senses. If Becky has a sea shell in her closed hand and moments later it has disappeared, Mikey as a toddler can infer that Becky must have put the shell somewhere. The same ability that enables toddlers to infer

things they don't actually see happen also enables them to store mental images of other people's actions, images that can later be used as models for deferred imitation. In addition, representational skills allow toddlers to engage in symbolic play, letting one object stand for another, as when Mikey uses a block of wood as a toy car. And, of course, representational skills underlie the use of language, in which groups of sounds are used to symbolize objects, qualities, and actions.

With representational skills comes an awareness of the self as an agent and an object. Children such as Mikey, Malcolm, and Meryl become aware that it is "I" who shakes this object, "I" to whom Mommy talks, "I" who wants to find the object that has been hidden away. Hand in hand with this emerging awareness of self comes an understanding of others as independent agents with their own wishes and intentions. Mikey, for instance, now recognizes that his intentions (such as a desire to continue playing) may be different from or even in conflict with those of his mother (who may want to put him to bed). Language helps Mikey to communicate about this clash of intentions, to exert his own autonomy in the situation, and to find compromises (such as complying with his mother's wishes but going "by myself").

Not surprisingly, with these new understandings about the self and others comes the emergence of new emotions. Recognizing the self as a separate, autonomous individual, the toddler is now capable of having negative feelings about the self, of experiencing shame and vulnerability. By the same token, the toddler is also capable of positive self-evaluations. When DeeDee hugs Malcolm and praises his actions, we can imagine Malcolm's feeling of being positively valued. This is the forerunner of genuine pride. Differentiation of the self from others likewise enables toddlers to experience new interpersonal emotions, such as affection. While love pats of parents and dolls are rare at age 12 months, they are common at 18 months of age (Sroufe, 1979a).

Just as a toddler's growing autonomy helps to foster new emotions, it also helps to bring about major changes in the parent-child relationship. Parents in our culture expect a toddler to show increasing self-reliance. At the same time, they expect the child to begin complying with the various rules and limits that they set. As an increasingly active participant in the parent-child relationship, the toddler exerts a stronger and stronger force in determining the relationship's course. Although personality is certainly not fully formed in toddlerhood, children this age are less malleable than they were as infants. Toddlers have rather firm expectations about their parents' availability and actions, and these expectations in turn affect children's customary ways of responding.

Change in the parent-child relationship is always possible, of course. Parents who were unresponsive or inconsistent toward their children as infants can make a special effort to turn the relationship around. These efforts at first may be somewhat puzzling to a toddler who doubts a parent's new availability and questions the new firmness. Such a toddler is apt to be whiny and negative, having learned in the past that only through such behavior would the desired response from the care giver be achieved. It takes time and resolve to change the negative patterns of adaptation that have become established over the previous months. In the end, however, even "difficult" toddlers generally respond to reassuring firmness from their parents. We may be seeing the beginning of such a change in Meryl. What can we say about her adaptation as a toddler and those of Mickey and Malcolm?

Three Children as Toddlers

All three of our children continue to show normal development in terms of the major milestones we have just reviewed. All are walking, talking, and becoming more autonomous in their thought and behavior. Although Meryl is progressing more slowly than the other two, she is well within the normal range. Each child, however, continues to develop an individual style, a style consistent with his or her past. Despite dramatic changes as they grow older, all three children are building upon foundations laid down in the prior developmental period.

You can see this clearly in Mikey, whose development is proceeding well. He seems to be an easygoing toddler who has taken day care in stride. Given his history of secure attachment, his mother's continuing nurturance and availability, and the high-quality day-care program in which he is enrolled, this is not surprising. An additional ingredient in Mikey's positive adjustment is his father's strong interest in and involvement with him. Frank is quite responsive to Mikey's emerging capacities, and much mutual enjoyment marks their relationship. We also see in Frank the beginnings of a serious concern about his son's gender "appropriate" behavior. This is a common paternal influence in the socialization of boys. We will return to it when we discuss the preschool child.

As well as things are going for Mikey, there is also growing trouble in the Gordon family. Partly because of the stress of Frank's insecurities at work, partly because of their sharply differing views about women working outside the home, Christine and Frank are experiencing conflict. They also show less parental unity than many couples do. What one thinks is good for Mikey the other often opposes. Most troublesome of all, they frequently center their arguments around the child. How this will affect Mikey's future development bears watching.

Like Mikey, Malcolm is also developing well. As you might have expected of this robust baby, he has become a live wire of a toddler. He is exuberant, energetic, and into everything.

The members of his family, however, continue to view his liveliness in a very positive light. Momma Jo delights in telling a friend what a "pile of mischief" Malcolm gets into. For her, as for DeeDee and John, Malcolm is a source of great joy and pride. It is doubtful that in a family with fewer social and psychological resources Malcolm's style of responding would be valued so highly. In other circumstances he might be considered a "difficult" child. Notice, too, how the Williams' network of mutual caring and support more than makes up for the stresses they face as a moderate-income, urban, minority-group family. Malcolm reaps the benefits of this rich social network. DeeDee, John, Momma Jo, Denise, Theresa, and John, Jr., are all actively involved with him and part of his ongoing feelings of security and acceptance.

Things are not going as well for Meryl as they are for Malcolm and Mikey. Meryl is in many ways a difficult toddler. She is lagging in terms of achieving self-reliance; she is easily stressed and unusually needy of adult contact; she can be whiny and negative, and she is prone to tantrums. In addition to being difficult, Meryl also shows signs of being what Alexander Thomas and Stella Chess (1977) call a "slow to warm up" child. This means that she is timid and hesitant in new situations, as when she refuses to try out the new seesaw at Mrs. Jaspers'. It was predictable that entering day care would be difficult for Meryl and a challenge to the relationship between Karen and Meryl.

There are, however, some seeds of positive change for Meryl. Karen seems to be settling into a happier and more stable life. The détente with her own mother has been a big help. Karen can now draw on her mother's emotional support, counsel, and day-to-day assistance in caring for Meryl. Mrs. Jaspers is also a source of emotional support for Karen, as well as a model from whom she can learn. Karen clearly seems to care about Meryl and wants to do well as a mother, as evidenced by her attentiveness to Mrs. Jaspers' suggestions and the way that she keeps trying despite her struggles with Meryl. There are also seeds of positive change in Meryl herself. We see her actively trying to cope with her anxieties through play. With the stuffed bears she works and reworks her concerns about Karen's availability, thus creating feelings of mastery that may counteract her feelings of vulnerability. Such active mastery is made possible by the representational skills that Meryl has developed. It is also supported by the increased stability in her life and the improved quality of care she is receiving. Let's see if these seeds of positive change take root in Meryl's preschool years.

Part Four

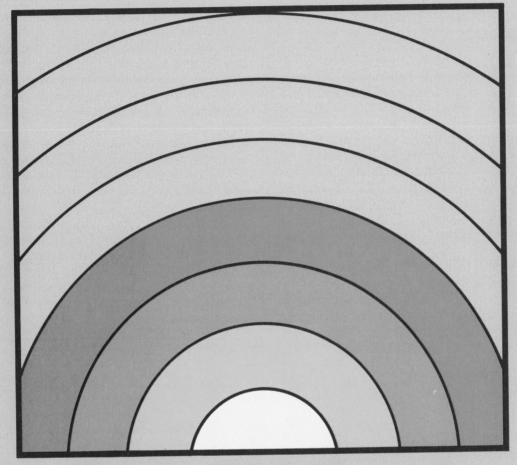

Early Childhood

Three Children in Early Childhood

Malcolm Williams

"C'mon, Motor Man. You want this horse? You jump for it!" John, Jr. told his little brother. Malcolm reached an arm as high as he could and jumped with all his might, but the toy horse remained tantalizingly just outside his reach. "Now how you ever gonna make the pros with jumps like that, man," JJ kept on teasing. "Let's see a real jump!" This time Malcolm jumped so hard he fell over backward as he landed. "Gimme!" he yelled in frustration. "Gimme it!"

"You give that horse to your brother right now!" said Momma Jo, as she strode into the room. "What are you tryin' to do makin' him jump and fall all over the place? He's only four years old. Treat him like your brother, not your dog!"

"We were just havin' fun," JJ protested. "He didn't hurt himself none."

"I'm four *and a half*," chimed in Malcolm. "And I'm gonna be the greatest basketball player ever!"

"Hey, Motor Man," said JJ, pretending to dribble a ball in front of Malcolm. Malcolm raised both arms and waved them frantically in a childish imitation of a guard blocking a shot. As Momma Jo's expression changed from annoyance to amusement, the front door opened and John Williams walked in. "Daddy!" yelled Malcolm, running over to his father. "Hey, my man," John Williams answered, picking Malcolm up and holding him above his head. "What's happenin'?"

"We're playin' basketball!" said Malcolm. "An' I'm the best!"

"Oh, yeah?" his father smiled. "I bet you are."

At dinner that night Malcolm was in high spirits. With great gusto he told the family about a man that he and Momma Jo had seen in the park flying a model airplane. "An' he had this box an' he prested a button an' the plane went just like this—see?" Malcolm's hands illustrated a sharp upward climb. "Then he prested again, an' the plane went round an' round." Malcolm's whole body circled around to help make the point. "An' you know what? The man said the box *told* the plane what to do, but you couldn't hear it talk!"

"That's called remote control, Malcolm," John Williams told his son. "The box sends out signals, and the plane does what the signals tell it."

"Yeah," said JJ, "that's what Momma Jo's gonna get for you, Motor Man, to help keep track of you." The whole family laughed.

"You know," DeeDee said to John as they sat in the living room later, "I've been wondering whether public school is the best place for Malcolm to start out."

"They might take him at St. Dominic's," John answered. "I'd rather he go there than to the public school. They're strict at St. Dom's, and that would be good for Malcolm."

St. Dominic's was the nearby Catholic school that Theresa went to. It had a good reputation, and the tuition was reasonable.

"Well, if we can afford it for Theresa we can find some way to manage for Malcolm too," DeeDee concluded. "I'll check into it tomorrow."

"Hold still now, Malcolm, while I take your picture," DeeDee said smiling. "You look so fine and grown up in your new school clothes."

"I gotta go to the bathroom, Momma," Malcolm complained, hopping from one foot to the other.

"This'll just take a second, honey. Stop holding yourself, Malcolm. You can go to the bathroom in a minute. There. That's better. Now you can run along. Theresa? Hurry up, sugar, or we'll be late."

An hour later DeeDee stood with 22 other mothers in the large, sunny kindergarten room.

"The mommas have to leave now," she told Malcolm, placing a hand on each of his shoulders. "You be good and *mind* your teacher. Bye-bye, honey. You can tell me all about it tonight." And with that DeeDee turned and walked quickly out the door. Malcolm, in his new navy blue shorts and spotless white shirt, was left alone, wide-eyed with wonder, for his first day at school.

It didn't take Malcolm long to adjust to school life. Every morning he was eager to be off to his classroom. He loved having so many other children to play with. His "best friend in the whole world" was a large, good-humored, red-headed boy with a face full of freckles. His name was Patrick Coleman, called Pug for short. As soon as Mrs. Hennessy, their teacher, announced outdoor play, Malcolm and Pug would race to the door so they could claim the two blue tricycles kept in the schoolyard. On one particular Wednesday late in October, Malcolm and Pug rushed out the door and climbed on the bikes as usual. Pug pedaled furiously down the path, but before Malcolm could get started April Kaid stepped out in front of him.

"I wanna ride," April said. "It's my turn. Let me ride."

"I was here first!" Malcolm answered. "Get outa my way! It's my bike."

"No, it's not!" April said, gripping the handlebar with both hands. "You get off or I'll tell Mrs. Hennessy."

"Get outa my way," Malcolm repeated, trying to pry her fingers off the bike. Finally, when April refused to let go, Malcolm made a fist and punched her in the chest. April wailed and ran to the teacher.

"What does she *mean*, a little hyperactive?" John Williams asked indignantly as DeeDee told him about her meeting with Mrs. Hennessy.

"Hyperactive, indeed!" Momma Jo added. "That child's just full of pep, that's all. What he needs is a firm hand from a good teacher."

"Now, Momma," DeeDee answered, "Mrs. Hennessy *is* a good teacher. She said that Malcolm is a real smart boy and a leader in the class. He just has to work harder at controlling himself sometimes. He's got so much energy

inside him, we all know that. But he's gotta learn he just can't go hittin' other kids when he doesn't get his way."

"Well look who's here," said John as Malcolm burst through the door ahead of his brother JJ. "Just the man we're talkin' about."

"Uh-oh, Motor Man. You're in for it now," JJ cautioned as he walked off toward the kitchen, sniffing the aroma of chicken in the oven, his basketball tucked under one arm.

"I went to see your teacher today," DeeDee said to Malcolm, "and she told me you hit a little girl."

"Yucky April Kaid," Malcolm answered. "She wouldn't let go of my bike!"

"It wasn't your bike, boy," Malcolm's father cut in sharply. "It belongs to the whole class. And even if it had been your bike, you still shouldn't have hit her. Men don't hit women, you hear me. Your momma had to leave work to go talk to your teacher. I don't want that ever happenin' again!"

Malcolm started to sniffle as tears welled up in his eyes.

"Now you just dry up, boy," John Williams admonished. "I mean dry up right now."

"Malcolm," DeeDee added, "you've gotta learn to share. You can't always get what you want and do what you want. Do you understand me?" Malcolm nodded slowly as he wiped his eyes with his hands. "OK," his mother concluded, "go wash up for supper."

Mikey Gordon

The boys stood back, gazing at their masterpiece. "Wow!" said Mikey in admiration. "That's tall!" The tower of blocks was indeed impressive. It stood as tall as the boys could reach. Some oddly angled pieces formed the base, making one wonder why the whole thing didn't topple over.

"I'm gonna put this purple one on the very top," Justin Davis announced, picking up a large pyramid-shaped block.

"No!" said Bryan Packer, pushing Justin's hand away. "I'm gonna put this green one there."

"I thought of it first!" Justin answered angrily, pushing Bryan back.

"Hey, I got it! Let's make a spaceport at the top!" Mikey suggested.

"Yeah! That's neat!" the other two agreed, forgetting their momentary tussle. "Go get the rocketship!"

Once again 4-year-old Mikey Gordon had warded off a fight among his playmates at day care. Mikey always seemed eager to avoid unpleasant incidents. He was successful at defusing trouble often enough that his teachers fondly called him the class peacemaker. Mikey was one of the most popular children at the center. A friendly, athletic, competent preschooler, with an infectious giggle, he was also intellectually curious. Even at the age of 3 he could solve puzzles that some 5-year-olds had trouble with. The other children looked up to him.

"Mikey," called out Sue, one of the day-care workers, "your mom's here. Time to go home."

"Gotta go," said Mikey to his friends, as he ran toward the door where his mother was waiting. "Seeya guys."

"Late as usual," Frank Gordon grumbled, sliding into his customary place at the head of the dinner table. "Pretty soon you're gonna be starving us 'til midnight."

"Oh come on, Frank," Christine answered, trying to keep things light. "It's not even six o'clock."

"Yeah, but it's later and later every night. We're hungry, aren't we kids?"

Three pairs of eyes kept staring down at the table. No one said a word.

"Well *I'm* hungry," Frank persisted irritably, rising slightly from his chair so he could reach the large platter of fried chicken.

"Janie, pass Daddy the biscuits please, honey, and the butter," Christine asked of her youngest daughter.

"Yeah, I guess I'll have some of those," Frank remarked unenthusiastically. "But they're not as good as the ones you used to make from scratch. You kids remember when Mommy used to have time to bake good things for us?"

"I like *these* biscuits," piped up Mikey. "They're yummy!" As if to prove it he placed an extra large glob of butter in the steamy center of the biscuit he had just broken open.

"Thank you, Mikey," Christine answered. "Would you like to tell Daddy about the tower you built at day care today?"

"Yeah!" said Mikey. "It was neat! It was so high it almost hit the ceiling! An' you know what? When I was runnin', Justin grabbed my back pocket and ripped it almost off! Wanna see?" And he stood up to display a flap on the back of his jeans that used to be a pocket.

"You're gonna have to wait a long time for Mommy to fix *that*," Frank commented. "I've been waiting months for her just to sew a few lousy buttons back on my shirt. But she doesn't have the time these days. She can find time to sew for a bunch of strangers but not for us!"

Mikey's face fell as he climbed back onto his chair. He began to fidget with a chicken bone on his plate. Across from him his sisters ate silently, eyes cast downward. As Mikey hit the end of the bone with his finger, it flipped up and fell to the floor.

"Woops," said Mikey. And he climbed back down from his chair to find the drumstick. Seconds later his face appeared grinning above the edge of the table. Clenching the chicken bone between his teeth, he began to growl like a dog.

"Oh, Mikey," Christine laughed. "Aren't you a silly boy!"

The girls looked up and started to giggle at Mikey's clowning. Even Frank stopped his griping and helped himself to another biscuit. Mikey got back up on his chair. Temporarily, at least, the tension had eased.

"A man's got to feel like he's the provider, Chrissie. It's only natural. Your father was the same way. You made your bed when you decided to take that job of yours. Now you've got to lie in it."

"But, Mom," Christine said with the phone under her chin as she washed dishes, "I've got *my* life. It can't always be what he wants."

"If you ask me, your life is with Frank and the children. This job is only a sideline. Think of what's really important to you and work harder at being a good wife."

"I've gotta go now, Mom. Frank's coming. I'll talk to you later."

"So your mom sided with me again," Frank said smugly as he sauntered into the kitchen for a beer.

"Oh, shut up," Christine answered, defeated. She was not up to another fight.

"That's a hell of a way to talk to your husband," Frank shot back. "What's eatin' you?"

"Nothing. Just leave me alone, will you? I'm tired."

"You wouldn't be half so tired if you quit that stupid job of yours," Frank continued, spotting his opening.

"Look. Not tonight, OK? I'm not gonna be dragged into another argument with you."

"I'm not arguing," Frank answered. "I'm just tellin' ya what's what."

"Well I wouldn't be half so tired," Christine snapped, "if you'd take one-tenth the effort you put into griping and put it into helping me around here!"

"Why should I help?" Frank persisted, popping the top off his beer can. "It's your damn job to take care of the house and kids."

"Oh, so you don't live here too," Christine shouted. "You don't dirty the clothes or eat the food or mess up or anything else, huh?"

At the top of the stairs Mikey sat listening to his parents' voices growing louder and louder. He hugged his legs tightly with both arms and rested his chin on his knee. This was a scene he had heard enacted countless times before.

"What are you doing, Mikey?" Christine asked the next day as she was making dinner. As he often did, he was playing with trucks on the kitchen floor, but this time the trucks were crashing into each other.

"The trucks just ran over a boy," Mikey responded. "Here comes the ambilenz. Take'm to the hospital, quick!"

Christine was disturbed at Mikey's answer. "That's an awful story, Mikey," she said. "Where are the little boy's mommy and daddy? They wouldn't let that happen."

"They was drivin' the trucks," Mikey explained, "an' the boy fell out by accident."

My God, thought Christine to herself. Are Frank and I the cause of this?

Meryl Polonius

"Mommy, pick me up! Hold me so I can see what you doing."

"Not now, Meryl," Karen answered as she stirred a large pot on top of the stove. "Why don't you go play with your new Pound Puppy for a while."

"Nooo!" whined Meryl, tugging the leg of Karen's pants. "I don't waaant to. Pick me up!"

"I'm cooking dinner, Meryl, and I can't cook and hold you at the same time. Now go and play."

"No!" said Meryl, stamping her foot and scowling. "I want to seeee!"

"Now *stop* it, Meryl," Karen snapped, losing her temper. "Don't be such a pest!"

Meryl's face puckered, and she ran to the kitchen table. Placing her head on one of the chairs, she began sobbing.

"Oh, Meryl, I'm sorry," Karen relented. "Come here, honey. It's OK. Mommy's sorry."

But Meryl was not to be appeased. "No!" she shouted, clenching her hands into two tight fists. "I won't!"

Before Karen could answer, the back door swung open and Joe Turner walked in. "Hi," he said, smiling at Karen, and then to Meryl: "What's the matter, honey?"

"Go 'way!" Meryl pouted as Joe approached her. Then turning her back she started sucking her thumb.

"Don't ask me how my day was," Karen said, returning Joe's affectionate kiss. "This is the high point!"

Karen and Joe had been living together for nearly a month now. Seven months before, right after Meryl turned 3, another waitress at The Green Door had introduced them. Joe worked as a reporter for the local paper and was 6 years older than Karen. At first she had not been very interested in him. There was something soft and vague looking about Joe Turner. As far as looks were concerned, he was certainly no Jeff. Even at 26 his hair was thinning, and Karen suspected he would soon have a fair-sized bald patch. But there was also something about Joe Turner that made Karen feel warm and comfortable. With him she didn't have to pretend to be anyone other than exactly who she was. In time she grew to love Joe for making her feel so special and also for his genuine fondness of Meryl.

"Do you think Meryl will ever get over these awful tantrums?" Karen asked doubtfully after mother and daughter had staged yet another battle of wills, this time over whether Meryl would go to bed on time.

"Of course," said Joe. "Do you think 10 years from now you're going to have a teenager who stamps her feet and pouts?"

"Yes," laughed Karen. "That's *exactly* what I'm afraid I'm going to have! Don't joke about it."

"Honey, give it time," Joe smiled. "I think maybe it's all the changes she's been through. We dragged her off to this new apartment just when she was finally settled at your mom's. You've gotta expect a few problems. Just don't keep blaming yourself all the time. You have a right to get angry at her once in a while. She could try the patience of a saint when she gets that little scowl on her face," he chuckled, imitating Meryl's pursed lips and deeply furrowed brow.

"Yeah, she's a stubborn little thing sometimes," Karen said, smiling. "But seriously, how can I do things better?"

"Well, you might try not waffling quite so much," Joe suggested. "I don't mean to criticize you, honey, but you do go back and forth a lot. First you tell her she can't have something, then you give it to her anyway. Next you tell her she can't sit on your lap, then you pick her up when she pouts. She's not gonna die if she doesn't get her way all the time, you know."

"I know," agreed Karen. "It's just that when she gets upset I think I must have done the wrong thing, so I turn around and do the opposite. I know it doesn't help. Mrs. Jaspers told me that too. She said I just have to mean what I say more."

"I think she's probably right," said Joe, taking hold of Karen's hand.

In the weeks that followed Joe not only advised Karen about dealing with Meryl, he also showed her. One day when Karen was in the living room, she overheard Joe and Meryl in the kitchen. "I want another cookie," Meryl demanded. "No," Joe said firmly, "one is all you get until dinner. Now you just play there with your farm until I get these dishes put away." In a voice that sounded as sweet as an angel's Meryl answered, "OK." How could it be so easy for him and so hard for me, Karen

wondered. "I think it's partly because she doesn't know any different with me," Joe said later. "Give it time. Things'll work out."

And in time things did work out. After about 4 months of the new living arrangements, Meryl was far more cheerful and cooperative. Karen thought Joe was the major reason. He read Meryl stories and played with her a lot. To Meryl these enjoyable pastimes were much more interesting than pouting and clinging. Joe also assured Karen that she seemed more confident and that this confidence was coming through to Meryl. Meryl's fourth birthday was a real celebration for them all.

"I have a surprise for you, sweetie," Karen said to Meryl, as she put her to bed after a party with ice cream and cake. "Joe and Mommy are getting married. That means we're going to have another party—just like a birthday party only without the balloons. And you'll get a new little dress to wear. What do you think of that?"

"Oh, boy!" said Meryl. "Can I have flowers?"

"Of course," smiled Karen. "We'll get you flowers to wear in your hair."

"You know," said Joe as he and Karen walked arm in arm to the living room, "after we're married I'd like to adopt Meryl. I feel like her father already and adopting her would make it all legal. I think it would mean a lot to Meryl, too, especially when she's older."

"That'd be wonderful," Karen answered, thrilled with the idea. "It would make us a real family."

Meryl Polonius Turner stood shy and hesitant in the room full of kindergarten children. She looked down at her new unscuffed shoes and began wriggling her toes.

"Would you like to come play in the store, Meryl?" Mrs. McBrier asked in a kind, encouraging voice.

Meryl walked slowly toward her without saying a word and stood in the doorway of the large cardboard structure. Inside were shelves stocked with brightly colored boxes, just like in a real supermarket. To one side was a counter and a toy cash register. Two little girls toting bright red shopping baskets were busily inspecting the wares. One had on a long string of beads, the other a pair of large purple sunglasses. Meryl smiled slightly and glanced up at the teacher.

"We need someone to work at the checkout counter, Meryl. Would you like to do that?"

Meryl walked quietly behind the counter. She pressed one of the buttons on the cash register and the drawer flew open, revealing a tray crammed full of make-believe money. Meryl's smile grew bigger. She had never seen such a wonderful play store in her life.

One of the shoppers approached Meryl with her "purchases." "Do you have any coupons?" Meryl asked shyly, just as she had heard checkout clerks asking her mother.

The shopper looked disappointed. "No," she said, adjusting the sunglasses on her nose. "I just have money."

"Don't worry," said Meryl. "We give coupons." And ripping some strips of paper from a brown paper bag, she handed them to the shopper.

"Thanks!" said the shopper, smiling happily at Meryl. "My name's Amy."

From that morning on, Meryl and Amy were always together at school.

10

Cognitive Development in Early Childhood

"Mommy, who was born first, you or me?"

"Daddy, when you were little, were you a little boy or a little girl?"

"Why do they put a pit in every cherry? We have to throw the pit away anyway."

"When the sun sets into the sea, why isn't there any steam?"

These are all questions actually asked by preschool children in the Soviet Union (Chukovsky, 1941/1971). Children this age in every country ask exactly the same kinds of questions as they strive to understand their world. Some of the strange and humorous things about preschoolers' ideas stem from a simple lack of information. We might imagine extremely intelligent aliens from another planet making some of these errors just because they didn't yet have all the relevant facts. However, it also appears that young children's thinking itself differs in basic ways from the thinking of adults, and this is what makes preschoolers so interesting. One of the goals of this chapter is to

The preschooler wants to know why. *(Patrick Grace/ Photo Researchers, Inc.)*

describe and analyze the distinctions between the two modes of thought. The thinking of a preschooler is particularly fascinating because it possesses both mature and immature qualities. It is sufficiently different from the thinking of an adult so that we notice its magical elements. Yet it is close enough to adult thought to enable the construction of complex ideas and to allow us to observe developmental continuities.

As you explore preschool cognitive abilities you will notice an important change in the child's approach to learning about and mastering the environment. Infants understand the world strictly by perceiving it and acting on it. Then, during toddlerhood, representational thought emerges in the context of developing concepts and learning a vocabulary. Toddlers can imagine the consequences of an action without actually carrying it out, and they can combine symbols. These new acquisitions provide the foundation for further aspects of language development, such as putting several words together in simple sentences. In this chapter you will see preschoolers (which includes children 2½ to 5 years old) trying to understand the world at an even more advanced level—attempting to explain how things work and why events take place. When Malcolm strives to grasp the workings of a remote-controlled model plane, he is functioning in a way that no toddler can.

You will encounter some of the same themes you met in earlier chapters. First, preschoolers continue to be *active participants* in their own development. By this we mean not only that they actively explore the world but also that they actively construct an understanding of what they discover. Preschoolers progress from observing and describing events to trying to explain them. An important part of this active mental participation in development is a continued search for *general patterns and rules.* Just as toddlers search for patterns in forming early concepts, so preschoolers do the same in trying to master new cognitive challenges. For instance, you know that Malcolm has identified a general pattern when he uses the word *goed.* Although this is not the way adults form the past tense of the irregular verb *to go,* Malcolm's error can be thought of as a "smart" mistake. It shows that he is striving to impose order on what he learns, something that all children do.

A second major theme is the continuing interplay between the child's unfolding capacities and the environment in which he or she grows up. Children's advancing cognitive skills allow them to engage the environment in new ways and draw forth new types of parental interaction. Peers as well as parents are now sources of information about solving problems and engaging the environment, and both provide continuing feedback.

In addition to these two major themes, you will encounter three limitations characteristic of young children's thinking. One is the difficulty preschoolers have integrating multiple pieces of information. For example, when asked which of two cars is going faster, 4-year-old Mikey is apt to consider only which car is currently ahead. He is not likely to integrate this piece of information with knowledge of how far apart the cars were when they started moving. This tendency to consider only one piece of information when multiple pieces are relevant is called **centration.** A second limitation of young children's thinking is the difficulty they have distinguishing between appearance and reality. For instance, when 3-year-olds look at a white object, look at it again through a blue filter, then remove the filter, and so forth, they think that the object is really changing color, not just *appearing* to change (Flavell, 1985). This tendency to define reality by surface appearance is called the **appearance-reality problem.** A third limitation you will encounter in this chapter is preschoolers' difficulty with tasks that require memory strategies or other activities to enhance memory. Meryl is beginning to understand the value of some memory strategies when she holds on to her sweater after her mother has told her not to forget it as they are preparing to leave the house. But preschoolers do not usually know about strategies that could be used in remembering, and even when they do know such strategies they don't often use them.

We must be cautious when discussing young children's cognitive limitations, however. In the past some researchers believed that preschoolers totally lacked certain cognitive capabilities, only to find out later that these abilities may be present to some extent by the middle preschool period. Whether young children display certain skills depends in part on the difficulty of the tests they are given. For example, Jean Piaget once found that 4-year-olds, allowed to inspect a large model of a mountain range, could not pick out a picture of the model that showed the view as seen by a person sitting on the opposite side from the child. On the basis of this and other studies, Piaget argued that preschoolers are **egocentric:** They see the world from their own viewpoint and are unable to take the perspective of another person. Today we know that egocentrism is not absolute in young children. In less complex situations, preschoolers can sometimes take another person's perspective in a limited way. This perspective-taking ability unfolds gradually during the preschool years and is applied in an increasing number of contexts. Thus, understanding preschool cognitive development demands attention both to how new skills are acquired and to how existing skills become more widely used.

The new capabilities that emerge during the preschool years depend in part on the acquisition of new knowledge. At the same time, this acquisition of knowledge is fostered by the development of new cognitive skills. Counting and measuring are examples of such skills, which mark movement toward more abstract characterizations of the world. Although these emerging skills are not yet integrated into fully logical systems of understanding, within limited contexts they allow preschoolers to solve problems that a toddler could not. For example, both a toddler and a preschooler can discriminate a triangle from a square, but only a preschooler is likely to report that an important difference between them is the number of sides. Preschoolers' improving understanding of other people's perspectives allows older preschoolers to communicate and learn from others more effectively.

The first major section of this chapter examines the general characteristics of preschoolers' thought. We begin by exploring how preschoolers reason and how they try to explain the causes of things. Here you will learn that a young child's understandings are often quite different from those of an adult. Next we explore some conceptual tools that are extremely valuable in learning about and dealing with the world. To what extent do preschoolers possess these abilities? Recent research has yielded some fascinating results. In our next major section we examine the preschool child's cognitive skills from an information-processing perspective. In particular, we describe preschoolers' skills for directing their attention and managing their memory. Finally, we take up the subject of social cognition, exploring how cognitive advances of preschoolers promote more effective communication and social interaction and how social relations promote cognitive development and performance.

GENERAL CHARACTERISTICS OF PRESCHOOLERS' THOUGHT

Causal Reasoning

Jean Piaget was very interested in how children's reasoning changes as they grow older. In his early work he used interviews to explore this topic. He asked children questions, such as "Why do clouds move?" and searched for developmental trends in their answers. Here are examples of children's responses at four different developmental levels.

Level 1
Adult: What makes clouds move?
Child: When we move along they move along too.
Adult: Can you make them move?
Child: Yes.
Adult: When I walk and you are still, do they move?
Child: Yes.
Adult: And at night, when everyone is asleep, do they move?
Child: Yes.
Adult: But you tell me that they move when somebody walks.
Child: They always move. The cats, when they walk, and then the dogs, they make the clouds move.
(Piaget, 1930/1969, p. 62)

Level 2

Adult: What makes the clouds move along?
Child: God does.
Adult: How?
Child: He pushes them.
(Piaget, 1930/1969, p. 63)

Level 3

Adult: What makes the clouds move along?
Child: It's the sun.
Adult: How?
Child: With its rays. It pushes the clouds.
(Piaget, 1930/1969, p. 65)

Level 4

Adult: What makes the clouds move along?
Child: Because they have a current.
Adult: What is this current?
Child: It's in the clouds.
(Piaget, 1930/1969, p. 72)

What makes the clouds move? *(R. B. Sanchez/The Stock Market.)*

In the first response, which is characteristic of preschoolers, the child reports that when we move along the clouds move along too. At first this answer may be perplexing to you. Where did the youngster get such a strange idea? To understand, stop and think about how objects appear in relation to us as we walk along. We first approach nearby objects, which then recede into the distance after we pass them by. This is not true of things that are very far away, however, such as the sun, moon, or clouds in the sky. These very distant objects never seem to get any closer or farther away. For instance, if you start out on a walk and the sun is directly overhead, it will still be in virtually the same position an hour later, during which time you could have walked four miles. The same is true of clouds far in the distance. As you walk, the clouds remain in approximately the same position, even though nearer objects come and go. Young children often notice this phenomenon and interpret it to mean that the sun, moon, and clouds must be moving with them. As one Soviet preschooler on a trip to the mountains described the moon's behavior: "The moon flew along as we went on the train. She wanted to see the Caucasus too!" (Chukovsky, 1941/1971, p. 20). Notice how the child is using observations to construct an understanding of the world. The child can be said to be actively constructing his or her own reality. We adults do *not* perceive the sun, moon, and clouds to be moving with us, because our understanding of reality differs from that of preschoolers. Notice, too, that for a child at this level, reality is defined by the superficial appearance of things. This is one of the cognitive limitations of early childhood that we mentioned earlier.

As children grow older, their interpretations of things change, and with these changes come different understandings of the world. Returning to Piaget's levels of causal reasoning, at level 2 the child often appeals to an all-powerful force controlling objects and events. This omnipotent force may be called God, or perhaps Mommy or Daddy. While many adults believe in God, they generally do not believe that the existence of

Lack of knowledge concerning causality sometimes leads the preschooler to ideas that adults find amusing or even magical. These children seem to be planting rocks in a garden to see if they will grow. *(Kathleen Brown/West Stock.)*

an all-powerful being is a sufficient explanation for why things happen as they do. At reasoning level 3 the child begins appealing to causes in nature to explain natural phenomena. At this stage, however, those causes may be quite improbable (the rays of the sun pushing clouds along, for instance). Finally, at level 4, the child is approaching an adult explanation, even though that explanation is still incomplete.

Although Piaget did not find mature causal reasoning until well into middle childhood, other researchers have shown that the level of reasoning is partly a function of the kinds of problems posed. For instance, if young children are asked for explanations of things they are familiar with (such as how a bicycle works), their responses are more mature (Berzonsky, 1971). These results make two important points about preschoolers' cognitive abilities. First, preschoolers have the skills to give good explanations if the thing to be explained is simple and familiar. Second, preschoolers do not yet understand what constitutes a "good" explanation, so when they don't know the reason for something they may invent one that seems fanciful or even absurd to adults. Preschoolers, in other words, lack an abstract idea of what can constitute a cause.

Conceptual Tools

As an adult you have many implicit understandings about how objects and events are related. You know, for example, that when a tall glass of water is poured into a very flat dish, the amount of water does not diminish even though it becomes very shallow. Psychologists say you possess the conceptual tool of **conservation** of liquid volume. You also possess the conceptual tool of **classification.** You can easily sort things by size, shape, make, color, price, and so forth. You think nothing of classifying along several dimensions simultaneously, as when you group together all the high-priced, mid-sized, foreign-made cars. Another conceptual tool you take for granted is **seriation,** the ability to arrange things in a logical progression, such as organizing a batch of newspapers from earliest to latest. You also take for granted the conceptual tool of **transitive inference,** the ability to infer the relationship between two objects by knowing their respective relationships to a third. When you know that two boards are equal in length because they both measure 32 inches on the same yardstick, you are using a conceptual tool that you have learned through experience. Very young children have not yet acquired these implicit understandings. Conservation, classification, seriation, and transitive inference only begin to develop during the preschool period. What's more, centration and the appearance-reality problem in preschoolers place limits on all four capacities.

PRESCHOOLERS' UNDERSTANDING OF QUANTITY

One tool used to understand the world is quantification. Even before they fully understand the answers, preschoolers can be heard to ask questions about "how big," "how little," "how fast," "how many," and "how much." But preschoolers' knowledge of quantification is not systematic and includes both surprising abilities and inabilities. We will begin by examining one of the surprising inabilities: failure to understand conservation.

Much of our knowledge about the physical world can be expressed by **rules of conservation,** which state that certain characteristics remain unchanged despite transformations carried out on them. You probably know of Einstein's famous equation, $E = mc^2$. It is a formula about the conservation of mass and energy which says that while mass and energy can be transformed from one to the other, their *total* amount is fixed. That total amount, in other words, is conserved; a transformation produces neither an increase nor a decrease. Although to physicists this idea seems intuitive and obvious, many adults find it difficult to grasp. In the same way, concepts of conservation that seem obvious to adults are not at all obvious to preschoolers.

One such concept is the conservation of liquid volume, the idea that the total amount of a liquid remains the same despite being poured from one container to another. To investigate when children acquire this concept, Piaget presented youngsters of different ages with two glasses of equal size and shape filled with identical amounts of water (see Figure 10.1, part A). He then asked each child which glass had more water, a or b, or whether the two had just the same amount. Most children said that the two had just the same, although for some, small adjustments had to be made before they declared the amounts to be equal. Next, while the child observed, Piaget poured the water from glass b into another glass (c), which was wider and shorter than the other two glasses (see Figure 10.1, part B). The child was then asked if glass a had more water, if c had more, or if they both had the same. Preschoolers almost invariably answered that a had more. When asked why, they pointed out that the water in glass a rose to a higher level.

Piaget concluded that preschoolers lack the concept of conservation of liquid volume. They do not seem to grasp that a volume of water remains the same regardless of the size and shape of the container into which it is poured. In addition, this experiment illustrates the two limitations on preschoolers' thought that we mentioned earlier. First, the children are misled by the appearance of the liquid in the tall, narrow

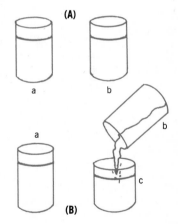

Figure 10.1
Conservation of Liquid Volume
When glasses a and b are filled to equal heights, preschoolers judge that they have equal amounts of water. However, when the water in glass b is poured into glass c, which is shorter and wider, they judge glass c to have less than glass a. This is an example of preschoolers' failure to conserve.

glass; they mistake superficial appearance for reality. Second, the children focus on only one aspect of the stimulus, the height to which the water has risen. This shows their tendency toward centration.

Piaget studied the development of various concepts of conservation. Three examples are:

Conservation of number	Items in a group remain the same in number despite being rearranged.
Conservation of mass	A ball of clay rolled out into a long, thin snake does not change in mass.
Conservation of length	A coiled up string pulled out full length does not grow any longer.

Most preschoolers do not understand any of these concepts. An understanding of conservation usually doesn't emerge until the elementary-school years. Moreover, children do not come to grasp concepts of conservation all at once. Some of these concepts are learned well before others. It is as if the child approaches each concept as a relatively new problem. This makes sense when you consider that whether or not a quantity will be conserved despite a transformation depends in part on the particular transformation being made. For instance, if you cut out 16 one-inch squares of paper and assembled them into different patterns, the area of those patterns would always be 16 square inches; area would be conserved. However, if you tied together the ends of a 22-inch piece of string and pulled the string into different shapes, the area within the string would vary greatly; it would *not* be conserved. If the string formed a circle, the area inside it would be 38.5 square inches. If the string formed a rectangle 1 by 10 inches, the area inside would be only 10 square inches. With such seeming inconsistencies, no wonder it takes time for children to master concepts of conservation.

Concepts of conservation are intimately connected to concepts of measurement and questions of "how much." If you thought that the amount of liquid changes when poured from one container to another, what would be the sense of using a measuring cup? Piaget believed that learning about conservation of liquid volume, conservation of number, length, mass, area, and all the other related concepts, requires a common underlying cognitive skill. That underlying skill, Piaget argued, is absent in the preschooler.

As another example of how preschool children perform on conservation tests, consider a test of conservation of number. The researcher assembles two rows of seven pennies each, both rows of equal length. The child is then asked if one row has more pennies, or if the number of pennies is just the same in each. After the child declares that both rows have the same number, the coins are spread out in one of the rows so that that row becomes longer. The child is asked again which row has more pennies or if they both have the same number. Typically the preschooler answers that the longer row has more. It is as if the child confuses apparent length with number, just as height was confused with amount of liquid in Piaget's experiment.

Researchers have devoted much effort to finding out whether preschoolers really do think that the number of objects has changed because of a rearrangement, or whether they are giving a wrong answer for some

Figure 10.2
Number Conservation
Children were asked which row of dolls fit in the beds with no dolls left over and no beds left over. Preschoolers' inability to conserve number on this task illustrates that their failure is not caused by a misunderstanding of the words *more, less,* and *equal.*

other reason. They might, for instance, have simply misunderstood the question. When people are asked a question about some object, followed by an action carried out on that object and a repeat of the same question, they usually assume that the action was relevant to the question and therefore that the answer should change. Preschoolers may have already learned this convention and so change their answer in the only way that seems plausible. Why would the researcher repeat the question, young children may wonder, if spreading out one of the rows didn't make that row get more?

To rule out this explanation, researchers have presented preschoolers with other conservation tasks—tasks that make it clearer that the experimenter's actions don't necessarily mean the child's answer should change. In one such study, illustrated in Figure 10.2, children were shown a row of doll beds and two rows of dolls (Cooper, 1976). One of the rows of dolls contained the same number of dolls as there were beds, and this row was initially arranged to be the same length as the row of beds. The child was asked which row of dolls fit into the beds with no dolls or beds left over. After choosing the correct row, the child was instructed to put the dolls in that row into the beds to be sure this answer was right. The experimenter then removed the dolls from the beds and lined them up again so that again they formed a row equal in length to the row of beds. Again the child was asked which row of dolls just fit into the row of beds, and again the child answered correctly. Next the experimenter manipulated *both* rows of dolls, either spreading them both out to become longer or compressing them both to become shorter. Again the child was asked which row fit into the beds, and this time the child answered incorrectly. He or she responded as if equality of length indicated equality of number. But note that the number of wrong answers given could be greatly reduced by decreasing the number of items in each row. With rows containing only two or three dolls instead of six or more, 4-year-olds made errors only 27 percent of the time.

Other studies have demonstrated that preschoolers do develop substantial understanding of small numbers *before* they fully master conservation concepts. Consider a study conducted by Rochele Gelman (1972), who is well known for her work in this area. Gelman presented young children with two plates, each containing toy mice fastened to a Velcro strip. One of the plates had a row of two mice, the other a row of three. The children were told that they were going to play a game in which they had to identify the "winning" plate. Gelman pointed to the plate with three mice and said that it would always be the winner, but she never described the plate in any way. The children had to decide for themselves which characteristic—number of mice or length of the row—made that plate the winner. Next Gelman covered each plate with a large lid and shuffled them. Each child was then asked to pick the lid under which the winning plate lay. Whenever the child picked the three mice plate, he or she was given a small prize. After several rounds of shuffling and picking, Gelman made the critical transformation. She surreptitiously changed the three mice plate, either by moving the mice closer together or farther apart or by removing one mouse entirely. Because these changes were made without the child's knowledge, this experiment has been dubbed the "magic" study.

Gelman's findings showed that even 3- and 4-year-olds defined the winning plate by the number of mice, not by the length of the row. Almost no children claimed that a change in the length of the three mice row disqualified the plate as a winner. Many failed even to notice such a change. In contrast, almost all the children noticed removal of a mouse. Many showed great surprise that one of the mice was missing, exclaiming "Where is it?" "Where'd it go?" and searching for the missing toy. The overwhelming majority doubted that a three mice plate with one of its mice missing could still be considered a winner. Over two-thirds emphatically declared that the plate was now a loser. The only way to fix things, they said, would be to add another mouse. These children clearly understood something about the effects of addition and subtraction on number. Other studies have similarly shown that preschoolers know something about the ways that adding and subtracting change number even *before* they can correctly solve conservation problems involving numbers greater than 6 (Cooper, 1984; Starkey and Gelman, 1982). These findings require modifications of Piaget's early writings in which he argued that although preschoolers have an "intuitive" grasp of small numbers, they do not develop a true concept of number until they understand number conservation (Piaget, 1952).

Preschoolers also show an intuitive grasp of measurement before they correctly solve conservation problems. For example, Kevin Miller (1983) has shown that they will divide a string in half by holding it near the center and adjusting the held position until the length of the two string segments is equal. Also, children will form two equal groups of cookies by dividing a large group a pair at a time (Cooper, 1984). Therefore, children make measurement errors when the appearance of two equal quantities makes them look unequal, as when one row of pennies is spread out. But in the absence of misleading perceptual information, they frequently perform reasonable measurement activities. What is missing for preschoolers is a systematic understanding of quantity that justifies these measurement activities. In the section on reasoning about order, you will see one of the missing tools that limits developing such a system.

We can summarize what we've discussed about quantitative concepts in preschool children with three basic points. First, preschoolers do not usually display an understanding that quantities are conserved despite some transformations that change their appearance. Second, when preschoolers fail to demonstrate a grasp of conservation, they tend to focus on only a single aspect of the stimulus. They look at the height of the water in the glass and ignore the narrower width; they look at the length of a row overall and ignore the spacing between objects. To them the immediate appearance seems to be what counts. Third, failure to understand conservation does not prevent preschoolers from learning a substantial amount about measurement and about small quantities and how they can be changed through addition and subtraction.

UNDERSTANDING CLASSES AND COLLECTIONS

When we group things by shared characteristics, we are engaging in classification. A **class** is any set of objects or events that we think of as having certain features in common and therefore as being the same in certain ways. Joe Turner, for example, classifies objects as he empties the dishwasher, putting glasses in one cupboard, plates in another, and silverware in a drawer. If Meryl, after watching him, takes one of her toy spoons and puts it into the silverware drawer, we can say that she seems to understand the class silverware.

When do children first display classification skills? Infants show an implicit form of classification when they treat certain stimuli as the same based on shared characteristics. For instance, if you give a baby bottles of slightly different sizes with different colored nipples, the child will ignore these perceptual variations and treat the bottles similarly. Although the child is certainly not aware of this implicit classification, he or she is nevertheless showing a primitive form of this skill. In time the child begins to "group" more intentionally. Before they are 2, toddlers can be seen actively sorting objects on the basis of common properties (Flavell,

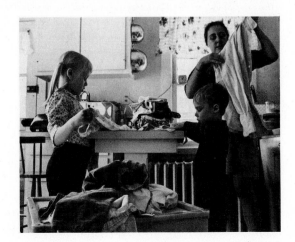

The preschooler has some ability to "help" with a complex sorting task. The younger child could pick out all of the socks (a class based on shape). But simultaneously sorting socks in terms of *both* color and size would be beyond his capacity. That would be systematic sorting, which is especially difficult. (*Mimi Forsyth/Monkmeyer Press.*)

1970). Meryl as a toddler, for example, loved to explore a lower kitchen cupboard and sort the pots from the lids. However, not until the preschool years are children able to classify objects consistently when they are asked to do so.

Piaget studied classification in preschoolers by giving them several tasks (Inhelder and Piaget, 1964). He presented children with different colored shapes, instructing them to sort the things that "go together" into separate groups. In the simplest form of this task there were only two colors (such as red and blue) and only two shapes (such as circles and squares). Piaget found that the youngest preschoolers would sometimes sort correctly along one dimension. They might put all the red circles and squares in one pile and all the blue ones in another. However, it was not unusual for a 3-year-old to start sorting on the basis of color and then to switch suddenly by matching the *shape* of the last object added to a pile. Older preschoolers were more consistent in their sorting, until by age 5 they were quite consistent in classifying along one dimension. But note that even the 5-year-olds still focused on only a single characteristic (color alone, for example, not color *and* shape). A 10-year-old, in contrast, would sort using both dimensions simultaneously, putting all the blue squares in one pile, all the blue circles in another, all the red squares in a third, and all the red circles in a fourth. Piaget saw this difference as another example of the preschoolers' centration.

Later research, however, has shown that this centration is not completely rigid. Two-dimensional sorting can be encouraged in preschoolers by giving them experience in classifying objects. In one study, children who had been trained to sort along single dimensions showed substantial two-dimensional sorting by age 4 (Watson, Hayes, and Vietze, 1979). Other researchers have likewise found that training can prompt older preschoolers to classify along two dimensions (see Cooper, 1973). But note that preschoolers seldom spontaneously use these more complex classification schemes to organize objects in their everyday environments. Although centration on a single dimension can be somewhat overcome by training, preschoolers return to this narrower focus in situations that differ from the training examples.

While classification requires that people impose some kind of organization on stimuli, many of the things we perceive as grouped together in the everyday world already seem to be organized for us in time or space. Such natural groupings are called collections. A **collection** is any entity composed of subparts which, because of their proximity to one another, seem to be automatically related. Examples are a forest composed of many trees or a herd of cattle made up of many cows. Such collections have a natural unity; we do not need to sort and organize the subparts by shared characteristics. Preschoolers seem to reason in more advanced ways when asked questions about collections than when asked questions about classes. For example, Ellen Markman (1979) presented number conservation problems to 4- and 5-year-olds using either class terms (trees, soldiers, birds) or collection terms (forest, army, flock). The children were much more likely to answer correctly when collection terms were used. Referring to a group of trees as a forest seems to help preschoolers focus on the whole group as an unchanging entity, whereas using the term trees leads them to focus on characteristics of the individual units. Apparently because of its natural unity, a collection is easier for young children to think about. A class, in contrast, is often a more abstract concept, requiring more mental effort to organize and define.

The major limitation of preschoolers is not in classes but in reasoning about classes and the interrelationships among classes. These limitations stem from centration—considering only one class or one characteristic that differentiates two classes at a time. In fact, the difference in performance between using class and collection terms can be interpreted based on centration: The class term leads preschoolers to focus on the individual entities, while the collection term leads them to focus on the whole group. We will say more about the development of an understanding of classes in our unit on middle childhood.

UNDERSTANDING ORDERING

Seriation is the arrangement of things in a logical progression, such as from oldest to newest. Piaget was interested in seriation in children because he believed that the ability to order objects according to some dimension indicated an underlying cognitive skill required to appreciate numbers and to measure effectively. Piaget (1952) studied seriation by asking children to arrange a group of sticks in a row from smallest to largest. If the child succeeded in organizing the sticks into an orderly progression, the youngster was given another stick of intermediate length to insert at the appropriate place in the series. Piaget discovered that young preschoolers can find the largest or the smallest stick in a group, but they have great difficulty constructing an ordered series of seven sticks. By age 6 or 7, however, most children can easily construct such a series, and they can also insert an additional stick in the correct location.

Interestingly, when the number of sticks to be ordered is smaller, preschool children perform much better on this task (Blevins and Cooper, 1986; Cooper, Leitner, and Moore, 1977). Why would decreasing the number of sticks make any difference? The answer lies in the way in which preschoolers approach the seriation task. If you were given this task you would probably start by finding the smallest stick and putting it on the left, finding the next smallest and putting it second, and so on until all the sticks had been arranged. This planned course of action requires that you grasp the nature of a seriated set of sticks before you begin to work. Such an overall understanding guiding each move is not apparent in the behavior of young children, even when they are organizing only a small number of sticks. Instead, preschoolers seem to arrange the sticks more or less at random and then check to see if the results look right. This trial-and-error strategy can work for a small number of sticks, such as three or four, which can be arranged in only a very limited number of ways. With seven sticks, however, the alternatives are far more numerous, and trial-and-error is less likely to lead to success.

The preschooler's approach to seriation tasks illustrates the two cognitive limitations we talked about earlier. First, we see the appearance-reality problem in a slightly different form. The preschool child cannot conceive of the reality of an ordered set in the absence of the immediate appearance of one. Second, some of young children's attempts to order a set of seven sticks show evidence of centration. Notice in part B of Figure 10.3 that the top ends of the sticks are seriated, but the bottoms vary

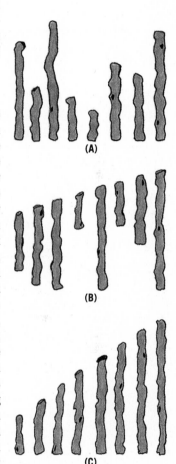

Figure 10.3
Development of Seriation
When young preschoolers are asked to order a set of sticks from smallest to largest, they frequently produce a random order, such as that shown in (A). Older preschoolers sometimes centrate on the top ends of the sticks and produce an arrangement like that in (B). Usually between 5 and 7 years of age, children can produce the correct ordering shown in (C).

randomly. It is as if the preschooler who constructed this series could not coordinate the information from the two ends simultaneously and so focused on the tops only.

TRANSITIVE INFERENCE

Transitive inference is a reasoning process for drawing conclusions about the relative characteristics of two objects by knowing their respective relationships to a third object. For example, if you know that A equals B and that B equals C, you can conclude by transitive inference that A and C are equal. Transitive inference can also be used to reason about inequalities. If you know that Mikey is taller than Jeff, and Jeff is taller than Richie, you know by transitive inference that Mikey is the tallest of the three.

In Piaget's initial studies, children were unable to solve transitive inference problems until middle childhood (Piaget, 1970). More recent research challenges this conclusion, however (Bryant and Trabasso, 1971; Riley and Trabasso, 1974). Tom Trabasso and his colleagues have shown that even 4-year-olds can succeed at these problems if they are given sufficient training to remember the premise conditions (such as Mikey is taller than Jeff, and Jeff is taller than Richie). To rule out alternative explanations as to why 4-year-olds succeed, Trabasso has had to train his young subjects regarding five premise pairs, all involving relationships between pairs of real objects. It takes a very long time to get 4-year-olds to master these five pairs, but in the end they can answer questions such as "Who is taller, Mikey or Richie?" even though they have never been directly taught that relationship.

There is still disagreement about exactly what 4-year-olds have learned when they demonstrate such knowledge of between-pair comparisons (Breslow, 1981; Russell, 1981). One criticism has focused on a frequently used component in the training procedure. Early in training, the children learn the five premise pairs in the proper order. For example, first they learn that Mikey is taller than Jeff, then that Jeff is taller than Richie, and so on. It has been suggested that this might allow a child to learn the serial order of items without the skills underlying transitive inference. Even so, it is still impressive that preschoolers can make correct judgments about relative size based on a mental representation they have formed of a series. This feat shows that they can accomplish an important part of transitive inference.

Despite the accomplishments 4-year-olds made in Trabasso's studies, they clearly face cognitive limitations that older children do not. For instance, preschoolers have a dramatically harder time learning Trabasso's premise pairs than do school-age youngsters. To understand why, consider the series A>B>C>D>E. Is C big or little? To answer this question you would probably compare C simultaneously to B and D, concluding that it is small relative to one and big relative to the other. But as you know, performing two comparisons at once is usually beyond the capabilities of a preschooler. This is partly the result of centration. To a 4-year-old, then, the premise pairs in this series may seem confusing and inconsistent. Sometimes an object is the big one; other times it is the little one. Coordinating all this information is extremely difficult for a preschooler.

The preschooler knows well that objects come in different sizes and can identify which object in a pair is bigger. But he or she does not have the idea of seriation and therefore has difficulty with problems involving transitive inference. The preschooler finds it hard to keep in mind that the same object can be both small and big, depending on what it is compared to. *(Joseph Schuyler/Stock, Boston.)*

SUMMING UP

In the previous sections we examined four capabilities that Piaget believed were immaturely developed, if not completely absent, during the preschooler period. In each case, however, we found that at least some aspects of the skill in question were present by age 4. It is not yet clear how to explain the 4-year-old's partial successes at tasks once thought to be the province of older children. Currently the claim that these skills may actually emerge much earlier than Piaget thought is at the center of much controversy. The only safe conclusion for now is that the precursors of these skills can be seen by age 4. But at this age the child is still hampered by centration and by a confusion of superficial appearance with reality. These limitations make the cognitive performance of a 4-year-old markedly less advanced than that of a school-age child. If a 4-year-old indeed possesses more than just the precursors of conservation, classification, seriation, and transitive inference, these skills are so fragile as to be of little use in the child's day-to-day quest to understand the world.

PRESCHOOLERS' ATTENTION AND MEMORY ABILITIES

This section will examine preschoolers' abilities to select information, store it in memory, and retrieve it. In contrast to the previous section, which dealt mainly with issues raised by Piaget, the focus here is on issues raised by information-processing approaches.

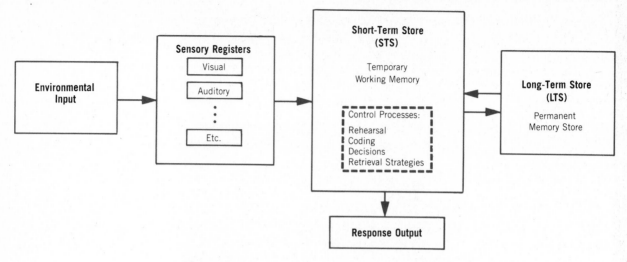

Figure 10.4
Atkinson and Shiffrin's Information Processing Model
In this model of human information processing, information first enters the sensory registers, which have a large capacity. Information picked up here fades in less than one second. Before it fades, however, some is transferred to short-term store, and part of this in turn is transferred to long-term store, or permanent memory.
Source: Adapted from Atkinson and Shiffrin, 1968.

According to many information-processing theorists, data that are available for memory go through the various steps of processing shown in Figure 10.4. Information (environmental input) first enters the *sensory registers*, where immediate experience is very briefly stored (less than one second). Then, whatever information is consciously noted is moved to *short-term memory*, or short-term store, which is of more limited capacity but lasts longer (about 20 seconds). Some of the information in short-term memory is moved to *long-term memory*, or long-term store, which is very long-lasting and has a very large capacity. Most of us have learned various memory strategies, such as going over material a number of times, to increase the likelihood that information will be stored in long-term memory.

From the perspective of the information-processing model just presented, preschoolers' attentional skills refer to the processes that control the transition of information from the sensory register to short-term memory. Memory skills, in contrast, are those processes that control the transition from short-term to long-term memory. All information-processing models focus on attentional and memory skills, that is, on skills for processing information.

Deploying Attention

In a kindergarten class where a teacher was instructing the children about the names of different shapes, one child was paying no attention to the teacher but instead was observing a red-tailed hawk that was hunting in a field just outside the window. After several minutes, the teacher noticed that the child was looking out the window and said, "Jimmy, pay attention." Of course, Jimmy had been paying careful attention for several minutes, but his attention was focused on the hawk, not on the teacher. The tasks of selecting information, maintaining focused attention, and ignoring irrelevant stimuli all pose challenges to preschoolers. As the above example illustrates, they can pay attention to interesting events very well, but research indicates that their attentional system is not yet fully developed.

In a classic study, Elaine Vurpillot (1968) showed children pairs of houses like those illustrated in Figure 10.5 and asked them to determine if the two houses were the same. Half of the houses were identical, while the other half differed in the way the windows looked: One, three, or five of the six pairs of windows were different. The children's eye movements were filmed as they made their judgments; the film recorded where they were looking to gain the information they used in deciding if the houses were the same. Compared with older children, preschoolers looked at fewer windows before deciding (an average of only seven out of the 12 windows). Also, preschoolers continued to scan the windows even after they had looked at a pair that differed and that should have given them sufficient information for a decision. Thus, although the judgments of preschoolers were frequently correct, they made more errors than older children because they did not employ systematic and organized scanning strategies.

Another difference between the scanning strategies of preschoolers and older children was noted by Mary Carol Day (1975). When unfamiliar pictures are presented to 6-year-olds and older children, they typically begin scanning at the top and continue downward. Preschoolers, however, have a tendency to begin their scanning from the focal point of the picture and scan downward. The focus of the picture captures their attention, and they scan from that point onward, again missing important information in the picture.

Although preschoolers appear less advanced than older children, their attention deployment is different from that of toddlers. For example, Daniel Anderson and Stephen Levin (1976) observed 2- to 4-year-old children while they were watching the TV program "Sesame Street." The youngest children spent the least amount of time viewing the screen. This was especially true when toys were placed in the same room. They often wandered around the room, playing with the toys and talking with other people. The older children also played with toys, but they were more likely to divide their attention between the television and the toys.

Preschoolers' Memory

One Friday evening when Mikey was 3, his parents decided to take the family to the beach the next day. Mikey was very excited but did little planning for the trip. If Christine hadn't made a list of what to take along, Mikey would have forgotten most of his favorite toys. Three years later, when Mikey was 6, another trip to the beach was planned. This time Mikey thought about what he wanted to take with him, and he hoped he wouldn't forget anything. When he saw Christine putting together a group of things to take, he gathered his toys and added them to the pile. Three years later, when Mikey was 9, his father and he would often go to the beach on summer days. At this age, Mikey was much more organized in

Different Houses

Identical Houses

4-Year-Olds' Fixations

8-Year-Olds' Fixations

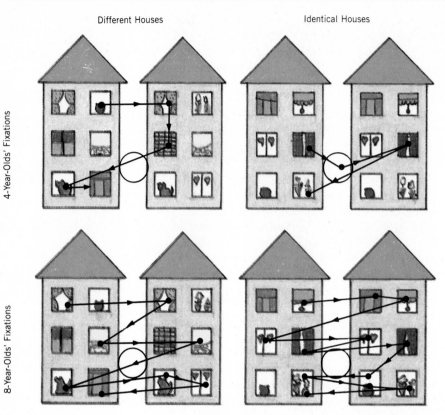

Figure 10.5
Vurpillot's Study of Children's Eye Movements
Children were asked if houses were the same or different. Preschoolers compared only a few of the windows, whereas older children scanned back and forth more systematically.
Source: Vurpillot, 1976.

his efforts to remember. The night before, on his own, he would place his kite and fishing gear at the front door to make sure he would see them on his way out.

This example illustrates many key features of memory development. Often, young preschoolers, such as Mikey at age 3, are oblivious to the memory demands of a situation. Thinking about the need to remember doesn't even occur to them. By the end of the preschool years, however, children are often aware that a particular task requires remembering. But 6-year-olds are not very good at generating a *plan* to facilitate memory. Although he did not generate his own plan, Mikey could recognize that his mother's plan was effective and so he did the same thing. Finally, by age 9, we see intentional memory strategies emerging spontaneously. Mikey piles up the things he wants to take in a place where he knows he'll see them. This description highlights many components of memory that show substantial developmental change during middle childhood. We will focus on these changes in Chapter 12. Here we will address preschoolers' memory development, which includes the beginning use of memory strategies and the ability of youngsters to guide their own learning.

In Chapters 5 and 6 the recognition memory skills of infants were amply demonstrated. By the toddler period, children have some **recall** memory skills; that is, their ability to remember something is not always based on the presence of some obvious cue. For example, they can get a toy they just left in another room, when they need it for play. Preschoolers demonstrate both recognition and recall in all their daily activities, although it frequently appears that they do not remember as well as adults. One measure of recall is the digit span test, in which numbers of increasing length are read to children (or adults) at a rate of one digit per second, and then they are asked to repeat the number. If they succeed, a number that is one digit longer is read. Thus, this test measures the longest number that can be remembered from a single reading. Average performance for preschoolers is four digits; for 6- to 8-year-olds, five digits; for 9- to 12-year-olds, six digits; and for college students, eight digits (Chi, 1978).

One possible explanation for the poor memory performance of preschoolers is that they are less familiar with the number names they are asked to remember. When they do know as much as older children, however, and when the memory task does not require strategies, they sometimes remember as well as older children. For example, in a study in which the subjects were asked to recognize pictures of cartoon characters that were viewed in a cartoon the day before, preschoolers remembered as well as older children and adults (Chi and Ceci, 1987). Although familiarity with the material to be remembered is one explanation of this result, another is that the subjects were not told of the need to remember the characters. In studies where children are instructed to remember presented material, older children almost always perform better than preschoolers (Flavell, 1985), no doubt partly because they know better how to go about remembering.

How can we demonstrate that preschoolers have any intention to remember? One group of researchers asked young preschoolers to remember where a toy dog was hidden (Wellman, Ritter, and Flavell, 1975). They then hid the dog under one of several containers (so it could not be seen) and left the room. The children's behavior was observed through a one-way mirror. Three-year-olds exhibited such behaviors as looking fixedly at the correct container, moving the container away from the others so it was easy to recognize, and resting their hand on the container. All these appear to be effective memory strategies, and children who used them performed better than children who did not.

When parents ask their preschooler the whereabouts of a toy he or she was playing with earlier, the child frequently responds, "I don't

Preschoolers begin to develop the capacity to divide their attention. *(Frank S. Balthis/Jeroboam.)*

Only very simple strategies for remembering are available to preschoolers. This child holds on to his stuffed toy, so as not to forget it on a trip to grandmother's house. *(Danny Lyon/Magnum Photos, Inc.)*

know." It sometimes seems that preschoolers make no attempt to keep track of their toys. However, the results of a study in which a child was asked to help find a lost camera that had recently been used to take the child's picture suggest that preschoolers can make use of past knowledge in guiding their search behavior (Wellman, Sommerville, and Haake, 1979). The child's picture was taken first at location 1, then 2, then 3. Children 3½ years and older were much more likely to begin their search at location 3 than 1 or 2. Thus, in guiding their search they made use of logical constraints on where the object might be, rather than simply looking in places where they had seen it before.

Despite these successes in demonstrating an active approach to memory by preschoolers, there have also been many failures. For example, when 5-year-olds were asked to remember the objects they saw in a set of pictures, they did not do anything different and did not remember any better than if they were just asked to look at the pictures (Appel et al., 1972). It has been suggested that children younger than 5 do not rehearse information (Perlmutter and Myers, 1979). Harriet Waters (Waters and Andreassen, 1983) has proposed that initial memory strategies tend to be limited, context-specific, and inconsistently used, and that with development they become more general and more consistently used. Preschoolers' occasional successes at demonstrating active efforts to memorize or search for information systematically are the exception rather than the rule. They depend on a situation that fosters simple memory-related activities and frequently on guidance from adults.

V. S. Vygotsky, a prominent Russian psychologist, proposed a concept that provides perspective on the memory performance of preschoolers (Vygotsky, 1978). He focused on the gap between a child's current performance and that child's *potential* performance if given guidance by someone more skilled. Vygotsky called this gap the **zone of proximal development,** "proximal" meaning near the point of origin or near the level of understanding that the child currently possesses. Vygotsky emphasized the role of more knowledgeable others in helping children make progress within their zones of proximal development by building on the prerequisite skills the youngsters already have.

The concept of the zone of proximal development applies to the memory performance of preschoolers. Their memory skills are limited, and a gap exists between their usual memory performance and their potential. In many circumstances preschoolers do seem to realize that activity to improve memory could be useful and that forgetting is possible, but usually they do not know what to do. If the situation is structured so the required activity is very simple or so the adults' behavior suggests the appropriate activity, then their memory performance is more mature (Waters and Andreassen, 1983). Preschoolers are just beginning to use memory skills that become more elaborate and more consistently used during middle childhood, as we shall see in Chapter 12.

SOCIAL COGNITION

As memory skills and other aspects of thinking improve during the preschool years, what impact does this have on the child's social relationships with peers and parents? This is one of two basic questions defining the field of social cognition. It has guided the work of theorists such as Marilyn Shatz (1978). The other question—the other side of this same coin—concerns the role of social interaction in supporting cognitive development. This question was emphasized by Piaget. It is now clear that the developmental relation between the two types of skills is a two-way street. The increase in cognitive skills that have already been described in this chapter provides the underlying support for social interaction more complex than that of infants or toddlers. Increasingly complex social interaction, in turn, is a potent source of new information for fostering cognitive growth. This interdependence will become obvious when we look at egocentrism. Social experience is necessary for a preschooler to discover that other people have different perspectives. This discovery—that people's experience of the world differs—then allows the preschooler to interact more successfully.

Egocentrism in Preschoolers

One of the most interesting characteristics of human thought is egocentrism, the failure to differentiate the perspective of others from one's own point of view. Egocentrism is a cognitive limitation that appears at all levels of development (Elkind, 1967, 1978), but it is most easily seen and most often studied during the preschool years. One of the authors of this book once saw a 4-year-old girl put her fingers in her ears and then ask her father, "Can you hear me?" When he responded "no," she then raised her voice and asked, "Can you hear me now?" There are two illustrations of egocentrism in this example. First, the little girl apparently believed that because she put her fingers in her own ears she made it hard for her *father* to hear. She was not differentiating her own perceptual experience from that of her father. Second, when the father answered "no" to the child's first question, she repeated the question, only louder, showing lack of awareness that a "no" meant the father *must* have heard her. Here the little girl failed to take into account her father's cognitive perspective and realize that in this situation he was only teasing her. This second kind of egocentrism is not overcome until middle childhood. The first kind, in contrast, is gradually conquered during the preschool years.

Other examples of egocentrism abound in the early and middle preschool period. One day when 4-year-old Meryl was excited about a new pair of shoes, she asked Karen if she could call her grandmother to tell her about them. "Look, grandma," Meryl said into the receiver, as she held up one foot. "Aren't they beautiful?" Four-year-old Mikey did much the same thing one evening as he looked through pictures of airplanes in a new book. "These planes are neat!" he exclaimed to his father, who was sitting at the other end of the sofa. And without bothering to turn the book so Frank could see it, he asked, "Which do you like best?"

Piaget studied perceptual egocentrism with his mountain-range model, mentioned at the beginning of this chapter. Four-year-olds were unable to pick out a picture that showed the view as seen by someone on the model's opposite side. In a similar study it was not until age 4 to 5 that children became aware that a picture lying on a table and appearing right-side-up to them would look upside-down to someone sitting across the table (Masangkay et al., 1974). Because perceptual egocentrism is so obvious and strikes us as so odd, we tend to notice instances of it when they occur. But other, less obvious forms of egocentrism are equally common in preschoolers. Egocentrism permeates the ways that young children think and deal with their social worlds.

John Flavell has studied egocentrism in children's assessments of the wishes of others. He asked youngsters age 3 to 6 to select gifts for various people—their mother, their father, a brother or a sister if they had one, their teacher, and themselves (Flavell et al., 1968). The gifts to choose from included silk stockings, a necktie, a toy truck, a doll, and an adult book. Three-year-olds showed much egocentrism by often selecting dolls and trucks for their mothers and fathers. They failed to differentiate their own desires from those of adults. If *they* wanted a doll or a truck, everyone else was presumed to want one too. In contrast, the 4-year-olds seemed to be aware that everyone in the world might not want what they want, but they still had trouble taking an adult's perspective and picking out an appropriate gift. Interestingly, they were more egocentric in making a gift choice for their teacher than they were in making choices for their parents, perhaps because they knew more about what parents buy for themselves. It was not until age 5 that 50 percent of the subjects chose appropriate gifts for everyone on the list. And it was not until age 6 that all of the children chose appropriately. This study shows that during the preschool period youngsters come to realize that others may have desires different from their own and begin to take another person's perspective in trying to determine what that person's wishes might be.

Flavell has analyzed the cognitive components needed to overcome egocentrism and to attain these important capabilities (e.g., Flavell, 1985). One is a knowledge that other people have motivations, thoughts, and viewpoints that may not coincide with one's own. Flavell calls this a *knowledge of existence*. In addition, children need to realize that it can be useful to consider the perspective of another person, that doing so can facilitate social interaction and communication. Flavell refers to this cognitive component as an *awareness of need*. Finally, children must

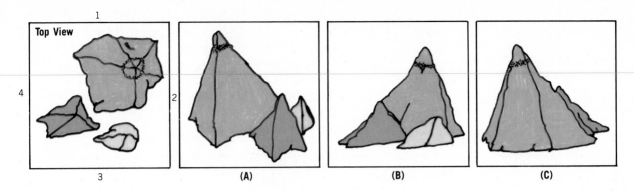

Figure 10.6
Piaget's Three-Mountain Problem
A child is sitting in position 1 (in the overhead view) looking at this three-mountain display. When asked which picture, (A), (B), or (C), demonstrates how the display would look to a child sitting in position 4, most preschoolers would often incorrectly select their own view (C) rather than correctly choosing (A).

become skilled at *social inference*. They must be able to "read" another person's actions and imagine that person's viewpoint to determine what the person desires in a given situation.

The same cognitive components enable children to understand the feelings and emotions of another person. This is why very early signs of sensitivity to other people's feelings should not be considered indications that the child truly comprehends the others' emotions. The fact that infants often cry when they hear another baby crying is best described as simple "contagion," with no conscious awareness on the infant's part. Even the social referencing of early toddlerhood, in which the child takes cues from the care giver's face in a novel situation, involves only a primitive awareness of the care giver's feelings (see Chapter 9). Not until about age 4 do children interpret facial expressions in general categories, such as "feels good" and "feels bad" (Shantz, 1975). More fine-tuned interpretations of other people's feelings take substantially longer to develop. Even adults often seem to have trouble with the inference part of this process. They recognize the existence of other people's emotions and the need to assess them, but they aren't always correct in deducing what those emotions are. In preschoolers the emerging ability to grasp other people's feelings does not imply that the child uses this new skill regularly. At this age a spontaneous tendency to consider the emotions of others appears to be still quite limited (Flavell, 1985). We will return to this topic of understanding someone else's feelings when we discuss the development of empathy in Chapter 11.

Communication and the Decline of Egocentrism

Communicating with others involves more than simply having a vocabulary and knowing how to put words together; it also involves an understanding of how to participate in conversations. How much information do others require to understand your meaning? Which of your ideas must you spell out in detail and which can be inferred by the listener? How do you know when clarifications are needed in the messages you express?

These children appear to be playing together. Actually, each is involved in his or her own activity, and what one says may not take the other's activities into account. More speech occurs, however, because the other is present. And, of course, preschoolers do at times share activities. *(Guy Gillette/Photo Researchers, Inc.)*

These and similar understandings about social communication are something children start to acquire in the preschool period. One way to conceptualize the preschooler's progress in this area is to think of it as part of a general decline in egocentrism. When a child's speech begins to reflect more than just the youngster's own perspective, that child is on the way to being a more effective communicator.

One form of egocentric speech occurs when children talk to themselves. For instance, one day when DeeDee was in the living room she overheard 3-year-old Malcolm in the kitchen playing with a toy truck. Malcolm was providing a running commentary on what he was doing and thinking: "Now I go here. I have a truck. Go fast. Go fast! Crash! Again. Again! That's fun. Get a bigger truck." Such speech directed solely to the self is very common among preschoolers. A more social example of egocentric speech is the **collective monologue.** Imagine 4-year-old Meryl at day care, standing next to a little boy about the same age who is wearing a Styrofoam crash helmet. Meryl is busily beating a wooden spoon inside a plastic bowl. "What would you like for dinner?" Meryl asks. "Get ready to take off," the little boy announces. "I'm gonna light the engine." "I'm making pancakes," Meryl continues. "With lotsa syrup." "Blast off!" the other child says. If you viewed these two from a distance you might think they were playing together, but closer inspection shows they are in entirely different fantasy worlds. Such episodes do have a social component, however, in that preschoolers are more likely to be vocal in this way if there is another child nearby to listen.

Researchers have documented children's egocentric speech. For example, Sam Glucksberg and Robert Krauss (1967) had two children sit at opposite sides of a screen, with identical sets of blocks in front of them. Each block had on it one of the abstract figures shown in Figure 10.7. The children's task was to stack the blocks in exactly the same order without ever seeing what the other one was doing. One of the children was given the job of describing each block to the other youngster so that the latter could pick it out of the pile and add it to his or her stack. Four-

Figure 10.7
Pictures on Blocks in Glucksberg and Krauss's Communication Experiment
Preschoolers had great difficulty communicating orally the nature of these abstract designs.
Source: Glucksberg and Krauss, 1967.

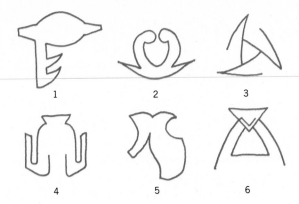

and 5-year-olds performed very poorly on this task because they gave so many egocentric and uninformative descriptions: "A yellow part of a pipe," the speaker might say, or simply "The first one." That children this age can be egocentric in describing unfamiliar things was confirmed in a similar experiment. In this study, the two children on either side of a screen had identical sets of pictures in front of them. The task again was for the listener to figure out which picture the speaker was describing. Here is one sample "solution":

First child points to a picture in front of him and says "It's this one."

Second child points to a picture in front of him and asks "You mean this one?"

First child answers "That's right."

Initially these results were thought to indicate that preschoolers cannot analyze what a listener needs to know to foster effective communication. This conclusion should not be overstated, however. Under different circumstances preschoolers *can* convey their perceptions to others in ways that are understood. For instance, when the abstract figures on the blocks in Glucksberg and Krauss's study were replaced with simple geometric shapes (a yellow circle, a blue square, and so forth), preschoolers were much more successful at describing them to another child. Similarly, when preschoolers had eye contact with their listeners while engaging in two-way conversations, their speech again was significantly less egocentric (Hoy, 1975).

One aspect of communicating effectively with others is adapting your vocabulary and style of speech to suit the age and other characteristics of your audience. Do preschoolers modify their speech in this way to aid communication? Some early experiments by John Flavell and his colleagues suggested they do not (Flavell et al., 1968). In one of these experiments children were told the fable of "The Fox and the Grapes" and then asked either to retell it or to read it to an adult or to a young child. Since the fable contained many words beyond the comprehension of very young children, the researchers were interested in knowing if their subjects would simplify the wording when conveying the story to young listeners. It wasn't until age 11 or 12 (the sixth-grade level) that subjects consistently did this. In another experiment, the same researchers taught children to play a simple board game and then asked them to teach the game either to a blindfolded person or to someone who could see. Again, it wasn't until middle childhood that the subjects took into

Preschoolers do adapt their speech to the level of the partner. For example, they talk in simpler terms and check in more with younger children. This is the beginning of perspective taking. They recognize that communication at times must be adjusted to accommodate the listener. *(Gabe Palmer/ The Stock Market.)*

account the special needs of the blindfolded listener and taught that person appropriately.

Other studies raise cautions about these early findings, however, encouraging us not to conclude that preschoolers never adapt their speech. In one such study, for example, 4-year-olds were observed to speak in shorter sentences with a simpler vocabulary when addressing 2-year-olds than when addressing peers or adults (Shatz and Gelman, 1973). Here they adapted their speech to suit the age of their listeners. In another study preschoolers spontaneously adapted the amount of detail in their explanations to suit the knowledge of their listeners. This study involved exposing 4-year-olds to a staged "accident" in which an adult spilled a cup of liquid. When asked a week later why the empty cup was in the room, the children varied their answers depending on whether they were speaking to the adult who had knocked the cup over or to another person who knew nothing about the previous incident (Menig-Peterson, 1975). Clearly, preschoolers can sometimes take another's perspective into account when deciding what to say (see Shatz, 1983).

If preschoolers have some ability to modify their speech in accordance with a listener's needs, why did they perform so poorly in early experiments like those of Glucksberg and Krauss or Flavell and his colleagues? The answer may lie in the difficulty of the tasks presented. The figures on the blocks in the Glucksberg and Krauss experiment were abstract and hard to describe. Some of the words in "The Fox and the Grapes" fable were a struggle even for second and third graders to understand. It may be that when a task is very difficult it uses all the cognitive capacity of a young child, leaving nothing for the child to use in determining an appropriate form or level of speech. As a result, the youngster lapses into egocentric wording, which doesn't take into account the particular needs of the listener (Shatz, 1978). This explanation should remind you of theories we discussed in Chapter 6 on cognitive development in infancy. Some researchers think that the major constraints imposed on a baby's mastery of new skills have to do with limitations on working memory. When a task exceeds the present capacity of working memory, the infant either fails to perform that task or performs it very poorly.

This notion that performance of tasks consumes cognitive resources suggests something important about studying children's abilities. To determine a child's *maximum* skill at any task, you should limit all other cognitive demands as much as possible. However, if you want to know how children *typically* perform regarding some behavior, you should make sure that they are in an environment with all the demands and distractions usually found in a natural setting. That both these approaches can reveal worthwhile information was demonstrated in a recent pair of studies. In the first, researchers listened in on arguments between pairs of preschoolers in a laboratory setting (Eisenberg and Garvey, 1981). Usually the arguments arose over one child's refusal to agree to the request of the other. In addition to simple insistence and the use of force, the researchers also observed the children offering explanations to one another and suggesting compromises. These latter strategies were the most effective in resolving the conflicts and they were also the most advanced in that they required taking the perspective of the other person.

Do preschoolers use reasoning and compromise to settle arguments in natural settings? Other researchers have found that generally they do not (Genishi and Di Paolo, 1982). Apparently the added complexity and demands of a natural setting usually prevent preschoolers from demonstrating their most advanced communication skills. Thus it should come as little surprise that we portrayed 4-year-old Malcolm as solving a difficult conflict on the playground by resorting to force.

Limited Cognitive Resources and Communication

The ability to handle environmental complexity *and* engage in effective communication increases with age. This fact can be seen in some recent studies of children working together to solve problems (Cooper, 1980; Cooper and Cooper, 1984). In one of these studies two preschoolers were ushered into a quiet room and seated before a balance scale (one with a fulcrum at the center, supporting a pan on either side). Their task was to find pairs of blocks of equal weight. Even in this quiet setting, language served the important function of maintaining the children's focus on the task. If they digressed onto other topics, their performance suffered significantly.

In another study, older children observed in a busy classroom proved better able to tolerate conversational digressions without negative consequences on their work. Overall, these older children were more skilled in using language to attract and maintain another's attention ("Hey Bill. Bill! I need your help!"), as well as to express their own needs and negotiate to have those needs met ("Do you want to go to the library? After you finish your math with Ellen? OK"). These older children also were better at modifying a message to make it clearer or more acceptable to peers ("This math sure is hard for me . . . . I wish someone could help me . . . . Frank, could you help me with number 6?"). Apparently preschoolers, when faced with an unfamiliar task, find it hard to simultaneously engage in normal conversation. They do not maintain focus for long in a distracting classroom environment. The demands of communication seem to draw on resources that are needed to master the new skill.

What is it that older children have acquired that makes communication less cognitively demanding for them? One possibility is found in the concept of **scripts** (Myles-Worsley, Cromer, and Dodd, 1986; Nelson and Gruendel, 1979; Schank and Abelson, 1977). A script is an abstract representation of a sequence of actions needed to accomplish some goal. For example, most older children have a mental script for the task of participating in "show and tell." This script involves walking to the front of the classroom, holding up the object, telling where it came from, and demonstrating what it can do. With such a script firmly in mind it becomes much easier to engage in the appropriate behaviors.

Although most preschoolers lack a "show-and-tell" script, they do have knowledge of other sequences of behavior they experience in their daily lives (e.g., eating in a restaurant, going to a birthday party, or shopping in a supermarket). Here is a conversation between two 4-year-olds which shows that they certainly have acquired the basics of a "talking-on-the-phone" script.

Gay: Hi.
Daniel: Hi.
Gay: How are you?
Daniel: Fine.
Gay: Who am I speaking to?
Daniel: Daniel. This is your daddy. I need to speak to you.
Gay: All right.
Daniel: When I come tonight, we're gonna have . . . peanut butter and jelly sandwich, uh, at dinner time.
Gay: Uhmmm. Where're we going at dinner time?
Daniel: Nowhere. But we're just gonna have dinner at 11 o'clock.
Gay: Well, I made a plan of going out tonight.
Daniel: We're going out.
(Nelson and Gruendel, 1979, p. 76)

Katherine Nelson, one of the researchers who recorded this conversation, believes that scripts like this one can be learned by firsthand experience or by observation of others. Meryl's acquisition of a "going shopping" script, seen in our earlier story, would have been acquired by watching her mother and checkout clerks at the supermarket.

When young children communicate with adults instead of with peers, a knowledge of scripts is probably less essential. This is because in adult-child conversations the adult takes responsibility for seeing that the dialogue progresses smoothly, that intended meanings are understood and confusions eventually clarified (Ellis and Rogoff, 1986). This again is an example of the role of more knowledgeable others within the zone of proximal development. In peer interactions, in contrast, children must monitor and coordinate their own conversations. Here having shared understandings of the scripts for various activities can greatly facilitate communication. The learning of such scripts steadily increases across the childhood years and with it the effectiveness of peer communications. Still, there remain substantial individual differences in children's skill at conveying their ideas and feelings to others, as well as their skill at understanding what others are trying to say. These individual differences, which persist into adulthood, help explain differences in social acceptance or rejection.

AN OVERVIEW OF PRESCHOOL COGNITIVE DEVELOPMENT

The infant knows the world only through perception and direct action. The toddler shows a major advance in being able to represent actions and events mentally. The toddler can imagine an action taking place and imagine outcomes without actually carrying out the action. But the toddler's imagination is still tied to past direct experience and has very limited skills for organizing information.

Preschoolers quickly learn the format of a birthday party. You arrive, you play games, you have cake and ice cream. Such an abstraction is called a "script." Scripts serve to reduce the cognitive requirements of a situation. Just as knowing the plot of a story makes it easier to follow, having a general understanding of events frees the child's cognition for other tasks. *(Rameshwar Das/Monkmeyer Press.)*

The preschooler makes large strides beyond the toddler toward mature thought. First, preschoolers are actively seeking explanations for things (thus the endless "why" questions). They understand that there are problems to be solved. Moreover, preschoolers evolve a number of advanced skills for organizing information. And they are beginning to understand that their thought processes are something that can be managed. Still, their repertoire of skills remains quite limited. Beyond this limited set of skills, they often don't recognize the need for cognitive strategies such as aids for remembering, and they don't select well from the strategies they do have available. They don't seem to have the basic understanding that some ways of organizing information are better than others, especially for attacking particular problems. They aren't skilled at evaluating effective and less effective approaches. Finally, they are still somewhat bound by the appearance of things, and they are prone to errors when appearance and reality are in conflict. All of these limitations will be substantially overcome in middle childhood.

Chapter Review

1. The preschool years provide excellent examples of how children are active participants in their own development. Part of this participation involves actively constructing understandings of things in the environment. Preschoolers search for general patterns in what they see and hear, and then they use these patterns as a basis for explaining and organizing their world. The preschooler's thought is still quite immature, however, because of three cognitive limitations. The first is a tendency to equate superficial appearance with reality, called the **appearance-reality problem.** The second is a tendency to focus on only one piece of information at a time, referred to as **centration.** The third is poor skills for managing their own attention and directing their memory activities.

2. Preschoolers from different cultures exhibit similar kinds of errors or immaturities in the causal explanations of physical events, such as the movement of clouds. Preschoolers frequently focus on surface perceptual features or make reference to a powerful being (God or Daddy) as the cause of events. However, if the event is something with which they are familiar, such as the movement of a bicycle, they sometimes provide more mature explanations. Even when they make errors, preschoolers are remarkable for their active effort to interpret and construct explanations for the world in which they live.

3. Adults have many implicit understandings about how objects and events are related. These implicit understandings provide important conceptual tools for dealing with the world. Among these tools are **rules of conservation,** which state that certain characteristics remain unchanged despite various transformations carried out on them. Other conceptual tools are **classification** (the ability to group things according to shared features), **seriation** (the ability to arrange things in logical progressions), and **transitive inference** (the ability to infer the relationship between two objects by knowing their respective relationships to a third). Although preschoolers fail to demonstrate these abilities in standard laboratory tests, evidence suggests that the precursors of these skills may be present by 4 years of age.

4. Preschoolers have difficulty selectively paying attention to stimuli in their environment. They scan less systematically and are more distracted by irrelevant information. Improvement in maintaining focused attention is seen during the preschool years, and it seems to depend more on the intrinsic interest of that which is being attended to. Older preschoolers

are just beginning to exhibit more active control over their own attention.

5. Preschoolers do not remember information as well as older children or adults do. One explanation for their poorer memory is that they are frequently less familiar with the information to be remembered, and hence find it more difficult. Another is that they usually do not have any strategies to improve their memory. However, under optimal circumstances, preschoolers show an intent to remember and perform activities that increase the likelihood that they will remember. Thus, if adults structure the memory situation properly, preschoolers' performance appears much more mature. This improved memory performance is an example of Vygotsky's concept of the **zone of proximal development,** that area of performance just barely within the child's potential, which can be realized with proper support.

6. An interesting characteristic of human thought is **egocentrism,** the failure to differentiate the perspective of others from one's own point of view. Egocentrism appears at all developmental levels, but it is particularly pervasive and apparent during the preschool years. Preschoolers show egocentrism when they try to assess other people's perceptions, feelings, and wishes. Flavell has identified three cognitive factors needed to overcome egocentric thought. First, the child must develop a simple knowledge that other people have motivations and viewpoints different from his or her own. Second, the child must realize that it can often be very useful for effective communication to consider the other person's perspective. Finally, the child must gradually gain skill at social inference, the ability to interpret other people's thoughts and feelings.

7. During the preschool years, children begin to learn about how speech can be used effectively in social communication. One way to conceptualize the preschooler's progress in this area is to think of it as part of a general decline in egocentrism. During the preschool years, children begin to show some ability to adjust their speech in accordance with a listener's needs. Such adjustments require cognitive effort, however, so when a task is very difficult, young children often lapse into egocentric wordings. It is as if the difficulty of the task uses all their cognitive capacity, leaving nothing for the children to use in determining an appropriate form or level of speech.

8. Why are older children better able to combine the performance of difficult tasks with effective communication? Part of the answer may lie in the greater number of cognitive scripts they possess. A **script** is an abstract representation of the sequence of actions involved in accomplishing some goal. With a script in mind it becomes less cognitively demanding to go through the motions of a task, thus leaving some cognitive capacity for monitoring the effectiveness of one's speech.

11

Social Development in Early Childhood

Five-year-old Mikey, his first day at kindergarten, stands in line with 20 other children. Beside him are two boys from his neighborhood—Justin and Bryan. Although the three friends are eager to be out on the playground, they wait for the teacher to swing open the large exit door. Then, without any pushing, they walk quietly, though quickly, out with the class. Once in the warm September sunshine, however, their self-restraint breaks down. Shouting with glee, they race toward the play equipment. "Hey! It's a boat!" Mikey calls out, pointing to a large climbing apparatus in the center of a sand-filled area. The structure, made of wood, ropes, and old car tires, looks nothing like a boat, but its placement in the middle of the sandlot inspires the boys' imaginations. "C'mon! Let's climb on!" Mikey squeals, and the other two scramble up behind him. There they play joyously for a time, taking turns being captain at the "wheel." Just when their excitement has begun to subside, Justin yells in mock alarm: "Oh no! We're sinkin'! Swim for it!" With that, he jumps into the sand and begins spinning his arms and

The preschooler's curiosity is boundless. *(Index Stock International.)*

kicking his legs. Laughing and shouting, the others jump off too, and the trio makes its way to "shore."

This episode illustrates much about the social achievements of early childhood. First, Mikey and his friends demonstrate that youngsters between the ages of 2½ and 5 experience a dramatically *expanding world*. Day care, nursery school, and kindergarten take the preschool child increasingly away from home and parents. In these new settings the youngster is propelled by a natural curiosity to explore. No one has to tell Mikey and his friends to play in the sandlot. The motivation and ideas for their activities come from themselves. Notice too how the boys' world is enlarged by their rich interactions with one another. Early childhood is the age when true peer relationships emerge, relationships that have far-reaching influences.

Second, the example of Mikey and his friends illustrates that early childhood is a time of notable developments in *self-control and self-management*. It is hard to imagine a large group of toddlers forming a line and waiting patiently for a teacher to usher them outdoors. Yet just a few years later children are routinely expected to tolerate minor delays and frustrations. They are also expected to control aggressive impulses, such as pushing, shoving, and hitting. These new expectations have significant effects on youngsters' developing self-concepts. Whether children think of themselves as capable or incapable, mean or kind to others stems in part from how they meet adults' demands for self-management.

Finally, our opening example shows that during early childhood youngsters begin to explore various adult roles. Mikey and his friends take turns being captain of a ship, a role they have heard about in stories and seen on television. This exploration of roles takes place during play, especially social fantasy play such as that involving the three boys. Typically preschoolers try out roles that are important to them: mother, father, teacher, grocery store clerk, and so forth. When children not only mimic adults but also strive to be like them in feelings and values, developmentalists say the youngsters are *identifying* with the grownups.

In the first major section of this chapter we look in more detail at the key social developmental changes of early childhood. In the second major section we turn to the topic of the parents' role in helping promote favorable development during the preschool period. From here we look at the causes of some individual differences. What makes one preschooler friendly and self-reliant while another is reticent and emotionally dependent on adults? Researchers look for answers in the interaction of various influences. Finally, we examine the coherence of behavior in preschool children. Here you will discover that by early childhood each youngster is an individual with characteristic ways of responding to different situations; in short, he or she has become a more complete *person*.

Fantasy play is fun. It also provides opportunities to practice social skills and to explore roles. (*B. Griffith/ The Picture Cube.*)

DEVELOPMENTAL CHANGES IN EARLY CHILDHOOD

The Child's Expanding World

One of the major enterprises of early childhood is expansion of the child's world beyond the home and family. With this widening of horizons come new opportunities to explore and master the environment, to be more self-reliant, and to form relationships with peers.

EXPLORING THE ENVIRONMENT

Developmentalists are keenly interested in children's curiosity and exploration. The quest to discover for its own sake is a basic human motivation. Humans and other primates are drawn to novelty and will engage in difficult tasks merely to have a new experience (Berlyne, 1966; Harlow, 1953; White, 1959). This innate motivation has been advantageous for the survival of our species. Although individual acts of exploration and discovery may sometimes seem of little value, together they provide a broad range of experience from which people can later draw when problems arise (Breger, 1974).

A given child's level of curiosity and exploration is an important indicator of overall adjustment. Normal preschoolers are always into things. They spend much time exploring and discovering (Banta, 1970; Coie, 1974; Henderson and Moore, 1980; Minuchin, 1971; Nezworski, 1983). In contrast, lack of interest in the world and limited enthusiasm for mastery are generally considered signs of maladjustment. Curiosity and exploration have been found to be related to a number of positive characteristics in preschoolers. In one study, boys high in curiosity showed more self-reliance and greater self-regard (Maw and Maw, 1970). In another study, highly curious children were observed to be more socially competent (Minuchin, 1971). High or low curiosity in a child tends to be fairly consistent over time, across situations, and regardless of the measures used (Arend, Gove, and Sroufe, 1979; Nezworski, 1983). Therefore, we are not surprised to see a child like Mikey show his high level of curiosity both at home and on the playground.

MOVING TOWARD GREATER SELF-RELIANCE

Accompanying the preschooler's entry into a broader world is the development of greater self-reliance. This important development is supported by a number of capacities that 3- and 4-year-olds possess. First, children this age have very impressive motor skills; they can run, jump, climb, and manipulate all kinds of objects. Their skills allow them to do many things for themselves. Preschoolers also have language and other cognitive abilities that enable them to think and plan in ways they could not before. These abilities promote the solving of problems that would have baffled the child just a year or two ago. Improved problem-solving skills are further aided by a growing ability to tolerate delays and frustrations. Compared with toddlers, preschoolers are much better able to stick to a task despite obstacles and setbacks. Finally, an emerging capacity for imagination and fantasy play allows preschoolers to maintain a sense of power in a world generally controlled by adults. This sense of power is an important psychological foundation for strivings toward autonomy.

Some children, of course, have trouble moving toward this greater independence. For them, infantile dependency is hard to leave behind. We see this problem in Meryl as a 3-year-old when she whines and tries to cling to Karen. Why is Meryl at this age so much less autonomous than Mikey or Malcolm? For several decades researchers have been searching for the origins of such overdependency (e.g., Beller, 1955; Hartup, 1966; Sears, Maccoby, and Levin, 1957).

In studying overdependency we must first define this term carefully. When psychologists talk about overdependent preschoolers, they are talking about children who show excessive **emotional dependency:** The youngsters need continual reassurance and attention from adults in order to function. Like Meryl, emotionally dependent preschoolers frequently demand physical contact from the care giver, such as being picked up or held in the grownup's lap. Note that such contact and reassurance is *not* needed just when the child is upset; instead, the child requires attention virtually all the time. Emotional dependency must be distinguished from **instrumental dependency,** a need for adults to help the child solve complex problems or perform other difficult tasks (Sears, Maccoby, and Levin, 1957). When Malcolm is trying to find a certain toy and has run out of places to look, he has to seek assistance from a member of his family. Although he is showing instrumental dependency in this situation, he does not have a dependency problem. Unlike Meryl's actions, Malcolm's are appropriate to his stage of development.

Emotional overdependency in preschoolers seems to have its origins in the quality of the early relationship between child and parent. Researchers have found that a child who experiences secure attachment in infancy is likely to develop into a relatively self-reliant preschooler (Sroufe, Fox, and Pancake, 1983). This finding makes sense when you recall what you already know about the nature of a secure attachment. A secure attachment means that the infant has developed an expectation that adults will be available when needed, that they will provide appropriate comfort and care. Accompanying this expectation is the development of a more general belief in the ability to affect the environment. By gaining confidence that adults will respond to their signals, children acquire a sense of being able to *make things happen.* John Bowlby (1973)

Some children need a great deal of support from and contact with their preschool teachers. *(Lawrence Migdale/ Photo Researchers, Inc.)*

refers to such expectations about the world as the child's **inner working model.** These models are carried forward into the preschool period; from confidence in the care giver grows confidence in the self.

As you might expect, degree of independence is related to a child's level of curiosity. In one study, researchers observed preschoolers playing with a "curiosity box" (Henderson and Moore, 1980). Children judged from classroom behavior to be high in curiosity explored the novel box extensively whether their mothers were present or not. In contrast, children judged to be low in curiosity explored the box extensively only when their mothers were nearby. Apparently, the low-curiosity children had the same basic motivation to discover, a motivation that is probably innate. However, this tendency was hampered by wariness if the mother wasn't there to provide emotional support. Highly curious preschoolers seem to have progressed beyond this need for constant reassurance. Their past experience with supportive care givers may have been the reason. Children with secure histories do tend to be high in curiosity as well as low in emotional dependency (Sroufe, 1983).

INTERACTING WITH PEERS

The expanding world of the preschooler encompasses more than just new places and physical objects to explore. The expanding world also encompasses new people, especially peers. Peers are of great interest even to toddlers, as you learned in Chapter 9. Often by age 2, and certainly by age 3, children show the rudiments of social turn-taking (Garvey, 1977; Mueller and Lucas, 1975). They speak or do something to their partner, wait for a response, and then repeat the cycle. However, most of this early turn-taking is centered around objects, and only sometimes do the toddlers really respond to each other's specific intentions (Bronson, 1981; Mueller and Vandell, 1979). Not until the preschool period, with children's growing mastery of language, do their interactions become highly coordinated mutual exchanges.

To see the difference between peer interactions among toddlers and among preschoolers, consider two examples. The first is a "conversation" between two boys, 13 and 15 months of age (Mueller and Lucas, 1975). Bernie, the younger, initiates the exchange by turning and looking at Larry, who has been watching him while mouthing a toy. Bernie then "speaks" to Larry.

> *Bernie:*　Da. . .Da.
> *Larry:*　(Laughs very slightly as he continues to look.)
> *Bernie:*　Da.
> *Larry:*　(Laughs more heartily this time.)
> The same sequence of Bernie saying "da" and Larry responding with laughter is repeated five more times. Then Larry looks away and offers an adult a toy. Bernie pursues him:
> *Bernie:*　(Waving both hands and looking directly at Larry.) Da!
> *Larry:*　(Looks back at Bernie and laughs again.)
> The sequence of "da" followed by laughter is repeated nine more times. Finally, Bernie turns away abruptly and toddles off. Larry laughs once more in a forced manner and then silently watches Bernie depart. (p. 241)

Children learn a great deal from each other. *(Tom Dunham.)*

Now consider a second conversation, this one between a boy and a girl, both 5 years of age (Garvey, 1977). The boy is testing the girl's competence, and the girl is rising to the challenge.

Boy: Can you carry this? (Shows girl a toy fish.)
Girl: Yeah, if I weighed 50 pounds.
Boy: You can't even carry it. Can you carry it by the string?
Girl: Yeah. Yes I can. (Lifts fish overhead by string.)
Boy: Can you carry it by the nose?
Girl: Where's the nose?
Boy: That yellow one.
Girl: This? (Carries it by the nose.)
Boy: Can you carry it by its tail?
Girl: Yeah. (Carries it by tail.).
Boy: Can you carry it like this? (Shows how to carry it by fin.)
Girl: (Carries it by fin.) I weigh 50 pounds about, right?
Boy: Right. (p. 59)

As socially competent as Bernie and Larry are for toddlers (perhaps because they are longtime acquaintances), there is no comparison between their interaction and that of the 5-year-olds. The 5-year-olds can share a fantasy, make elaborate rules for a game, respond to each other's questions, demonstrate novel procedures, and in general coordinate their behaviors in ways far beyond the abilities of any pair of 1-year-olds.

Assessing Social Competence. The child who engages with peers, is highly regarded by them, and is able to sustain the give-and-take of peer interaction is said to be **socially competent.** But as simple as it is to describe such a youngster in general terms, social competence is not so simple to measure (Waters and Sroufe, 1983). You cannot measure it merely by counting a child's contacts with peers, for if contacts are mostly aggressive or consistently asymmetrical (with the child always in the role of follower) even a large number of contacts does not imply social competence. The absence of peer rejection is likewise a poor measure of social competence, for an unrejected child may simply be of little interest to peers. How, then, do researchers go about identifying the most socially competent children in a group?

One way is through teachers' judgments. Teachers have the opportunity to observe children in a variety of contexts so they are not apt to be influenced by a single experience. To provide assessments teachers can either rate individual children (on a scale of, say, 1 to 7) or they can rank order all the class members. Such assessments have proved to be quite useful, agreeing well with other measures of social competence (LaFrenier and Sroufe, 1985; Vaughn and Waters, 1980).

But in some cases teachers who are assessing an individual child are responding to the child's social competence with *them*, not with peers. Consequently, it is wise to supplement teachers' judgments with the judgments of children themselves, a procedure usually referred to as **sociometrics.** Preschool children may be asked whom they "especially like" (acceptance) and whom they "do not especially like" (rejection). By subtracting how often a given child is rejected from how often that child is accepted, the researchers can produce an index of social status in the group (e.g., Asher et al., 1979).

Insights into social competence can also be obtained by carefully observing children. Different investigators have used a variety of observational approaches. Some have stressed the frequency of certain social behaviors, such as solitary, parallel, and cooperative play (Parten and Newhall, 1943). Others have emphasized the quality of the emotions expressed in interactions with peers (Leiter, 1977). Still others have focused on physical dominance within groups, such as the ability to win struggles over objects or to have others follow your lead (Strayer and Strayer, 1978). Another focus has been on the amount of attention each child receives from other children, high attention getters presumably being more socially competent (Abramovitch and Grusec, 1978; Vaughn and Waters, 1980).

All the various ways of identifying socially competent youngsters tend to single out the same children within a group (LaFrenier and Sroufe, 1985; Vaughn and Waters, 1980). In addition to being seen as socially skilled by their teachers, these children are also liked and admired by their peers. In their everyday actions, they are friendly and emotionally positive and tend to get group attention and win struggles over objects without being hostile (LaFrenier and Sroufe, 1985; Leiter, 1977; Sroufe et al., 1984; Vaughn and Waters, 1980).

Our chapter-opening example illustrates the socially competent preschooler, especially the positive emotions such a child expresses toward peers. Mikey conveyed his excitement about seeing the play apparatus as a boat through his tone of voice, his body posture, and his facial

Being a peer leader involves more than being the biggest and strongest. Leaders know things that are fun to do, and they have a contagious enthusiasm. *(Kathy Sloane/ Black Star.)*

expression. If he had suggested the boat idea in a flat, matter of fact way, the other two boys might have ignored it. But Mikey's enthusiastic "Hey! It's a boat!" brought the other two running. His enthusiasm captured their interest and was contagious. This ability to have fun and to share that fun with others is one reason why such a child is popular with peers.

The Importance of Relations with Peers and Siblings. Competence with peers is important not just for the fun it brings. The child who is well liked by peers and often engaged with them can learn much from the peer group. As we mentioned in Chapter 3, the peer group is a major setting for learning about the concepts of fairness, reciprocity, and co-operation. It is also a critical setting for learning to manage interpersonal aggression (Hartup, 1983), as our earlier story of Malcolm illustrated. In peer groups, too, children learn a great deal about cultural norms and values, such as the roles associated with being male or female. Finally, experiences within the peer group—whether positive or negative—can greatly affect a youngster's self-concept and future dealings with others.

Increasing peer interactions can also sometimes help children overcome developmental problems. This idea was first suggested in a study by Stephen Suomi and Harry Harlow (1972). They took young monkeys that had previously been raised in social isolation and placed them with more normally raised young peers. In time, the socially deprived monkeys were functioning much better, and such effects persisted (Novak, 1979). Apparently, contact with young peers partially reversed the negative effects of being reared without a parent. We do not know if this would also be true of humans. However, the famous case of orphans raised together in concentration camps, which we mentioned in Chapter 7, suggests some parallels (Freud and Dann, 1951). The bonds among these children were clearly very important to their functioning. A more recent study of socially withdrawn preschoolers likewise suggests the potential importance of peers in fostering healthier adjustment (Furman, Rahe, and Hartup, 1979). When these withdrawn youngsters interacted one on one with somewhat younger children in a series of special play sessions, they became more outgoing in their regular classrooms. Here, having the chance to interact successfully with a peer seemed to enhance both social skills and confidence concerning peer relations. Interacting with a more competent, but tolerant, peer (or even an older sibling) also would be expected to enhance social competence.

Sibling relationships are important not just for what the younger child can draw from and learn from the older but also for what the older child learns in being in the more responsible leadership role. Moreover, sibling relationships are special because of their enduring nature and their special emotional properties (Dunn and Kendrick, 1982). We have argued that parents provide a context and framework within which the child develops. But older siblings do so as well, at times uniquely so. Judy Dunn (1985) reports that young preschoolers can engage in joint fantasy play with a nurturant older sibling in a way they cannot do with their mothers. As will be discussed further in Chapter 12, such provision of contexts that support development, whether by parents or siblings, is referred to as "scaffolding" (Fischer and Bullock, 1984). We will present a more extensive discussion of sibling relationships in Chapter 13.

Self-Control and Self-Management

Not only does the child's social world expand during the preschool years, but he or she also assumes a more active role in self-control and self-management. Acquiring the ability to monitor and direct one's own behavior is another major development of the preschool period (Flavell, 1977; Kopp, 1982).

Self-control and self-management are relatively absent during early toddlerhood. Twelve-month-old Malcolm may suddenly decide that it is time to scale the staircase and go right ahead despite previous prohibitions by adults. Malcolm does not reflect on the hazards of this action or on the "naughtiness" of disobeying a rule. His behavior shows no efforts at self-restraint. Often, too, it lacks logical organization. He does not plan the best way to accomplish objectives or think about all the consequences of his acts. Instead, Malcolm's activities at 12 months of age are guided largely by the satisfaction of immediate desires and needs. By age 24 months, however, we see clear advancement in Malcolm's ability to exert self-control. After Momma Jo forbids him to reach for a leaf in the pool, 2-year-old Malcolm starts to stretch for it again but then stops himself, a common reaction in 2-year-olds (Maccoby, 1980). This is the beginning of self-management of behavior.

By the end of the preschool period children are much more able to exercise self-control and reflect on what they are doing. Psychologist

The preschooler can be expected to exercise care and self-control. *(Erika Stone/ Peter Arnold, Inc.)*

Eleanor Maccoby (1980) has listed some of the specific advances that illustrate this developmental change:

1. Older preschoolers are able to weigh future consequences heavily when deciding how to act.
2. Children this age are able to delay many pleasurable activities until they are more appropriate or until they will have better outcomes.
3. If blocked by some obstacle when pursuing a goal, older preschoolers are able to stop and think of possible ways around it.
4. Children this age are better able to control emotions when goal-directed activity is blocked, thus greatly decreasing the likelihood of tantrums.
5. Older preschoolers are able to do more than one thing at a time, as long as those things are not incompatible or highly complex.
6. Children this age are better able to concentrate—that is, to block out irrelevant thoughts, sights, and sounds and to focus instead on what is needed to reach a desired objective.

These capacities, of course, are not fully developed by the end of the preschool period; further advances will be made as the children grow older. Nevertheless, the preschool years are a time of great progress in exercising management and control over the self.

Reviewing Maccoby's list of specific advances in self-control and self-management, you can see that these advances depend on a number of general abilities. One is the ability to inhibit physical actions, another the ability to delay gratification (wait for rewards), a third the ability to tolerate frustration, and a fourth the ability to adjust behavior to suit situational demands. Let's examine the preschooler's progress in acquiring each of these.

INHIBITING ACTIONS

Imagine that Frank Gordon is organizing a race between 3-year-old Mikey and his neighborhood playmates Justin and Bryan. The children are to run across the yard, touch the trunk of the big oak tree, and then run back to the starting line. Frank gives the signals "Ready . . . get set . . ." But before he can say, "go," Mikey bolts off toward the oak tree, and the other two quickly follow. It takes Frank five recalls before he can get all three boys to wait until they hear the word "go." Are they just not listening to his instructions? Or are they really having trouble following this seemingly simple request?

A developmental psychologist could tell the greatly exasperated Frank that the second explanation is correct. Research shows that the ability to inhibit a physical action until given a signal to proceed is something that emerges gradually during the preschool years (Fuson, 1979). The Soviet psychologist A. R. Luria (1961) studied this ability in children ages 2 through 4. When a green light came on, the youngsters were to press a rubber bulb held in one hand, and when a red light came on, they were not to press. The 2-year-olds made many mistakes, pressing away for red lights as well as for greens. Not until age 4 could most children reliably inhibit a response to the "wrong" color. Later studies have shown that it is not just that 4-year-olds understand the instructions better (Miller,

Shelton, and Flavell, 1970). The 2-year-olds realize they are not to press on red, but somehow they just can't stop themselves.

During the preschool period the ability to refrain upon request from engaging in some pleasurable activity also improves dramatically. It is very hard to tell a toddler to "wait until after supper" before playing with a brand new toy. Insistence is likely to prompt a tantrum. A few years later, however, much more self-control can be expected of the child. This developmental advance has been confirmed through research. In one study experimenters asked children 18 to 30 months of age to temporarily inhibit some very enjoyable action (Kopp, Krakow, and Vaughn, 1983). For instance, they were shown an attractive toy telephone but were told "not to touch it until I come back," and they were presented with a brightly wrapped gift but were instructed "not to open it until I finish my work." Given such clear prohibitions and the presence of the youngsters' mothers, even the 18-month-olds were able to control themselves for a short while. But the 25-month-olds were a great deal better at inhibiting their behavior, and the 30-month-olds were better still. Although not studied in this experiment, the performance of 3- and 4-year-olds would be even further advanced on such tasks (Arend, 1983). Children by this age should be able not only to withhold a response longer but to do so with fewer external reminders, such as a mother's watchful eye.

Preschoolers begin to develop patience and self-control in a variety of areas. A year ago this child would have been much less skillful with this toy, which requires complex physical coordination. *(Larry Voigt/ Photo Researchers, Inc.)*

As the capacity for self-control emerges, children start to show consistency regarding it. For instance, by age 2½ a positive relationship can be shown between a child's ability to resist touching one attractive object and his or her ability to resist touching other attractive things. In the experiment described above, those 2½-year-olds who could keep themselves from tearing into the present were also likely to refrain from touching the toy phone. Conversely, those who had trouble ignoring the telephone were also likely to have trouble resisting the pretty gift. In short, by 2½ a child's capacity for self-control tends to be fairly consistent from one situation to another. Thus, individual differences in level of self-control will begin to be apparent by the age of about 3 (Kopp, Krakow, and Vaughn, 1983). These individual differences have been found to be quite stable even into middle childhood and adolescence (Block, 1987; Block and Block, 1980). The relatively impulsive 4-year-old is likely to be relatively impulsive at age 7 or 8 and even at age 14 or 18.

DELAYING GRATIFICATION

Closely related to the ability to inhibit behavior is the ability to forgo something attractive at present in order to receive something better at a later date. This ability is called **delay of gratification.** You have probably exhibited it many times yourself. Whenever you stop yourself from buying something you want at the moment in order to save for a more expensive and desirable future purchase, you are delaying gratification. Delay of gratification is widely viewed as an important aspect of self-control.

Preschoolers can delay gratification much better than toddlers, but they are dependent on assistance from adults. When on their own, they still have great difficulty. In a typical experiment children are given the choice between a modest gift now (such as a small candy bar) or a much

Preschoolers can maintain organized behavior in the face of hard problems. One reason is that they have the patience to wait for a reward. *(Miro Vintoniv/The Picture Cube.)*

better gift later (such as a large candy bar). The youngsters are not prohibited from taking the immediate pleasure, but they *are* rewarded for being able to wait. Do preschoolers left by themselves exert this form of self-control? Except under special circumstances, most of them do not (Mischel and Underwood, 1974). Even children as old as 5 tend to take what is offered here and now. We will discuss the development of this interesting capacity further in our unit on middle childhood.

TOLERATING FRUSTRATION

Another important aspect of self-control is the ability to tolerate frustration, that is, to avoid becoming so upset in a frustrating situation that emotions get out of control and behavior becomes disorganized. Research shows that this ability begins to appear by about age 2. In one experiment toddlers were allowed to play with an attractive toy for several minutes, after which the mother put the toy into a big Plexiglas box with a latch too difficult for the child to open (Van Lieshout, 1975). When placed in this situation at age 18 months, many of the children had tantrums. They kicked and pounded on the box while crying loudly in anger. At age 24 months, in contrast, notably fewer of the same children had tantrums directed toward the box, and the girls demonstrated a sizable reduction in angry outbursts toward the mother. Other researchers have shown that the ability to tolerate frustration improves even further over the next year and a half. For example, in an experiment in which 3½-year-olds were kept from playing with desirable toys, only a small proportion called out for the mother or tried to leave the room to find her, and virtually none of the children became seriously distressed (Arend, 1983).

Although tolerance for frustration improves during early childhood, researchers do not know what allows this advance. Probably, youngsters are acquiring the ability to suppress their feelings to some extent, so that outwardly they do not seem so upset (Maccoby, 1980). At the same time, they are learning strategies that help them limit the build-up of tension that tends to accompany a frustrating situation. For instance, in the experiment in which the toy was locked inside the Plexiglas box, the children were more inclined to make positive overtures toward the mother at 24 months of age than they were at 18 months. During the 6-month interval they apparently became more aware that the mother could be used as a problem-solving tool. Turning to her was a way to deescalate their mounting tension (Van Lieshout, 1975). During late toddlerhood and the early preschool period, children seem to learn other strategies to cope with "unsolvable" problems when the mother is not around. One such strategy is simply turning away and attending to other things; another is redefining the situation so the problem no longer exists. As an example from another situation, one 3½-year-old drew a picture of a person, but the triangular arms turned out to look more like wings. He studied his creation for a moment and then proclaimed with joy: "It's a bee!" A bee would do, and he could proceed happily.

ADJUSTING SELF-CONTROL TO THE SITUATION

The abilities to inhibit behavior, delay gratification, and tolerate frustration are all important aspects of self-control that develop during the preschool years. But such control would not be very adaptive if children couldn't adjust its level to suit particular situations. Some situations demand much self-discipline, while others allow children to be as impulsive as they want. The ability to modify self-restraint as circumstances require has been referred to as **ego resiliency** because the ego, or self, is showing the capacity to be flexible in its control over behavior. Mikey is showing ego resiliency in the scene at the start of this chapter. He is able to line up quietly when the teacher requests, but he also runs, shouts, and plays gleefully during outdoor recess. Like all ego-resilient children, Mikey can be spontaneous and expressive in some settings, reserved and self-disciplined in others. The behaviors he shows at any given time depend on the particular situation.

Psychologists Jeanne and Jack Block at the University of California have devised ways to assess a child's level of ego resiliency. They have found individual differences in ego resiliency beginning at age 3½ (Block and Block, 1980). These individual differences tend to remain fairly stable throughout childhood. Other researchers have found that ego resiliency during early childhood is related to both secure attachment during infancy and effective problem solving during toddlerhood (Arend, Gove, and Sroufe, 1979; Sroufe, 1983).

Aggression and Prosocial Behavior

Aggression and prosocial behavior (deliberately directing positive feeling and actions toward other people) are closely related to self-management. When Malcolm hits April Kaid in order to get possession of the bike, he is letting go of self-restraint and acting on impulse. Aggression in general involves relinquishing self-control and spontaneously striking out. Like controlling aggression, prosocial behavior involves self-management, but in a different way. In order to help someone else you must often make a conscious effort to put aside your own desires and enter into the other person's needs and point of view. This requires a substantial amount of

The ability to redefine situations allows the preschooler to take pride in his work. *(Doug Wilson/Black Star.)*

self-regulation. Thus, as the capacity for self-management unfolds in children, we would expect to see changes in both aggression and prosocial behavior, and this is precisely what happens.

DEVELOPMENTAL CHANGES IN AGGRESSION

When 12-month-old Mikey roughly pushes away his mother's hand to get at his favorite toy, it is not technically correct to describe this as aggression. Although his behavior is assertive and purposeful, he does not intend to cause physical or psychological harm. Intent is central to true aggression. Only when Mikey is cognitively advanced enough to appreciate the consequences of his actions can he engage in genuine aggression (Maccoby, 1980). This ability develops some time during toddlerhood, when representational thought emerges. During toddlerhood we see more angry outbursts in response to constraints that parents impose, as well as more negative behavior directed toward peers (Fawl, 1963; Goodenough, 1931). Most of this negative peer interaction is object-centered, however, with each child pulling on a plaything in order to possess it. Such behavior lacks the negative *personal* intent needed to qualify as true aggression (Bronson, 1981). Not until the preschool period, when the child better understands both the self as an agent and the concept of fairness, does truly aggressive behavior become common (Hartup, 1974; Maccoby, 1980; Patterson, Littman, and Bricker, 1967).

During the late preschool and early elementary school years aggressive behavior changes. Children's overall level of aggression declines because of a drop in aggression aimed at possessing objects (Hartup, 1974). This so-called **instrumental aggression** is what 5-year-old Malcolm engages in when he tries to wrest the tricycle from April's grip. In another year or so Malcolm will be much less likely to become involved in such a squabble. The reason is that, by the end of the preschool period, children have learned alternative ways to settle disputes over objects. But though instrumental aggression drops sharply in middle childhood, **hostile aggression** (aggression aimed purely at hurting someone else) does not. Most acts of hostile aggression during middle childhood are concerned

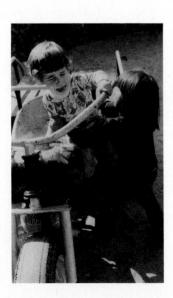

Preschoolers have the capacity for both aggression and cooperation. *(Elizabeth Crews.)*

with "getting even." Youngsters lash out when they perceive their rights have been violated or their egos threatened (Maccoby, 1980). Over the elementary school years hostile aggression changes dramatically in form. Older children become much more prone to verbal insults than to hitting. If April calls Malcolm a big bully and Malcolm retaliates by calling her a stupid tattletale, they are engaging in hostile aggression more typical of older children.

THE DEVELOPMENT OF EMPATHY AND ALTRUISM

Empathy and altruism are two forms of prosocial behavior. **Empathy** is the ability to experience the thoughts and emotions of another person. **Altruism** is the practice of acting unselfishly in order to aid someone else. Both follow a developmental course parallel to that of aggression because the same cognitive factors underlie all three. To engage in true aggression, altruism, or empathy, children must understand that they are independent agents responsible for their own actions. The child must also grasp that the actions of the self can cause feelings in other people that are different from the feelings the self is experiencing.

Researchers have suggested several phases in the development of empathy and altruism (Hoffman, 1979; Radke-Yarrow, Zahn-Waxler, and Chapman, 1983). In the first phase, during infancy, the child shows a primitive capacity for empathy by crying when another person is distressed. But the child as yet has little understanding of who is actually upset. Upon hearing another baby cry, 8-month-olds will often crawl over to their own mother and seek contact with her (Hoffman, 1979). Apparently, the distinction between self and other is not yet clear in children's minds. At this stage, crying when another person cries is more aptly described as "contagion."

In the second phase, during early toddlerhood, advances in the concepts of self and other enable the child to engage in more purposeful helping behaviors. Children may hug or pat another child who is crying, bring their mother to the crying youngster, or bring the child a favorite toy. But these actions do not take into account the needs of the other child. Instead, toddlers do what would be helpful to *them* in that situation; they bring their *own* mother, their *own* favorite toy, and so fourth.

In phase three, during early childhood, the capacity to take the role of others, and with it a growing ability to respond to others' needs, increases dramatically (Borke, 1971; Selman, 1971). Research shows that the capacity for empathy and altruism is widespread among preschoolers (e.g., Leiman, 1978; Radke-Yarrow et al., 1983). In natural settings, however, displays of helping are relatively rare. Just because a child can experience the distress of others does not guarantee that the child will immediately offer comfort or assistance (Iannotti, 1985). Also, preschoolers sometimes do not come to the aid of others because they know that adults will often offer help.

How have researchers studied empathy and altruism in young children and discovered these various phases? The work of Marion Radke-Yarrow deserves special mention because it shows how naturalistic observations and laboratory studies can be used together (e.g., Radke-Yarrow and Zahn-Waxler, 1984). Radke-Yarrow asked 41 mothers to record in detail their young children's reactions to distress in others. This focus on reactions to real-life situations guaranteed that the findings applied to the everyday world. Because of the possibility of bias in the mothers' reports, assistants sometimes observed and recorded the same incidents that the mothers did. In addition, Radke-Yarrow supported all of her findings with laboratory experiments.

Not only did Radke-Yarrow's data reveal the developmental phases outlined above, but they also suggested that a parent's style of care giving greatly influences a child's prosocial behavior. Specifically, a young child's tendency to show empathy is related to experience with nurturant care givers who also provide models of empathy and helpfulness toward others. Just scolding a child for hurting others is apparently not enough. The parent must also clearly state the consequences for the victim, explain to the child the principles and expectations regarding kindness, and convey the entire message with intensity of feeling about the issues involved. Not surprisingly, then, a secure attachment in infancy is associated with a high level of empathy in the preschool years (Sroufe, 1983). It makes sense that the same responsive, nurturant parents who foster secure attachments would also show the various supports for prosocial behaviors that Radke-Yarrow talks about. In being part of an empathic care-giving relationship, children not only learn how to be cared for but to care as well.

WHAT INFLUENCE DOES TELEVISION HAVE?

Children spend a great deal of time watching television. It has been estimated that 3- to 4-year-olds watch two or more hours of television each day (Stein and Friedrich, 1975; Williams, 1986). What are the effects of all this television viewing on children's behavior? For example, does exposure to TV violence increase aggression? On the basis of powerful evidence for modeling effects in general (Bandura, 1977), one would expect some influence. However, such questions have proved difficult to answer because researchers can seldom control what programs children watch in their everyday lives. Nevertheless, the evidence we have is suggestive concerning TV influences, though only in interaction with other factors.

Demonstrations of *immediate* short-term effects of viewing violent TV content are rather conclusive. In one such landmark study (Friedrich and Stein, 1973), researchers first observed the amount of aggression that young children showed in their nursery school classroom. Then they exposed some of the children to aggressive TV programs, such as Superman and Batman cartoons. Other children spent the same amount of time watching "Mr. Rogers' Neighborhood," a program with a prosocial message. The children in the aggressive program group showed a greater rise in aggressive behavior in the classroom than the other children did. TV violence apparently can promote aggression. But note that a significant increase in aggression as a result of viewing TV violence occurred only for youngsters already rated high in aggressiveness. Children rated low in aggressiveness were much more immune to the negative impact of television. Clearly, TV violence is not the only factor that promotes aggression in children.

Other studies with older children support these findings. Ross Parke and his colleagues (1977) showed some juvenile delinquents violent films, while other delinquents saw equally engaging but nonviolent films. Following this, those exposed to the violent films engaged in more fights and other aggression.

Such experimental studies leave open the question of the long-term consequences of TV violence in the normal home life of children. Here, ethical considerations preclude deliberately exposing children to violent content over time. Researchers therefore rely on correlational approaches: trying to determine how much individual children are exposed to (or "prefer") violent TV programs and independently looking at the children's aggressive behavior. A problem, of course, is that such a correlation could mean only that aggressive children like to watch violent programs (Freedman, 1984; Wiegman, Kuttschreuter, and Baarda, 1986). A partial solution to this problem is to look at viewing patterns at one age (for example, as reported by parents) and aggression later (for example, as reported by peers). If such a correlation is significant and higher than the correlation between early aggression and later viewing preferences, one can infer that TV viewing causes aggression rather than the other way around. Such findings were indeed reported by Leonard Eron and his colleagues (e.g., Huesman and Eron, 1986). However, this study has been criticized because it used different measures at the two ages and other investigators obtained weaker results, suggesting that aggression and TV violence are modestly related, with the cause being in *both* directions (Milavsky et al., 1982).

The issues here are complicated. Aggression clearly is influenced by many factors, including parenting practices (see Chapter 13). Also, violence on television is a reflection of society as much as it is a societal influence. At present, some fair-minded, thoughtful reviewers have concluded that negative influences of TV violence have been demonstrated (Friedrich-Cofer and Huston, 1986), and others have concluded that they have not (Freedman, 1986; Wiegman, Kuttschreuter, and Baarda, 1986).

If watching TV violence increases aggression in some children, it also seems likely that watching prosocial programs could make children more thoughtful toward others. Again, experimental research shows short-term influences. Even preschoolers can understand prosocial messages on television (Stein and Friedrich, 1975); and youngsters of all ages are inclined to imitate models whom they admire, including prosocial models (Bandura, 1977). In the study of nursery school children we described earlier, those who were exposed to "Mr. Rogers' Neighborhood" became more cooperative and helpful in the classroom. Such a link also has been demonstrated with older children (Sprafkin and Rubenstein, 1979). Television apparently can be a positive influence as well as a negative one (Williams, 1986). But again, long-term influences are more difficult to demonstrate.

From Imitation to Identification

You have seen that preschoolers differ from toddlers in the breadth of the worlds they explore and in their capacities for self-control, aggression, and altruism. Preschoolers also differ from toddlers in how they relate to parents and other adults in their lives. While toddlers often imitate others around them, mimicking specific actions, preschoolers go further by iden-

Researchers continue to investigate the consequences of repeated exposure to violence and prosocial behavior on television. Educational programming can present prosocial behavior while teaching other skills. *(Michael McGovern/The Picture Cube.)*

tifying with adults who are important to them. As we said earlier, **identification** involves striving to be like someone else not only in actions but in thoughts, feelings, and values as well. Thus, imitation may be the starting point for identification, but the two are distinct processes.

The concept of identification is one of the most compelling aspects of the psychoanalytic view of early childhood development (Breger, 1974). Consider the process from the youngster's point of view, say, from the viewpoint of Mikey Gordon at 2 years of age. In moving away from the great dependency of infancy, Mikey strives to exercise the limits of his new autonomy. At first he sees no boundaries to his abilities. Overflowing with excitement at each new achievement, he feels all-capable and all-powerful. Inevitably, however, clashes of will with his parents bring Mikey face-to-face with limits to his independence. However resistant he might be to his parents' wishes (and children this age are often testimony to the strength of the human spirit), he cannot hold out indefinitely against overwhelming evidence—his parents are more powerful than he.

What is Mikey to do in this situation? Relinquish his new-found autonomy? Return to his earlier dependency? Surely not. Psychoanalytic theory proposes another solution, made possible by Mikey's cognitive development in early childhood. Mikey can identify with his parents, incorporating their attributes into his own self. In this way he becomes more like his parents and so more powerful, as they are. Notice how instead of relinquishing his newly formed self, Mikey's sense of self is developing further. He internalizes characteristics he perceives in his parents and thus acquires new feelings, beliefs, and values. The period that follows—from age 3 or 3½—is often considered a paradise by parents. The child shows more confidence and security, a new level of cooperation, and a closer alignment with the parents, especially the parent of the same gender.

Identification is not possible until a child has some ability to understand the parents' attitudes and feelings, not just observe their actions. Identification therefore does not occur until the early preschool period, at the same time that we begin to see true aggression and empathy as well as a marked increase in self-regulation. All of these developmental changes are intimately connected. Self-control, for example, partly involves internalizing parental controls, using them as standards and guides for behavior.

It is difficult to carry out research on identification because the cognitive and emotional components of the process are so complex. In the past, therefore, researchers focused on imitation. These researchers found that children are more likely to imitate those who are warm and nurturant as well as those who are relatively powerful (Hetherington, 1965; Hetherington and Frankie, 1967; Zahn-Waxler, Radke-Yarrow, and King, 1979). If two models are hostile rather than nurturant, the child will tend to imitate the dominant of the two (Hetherington and Frankie, 1967).

When it comes to identification with parents, children probably identify with both their mother and father, whatever their characteristics. Just as attachment will occur regardless of treatment, so will identification. Identification with abusive parents, or split identifications between two parents who are incompatible, can be a source of great conflict for a child.

Partly for this reason Freud argued that neuroses (anxiety-related psychological problems) stem from this developmental period. Before this time, children have not internalized norms or values and so cannot have mental conflict over them. These ideas are supported amply by clinical case studies and by some research. For example, Judith Wallerstein and Joan Kelly (1982) interviewed a large number of 3½- to 6-year-olds following their parents' divorce. The children's predominant reaction to this family disruption was self-blame. Younger children probably could not have had such a reaction.

Sex-Typed Behavior and Gender Concept

One part of the process of identification is to pay close attention to the parent of the same gender, gradually adopting that parent's gender-related behaviors, attitudes, and values. At the same time, children also gradually acquire a **gender concept,** that is, a sense of being male or female.

The development of sex-typed behavior and a gender concept follows a series of phases that is closely tied to cognitive development. By the age of 2, children are already showing gender-related preferences in toys. Boys have learned to play largely with trucks and cars, while girls have learned to gravitate toward soft, cuddly toys (Smith and Daglish, 1977). These early preferences are not absolute, however, as we illustrated in our story of Mikey who at age 2 became very attached to a Raggedy Ann doll. Research shows that at this young age children as yet have very little understanding of gender. Although they know that certain objects go with mommies or daddies (lipsticks versus neckties, for example), they do not yet understand that they share a gender with one of their parents (Thompson, 1975).

By age 3 or 4, sex-typed behavior greatly increases (Connor and Serbin, 1977). Boys in nursery school classes engage in more rough-and-tumble play than girls do, often despite teachers' protests (DiPietro, 1981). Conversely, girls as young as preschool age show more interest in and nurturance toward infants than their male peers do (Edwards and Whiting,

The preschooler learns gender identity by observing those around him. *(Mimi Cotter/International Stock Photo, Ken Karp.)*

1977). The fact that similar sex-typed behaviors are seen in young monkeys suggests some biological basis (Suomi, 1977). However, we humans also actively teach gender stereotypes. Even during infancy most parents dress boys and girls in different clothing, decorate their rooms differently, give them different playthings, and interact with them differently (Fagot, 1978; Rheingold and Cook, 1975). By preschool age if children behave in gender-inconsistent fashions, parents and peers are quick to give negative feedback. Judith Langlois nicely illustrated this feedback process by getting preschoolers to play with gender "inappropriate" toys and then inviting in the mother, father, or peers to watch (Langlois and Downs, 1980). Fathers reacted very negatively to gender "inappropriate" play, especially to the sight of their boys playing with "feminine" toys, and milder negative reactions also occurred in peers. Just as Mikey is encouraged by his father to shun "sissy" playthings, so other preschoolers are channeled into sex-typed behaviors.

The marked increase in sex-typed behavior during the preschool period is accompanied by increased understanding of gender as well as by a rather strict gender segregation in the classroom (Strayer, 1977). The fact that 4-year-old Mikey's favorite playmates at day care are two other boys is no accident. Children this age know that they are boys or girls, they know that these are categories of people, and they see themselves as members of one category or the other (Thompson, 1975). Hence they are attracted toward interacting with others of their own gender.

Striking evidence that a sense of gender emerges during the preschool period comes from studies of children whose genitals were ambiguously formed at birth (Money, 1975). Such children are sometimes assigned to the wrong gender; that is, baby boys are mistakenly identified as girls, and baby girls are mistakenly thought to be boys. If the error is discovered before age 2½ and the child from then on is raised as the biologically correct sex, problems rarely arise. The toddler accepts the new sexual identity with little distress or resistance. However, if reassignment to the opposite sex is made in later childhood, it tends to be very hard for the youngster. Such children may grow up still thinking of themselves as belonging to their "original" gender, including a preference for what would have been the opposite sex had their gender not been reassigned. Thus, there seems to be a sensitive period for beginning to develop a sense of gender.

One important aspect of children's developing sense of gender is an understanding of **gender constancy** (Emmerich et al., 1976; Kohlberg, 1966; Slaby and Frey, 1975). By this we mean an understanding that gender is permanent despite changes in age, in dress or hair style, or in behavior. Three-year-olds know that they are boys or girls, and they know the things usually associated with their gender. But they still think that changes in superficial characteristics (boys wearing dresses and playing with dolls, girls cutting their hair short and playing with footballs) can produce a change in gender. They are also still unaware that they will always be the same sex. To them gender may be capable of varying.

By age 5, children are beginning to understand gender constancy, and by age 7, their understanding is even more firmly established. This developmental change has implications for children's behavior. In one study, boys who understood gender constancy consistently preferred to look at slides of men over slides of women (Slaby and Frey, 1975). Apparently, the realization that they would *always* be male prompted a greater curiosity about adult men. In another study, girls with a newly emerging grasp of gender constancy were found to have the strongest preference for playmates of the same sex (stronger than that of girls still unaware of gender constancy and even stronger than that of girls who understood gender constancy very well). Thus, a developing sense of gender can motivate children "to seek social contexts in which to acquire and practice sex-appropriate behavior" (Smetana and Letourneau, in press, p. 1).

Changes in Children's Play

Play is the province of the child. It is the "laboratory" where the child learns new skills and practices old ones. Play is also the child's social workshop, the arena for trying out roles alone and with other children. When more fundamental needs are met—when the child isn't eating or sleeping or seeking attention from adults—the child will play, often for hours on end (Sutton-Smith, 1971). Even emotionally disturbed children play, although the quality of their play is notably affected. The absence of play is considered a sign of extreme abnormality (see Chapter 16). This intrinsic motive to play shows how much of children's behavior lies outside the influence of reinforcement. No one has to teach children to play; they do so naturally. No one has to reward children for playing; play is its own reward. Contemporary researchers stress this view of children as active explorers of their environments, active creators of new experiences, and active participants in their own development. Let's briefly examine some of the ways in which play is involved in this active learning process.

MASTERY OF CONFLICT

By the preschool years play becomes the child's foremost tool for dealing with conflict and mastering what is frightening or painful. One illustration of this point appears in a film that Jeanne Block and her colleagues at Berkeley made during the civil disorders of the 1960s. The sandbox play of children at that time was filled with police officers and civilians in conflict. We illustrated this at the end of our story about Mikey, when anxiety surfaces in his fantasy play. The little boy in Mikey's make-believe drama is caught in the midst of his parents' crashing cars, just as Mikey is caught in the middle of Frank and Christine's persistent clashes. Another 4-year-old was observed by her mother to dwell upon a current fear in her play. The day after she was frightened by a large dog, she pretended to be a dog terrorizing a group of dolls. She barked ferociously while crawling on the floor and then reassured the dolls by saying: "It's OK. He won't hurt you." In such ways preschoolers work their anxieties into play and thereby master them. In fact, play often centers on the most frightening of topics, such as being lost or having to fight off "monsters" (Rosenberg, 1984). Apparently, the motive to master fears and conflicts is very powerful.

And not just transient concerns appear in children's play. Play is also an arena for working through ongoing developmental issues. Consider

As gender constancy develops, children understand that gender is not subject to change. This is reflected in their choice of play activities, choice of playmates, and other behaviors. (*Paul Fusco/Magnum Photos, Inc.*)

Through play, children can express and work through conflicts in a safe setting. *(Alice Kandell/Photo Researchers, Inc.)*

the process of identification through which children resolve the conflict arising when they realize they have limited power compared with parents. On a day-to-day basis this resolution is often worked out in play (Breger, 1974; Rosenberg, 1984). In play the child can safely turn the tables and become the powerful one. A common game that preschoolers initiate with parents is "you be the baby and I'll be the mommy (or daddy)." The child might say: "Now you go right to bed!" (Parent: "Can I read?") "No, you have to go right to sleep!" The power roles are reversed in play, and the parent is charmed, not infuriated. Or consider another 3½-year-old, told by her mother to fasten her seatbelt. This demand earlier had been the start of impressive struggles of will. This time, however, the child buckles up cooperatively. She then informs her mother that the stuffed bear beside her is very mad at her mother about this. "But *I'm* not mad," she assures mother. "I love you, Mamma."

No wonder 3-year-olds and their parents usually get along so well. The children can express anger and defiance in their play while otherwise accepting the parents' authority. Pretending, which begins in the late toddler period and expands rapidly during the preschool period (Dunn, 1985), allows the expression of forbidden behaviors and feelings that might not only be punished but might also cause the child guilt. Remember that the preschooler has started to internalize the parents' values and so is capable of feeling guilty when he or she does wrong. Play opens up an escape valve at this stage of development. In play the child can pretend to be destructive, disobedient, or uncooperative without reprisals from either parents or conscience.

In research on preschoolers' fantasy play, Deborah Rosenberg (1984) found that the complexity, flexibility, and elaborateness of play were positively related to a history of secure attachment. She also found that in their play those with secure histories significantly more often brought negative themes to successful resolution ("Oh no! He got his leg broken! Here comes the ambilenz. They take him to the hospital. They fixed it!"). Rosenberg further found that children who as infants showed the avoidant pattern of attachment later revealed a virtual absence of play about people, in stark contrast to most children. This work illustrates the importance of play as an entrée to the child's inner world and as an indicator of positive adaptation during the preschool period.

Pretend solutions are usually a healthy outlet for the preschool child. Because they involve active confrontation of a problem, they provide a kind of prototype for more mature solutions in later years. Recognizing a conflict and doing something about it (rather than denying it) is a growth-enhancing response (Breger, 1974). With further development, of course, pretend or play solutions must be left behind. Nevertheless, they represent the beginnings of active mastery of conflict.

ROLE-PLAYING

Preschoolers' play serves important functions beyond the mastery of conflicts. One is providing the opportunity to try out social roles. In play, children can be mommies and daddies, doctors, police officers, or robbers. In play, they can act out their aspirations as well as their fears (Fein, 1978). Dressing up in grownup clothes and playing at grownup jobs are also an important part of identifying with parents and exploring gender roles. When preschool boys and girls play "robbers," with the boys always being the robbers and the girls taking flight and hiding, they are working on developmental issues beyond their conscious understanding.

One recent study found that, generally speaking, the greater the amount of social fantasy play in which a preschooler engages, the greater that child's social competence as judged by teachers (Connolly and Doyle, 1984). Rosenberg (1984), in the study we discussed above, found that her qualitative measures of play (elaborateness, flexibility) were related to a variety of measures of social competence in the classroom, including peer sociometric status. We have portrayed this correlation in Mikey, who is both greatly liked by peers and very skilled at social fantasy play. Does skill at social fantasy play promote acceptance among other preschool children? Or do popular preschoolers simply have more opportunities for this kind of play? A correlational study alone cannot answer such questions. These findings, however, do reveal the importance of social fantasy play as an indicator of a child's overall quality of adjustment during the preschool years.

Further Development of the Self

You know from Chapter 9 that a sense of self emerges along with increased autonomy. Doing things on one's own inevitably leads to an understanding that "I am the author of my acts" (Keller, Ford, and Meacham, 1978). These first perceptions of self are followed by repeated acts of self-assertion. In time, however, children come to the realization that their powers are limited; they cannot always do what they want. Parents, they discover, have rules and expectations about behavior. Preschoolers internalize these rules and expectations through the process of identification. Children now begin to feel guilty when they do something forbidden. They strive to adhere to their internalized standards, to coordinate them with their personal needs and wishes. These experiences lie at the heart of their self-regulation and self-concept.

Louis Sander (1975) has described an important aspect of the developing self, what he calls a sense of **self-constancy.** By this he means the perception of a stable self, a self that endures despite varied behaviors and varied responses from others. In Sander's view a sense of self-constancy is the natural product of interactions between children and their parents over the first three years of life, especially after the age of about 18 months.

To understand the emergence of a sense of self-constancy, picture Malcolm, who has just turned 3. He is eyeing the cords of the window blinds, which he loves to play with but is forbidden to. DeeDee, who is cleaning a nearby closet, glances over at him. Malcolm is aware not only of his own intentions to pull on the cords but also of his mother's knowledge of these intentions. Such awareness, which depends on a certain level of language and cognitive development, paves the way for Malcolm to upset the relationship with DeeDee deliberately by doing what he *knows* is counter to her wishes. In this case he grabs the cords and begins to pull them vigorously, knowing full well that his mother sees his actions as both bad and deliberate. "Malcolm!" says DeeDee sharply. "You stop that right now!" This response is just what Malcolm expects. Notice how his awareness of someone else's view of his thoughts and motives helps to consolidate his developing sense of self. Malcolm also understands that the self who has just done something wrong and who is being scolded is the same self who a moment before was in harmony with DeeDee. Equally important, Malcolm knows that he can reinstate the former harmony at will by "making up" with his mother, for example, by saying he is sorry. Malcolm, in short, understands the continuity of his self in relation to his mother—quite an accomplishment for a 3-year-old.

Although all children come to acquire a sense of self-constancy, not all come to think of the self in exactly the same way. Each child develops a particular view of the self based on his or her unique experiences. These thoughts and feelings about the self are referred to as **self-esteem.** Our earlier story of Malcolm suggested he has high self-esteem or at least a high evaluation of his own physical abilities. ("I'm the best!" he tells his father.) Most developmentalists think that such favorable self-evaluations stem from a history of positive exchanges with others, especially with care givers. When adults communicate warmth, empathy, and positive regard for a youngster, they encourage high self-esteem in the child (Coopersmith, 1967). We will say more about self-esteem in Chapter 13.

THE PARENTS' ROLE IN EARLY CHILDHOOD DEVELOPMENT

As children undergo rapid and far-reaching changes during the preschool years, parents must adjust their behavior so as to continue fostering favorable development. The tasks of both children and parents in the preschool years are summarized in Table 11.1. In general, parents must gradually give the child more responsibility, while still being available to step in and help if his or her resources are exceeded. According to Erik Erikson, the preschool period is a time when children may attempt to do too much as they strive for mastery. If parents ridicule or punish

TABLE 11.1   Tasks for Preschoolers and Their Parents

Parents' Tasks	Children's Tasks
Nurturance	Accepting care and developing trust
Training and channeling of physical needs	Complying and controlling
Teaching and skill training	Learning
Orienting child to family and peers	Developing a general understanding of the social world
Promoting interpersonal skills, motives, and control of emotion	Role taking
Guiding formation of goals, plans, and aspirations	Achieving self-regulation
Transmitting cultural values	Developing a sense of right and wrong

Source: Adapted from Clausen, 1968.

failures unduly, preschoolers may be vulnerable to pervasive feelings of guilt (Erikson, 1963). Thus, parents must neither push preschoolers too fast nor thwart their efforts. This role is similar to the one parents played with the child as a toddler, but now they are dealing with a much more mature and competent youngster. Parents must also be aware of the models they provide for the preschooler, since this is the age of identification. The parents must try to manifest clear roles and values in their own actions and also show the flexible self-control they hope to promote in their child.

Louis Sander (1975) has described this critical parent-child interaction as a process whereby dyadic (two-person) regulation becomes self-regulation. At first the parent almost single-handedly coordinates activities with the baby by tailoring responses to suit the child's biologically based states and behaviors. Soon, however, parents must make room for initiatives on the child's part. The older baby initiates exchanges (vocalizing, showing a toy), and the parents follow so that coordination is maintained. By the end of the first year the infant becomes more active in making intentional bids toward the parents. Continued responsiveness on the parents' part helps the child become increasingly aware that he or she can control important elements in the environment (Sroufe, in press). Then in the toddler period, when the child can intentionally initiate actions that oppose the parents' wishes, the parents' acceptance of the child's autonomy coupled with appropriate limits deepens the child's awareness of his or her own motivational states. As the child becomes aware of these states and their accompanying feelings, he or she can be guided by them; this is the basis for self-regulation. Finally, if the parents reinstate a harmonious relationship after the child expresses anger or aggression, the child can experience a continuity of the self, which is the key to flexible self-management. In Sander's view, therefore, unresponsiveness toward an infant, harsh treatment of negativism during toddlerhood, or failure to confirm for a child that the relationship with the parents remains intact despite the child's feelings of anger or destructiveness can all compromise healthy development.

Some of the same conclusions derive from the research of Diana Baumrind, who has approached the issue of the parents' role in a more empirical manner. Baumrind (1967) began by identifying three basic personality profiles among nursery school children on the basis of 14 weeks of observation. Children in group 1 were energetic, emotionally positive toward peers, and high in curiosity, self-reliance, and self-control. Children in group 2 were moody, apprehensive, easily upset, passively hostile, and either negative in their relations with peers or socially withdrawn. Children in group 3 were impulsive, undercontrolled, and low in self-reliance but more cheerful and resilient than those in group 2. Baumrind then assessed the parents of these children through personal interviews, home observations, and laboratory studies. She found three distinctive styles of care giving. Parents of group 1 children were more nurturant and responsive and less punitive than parents of group 2 and group 3 children. In addition, they were firm in setting limits and were not easily manipulated by their youngster (what Baumrind calls **authoritative**). Yet group 1 parents were also flexible in their attitudes and outlooks and encouraged their child toward independence. In contrast, parents of group 2 children were unresponsive to their child's wishes, inflexible, and harsh in controlling behavior. Such parents have also been described by Gerald Patterson (Patterson and Dishion, in press), who has linked such treatment to later aggressiveness in children. Parents of group 3 children were somewhat nurturant, but they totally failed to set firm limits or to require appropriately mature behavior, thus hindering their child's development of self-control. We need only assume continuity of these parenting styles over time to see complete agreement with Sander's ideas. Such evidence is now available (Patterson and Dishion, in press; Pianta, Egeland, and Sroufe, in press).

Baumrind's conclusions have been supported by other researchers (Maccoby and Martin, 1983; Roberts, 1983). W. L. Roberts obtained assessments of social competence among a group of preschoolers, while also assessing the care-giving styles of these children's parents. He found that excessive use of power on the parents' part was related to lower social competence. High social competence was associated with parents who were warm and nurturant. Eleanor Maccoby (Maccoby and Martin, 1983) studied the relationship between parenting style and cooperativeness in young children. She found that when a mother followed her child's lead in a playroom setting, the child was later more willing to comply with her directions on another task. Apparently, total unresponsiveness to a child's wishes tends to breed resistance on the child's part. A similar conclusion comes from the experimental work of Leon Kuczynski (1984). He found that when parents are given the long-term goal of having their child comply with their directives even in their absence, they tend to rely more on reasoning and less on power assertion. Here a responsive, less punitive approach tends to foster self-management.

In summary, parents can encourage self-confidence, autonomy, and positive feelings toward others by means of responsive care coupled with firm limits appropriate to their child's age and level of self-management.

"Come let us reason to-gether." *(Ellis Herwig/The Picture Cube.)*

The child's temperament, of course, may also have to be considered. Some children are more challenging than others, especially for some parents. Nevertheless, responsive care, respect for autonomy, and clear limits when needed should lead to healthy development in all but the rarest of cases.

EXPLAINING INDIVIDUAL DIFFERENCES

You have seen that there are many individual differences in preschoolers' behavior. Some children are high in curiosity, independence, self-esteem, and peer competence, while others are low in these characteristics. Some children lack self-control and tend to be impulsive and aggressive, while others are just the opposite. You can see substantial differences along all of these dimensions in Mikey, Meryl, and Malcolm. Mikey is an eager, curious, well-liked child, who would cling to parents or teachers only if ill or injured. Meryl, in contrast, is very dependent, shy, and low in self-confidence. Malcolm, although more like Mikey than Meryl, differs from Mikey in his greater energy level. Where do all these individual differences come from? Psychologists now believe that they are a result of an interaction of factors in the child's developmental history, as well as current circumstances.

Interplay of Biology and Learning

Some researchers have offered biological explanations for many of the individual differences we see in preschool children's behavior, including differences in curiosity, exploration, aggression, empathy, sociability, and competence with peers (Haywood and Burke, 1977; Reznick et al., 1986; Schaffer and Emerson, 1964; Smith, 1978; Wender and Klein, 1986). To date, however, there is little evidence to support these ideas. It is the case that identical twins are more similar than fraternal twins on characteristics such as shyness, but the magnitude of such relationships generally is small (Daniels and Plomin, 1985). Biological factors alone do not seem sufficient to account for the dramatic differences among children in terms of these features of development.

As one alternative, some researchers have proposed that biology creates certain *general* differences in temperament, which then interact with experience to produce the different developmental outcomes that we observe. For instance, a child like Malcolm, who from infancy is highly active, may have parents who fail to set firm limits. Unlike Malcolm, such a child may then grow up to be seriously lacking in self-control.

Another way to look at the role of biology in children's behavioral differences is to say that human genetic inheritance provides certain capacities for behavior, which are then encouraged or dampened by day-to-day experiences. Aggression in children provides a good example. Aggression is undoubtedly a built-in part of the human behavioral repertoire. We all have the capacity to strike out at others, particularly when they have injured or frustrated us. This capacity may have evolved because it helped our early ancestors maintain a workable social structure and distribution of the population, thus increasing their chances of survival. The fact that aggression appears in children at a relatively fixed age suggests that it is partly under genetic control (Maccoby, 1980).

However, learning must also play a powerful role in aggression, especially in its individual differences. This conclusion is supported by studies of young monkeys (Suomi, 1977). Monkeys that have been isolated from others during infancy show the emergence of aggression at the usual time, but they tend to be more aggressive toward peers. Apparently, the inclination to respond aggressively is greatly influenced by early experiences. Among humans, some of these early experiences may have to do with reinforcement. Gerry Patterson (Patterson, Littman, and Bricker, 1967) has shown that some children who experience positive outcomes from aggression (getting the toy they want, for instance) tend to act aggressively again. Models provided by parents and others may also play a part, as may broader aspects of the child's care-giving history (see Chapters 13 and 16). Finally the great variation among cultures in aggression shows clearly that this capacity is open to learning. For example, among the Mundugumor, a New Guinea tribe that anthropologist Margaret Mead once studied, women as well as men are combative and aggressive, quick to perceive insults and avenge wrongs; other groups are far more peaceable (Mead, 1935).

In summary, biology provides an important context for development, a set of potentialities that experience then works upon. Our evolution has given us the capacity for aggression, but how much aggression we actually express is heavily influenced by learning. In the same way, we inherit capacities for empathy toward others, for curiosity and exploration, for autonomy and dependence, for sociability. Individual experiences as we develop, however, encourage or stifle those potentials, helping to make us noticeably different from one another. Chief among these individual experiences are our various care-giving histories, the lessons and outlooks we learned from interactions with our parents.

Care-Giving History

Research provides considerable support for the idea that care-giving history sets a context for the emergence of individual differences among preschoolers. We have already mentioned the role of parental nurturance in encouraging empathy in children. We have also mentioned the role of warm, responsive care in promoting high curiosity, competence with peers, and a positive overall emotional tone. This emphasis on nurturant, responsive care is closely related to our earlier emphasis on the importance of sensitive care during infancy. The sensitive care giver is in tune with the baby's needs and wishes and is responsive to them. He or she paces social interactions so that the child can deal with increasing levels of novelty and excitement without becoming disorganized and upset. Such care-giver support should lead not only to secure attachment but also to curiosity and confidence in engaging new aspects of the world.

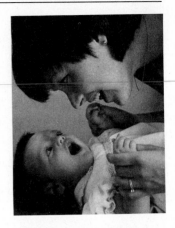

Sensitive care during infancy has been shown to promote confidence and curiosity in toddlers and preschoolers. *(Mimi Cotter/ International Stock Photo.)*

Researchers have found that these relationships do hold true. For instance, Richard Arend studied 26 5-year-olds who at age 18 months had been assessed for the quality of their attachment to the mother. Those who had been securely attached were found to explore a large, novel play box for a longer time, to manipulate more of the objects inside the box, and to engage in more in-depth manipulations (Arend, Gove, and Sroufe, 1979). In another study with similar findings, children assessed as securely attached at age 15 months were more often rated "curious about the new" at age 3½ years (Waters, Wippman, and Sroufe, 1979). Apparently, secure attachment during infancy and toddlerhood tends to set the stage for a confident, eager outlook in exploring the environment, provided of course that the environment continues to support such behavior.

Preschoolers with histories of secure attachment are also more competent with peers. They are described by their preschool teachers as "peer leaders" and "sought out by others," not as "hesitant to engage" or "socially withdrawn" (Waters, Wippman, and Sroufe, 1979). Mikey and Malcolm are portrayed as examples of such children. Research also shows that preschoolers with histories of secure attachment have a number of other positive characteristics as judged by teachers. Compared with youngsters who experienced anxious attachment in infancy, they have higher self-esteem, greater self-reliance, and more flexibility in their self-management. They also express more positive emotions toward peers and in their play, as well as more empathy for others and less aggression (Sroufe, 1983). The teachers' judgments regarding self-reliance, flexible self-management, positive emotion, and level of aggression have been supported by direct observations of preschoolers (Arend, Gove, and Sroufe, 1979; Sroufe, 1983; Sroufe et al., 1984).

The findings on the link between secure attachment and self-reliance are especially important because they show the inadequacy of simple trait notions regarding dependency. In one longitudinal study, children who had been securely attached (that is, effectively *dependent*) in infancy were judged by their preschool teachers to be dramatically less emotionally dependent on them than children who had been anxiously attached (Sroufe, Fox, and Pancake, 1983). Those children with a history of secure attachment were not aloof. Routinely they greeted teachers warmly, shared discoveries with them, and sought them out when injured or

Preschool teachers react differently to different children, and their reaction is related to each child's history. *(Jeffrey W. Myers/The Stock Market.)*

distressed. But such contacts were viewed by the teachers as flexible and appropriate, with the children quickly going on to other business. In sum, secure reliance on care givers in infancy predicted self-reliance in preschool.

In sharp contrast, children with a history of anxious attachment tended to be preoccupied with their teachers. They spent more time than their classmates eliciting guidance, support, and discipline from teachers (Motti, 1986) and more time sitting on the teachers' laps during group activities (Sroufe, Fox, and Pancake, 1983). We described such behavior in Meryl's early responses toward Mrs. Jaspers. Interestingly, this pattern does not only occur in preschoolers with a history of anxious-resistant attachment, such as Meryl. It is also seen in children who as infants developed an anxious-avoidant attachment. This finding may surprise you because in the laboratory situation where the mother leaves the baby, these children do not seek out the mother when she returns or show other obvious signs of dependency. Nevertheless, their ineffective attachment relationship apparently leaves them very emotionally needy as they enter the preschool years (Sroufe, 1983).

These findings do not mean that quality of attachment in infancy directly *causes* the child's behavior. Quality of care in the preschool years also predicts the child's functioning at that time (Baumrind, 1967; Erickson, Egeland, and Sroufe, 1985), and when quality of care notably improves, so does child behavior, even though the child was anxiously attached earlier (Erickson, Egeland, and Sroufe, 1985). This research result is congruent with Bowlby's ideas about the changeability of the child's inner working models of the world. However, quality of parental care tends to be consistent across this time period (Pianta, Egeland, and Sroufe, in press; Ward, Vaughn, and Robb, 1987), and the child has become a more active force in his or her own development (Sroufe, in press). Difficulties based on early experience may make current parenting harder; for example, a whining, dependent child may promote further rejection by a parent, leading to more demandingness in the child, and so forth.

Recent research illustrates this influence of the child on the social environment. Preschool teachers behave differently toward different children, and these reactions are related to attachment history (Motti, 1986). Teachers are warm and accepting of those with secure histories, hold out age-appropriate standards for them, and expect them to comply. However, they exercise little control over these well-managed children. They are quite controlling of children with histories of anxious-resistant attachment (such as Meryl). They also make allowances for them, accepting immature behavior, and they are nurturant toward them as much as one would be with a younger child. With children having an avoidant attachment history, teachers are controlling and at times even angry. They rarely expect compliance, and they discipline these children often. Thus, while the behavior of teachers no doubt can be a positive influence on children with troubled histories, it is also the case that children with troubled histories at times draw forth negative behavior from teachers, which confirms the children's preexisting models.

Therefore, while it is likely that current parental behavior has the strongest influence on the preschooler's behavior, nonetheless the behavior of both the child and the parent is predicted by earlier care, and change is often difficult to bring about. As Bowlby argues, the quality of adaptation at each period turns both on current circumstances *and* on development prior to that point, just as was the case during prenatal development (see Chapter 4).

THE COHERENCE OF INDIVIDUAL BEHAVIOR

One important aspect of preschool social development is how the various lines converge. Curiosity, self-reliance, peer competence, self-management, aggression, empathy, and so forth are all intricately related developmentally. The developmental process is organized and coherent. Likewise, by the preschool period if not before, each child is a coherent, unique person. Clusters of individual characteristics tend to go together as the result of a child's particular developmental history. For instance, children who have high self-esteem tend to have flexible self-control, to show more empathy for others, to be better liked by peers, and to be judged more socially competent by teachers (Sroufe, 1983). In contrast, children who show hostility do not show much prosocial behavior, nor do children who are highly dependent on their preschool teachers. The point is that children do not behave in a random, haphazard fashion. Their behavior reflects a coherent, underlying self.

Situational determinants of behavior are important, though (Epstein, 1983; Mischel, 1968). Children behave differently in different situations. But these differences across situations also are coherent. Thus, a child like Mikey who shouts and plays exuberantly on the playground but who can work quietly and diligently in the classroom is not being inconsistent

(Block and Block, 1980). Across situations he is showing a coherent pattern of flexible self-control.

How a child characteristically changes from one situation to another provides important insights into personality. Knowing that a child is never hostile toward other children under the teacher's eye but is routinely mean to vulnerable peers when the teacher isn't looking tells us much more about this child than either observation alone. How different this youngster is from another child who causes disruptions only when teachers *are* there to intervene and thereby grant attention. Also of interest are the ways in which each child defines situations. A situation, after all, is only what we construe it to be, and what we construe depends on our habitual ways of thinking and perceiving (Bowlby, 1973; Sroufe, 1987). Thus, a preschool classroom may be a garden of delights for one child and an alien environment for another, depending upon their respective outlooks. Children who isolate themselves, children who alienate others, and children who are preoccupied with their teachers have very different preschool experiences than those who actively and positively engage with peers (Sroufe, 1987).

The coherent sets of characteristics found in different children are greatly influenced by each child's developmental history, as you have already seen. For instance, preschoolers with a history of secure attachment in infancy—while varying in their social involvement, activity levels, and so forth—tend to have certain things in common (Sroufe, 1983). They have high self-esteem, are popular with peers, and show little negative emotion or hostile aggression. This is not to say that these preschoolers never use force. In fact, they tend to be quite assertive and sometimes display instrumental aggression in struggles over objects. You saw this in Malcolm's response to April Kaid as they struggled to possess the bike (LaFrenier, 1983; Maccoby, 1980). Such instrumental aggression will soon decline as Malcolm grows older. Preschoolers like Malcolm who have a history of secure attachment do not seek to injure other children either in response to frustration or without obvious provocation. Generally, they are empathic toward their peers. Their social involvement is reflected in their fantasy play, which tends to be complex and socially oriented (Rosenberg, 1984).

A very different behavioral profile emerges for preschoolers with a history of anxious attachment. These children in general have lower peer competence, lower self-esteem, and a lower capacity for flexible self-management; they also have a greater need for nurturance or discipline (Motti, 1986; Sroufe, 1987; Sroufe, Fox, and Pancake, 1983). Those with histories of avoidant attachment, for example, are often hostile and aggressive toward other children or are emotionally isolated. Some of these children show aggression that is calculated and without immediate provocation. At times it has a mean quality. For instance, in response to a playmate's remark that she had a stomach ache, one little girl jabbed her fist into the other child's stomach (Troy and Sroufe, 1987). When the playmate complained, "That hurt!" the girl punched her again. Similarly, one boy with a history of anxious-avoidant attachment systematically cruised the classroom, disrupting other children's play. When one of the victims became upset (generally another child with a history of anxious attachment), he would intensify his attack on that particular youngster.

Lying, blaming others, and defiant behavior are also common in some of these children. Yet these same antisocial children, as well as the isolated ones, show strong dependency needs. During group activities or when it's time to go home, their efforts to seek contact with the teacher often have a desperate quality. Yet ironically, when greeted by a teacher or when very upset, they deliberately turn away. This pattern of behavior, though at first glance seemingly inconsistent, is in fact coherent and understandable. The hostility or isolation, the desperate dependency, coupled with avoidance when contact with adults is appropriate, can all be interpreted as reflecting low self-esteem, general mistrust, and unresolved needs for nurturance. In other words, these behaviors can all be thought of as the product of the same inner working model of the self in relation to others. Even such children, however, are found to be responsive to the persistent efforts of caring teachers (Sroufe, 1983).

Chapter Review

1. Dramatic developments in social and emotional behavior occur during the preschool period. For one thing, children become more self-reliant and begin to explore a much wider world. Included in their broader social environments are true peer relationships. Positive peer interactions are extremely important because during childhood so much is learned within the peer group.

2. Preschoolers also begin to achieve notable self-regulation. They can inhibit actions, delay gratification, and tolerate frustration much more than toddlers can. Parents begin to expect children at this age to "behave" and obey certain rules even when adults are not there to watch them. Developmentalists are especially interested in children's capacity to appropriately modify self-restraint depending on the situation, a capacity called **ego resiliency.**

3. Closely related to advances in self-regulation is the emergence of true **aggression, empathy,** and **altruism.** All these behaviors require that children understand the self as an independent agent and grasp that one can cause feelings in others that are different from the feelings one is experiencing.

4. During the preschool period a major change takes place in children's relationships to their parents. While toddlers often imitate specific actions of their parents, preschoolers go further by identifying with them. **Identification** involves striving to be like the parents not only in actions but also in thoughts, feelings, and values. In psychoanalytic theory, identification resolves the conflict that arises when newly autonomous 2-year-olds discover that parents are more powerful than they are and insist on imposing rules. Through identifying with their parents and becoming more like them, preschool children acquire some of their parents' power and competence.

5. One part of identification is adopting the gender-related behaviors, attitudes, and values of the parent of the same sex. At about the same time, children also gradually acquire a **gender concept,** or sense of being male or female. An important aspect of this new self-awareness is the understanding that gender remains permanent despite superficial changes in appearance or behavior. This grasp of **gender constancy** starts to emerge by the end of the preschool period.

6. Preschoolers' play differs notably from that of young toddlers in the rich and complex forms of fantasy it involves. This **fantasy play** is a child's foremost tool for dealing with conflict and mastering what is frightening or painful. Fantasy play also gives preschoolers the chance to try out a large variety of social roles.

7. The child's sense of self undergoes further development during the preschool years. By the age of about 3, youngsters have acquired a sense of **self-constancy,** the perception of a stable self that endures despite varied behaviors and varied responses from others. During the preschool period children also acquire specific thoughts and feelings about the self, either positive or negative ones. These self-evaluations are referred to as **self-esteem.**

8. As children undergo so many important changes during the preschool years, parents must adjust their own behavior to continue fostering favorable development. Parents must gradually give the child more responsibility, while still being available to step in and help when the youngster's resources are exceeded. Research suggests that parents should also set clear limits on what the child is and is not allowed to do. Warmth and nurturance continue to be important parental characteristics, as is a respect for the child's needs and point of view.

9. Developmentalists want to understand how individual patterns of behavior among preschoolers evolve from the children's earlier adaptations. An important influence appears to be care-giving history. A history of secure attachment during infancy and early toddlerhood tends to lead to greater curiosity, more competence with peers, higher self-esteem, greater self-reliance, and more flexible self-management (ego resiliency) during the preschool years. In contrast, a history of anxious attachment tends to be linked with a number of behavorial problems. Children who formed an anxious-resistant attachment are often either high-strung and easily frustrated as preschoolers or reticent and overly dependent. Children who formed an anxious-avoidant attachment are often either hostile and aggressive or socially withdrawn and lacking in emotional expression. These findings suggest that by the preschool period, if not before, each child is a coherent individual with characteristic ways of responding to the world.

Early Childhood

Development continues at an explosive pace during the preschool period, ages 2½ through 5. Preschoolers do not simply learn more facts and acquire additional skills. They also undergo qualitative changes—transformations in how they think and act. While development during this period certainly builds upon what has preceded, the 5-year-old is a fundamentally different person from the 2-year-old. The 5-year-old, for instance, is using language fluently, in contrast to the short, two- or three-word sentences of the 2-year-old. The 5-year-old is also reasoning about the world in ways far beyond the 2-year-old's capacities. Although the 5-year-old's explanations for why things happen often charm us with their magical qualities, the very fact that 5-year-olds are so preoccupied with how things work sets them distinctly apart from children who are only 2. In independence from parents 5-year-olds are also markedly different from toddlers, who are just discovering their autonomy. Similarly, 5-year-olds exert a degree of self-management not to be found in children 3 years younger. We could go on and mention many other differences that you have read about. It is no exaggeration to say that a 5-year-old is in some ways more similar to an adult than to a 2-year-old. To prove this to yourself, try reasoning with a 5-year-old and a 2-year-old.

What underlies these dramatic qualitative changes during the preschool period? Much of the answer has to do with cognitive development. Compared with toddlers, preschoolers have a more advanced capacity for mental representation. Preschoolers can imagine combinations of things they have never actually experienced. For instance, after spotting some candy on a shelf that is too high to reach, a preschooler might imagine stacking some nearby boxes to form a makeshift set of steps. Representational skills of this sort account for more effective problem solving. The child can "see" the solution without engaging in a random trial-and-error approach. Compared with toddlers, preschoolers also have a much greater capacity for using and manipulating symbols, including the words of their native language. This more advanced symbolic capacity facilitates communication and learning. Preschoolers can describe their current understandings, ask questions of adults, and learn from verbal explanations. Their endless "whys" result in the accumulation of a great deal of knowledge that they could otherwise acquire only through firsthand experience.

The preschooler's cognitive advances have far-reaching consequences for social and emotional development. Improvements in language and the ability to take another person's perspective provide the basis for rapid advances in peer relationships. Representational skills and imagination make possible fantasy play, which in turn helps the child to resolve conflicts, practice new skills, and try out social roles. Representational skills also enable identification with parents, while contributing to the child's growing ability to delay gratification, inhibit responses, tolerate frustration, and otherwise exert self-management.

Cognitive advances also help promote a change in the parent-child relationship. Parents

Issues in Early Development

Phase	Age in months	Issue	Role for care giver
1	0–3	Physiological regulation	Smooth routines
2	3–6	Management of tension	Sensitive, cooperative interaction
3	6–12	Establishing an effective attachment relationship	Responsive availability
4	12–18	Exploration and mastery	Secure base
5	18–30	Individuation (autonomy)	Firm support
6	30–54	Management of impluses, sex-role identification, peer relations	Clear roles and values, flexible self-control

Source: Sroufe, 1979.

begin to expect more mature behavior from the child, and those expectations help encourage the very behaviors that the parents deem appropriate.

Just as cognitive advances influence social and emotional development, so the reverse is also true. The way that a preschooler interacts with and feels about other people can greatly affect opportunities for cognitive stimulation and growth. A good example can be seen in peer relationships. Children learn a great deal about the world from one another, making the peer group an important source of knowledge. Moreover, interactions among peers also afford extensive opportunities for preschoolers to practice language and other cognitive skills.

All these examples underscore the intimate connections between different aspects of development. When we see a change in a child's way of thinking and reasoning, we usually see a parallel change in the youngster's social interactions. For instance, you learned in Chapter 10 that preschoolers begin acquiring abstract representations of the sequences involved in accomplishing various goals (such as going to a birthday party or making a telephone call). These abstract representations, called scripts, are an important part of cognitive development. In a parallel fashion preschoolers also develop abstract representations of themselves in relation to others. More specifically, they acquire expectations about how others are likely to respond to them when they engage in various behaviors (such as asking another child to play or requesting help from a parent).

Bowlby refers to these social representations as inner working models. Countless other parallels between cognitive and social development are mentioned throughout this book. The point is that the various aspects of human development do not proceed in isolation. Each is linked to the others; development is organized and coherent.

Continuity and Change

Individual development is likewise coherent. By the end of the preschool period we see individual adaptations that have evolved in a logical way from the adaptations that emerged during infancy and toddlerhood. These individual adaptations, or patterns of personality, are intimately related to the care-giving system in which the child has been raised. The extent to which temperament shapes parent-child interactions is difficult to gauge. By the time behavioral differences in children become stable, the youngsters have long since had numerous social experiences that could be influencing the observed behavioral patterns. Thus, by the preschool period temperament and experience, whatever their respective roles, have both become incorporated into the total child.

Continuity in development proceeds beyond the preschool period. For instance, evidence now suggests a link between the child's self-control as a preschooler and the same child's self-control at ages 7, 11, 14, and 18 (Block, 1987). For girls, the correlation between self-control at age 4 and self-control 10 years later is particularly strong. Researchers have even been able to predict the likelihood of teenage drug abuse from earlier measures of self-control versus impulsiveness (Jack Block, personal communication). In a similar vein psychologist Walter Mischel has found that measures of a 5-year-old's ability to delay gratification can be used to predict related aspects of behavior at 12 years of age (Mischel, 1983). Complex issues are involved in conducting such longitudinal studies. Often the researchers must look at very different behaviors over time, behaviors appropriate to the child's developmental level and the particular situation to which the child is responding (Sroufe, 1987). Nevertheless, as developmental research becomes more conceptually sophisticated, increasing evidence of a marked coherence to human personality is emerging. Children are not chalkboards to be erased and written on anew. Current development unfolds in a logical fashion from what has gone before.

Three Children as Preschoolers

Both continuity and change are apparent in the lives of all three of our children. As far as fundamental change is concerned, all three are dramatically different from the toddlers we met in Part III. All are now using language fluently; all are now thinking and reasoning on a different level than they did just a few years ago. Socially they have all entered the world of peers, and all can be seen engaging in the rich fantasy play of the preschooler. But again we see each child as an individual. Some of the things that happen to Meryl are not likely to happen to Mikey or Malcolm and vice versa. Each of the three children is a coherent person. Let's review the various factors that help make them who they are.

Mikey is tackling the developmental issues of the preschool period with ease. He is a capable, self-reliant child who shows all the signs of readiness for school. He is interested in cognitive activities and is responsive to his preschool teachers. At the same time he has moved smoothly into the world of peers, becoming a peer leader who is greatly liked by others.

But despite all these positive developments, Mikey may encounter some problems. Because he is such a bright, sensitive, perceptive child, he is vulnerable to internalizing the conflicts between his mother and father, which are now intensifying. The role of peacemaker we see him playing is not really a new one for Mikey. Earlier Christine and Frank used Mikey's behavior as an excuse to become distracted from their differences. Now Mikey deliberately distracts them from their arguments with his words and antics. While his awareness of interpersonal tension is impressive in a child this age, it is also worrisome. Mikey is too young to be mediating conflicts between others, especially between his parents. He is essentially assuming responsibility for his parents' needs rather than the other way around. This role reversal is a burden for any child (Minuchin, in press). Unless the marital conflicts are resolved, Mikey may face some difficulties ahead.

When we last saw Malcolm, the active, precocious toddler had become a lively and engaging preschooler. Malcolm is curious, confident, full of energy and good humor. His language and thinking skills are well developed when he enters kindergarten. Being big for his age and very outgoing, Malcolm quickly makes friends in his classroom.

At home Malcolm's social environment continues to be warm and supportive while still providing him with clear-cut standards of behavior. His mother, father, and grandmother nicely illustrate Baumrind's authoritative parenting: high expectations and firm limits combined with a great deal of love. Their handling of the incident on the playground is a case in point. DeeDee, John, and Momma Jo cherish Malcolm, including his great exuberance. Behavior that to others might seem slightly hyperactive is to them an indication of his simply being full of pep. Yet they do not take Malcolm's physical aggression lightly. They demand of him more self-control and concern for other people. In a family less able to handle Malcolm and less willing to go to bat for him, this incident could have been a negative turning point. But instead, Malcolm's parents take the event in stride and turn it into a valuable learning experience for him. We can imagine Malcolm in the future striving to heed what his parents have said by resolving peer conflicts more peacefully. If the Williams family continues to be this supportive of Malcolm's development, we would expect him to continue to flourish as he enters middle childhood, a time that poses special challenges for urban, minority-group children.

The preschool period for Meryl, as we have said, marks a significant turnaround. She is showing more independence and self-management. When functioning at her best (as in the classroom episode with Amy), she seems every bit as competent as Mikey and Malcolm. More than likely this notable improvement is due in large part to Meryl's more stable and responsive home environment. In offering Karen his love and support, Joe Turner has helped her to become a more effective mother. Now potentially stressful situations with Meryl seem more benign to Karen. She can respond to Meryl more firmly and consistently, following the model that Joe provides. Joe has also made a direct contribution to Meryl's improvements by

handling her in an affectionate but authoritative way. In these new circumstances Meryl has become more cooperative, self-reliant, and confident about herself. She is breaking away from the overly passive, weak, and dependent profile often found in children with a history of anxious-resistant attachment.

We cannot say that Meryl is suddenly an entirely different person, however. Her new self and her past one show clear continuities. While perhaps no longer a "difficult" child, she is still initially hesitant with peers; she is still reluctant to try new things; and transitions continue to be hard for her. Under stress she may revert to her earlier patterns, but given time she can adapt well to new situations. As with our two other children, we can be optimistic about Meryl's ultimate adjustment to school.

Our three cases are, of course, fictionalized, and they are written in a way that simplifies reality somewhat. Nonetheless, the coherence we describe in each case is supported by an emerging body of research.

Part Five

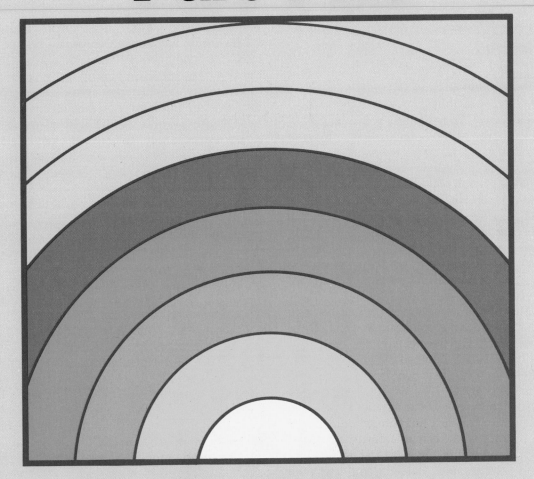

Middle Childhood

Three Children in Middle Childhood

Malcolm Williams

"Here are the arithmetic tests you took yesterday," announced Mrs. Singleton to her class of fourth graders. "Four of you scored 90 or above: Gretchen, Andrea, Kevin, and Malcolm." Malcolm felt a glow of pride as the teacher handed him his paper. He sneaked a look at Tammy Wilson, who sat diagonally in front of him. She had been watching Malcolm, but she quickly turned away as soon as he glanced in her direction. She stared down at the paper on her desk, and her mouth broke into a smile. Two large dimples appeared on either side of her face. Malcolm quickly turned back to his own paper. He wanted to look again at Tammy, but he didn't dare. His friends would tease him to death if they knew he liked her.

The rest of the afternoon dragged endlessly for Malcolm. By 3:02 he was in his coat and hurrying down the stairs, trying as best he could not to break the "no running" rule. Down the corridor, past the cafeteria, turn right by the main bulletin board; the short trek to freedom seemed interminable. Malcolm could feel the cool March air rushing in through the open door. The breeze was like a shot of adrenaline to him. Veering around the other children he raced out the door and down the path, his math test flapping in his tightly closed fist.

"Hey, Malcolm, wanna shoot some baskets?" shouted Andy, a neighborhood friend in Mr. Denning's class.

"I gotta get home!" yelled Malcolm over his shoulder, never slowing his pace.

Despite Malcolm's excitement at getting a good grade on the test, doing well in school was not really new for him. Malcolm could be an excellent student when he applied himself. He was nowhere near as diligent as his sister Theresa, but his quick mind and enthusiasm for learning earned the praise of his teachers. "If he would just channel more of that energy into his school work," Mrs. Singleton told DeeDee, "Malcolm would routinely be near the top of the class." But channeling his energies into any one thing for long didn't come easily to Malcolm. He was a child with as many interests as there were hours in the day. Collections of everything imaginable cluttered his untidy room. It seemed that every week he was announcing something else he wanted to do when he grew up. All the members of his family took great pleasure in Malcolm's endless plans and projects. They were convinced that this child, with his buoyant high spirits, was a very special one.

"Momma Jo!" called out Malcolm loudly, as he ran up the front steps two at a time, still clutching his arthmetic test. "Momma Jo!"

"What is it?" Momma Jo asked. "What's got you so near burstin'?"

"Look!" said Malcolm excitedly, stopping at last to catch his breath, and he extended the precious, now crumpled piece of paper to his grandmother.

"Well, will you look at that! No wonder you're so proud of yourself."

"It was one of the best grades in the whole class!" Malcolm added.

"I wouldn't expect any less from such a bright chil' as you," Momma Jo answered. "Now come on here into the kitchen and tell me all about it. Your momma and daddy are gonna be so proud of you when they get home!"

The next two years of Malcolm's life seemed to pass quickly. In the sixth grade he was still doing well at school, though concentration remained a problem he constantly had to work on. Malcolm also continued to be popular with his classmates. Because he was filled with enthusiastic schemes for new ways of having fun, other children admired him and often followed his lead. Malcolm's best friends were three other boys from his neighborhood: Andy,

Leon, and Curtis. After school "the gang of four," as Theresa called them, would usually head for the park. Or, if the weather was bad, they would often congregate in Malcolm's room to play with his model trains. DeeDee marveled at how grown up the boys were becoming. Beginning this year they had started to ride the bus across town by themselves in order to look through the shelves of their favorite hobby shop. Given how independent Malcolm normally was, it seemed strange when he began to ask his father if he could catch a ride to school in the morning on his father's way to work. Malcolm himself was a little embarrassed by this new arrangement. He didn't want the other kids to think he was a baby, coming to school with his daddy. But he wanted to avoid tangling with a group of older boys who hung out near the video arcade. They had been hassling him on the way to school for weeks now. Malcolm was not about to tell his parents what the problem was. If his father tried to interfere, it would only make things worse.

One morning Malcolm decided to take his Swiss army knife with him to school—just for protection in case he met the older boys on his way home. On the playground he slipped the bright red pocket knife out of his jacket and secretly showed it to Andy. "Let 'em mess with me," he said with false bravado. "I know how to take care of myself!"

"What ya got?" asked Derek Sanders as he came up behind Malcolm and Andy and peered over their shoulders. "Hey, Malcolm, you're not supposed to have a knife in school. You're gonna get in trouble!"

"It's just for self-defense, turkey," Malcolm answered. "Everybody has a right to self-defense. It's in the Constitution. Come on, Andy. Let's go. Derek's being a jerk."

"Will you speak more slowly, Malcolm? I can't understand what you're saying." John Williams sat on the edge of a desk at the post office, listening into the phone.

"It was just for self-defense, Dad. Honest it was. To show those gang kids I'm not afraid of them. Only Derek *ratted* on me. He told Mrs. Singleton. I can't believe he did that! No one ever rats. I never would. Andy never would.

You just don't rat on guys!" Malcolm's voice was high-pitched and very emotional. He sounded on the verge of tears.

"OK, Malcolm, OK. I get the picture. Now put your principal back on the phone so I can set up a meeting with him. We'll talk more about this when I get to the school."

"Do you know why taking the knife to school was wrong?" DeeDee asked, as she and Malcolm sat at the kitchen table that afternoon.

"'Cause it's against the rules," Malcolm answered, his head hanging, his voice soft and contrite.

"And why is it against the rules?"

"'Cause people could get hurt."

"*You* could have gotten hurt; do you know that?"

"Yes."

"That's why your daddy isn't giving you back that knife until he knows you can be more responsible with it. You're lucky Mr. Esquallo understood the situation and let you off as lightly as he did."

"I don't feel lucky," Malcolm said. "I hate Derek. I hate all white people. You can't trust 'em."

DeeDee put a hand on Malcolm's shoulder and looked at him for a while. "Let me ask you something," she said softly. "What color were the boys who've been hassling you?"

"Black," answered Malcolm, fingering a small hole in the knee of his jeans.

"So you don't put down all black people just because those boys are bad. Why do you put down all white people because of Derek?"

"Because whites have been puttin' down black people for hundreds of years," Malcolm answered.

"That may be so," said DeeDee. "But it doesn't mean that *all* white people act that way. You've got to judge people by what they're like inside, not just by their color."

"I guess so," said Malcolm grudgingly, reaching for his glass of milk. "But you know, Momma, when a white guy's a jerk, he's the biggest jerk of all."

DeeDee smiled and shook her head. "Some lessons are learned in small steps," she thought to herself.

Mikey Gordon

"Would you read the next page for us please, Mikey," Mrs. Clayton asked.

Mikey swung his gaze back from the window as soon as he heard his name. He looked confused, then embarrassed. "Jimmy . . . ran . . . with the . . . kite," he began hesitantly.

"Mikey, Katie just read that part," Mrs. Clayton corrected gently, as the other children in the reading group started to giggle. "Begin at the top of the next page."

Mikey flushed and fumbled to turn the page. Everyone's eyes were on him. What's wrong with this child? Mrs. Clayton wondered as she showed Mikey where to start. On days like this he hardly seemed the same little boy who eight months ago was one of the best readers in her second grade class. Mrs. Clayton was also concerned about Mikey's relations with his classmates. He no longer seemed the leader that he used to be. On the playground he was usually content to follow what the other boys suggested. "I'm a little worried about Mikey," Mrs. Clayton told Christine at a parent-teacher conference toward the end of the school year. "Sometimes he's his old fun-loving self. But at other times he seems moody, even a bit lost. Is everything OK at home?"

"Things are fine at home," Christine answered all too quickly. But she knew in her heart that her marriage was going from bad to worse and that Mikey was a barometer of the conflict. Frank now stayed out late two or three nights a week. When he came home, he had always been drinking heavily, and when he was drunk, he was also surly. Christine had to treat him gingerly for fear of being struck. One day in March Frank's boss had called at lunchtime to ask where Frank was. Christine was taken aback and didn't know what to answer. Finally, she had blurted out some vague story about a possible doctor's appointment. She sensed that Frank's boss knew she was lying. That night when she asked Frank where he had been, he said it was none of her damn business. "But you'll lose your job," Christine had shouted. "*That's* my business." Frank laughed cynically and looked at her with contempt. "What the hell's the difference?" he asked angrily. "You don't need my paycheck. You're doing just fine

at your high 'n mighty shop!"

In the end Frank and Christine rarely talked except to argue. The best they could do was to try to ignore each other. Mikey, sensing the widening rift between his parents, began to fill the tense silences with hilarious imitations of some of the teachers at his school. He also began praising one parent to the other. When he was with his mother, he would talk excitedly about what he had done with his father; when he was with his father, he talked in glowing terms about his mom. But even these poignant efforts had no effect on Christine and Frank. The gap between them had become a canyon. There was no bridging it now.

The voices first came to Mikey as if in a dream. His parents were arguing, yelling angrily at each other. The voices grew louder and more filled with heated emotion. Eight-year-old Mikey could feel himself drawn from sleep into consciousness. He lay in bed with his eyes wide open. The voices were even clearer now, their tone even sharper. This was not a dream. Mikey got out of bed and pulled his door open. There sat his two sisters huddled in their nightgowns at the top of the stairs. Becky and Janie glanced at Mikey and then looked back down the stairs. Mikey walked over and squatted beside them. "They're going to kill each other this time," Becky whispered in her 14-year-old wisdom. "This is really a bad one."

The trouble had started hours earlier, as Frank sat drinking with four of his buddies at the Riverside Tavern. Matt had made a comment about men who couldn't "handle" their wives. The others had laughed and begun ribbing Frank. What was it like being married to such a women's libber George wanted to know. When Frank protested, Pete pointed out that Christine had him "well trained." Then Phil began to speculate about all those trips that Christine had been taking to New York. "It's pretty swinging down there, ya know," he went on relentlessly, "even if most of the guys are really more like girls." By the time Frank left he was very drunk and very humiliated. As soon as he walked through the door, he let the anger spill out.

"What do you want me to *do*?" Christine pleaded, knowing that she shouldn't try to reason with him when he was in this condition.

"Be the wife that you're supposed to be, damn it! Don't think I don't know what goes on in New York."

"Frank, that's crazy. I rush back home the same day just to try to keep you happy."

"Don't call me crazy!" Frank shouted, and he pushed her against the wall.

"That's it! I've had it!" Christine shouted back and she ran to the hall and started up the stairs. As she looked up, she was startled to see her three children silently watching, all with strangely calm expressions on their faces. "Get your coats," she instructed sharply. "And be quick about it! We're going to Grandma's." Two weeks later Christine filed for divorce.

"So how's it been goin' at home?" Frank Gordon asked his son as the two settled into a booth at Burger King.

"OK, I guess," said Mikey unenthusiastically. It had been almost a year now since the separation, and divorce proceedings were well underway. The time had been a difficult one for Christine and the three children. She had rented a small house near her mother's, and everyone despised the cramped quarters. The girls constantly complained that the bedroom they shared was too small even for a pair of ants. There was just no privacy, they said. Christine had given the second bedroom to Mikey, leaving herself with a fold-out couch in the living room to sleep on. Being so crowded only intensified the stress of a difficult situation. Then the girls began to complain that their father was always taking Mikey on weekend outings (fishing trips, baseball games, camping excursions) that didn't include them. When Christine insisted that Frank treat the children more fairly, he relented and began asking the girls along. But the girls then said they weren't interested in "a bunch of slimy fish" or living in a tent where you couldn't even plug in your hair dryer. In exasperation Christine let them go their own ways. After all they were 15 and 13 now. The girls spent most of their free time with their friends, and their sense of being female seemed to heighten with every passing month. Both were very clothes conscious and even seventh-grade Janie was starting to wear makeup when she went to parties.

But it was Mikey who gave Christine the greatest worry. Some days he seemed lethargic and depressed. When she tried to talk to him about the divorce, he would pick at his fingernails and mutter one-word responses. His school work also continuted to suffer, just as it had before the separation. He had trouble paying attention in class, and many mornings he insisted that he couldn't go to school because he had a bad stomach ache. It was only by promising to have him tutored in the summer that Christine prevented Mikey from repeating the third grade. Finally, toward the end of the summer, things seemed to improve a little. Mikey was happier as he looked forward to a two-week vacation he and his father were going to take in Maine. He smiled more often and spent less time alone in his room. Despite this more cheerful exterior, however, worries lay just beneath the surface. Mikey couldn't shake the idea that somehow *he* was to blame for the divorce. He kept thinking that in some way he had let his parents down. His secret dream was that one day they would get back together.

"Hey, what's up? You're a million miles away." Frank's voice, slightly muffled as he chewed his Whopper, interrupted his son's thoughts. "We're still goin' fishin', aren't we?"

"Sure," said Mikey, brightening a little.

"Good. 'Cause there's someone I'm gonna bring along. Someone I want you to meet. Her name's Nancy and she works in the office at the construction company. You'll like her. She's OK." Mikey looked blankly at his father, as if he understood the words but not their meaning.

"Hey, aren't you gonna eat the rest of those fries?" Frank asked, reaching over to help himself to one.

Meryl Polonius Turner

This summer I got a new brother. He cries a lot. Mommy says all babies cry. Sometimes I make a face and he stops crying. When he gets bigger I'll show him my toys. We can play together. I like having a brother most of the time.

"Why that's *very* good!" Karen exclaimed after reading the story that Meryl had written during her first day in third grade. "And look, you've done a picture of the whole family. There you are holding Daddy's hand, and here I am holding little Joey. You even drew my frowzy blue bedroom slippers. Are they really that big and blue?"

"They're pretty big, Mommy," Meryl said, considering the picture soberly.

"Well, we'll just have to hang this right up on the refrigerator where everyone can see it!"

"You can take down the one with the pussy willows to make room," Meryl suggested. "That one's old and I don't like it that much any more. I can draw a lot better now."

Karen was astounded at how much better Meryl did everything these days. Around the house Meryl was a real little helper. She would stand by ready to pass the soap and towel when Karen was giving Joey his bath. She meticulously set the table for dinner, making sure the silverware was neatly aligned. Meryl's second grade teacher had called her a "joy to have in the class." Although Meryl was not the brightest of her pupils, she worked hard, listened carefully, and cooperated well with others. Karen could hardly believe this was the same little girl who used to throw tantrums that could inspire awe in even the most seasoned of parents.

But looking beneath the surface, Karen could see threads from Meryl's past. Meryl was still shy when it came to strangers and new situations. Take the time that Joe had tried to teach her to ride a bicycle. Meryl had just turned 6 and was starting first grade. Other children her age were riding two-wheelers, and Joe knew that Meryl wanted to learn how. But she staunchly refused to let him remove the training wheels from her bike. "I'll fall off," she insisted. "I *know* I'll fall off!" In the weeks that followed Meryl would study other children on their bikes. She watched them pedal, mount and dismount, turn corners and circles. Then one day shortly before Christmas she suddenly announced to Joe: "I'm ready to ride that bike now." Joe removed the training wheels, and Meryl gingerly climbed on. "Don't let go," she instructed. "You promise?" Joe assured her he would run along right beside her, holding the seat until she was ready to solo. Within a week she was riding with confidence, as if she had been doing it for years. The following spring

she tried roller skating. At first she would inch her way from tree to fence post, clutching onto anything that could give her support. But soon she was skating with remarkable skill, even taking the cracks and bumps in stride. It seemed as if every month now she was ready to try something new.

But what pleased Karen the most was Meryl's friendship with Amy. The two girls played together every chance they got. Amy would call Meryl on Saturday morning and they would make plans for the weekend:

"Why don't you come over here and we can play in the pool. My dad's fixing it up today."

"OK. I'll bring my Barbie doll and her beach stuff." Later that day the two would be back at Meryl's, asking if Amy could stay for dinner. Soon they would be calling Amy's mother to ask if Amy could stay overnight. Because both girls had blonde hair, strangers sometimes asked them if they were sisters. "No," Meryl and Amy giggled, putting an arm around each other's shoulder. "We're just *best* friends."

The summer after Meryl finished fourth grade, the Turner family moved into a new house. Meryl was delighted with her new room. She and Amy spent hours picking out a new bedspread and curtains and deciding what color to paint the walls. But Meryl's "most favorite" part of the house was the area under the back deck. It was high enough for a 10-year-old to stand up in but much too low for an adult. Meryl and Amy called it their "apartment." They hung old blankets from the deck to form makeshift walls, and they posted a sign that said in large letters: "PRIVATE. KEEP OUT!" When 2-year-old Joey dared to peek in, the girls abruptly shooed him away despite his tears and protests. That summer everything had seemed perfect to Karen. Two beautiful children, a house of their own—finally some of the good things in life. Neither she nor Joe realized what a heavy strain a large mortgage could place on their marriage and family.

"Meryl, honey, are you going to stay in *all* Saturday? It's so beautiful out. Why don't you call Amy and see what she's up to?" The day was truly a beautiful one, particularly warm and sunny for November.

Meryl briefly looked up from the picture she was drawing of a mother dog and her puppies.

"Amy's probably playing with that stupid Jeannie Lewis who moved in next door to her," Meryl said jealously. "She's always trying to butt in and I don't like her much. She's not very nice."

"Well, why don't you ride your bike over there and see if all three of you can't play together," Karen persisted. She was concerned that Meryl had been spending too much time alone lately. Often she stayed in her room for hours, sprawled on the floor with her crayons spread around her, slowly and carefully drawing. Puppies with their mothers was a frequently repeated theme. But what worried Karen most was the way that her daughter was talking right now. She was disturbed to see the old negative, insecure Meryl emerging once again.

"I'm busy," answered Meryl, turning back to her drawing and picking up a brown crayon. "And anyway," she added with a touch of bitterness, "who needs them."

Karen knew her daughter too well to think this change had sprung from nowhere. Whenever there were problems that touched on Meryl's life, she tended to withdraw. Karen had seen this reaction when Meryl's third grade teacher turned out to be stern and critical. Meryl had become very dejected but refused to talk about it. Finally, Karen coaxed the problem from her, and Joe had solved it by insisting that Meryl be transferred to another class, the same class Amy was in. This time the old withdrawal and insecurity were reoccurring for a different reason. The strain of a high mortgage was taking its toll on Joe and Karen. Their credit cards were overdrawn. The bills were piling up. Even going to the supermarket had become an ordeal for them because they agonized over everything they bought. Did they really need that bag of cookies? Could they get Meryl to eat that no-name brand of peanut butter? One evening Joe exploded because Karen had splurged on a sirloin steak for dinner.

"I was only trying to do something a little special," Karen protested, tears in her eyes.

"Will you stop that crying," Joe had shouted. "I'm sick and tired of being the only adult around here. Let's just sell this damn house! I'm fed up with living this way."

Meryl, who was sitting at the kitchen table, visibly shrank. Later she told her mother she didn't feel good, and she shut herself in her room. It was then that Karen decided that she and Joe couldn't go on the way they were. Gradually, they began to talk about the problem in a more rational way. They decided that they really loved the house and wanted to keep it. The best solution would be for Karen to find a job. After some thought Karen hit on the idea of getting a real estate license and going to work with her mother. The idea buoyed her spirits, and she threw herself into studying for the exam. It was a happy day the following April when she took her first clients house hunting. But the best part of the story in Karen's eyes was the change she could see in Meryl. Meryl was thrilled with her mother's new "business." She was constantly asking questions about the office, poring through Karen's book of listings, and saying which houses she thought were the prettiest. Meryl's friendship with Amy was also rekindled and became stronger than ever. Meryl was even confident enough to allow Jeannie along on some of their weekend bike hikes.

"It's only fair," Meryl told her mother. "Jeannie's new in school and she doesn't have any best friends."

Karen smiled and brushed back a lock of Meryl's hair. She was pleased with the way her daughter was growing in so many ways.

12

Cognitive Development in Middle Childhood

The following three jokes are taken from a study of children's humor conducted by Paul McGhee (1976). If they don't strike you as hilariously funny, you are out of step with youngsters in the middle years of childhood.

Mr. Jones went to a restaurant and ordered a whole pizza for dinner. When the waiter asked if he wanted it cut into six or eight pieces, Mr. Jones said: "You'd better make it six. I could never eat eight!"

"Please stay out of the house today," Susie's mother said. "I have too much work to do." "Okay," replied Susie as she walked to the stairs. "Where do you think you're going?" her mother asked. "Well," said Susie, "if I can't stay in the house, I'll just play in my room instead."

Mr. Barley teaches first grade. One day his class was talking about religion, so Mr. Barley asked how many of the children were Catholic. When Bobby didn't raise his hand, the teacher said, "Why Bobby, I thought you were Catholic too." "Oh no," said Bobby. "I'm not Catholic; I'm American."

The typical 8- or 9-year-old finds these jokes very funny. The first one involves a misunderstanding about conservation, a concept we discussed in Chapter 10. Mr. Jones apparently thinks that the amount of pizza increases if it is cut into more slices. The other two jokes involve misunderstandings about classification. Susie is confused over the relationship between the subordinate concept of room and the larger concept of house; Bobby doesn't realize that he can simultaneously be classified as both a Catholic *and* an American. Each of these errors in reasoning is conquered during middle childhood, which is why children this age find these jokes so funny: The punch lines deal with skills that 8- and 9-year-olds have recently acquired. Preschoolers, in contrast, do not find these jokes funny because they don't understand that Mr. Jones, Susie, and Bobby have committed errors in reasoning. Adults don't find them very funny because they involve concepts mastered long ago. For jokes to be funny they must involve a certain amount of cognitive effort.

The riddles that children tell show a similar pattern of humor stemming from the exercise of newly mastered skills. Here is a riddle that might be told by an 8- or 9-year-old:

> *Question:* Why should you always wear a watch in the desert?
> *Answer:*   Because a watch has springs in it.

Preschoolers would not understand this riddle because it requires that they simultaneously consider two meanings of the word "spring." Remember from Chapter 10 that preschool thought is characterized by centration, the tendency to focus on only one piece of information at a time. Because preschoolers do not "get" this joke, most of them would have trouble retelling it. A 5-year-old might repeat the joke this way:

> *Question:* Why should you always wear a watch in the desert?
> *Answer:*   Because the desert gets hot.

Even when it is told correctly, adults seldom laugh at a riddle like this one because they mastered the riddle format and the ambiguity of double meanings long ago. Such riddles no longer present the element of surprise or cleverness to adults that they do to elementary-school children.

Why between the ages of 5 and 8 does telling jokes and riddles take on such fascination? We might argue it is because a child this age is more exposed to jokes and riddles, especially through interactions with peers. This is a social learning explanation of joke telling: The behavior is acquired largely through observation of others. Alternatively, we might argue that the emergence of joke telling marks an important shift in the child's cognitive development. Youngsters this age acquire the cognitive skills needed to understand such humor, and so they take great pleasure in exercising these new-found abilities. This is a Piagetian explanation. A third possibility is that between the ages of 5 and 8 all the various skills needed to understand and tell jokes have become practiced and refined enough for the child to integrate them into an effective joke-telling sys-

In middle childhood, children become interested and skilled in telling jokes. (*Lynn Johnson/Black Star.*)

tem. This is an information-processing explanation. In searching for the roots of cognitive changes during middle childhood, we will use a combination of all three of these approaches.

Piaget saw the age of 7 as a major cognitive turning point. At around this age, he argued, children make the important transition from the so-called preoperational subperiod to the more advanced concrete operational one. This proposed transition has been the focus of challenges to Piaget's theory (see Gelman and Baillargeon, 1983). Many theories of cognitive development now see a major developmental reorganization at the age of about 4, rather than several years later (Bickhard, 1978; Fischer and Bullock, 1984). We presented this more modern viewpoint in Chapter 10, where we talked about the early precursors of many concrete operational skills. This chapter, continuing that perspective, examines how the major cognitive changes occurring during the elementary-school years involve refinements in and more widespread use of skills that were present in primitive form during early childhood. The picture we present differs from the more traditional Piagetian view that middle childhood marks the emergence of an entirely new system of logic.

Despite debates over the question of when certain cognitive skills begin to appear, developmentalists generally agree that youngsters in middle childhood function at a more advanced level than preschoolers do. For instance, elementary-school children have a greatly enhanced ability to think systematically using multiple pieces of information. In other words, children this age exhibit a marked decline in centration compared with preschoolers. This decline is associated with the emergence of skills for logically interrelating information. In addition, youngsters in middle childhood become much more capable of perceiving underlying reality despite superficial appearance (Flavell, 1985). This advance in overcoming the appearance/reality problem helps them to think far more maturely about transformations, such as the one that occurs when water is poured from a short, wide container into a tall, thin one. The child is now able to see that no real change in quantity has occurred despite a change in the height to which the water rises. This new understanding involves a grasp of **reversibility,** the realization that if the water were poured back

Youngsters in middle childhood understand the distinction between appearance and reality. When the distinction is puzzling, as in the apparent bending of the straw in this picture caused by the refraction of light, it causes increased interest and exploration. (*George Goodwin/Monkmeyer Press.*)

into the first container it would look just the same as before. Finally, youngsters in middle childhood come to think much more effectively about their own knowledge and thought processes. This capacity to think about thinking is called **metacognition.** Needless to say, metacognition greatly increases the ability to plan effective problem-solving strategies.

Elementary-school children are still constrained by some cognitive limitations, however. First, they lack the broad base of knowledge that adults possess. This absence of information sometimes makes their reasoning seem immature. For instance, the summer that Mikey turned 10, he and his friends decided that they would build a raft out of pieces of Styrofoam held together by string and large thumbtacks. The raft, of course, fell to pieces as soon as the boys launched it in a nearby stream, much to their disappointment. Second, elementary-school children have only recently acquired some of their thinking skills and have had relatively little chance to practice them. As a result they sometimes have trouble using a skill they possess as part of a larger problem-solving system. For instance, one day when they were 8 years old, Meryl and her friend Amy got into an argument over whether a large chocolate rabbit that Amy had received for Easter was more than a foot high. The girls searched for a ruler, but couldn't find one. All the while a teddy bear that Amy knew to be 12 inches tall lay on a corner of her bed. Using transitive inference to settle the debate simply didn't occur to either child, even though they both understood the basics of this reasoning process. Finally, limitations exist on elementary-school children's thinking in that they cannot reason maturely about abstract and hypothetical problems. Their reasoning tends to be confined to the concrete here and now. For example, if 9-year-old Malcolm were presented with the hypothetical problem "What would you do if your train set wouldn't run one day?" he could not construct a comprehensive picture of all the things that *might* go wrong and then systematically set out to test each one, both alone and in various combinations. Such sophisticated and abstract reasoning does not emerge until adolescence.

As you read this chapter, you will learn much more about both the cognitive advances and limitations of middle childhood. In the first section we describe three major areas of cognitive development: concepts of conservation, classification skills, and memory abilities. In each case you will see how capacities that emerged during the preschool period set the stage for later, more mature accomplishments. Next we turn to factors that can facilitate or inhibit cognitive development during middle childhood. Here we highlight the potential role of peers and adults in promoting cognitive growth. Finally, we discuss individual differences in cognitive functioning, especially as measured by IQ tests. Intelligence, like many other individual differences, can best be viewed as arising from an interaction of genes and environment.

MAJOR COGNITIVE DEVELOPMENTS OF MIDDLE CHILDHOOD

Concepts of Conservation

Concepts of conservation were introduced in Chapter 10, where we talked about some of the difficulties preschoolers have in reasoning about quantities. Here we will explore the topic in more detail, focusing on how an understanding of conservation develops during middle childhood and how this understanding is related to other cognitive skills. Remember that an understanding of conservation involves the knowledge that some quantity remains unchanged despite certain transformations carried out on it. A volume of water, for instance, remains the same despite being poured into containers of different shapes and sizes. During middle childhood most youngsters come to understand conservation of physical quantities such as number, length, liquid volume, area, and mass. Figure 12.1 shows how researchers assess children's knowledge of some of these conservation concepts.

It is hard to overestimate the importance of acquiring conservation concepts. Try to imagine what it would be like not to understand that quantities like number and weight are permanent unless changed through addition or subtraction. For example, it would be meaningless to ask for a pound of cheese at the store if you didn't realize the amount would stay the same whether left in a chunk, cut into slices, or melted to make a sauce. An understanding of conservation is clearly essential to our sense of a relatively stable world.

The development of conservation has been studied intensely during the past 20 years. It is the most frequently used marker of the transition from the preoperational subperiod in Piaget's theory to the concrete operational subperiod. Thus, it has been a major focus for those who support Piaget's account of cognitive development. It has also been of interest to those who offer alternatives to Piaget's view. For instance, both neo-Piagetians and information-processing researchers have studied conservation and offered their own theories about its development. We will consider some of these alternative viewpoints a little later in this chapter.

MASTERING CONSERVATION: AN OVERVIEW

To provide a general picture of the development of conservation, let's look at how youngsters from 4 to 8 acquire an understanding of conservation of liquid volume. You may recall from Chapter 10 that in the

A

B

1. Conservation of Number
Two rows of chips are placed in one-to-one correspondence. The child admits their equality.

One of the rows is stretched out. The child is asked whether each row still has the same number.

Figure 12.1
Assessment of Conservation
Researchers use tasks such as the ones shown here to assess children's understanding of conservation during middle childhood.

A

B

2. Conservation of Length
Two sticks are presented to the child. He or she admits their equality.

One of the sticks is moved to the right. The child is asked whether they are still the same length.

A

B

3. Conservation of Area
The child and the experimenter both have identical sheets of cardboard. The experimenter places wooden blocks on these in identical positions. The child is asked whether each cardboard has the same amount of space remaining.

The experimenter scatters the blocks on one of the cardboard sheets. The child is asked the same question.

A

B

4. Conservation of Substance
The experimenter presents two identical clay balls. The child admits that they have equal amounts of clay.

One of the balls is rolled out. The child is asked whether they still contain equal amounts.

A

B

5. Conservation of Volume
Two balls of clay are placed in two identical glasses with an equal amount of water. The child is asked whether they displace equal amounts of water.

The experimenter changes the shape of one of the balls and asks the child the same question.

standard study of this topic the researcher begins with two identical containers, each holding the same amount of water. The researcher makes sure that the child agrees the two quantities of water are equal. Then the water from one of the containers is poured into a third container, which is taller and thinner than the other two. The child is asked the critical question: "Which of the containers now has more water, or do they both still have the same?" In what Piaget called stage 1 of acquiring conservation (which includes virtually all 4-year-olds), children are "nonconservers." They judge the amount of liquid by the height to which it rises, thus declaring the taller, thinner container to have more. By the same token, if the water was next poured into a wide and shallow container, the stage 1 child would now judge it to have less. Note two things about this stage in the understanding of conservation: First, stage 1 children are limited by centration. They look only at the height of the water, failing to take width into account. Second, stage 1 children are using a consistent rule to judge the amount of liquid. Although this rule is wrong from an adult's point of view, nonconservers are perfectly happy with it. They are quite sure their answers are correct and have no motivation to change their thinking.

In what Piaget called stage 2 of acquiring conservation, children enter a transitional period. Regarding the concept of conservation of liquid volume, stage 2 typically spans the ages 5 to 6 years. Now youngsters are less decisive in answering questions about which container has more. They may first say that the taller one has more water, but then wonder if the second container doesn't have more because it is wider. They may also begin to notice the fact that if the "high" water is poured back into its original container, both amounts of water are once again equal. Thus children in transitional stage 2 seem to be displaying two underlying changes: First, they appear to be aware that their answers to the experimenter's questions may be wrong, and they seem motivated to find a consistent and correct basis for responding. Second, the cause of this awareness apparently is the ability to bring new information to bear on the problem. Children in stage 2 are no longer limited by centration on a single perceptual dimension. They can consider more than one dimension, at least sequentially (height, then width, then back to height again). For this reason they vacillate in making a decision. Stage 2 children are also able to use information about how the water changes over time, rather than merely considering how it looks at a particular moment. Here we see the increased information-handling capacity of the 5- to 6-year-old, which allows skills that emerged during the preschool years to be further developed and integrated into more complex problem-solving systems.

In Piaget's stage 3, mature conservation, children answer the experimenter's questions quickly, confidently, and correctly. Conservation of liquid volume is usually understood at about age 7, when youngsters frequently feel the answer is so simple and obvious that it is "dumb" to ask which container has more water. The experimenter may challenge them to justify their answer by asking, "How can both have the same when this one is so much higher?" To this, a stage 3 child might reply: "This one is higher, but it's narrower too; the other is shorter, but wider. So they're both the same." This kind of justification is called **compensation** because the child realizes that two dimensions have been affected, with an increase in one compensated for by a decrease in the other. Depending on how stage 3 children are questioned, they may offer other justifications too (Goodnow, 1973). Sometimes they appeal to reversibility by pointing out how the effects of the transformation could be undone (for example, by pouring the water back into the original container). Other times they focus on a **constant identity** ("It's still the same water") or on the lack of a relevant change—the so-called **nothing added or subtracted criterion** (Peill, 1975).

The ability to provide explanations of conservation marks a new kind of understanding that begins to be more common during middle childhood. This new kind of understanding is embodied in the notion of **necessary truth,** a concept that differs from another form of understanding called **contingent truth** (Campbell and Bickhard, 1986; Inhelder and Piaget, 1964; Moshman and Timmons, 1982). To illustrate these two kinds of knowledge, consider first how you answer the question "Is it raining out?" You would probably look out the window to see if you observe raindrops, or you might listen for the sound of rain falling on the roof. Your answer is contingent on information you gather through your senses; hence it is referred to as contingent truth. Notice that contingent truth is empirically based: You hear or see raindrops; therefore it is raining. Now suppose you are told that two groups of people are equal in number, and that one of the groups decides to form a long, single-file line, while the other forms a circle. You are then asked: "Which group now has more people, or are they both the same?" Even without counting the number of people, measuring how long the line is, or seeing the two groups for yourself, you know that they must still be equal because no one has been added or subtracted. Your knowledge in this case is a necessary truth, meaning it is a logical necessity.

Conservation of number is one example of a necessary truth that elementary-school children know. Notice how this understanding helps to free youngsters from the constraints of the appearance/reality problem we talked about in Chapter 10. Children can now look beyond superficial appearance (such as the length of a line of objects) and see the underlying factors that logically determine reality. During middle childhood such knowledge "by necessity" tends to be limited to concrete characteristics, such as number of people or volume of liquid. Children this age find it very hard to grasp the necessary truths of more abstract concepts. You'll see this in a later section, where we talk about classification.

Piaget argued that the same logic skills provide the basis for understanding all the concepts of conservation. Granted, some of these concepts are acquired before others, but Piaget believed this was due merely to the fact that children learn the specific characteristics of different kinds of quantities at different times. Table 12.1 shows the age at which 50 percent of the children tested succeeded at different types of conservation tasks. Because this table is based on a large number of different studies, many with different criteria for having attained conservation, a range of ages is reported for many of the types. Nevertheless, the table presents a fair picture of what we know about the order in which conservation concepts are mastered. For example, conservation of number is acquired relatively early, conservation of weight is intermediate, and conservation of displaced liquid volume is acquired relatively late.

Together the various concepts of conservation allow children to think logically about many quantitative issues. For instance, conservation concepts are prerequisites for performing well on many of the arithmetic problems given in elementary school. If you looked at elementary-school curriculums, you would discover that problems dealing with such issues as amount of liquid come after the age at which we would expect an understanding of the relevant conservation concept. In general, a close connection exists between the emergence of certain cognitive skills during middle childhood and the age at which societies begin formal schooling of youngsters.

ALTERNATIVES TO PIAGET'S THEORY

A number of developmentalists have offered modifications to Piaget's theory of conservation, and others have offered alternative views that

TABLE 12.1   Age Range When Most Children Begin to Pass Tests of Conservation

	Age							
	4	5	6	7	8	9	10	11
Number	▬▬▬▬▬							
Substance			▬▬▬▬▬▬▬▬▬▬					
Length		▬▬▬▬▬▬▬▬▬▬▬▬▬▬						
Continuous Quantity			▬▬▬▬▬▬▬▬					
Area				▬▬▬▬▬▬▬▬				
Weight					▬▬▬▬▬▬▬▬			
Liquid Volume							▬▬▬▬▬	

Source: Adapted from Gross, 1985.

differ substantially from Piaget's. Among the latter is information-processing theory. Remember that information-processing researchers seek to describe in detail the various steps involved in performing a cognitive task—from inputting sensory data, to performing various mental operations, to producing a solution or other form of output. As children mature, their methods of processing information, including their methods of processing problems of conservation, undergo change.

Figure 12.2 illustrates an information-processing approach to conservation using five rules (Siegler and Robinson, 1982). These rules underlie children's judgments about the effects that various transformations have on two groups of objects initially equal in number. The transformations include additions and subtractions as well as spatial rearrangements of items in a row (either spreading the items out or moving them closer together). Rule I underlies the typical performance of a preschooler. For spatial rearrangements, length is the basis for responding, and the row that is longer is said to have more. For small collections, the group added to is judged to have more, or the group subtracted from is judged to have fewer. Rule II differs from rule I because in transformations involving addition or subtraction, the group added to is judged to have more, while the group subtracted from is judged to have fewer regardless of the size of the collections involved. For small collections, rule III is the same as rule II. For large collections, if an addition or subtraction occurs, the group added to is judged as having more or the group subtracted from is judged as having fewer, but if a rearrangement transformation occurs, the longer row is judged as having more. Rule IV represents an empirical approach to both spatial rearrangements and additions/subtractions. Either judgment is based on counting the items after the transformation. This method of correctly solving conservation of number problems is not included in Piaget's theory. Notice that it involves contingent truth: The child counts the items in each group to decide which group has more. Rule V represents a more advanced approach to conservation, one based on necessary truth. Here the child understands that only when something

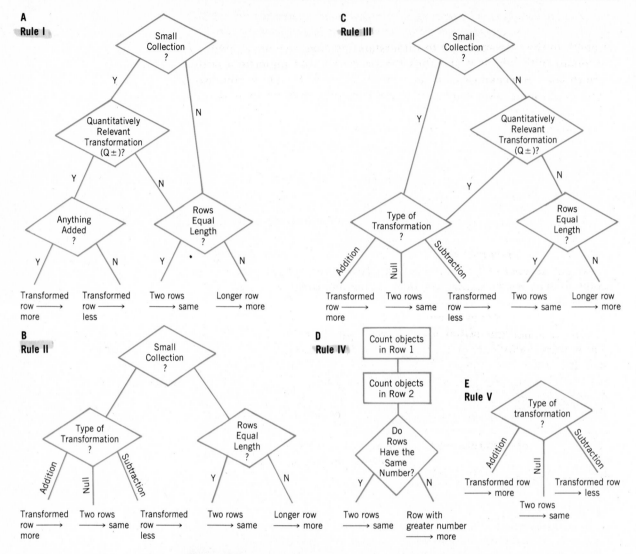

Figure 12.2
Rules for Number Conservation
These five rules describe the developmental changes in the acquisition of number conservation, which Siegler and Robinson describe as occurring between ages 3 and 9. Each diamond in the rule represents a question, and each path below the diamond, a possible answer.
Source: Siegler and Robinson, 1982

is added or taken away can a quantity change. The concept is grasped as a logical necessity. No longer must the youngster count the number of items to find out if they are different or the same.

To summarize this information-processing approach to the development of conservation, we can say that progress depends on modifying the rules by which judgments are made. The rules just presented apply to conservation of number tasks. In making judgments about other kinds of conservation (such as conservation of liquid volume or conservation of weight) the most mature approach is often that of rule V in Figure 12.2. While the intermediate rules frequently differ according to the type of conservation, a child's rate of development in acquiring the concept always depends on his or her progression through various rules. A strength to the rule approach to understanding cognitive development is the detail with which it specifies the processes that underlie a child's performance. A weakness is the lack of information about how youngsters construct new rules and then organize them into systems such as those we just described.

The rule approach to understanding cognitive development has been used extensively. In one study, for example, it was employed to explore how children develop solutions to addition and subtraction problems (Cooper, 1984). The children were presented with groups of objects that at first were either equal in number, differed by one, or differed by two. The experimenter then sometimes added an object to one of the groups or took an object away. The children were to determine which group had more or less after the transformation. The youngest children used what can be called a **primitive rule** for making their judgments. They ignored the initial number of items in each group and always said that the one added to had more, while the one subtracted from had fewer. (This corresponds to rule II in Figure 12.2.) Next the children acquired what can be called a **qualitative rule.** With this rule, the youngsters took into account whether the initial groups were equal or not, but if the two groups were initially unequal they ignored the magnitude of the difference. It was as if they encoded the arrays in purely qualitative terms: less than, equal to, or more than. This rule led to errors when the initial arrays differed by more than one. For instance, if one group had 5 and another had 7, and 1 more was added to the smaller, a child using this rule would then declare the two groups to be equal. Finally, the oldest children had developed a **quantitative rule,** which led to consistently correct responses. These youngsters always took into account quantitative differences between the initial groups.

How does use of these three rules relate to the development of conservation of number? Children who use the primitive rule for addition/subtraction tasks do not show any grasp of number conservation, while those who use the qualitative rule appear to be transitional (at Piaget's stage 2). Among those who employ the quantitative rule, all exhibit number conservation; they have reached Piaget's stage 3. Thus, Piaget seems to have been correct in his belief that children's understanding of number conservation is related to their general understanding of numbers. In other ways, however, Piaget's perspective on this developmental process is less accurate. Many studies show that the acquisition of number concepts begins earlier and extends longer than Piaget suggested (Gelman and Baillargeon, 1983; Gelman, Meck, and Merkin, 1986).

CAN CONSERVATION BE TAUGHT?

American developmentalists have been fascinated by the question of whether concepts of conservation can be taught to young children. In Piaget's view, such efforts should not have much success, because a child's current stage of mastering conservation depends on an interaction of physical maturation and experience in the world. We cannot simply *tell* a 4-year-old that the water in the beaker remains the same and expect the child to grasp the underlying concept. In keeping with Piaget's expectations, the earliest attempts to teach conservation were not successful (see Flavell, 1963). Subsequent studies, however, have met with more success. For example, Jerome Bruner has shown that when the learning situation is constructed to help youngsters overcome cognitive limitations, many can be taught to "discover" conservation before they normally would.

In one study (Bruner, Olver, and Greenfield, 1966), Bruner and his colleagues first presented children with the standard conservation of liquid volume task. This phase of the study was a pretest to find out what the youngsters already knew about conservation. Next Bruner modified the standard conservation task: He screened the containers so that the children couldn't see the height to which the water rose after it was poured from one container to another. His hope was that this technique might help youngsters overcome the appearance/reality problem. Finally, Bruner conducted a posttest using the standard conservation task again. The posttest allowed him to see if the modified task had significantly changed the children's general level of thinking.

Bruner found that 4-year-olds didn't conserve on either the pretest or the posttest; they consistently said that the higher water was more. On the screened test the 4-year-olds performed randomly: They were right 50 percent of the time and wrong 50 percent. Apparently, they depended on appearance in making their judgments about quantity, and when the look of the water was hidden from view they resorted to simple guessing. More interesting were the responses of 6-year-olds, who in the pretest were in Piaget's transitional stage 2. When they were presented with the screened task, their performance improved dramatically. It was as if they were able to consider the underlying concept of conservation when no longer distracted by contradictory perceptual information. Apparently they were on the verge of grasping conservation, but they had trouble overcoming the final hurdle of the appearance/reality problem. With that problem hidden, they could reason more maturely. On the posttest, moreover, these children maintained their improved performance. It was as if they were able to handle the perception of the water's height once they had had a chance to think through the situation with that distraction eliminated. In other words, Bruner's training session enabled them to make the appearance/reality distinction on their own.

In a more recent study, young nonconservers (average age 5½) were trained to use the strategy of counting in order to judge the number of items in each of two groups (Gold, 1978). This training led 20 out of 29 children to overcome centration on appearance or length and solve conservation of number problems correctly. Using even younger children as subjects, Rochele Gelman also had success encouraging conservation of number with a different training technique (Gelman, 1982). In her study, all the children showed improvement on number conservation tasks. The younger preschoolers, however, didn't retain this improvement on a posttest several weeks later.

Thus, older preschoolers and very young elementary-school children probably can be trained to succeed with problems that they wouldn't usually solve until a year or more later. We suspect that in these cases, the training procedures are merely speeding development along its normal course. For younger preschoolers, however, such learning is unstable because these children haven't yet acquired a large enough framework of understanding into which they can fit new conservation skills. This point emphasizes that a grasp of conservation is only one part of an overall cognitive system. As children attempt to solve problems and to understand how things work, their various cognitive capabilities need to support a consistent view of the world. Cognitive developments, in short, are interdependent. Consequently, inducing unusually early acquisition of just a single skill is hard.

Classification Skills

Piaget believed that classification, like conservation, was central to the development of concrete operations (Inhelder and Piaget, 1964). Classification skills are also prominent in the theories of researchers who take an information-processing perspective (Klahr and Wallace, 1976; Siegler, 1983). Classification is considered important because it allows children to impose structure on the many things around them. It is also closely related to the ability to learn language and to communicate effectively. In addition, classification skills provide part of the basis for logical thinking itself. The logic of contradiction, for example, would not be possible unless we could separate "A" from "not A" in a consistent and unambiguous manner. By exploring the classification skills that youngsters possess, we can thus gain insights into their thinking processes.

At the beginning of middle childhood, children show rapid development of their understanding of numerical concepts, especially of their knowledge of number facts (e.g., 2 + 3 = 5). (*Elizabeth Crews.*)

Placing objects in groups, which is part of classification, is not new to middle childhood. As we discussed in Chapter 6, even infants categorize objects to some extent. During the toddler and preschool years, early systems of categories are further differentiated into a larger and larger number of classes, each making increasingly more subtle distinctions among things. In Chapter 10 we described how the use of categorization becomes more systematic during early childhood. For example, preschoolers can readily sort things along one dimension, such as separating all the red blocks from the blue ones. But Piaget maintained that not until the concrete operational subperiod, beginning around age 7, can children understand the interrelationships among categories in a more complex classification system.

Piaget described two kinds of classification systems that youngsters become able to understand during early middle childhood. One is **hierarchical classification,** which, he argued, depends on the ability to *add* classes. The other is **matrix classification,** which depends on the ability to *multiply* classes. Addition and multiplication of classes are two of the eight different operations that make up the logical structure of concrete operations in Piaget's theory. However, because much of the recent research on classification has not been conducted within a Piagetian framework, we will describe the development of these two important skills relatively independently of Piaget's theory.

HIERARCHICAL CLASSIFICATION

Hierarchical classification systems are often used in organizing bodies of knowledge. Consider how we organize our knowledge of animals, for instance. The Gordon family has a dog named Sam, which belongs to the breed golden retriever. This breed, in turn, is a type of domesticated dog, belonging to the species canine, along with such other animals as wolves, jackals, and coyotes. Canines, of course, are classified as a type of carnivore, which is a type of mammal, which in turn is a type of animal (see Figure 12.3). As we move up this hierarchy of classification, each term is broader and more inclusive. Notice, too, that each higher class is composed of *all* the classes at the level just below it. The concept domesticated dog, for example, is produced by adding all the various breeds of dog together (golden retriever, poodle, cocker spaniel, and so forth). For this reason, Piaget said that hierarchical classification involves the addition of classes.

Researchers use a task called **class inclusion** as the standard test of whether a child understands hierarchical classification. The child is presented with a group of objects, say, six petunias and three begonias. The investigator questions the child to make sure that he or she knows petunias and begonias are both flowers. The youngster is then asked, "Are there more petunias or more flowers?" You may be surprised to learn that most 6-year-olds say there are more petunias. They seem to be comparing the two subordinate classes, petunias and begonias. Not until age 8 or 9 do most children start to give the correct answer by comparing one of the subordinate classes (petunia) to the superordinate class (flower).

Many studies have documented the same results for children given the standard class-inclusion test. Researchers have offered various opinions of why children age 6 and younger tend to fail at such tasks (see Gelman and Baillargeon, 1983). Youngsters this age seem to have difficulty thinking about a subclass and its superordinate class at the same time. You might think of this as a kind of centration, one of the limitations of preschool thought. Failure on the standard class-inclusion test doesn't mean, however, that 6-year-olds can't learn hierarchical classification schemes. By the age of 5 or 6, Mikey certainly knew that Sam is a golden retriever and that this is a type of dog. But children this age lack a genuine understanding of a hierarchy's structure and its logical implications. They are able to learn certain hierarchies of classes, but they don't yet grasp all the useful characteristics of the classification scheme.

Ellen Markman has shown that even when children can answer the class-inclusion question correctly, they still may not know that their answer is logically required by the nature of classification hierarchies. That is to say, an 8- or 9-year-old may not yet realize that a subclass, by definition, cannot contain more elements than its superordinate class (Markman, 1978). She demonstrated this by asking children older than 8 the class-inclusion question about objects they could see. Most answered correctly. However, when the children were then asked a hypothetical question about classification hierarchies ("Suppose we added 100 more petunias; would there be more petunias or more flowers?"), those younger than 11 often gave the wrong answer. Apparently, not until adolescence nears do children grasp the more abstract, logical structure of classification hierarchies. In the earlier years of middle childhood, a knowledge of hierarchical classes seems to be tied to concrete objects and situations. Such knowledge is based on contingent, not necessary, truth.

How, then, can we characterize the progress that is made between the preschool years and middle childhood? We can say that, at first, skills

Figure 12.3
Hierarchical Classification
This hierarchy is part of the classification system for mammals. Each intersection, or node, represents a class (e.g., the class of domesticated dogs, which is composed of the subordinate classes of golden retriever and all other domesticated dog breeds). Understanding the relationships between subordinate and superordinate classes develops during middle childhood.

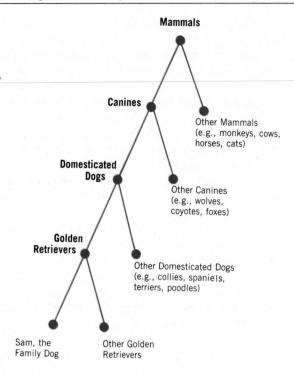

which started to develop during the preschool period become more effective tools for organizing information and solving problems. Preschoolers learn hierarchical structures, as you saw in our example of 5-year-old Mikey's learning the relationship between Sam, golden retrievers, and dogs. But youngsters don't begin to use the structure of such hierarchies effectively until middle childhood. Effective use seems to involve the ability to consider simultaneously different levels in a classification system. Nine-year-old Mikey must be able to compare the subclass retriever with the superordinate class dog in order to answer the question "Are there more retrievers or dogs on your block?" This skill exactly parallels the reversible thinking skill discussed earlier with respect to the acquisition of conservation. Mikey must be able simultaneously to decompose and recompose the superordinate class dog and the subclass retriever.

Interestingly, when the superordinate term is a naturally occurring collection rather than an abstract class, youngsters in early middle childhood have an easier time thinking about the relationship between levels in the system. Remember from Chapter 10 that a collection is an entity with subparts that seem automatically to go together because of their proximity. *Forest,* for example, is a term that refers to a collection of trees. Markman and her colleagues asked 6- and 7-year-olds the standard class-inclusion question versus a modified version that used a collection for the superordinate class (e.g., Markman and Siebert, 1976). For instance, the child might be shown a picture of a forest with 20 oaks and 10 pines, and asked either "Are there more oaks or more trees here?" or the alternative "Which has more, the oaks or the forest?" Quite often 6- and 7-year-olds were able to answer the second type of question correctly even though they had failed on the first. Apparently, use of the collective term *forest* helped them to consider different levels simultaneously in this classification system.

The final step in mastering hierarchical classification is acquiring the ability to grasp the logic that underlies hierarchies. This skill, as you learned, is something that begins to emerge after the age of about 11. The relatively late development of this ability is consistent with a general characteristic of middle childhood thought: The cognitive skills of youngsters during most of the elementary-school years are adequate for dealing with specific concrete situations, but are not yet advanced enough to deal with abstract concepts and hypothetical questions. These more difficult challenges aren't mastered until the teenage years.

MATRIX CLASSIFICATION

Although hierarchical classification systems are very useful for organizing some kinds of information, other data are better organized in a matrix system. Suppose you are asked to organize bolts for sale in a hardware store. The bolts come in a range of diameters and lengths. You might arrange them in a set of drawers in which the top row has bolts one-quarter inch in diameter, the second row three-eighths inch in diameter, the third row one-half inch in diameter, and so on, working downward in ascending order. Similarly, you would put the shortest bolts, say one-half inch long, in the column of drawers farthest left, the next shortest bolts in the second column, and so forth, until the longest bolts were in the column farthest right. In the end you would produce a matrix of diameter × length. The bolts in each cell of the matrix would always be the product of the diameter assigned to that particular row and the length assigned to that column. Piaget therefore called the underlying mental operation a multiplication of classes: One classification dimension (diameter) is being multiplied by another (length).

One way that researchers study the development of matrix classification is to ask children to sort objects that differ along two or more dimensions. For instance, a child might be given a pile of small and large blocks, some of which are red, others green. The child is asked to put the blocks into separate piles so that all the blocks in each pile "go together." Preschoolers typically sort along one dimension only (size or color), as if centration keeps them from noticing the other dimension. During the transition between the preschool period and middle childhood, youngsters frequently sort first along one dimension and then subdivide the blocks in each of the two resulting piles along the second dimension. This behavior suggests that they notice both dimensions, and so are no longer centrated, but that they are able to categorize only one dimension at a time. Finally, by age 8 or 9, children approach this task much as adults do. They sort along both dimensions simultaneously to produce the appropriate classification matrix.

A second method of assessing children's understanding of matrix classification is to ask youngsters to place objects in a matrix that is already partially completed. This task is illustrated in Figure 12.4, which shows a matrix classification system that sorts circles, squares, and triangles of three different colors. A number of studies have confirmed Piaget's original findings that preschoolers tend to pick an object that is correct along only one of the two dimensions—a green triangle, for ex-

Figure 12.4
Matrix Classification
The objects in this matrix classification scheme are sorted by shape and color. One way to assess a child's understanding of matrix classification is to ask what the shape and color of the missing object should be.

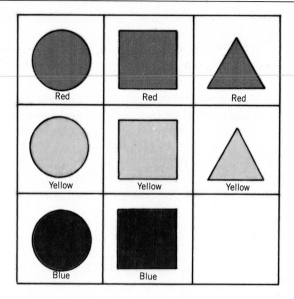

ample, or a blue square (e.g., Jacobs and Vandeventer, 1968; Overton and Brodzinsky, 1972). By age 8, in contrast, most youngsters can successfully solve an easy matrix classification problem like this one.

Several researchers have also shown that children as young as 6 can be taught to solve such problems (Jacobs and Vandeventer, 1971a; Resnick, Siegel, and Kresh, 1971). The youngsters are trained to use a sequential strategy in which they deal first with one dimension and then with the other. This training overcomes two limitations that preschool children normally encounter. First, it provides them with a ready-made approach to the problem. They do not have to formulate their own plan for using the classification skills they possess. Second, the training allows youngsters to get around the constraints of centration. Even though they focus on only one dimension at a time, they solve the problem anyway by using a two-step process.

Matrix completion tasks are used not only to assess an understanding of matrix classification but also to assess individual intelligence. For instance, the Raven Progressive Matrices Test consists of a set of matrices in which one cell is left vacant for the subject to fill in. For subjects older than 9 the difficulty of the test comes not from trying to understand the logic of a classification matrix, but from trying to infer the dimensions of classification being used in the particular problem. We will say more about intelligence and intelligence testing later in this chapter.

A third way of assessing children's understanding of matrix classification is to present them with games in which the use of this skill is very helpful and then to see what playing strategies the youngsters adopt. In one study, for instance, researchers asked children to play the game of "twenty questions" (Mosher and Hornsby, 1966). The experimenter began by thinking of some object or event that the child then had to guess by asking a maximum of 20 questions, which could be answered only with a yes or a no. In one version, the child's task was to determine which of 42 pictures the experimenter was thinking of (see Figure 12.5). In a second version, the experimenter posed problems such as the following: "As a man was driving, his car went off the road and hit a tree. Find out how it happened.'' Or: ''A boy leaves school in the middle of the morning. How come?'' Remember that the experimenter is allowed to answer questions only with a yes or a no.

Two kinds of approaches can be used in playing twenty questions. With the first, called **hypothesis scanning,** each question the child asks is a single, self-contained hypothesis, unrelated to previous questions. For instance, in the version of the game using the 42 pictures, the youngster might simply ask: ''Is it the apple?'' If the experimenter *is* thinking of the apple, the child has won the game. But if apple is wrong, the child has used up a question and eliminated only one of the 42 possible choices. The hypothesis scanning approach is dominant among 6-year-olds and decreases with age. As children grow older, they become more

Figure 12.5
Using Matrix Classification to Play Twenty Questions
A child is told that one of the pictures in this set is ''correct.'' The child's task is to determine which one by asking yes/no questions. Questions such as ''Is it a tool?'' are more efficient than ''Is it a saw?'' for zeroing in on the correct object. Such constraint-seeking questions begin to occur frequently around age 9 and predominate by age 11.

Adapted from Bruner, Olver, and Greenfield, 1966.

and more likely to use an approach called **constraint seeking.** Here the child tries, with each consecutive question, to narrow down the range of possible alternatives. For example, the child might ask, "Is it bigger than a television?" and when given the answer no, go on to ask, "Is it something you can eat?" If the answer turns out to be yes, the child has eliminated all but four possible choices in the 42-picture game (apple, carrots, fish, and pie). To limit the choices to two, the child might ask next, "Is it something you could grow in a garden?" Notice that this strategy multiplies dimensions of classification (small object × edible × garden-grown) in order to reduce the alternatives. By age 11 children use this strategy about 80 percent of the time.

We can summarize the development of classification skills in children by reviewing a few key points. First, children begin to classify objects very early in life, but it is not until middle childhood that they make effective use of relationships among classes when organizing information. At this point in the emergence of classification skills, youngsters start to answer class-inclusion questions correctly and they begin to use a constraint-seeking strategy more extensively in games like twenty questions. Second, in searching for the reasons why preschoolers perform poorly on classification tasks, one must consider centration—either centration on a single dimension of classification or centration on a single level in a classification hierarchy. During middle childhood, youngsters largely overcome the limits imposed by centration. Finally, although elementary-school children make great progress in classification skills, they still do not entirely grasp the logical necessity of classification structures. For them an understanding of classification is not abstract; it is applied to concrete objects and situations. Another way of saying this is that their knowledge derives from contingent, not necessary, truth.

Memory Abilities

Chapter 10 described the development of memory and the emergence of the intention to remember. This section will explore the development of memory during middle childhood, which is most notable for the increase in variety and effectiveness of memory strategies and the child's increasing awareness of the nature of memory. To explore the major aspects of memory that develop during middle childhood, we will employ a framework that divides memory into various parts. Such a framework has been suggested by John Flavell, who has studied memory development extensively. Flavell (1985) lists four aspects of memory that we need to consider in understanding how memory skills change during the elementary-school years. The first he calls *basic processes,* the second *knowledge,* the third *memory strategies,* and the fourth *metamemory.* In the following sections we will explore each of these factors.

BASIC PROCESSES

Basic memory processes include the most fundamental aspects of remembering things: the routine acts of storing and retrieving information. These are the processes that enable an infant to recognize something as familiar when it is seen again and again. These are also the processes that enable toddlers to recall their first words, or preschoolers to remember the route to a friend's house. Basic memory processes may develop further during middle childhood, but only minor refinements, not dramatic improvements, are involved.

KNOWLEDGE

Knowledge is what Piaget once called "memory in the wider sense" (Piaget and Inhelder, 1973). By this he meant the vast networks of accumulated information that people have stored in memory during their lives. Knowledge greatly affects what we are currently able to learn and remember. In one study that demonstrated this fact, researchers compared the memory performance of chess masters and amateur players (Chase and Simon, 1973). If the chess pieces were arranged randomly on the board, the masters were no better at remembering their locations than the amateurs were. However, if the pieces were arranged in patterns that might occur during an actual game of chess, the masters were much better than the amateurs at recalling the arrangements. Apparently the chess masters' extensive knowledge of the game gave them an advantage. They were able to encode arrangements of pieces in terms of layouts they had already stored in memory through their playing experience. The same results have been obtained in a study that used excellent elementary-school chess players as the experts and novice adult players as the amateurs (Chi, 1978). Again the experts outperformed the novices when the arrangements of the pieces on the board "made sense" in terms of what would be expected in a real game. Clearly, knowledge is the factor causing this memory advantage.

Much of the research on the knowledge component of memory has involved what is called **constructive memory**—recall of new information that is only partly the product of the actual data just processed. Recall of new information is also the product of inferences made on the basis of data previously stored in memory. To better understand what we mean by this, read the following paragraph from a study by Scott Paris (1975):

> Linda was playing with her new doll in front of her big red house. Suddenly she heard a strange sound coming from under the porch. It was the flapping of wings. Linda wanted to help so much, but she did not know what to do. She ran inside the house and grabbed a shoe box from the closet. Then Linda looked inside her desk until she found eight sheets of yellow paper. She cut up the paper into little pieces and put them in the bottom of the box. Linda gently picked up the helpless creature and took it with her. Her teacher knew what to do.

Now test your memory of the information in this paragraph by trying to answer the eight questions that Paris asked his subjects. Don't look back at the paragraph as you answer these questions.

1. Was Linda's doll new?
2. Did Linda grab a match box?
3. Was the strange sound coming from under the porch?
4. Was Linda playing behind her house?
5. Did Linda like to take care of animals?

6. Did Linda take what she found to the police station?
7. Did Linda find a frog?
8. Did Linda use a pair of scissors?

Questions 1 through 4 can be answered directly from information contained in the paragraph, while questions 5 through 8 require inferences based on general knowledge of children's characteristics, where teachers are normally found, what kinds of animals have wings, and how paper is generally cut into pieces. Paris's study showed that youngsters in middle childhood automatically make these kinds of inferences in the process of storing and remembering information. Paris also found that this inference drawing, or constructive memory, is an overall aid to better recall. In another similar study, Scott Paris and Laurence Upton (1976) learned that the best predictor of how well children would remember information was how well they did on inference questions like 4 through 8 above. Apparently if children can integrate new information into meaningful structures they already have stored in memory, they are more likely to recall the new information.

New experiences provide children with information to add to their network of constructive memory. (*Gabe Palmer/The Stock Market.*)

When do constructive memory abilities emerge in children? The evidence is good that substantial development of this capacity occurs during middle childhood (e.g., Bisanz, Vesonder, and Voss, 1978; Paris, Lindauer, and Cox, 1977). Paris and Upton have argued that even preschoolers possess this skill to some extent, although others have questioned that conclusion (Liben and Posnansky, 1977). It is our belief that preschoolers do have constructive memory capabilities; however, these capabilities are often hard to demonstrate because of the limited general knowledge preschoolers possess and because of their often "illogical" inference processes. In the elementary-school years, constructive memory really comes into its own, allowing children to make accurate inferences. Here we see another example of middle childhood as a time when youngsters expand and refine cognitive skills that began to emerge in an earlier period of development.

The effect of knowledge on memory continues to expand as what is known changes, so this component of memory develops long past middle childhood. You can demonstrate this fact to yourself by considering what a 12-year-old boy would learn from a technical lecture on high-energy physics. If he has an average knowledge of physics for a child this age, he would probably learn very little. But 10 years later, as a physics major in college, he would probably learn a great deal. What we know influences what we can learn and the ease with which we assimilate new information. The fact that what children know increases across the elementary-school years accounts for some of the development in memory abilities we see during this period.

MNEMONIC STRATEGIES

The term *mnemonic* comes from the Greek word for memory, so **mnemonic strategies** are simply cognitive ways of facilitating memory. In the example in Chapter 10, Mikey used a mnemonic strategy when he piled up the things he wanted to take with him by the front door. His mother used another mnemonic device when she made a list of items she wanted to pack. Another common mnemonic strategy is called **rehearsal,** delib-

In learning to play chess children develop memory strategies to help recall the moves that each piece may make. (*Elizabeth Crews.*)

erately repeating over and over something you want to remember. When you repeat a telephone number you just looked up before beginning to dial, you are using the tactic of rehearsal. A huge variety of thoughts and actions can serve as mnemonic devices (Kail, 1979). Each is an intentional, goal-oriented behavior designed to improve memory.

In one of the earliest studies of mnemonic strategies used by children, researchers showed a set of seven pictures to 5-, 7-, and 10-year-olds (Flavell, Beach, and Chinsky, 1966). The experimenters then indicated a subset of either two or five pictures that the child was to recall. During the interval between seeing the pictures and the time when the recall test was to start, each child was observed for evidence of rehearsal. The rate of rehearsal increased from only 10 percent among the 5-year-olds, to 60 percent among the 7-year-olds, to 85 percent among the children 10 years of age.

In another study researchers investigated what effect training in rehearsal would have on the memory performance of children who didn't yet use this mnemonic strategy (Keeney, Cannizzo, and Flavell, 1967). The youngsters, a group of first graders, were told to whisper the names of objects over and over until it was time for a recall test. This training was effective in two ways: First, whereas the children previously had not used rehearsal at all, they now used it during 75 percent of the trials. Second, the memory performance of these youngsters improved to the level of first graders who spontaneously rehearsed without having to undergo training. At the end of the experiment all the children were told that they didn't have to rehearse any longer, but could do whatever they wished to remember a new set of pictures. Of the 17 children who had been trained to rehearse, ten reverted to not rehearsing, and their memory performance declined. We will consider the implications of this last finding in our section on metamemory.

The question of when children first use mnemonic strategies on their own is difficult to answer. Much depends on the nature of the task and the setting in which it is presented (Naus and Ornstein, 1983). Nevertheless, Robert Kail and John Hagen (1982) offer these generalizations based on current knowledge. First, 5- and 6-year-olds do not spontaneously use mnemonic strategies often. They may feel it is important to remember something, but they seldom turn this motivation into a deliberate effort to try to improve memory. Second, the period between 7 and 10 years of age seems to be a transitional stage during which mnemonic devices increasingly develop. Exactly when a particular strategy emerges depends on both its nature and the context in which it is to be applied. Finally, beginning at about age 10, the child shows the first inklings of using mnemonic devices maturely.

What are some of the memory strategies, besides rehearsal, that youngsters gradually come to use? One is an effort to organize information, for good organization in storing data facilitates later recall. In one study of children ages 6 to 11, researchers found a large increase in the use of a simple organizational technique, in that the youngsters tended to group together by subject various pictures that were to be remembered (Moely et al., 1969). An 11-year-old, for instance, was much more likely than a 6-year-old to separate pictures of animals from pictures of plants and then to store each as a separate group. The greatest increase in this tendency came between the ages of 9 and 11, by which time most children have acquired the classification skills needed to carry out this process. The tactics of organizing, classifying, and summarizing data to be learned continue to develop throughout adolescence and into the college years (Brown et al., 1983; Rohwer, 1973; Wellman, 1983).

METAMEMORY

A fourth aspect of memory is something psychologists refer to as metamemory. **Metamemory** is simply knowledge about memory and memory processes. When you think about the need to remember and how to go about remembering, you are using metamemory capabilities. Also included in the concept of metamemory is knowledge of your own strengths and weaknesses in remembering. (Are you good at remembering faces, poor at remembering names?) In addition, metamemory entails the ability to monitor your own memory performance in a given situation. When you study for a test, do you know at what point you have learned the material? If so, this aspect of metamemory is well developed in you. Metamemory is one of many so-called metacognitive skills that show substantial advancement during middle childhood.

John Flavell and his colleagues examined one component of metamemory by asking children to predict how many pictures they would be able to remember (Flavell, Friedrichs, and Hoyt, 1970). On the first trial each child was shown only one picture. That picture was then covered and the child was asked if he or she could remember it. On each subsequent trial the number of pictures was increased to a maximum of ten. In the first phase of the experiment, the subjects were not required to actually remember the pictures, just to say whether they thought they could remember them. Then, in the second phase, actual recall tests were given. Table 12.2 shows both the children's self-predictions and their actual performance. Notice that the preschoolers were quite poor at remembering, the second graders were better, and the fourth graders were quite good. Notice, too, that for the younger children there was no correspondence between self-predicted memory performance and actual performance. The younger children were repeatedly overoptimistic about how well they could recall. The older children, in contrast, showed a

TABLE 12.2 **Children's Predictions of the Number of Items They Could Remember and Their Actual Performance**

	Predicted Memory Span	*Actual Memory Span*
Preschool	7.21	3.50
Kindergarten	7.97	3.61
Second Grade	6.00	4.36
Fourth Grade	6.14	5.50

Source: Flavell, Friedrichs, and Hoyt, 1970.

significant positive correlation between predicted and actual memory performance. Apparently, knowledge about one's own memory ability increases greatly during middle childhood.

Several other studies have shown similar improvements in metamemory skills over the elementary-school years (Flavell and Wellman, 1977; Waters and Andreassen, 1983; Wellman, 1986). For instance, in the study on training first graders to use rehearsal that we described earlier, we said that many of these youngsters reverted to not rehearsing after the training sessions were through. Many 6-year-olds seem not to realize that this strategy improves their memory performance. They lack the metamemory skill of monitoring how well they are doing on a set of memory tasks. Thus, metamemory may be an important factor in successfully learning and using mnemonic strategies.

The findings we have discussed so far should not be taken to mean that 6-year-olds and younger children have no metamemory capabilities. Flavell has argued that the beginnings of metamemory occur during the preschool years, but these beginnings are greatly overshadowed by the dramatic progress made in middle childhood. For instance, even kindergarteners and first graders know that increasing the number of items to be remembered makes a memory task harder; they are aware, in other words, of certain factors that can influence memory performance (Kreutzer, Leonard, and Flavell, 1975). And yet these same children are very poor at predicting how much they will remember when presented with increasing amounts of information to recall. It is as if they have trouble making use of the bits of metamemory knowledge they possess. Among older children, in contrast, metamemory knowledge not only becomes much more extensive but also becomes much more useful. For example, when presented with a memory task, many 5- and 6-year-olds can think of a strategy to help them remember, but older children are able to think of many more that could be of assistance (Kreutzer, Leonard, and Flavell, 1975). What's more, older children are also far more likely to use these memory strategies spontaneously, as you learned earlier. Thus, we again have a picture of middle childhood as a time when cognitive skills that began to emerge earlier are refined, elaborated, and made into more effective practical tools.

SOCIAL INTERACTION AND COGNITIVE DEVELOPMENT

How does a child's interaction with others influence cognitive development? In the previous sections you saw how training programs can sometimes encourage cognitive skills to appear before they normally would. This was true in our discussions of conservation, classification, and memory capabilities. In many cases, however, we had reason to suspect that the resulting cognitive "development" was different from what usually occurs. In this section we turn our attention to interactions with others in more natural settings. We ask what everyday interactions with peers and teachers can do to promote cognitive advances in children. We will be concerned with two kinds of learning situations: In the first a knowledgeable teacher, either an adult or another child, who already knows how to solve the problem, helps the learner understand what's involved. We call this a *didactic* situation, didactic meaning that it involves deliberate teaching. In the second kind of learning situation, two learners at approximately the same level interact with one another, and no knowledgeable teacher is present. We call this a *cooperative* situation because the children learn from each other.

The acquisition of concepts such as conservation of length are facilitated by discussions among peers. (*Elizabeth Crews.*)

What Children Can Learn from Children

Piaget believed that peer interaction can reduce egocentrism because it gives children the chance to experience conflict between their own ideas and those of others (Piaget, 1965). Frank Murray (1972, 1981) has explored the role of peer interaction in the development of conservation. He paired one child who understood conservation with a second child who did not and asked the two to come to a consensus about various conservation questions. Even though the children were similar in age, it was a didactic learning situation because one of the youngsters already knew the correct answers. The consensus reached by the two children almost invariably favored conservation; that is to say, the viewpoint of the more advanced child prevailed. And it was not simply a matter of one child's going along with the other out of sheer conformity. Genuine learning had apparently occurred. When the previously nonconserving children were later tested alone, they continued to give correct responses to conservation questions.

A series of studies by a group of Swiss researchers gives a much more detailed picture of the role that peer interaction plays in improving children's performance on cognitive tasks (Mugny, Perret-Clermont, and Doise, 1981). The researchers allowed children to cooperate on a broad range of tasks over an extended period of time. They found that when cooperation led to improvement on one task, that advancement in understanding often generalized to related tasks. Progress in understanding number conservation, for example, helped to foster progress in understanding conservation of liquid volume. The researchers also showed that the gains the children made were not simply the result of one youngster's imitating another. When children who had made cognitive progress explained the principles underlying some solution, they often gave slightly different explanations than ones they had previously heard. The children, in other words, could rephrase the fundamental concepts, which suggests that they truly grasped them. Interestingly, in order for interaction with a peer to promote cognitive progress, that interaction did not need to be with a more advanced child. In one case, for example, a child who couldn't yet solve number conservation problems but who understood one-to-one correspondence and could count accurately interacted with a child who was less advanced in these areas. Through discussing number conservation with the less competent child, the more advanced one acquired a grasp of this concept.

If relative competence among the two interacting children is not essential in promoting cognitive advancement, what might be the key factors underlying this developmental progress? In the Swiss studies just described, two conditions seemed necessary: First, at least one of the children had to possess certain prerequisite skills. Second, the interactions between the two youngsters had to involve a sustained give-and-take; there could not just be one child asserting an opinion and the other child complying. Other researchers have proposed additional factors that facilitate cognitive advancement in peer interactions. Three conditions have been suggested as being particularly important (Foreman, 1982). First, there should be a concrete task for the children to work on, one that provides a rich source of relevant information. Second, the information available must be somewhat ambiguous; it must be able to support at least two different conclusions. (Here we see something of the cognitive conflict, or disequilibrium, that Piaget stressed.) And third, the peers must consider reaching a consensus as a goal of their interaction.

In Chapter 10 Vygotsky's (1978) concept of the zone of proximal development was introduced, and it will again be used in considering factors that influence and support cognitive growth. Jerome Bruner (1975) has described one means of fostering advancement within a child's zone of proximal development, a means that involves the concept of scaffolding. **Scaffolding** refers to the support system that others can contribute to the learning process by observing the learner's behaviors, providing guidance, hints, or advice, and offering feedback about the performance, as well as correction when needed. Scaffolding suggests the use of strategies that the teacher progressively alters as the learner advances; initial approaches are replaced gradually with ones that enhance the mastery of more complex understandings (Cazden, 1983). Scaffolding is probably more common in didactic learning situations, where the teacher knows more than the pupil does (Cooper, Marquis, and Edwards, 1986). However, the teacher need not necessarily be an adult. Scaffolding has been observed in fifth graders who are tutoring second graders, so we know it is a skill that emerges in middle childhood (Allen, 1976). Scaffolding is a strategy for helping others learn, just as rehearsal is a strategy for promoting learning in oneself. While the selection of effective mnemonic aids requires metamemory, the selection of effective scaffolding approaches requires metacognitions about what others think and understand. Thus, the age of the teacher can be a significant factor in how effective scaffolding is. Let's look at some other ways in which age can influence the kind of learning fostered by social interactions.

Age, Interactions, and Learning

Catherine Cooper and her colleagues looked at the issues of age, peer interactions, and the fostering of learning in a study of 5- to 12-year-olds at a Montessori elementary school (Cooper, Marquis, and Edwards, 1986). This Montessori program was particularly active in encouraging peer interactions as a means of promoting learning. Cooper and her colleagues observed the children in the classroom, conducted interviews with them, and gave them cooperative tasks to perform in an experimental study. The researchers identified several forms of learning among their subjects: solitary learning (choosing to work alone), onlooking (learning simply by watching others), parallel-coordinate learning (involving two children working side-by-side, often briefly exchanging task-relevant information), guidance (a kind of didactic learning because one child is telling another how to accomplish some goal), and collaborative learning (in which the children share power in directing the course of the interaction). The study concluded that effective didactic and collaborative peer learning emerges early in middle childhood. Compared with older elementary-school children, younger ones tend to engage in more symmetrical collaborations. They are also more likely to use physical demonstrations and simple announcement of solutions as teaching tactics. With their increased metacognitive skills, older elementary-school youngsters become better able to plan long-term collaborative projects, to engage in more elaborate and extended arguments, to offer more effective teaching approaches, and to progressively adjust the guidance they provided as teachers.

The interpretation of behavior in a classroom as cooperative learning or as cheating may depend as much on the attitudes of the teacher as it does on the behaviors of the children. (*Elizabeth Crews.*)

Shari Ellis and Barbara Rogoff (1982) have examined the differences in teaching styles between elementary-school children and adults. All the children in this study (both the learners and the teachers) were age 8 or 9, while all the adults were women who had children this age. The learners had to master a relatively complex classification task in which photos of common objects were to be sorted into appropriate categories. Ellis and Rogoff identified three things that the teachers needed to accomplish in order to be successful: First, they had to physically sort the photos into the appropriate categories. Second, they had to assist the learner in understanding the underlying classification scheme. And third, they had to take primary responsibility for managing the social interactions between themselves and their learners. How did the two kinds of teachers—8- to 9-year-old children and adults—compare in handling these three essential tasks?

The child teachers tended to focus simply on getting their learners to accomplish the sorting task. They concentrated less than the adult teachers did on communicating the underlying classification scheme. Yet, when interviewed following the instructional session, they showed a knowledge of the categories involved and could give those categories appropriate names. Apparently, the job of coordinating all three tasks listed above was too complex for children this age. They couldn't put together an integrated teaching plan—one that simultaneously demonstrated how to sort, conveyed the underlying categories, and controlled the social give-and-take. As a result, the child teachers were less effective than the adult teachers. The fact that the participants in this study were relative strangers to one another probably added to the difficulties for the child teachers (Cooper and Cooper, 1985). Peer learning is most effective when the children involved are well acquainted and have worked out a smooth interaction system.

INDIVIDUAL DIFFERENCES IN INTELLIGENCE

So far in this chapter we have described cognitive skills common to youngsters in middle childhood. Our stress has been on *general* cognitive characteristics that most children in this age range share. In this section we shift our focus to cognitive *differences* among children. We discuss cognitive differences in more depth in this chapter than in earlier ones because a child's level of intellectual competence takes on special importance when he or she enters school. A high level of intelligence and good performance in school tend to go together, although there are exceptions. Since we want to present some general information about intelligence and its origins, we will not always be concentrating exclusively on middle childhood. This broader focus, however, will help you understand some of the key issues in the study of human intelligence.

Conceptions of Intelligence

Discussions of individual intelligence are always hampered by lack of agreement about what intelligence is. That is why we begin this section with a look at some of the different definitions of this elusive concept. It is useful to consider both informal conceptions of intelligence (those that the "average" person holds), as well as more formal conceptions embodied in the content of standardized intelligence tests.

INFORMAL CONCEPTS OF INTELLIGENCE

How do you define intelligence? What qualities do you think of as associated with it? In one recent study, Steven Yussen and Patrick Kane (1983) asked these questions of first, third, and sixth graders. They found that the older children had a more differentiated view of intelligence than the younger ones. Increasingly with age children thought of intelligence as an internal information-processing skill. Older children were less likely than younger ones to associate a person's external characteristics with his or her intelligence. Older children were also more likely to stress academic skills as part of intelligence, whereas younger ones put more emphasis on social abilities.

In a recent study, researchers explored people's concepts of intelligence across a broader age range—6 to 22 years (Nicholls, Patashnick, and Mettetal, 1986). These investigators identified three age-related views of intelligence. The first, which is characteristic of children ages 6 to 9, holds that intelligence is related to the ability to perform difficult tasks. At this stage the judgment of "difficult" is subjective: What is hard for the child is considered generally hard. The second view of intelligence is characteristic of children ages 10 to 13. It holds that intelligence involves acquiring information and making an effort to learn. At this stage a person's level of intelligence is seen as largely dependent on the amount of information acquired through memorization. The third view of intelligence is characteristic of people age 14 and older. It sees intelligence as made up of two components: One consists of abstract skills related to solving problems, reasoning, and exercising common sense; the other consists of verbal skills, vocabulary level, and accumulated information. These are seen as more easily improved through training than are the abstract thinking abilities.

Notice that the third, most mature view in this study integrates increasingly sophisticated versions of views one and two. The two components that make up the third view correspond to what psychologists call fluid intelligence and crystallized intelligence. **Fluid intelligence** reflects processes of thinking and reasoning that are measured by analogy problems, series completion tasks, problems in classification, and so forth. **Crystallized intelligence,** in contrast, is assessed by measuring what a person knows, such as vocabulary size, general information, and reading comprehension (Cattell, 1971; Horn, 1968, 1982). This distinction is particularly important to those who are interested in development throughout the life span. Performance on measures of fluid intelligence generally improves until late adolescence and then slowly declines; but performance on measures of crystallized intelligence continues improving until around the age of 60 (Horn, 1982).

Coordination and creative problem solving are both generally understood to be characteristics of intelligence. (*Wayne Miller/ Magnum Photos, Inc.*)

Another way of studying conceptions of intelligence and how they change over time is to ask subjects what they think constitutes intelligence for people of different ages. In one such study researchers found that for 6-month-old babies people tend to associate intelligence with such characteristics as alertness, coordination, awareness of people, and the tendency to vocalize (Siegler and Richards, 1982). For 2-year-olds the list was modified to include verbal skills, learning ability, and curiosity. For 10-year-olds verbal skills were given top importance, followed by learning, problem solving, and reasoning abilities. For adults the list was very similar to the one for 10-year-olds, except that reasoning ability was placed first and verbal skills second. Thus, as people consider increasingly older subjects, they tend to conceptualize intelligence as more cognitive and more academic.

FORMAL CONCEPTS OF INTELLIGENCE

Formal concepts of intelligence are those embodied in the theories and tests psychologists develop. In order to create a way of measuring intellectual differences, researchers must first decide what they think intelligence entails. Therefore, a brief look at the history of intelligence testing reveals how formal ideas about intelligence have changed over the years.

The first modern intelligence test was developed in France at the beginning of the twentieth century. Administrators of the public school system wanted a way of differentiating normally intelligent children from those requiring special help. In this way all children would be given education suited to their abilities and needs. The minister of education called upon Alfred Binet, a well-known French psychologist, and his colleague Theodore Simon to develop a reliable test. The process included constructing a large number of potential test items and then evaluating them against a set of critical criteria. For instance, performance on test items had to correlate with school performance, and the likelihood of answering any item correctly had to increase with age. The test items chosen included word definitions, arithmetic problems, verbal reasoning tasks, questions on general information, and tasks requiring an understanding of complex spatial relationships. Within each type of item the questions were ordered from easiest to hardest.

An English version of Binet's test was first published in 1916 by Lewis Terman at Stanford University. This test, called the Stanford-Binet, was designed for children between the ages of 3 and 18. Scoring of the test involved the concept of **mental age (MA),** the average age of children correctly answering the same number of items that the tested child answered. For instance, if a child correctly answered as many questions as the average 12-year-old, that child would be said to have a mental age of 12. Mental age was then divided by chronological age (CA) and multiplied by 100 to produce an **intelligence quotient,** or **IQ.** (MA/CA $\times$ 100 = IQ.) If our child with a mental age of 12 was also 12 years old, that child would be exactly average and would be assigned an IQ of 100 (12/12 $\times$ 100 = IQ 100). If, on the other hand, this child was only 10, his mental age would be above his chronological age and his IQ would be higher than average (12/10 $\times$ 100 = IQ 120). By the same token, if the child was 14 and had a mental age of 12, his IQ would be below average (12/14 $\times$ 100 = IQ 86). This simple method of computing IQ score is no longer used; a more complex calculation has taken its place. Nevertheless, IQ scores are still determined by comparing an individual's performance with the performance of others who are the same age.

Notice how Binet's approach entails a unitary conception of intelligence. Each person has an intelligence that can be measured by a single IQ score. People are not thought of as having many different kinds of intelligences. Instead, intelligence is considered a *general* intellectual capability. In England during the early part of the twentieth century, an educational psychologist named Charles Spearman was also sympathetic to the concept of a general intelligence. In his approach this general reasoning ability was labeled "g." But Spearman (1927) believed that performance on an intellectual task depended not only on "g" but also on specific knowledge, abilities, and aptitudes—that is, specific to the particular problem or question at hand. Thus, Spearman would have argued that your level of performance in a college algebra class would be determined in part by your general reasoning ability and in part by your specific aptitude for math.

Many contemporary intelligence tests are based on a combination of Binet's and Spearman's conceptions of intelligence. One example is the widely used Wechsler scales, which include separate tests for adults, for children ages 6 to 16, and for children ages 4 to 6. The Wechsler scales provide IQ scores that summarize overall performance, so in this regard they use Binet's global approach to intelligence. At the same time, however, the Wechsler scales are made up of a variety of different kinds of subtests (for example, vocabulary, arithmetic, and general information, mazes, block design, and object assembly). This variety minimizes the contribution to overall performance made by any one specialized skill. The test taker also receives a separate subscore for each of the various

Group IQ tests are part of most children's educational experience in the United States. Individual IQ tests, such as the Stanford-Binet and the Wechsler Intelligence Scale for Children, are administered less frequently. (*Elizabeth Crews.*)

subtests, a procedure that acknowledges Spearman's stress on specific abilities in addition to general intelligence.

An alternative to the approaches of Binet and Spearman is found in the work of L. L. Thurstone, an American psychologist. Thurstone (1938) rejected the concept of general intelligence. He argued instead that intelligence is composed of seven primary mental abilities: verbal meaning, inductive reasoning, perceptual speed, number facility, spatial relations, memory, and verbal fluency. Thurstone saw these primary mental abilities as relatively independent of one another, with none predominant over the others. From Thurstone's ideas, the Primary Mental Abilities Test was developed. It yields separate scores for each of the seven abilities (although provision is made for calculating an overall score as well). Other researchers have proposed even more than seven components to human intelligence. French (1951) has suggested a list of 20, and Guilford (1967) a list of 120. Figure 12.6 shows the three dimensions along which Guilford categorizes his various components of intelligence. Although such approaches may have value for trying to understand the multifaceted nature of human intelligence, approaches that treat intelligence as unitary or composed of a few components have been used more effectively in developmental contexts.

Exploring IQ Differences

Now that we have examined the concepts of intelligence embodied in IQ tests, let's turn to the topic of IQ differences. Virtually all American children, at some time in their school careers, are given at least one intelligence test. Most scores range somewhere between 70 and 130, although there are a few lower or higher on the scale. What are the origins of these IQ differences? Is a person born with a certain IQ level, or is IQ more the product of experience? And what significance does a child's IQ have? Can it predict whether he or she will go on to college or find a good job as an adult? Can we even expect a person's IQ to remain stable over time? These are some of the issues we'll be exploring in the rest of this chapter.

IQ, HEREDITY, AND ENVIRONMENT

The question of how much heredity and environment each contribute to IQ differences has aroused controversy for decades. One of the things

Operations

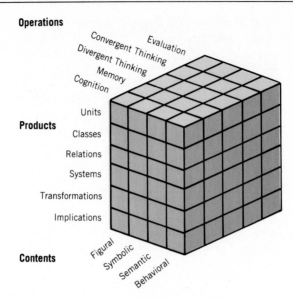

Products

Convergent Thinking
Evaluation
Divergent Thinking
Memory
Cognition

Units
Classes
Relations
Systems
Transformations
Implications

Contents

Figural
Symbolic
Semantic
Behavioral

Figure 12.6
Guilford's Model of
Intelligence
J. P. Guilford (1967) described the components of intelligence as varying along three dimensions: operations, products, and contents. This model defines 120 distinct components of intelligence.

developmentalists agree on is that the influence of heredity on intelligence involves *many* genes. No single gene, or small set of genes, makes a person smarter than others. In addition, even the staunchest proponent of a strong role for heredity in intellectual differences acknowledges that the environment also plays an important part. Let's examine some of the evidence for the contributions of both heredity *and* environment.

The evidence for a genetic contribution to IQ differences comes primarily from studies of twins and adopted children. By looking at Table 12.3, you can see that the median correlation between the IQs of two people increases as a function of how close genetically those individuals are. Such data have been used to support the claim that heredity contributes to the differences in intelligence among people. At the same time, however, these figures also show a powerful role for environment. For instance, identical twins who share identical genes do not have identical IQs, and the divergence in scores is greater if they are reared separately. It seems that a complex interplay of genes and environment shapes IQ differences.

This complex interplay was illustrated in an early study of adopted children (Skodak and Skeels, 1949). The biological mothers had below-average intelligence (the mean IQ was 85.7), while the adoptive parents had above-average intelligence (the mean IQ was about 120). The children were placed in their new homes before 6 months of age, so the rearing environments they experienced were largely those of their adoptive families. The researchers tested the children several times over a period of years. They found that their mean IQs ranged from 107 to 116. This is 20 to 30 points above the mean IQ of the biological mothers, a very significant difference. However, at age 7 the average correlation between a child's IQ score and the score of his or her adoptive parents was only .16, as opposed to a .36 correlation between the child's and the biological mother's IQs. By the age of 13, the child–adoptive parent IQ correlation had dropped to .04, while the child–biological mother correlation still averaged .38. What is the meaning of these findings? Apparently, the mean IQ of all the children considered as a group was raised by their being placed in more advantaged environments. However, individual differences among the youngsters were more predictable from information about their genetic endowments.

These early findings are consistent with those of many later studies. For instance, several studies have shown higher IQ correlations between children and their biological parents than between children and their adoptive parents (e.g., Honzik, 1983; Scarr and Weinberg, 1983). Other studies have shown substantial IQ gains for children who are placed in more enriched environments than would normally be provided by their biological parents (e.g., Ramey and Campbell, 1979; Ramey and Haskins, 1981).

The concept of reaction range can help you better understand the interaction of genes and environment that underlies findings like these. **Reaction range** refers to the limits within which the effects of genes can vary depending on environment. Genes, in other words, set outer limits to the traits a person may show, with environment then determining where within those limits the person actually falls. In the case of intelligence, genes can be thought of as setting a lower and an upper limit on potential IQ. If a person is raised in a very stimulating environment, an IQ near the top of the range will likely result, but if the person is raised in a deprived environment, we can expect an IQ near the range's lower end. Since the studies mentioned earlier involved bringing children from relatively poor environments into much more supportive ones, they provided a rough estimate of the size of the IQ reaction range. That range seems to be between 20 points or so. Of course this is the range of potential IQ change given "normal" variations in environment. If a child began in a *highly* deprived setting (such as being locked away in social isolation), we would expect the range of potential IQ difference to be even greater.

We have seen that a child's IQ score can change substantially with alterations in the quality of that child's environment. Once such changes

TABLE 12.3 **Correlations of IQ Scores for Individuals with Differing Biological and Experiential Similarity**

Number of Samples	Biological Relationship	Condition of Rearing	Median Correlation
15	One-egg twins	Same family	.88
4	One-egg twins	Separate families	.75
21	Two-egg twins	Same family	.53
39	Siblings	Same family	.49
3	Siblings	Separate families	.46
7	Unrelated	Same family	.17

Source: Estimated from Figure 3 of Jarvik and Erlenmeyer-Kimling, 1967.

in IQ have come about, how stable are they? If there is early intervention, such as a special remedial program, but *no* follow-up, the IQ gains caused by the intervention seem to regress (Gray, Ramsey, and Klaus, 1982; Lazer et al., 1982). Although this is disappointing from the standpoint of those who are trying to assist disadvantaged children, it makes sense in terms of the concept of the reaction range. To maintain a rate of intellectual development toward the top end of the range would seem to require continued environmental support.

PREDICTING A CHILD'S IQ

But what about the majority of children, who don't experience wide fluctuations in their intellectual environments? Can we expect their IQ levels to remain relatively stable over many years? Knowing a child's IQ score at age 6, can we predict IQ 6 or even 12 years later? And how early can we begin to make accurate predictions? Can a child's performance on intellectual tests in infancy and toddlerhood be used to estimate performance during the elementary and high-school years?

In trying to estimate the relationship between early competencies and later IQ scores, psychologists have developed a number of tests for infants and toddlers. These include the Bayley Scales of Infant Development, the Gesell Developmental Schedules, and the Cattell Intelligence Tests for Infants and Young Children. The Bayley scales, originally developed in 1933, were revised and restandardized in 1969. Table 12.4 shows some of the items they contain. Notice that the items designed to assess younger infants measure attention and sensorimotor coordination, while those designed to assess older infants and toddlers include yardsticks that are more cognitive in nature.

In a longitudinal study that took many years to complete, Nancy Bayley (1949) tested a group of children from age 3 months to age 18 years. She found that test scores at different ages did not reliably correlate with one another until after a child was 4 years old. Many other researchers have made similar findings: Measures of intellectual ability made in infancy and toddlerhood are not very predictive of later IQ (e.g., Honzik, 1983). Figure 12.7 shows the general increase in predictability of adult IQ as children grow older. By middle childhood this predictability has become quite good, suggesting that at this point intelligence tests are measuring relatively stable aspects of cognitive functioning.

Why are infant assessments of intelligence such poor predictors of adult intelligence? Does it mean that cognitive functioning early in life is extremely variable? Recently some researchers have offered a different explanation by proposing that traditional tests of infant intelligence may simply be measuring the wrong behaviors (Bornstein and Sigman, 1986; Fagan and McGrath, 1981). These newer studies use habituation measures to assess a baby's processing of information, since habituation measures are thought to provide a reasonable estimate of how easily the child can construct a mental representation of things. Correlations between infant habituation scores and measures of IQ in middle childhood are around .5. This suggests moderate developmental stability in at least some of the factors that influence performance on intelligence tests.

TABLE 12.4   **Select Items from Bayley Scales of Infant Development**

To score: Check P(Pass) or F(Fail). If other, mark O(Omit), R(Refused), or RPT(Reported by mother).

Item No.	Age Placement and Range (Months)	Situ-ation	Item Title	Score			Notes
				P	F	Other	
1	0.1	A	Responds to sound of bell				
2	0.7 (.3-2)	E	Eyes follow moving person				
3	1.6 (.5-4)	F	Turns eyes to light				
4	1.9 (1-4)		Blinks at shadow of hand				
5	2.4 (1-5)	E	Reacts to disappearance of face				
6	3.1 (1-5)	D^1	Reaches for dangling ring				
7	3.8 (2-6)	D^1	*Inspects own hands				
8	4.1 (2-6)	H	Reaches for cube				
9	4.4 (2-6)	H	Eye-hand coordination in reaching				
10	5.4 (3-12)	K	Smiles at mirror image				
11	5.8 (4-11)	L	Lifts cups with handle				
12	7.1 (5-10)	D^2	Pulls string adaptively: secures ring				
13	8.1	H^1	Uncovers toy				
14	9.1 (6-14)	N	Responds to verbal request				
15	10.4 (7-15)	M	Attempts to imitate scribble				
16	12.0 (8-18)	Q	Turns pages of book				
17	12.5 (9-18)	N	*Imitates words (Record words used)				
18	14.2 (10-23)	G^3	*Says 2 words (Note words)				
19	16.7 (13-21)	H^1	Builds tower of 3 cubes				

*May be observed incidentally.

HOW MEANINGFUL ARE IQ SCORES?

Ever since IQ scores were first introduced, people have debated their value. If Malcolm gets 110 on an IQ test and Mikey gets 120, what exactly does that tell us about these two children? Part of the controversy over IQ scores centers on the issue of cultural bias in the tests. Controversy also arises over the question of just what an IQ score can predict.

The Issue of Cultural Bias.   How well do you think you would perform on Binet's original intelligence test? Since this test was given in French, you might predict you would do very poorly. And even if you are fluent in French some of the general-information questions asked at the turn of the century might be obscure today. The fact is that any IQ test is the product of a certain culture, and knowledge of that culture affects how well a test taker does. To demonstrate this to yourself, try taking the test

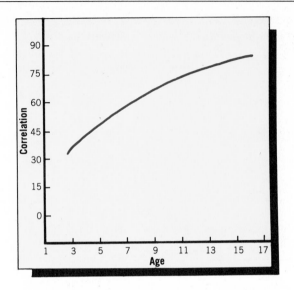

Figure 12.7
Correlations Between IQ Scores Obtained at Maturity and Those Obtained at Early Ages
The graph line illustrates the approximate substantial power of tests obtained during early childhood to predict later performance.
Source: Bloom, 1964.

in Figure 12.8. If you are an average white American you will probably be able to answer very few of the questions. This test was constructed by a black sociologist as a reminder that an IQ score may reflect more about a person's cultural background than it does about that individual's underlying intelligence (Dove, 1968).

To overcome the problem of cultural bias, a number of psychologists have tried to develop **culture-free** or **culture-fair IQ tests.** The Raven Progressive Matrices Test mentioned earlier in this chapter is one such attempt. Because the problems on this test require analysis of visually presented information and are not expressed in language, it was thought that cultural differences among test takers would affect individual scores to a minimum extent. However, it has been found that, for adults, educational level is a good predictor of performance on this test. This finding suggests that the test still has some cultural bias.

The idea of a culture-free IQ test is based on the assumption that intelligence is something inherent in a person, something independent of context. Interestingly, the efforts to develop a culture-free test have led developmentalists to just the opposite conclusion. It has become apparent that intelligence *always* exists in some kind of context and that high intelligence helps people adapt to the context in which they live. This makes intelligence tests effective means of comparing the abilities of individuals *within* the same culture or subculture. For comparisons *across* cultures, IQ tests still have their uses, but they must be interpreted cautiously.

In general, IQ tests are fairly good predictors of a person's success in school, at least in the schools created by the same culture that developed the tests. In this country the average correlation between IQ score and school grades is about .7, quite a close relationship (McClelland, 1973; Sigler and Berman, 1983). This makes sense when you consider that prediction of school performance is the purpose for which IQ tests were originally constructed. Most IQ tests, however, are not meant to be a measure of some inherent, underlying intellectual potential, independent of a person's environmental experiences. This is why your score on

Binet's test would not tell us very much about how "smart" you are, even though it would give us a very good idea of how well you would do in the Paris schools of 80 years ago.

IQ and Performance.   IQ scores are relatively good indicators of success in school, but what else can they predict about a person's performance? Data from one longitudinal study indicated a moderate correlation be-

---

1. Who did "Stagger Lee" kill?
   (A) His mother, (B) Frankie, (C) Johnny, (D) His girlfriend, (E) Billy.

2. A "gas head" is a person who has a. . .
   (A) Fast-moving car, (B) Stable of "lace," (C) "Process," (D) Habit of stealing cars, (E) Long jail record for arson.

3. If a man is called a "blood," then he is a. . .
   (A) Fighter, (B) Mexican-American, (C) Negro, (D) Hungry hemophile, (E) Redman or Indian.

4. If you throw the dice and 7 is showing on the top, what is facing down?
   (A) Seven, (B) Snake Eyes, (C) Boxcars, (D) Little Joes, (E) 11.

5. Cheap chitlings (not the kind you purchase at a frozen-food counter) will taste rubbery unless they are cooked long enough. How soon can you quit cooking them to eat and enjoy them?
   (A) 45 minutes, (B) 2 hours, (C) 24 hours, (D) 1 week (on a low flame), (E) 1 hour.

6. "Down home" (the South) today, for the average "soul brother" who is picking cotton (in season) from sunup until sundown, what is the average earning (take home) for one full day?
   (A) $.75, (B) $1.65, (C) $3.50, (D) $5, (E) $12.

7. A "handkerchief head" is. . .
   (A) A cool cat, (B) A porter, (C) An Uncle Tom, (D) A hoddi, (E) A preacher.

8. "Jet" is. . .
   (A) An East Oakland motorcycle club, (B) One of the gangs in "West Side Story," (C) A news and gossip magazine, (D) A way of life for the very rich.

9. "And Jesus said, ' Walk together, children. . .'"
   (A) "Don't get weary. There's a gret camp meeting," (B) "For we shall overcome," (C) "For the family that walks together talks together," (D) "By your patience you will win your souls" (Luke 21:19), (E) "Mind the things that are above, not the things that are on earth" (Col. 3:3).

10. If a pimp is up tight with a woman who gets state aid, what does he mean when he talks about "Mother's Day"?
    (A) Second Sunday in May, (B) Third Sunday in June, (C) First of every month, (D) None of these, (E) First and fifteenth of every month.

11. Jazz pianist Ahmad Jamal took an Arabic name after becoming really famous. Previously he had some fame with what he called his "slave name." What was his previous name?
    (A) Willie Lee Jackson, (B) LeRoi Jones, (C) Wilbur McDougal, (D) Fritz Jones, (E) Andy Johnson.

12. What is Willie Mae's last name?
    (A) Schwartz, (B) Matsuda, (C) Gomez, (D) Turner, (E) O'Flaherty.

13. What are the "Dixie hummingbirds"?
    (A) A part of the KKK, (B) A swamp disease, (C) A modern gospel group, (D) A Mississippi paramilitary group, (E) Deacons.

14. "Bo Diddley" is a. . .
    (A) Game for children, (B) Down home cheap wine, (C) Down home singer, (D) New dance, (E) Mojo call.

15. "Hully Gully" came from. . .
    (A) East Oakland, (B) Fillmore, (C) Watts, (D) Harlem, (E) Motor City.

16. Which word is most out of place here?
    (A) Slib, (B) Blood, (C) Gray, (D) Spook, (E) Black.

2. (C) 4. (A) 6. (D) 8. (C) 10. (E) 12. (D) 14. (C) 16. (C)
1. (E) 3. (C) 5. (C) 7. (C) 9. (A) 11. (D) 13. (C) 15. (C)
The Answers

Figure 12.8
A Black-Biased IQ Test
This "intelligence test" was created by Adrian Dove, a black sociologist, to illustrate, with humor, how information and vocabulary common to one culture might be entirely foreign to another.
Source: Dove, 1968.

tween IQ in childhood and later occupational success (McCall, 1977). An older study, conducted by Lewis Terman beginning in the 1920s, drew even broader conclusions. Terman selected a large number of highly gifted children (IQs over 135) and followed them through life (Terman, 1925; Terman and Oden, 1959). He found that many of the participants achieved great success in their chosen fields. As a group they had occupational and income levels significantly higher than people of average intelligence, and they also seemed generally better adjusted. For instance, their average rates of divorce, alcoholism, mental illness, and trouble with the law were lower than those of people with lower IQs. Thus, at the group level, IQ appears to be a reasonably good predictor of overall success in life. There are, however, many individual exceptions to this pattern. A high IQ is certainly no guarantee of high achievement and happiness.

Chapter Review

1. Middle childhood is a time when cognitive skills that began to emerge in the preschool period become increasingly refined and elaborated, making them much more effective problem-solving tools. Compared with preschoolers, elementary-school children are much more able to think systematically about multiple pieces of information—that is, they show a marked decline in centration. Youngsters in middle childhood also make strides toward overcoming the appearance/reality problem. They are much more able to ignore superficial appearances and focus instead on underlying truths. At the same time, they are able to think more effectively about their own knowledge and thought processes, an ability called **metacognition.** Elementary-school children still face some cognitive limitations, however. Their general lack of knowledge and practice in using new skills make them appear less competent than older children. They also have trouble reasoning maturely about abstract or hypothetical questions, an ability that doesn't emerge until adolescence.

2. Among the major cognitive developments of middle childhood is mastery of conservation concepts. Piaget believed there are three stages in this developmental process: In the first, children are nonconservers, still limited by centration on superficial appearance. In the second, youngsters enter a transitional stage, during which they begin to notice more than one dimension of the problem. In the third, a mature understanding of conservation emerges, and the children grasp the reversibility of superficial transformations. They understand by logical necessity that quantities do not change unless something is added to or subtracted from them. Such an understanding is based on **necessary truth.** In contrast to Piaget's stress on fundamental changes in the structure of children's thinking as conservation develops, information-processing theorists see a set of gradual changes in the rules youngsters use to solve conservation problems. A strength of the rule approach to understanding conservation is the detail with which it specifies the thought processes that underlie a child's performance.

3. Piaget described two kinds of classification that youngsters become able to understand during middle childhood. One is **hierarchical classification,** which involves addition of classes. The other is **matrix classification,** which entails multiplication of classes. It is not until age 8 or 9 that children are able to pass the standard **class-inclusion** test of hierarchical classification by simultaneously comparing a subclass with its superordinate class. It is at this age, too, that children are first able to solve matrix classification problems by sorting items simultaneously along two or more dimensions (color *and* shape, for example). In both these cases we see the child overcoming centration—either centration on a single classification dimension or centration on a single level in a hierarchy. Still, 8- or 9-year-olds may not yet grasp the more abstract logic of classification schemes. Until about age 11 an understanding of such systems seems to be tied to concrete objects and situations.

4. During the preschool years children show marked improvements in their ability to remember things. Some of these improvements come from an expansion of youngsters' knowledge, for what we know provides mental structures that ease assimilation of new information. In fact, what we recall about new information is only partly a product of the actual data we encountered. Recall is also the result of inferences made on the basis of what we already know. This inference process is referred to as **constructive memory.** During middle childhood constructive memory comes into its own, allowing children accurately to infer more than they are told. The memory abilities of elementary-school children also improve through better use of **mnemonic strategies** such as rehearsal. Whereas 5- and 6-year-olds don't spontaneously use mnemonic strategies very often, children between the ages of 7 and 10 increasingly do. Another aspect of remembering that improves during middle childhood is **meta-memory,** a person's knowledge of memory and memory processes. For instance, by the age of about 9, children are much better at predicting how likely they are to remember something and what kinds of memory strategies are apt to aid recall. This may help explain their increased use of mnemonic devices.

5. Children can learn a great deal from other children, as well as from adults. For instance, when a child who does not yet understand conservation is presented with a conservation problem to solve in conjunction with a more knowledgeable child, the less competent youngster will often make genuine progress in understanding the concept. Even interacting with a peer of equal competence in solving a conservation task can sometimes prompt discovery of the underlying principle if one of the children has the prerequisite skills. Piaget believed that an important factor promoting such socially fostered learning is the chance for children to experience conflict between their own ideas and those of other people. He emphasized the role of others in helping children make progress building on already-developed skills. One means of doing this is called scaffolding. **Scaffolding** involves a set of strategies that a teacher progressively alters based on an awareness of the learner's progress. Fifth graders have been observed to use scaffolding in tutoring younger children, one sign of the tutors' growing metacognitive skills.

6. **Intelligence quotients,** or IQ scores, are determined by comparing a person's performance on a set of cognitive tasks with the performance of others similar in age. Psychologists who develop IQ tests often have different conceptions of intelligence, from a unitary concept (seeing intelligence as a *general* capacity) to a multifaceted concept (seeing intelligence as made up of many separate and largely independent mental abilities). No matter how it is defined or measured, researchers agree that intelligence is a product of heredity interacting with environment. The concept of **reaction range** is useful in describing this interaction process. It refers to the limits within which the effects of genes can vary depending on environmental influences. Given normal variations in intellectual environments, the reaction range for IQ seems to be 20 points or so. Critics have questioned how meaningful IQ scores are, given that these tests almost inevitably have some cultural bias. Others have answered that IQ tests are relatively good predictors of school performance, the purpose for which they were originally created. When comparing children from different subcultures, however, we must be very cautious in interpreting IQs. These tests should not be taken to be measures of some enduring innate intellectual ability.

13

Social Development in Middle Childhood

Ten-year-old Malcolm and his buddies Andy, Leon, and Curtis pass Tammy Wilson on the sidewalk with her friends Vanessa and Lorraine. It is as if two powerful force fields have collided. The girls fall silent; the boys get "cool." Vanessa nudges Tammy in the ribs with her elbow. Tammy slaps her arm away but continues looking straight ahead. Lorraine suppresses a giggle. As each group goes in its own direction, Vanessa turns around and yells: "Hey, Malcolm, Tammy likes you!" Tammy covers her face and runs up the street. All three of Malcolm's buddies turn on him:

"Uuuh-ahh, Malcolm, you sweet on her!"

"Yeah! Malcolm got a girlfriend!"

"Why don't you go kiss her, Malcolm!"

Malcolm shoves each of them and shouts defensively, "No way, man! Get outa here," Then with laughter, shouting, and playful fighting the boys proceed to the candy store.

Middle childhood was once considered an uneventful phase of development. Given the whirlwind pace of changes during infancy, toddlerhood, and the preschool period, this view is understandable. The physical growth of school-age children slows to a few inches yearly, and their cognitive and social advances no longer seem so dramatic. Freud went so far as to label middle childhood a **latency period.** He believed that children's sexual urges lie relatively dormant at this time, awaiting their great reawakening in adolescence. Others took Freud's view to mean that little of importance in social and emotional development happens during the middle childhood years. Partly for this reason social and emotional development in middle childhood has until recently been one of the least studied topics in all of child psychology.

This lack of attention to social and emotional changes during middle childhood is unfortunate. From a developmental perspective, to ignore any period creates serious gaps in our knowledge of how children grow. Ignoring middle childhood also hinders our ability to understand how youngsters handle the critical challenges of adolescence, for developmental outcomes in this later period build on those of the earlier one (Blos, 1970). But perhaps most important of all, research into middle childhood has shown very clearly that it is *not* an uneventful time. Much social and emotional development goes on from ages 6 through 12.

We can glimpse some of these changes in our opening example. Here we observe boys and girls interacting in ways never seen among preschoolers. While strict separation of the sexes generally prevails (Huston, Carpenter, and Atwater, 1986), the beginnings of mutual attraction lie just beneath the surface. In fact, the energy devoted to maintaining a boy-girl separation makes clear that sexual issues are not completely latent. However, middle childhood is a period of development in which other issues take precedence—issues such as consolidating a sense of self and working out the rules of friendship with members of the same sex.

Several theorists have tried to summarize the central socio-emotional issues facing children at this time. For instance, Erik Erikson (1963) has argued that during these years children begin to learn in earnest many adult skills. Successful adaptation to this challenge gives rise to what Erikson calls a **sense of industry,** that is, a basic belief in one's own competence and ability to master the world coupled with a tendency to initiate activities, to seek out learning experiences, and to work hard to accomplish goals. You saw some good examples of this new sense in our earlier stories of Meryl and Malcolm. These children and their friends feel pride in being able to carry out projects, and they are busy setting new challenges and objectives for themselves. The sense of industry does not derive from the frequent fantasy play of the preschool period, which declines now (Doyle et al., 1984). Rather, it is based on concrete achievements in the real world, achievements that bring deep feelings of competence and self-worth. In contrast, repeated failure to master skills, in Erikson's view, leaves the child with the opposite feelings of incompetence and inferiority. To see where this challenge of middle childhood fits into Erikson's overall theory, turn back to Table 2.1.

Erikson focuses on the practical skills that children seek to master during middle childhood and on the effects that their overall success or failure has on the developing sense of self. The process he talks about,

Single sex groups are the major social milieu of middle childhood. *(Naoki Okamoto/Black Star.)*

however, can be viewed as one critical part of an even broader developmental challenge. During the elementary school years children begin to pull together their histories of experience as a social partner, a "worker," an initiator, a boy or a girl, a problem solver, a coper, and so forth and to integrate them all into a coherent self-concept. In other words, in middle childhood a self-image with many dimensions becomes consolidated in the child's mind (Damon and Hart, 1982). It is crucial that this consolidation be well advanced before the dramatic changes of adolescence, when so much will be demanded of the child. Because the maturing sense of self is so important, we will consider it first in this chapter.

Middle childhood is not simply a time of turning inward to consolidate an image of the self, however. It is also a period of expansion, of reaching outward toward new experiences. The peer group is the setting for many of these experiences. In middle childhood children first form what can be called true friendships, peer relations based on mutual trust, loyalty, and support, such as the relationship between Meryl and Amy. Middle childhood is also the time when children develop a genuine understanding of what it means to be part of a group and adhere to group norms. Meryl and Amy's creation of their own private "apartment" and Malcolm's strong belief that peers shouldn't "rat" on one another are both outgrowths of this developmental change. At the same time that new perspectives and experiences are emerging in the peer group, the classroom is offering children additional new horizons. At school, children encounter new people, new activities, and new expectations for behavior. We will examine the child in both the peer group and the classroom in this chapter.

We will also examine the continuing influence of the family in middle childhood. Parents' styles of discipline, their attitudes toward sex roles, and the existence of marital conflict, separation, and divorce can all have an impact. But before turning to the family as a continuing setting for human development, we want to give you a better idea of how school-age children differ socially and emotionally from preschoolers. Let's begin by trying to step inside the mind of school-age youngsters to observe the new ways in which they think about themselves.

DEVELOPMENT OF THE SELF

Advances in Self-Understanding

The challenge of understanding the self continues throughout childhood and on into adulthood. During the preschool years, as you learned in Chapter 11, a sense of self-constancy emerges and a concept of gender begins to form. Then, during middle childhood, youngsters start to broaden their self-understandings to include not just physical self-conceptions but mental and emotional ones as well (see Table 13.1). At the same time they become increasingly able to see the self within a social context and to assess personal abilities by making comparisons with peers. These developmental changes lay the groundwork for assembling a more complete, well-integrated, and mature view of the self.

FROM THE PHYSICAL TO THE PSYCHOLOGICAL SELF

Preschoolers' notions of the self are very different from those adults hold. For one thing, preschoolers' self-concepts are highly physical in nature. Psychologist John Broughton (1978) asked children of different ages such questions as "What is the self?" "What is the mind?" and "What is the difference between the mind and body?" He found that preschoolers tend to think of the self as a concrete entity, often synonymous with the brain, the head, or sometimes the entire body. As a result, they tend to think of nonhumans as having "selves" as well. A 4-year-old would insist, for example, that a dog or a bird or perhaps even a tree or a flower has a self. In keeping with this kind of thinking, preschoolers also tend to distinguish themselves from others in terms of physical attributes. "I'm different from Madeline because I have curly hair," a 5-year-old might explain; or "I'm different from Kevin because I have a red sweater." Similarly, when preschoolers are asked to list things about themselves, they usually dwell on their physical activities. "I play on the swings," a 4-year-old might say; or "I go to nursery school" (Keller, Ford, and Meachum, 1978). Apparently, during early childhood the concept of self remains closely tied to the child's body. Even motivations arise from a physical entity in the typical preschooler's mind. As one young child charmingly explained the notion of individual free will: "I am the boss of myself . . . [because] my mouth told my arm and my arm does what my mouth tells it to do" (Selman, 1980, p. 95).

By the early elementary school years this physical view of the self is changing. Eight-year-olds begin to show an understanding of the self's subjective nature, an awareness that the mind and body are not one and the same (Broughton, 1978). Increasingly with age elementary school children begin distinguishing themselves from others not just in terms of physical traits but also in terms of thoughts and feelings. This more sophisticated outlook brings with it a firmer understanding of the self's uniqueness. As one of Broughton's 10-year-old subjects explained it: "I am one of a kind. . . . There could be a person who looks like me or talks like me, but no one who has every single detail I have. Never a person who thinks exactly like me" (Broughton, 1978, p. 86).

The same trends in self-understanding have been revealed in other

TABLE 13.1   Children's Conceptions of the Self

Level 0: The Self as a Physical Entity

View of Self: overt behavior defines inner experiences
Personality: overt, physical appearance

CHILD: I am a good boy.   Age 5
INTERVIEWER: Why?
CHILD: Because I am big.

Level 1: The Self as an Intentional Subject

View of self: motives and thoughts underlie behavior; feelings are not easily hidden
              (people are taken at face value)
Personality: abilities and skills

I: How does Mike feel inside?   Age 8
C: Sad.
I: How do you know?
C: Because of the way he looks.
I: Could he look sad and be happy inside?
C: He could but you would be able to tell if you watched him long enough; he'd
    show you he was happy.

Level 2: The Individual as an Introspective Self

View of self: self-reflective; person can conceal inner reality; multiple but separate
              feelings toward one object
Personality: feelings, moods, and actions   Age 10

I: Could a person feel happy and sad at the same time?
C: A gift of a new puppy can make one happy because one wants a puppy and sad
    because it reminds one of one's old dog.

Level 3: The Self as a Stable Personality (Adolescence)

View of self: self can observe its own reflections; can experience mixed feelings at
              the same time
Personality: relatively stable and unchangeable; focus on individuality

studies. In one, researchers asked children between the ages of 6 and 9 questions designed to tap their sense of themselves as unique and enduring individuals. Most of the children had a stable sense of self-identity, but the basis for this sense became much less physical with age. Whereas a 6-year-old may assert that he will be the same person when he grows up because he will still have red hair and be named Tim, a typical 9-year-old will answer quite differently. As one child who had just turned 9 put it: "'Cause I'll just be the same. I don't change anything." (Interviewer: "What will be the same?") "Me. I just don't turn into anything. I just stay the same and stuff, and I grow" (Guardo and Bohan, 1971, p. 1919). The same developmental change emerged in responses to the question of why the children couldn't take on the identity of another animal, say, a dog. Whereas 6-year-olds generally focused on external, physical reasons ("I don't bark and I don't have four legs"), 9-year-olds appealed to deeper, more psychological factors. "I am a human being," said one of the older subjects. "A human being can learn more things than dogs" (p. 1916). Clearly, older children have more sophisticated, less physically based notions of the self.

Psychologist Robert Selman (1980) has shown how the emergence of a child's sense of an *inner, private self* parallels a growing awareness that all people have internal thoughts and feelings that are often hidden from others and sometimes even from themselves. Selman explored this topic by presenting children with dilemmas such as the following one:

> Tom has just saved some money to buy Mike Hunter a birthday present. He and his friend Greg go downtown to try to decide what Mike will like. Tom tells Greg that Mike is sad these days because his dog Pepper ran away. They see Mike and decide to try to find out what Mike wants without asking him right off. After talking to Mike for a while the kids realize that Mike is really sad because of his lost dog. When Greg suggests he get a new dog, Mike says he can't just get a new dog and have things be the same. Then Mike leaves to run some errands. As Mike's friends shop some more they see a puppy for sale in the pet store. . . . Tom and Greg discuss whether to get Mike the puppy . . . . What do you think Tom will do? (p. 175)

Selman then presented a number of more specific questions related to the story. Did Mike mean what he said? Can someone say something and not mean it? Did you ever think you'd feel one way and then find out you felt another? How can this happen? Can you ever fool yourself?

Selman found that very young children do not seem to distinguish between people's inner psychological experiences and their external words and actions. Many 5-year-olds concluded that Tom should not buy Mike the puppy because Mike doesn't want another dog. They knew this, they said, because Mike *told* Tom so. In contrast, by about age 8 or 9 an understanding of the internal self had usually emerged. Now children recognized that what people say and do need not necessarily conform to what they think and feel. Mike may insist that he doesn't want a puppy, and he may even make himself believe this. Yet underneath it all, his inner, private self could want a new dog very much. Such insights into the private, psychologically based self show that children make great strides in self-understanding during the elementary school years.

DEVELOPMENT OF THE SOCIAL SELF

Another advance in self-understanding that occurs during this period is often referred to as development of the **social self** (Damon, 1983). By this psychologists mean an awareness that "who I am" is often intimately tied to "the many other people around me." During the elementary school years, children's ability to adopt this perspective changes significantly.

What evidence do we have of this advancement? For one thing, school-age children begin to define themselves in terms of traits they usually exhibit in their dealings with others (Benenson and Dweck, 1986). Ideas such as "I am kind," "I am friendly," "I am tough," or "I am shy" begin to enter their self-concepts. In addition, school-age children begin to incorporate social group membership into their self-descriptions (Damon, 1983). When asked to tell about himself, 10-year-old Mikey's answers might include that he is a fifth grader, a Boy Scout, and a member of a Little League team. Such references to social group membership are very prominent in the self-descriptions given by adults. Their emergence in middle childhood tells us that youngsters are increasingly placing the concept of self within a social context.

THE SELF IN COMPARISON WITH OTHERS

Closely linked to the inclination to define the self in terms of relationships with others is the tendency to use others as a source of comparison in making self-evaluations. In one set of experiments, for instance, children ages 5 to 10 were given feedback about their performance on some difficult tasks (how many hits or misses they made, or how many correct and incorrect responses they gave). In addition, they were given information about how well other children had done on the same tasks (Ruble et al., 1980). The researchers found that youngsters did not begin to evaluate their own performance in comparison with that of others until age 7 or 8. And not until age 9 or 10 did they consistently and systematically use comparative information in making self-assessments. Again, we see the age of about 8 or 9 as a turning point in social development.

Comparing oneself with others is an important influence on the developing concept of the self. *(Ellis Herwig/The Picture Cube.)*

Younger children do sometimes compare themselves with peers, but their earliest social comparisons are usually motivated by tangible objectives, such as making sure that they receive a fair share of rewards (Masters, 1971). In the experiments just described, in contrast, social comparisons were used to make a much more abstract self-evaluation: How well did I perform on this new task? In part, the child's advancing cognitive development underlies this trend toward using social comparisons to answer more abstract questions about the self. Teachers may also encourage it by stressing each student's academic progress relative to that of classmates (Ruble et al., 1980). You saw this kind of encouragement in our earlier story of Malcolm, whose teacher made a point of telling the four highest test scorers that they had performed better than others in the class.

The effects of social comparison on self-evaluation can be seen in older children's self-descriptions (Lively and Bromley, 1973; Secord and Peevers, 1974). Whereas preschoolers tend to describe themselves in terms of their physical activities ("I play baseball; I run around the bases"), 8- to 9-year-olds tend to make comparative judgments about their abilities ("I play baseball better than Jeff or Richie; I am the fastest runner in my class"). The developmental change here is from a focus on typical activities, with relatively little self-evaluation, to a focus on the child's own competencies as measured through comparisons with peers. Such social comparisons further sharpen the child's differentiation of the self from others (Damon and Hart, 1982).

Self-Esteem in School-Age Children

The kinds of self-evaluations children make contribute to their levels of self-esteem. Psychologists measure self-esteem in school-age youngsters by using a number of different techniques. Sometimes they ask children to judge their overall self-satisfaction ("How happy are you with the kind of person you are?" "Do you often wish you were someone else?"). At other times they ask more specific questions about self-attitudes and personal talents ("Are you proud of your school work?" "Do you make friends easily?"). In still other cases they use more formal self-esteem scales (Harter, 1983). Observation of children assessed by these various methods reveals that those high in self-esteem tend to have very positive approaches to the world. These positive approaches, in turn, are related to success in many areas. For instance, high self-esteem predicts success in school, including reading ability (Markus and Nurius, 1984). Not surprisingly, youngsters high in self-esteem are also very confident, not only in their own abilities but also in their own ideas. Stanley Coopersmith (1967), who has extensively studied self-esteem in fifth and sixth graders, describes these children this way:

> [They] approach tasks and persons with the expectation that they will be well received and successful. They have confidence in their perceptions and judgments and believe that they can bring their efforts to a favorable resolution. Their favorable self-attitudes lead them to accept their own opinions and place credence and trust in their reactions and conclusions. This permits them to follow their own judgments when there is a difference of opinion and also permits them to consider novel ideas. (p. 80)

High self-esteem in middle childhood and its accompanying characteristics tend to be stable over time (Rosenberg, 1979), and they are predictable from patterns of adaptation in preschool and from quality of attachment in infancy (Sroufe and Jacobvitz, 1987). For instance, a child like Malcolm who was self-confident as a preschooler and has high self-esteem at age 10 is likely to have high self-esteem as a teenager and even an adult. Later in this chapter we will explore how parenting practices help encourage high self-esteem in youngsters.

Locus of Control and Self-Management

One important accompaniment to high self-esteem is belief in one's personal effectiveness. By this we mean a sense that you can do things well, that you can master and prevail in challenging circumstances, and that your successes come from resources *within* yourself (Hrncir, 1985). Psychologists call this sense an **internal locus of control** (Rotter, 1966).

Most children acquire an internal locus of control, but it does not emerge suddenly and completely. Instead, a sense of internal locus of control evolves step by step (Benenson and Dweck, 1986). For instance, Susan Harter (1980) has found that while most preschoolers believe their physical and cognitive accomplishments are the result of their own efforts, social success at this age is viewed as a chancier matter. When asked, "How do you find a friend?" a preschooler might answer, "You go up and ring someone's doorbell" or "Maybe a policeman can help you." In contrast, by school age, most children feel that social successes, like physical and cognitive ones, depend on one's own actions. As one 8-year-old girl replied when asked how you get someone to like you: "Be nice and you'll get niceness in return" (Damon, 1977, p. 160). Some school-age children, however, persist in thinking that social successes, as well as cognitive and physical achievements, are beyond their personal control. Instead, they see what happens to them as governed largely by external factors. This negative outlook, called an **external locus of control,** tends to be shaped by children's past experiences. We will discuss its development further in a later section.

Since children with an internal locus of control believe that what happens to them depends on their own actions, they tend to perform quite well on tasks requiring self-control. For instance, when given the choice of accepting a small reward immediately or waiting for a much larger one later, and when told that certain actions carried out in the meanwhile will shorten the waiting period, children with a strong internal locus of control tend to busy themselves with the prescribed behaviors and are able to wait substantial amounts of time (Mischel, Zeiss, and Zeiss, 1974). The reason for their success at delaying gratification lies in their way of thinking. They are convinced that what they do *will* matter, that it will hasten the arrival of the larger reward. In contrast, children with an external locus of control are unlikely to exert this kind of self-discipline. For them, future outcomes seem so chancy that they quickly grab what is offered here and now.

Although the ability to exert self-discipline often varies with a child's locus of control, the capacity for self-management greatly improves with age for virtually *all* youngsters. Many experiments have demonstrated this fact. For example, when children are given the simple choice between a small candy bar now and a much larger one later, delay of gratification increases markedly between the ages of 5 and 12. In one study, 72 percent of kindergarteners and 67 percent of first and second graders decided to take the immediate reward, whereas only 49 percent of third and fourth graders and only 38 percent of fifth and sixth graders did so (Mischel and Metzner, 1962). Perhaps the older children had learned that by turning their thoughts elsewhere they could minimize frustration during the waiting period. The younger children, in contrast, may have found it hard to stop thinking about how good a candy bar would taste (Mischel and Mischel, 1983).

Children's thoughts about themselves develop rapidly in middle childhood, as their social experience widens and their cognitive abilities mature. *(© Naoki Oka-moto/Black Star.)*

PEER RELATIONS

Willard Hartup (1983), who has extensively studied peer relations among children, asserts that the peer group is rivaled only by the family as the child's major developmental setting. Most developmentalists agree with this viewpoint. What gives peers such great significance? Why do they have such a marked influence on children? One reason is the sheer amount of time that peers spend together. The number of hours spent with other children increases sharply once a youngster enters school. And by the age of about 11 the typical American child spends as much time with peers as with adults (Wright, 1967).

But time spent together is not the whole story. Peers are also influential because of the unique learning experiences they provide. Adult-child relationships are limited in what they can teach about such things as reciprocity, cooperation, and aggression. The reason is that adult-child relationships are inherently unequal. The adult always holds ultimate authority over the child: The adult has the right to *tell* the child what to

Cooperation, reciprocity, and equity are important principles that are learned in interaction with peers. *(Mike Mazzaschi/Stock, Boston.)*

do, and the child is expected to listen. In the peer group, in contrast, relationships are far more equal. The very word *peer* means equal standing. This makes the peer group highly conducive to learning firsthand about the rules and expectations that will guide one's behaviors with others later in life. Peer relations may be especially important for learning to regulate aggression and for understanding the principles of reciprocity and equity (Hartup, 1980; Suomi, 1977b; Youniss, 1980). When Malcolm and Andy debate how to "get even" with Derek or when Meryl and Amy discuss how to share a new toy, they are tackling principles that can best be learned within the peer group.

Finally, the fact that children have not yet acquired all the social skills that adults have means that youngsters challenge one another's developing capacities for interaction (Hartup and Sancilio, 1986). Children must work to make peers grasp what they are thinking and feeling, and they must also struggle to see the points of view that other children hold. Through such efforts toward mutual understanding, children gain in social competence throughout the elementary school years.

Developmental Changes in Peer Interaction

During the elementary school years children acquire new ways of relating to one another. These developmental changes in peer interaction can be seen in many different areas. For instance, school-age children become increasingly effective in their communication skills, and they also begin to express their prosocial and aggressive tendencies differently. At the same time, the meaning of friendship alters substantially across the middle childhood period. We will explore each of these changes in the following sections.

ADVANCES IN COMMUNICATION SKILLS

Six-year-old Mikey is trying to teach a younger boy how to tie his shoes. Mikey squats down by Gary, unties his own laces, and launches into a verbal and visual demonstration:

> *Mikey:* It's easy. First you pull the two strings, see. Then you make the loop, an' wrap around, an' push through, an' pull. See? That's all there is to it. Now you try.
>
> *Gary:* First you pull the strings. . . .
>
> *Mikey:* No, no. You've gotta wrap 'em first.
>
> *Gary:* Like this?
>
> *Mikey:* No! That's the loop part. You wrap 'em like twist 'em first. . . . No! Not *that* way. Here, let me do it.

Mikey's efforts, however well intentioned, are not very effective. He lacks the ability to take the younger, less competent boy's perspective. Difficulty in adopting another person's viewpoint continues from the preschool period into the early elementary school years. Soon, however, Mikey's communication skills will improve significantly. By the end of middle childhood youngsters are quite adept at conveying their thoughts and feelings to one another.

Researchers have studied these improvements in peer communication within the laboratory. In Chapter 10 we examined one of these studies in some detail. Two children, separated by a screen, were given identical blocks, each with a different abstract picture on it. One child was asked to describe each block to the other child, so that the two children could ultimately stack their blocks in the same order (Krauss and Glucksberg, 1969). As you know, preschoolers performed poorly on this task; they tended to give very egocentric descriptions ("Like the kitchen thing" a 5-year-old might say, or simply, "It's this one"). With age, however, children's skill at the game increased markedly. Fifth and sixth graders were quite good at considering the knowledge their listeners possessed and tailoring their descriptions accordingly.

The same developmental trend can be seen in natural settings. Older elementary school children are much better than younger ones at conveying information so that a particular listener will understand. Older school-age children are also more effective at understanding others. For instance, they are quite good at seeking the necessary extra information when a speaker's meaning is initially unclear (Alvy, 1968; Dittman, 1972). They are also reasonably good at interpreting the many nonverbal cues (gestures, intonations, expressions) that accompany speech.

CHANGES IN PROSOCIAL AND AGGRESSIVE BEHAVIOR

The improved ability of school-age children to communicate with one another and to consider one another's perspective influences both their prosocial behavior and their displays of aggression. For instance, elementary school children tend to be more altruistic than younger children, and they are also more likely to fashion prosocial responses in ways that take situational factors into account (Damon, 1983; Handlon and Gross, 1959). These developmental changes are undoubtedly tied to an increased capacity to understand another person's viewpoint.

Elementary school youngsters are less likely than preschoolers to engage in instrumental aggression—striking out in order to gain control of an object. School-age children, with their better communication skills, have acquired more sophisticated ways of getting what they want. They may barter to gain possession of a plaything, or they may appeal to the norm of sharing, mustering support from their peer allies.

But as instrumental aggression declines in middle childhood, some forms of hostile aggression increase. Hostile aggression, as you may recall, is aggression aimed purely at hurting someone else. Compared with preschoolers, elementary school children are much more likely to hurl verbal insults in order to cause each other psychological distress (Maccoby, 1980). This trend makes sense when you consider the developmental changes taking place in their understandings of the self and others. For instance, in order for Derek to be truly insulted upon being called a jerk, he must first have an image of himself as generally well liked and competent. At the same time, only when Malcolm is able to consider Derek's feelings about receiving such an insult will he genuinely understand how much the taunt can hurt.

Cognitive factors have been associated with individual differences in aggression as well as with developmental changes. In a series of studies, Ken Dodge has shown that aggressive children more frequently interpret others' actions to imply hostile intent, especially when cues are ambiguous (e.g., Dodge and Frame, 1982). This could be interpreted to mean that a cognitive "deficit" may be a cause of aggression. However, these children may in fact be basing their judgments on past experience, which for them may have consisted of repeated examples of hostile treatment. These children's interpretations may be inappropriate but still be accurate reflections of their experiences. Recent research shows that a history of avoidant attachment predicts such "errors" of interpretation (Suess, personal communication). Still, all of this research shows that how children think and how they behave are tied together in middle childhood.

Verbal hostility replaces physical hostility as the dominant mode for expressing anger or displeasure with a peer. *(Sybil Shelton/ Monkmeyer Press.)*

CHANGES IN PEER FRIENDSHIPS

Interviewer:	Why is Caleb your friend?
Tony (a preschooler):	Because I like him.
Interviewer:	And why do you like him?
Tony:	Because he's my friend.
Interviewer:	And why is he your friend?
Tony:	(slowly and emphatically with mild disgust) Because . . . I . . . chosed . . . him . . . for . . . my . . . friend.

(Rubin, 1980)

Tony's depth of understanding about friendship is fairly typical of children his age. Although preschoolers routinely label other children their "friends," these relationships lack the reciprocal support and loyalty, the shared intimacy and common interests of genuine friendships. Not until middle childhood do more mature ideas and expectations concerning friendships develop. This, in fact, is one of the major social accomplishments of middle childhood. By the end of the elementary school years most youngsters are involved in what psychiatrist Harry Stack Sullivan (1953) called "chumships"—very close and special friendship between two peers, such as that between Meryl and Amy.

The deepening of peer relationships that occurs in middle childhood is related to various advances in how children think (Bigelow, 1977; Hartup and Sancilio, 1986; Rubin and Krasnor, 1985; Youniss, 1980). During the elementary school years, as we said earlier, youngsters begin to conceive of both the self and others in less physical, more psychological terms. They become increasingly aware that people have inner thoughts and feelings that are not always expressed. With this awareness comes a broadened understanding of how friends can support one another. School-age youngsters no longer define a friend simply as "someone I like," "someone I play with a lot," and "someone who gives me toys." Friends are now seen as people who help and share with each other, especially in times of need. School-age children also focus more on the personal traits a friend possesses. Friends are described as nice, kind, and worthy of trust. This is how one 10-year-old girl compared her friends with her nonfriends:

(Why don't you make friends with Bernadette?) "'Cause we had a fight, a big one." (Why can't you make up?) "Because I don't know her phone number and I wouldn't apologize anyway." (How come?) "'Cause we're not good friends and I don't like her that much. She's not my kind of person. She's not my taste." (What's your taste?) "I like nice people. If they're not kind then they're not a friend." (Weinstock, quoted in Damon, 1977, p. 158)

By the end of middle childhood children's conceptions of friendship have become quite mature. Youngsters now recognize that the essence of friendship is mutual understanding and caring, as well as shared outlooks and interests (Rotenberg and Mann, 1986). One boy, who had recently turned 13, explained it this way:

(Why is Jimmy your best friend?) "I don't know, I guess it's because we talk a lot and stuff." (What do you talk about?) "Secret stuff, you know, what we

Close friendships often offer special opportunities for learning and development. *(Jeffry Myers/Stock, Boston, Michael Hayman/Photo Researchers, Inc.)*

think of him or her or whoever. And sports, things we both like to do." . . . (When did you get friendly?) "After we found out that we didn't have to worry about the other guy blabbing and spreading stuff around." (Weinstock, quoted in Damon, 1977, p. 163)

Clearly, this boy has a notion of friendship that in certain ways is approaching notions held by many adults.

Developmentalists are interested not only in how school-age children think about their friends but in how youngsters who are friends interact with one another. Numerous studies show that children behave differently with their friends than they do with mere acquaintances (Berndt, Hawkins, and Hoyle, 1986). For instance, in a study in which pairs of elementary school children were asked to build block towers in order to win rewards, those pairs consisting of friends showed more positive emotion (more laughing, smiling, exclaiming, and so forth) than did other pairs (Newcomb, Brady, and Hartup, 1979). The pairs of friends were also more likely to phrase ideas in mutual terms ("Let's do it this way." "Let's make sure it's straight."), and they were more concerned with equity in how rewards were distributed. Similar findings come from extensive research by John Gottman (1983) at the University of Illinois. He concludes that children who become mutual friends are better able to find common ground and shared interests. Their relationships are also characterized by amity—that is, by fun, humor, warmth, and harmony. But pairs of friends don't *always* cooperate. At times they may even be more competitive than nonfriends. This is especially true when the spontaneity typically found between friends causes an initially low-key competitive game to get out of control (Berndt, 1981a). But whether they are cooperating or competing, the thing that distinguishes friends' interactions the most is the deeper involvement that exists (Furman and Buhrmester, 1985). By middle childhood friendship demands a substantial investment of self.

In summary, cognitive development and interactions with friends during the elementary school years work hand in hand to lead children to a new understanding of social relationships. Although preschoolers also share things with one another, their sharing is not based on the same psychological foundations found in older children. By the age of about 8 or 9 giving and sharing become closely tied to rectifying inequalities. Meryl, for example, says that it's "only fair" to allow Jeannie to join in some of the bike hikes she and Amy take. Such stress on fairness is seen repeatedly in school-age youngsters. Fairness, equity, and reciprocity are cardinal principles of their relationships (Hartup and Sancilio, 1986; Rotenberg and Mann, 1986; Youniss, 1980).

Peer Groups in Middle Childhood

Elementary school children tend to play with relatively stable clusters of friends called **peer groups.** During middle childhood girls' peer groups become smaller, with each girl having one or two best friends (Lever, 1976; Waldrop and Halvorsen, 1975). This tendency is in keeping with the stress school-age girls place on intimacy, sharing of confidences, and mutual support (Rubin, 1980). Meryl and Amy with their private "apartment" are typical of girls at this age. Boys' peer groups, in contrast, tend to be larger, with an emphasis on loyalty and shared activities. Malcolm and his three buddies—Andy, Leon, and Curtis—provide a good snapshot of the kinds of peer groups school-age boys tend to form. Even more than in early childhood, elementary school peer groups are strongly segregated by gender. Except for the inevitable cross-sex teasing and chasing, rarely do school-age boys and girls regularly play together.

DEVELOPING A SENSE OF "GROUPNESS"

Like conceptions of friendship, conceptions of the peer group also change with age (see Figure 13.1). Preschoolers have very little understanding of groups as such. They have little sense of peer group members sharing a collective identity, only rudimentary feelings of "we" versus "they." By the end of the elementary school years, in contrast, children have a well-defined sense of "groupness" and readily distinguish between those inside and outside their own group.

What gives rise to this awareness of group boundaries and membership? Largely, it stems from the same cognitive advances that promote changing conceptions of the self and others. In addition, however, the joint activities in which members of peer groups engage tend to foster recognition of shared values and goals, accompanied by a sense of "we." This fact was dramatically demonstrated in a classic study of peer group formation among 11- and 12-year-old boys (Sherif et al., 1961; Sherif and Sherif, 1953).

In their study Muzafer and Carolyn Sherif recruited 22 boys to attend a summer camp. The boys were divided into two groups, each of which was housed at a different campsite so that at first neither group knew of the other's existence. Soon after settling in, each group was presented with a series of tasks that required cooperative effort. For instance, one evening the campers were given all the ingredients for dinner, but they had to prepare the meal themselves. Such tasks rapidly gave rise to clear

Your group helps define who you are and provides standards and feedback for evaluating yourself. (*Naoki Okamoto/Black Star.*)

hierarchical group structures, with some boys repeatedly serving as leaders and others acting as followers. The projects also encouraged a strong sense of group identity. Soon the boys were using group names—the Eagles and the Rattlers—and were fashioning other symbols of their "we-ness," such as group flags and banners. Thus, the act of repeatedly coordinating their activities toward mutually desirable goals transformed what were originally collections of strangers into two very cohesive groups.

The researchers next demonstrated that solidarity with a peer group can be strengthened significantly by intergroup conflict. They organized a series of competitions between the previously isolated groups (ballgames, races, tugs of war), for which the winners received valuable prizes. At first, these competitive pressures tended to cause upheaval within each group, especially following losses. Group members would blame one another for their frustrating failures, and angry incidents often resulted, sometimes leading to a change in group leadership. Soon, however, this initial reaction faded and the groups emerged more unified than ever. Group spirit reached a new high. Each group became the target for the other's hostility. Intergroup bickering, name calling, fights, and raids rapidly became the norm. This phase of the study clearly showed that relations *between* groups can strongly affect interactions *within* groups. It also revealed some of the ways in which intergroup prejudices and hatreds are fostered.

Finally, the Sherifs decided it was time to end the intergroup warfare. The task proved far from easy, however. Requests that each group try to see the other's good side met with no success. Neither did attempts to get the groups together for friendly, shared activities such as picnics, firework displays, and movies. These social events inevitably dissolved into chaos as the Eagles and the Rattlers hurled food and insults at each other. The one strategy that did work was a series of bogus emergencies. The camp truck presumably had to be repaired or else food could not be delivered. A supposed leak had to be found in the water pipes or else the entire water system would be shut down. These staged emergencies required cooperation among *all* the boys at the camp. Intergroup conflict sharply decreased and friendships began to form across group lines. Apparently, when enemies are forced to pull together for their own mutual good, they often begin to see each other in a new, more favorable light. The old prejudices and stereotypes are difficult to maintain when the person working next to you seems so much like yourself. Psycholo-

Figure 13.1
Age Changes in Children's Conceptions of the Self, Friendship, and the Peer Group.
The development of understanding of self and others increases notably during the middle childhood years.
Source: Adapted from Selman, 1980, p. 180.

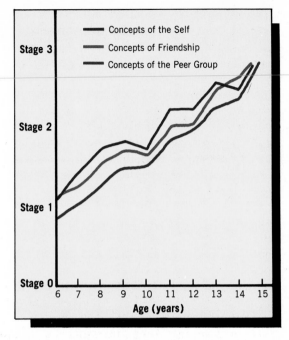

gists believe that this lesson in reducing intergroup conflict among school-age boys has application to people of all ages.

ADHERENCE TO PEER GROUP NORMS

If you have ever observed a group of elementary school children scrupulously dividing a large piece of candy so that all can receive *precisely* the same amount, you are aware of how concerned children this age are about enforcing peer group **norms,** or rules of conduct. Equity is a very important norm during middle childhood, perhaps because it helps maintain peer group harmony and cohesiveness (Streater and Chertkoff, 1976). Sometimes, of course, school-age children do divide things unequally. What is interesting about such cases is the basis on which they determine the allocations. Whereas preschoolers often allot rewards according to peripheral factors such as age or gender, school-age children often use performance as the basis (Graziano, 1984). Thus, Mikey and his Little League teammates might decide that the boy who scored the most runs in the game they just won deserves the remaining slice of the pizza they are sharing in celebration. If no one had clearly made a larger contribution to winning the game that day, the boys would probably be hard-liners in enforcing the equity standard. Such strict adherence to norms is common in school-age children. We saw one example in our story of Malcolm, who was amazed that Derek could ever break the code of not "ratting" on peers. Another example can be seen in school-age children's often rigid adherence to the rules of a game, as if the rules had sacred status. It is not until adolescence and even beyond that a person's conception of rules and norms becomes more relative and flexible.

Are school-age children total conformists then? No. The term *conformity* implies that people are simply going along with others, often in opposition to their own beliefs. But school-age children are not necessarily doing this when they adhere so closely to peer norms. In fact, research shows that in certain circumstances children's conformity to peer group opinion actually decreases throughout middle childhood. This is particularly true when the peer group has clearly made an incorrect choice (Hoving, Hamm, and Calvin, 1969). For instance, if 10-year-old Mikey can plainly see that Richie hits more runs than Jeff, he will probably stick to his judgment that Richie is the better hitter no matter how many peers try to tell him the opposite. Thus, school-age children are not necessarily conformists, even though they do tend to be norm-conscious and very literal interpreters of norms.

Some people express concern that the norms in children's peer groups are at odds with those supported by adults. According to this view, adult norms in America center around work and achievement, whereas peer norms center around play and having fun. The two are therefore said to be at odds. Although parents and teachers argue that such normative conflict is pervasive, little research substantiates this view. On such important issues as moral standards, self-control, and life aspirations, peer and parental values are usually in agreement (Hartup, 1983).

SOCIALIZATION WITHIN THE PEER GROUP

Since peer group norms are generally in agreement with those of the family and community, the peer group must be considered a major agent of childhood socialization. Socialization, as you may remember from Chapter 9, is the process of instilling in children the rules, standards, and values of their society. Although adults are the ones who initially teach youngsters how they are expected to behave, children themselves do much to ensure that those expectations are carried out. Friends and playmates tell each other when they are doing things "wrong," and children who refuse to follow the rules are often ostracized. The peer group, in short, is one of the mainstream culture's great watchdogs and enforcers. Partly through peer group vigilance, cultural norms and values become deeply engrained.

One area of socialization in which the peer group's influence stands out clearly is that of learning gender roles. Children model appropriate gender behavior for one another, and these models are closely followed (Langlois and Downs, 1980; Wolf, 1973). Elementary school children are particularly diligent in their efforts to ensure that children do not stray too far across gender boundaries. Chase games between the sexes may be acceptable, but a boy who tries to enter a girls' game of jump rope will usually be shunned as intensely by the girls as he is ridiculed by the boys. Researcher Barrie Thorne (1986) has called these rituals of teasing and ostracism "border work," because the children are defending the boundaries of their gender-segregated groups. This is what Malcolm's friends are doing in the scene at the beginning of this chapter. Their teasing clearly keeps Malcolm from showing any reciprocal "liking" for Tammy. Such self-imposed gender segregation is common in middle childhood throughout the world (Edwards and Whiting, 1980; Mead, 1939). One function it may serve is to protect young children from premature sexual contact. In this way they have a chance to first work on establishing intimacy with peers within the safety of their own gender

Girls and boys expend much energy trying to show that they don't want to have anything to do with each other. Virtually every 10-year-old, when asked about a recent day camp experience, said the only thing they didn't like was "the boys" or "the girls." Despite such protests, it is clear that cross-gender interest runs high. *(David Strickler/Monkmeyer Press.)*

groups. During adolescence and adulthood intimacy will then be extended to opposite-sex partners.

STATUS AND POPULARITY IN THE PEER GROUP

Not all children have equal status within their peer group. Some children seem to emerge naturally as leaders, while others are more inclined to follow. Some are highly popular, while others are less well liked. Among less popular children, some are actively rejected by their peers, while others are merely neglected or ignored (Asher and Wheeler, 1985; Rubin et al., in press). Developmentalists have conducted many studies to determine the type of children who tend to fall into each of these categories.

Research shows that status and popularity in children's peer groups are related to a number of personal characteristics, including self-esteem, kindness, an outgoing nature, the giving and receiving of positive reinforcement, and knowledge about how to make friends (Cox, 1966; Dodge et al., 1986; Gottman, Gonzo, and Rasmussen, 1975; Sroufe et al., 1984). It is also interesting to note the characteristics that are *not* on this list. Those who enjoy social influence in the peer group are not necessarily the biggest, the toughest, the most physically aggressive children. Instead, leadership and popularity generally accrue to those who have traits that are instrumental in achieving group goals. During middle childhood the most important group goal is usually that of organizing and directing enjoyable play.

Once a child has high or low status among peers, his or her resulting behaviors tend to reinforce peer attitudes and so perpetuate the child's level of popularity. A recent study of third and fourth graders supports this notion (Ladd, 1983). Children assessed as popular, neglected, or rejected by their peers were carefully observed on the playground. Rejected children spent more time isolated from others or engaged in negative behavior such as aggression. Neglected children spent more time watching other youngsters playing; they merely stood on the sidelines and didn't participate. Popular children spent much of their time in relatively large, heterogeneous play groups that included their friends and other popular youngsters. We cannot say for sure that the different behavioral styles of these children initially caused their different statuses among peers. But we can see how these different ways of acting might reinforce existing peer attitudes. Moreover, once patterns of behavior are established, they may tend to perpetuate themselves. Ken Dodge has shown that when children rated high or low in peer status are placed into a new group of youngsters, they will again be ranked by peers in the same way as before (Dodge et al., 1986). Apparently, children continue to behave in ways that encourage certain peer reactions (see Figure 13.2).

What are the roots of these different behavioral styles that children exhibit among peers? The answer is undoubtedly complex, involving the interaction of many different factors. However, one important influence seems to be a child's care-giving history. Susan Bergmann (cited in Sroufe, 1987) followed up 28 elementary school children whom other researchers had studied in earlier developmental periods. Colleagues who had no previous knowledge about the children observed them in their second and third grade classroom for several days. They then described various aspects of the children's functioning, including competence with peers. Some of the children were significantly more competent with peers— more poised, more involved, more inclined to show leadership ability. Bergmann found that these socially competent school-age children tended to be the very ones who as infants had enjoyed secure attachments to their care givers. This study does not settle the question of whether the benefits of secure attachment are being carried forward or whether care givers who promoted secure attachment continue to support development later. Probably both are true.

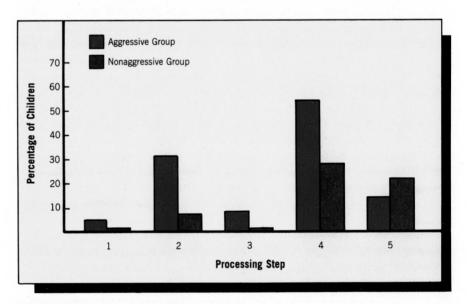

Figure 13.2
Aggression and Information-Processing Deficits
According to Ken Dodge's analysis, upon entering a new group, aggressive children show problems at each of five steps in the information-processing sequence: (1) encoding (using cues that are present); (2) interpreting cues correctly; (3) generating response options other than aggression; (4) evaluating the merits of appropriate responses, and (5) enacting a competent response to a provocation. This behavior leads these children to be negatively evaluated by peers.

Source: Dodge et al., 1986, p. 40.

Developmentalists have only begun to study the links between peer competence in the preschool period, acceptance by peers in middle childhood, and successful social functioning in adolescence and adulthood (e.g., Rubin and Daniels-Beirness, 1983). But even now it is clear that effective peer relations are important to healthy development. In one study, for instance, researchers collected achievement and IQ scores, attendance records, teachers' ratings, and measures of peer acceptance or rejection for a group of third graders (Cowen et al., 1973). The peer evaluations employed the "class play" technique, in which children are asked to nominate classmates for positive and negative roles in a fictitious play. Eleven years later the same subjects' mental health records were examined. Rejection by peers at ages 8 and 9 turned out to be the best school predictor of mental health problems in early adulthood. Other studies have confirmed a link between poor peer relations in middle childhood and social and emotional maladjustment later in life (Robins, 1978; Roff and Ricks, 1970). Of course, poor peer relations in childhood do not *destine* a person to later problems. Some children who are rejected by peers function quite well as adults, just as some adults who were popular as children become maladjusted. As we will discuss further in Chapter 16, poor peer relations in middle childhood is simply a risk marker: It suggests the *possibility* of later developmental problems.

FAMILY INFLUENCES ON DEVELOPMENT

The growing importance of friends in a school-age child's life does not lessen the developmental importance of the child's family. Family influences remain strong throughout middle childhood and on into adolescence. The primary family influence is usually exerted by the parents. In addition, however, many school-age children are also influenced by siblings, both older and younger ones. Let's look first at sibling relations in middle childhood before turning to the continuing impact of parents.

Sibling Relationships

Because relationships among siblings continue throughout life and are often deeply emotional, they are in some ways similar to parent-child relationships (Abramovitch, Pepler, and Corter, 1982; Stewart, 1983). By the end of middle childhood youngsters rate alliances with both parents and siblings as more enduring and reliable than those formed with people outside the family (Furman and Buhrmester, 1985). However, sibling relationships are far more equal in status than those between parents and children. In this sense, relationships among siblings are similar to those among peers, but they are different as well. The differences between peer and sibling relationships lie first in the age differences involved, which are usually accompanied by some differences in both power and privileges. Also, sibling relationships cross gender boundaries, whereas in middle childhood peer friendships rarely do.

EMOTIONAL QUALITIES OF SIBLING RELATIONSHIPS

Sibling relationships are quite complex, often involving both positive and negative feelings. Strong rivalry among siblings for their parents' attention and approval is a fairly common problem, especially in siblings of the same sex (Dunn and Kendrick, 1982; Minnett, Vandell, and Santrock, 1983; Pfouts, 1976). In fact, sibling conflict has been reported to be the most frequent reason for parental discipline of school-age children (Clifford, 1959). Sibling strife based on social comparison (who is better? smarter? faster? and so forth) intensifies after about age 8, when children develop the cognitive skills needed to compare themselves with others (Damon, 1983). Intermixed with this rivalry and conflict, however, are strong positive feelings among siblings. Younger siblings see older ones not only as controllers but also as facilitators; older siblings not only resent their younger siblings, but they also feel nurturant toward them (Abramovitch et al., 1982; Bigner, 1974; Bryant, 1982). Thus, although Malcolm's older brother often forbids him to do things, he also helps Malcolm to master new skills. And although Meryl initially feels some jealousy of her baby brother, she also fusses over him as if he were one of her dolls. Siblings, in short, show mixed emotions toward each other.

The overall quality of siblings' feelings toward each other varies from case to case. In one study, for example, the proportion of positive behaviors directed from an older sibling to a younger one was observed to range from 0 to 94 percent (Dunn and Kendrick, 1982). Researchers have explored many possible reasons for this wide variation. The relative ages of the siblings is one significant factor. Bigner (1974) has reported greater ambivalence between siblings when they are closer together in age, a finding that intuitively seems reasonable. Parents also seem to influence the quality of their children's relationships. For instance, how the mother prepares the first-born for the arrival of a new baby has an impact on the feelings expressed between the two siblings: The better the quality of the preparation, the better the quality of the later sibling relationship (Dunn and Kendrick, 1982). It has also been suggested, although not yet fully demonstrated, that parental unity tends to promote coalitions among siblings (Caplow, 1968; Kreppner, 1982). In contrast, antagonistic feelings between siblings can be encouraged when the parents meet the needs of one child but not the needs of the other (Bryant and Crockenberg, 1980; Ward and Robb, 1985).

How enduring is the quality of the relationship that develops between two siblings? At present we have little data with which to answer this question. However, there are signs that sibling relationships are to some degree stable, at least over a period of a few years. For instance, Judy Dunn found that a preschooler's positive interest in a newly arrived sibling tended to persist across a 3-year period and seemed also to be related to relationships with peers (Stillwell and Dunn, 1985). Much more research needs to be done on stability and change in sibling relationships as well as on the factors that give rise to these processes. In the next decade this is likely to be an active area of research.

WHAT SIBLINGS LEARN FROM EACH OTHER

The emotional ambivalence that often characterizes sibling relations has important implications for the learning opportunities that siblings provide each other. Siblings offer a unique opportunity to learn how to deal with anger and aggression in relationships. When siblings fight and become angry, they cannot simply decide to terminate all future interactions as peers can do. Whereas peers in conflict can simply refuse to see each other any more, siblings in conflict must continue to live in the same household. Siblings in conflict are also constantly encouraged by their parents to "get along" and to treat each other as brothers and sisters "should." As a result, sibling relationships are an excellent way to learn that expressing anger need not necessarily threaten mutual attachment in the long run (Bryant, 1982).

Some of the other lessons that children learn from their siblings depend on the youngsters' relative ages. For instance, in some cultures older siblings (generally girls) are explicitly assigned the role of caring for younger siblings (Liederman et al., in press; Whiting and Whiting, 1975). This care-giving role helps prepare the older children for later parenting, and it also increases the number of people to whom infants become attached. In our own culture school-age youngsters are seldom explicitly given the task of child care within the family. But in the growing number of households where both parents work, this role sometimes falls to older children by default. Moreover, even in traditional households older children frequently "look after" their younger siblings in an informal way. When Mikey was a toddler, for example, his older sister Becky kept a watchful eye out to make sure he didn't touch forbidden objects or venture into places off-limits to him. She also enjoyed helping him learn new things, such as teaching him new words. Such behaviors provide older siblings with experiences in role taking, in nurturance toward others, and in the teaching of skills (Bryant, 1982).

Younger siblings, for their part, also learn from these interactions. In learning to accommodate to an older sibling who is bossier and more punitive than parents and who is also more inclined to induce dependency, younger siblings learn to deal with dependency issues and to develop negotiation skills (Bryant, 1979, 1982; Bryant and Crockenberg, 1980). These experiences may play a part in fostering the greater social skills generally seen in second-born children compared with first-borns (Miller and Maruyama, 1976).

The Impact of Parents

Parent-child relationships continue to have a great impact on development during the elementary school period. However, over the years from early to middle childhood, parent-child relations change. This is partly due to the cognitive advances that youngsters are making. School-age children are more competent and more able to exert self-control, so parents begin to give them more responsibilities, often including participation in household chores (Goodnow, 1985). At the same time, parents are less inclined to use physical coercion and more apt to use reasoning in order to get their children to adhere to rules and values. In this way the parent-child system moves to what Eleanor Maccoby (1980) calls "co-regulation"—regulation that is shared by both parent and child. As in peer relations, there is also more concern now for equity and fairness in the parent-child relationship. The hallmark of effective parenting in this

While parents remain authorities for children, parent-child relations move more toward "co-regulation" in middle childhood. (*M. Nichols/The Picture Cube.*)

period is monitoring the child rather than always directing him or her (Hetherington, in press; Patterson and Dishion, in press).

PARENTING STYLES AND THEIR INFLUENCES

Although general changes in parent-child relationships take place in middle childhood, marked variations occur in the styles of parenting different mothers and fathers show. We can begin to conceptualize the many different approaches to parenting by using the scheme shown in Figure 13.3. This scheme classifies parenting styles in terms of two dimensions: (1) the degree of love versus hostility the parent shows the child and (2) the degree of control versus autonomy the parent imposes or allows (Schaefer, 1959). Certainly these two dimensions do not capture all there is to different parents' approaches, but they do provide a starting point for trying to understand the effects that different styles have on children.

Numerous studies using these dimensions have shown them to be reasonably good tools for predicting developmental outcomes. For instance, parents who are warm and loving and who often employ a reasoning approach to discipline tend to raise socially cooperative children who strongly internalize norms and values and take responsibility for their actions (Becker, 1964; Cole, Baldwin, and Baldwin, 1982). Parental warmth is also related to prosocial behavior, to high levels of self-esteem, and to a relative absence of behavior problems (Coopersmith, 1967; Hoffman, 1975; Radke-Yarrow and Zahn-Waxler, 1984; Rosenhan, 1969; Rothbaum, in press). In contrast, absence of parental warmth and a strong reliance on power-assertive discipline (shouting, physical punishment) tend to be associated with aggression and noncompliance in children, as well as with a tendency to project blame for negative outcomes onto other people (Caspi and Elder, in press; Egeland et al., 1981; McCord, in press; Patterson and Dishion, in press).

The degree of control exerted by parents versus the degree of autonomy they allow has likewise been found to be related to specific devel-

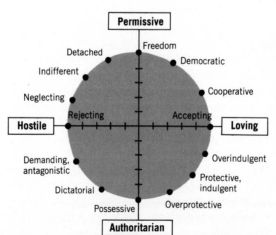

Figure 13.3
Dimensions of Parenting
Child-rearing practices can be classified along two dimensions: *affection*, which ranges from hostile to loving, and *control*, which ranges from permissive to authoritarian. Parents' relations with children can be said to be some combination of these two dimensions.
Source: Schaefer, 1959.

TABLE 13.2 **Summary of Research on Parental Warmth versus Hostility and Restrictiveness versus Permissiveness**

	Restrictiveness	*Permissiveness*
Warmth	1. Submissive, dependent, polite, neat, obedient (Levy; Symond) 2. Minimal aggression (Sears; McCord et al.) 3. Maximum rule enforcement, boys (Maccoby) 4. Dependent, not friendly, not creative (Watson) 5. Maximal compliance (Meyers)	1. Active, outgoing, creative, successfully aggressive (Baldwin) 2. Minimal rule enforcement, boys (Maccoby) 3. High in adult role taking (Levin; Sears) 4. Minimal self-aggression, boys (Sears) 5. Independent, friendly, creative, low projected hostility (Watson)
Hostility	1. "Neurotic problems" (clinical, anecdotal) 2. More quarreling and shyness with peers (Watson) 3. Socially withdrawn (Baldwin) 4. Low in adult role taking (Levin) 5. Maximal self-aggression, boys (Sears) 6. Matched-dependent behavior (McDavid and Hartup)	1. Delinquency (Glueck and Glueck; Bandura and Walters) 2. Noncompliance (Meyers) 3. Maximal aggression (Sears)

opmental consequences. In particular, parents who are very domineering and restrictive tend to foster inhibition in their children. The children may be polite and obedient, which are often viewed as positive traits, but they also tend to be shy and self-conscious, unusually dependent, and overly self-controlled (Block, 1971; Emmerich, 1977). The opposite extreme in parenting—great permissiveness toward children—has two-sided consequences as well. On the one hand, children of such parents tend to be sociable and expressive, but they are also frequently disobedient, irresponsible, lacking in persistence, and possessing short attention spans (Becker, 1964; Symonds, 1939).

These relationships, of course, are broad generalizations, and many exceptions exist. One reason is that we are isolating single dimensions when in reality any dimension is only one part of a larger configuration. Thus, more accurate developmental predictions can be made by assessing parental warmth and control simultaneously. The results of such studies are summarized in Table 13.2. Here we see that although permissiveness in a hostile context often gives rise to noncompliance and aggression, permissiveness in combination with parental warmth and caring is often associated with many positive outcomes, such as friendliness, independence, and creativity. Similarly, the consequences of restrictiveness vary significantly depending on parental warmth. When restrictiveness is combined with hostility, social withdrawal and neurotic problems often arise. But when restrictiveness is combined with love and affection, dependency and submissiveness are more apt to result (Becker, 1964).

Another dimension of parenting on which researchers have focused is the degree of anxious overinvolvement compared with a style of calm detachment. This dimension is useful in describing the difference between Christine Gordon and Karen Polonius as mothers when Mikey and Meryl were infants. Both women loved their babies and both allowed the children freedom to grow, but Karen was much more worried about doing things "correctly," and she constantly fretted over whether Meryl was progressing normally. Research suggests that an absence of such parental anxiety can have positive effects. For instance, parents who are restrictive yet warm and not anxiously overinvolved often raise children who are sociable and self-confident (Becker, 1964).

Efforts to tie children's characteristics to their parents' styles of child rearing have taught developmental researchers an important lesson: In order for parenting styles to predict developmental outcomes with reasonable accuracy, the models of parenting that are used must be quite complex. One-dimensional, two-dimensional, even three-dimensional models are not enough. Instead, we must try to assemble more inclusive and complex descriptions of parenting styles.

This goal led Diana Baumrind (1967) to compile the comprehensive parenting profiles we discussed in Chapter 11. Parents Baumrind labeled **authoritative** were nurturant and responsive toward their children. When disciplining, they often used reasoning rather than relying mainly on power-assertive techniques. Equally important, they were firm in setting limits and demanding maturity of their children, although they took care to respect the child's own point of view. Baumrind found that preschoolers raised by authoritative parents tended to be energetic, friendly, and self-reliant. In contrast, parents Baumrind labeled **authoritarian** tended to have preschoolers who were often irritable and conflict-ridden. These parents were harsh in their discipline and rigid in enforcing rules. Seldom did they try to understand the child's point of view.

A follow-up study of Baumrind's subjects conducted when they were 8 and 9 showed that authoritative parenting continued to have positive outcomes in middle childhood (Baumrind, 1977). School-age youngsters raised in authoritative homes tended to score higher than others in what is sometimes called **agency**—the tendency to take initiative, to rise to challenges, and to try to influence events. Interestingly, an added dimension to the parent-child relationship seemed to contribute to the development of agency in daughters, although not in sons. This was an argumentative quality in the girls' interactions with their parents, especially with their father. Baumrind proposes that these argumentative encounters may give girls the extra push needed to be more self-assertive.

In considering Baumrind's results how do we know that the parents are the ones who are exerting the major influences? Could it be instead that the child's personality is primarily causing the parents' behavior? One piece of evidence suggesting that this second interpretation is wrong comes from efforts to reduce problem behaviors in children by changing the child-rearing approaches of their parents. For instance, when authoritarian parents are encouraged to be firm but less power-assertive, their children typically become much better adjusted (Bernal, 1968; Patterson, 1976). Often, of course, the traits that have emerged in children serve to reinforce the parents' original behavior. The son of a harsh and rigid father, for example, may respond with irritability and so the father becomes even sterner and more demanding (Lee and Bates, 1985). This is why negative patterns of parent-child interaction can be so difficult to break. It seems unlikely, however, that personality characteristics in the children initially caused the parenting style to develop. Were this true we would not expect to find the notably consistent styles of parenting *across* siblings that we do (Dunn, Plomin, and Daniels, 1986; Ward, 1983). Of course, parents treat children differently in many specific ways, but with respect to broad patterns of parenting (warmth, responsiveness, and so forth) they tend to be consistent. In addition, parents' harsh discipline practices predict childhood aggression better than general levels of parental aggression (Patterson and Dishion, in press). Harsh discipline is a pattern found over several generations (Caspi and Elder, in press).

Baumrind's multifaceted descriptions of parenting styles are not the only ones that researchers have developed. For instance, Eleanor Maccoby and John Martin (1983) have offered a framework that emphasizes two factors: (1) the frequency of conflict over goals between child and parent and (2) the degree of balance or fairness in how parent and child tend to resolve their disagreements. The best developmental outcomes are said to occur when conflicts over goals are relatively infrequent (the parent is very supportive of the child) and when neither the goals of the parent nor the goals of the child always prevail (the parent both makes demands *and* accedes to the child's wishes, and expects the child to do the same). Like Baumrind's authoritative parents, these parents are responsive to their children and willing to negotiate with them, but they also require the children to respect parental views.

What sets the groundwork for this favorable style of parenting that Maccoby and Martin describe? They believe that the answer lies partly in the nature of parent-child interactions during earlier periods. In their view, a history of parental responsiveness to an infant, coupled with mutual exchanges in which the parents respect the baby's needs and feelings, serves as a form of "money in the bank" on which the parents can later draw. In toddlerhood, when it becomes more necessary to impose controls and refuse some of the child's wishes, the parents can draw on the child's store of confidence in the parents' concern and sensitivity (Maccoby and Martin, 1983). From this emerges a pattern of parent-child give-and-take that tends to endure over the years. At the same time, the early sharing of feelings that occurs in responsive families lays the groundwork for later empathy on the child's part. This is because, in observing empathic parents, the child learns not only specific behaviors but also a complementary set of roles characteristic of close relationships (Cottrell, 1969). As a result, the child should be more disposed to seek harmony with the parents, a point also made by Ainsworth and Bell (1974). Finally, cognitive development undoubtedly supports the school-age child's ability to accede to parents' wishes in many situations. As children move into middle childhood, they have a greater understanding of the legitimacy of parental authority (Damon, 1983). They come to grasp the fact that parents are far more experienced than they are and that parents' decisions are meant to be for their child's own good.

Children continue to require "monitoring," but they are much more able to carry out parental directives without direct supervision. One reason is that they are more accepting of parental authority. Another is that they are more able to follow through on plans themselves. (*Frank Siteman/The Picture Cube.*)

All these speculations about the origins of a favorable parent-child relationship await confirmation from ongoing research. However, given what we already know about the effects of care-giving history, it makes sense that we should look for the roots of current family relationships in a child's earlier experiences with parents. For instance, we know that children who were securely attached as infants are more competent with peers and less anxious as elementary schoolers than are children who were insecurely attached (Sroufe and Jacobvitz, 1987). Thus, it seems likely that a history of secure attachment and responsive care would also set the stage for healthy relationships between children and their parents during the elementary school years.

GENDER-ROLE TEACHING BY PARENTS

We have looked at how the family helps to shape the personalities that children show. Whether a child is outgoing, self-reliant, shy, dependent, anxious, or aggressive often depends partly on the family in which that child was raised. At the same time, the gender roles that children acquire are also partly a product of lessons learned within the family. We can see these lessons clearly in the Gordon family, where Mikey is actively encouraged to behave "masculinely."

While there is evidence that some of the behavioral differences between the sexes are biological in origin, parents in most cultures do prompt their sons and daughters to act in distinctive ways. Among other things, boys are allowed more freedom to explore and are encouraged to do more on their own (Huston, Carpenter, and Atwater, 1986). Girls, in contrast, are encouraged to stay closer to home, to be more involved in domestic activities, and to be more docile and dependent (Block, 1979). Parents' expectations for their sons and daughters also tend to differ. Boys more often than girls are expected to be ambitious, hardworking, achievement oriented, and assertive, whereas girls more often than boys are expected to be nurturant, kind, unselfish, and loving (Hoffman, 1977). In keeping with these different expectations, girls tend to place high value on socially oriented goals, such as showing concern for other people and being liked in return. When a girl's own achievements jeopardize her social acceptance, she is more likely than a boy to experience anxiety and a drop in her level of performance (Hoffman, 1972).

Not surprisingly, given the expectations that parents tend to have for them, sons have been found to have more powerful self-concepts than daughters. Males are more likely than females to think of themselves as self-assertive, inclined to take initiative, capable of influencing outcomes, and competent at getting things done (Block, 1979). These self-images are reflected in classic fairy tales, where the boys often perform extraordinary feats of cleverness and valor. Jack climbs the beanstalk and captures the goose that lays the golden eggs from the evil giant, while Peter saves the village by heroically plugging up the hole in the dike. In contrast, princesses in classic fairy tales are so delicate they can feel the pressure of a single pea beneath 20 mattresses! Parents not only tell these stories to their children, but they also subtly encourage them to internalize these gender ideals.

By the early part of middle childhood there is clear-cut evidence that children have accepted many gender-role stereotypes. In one study, for instance, William Damon (1977) told children ages 4 to 9 a story about a boy named George who liked to play with dolls despite the disapproval of his friends and parents. The children were then asked why people tell George not to play with dolls, whether he should continue playing with them if he wants, what will happen to him if he does, and other questions related to gender-role stereotypes. Their answers showed that by the age of 6 most children firmly believe that it is *wrong* for boys to play with dolls. And it is wrong precisely because it violates social standards. Children this age are quite rigid in applying these standards to others and to themselves. A few years later, however, youngsters come to realize that gender-role conceptions do not carry the weight of moral prescripts, such as laws against stealing, for instance. As a result, they also become more flexible in their attitudes toward gender-role deviance. It is not really *wrong* for George to play with dolls in the eyes of these older school-age children, but they strongly suspect he won't do it for long because other boys will ridicule and reject him.

Parents who hold egalitarian views regarding gender roles are often dismayed by their children's staunchly conventional attitudes during the early elementary school years. But this conservatism of early middle childhood does not necessarily mean that the youngsters will never adopt more flexible attitudes. Eleanor Maccoby (1980) has argued that "children may simply be exaggerating sex roles in order to get them cognitively clear. Perhaps cognitive clarity helps children establish their own sex identity firmly, and only after this identity is established can they become more flexible and less sex bound" (p. 237). Thus, if parents hold egalitarian attitudes regarding the two sexes and make those attitudes known to their children, it is likely that the children will incorporate those views as they mature.

Maccoby suggests that children who eventually acquire more flexible gender roles may be partly the product of parents who patiently stress egalitarian roles within the home. But what about youngsters who remain staunchly traditional in their sex-typed behaviors? Are they largely the product of parents who themselves adhere strongly to traditional gender roles? Research suggests that the answer is not this simple. Apparently, we must look at the family as a system to understand how extremely "masculine" or "feminine" behavior develops in children. Jeanne and Jack Block did just that in a study they conducted some years ago (Block, von der Lippe, and Block, 1973). They began by selecting a sample of adult subjects who had been participating since childhood in one of two long-term developmental studies. To obtain assessments of the subjects' parents the researchers looked at records collected many years earlier, before the parents had much of a chance to be influenced by their children's behavior. The researchers also asked the subjects to look back over their childhoods and to recollect the child-rearing style of each parent. Finally, the subjects themselves were assessed with a standard personality test administered in adulthood. Among other things, this test measured adherence to traditional gender roles and degree of socialization (how deeply the person had internalized cultural norms and values).

The Blocks' analysis of all this information is summarized in Table 13.3. On the basis of this summary, several conclusions seem warranted. First, both men and women who were low in their degree of socialization

Boys are given more freedom to be away from home and to be unsupervised than girls. Psychologists believe that such different treatment has important effects on personality development. *(Paul Fusco/Magnum Photos Inc.)*

TABLE 13.3 **Antecedents of Adult Sex Role and Socialization Patterns**

Males

1. *High masculine/high socialized*
These were "self-confident, competent, optimistic men with buoyant affect." The developmental history data for these men suggested that the *fathers* (who were most salient) were guarding of their autonomy and undemonstrative. But they were available and accepting, supporting their son's autonomy. The *mothers*, too, were accepting and noncoercive, and a "friendly, somewhat neutral atmosphere" prevailed.

2. *High masculine/low socialized*
Machismo, egotism, and impulsiveness characterized these men. Underneath the bravado was an insecurity and vulnerability. "The inability of these men to participate in a mutual interpersonal relationship appears to have alienated and isolated them from others" (p. 326). The *fathers* of this group were weak, neurotic, and somewhat rejecting. The *mothers* were resentful and dissatisfied in their marriage. "Reacting to both unsatisfied social and sexual needs, these mothers may have turned to their sons in a symbolically seductive bid for masculine attentions" (p. 327).

3. *Low masculine/high socialized*
These men were dutiful, productive, conscientious, and somewhat rigid. They were not viewed as "passive" or "feminine" but simply lacked the aggressive components often associated with masculinity. *Fathers* here were successful, ambitious, and socially adjusted. *Mothers* were relaxed, stable, and satisfied, and the marital relationship was positive.

4. *Low masculine/low socialized*
These men were characterized by vulnerability, insecurity, self-doubt, sensitivity to criticism, and feelings of victimization. *Fathers* were "distant" and "conflict inducing"; *mothers* were neurotic, apathetic, and "disaffected with their maternal roles."

Females

1. *High feminine/high socialized*
These women were conventional, controlled, and dependable. There was some anxiety, indecision, and personal dissatisfaction. *Mothers* were more salient, and the mother-daughter relationship was warm and close. A home-and-family-centered environment prevailed with traditional sex roles.

2. *High feminine/low socialized*
These women were hedonistic and self-centered, "rejecting both conventional and achievement-oriented values." As children, their *mothers* had been rejecting (of daughter and motherhood) and the *father*-daughter relationship was overinvolved, with a seductive element.

3. *Low feminine/high socialized*
These women were poised, outgoing, and relaxed. As girls they experienced stable, unconflicted homes, with caring from both parents. Intellectual and achievement values were fostered by both parents.

4. *Low feminine/low socialized*
These women were rebellious, critical, assertive, expressive, and decisive. Their *mothers* had been "neurotic, vulnerable, and martyred," uninvolved in marriage or motherhood. *Fathers* were active, authoritarian, power-oriented and uninvolved with their families. All relationships within these families were conflicted. Both parents rejected their daughter.

Source: Based on Block, von der Lippe, and Block, 1973.

came from homes in which the same-sex parent was uninvolved in child rearing or even actively rejected the child. At the same time, the opposite-sex parent was psychologically troubled or at least dissatisfied with life.

Second, an interesting mix of factors seems to encourage strong adherence to traditional sex roles in children. For instance, highly socialized men and women who are also very "masculine" or "feminine" seem to have internalized traditional sex-role stereotypes through strong identification with a competent same-sex parent. In contrast, men and women who are low in socialization but high in "masculine" or "feminine" traits seem to have acquired their gender roles through overinvolvement with a seductive opposite-sex parent. Such findings show how hard it is to trace the family origins of personality traits in children. We must consider not only the mother's and father's characteristics but also the relationship between the parents, each parent's relationship with the child, and the important fact of whether the child is a boy or a girl.

PARENTAL CONFLICT AND DIVORCE

Divorce in America is extremely widespread, as we discussed in Chapter 3. A million American children each year experience the effects of divorce or separation (Select Committee on Children, Youth, & Families, 1983). It has been estimated that if the current divorce rate continues, approximately 50 percent of all new marriages will eventually end in divorce, and nearly half of all the children now being born will spend some time in a one-parent household (Newberger, Melnicoe, and Newberger, 1986). Since not all unhappy marriages ultimately end in divorce, we can assume that the percentage of children experiencing serious family conflict will be even higher. Psychologists are greatly concerned about the effects that these experiences are having on American children.

Effects of Parental Conflict. Parental conflict rather than separation per se may be the key cause of the developmental problems sometimes seen in children of divorce. Psychologist Robert Emery (1982) points to several lines of evidence supporting this conclusion. First, children are much more likely to experience developmental problems when their families are broken through divorce than through death (Gibson, 1969; Gregory, 1965). In both cases the children are separated from a parent, but only in divorce is parental conflict usually involved. Second, longitudinal studies show that children suffer the same problems when their parents are together but in conflict as they do years later when the parents finally get divorced (Block, Block, and Gjerde, 1986). We illustrated this pattern with Mikey, who was troubled even before his parents separated. Finally, if parental conflict decreases sharply following a divorce, the children involved are usually better adjusted than are peers in intact families where parental conflict remains high (Hetherington, Cox, and Cox, 1978).

Researchers have tried to pinpoint the kinds of negative outcomes that family conflict tends to promote. Interestingly, boys in most cases are more obviously vulnerable than girls are, and they often respond in more disruptive ways. Common reactions in boys are increased aggression, troubled peer relations, and lack of impulse control (Block and Block, 1979; Block, Block, and Gjerde, 1986; Cole, Baldwin, and Baldwin, 1982). Although these negative outcomes may also be seen in girls, they are typically much milder and less pervasive than in boys (Block et al., 1986; Hetherington, Cox, and Cox, 1978). In addition, girls more often than boys respond to family turmoil with anxiety, inhibition, and withdrawal (Block, Block, and Morrison, 1981; Hess and Camara, 1979; Whitehead, 1979). Meryl's withdrawal during the period when her parents were having problems is a case in point. Since such reactions do not disrupt the home or classroom, they are more likely to be ignored or even overlooked.

Of course, none of these negative outcomes of family conflict are inevitable. Many children of both sexes manage to weather such storms quite well. Developmentalists are interested in learning why some children fare so much better than others in equally conflict-ridden homes. One mediating factor that often provides a buffer is a warm and close relationship with at least one of the parents (Hess and Camara, 1979; Hetherington, in press; Hetherington, Cox, and Cox, 1978; Rutter, 1971). In intact but conflict-ridden families, a good relationship with either parent can help the child through these difficult circumstances. In female-headed single-parent households, however, only a good relationship with the mother seems to offer a buffering effect (Hetherington, Cox, and Cox, 1978). This makes sense when you consider that the father in such families is absent on a day-to-day basis and thus often cannot provide psychological support when the child needs it most. The fact that Mikey had a good relationship with Christine at the time of his parents' breakup would probably help him through this developmental crisis.

The findings we have reviewed so far shed some interesting light on the common assumption that parents should always try to stay together "for the children's sake." When divorce ends severe marital conflict and helps make possible parental cooperation, the children involved usually fare better than those in conflict-ridden two-parent homes. On the other hand, if parental discord continues *after* divorce, children are likely to suffer even more developmental problems than they would from marital conflict alone (Hetherington, Cox, and Cox, 1978). The best advice to divorcing parents, then, is to reduce their levels of mutual hostility as much and as quickly as they can. In addition, if each parent maintains a warm and close relationship with the children, good adjustment is even more likely (Hetherington, in press). The meaning that children attach to divorce is also a critical factor. When a child feels abandoned by one parent and blamed by the other, negative consequences are apt to result. We can see this in Mikey, who feels strongly that he is responsible for his parents' breakup because he failed as a mediator between them. Such children need help in understanding that they are not responsible and that both parents will continue to care for and be involved with them.

Effects of Parent-Child Separation.   The emphasis placed on parental conflict as a cause of developmental problems in children of divorce does not mean that separation from a parent has no developmental effects. Studies have indeed linked various outcomes in children to the day-to-day absence of one of the parents, most often in divorce cases the father. But the nature and intensity of such outcomes vary greatly, depending on a number of mediating factors. These include the child's age and sex, the behavior of the custodial parent, and the degree to which the absent parent manages to remain involved.

Consider, for instance, the behavior of young boys in father-absent homes. Studies suggest that if the father leaves when the child is still a preschooler, during the years when gender identity is emerging and crystallizing, the boy may become less stereotypically "masculine" than peers raised in father-present households (Biller and Bahm, 1970; Hetherington, 1966). One reason for this pattern is that fathers tend to be more concerned than mothers about "appropriate" gender-role behavior in their preschool children, especially their sons (Langlois and Downs, 1980). Thus, not only does the typical male child of divorce lose a day-to-day masculine role model, he may also miss some very forceful early lessons regarding sex-appropriate behavior. Not surprisingly, research also shows that the sex-typed behavior of preschool boys tends to be related to the frequency of the divorced father's contact: the more contact, in general, the less the effect is found. In addition, this effect is also lessened when the mother is not overly anxious and restrictive toward the child and when she approves of the father as a role model for him (Hetherington, Cox, and Cox, 1978).

In summary, the effects of divorce on children are complex. The developmental impact of divorce is exerted not only through separation from a parent but also through the family conflict and many life changes that inevitably accompany marital breakups. As a result, numerous factors can magnify or reduce any "typical" outcomes. This is why there is no single answer to the question of how divorce affects children. It all depends on the particular circumstances and personal reactions involved. We will return to the topic of the effects of divorce on children in our unit on adolescence.

CHILDREN IN SCHOOL

The age of 6 is a momentous time for most American children because this is the age when they first enter elementary school. With that initial step inside the classroom, children's lives change dramatically. No longer are play and "good" behavior all that is expected of them. Now they must formally begin to learn the body of knowledge that adults deem important to master. For at least the next 12 years the children will be at school approximately 6 hours a day, 5 days a week. If influence is related to sheer time of exposure, schools must be considered a major developmental factor in American children's lives.

Children learn many things within the classroom beyond the subjects that teachers specifically teach. Most of our mainstream cultural norms and values are repeatedly reinforced through the way in which school activities are organized and the way in which rewards there are distributed. Schools encourage children to be competitive, to work hard, to strive for achievement; yet at the same time they require youngsters to obey authority, to observe rules and regulations, to be punctual, respectful of private property, and generally orderly and neat. The school, in short,

Children's self-esteem can be affected by the structure of the classroom, depending on whether the stress is on competition and comparison, or on cooperation and diversity. (© Milton Feinberg/The Picture Cube.)

Schools seem to reinforce gender stereotypes. *(David Hurn/Magnum Photos, Inc.)*

is a very powerful agent of socialization (Epps and Smith, 1984). At school, children are drilled in many of the behaviors that will be expected of them in the world of adults.

We can see this clearly in the area of gender-role learning. At the simplest level, teachers reinforce gender differences by organizing activities around gender. They create boys' lines and girls' lines, for instance, or they pit males against females for spelling and arithmetic contests (Thorne, 1986). They may also assign classroom chores in "gender-appropriate" fashion (Guttentag and Bray, 1977). Moving a table might be a boys' job, for example, while laying out cookies for a party a girls' job. The very hierarchy of the school emphasizes traditional gender roles as well. Men often occupy the most prestigious positions (curriculum coordinator, administrator, superintendent), while women tend to perform the rank-and-file jobs.

More disturbing are certain findings regarding boys' and girls' experiences in day-to-day classroom learning. Although girls more often than boys fit the stereotype of the "model pupil" (well-behaved, compliant, nondisruptive), there is evidence that many teachers are biased in favor of boys. In observational studies teachers have been found to interact more with boys and to give boys more positive feedback, whereas girls are more likely than boys to receive the teacher's criticism (Dweck et al., 1978; Sears and Feldman, 1966; Serbin et al., 1973). And ironically, high-achievement girls may be the most criticized of all. In one study of fifth graders, high-achievement girls received the least praise and positive feedback and the most disparaging remarks from the teacher than any other group of students. In contrast, when boys are criticized it is generally for misbehavior or lack of neatness rather than for lack of scholastic ability. Moreover, teachers tend to attribute poor performance by a boy merely to insufficient effort, whereas poor performance by a girl is more likely to be viewed as a sign of low aptitude (Dweck et al., 1978). Thus, there is reason to believe that many American schools are subtly discouraging intellectual achievement in girls (Block, 1979).

Schooling experiences are important because they can contribute to change in social and emotional adjustment. We illustrated this in describing the problems Meryl had during the third grade. When forced to deal with a demanding and critical teacher, Meryl reacted by becoming anxious and withdrawn.

The sensitivity of children to their school environments was clearly demonstrated in a study by Michael Rutter and his colleagues (Rutter, 1981; Rutter et al., 1979). Rutter assessed all the primary school children in one borough of London who were just about to enter the secondary school system. He measured their intellectual abilities and academic achievement, as well as their current social-emotional adjustment at home and in the classroom. He then followed the children through their secondary school careers (from ages 11 to 17). This part of the study included a very thorough assessment of attitudes, atmosphere, and teaching practices at the particular school each child attended. The pupils in these schools were extensively surveyed, the teachers were carefully interviewed, and detailed observations were made in many of the classrooms. Rutter found strong correlations between certain school qualities and certain outcomes in students by the time the students were ready to graduate. In particular, schools that emphasized academic achievement and provided incentives for good performance, schools with skilled teachers who allowed students to assume responsibilities, tended to turn out pupils with above-average records and few behavior problems. In contrast, children assigned to lower-quality schools faced an increased risk of performing poorly both scholastically and in terms of social adjustment. The conclusion? Schools seem to have substantial influence on children's behavior and achievements during late middle childhood and the adolescent years.

Chapter Review

1. During middle childhood youngsters begin to integrate their various ideas about the self into a coherent self-concept. Part of this process involves a growing awareness of the self as consisting of thoughts and feelings not always accessible to others. In contrast to the preschooler, who sees the self largely in terms of physical traits, the elementary school child has a much more psychologically based self-concept. Another advance in self-understanding that occurs during this period is development of what is called the **social self.** By this psychologists mean an awareness that "who I am" is closely tied to "the other people with whom I interact." For instance, elementary school children begin to define themselves in terms of the groups they belong to, and they begin to talk about themselves in terms of their social tendencies (I am shy, I am friendly, I am kind, and so forth). Closely related to this development is the tendency to use others as a source of comparison in making self-evaluations. By about 8 years of age children begin to think of themselves as more or less capable in relation to peers.

2. The kinds of self-evaluation children make contribute to their levels of self-esteem. High self-esteem tends to be related to a positive outlook and success in many areas. One important accompaniment to high self-esteem is an **internal locus of control,** the belief that one's ability to do things well comes from qualities within the self. Children who have an **external locus of control** persist in thinking that their achievements are caused largely by external factors such as luck or help from others. Such individual differences in self-esteem and

self-confidence may be predicted from the preschool period and, to some extent, even from the first two years.

3. During middle childhood the **peer group** becomes an especially important developmental setting. This is due partly to the large amount of time that school-age children spend with peers. It is also due to the unique learning experiences that equal-status peer relationships provide. The peer group is especially conducive to learning firsthand about such principles as fairness, reciprocity, and equity. Because school-age youngsters adhere so strictly to many such cultural norms and values, their peer groups must be considered major agents of socialization.

4. Among the changes that take place in peer interactions during middle childhood are advances in social communication skills as youngsters become much better at adopting the perspectives of other people. School-age children also become more altruistic and more able to fashion prosocial responses in ways that take situational factors into account. At the same time, youngsters are now more apt to express hostile aggression by verbally insulting peers, a change that once again shows their growing ability to grasp how other people think and feel. The nature of peer friendships also changes during middle childhood. Friendships become much deeper and are increasingly based on mutual loyalty and support as well as on common interests. Friends also develop a sense of "we-ness," an awareness of the boundaries of their special peer relationships. Popularity and status within a school-age peer group are related to such traits as high self-esteem, kindness toward others, and a friendly, positive nature. Such characteristics commonly arise from a child's developmental history, including presence or absence of maltreatment.

5. The growing importance of friends in a school-age child's life does not lessen the developmental importance of the child's family. Youngsters learn a great deal from their siblings, for example, including how to be nurturant, how to teach new skills, how to negotiate, and how to deal with anger without ending a close relationship. Parents continue to have a great impact on the school-age child. The styles of child rearing they adopt are closely related to many of the personality characteristics youngsters acquire. Developmentally important factors seem to be the amount of love the parents show, how much autonomy they allow, how responsive they are to their children's viewpoints, how anxiously overinvolved they are, and how much they rely on power-assertive techniques of discipline. In order to be reasonably accurate in predicting developmental outcomes from the behavior of parents, researchers must employ complex, multidimensional models of parenting.

6. The possible effects of marital conflict and divorce on children is another family issue that researchers have explored. It appears that conflict may be a key cause of the developmental problems sometimes seen in children of divorce. These problems can include increased aggression, lack of impulse control, and troubled relations with peers, especially among boys. Girls more commonly respond to marital conflict with anxiety, inhibition, and withdrawal. Of course, separation from a parent can also have negative developmental outcomes. The likely effects vary greatly, depending upon such factors as the child's age and sex and how he or she interprets the meaning of the marital breakup.

7. Children learn many things inside their classrooms besides the subjects teachers specifically teach. The school is a place where mainstream cultural norms and values are repeatedly reinforced. This can be seen in the area of gender-role learning. Teachers tend to stress traditional expectations regarding gender, including the expectation that academic achievement is more appropriate for boys than for girls.

Middle Childhood

Development continues to be rapid during middle childhood, roughly ages 6 through 12. The changes taking place, however, may not always be as obvious as those that occurred in earlier periods. Physical growth has slowed to a few inches yearly and is no longer as dramatic as it was in infancy and toddlerhood. Now the major developmental changes are largely internal—having to do with the child's way of thinking and feeling. Although these internal changes may not be very apparent to casual observers, they are nevertheless of great importance. In addition, the developments of middle childhood pave the way for the far-reaching changes that will occur in adolescence.

Like all developmental periods middle childhood involves qualitative change, major developmental reorganizations that boost children to higher levels of social and cognitive functioning. One such major reorganization occurs between the ages of 6 and 8 (Fischer and Bullock, 1984). At this time children acquire more sophisticated ways of thinking. They come to grasp the "logic" of concrete operations carried out on objects. Eight-year-olds understand most rules of conservation. They know, for example, that the mass in a lump of clay remains the same even though it is rolled and kneaded into very different shapes. Eight-year-olds also understand hierarchical classifications. If they are shown a group of objects that consists of toy dogs and toy cats, they know that fewer "dogs" than "animals" are present because they grasp the fact that the first of these two concepts is a subclass of the second. Similar advances occur in the area of social cognition. Youngsters are now much better at taking the perspective of others. They can also coordinate their knowledge of the various social categories that apply to people. For instance, a girl whose father is a doctor would now understand that she can be a patient and a daughter to him at the same time (Watson, 1981).

The age of 8 is also repeatedly mentioned as a milestone in social development. By this age children view the self in more psychological terms. They realize that "who they are" is partly what they think and feel, not just the physical traits they possess. They also begin to compare themselves to others in order to appraise their abilities; and they realize that how other people respond to them can depend on their own actions. By age 8 children also have a more mature view of friendship than preschoolers do. They begin to recognize that the basis of friendship lies in loyalty and mutual support, not just the sharing of playthings. With this advancement relations with peers take on much deeper meaning. In fact, the formation of close "chumships" is one of the hallmarks of middle childhood. In their interactions with friends school-age children also adhere very closely to peer group norms. Equity, fairness, and reciprocity are cardinal principles of their relationships. In addition, school-age children have a new understanding of the legitimacy of authority, including parental authority. This understanding coupled with their greater desire to conform to norms and values helps make the job of parenting easier than it was before. Markus and Nurius (1984) have summed up these many social advances this way: (1) school-age children acquire a relatively stable and comprehensive understanding of the self; (2) they acquire a refined understanding of how the social world works; and (3) they acquire a set of standards and expectations regarding their dealings with others.

Clearly, much development still lies ahead, and other major turning points will be reached in the years to come (Fischer and Bullock, 1984). Nevertheless, the fundamental changes of early middle childhood are highly significant. As in other developmental periods, all these changes are intimately interconnected; cognitive and social advancements influence each other. For instance, the cognitive abilities to understand different perspectives and to take on different roles help school-age children to interact more maturely with peers. At the same time, interactions with peers provide experiences that foster these cognitive skills. Social and cognitive development always proceed together, each helping to make possible advances in the other. Although it may have appeared in our earlier chapters that cognitive advances occasionally occur a little earlier than social ones, this appearance is partly the product of researchers' goals. Cognitive researchers often look for the first appearance of a particular skill, whereas social researchers often search for the age at which a certain ability is regularly used. Time and experience are typically needed before a new capacity is readily exercised. Thus, in their everyday behaviors children may not always show their highest levels of functioning.

Unevenness in Development

Repeatedly, we have stressed the orderliness and coherence of human development, whether we are talking about general developmental changes or the life of an individual child. This does not mean, however, that development is totally smooth and even. Several kinds of unevenness are often observed. First, development in different domains does not always proceed at the same pace. When Meryl was a preschooler, for instance, her social development lagged somewhat behind her cognitive progress. This is not unusual. In fact,

even within the same domain—cognitive or social—closely related developmental milestones may not be reached simultaneously. For example, a 6-year-old who grasps the concept of conservation of number may not necessarily also grasp conservation of liquid volume. Piaget called such unevenness in development *decalage*. As we have seen, some contemporary developmentalists have made this concept a central part of their theories (e.g., Fischer, 1980; Case, 1985).

In addition to the unevenness that occurs in general developmental changes, unevenness also exists in the progress of individual lives. Individual children experience developmental ups and downs. Life goes well for a time, but then they appear to be struggling. You saw this pattern especially in the development of Meryl and Mikey during the school-age years. It occurs in the lives of all children and in adults as well. What is important to recognize is that these ups and downs in the quality of individual adaptations are *not* incoherent and illogical. They make sense in terms of what is happening to the child at a particular time. Thus, the child may be responding to external circumstances, such as conflict in the family or a poor environment at school. Or the child may be reacting to internal changes, such as changes in health. Pulling back and retrenching before moving ahead again may even be the typical way in which children make developmental progress. Parents often notice that their children undergo a period in which they consolidate already acquired skills before moving forward to tackle new ones. In fact, much of middle childhood can be viewed as a period of consolidation, a gathering of potentials to be used during adolescence. Such a view gives new meaning to the concept of latency that Freud attached to this period.

Three Children in Middle Childhood

Our three children continue to unfold during middle childhood, often predictably, but sometimes taking unexpected turns. Although each continues to develop normally, each at times encounters problems. These problems illustrate the continuing need of school-age children for care, understanding, and guidance from adults.

For Mikey Gordon the elementary school years are a very stressful time. Divorce is especially difficult and painful when children are involved. Assessing the impact of Christine and Frank's divorce on Mikey—even saying whether it was good or bad for him—is complicated. On the one hand, things were going poorly even before the separation. The conflict between Christine and Frank had become intense, and Mikey was suffering ill effects both at home and in the classroom. Despite the best of intentions, Christine and Frank could not shelter Mikey from such a troubled marriage. On the other hand, the divorce was very hard on Mikey because he loved both his parents and desperately wanted them to stay together. Even more than most children a child such as Mikey would feel responsible for the breakup. Wasn't he supposed to be the peacemaker, the one who keeps conflicts from getting out of control? In the back of his mind the divorce meant that *he* had failed. Fortunately, Mikey is old enough to begin to understand that the divorce was not his fault. But he will need help to come to this realization. Since both parents clearly care deeply for Mikey, and Christine is the kind of parent who will talk to him about his feelings, we can be optimistic that Mikey will ultimately pull through this developmental crisis. In fact, in the long run the divorce may in ways be harder on Becky and Janie because it has shown so clearly the extent to which their father favors Mikey. They would probably feel more resentment toward Mikey if they did not have each other and were closer to Mikey's age. They cope largely by denying any interest in activities with their father and by becoming very involved with their friends. The effects on them are different from those on Mikey, but they are no easier.

It is tempting to see Frank as the villain in all of this. He is the one with the drinking problem, the one who can be physically abusive. He is also totally unsupportive of his wife's desire for a career outside the home. From a systems perspective, however, the situation is more complex than simply labeling Frank the "bad guy." Any interpersonal relationship is the product of two individual histories (Sroufe and Fleeson, 1986). Looking back at all we know about Christine, we can say that she seems to have been raised to take care of men. Her mother's only advice when the marriage became rocky was to work harder at being a "good" wife. It is also difficult for Christine to ask that her needs be met; she has been taught to be self-sacrificing. To cope with the mounting resentment Frank feels about her job, she strives to keep her working life separate from her life at home. As Frank's self-esteem is increasingly damaged by Christine's rise in the business world and as Frank's criticism of her becomes ever sharper, Christine keeps trying to mollify him. This reaction in Christine fuels the system as much as Frank's tendency to blame her does. And both of them, in their own way, put Mikey in the middle. The one thing that bodes well for the future is that through it all Frank and Christine remain devoted to Mikey. If this deep caring for their son can continue while they become disentangled from their problems, Mikey can still come out all right in the end.

Malcolm's development during this period is nowhere near as conflict-ridden as Mikey's is. Middle childhood for Malcolm seems to be a busy, productive, generally fun-filled time. But the incident with the knife at school illustrates how normal, healthy children sometimes get into trouble and sometimes cause their parents concern. The lovable exuberance of Malcolm bounding up the stairs stems from the same high-spirited energy that he sometimes expresses too impulsively. Malcolm hits upon the scheme of taking his pocketknife to school in a naive effort to defend himself from a gang of older boys. We see him becoming very emotional about Derek's "ratting" on him. But this is Malcolm's nature. He will not be upset for long. The incident will pass, and Malcolm will be fine again. In fact, he has probably learned some important lessons from it. In the long run there is more reason to be concerned about Derek, who has willfully broken a peer group norm, than there is to be concerned about Malcolm, whose infraction of a school rule was more unthinking than deliberate.

In Malcolm's life we also see the special challenges that inner-city children face: gangs to be dealt with going to and from school, interracial incidents that foster interracial mistrusts. Malcolm is fortunate that he does not have to deal with the additional challenge of a poor-quality school. Malcolm's teacher and principal recognize his talents despite his occasional impulsive behavior and difficulty concentrating. At the same time we once again see the benefits of Malcolm's large and constantly supportive family. Many ears listen to his reports of school achievements; many voices guide him when he gets into trouble. All this serves to encourage positive development in Malcolm.

Meryl also seems to be getting some good support at home. She has become a much more competent and self-confident child than we would have predicted from her infancy and toddler periods. She takes the arrival of her baby brother in stride and even seems to blossom in the role of big sister. She is generally doing well at school and has formed the normal close friendship characteristic of middle childhood. The only times we see vestiges of the old, hesitant Meryl are under conditions of stress. Her initial third grade teacher turns out to be harsh, and Meryl's schoolwork suffers. Karen and Joe have a period of tension, and Meryl becomes withdrawn. But even during the time of family problems Meryl works in her own way toward bolstering herself psychologically; we find her in her room drawing pictures of mother dogs caring for their puppies. As Karen and Joe resolve their difficulties, Meryl brightens once again and regains her confidence. With each developmental period she seems to be getting stronger.

Part Six

Adolescence

Three Children in Adolescence

Malcolm Williams

Malcolm could barely contain his excitement on the way home. He had just been offered an after-school job stocking shelves at Jewel's store. Now he would have money to cruise around with his buddies, to buy great-looking clothes, and—most important—to take Felicia out. But Malcolm knew that he would first have to get his parents' approval. Let's see; he would start by pointing out that he was almost 16, certainly no longer a kid. By the time his dad was 16, he'd had several jobs. Then there was the argument that jobs are good for keeping guys off the streets and out of trouble. Not that Malcolm was interested in joining one of the neighborhood gangs. He and his brother JJ were smarter than that, he thought. But it was a good point to bring up with his parents anyway. And, of course, he'd have to promise to keep his grades up. Malcolm was sure he could manage if he put his mind to it.

Leaping up the front steps two at a time, Malcolm pushed open the front door. Fantastic! His mother and father weren't home from work yet. That meant he could win Momma Jo over first and have her behind him when it came time to talk to his parents. Maybe Momma Jo didn't see too well anymore, but at 82 she was still one sharp lady. Everyone respected her judgment. In his eagerness to convince Momma Jo before his parents got home, Malcolm's words spilled out, his points becoming more and more jumbled. Momma Jo had trouble following what he was saying. By the time she was beginning to put it all together, DeeDee and John walked in. Oh no, thought Malcolm, now I have to work on all three at once.

When Malcolm finished presenting his case, his father looked doubtful. He felt that Malcolm had been a little less serious about his schoolwork lately. Momma Jo saw John's expression. "I remember seein' you nearly bustin'

with pride when you showed me your first pay slip," she said.

"Momma, I'm not saying that a job wouldn't be good for Malcolm," John answered. "I'm just concerned about him handling all the responsibilities that go with it."

"Oh, I'll be responsible, Dad," Malcolm assured him. "I won't ever be late for work, 'cause they dock your pay and..."

"Listen to me, boy," John cut in sharply. "I'm not talkin' about being late for work. I'm talkin' about your responsibilities right here at home. You've got to keep your school grades up so you can go to college, and you've got to do your chores around the house."

"Oh, I know *that*," said Malcolm quickly. "Sure, I'll do all those things. I'm not gonna mess up goin' to college. But I know I can do it."

DeeDee had been quiet all the while. Now she finally spoke. "What do you say we let him take the job on a trial basis? If his grades slip or his chores don't get done, the job goes—no second chances."

"That sounds OK to me," John said. "But remember what your momma said. No second chances."

"All riiiight!" crowed Malcolm. "Y'all are cool!" He hugged his mother and Momma Jo and punched his father on the arm. Then he charged out of the kitchen, heading for the phone to call the stockroom manager at Jewel's. Hallelujah, he thought. I got me a job!

The next morning Malcolm jumped out of bed, surging with energy. Appraising himself in the mirror he noticed with satisfaction his developing muscles, the smooth sheen of his brown skin, and the facial fuzz marking the beginnings of a mustache. I'm a man with style, he thought to himself. Felicia, you are one lucky lady!

When Malcolm came down to breakfast, he was ready for the affectionate teasing his family usually gave him about his clothes. This time it was his mother: "My, *my*. Someone would think you were entering a fashion show!"

"You dig my threads?" Malcolm grinned, pretending to model them for his mother. "I kind of appreciate them myself." And with that he slid into his chair at the table and began to wolf down his breakfast.

"Well, if you're so handsome and sophisticated," DeeDee continued, "maybe you'd like to come along with your daddy and grandma and me this weekend to show yourself off at the church retreat."

Malcolm's spoonful of cereal froze midway to his mouth. "Oh, no!" he said with exasperation. "Here we go again. I *told* you I didn't want to go to that thing! Why would I want to spend a whole weekend hanging out with the Geritol set? And anyway, I'll probably be working Saturday morning. Mr. Lacey and I are going to figure out my hours today."

DeeDee shook her head in resignation. "Well I'm not about to leave you here entirely on your own," she said. "I guess I'll see if JJ can come for the weekend—at least to stay over Saturday night."

"That's cool with me," Malcolm answered, digging into his cereal again. He knew his 27-year-old brother was not about to give him any trouble as far as his plans with Felicia were concerned.

When Saturday evening rolled around, Malcolm was relieved to see his brother show up all dressed to go out and party. "Hey, man," JJ said, "it's like this. I ain't gonna daddy you or nothing, 'cause I know this is a chance that don't come along too often. But I promised Momma that you would be cool, so whatever you do, don't have the neighbors calling over here. And don't let me know what you're planning to do, so that when I tell Momma everything was cool, I can say it without lying."

"All right, my man," agreed Malcolm. "We cool. I won't put you on the spot."

The brothers slapped hands as JJ headed for the door. "I'll be back around three," JJ added. "And hey, Motor Man. You all right!"

Malcolm smiled as he watched his brother go. As soon as the door closed, Malcolm ran to the phone and began to dial Felicia's number.

The next year of Malcolm's life passed quickly. True to his word, he kept up his grades and did his chores at home despite the added workload of his job at Jewel's. In fact, Malcolm seemed to thrive on the added responsibility. It forced him to think more about using his time wisely. Often now, if he found himself with a few spare hours on his hands, he would use them to get a headstart on some upcoming project, rather than just lounging in front of the television. DeeDee was impressed with this new maturity. She was also impressed with Malcolm's growing interest in the world beyond girls, clothes, and sports. Especially when the family conversation turned to racial prejudice or unfair treatment of the poor, Malcolm joined in eagerly, expressing very passionate views.

One evening in March of Malcolm's junior year at high school, his father brought up the subject of a new redevelopment plan. It seemed the mayor's office was proposing a scheme that would affect the neighborhood where the Williams family lived, and many area residents had great misgivings. They feared that lower-income people would be gradually forced out as the property values rose and rents spiraled. Malcolm was indignant at the thought of such a thing. How could they let people be pushed out of their homes just because a bunch of yuppies wanted to move in? "We have to *fight* this," he nearly shouted at his father.

"That's why the Community Action Committee is holding an open meeting next Tuesday night," John Williams answered. "If you feel so strongly about it, why don't you come along with me and let the mayor's staff know your views?"

"You *bet* I will," said Malcolm. "I'm not gonna let 'em get away with this!"

"But first you'd better read up on the subject," John Williams advised, passing Malcolm all the clippings and information he had accumulated.

"Right!" said Malcolm. "By Tuesday night I'll know this plan inside and out!"

The following Tuesday Malcolm and his father had front-row seats. Malcolm was fascinated by every facet of the discussion that took place. He leaned forward, soaking up every word. Finally, toward the end of the evening, he bravely raised his hand. The chairman of the committee nodded in his direction, and Malcolm rose to his feet.

"I've lived in this neighborhood all my life," he began in a strong, clear voice, "and I think that some change would be a good thing, but it's got to be *fair*. That low-income project you're talking about building way over on Melrose would be pushing poor people out of the center of this neighborhood. My grandma's 82 and if she had to walk to the stores from all the way over on Melrose, I don't think she could make it. And another thing that bothers me, my father always says that diversity is what made this country great. Well, I think that goes for communities too! All kinds of people living together is what'll make this neighborhood a good place to live."

Malcolm sat down abruptly and looked straight ahead. He was surprised to hear a murmur in the audience, and then a loud round of applause. John Williams placed his hand on Malcolm's shoulder and smiled proudly at him. "Good for you, son," he said softly. "You're gonna make your mark." Yeah, I am, thought Malcolm. I'm gonna be somebody. I'm gonna make a difference! With growing pride in himself as a black teen-ager in Chicago, Malcolm resolved to fight the odds and make an impression on the world.

Mike Gordon

"Mikey!" Christine's voice called out for the third time. Damn it, thought Mike, a guy can't get any privacy around here! "Coming," he yelled as he put out his cigarette and turned off his stereo. Bounding down the stairs two at a time, he reached the bottom quickly, swung nimbly on the end of the bannister, and headed for the kitchen. "What is it, Mom?" he asked.

"It's my car again. It doesn't start right. Would you take a look at it?"

"What do you mean it doesn't start right?"

"Well, you know. It sounds like it's going to start, but then it takes a long time to turn over."

"Do you have enough gas?"

"Of course. I've got almost a full tank."

"Does it ever make a real bad grinding kinda noise?"

"No. I haven't heard anything like that."

"Then it's probably your spark plugs or your distributor cap. I'll check 'em."

"Thanks, Mikey," Christine said. "I really appreciate it." Christine was truly grateful for her son's impressive talent with anything mechanical. It certainly helped to keep the cost of home repairs down.

"But Mom, could you remember to can the Mikey stuff? I've told you a million times, the name's Mike, okay? For cripes sake, I'm almost 15."

"Mike. Got it," Christine answered, pointing a finger in her son's direction. "Old habits die hard, I guess."

"Well, just bury them, will ya?" Mikey said as he headed out the back door.

Christine watched the wiry adolescent in jeans and T-shirt as he opened the hood of her car. He certainly was growing up fast these days, and she wasn't always happy with the way he was doing it. Since he entered senior high school last September, he had started hanging out with a different crowd of boys. These new friends dressed tough, talked tough, and acted tough. Christine was reluctant to criticize them to Mikey, for fear that that might only make him defensive and cement the friendships further. Christine was also displeased that Mikey had started to smoke on the sly. She was sure he must be drinking beer at parties and had probably even tried pot—who knew how many times? It bothered her, too, that Mikey was spending so much time alone in his room. She knew he wasn't doing schoolwork. Although his math and science grades were fair, his grades in English and history were barely passing. When she mentioned these problems to Frank, he just laughed them off, telling her that he had also "sown some wild oats" at Mikey's age. Christine suspected that part of the trouble stemmed from Mikey's feelings toward Nicholas, Frank's 4-year-old son by his second wife, Nancy. Frank was always trying to get Mikey and Nicholas together for joint outings, but Mikey would have no part of it. He referred to his stepbrother as "that obnoxious little brat," and would see his father only when Nicholas was left at home.

Desperate for a sympathetic man to confide in, Christine turned to her brother-in-law, Dan. Dan smiled when she told him her suspicions about what Mikey was doing behind that door with the large PRIVATE sign on it. He felt it was perfectly normal for a 14-year-old boy to spend time by himself looking at "girlie" magazines. "If I were you," he advised, "I'd be more worried about those kids he's hangin' out with. If Mikey really wants to go to college like his cousin Danny, he'd better stop hanging out with guys who are going nowhere, and pull his grades up. He needs a spark to set him in the right direction." Christine sighed, wondering where such a spark would come from. Mikey certainly wasn't about to listen to her. As it turned out, the spark came in Mikey's sophomore year, and as often happens, it came from an unexpected source.

"Did you know that early reptiles had large fins that soaked up solar heat and helped keep them warm?" Mike reached for a third pork chop and another helping of mashed potatoes. "I learned that in biology today."

Christine smiled with both pleasure and amusement. Ever since her son had entered Mr. Rosengren's class this fall, he had become an endless source of such information. What a difference a teacher can make, she thought. Mike pored through books on animal physiology and behavior as if they were sports magazines. For the first half of his sophomore year his grade in biology was a B+. This half of the year he was well on his way to earning an A.

"Aren't you interested in learning any *human* biology?" Janie asked. She was in her first year at Community College of Rhode Island, studying to be a nurse. To save money, she lived at home and commuted in a secondhand car.

"Sure, I am," said Mike defensively. "Probably more than you. I bet you didn't know that if you take a human heart out of the body and put it in the right kind of fluid it'll keep beating on its own."

"Yuck! That's disgusting," answered Janie. "Leave it to you to come up with something like that."

The school year ended as Christine had predicted. Mike received an A in biology, and his other grades were up somewhat as well. That summer Mr. Rosengren helped Mike get a job at the marine biology station where he worked. The experience opened up a whole new world for Mike. Although he was only washing bot-

tles and doing general cleanup, he felt that he was part of a very important research project on Narragansett Bay. Long conversations with Mr. Rosengren while driving to the station each day filled Mike's head with dreams of the future. *He* would end the ravages of pollution on marine life. *He* would invent new conservation-conscious methods of farming the seas. The entire world might even be saved by one of his discoveries!

On weekends that summer Mike began to confide his new hopes and ambitions to his Uncle Dan. Dan was helping Christine tend a backyard garden she had planted in return for a share of the vegetables. Mike knew his uncle was interested in gardening, so maybe marine biology would interest him too. Mike broached the subject hesitantly, however, fearing that Dan might react to the idea of a career in science just as his father would. (Frank always referred to scientists as eggheads.) But to Mike's delight his uncle was enthusiastic. "Hell, Mike," Dan had said as the two of them cleared out the pea patch to make room for some more spinach, "I think that sounds great! You've got the stuff to do whatever you want if you put your mind to it. You know, I got off on the wrong track when I was in high school—messin' around with a lot of losers. And I've kinda always regretted it since. I think I could have done a lot more with my life if I had buckled down and tried to go to college. But my dad didn't think it was important so I guess I didn't get the push I needed. Not that I've done so bad really. But I'd do things differently if I were your age again."

Mike was struck by the wistfulness in his uncle's voice. He had never thought that Uncle Dan would confide in him like this, and he had never imagined that he would feel so comfortable telling his uncle the things that he had. He would talk with his uncle often in the months to come.

In September of his junior year Mike returned to school determined to "set the place on fire." Mike, Mr. Rosengren, and Mrs. Miller, the guidance counselor, worked out a plan whereby Mike would be in a position to go on to college. Because Mr. Rosengren had gone to Amherst, Mike wanted to go there too. But he knew his family could never afford it if he didn't land a scholarship. Mike doggedly tackled the program he had set for himself. Christine was impressed with his tenacity and even more impressed with his grades: a B + both in English and in American history, an A − in advanced algebra, and an A in chemistry. These successes confirmed Mike's belief that he could do it if he really tried. He forged ahead with renewed determination, the goal of a scholarship to Amherst lodged firmly in his mind.

In order to appear "well-rounded" to the Amherst admissions board, Mike made time to keep up his participation in sports. That winter he went out for wrestling, much to his father's delight. ("That's a real man's sport," Frank had said with pride.) But though Mike was number one in his weight class at his own school, he often lost in competition with boys from other high schools. "Where's your killer instinct, Gordon?" the wrestling coach complained. "Yeah, yeah. I'll get'm next time," Mike would answer. But to him doing well at wrestling was just a means to an end. The varsity letter he earned that year put him one step closer to Amherst, he hoped.

For a varsity letterman who regularly made the honor roll, Mike dated very little. He went to parties and dances and would ask a girl out once or twice, but that was as far as he let things develop. He felt girls were trying to crowd him, wanting some kind of steady commitment, and he wasn't ready for that. "The next thing you know she'll be talking about getting married," Mike once remarked about a girl who seemed especially attracted to him. "And I don't want any part of that. I've got big plans for myself."

"There's a letter for you on the table," Christine said to her son as he walked through the back door late one afternoon in March of his senior year. "It's from Amherst."

"Did you open it?" Mike asked in excitement, hurrying over to the table.

"No, of course not. It's addressed to you. But it's thick. That's a good sign."

Mike's diligence in schoolwork had paid off this year. His grades remained in the B + to A range. He had taken the SATs in the fall and learned shortly before Christmas that he had received a 620 on the verbal—quite a good showing—and a 740 on the math—an outstanding score. Mike had already been accepted at the universities of Rhode Island and Massachusetts, his two "backup" schools. Now the long-awaited news from Amherst had finally arrived. With nervous fingers Mike tore open the thick envelope. His eyes raced across the top page, then he skimmed the page that followed. A gigantic grin spread across his face. Tossing all the pages into the air, he let out a rebel yell. "I made it!" he shouted ecstatically. "I'm going to Amherst with a scholarship!"

It was a proud family that watched Mike graduate from high school in June. Christine and Janie, now a nurse at Rhode Island Hospital, had front-row seats, as did Frank, Nancy, and their two sons, Nick and Tim. Becky also made the trip down from Boston, where she lived with her new husband, Mark. She had just been promoted to buyer at the Jordan Marsh store, and she came decked out in an ultra-high-fashion outfit. As he walked up to the podium to receive his diploma and a special award in science, Mike Gordon's eyes looked over the audience and beyond as if toward the future. Not quite 18—barely one-fourth of the way into his life—he smiled with the joy of someone eagerly awaiting new experiences.

Meryl Polonius Turner

"Close the door," said Meryl to her friend Amy as they hurried into Meryl's bedroom, schoolbooks clutched in their arms. "I don't want my little brother snooping. He'd tell Mom sure as anything."

Amy dumped her books on the bed, then went back and shut the door, locking it for good measure. "I don't know what you're so worried about," Amy said. "It's your hair. At 14 you have a right to do what you want with it."

Meryl reached into her large canvas handbag and pulled out a small cardboard box. The words "Drop of Sun" appeared in pale blue letters beneath the picture of a glamorous woman with long, light-blond hair. "Return to the natural blond you were born with," Meryl read aloud. "The golden glow of soft, healthy, natural-looking hair kissed by the sun."

"Anyway," Amy continued, "Your mom's never even gonna notice. It says natural-looking, doesn't it? I mean, you're blond already, Mer. So who's gonna notice a little lighter? It'll be just like the sun did it."

"I don't know," answered Meryl. "I don't feel so brave anymore. What if it turns my hair like *real* platinum? Everyone will notice then. They'll stare at me like I'm a freak or something. I already get stared at because my arms are so long. Have you ever noticed how my hands hang down so low?"

"What's wrong with your arms?" asked Amy, lying back on the bed and unwrapping a piece of gum. "They match your legs. And long legs are sexy. Everyone knows *that*."

"Uh-oh!" said Meryl, jumping up and looking out the window. "There's my mom in the driveway. I'd better hide this stuff somewhere."

Ever since Meryl had turned 13, she had been developing a new view of her mother. Suddenly her mom seemed like an obstacle blocking all the things that Meryl now wanted to do. "Sometimes my mom is *so dense*" Meryl confided to Amy. "She just doesn't understand what it's like to be my age." This new view led to frequent arguments between Meryl and Karen, especially where boys were concerned. Take the time Meryl was asked out on her first date to the movies. Meryl had attended many mixed-sex parties, but she had never gone out on a date alone before. "But Mom, you've just *got* to let me go," Meryl pleaded. "All my friends date. I'll be so embarrassed if you won't let me! Don't you see how unfair you're being?"

Karen searched for a compromise, suggesting that perhaps Joe could drive Meryl and her date to the movies. Meryl was horrified. "Have *Dad* drive us?" she asked in utter shock. "Don't you know *anything*, Mom?" Finally, Karen yielded to the inevitable. Meryl was a very pretty teen-ager. She couldn't keep protecting her from boys forever. But Karen remained strict about when Meryl could go out (never on a school night) and what time she had to be home.

"Amy's parents don't have all these dumb rules," Meryl complained. "She comes in whenever she wants. And she doesn't always have to say exactly where she's going, like she was some kind of prisoner or something."

"Well we're not Amy's parents," Karen answered. "Dad and I do things differently."

"But Mom, I'm 14," Meryl protested.

"That's just it. You're very grown up for 14, but you're still only 14. You're not old enough to make all your own rules yet. Teen-agers can get into trouble if they're left to do anything they please."

"Just because *you* got pregnant doesn't mean *I'm* going to!" Meryl blurted out. "It's not fair of you not to trust me because of something you did."

"It's not that I don't trust you, honey," Karen answered, knowing there was some truth to what her daughter said. "You handle yourself real well, and I'm proud of you for it. But I do worry. You've been seeing an awful lot of Jim lately, and I just think you have to slow things down a bit. You have your girlfriends to spend time with too."

Although Meryl often got angry during these talks with her mother, she felt better afterwards. Sometimes a few hours later she would seek her mother out and begin discussing other things that happened to be on her mind. She might tell Karen about some spat going on between two of her girlfriends, about how "dumb" one of her teachers was, or about how she just *had* to have a new sweater to wear Saturday night. And more and more Meryl would turn the conversation to her "real" father, Jeff. She wanted to know what he looked like, what her mother had felt about him, why he didn't want to get married, and where he might be now. Karen answered all those questions as honestly as she could. Later, she would ask Joe about Meryl's interest in Jeff, wondering if he thought it was OK.

"Don't worry about it," Joe would answer with a smile. "It's only natural. And it's no big deal to me. I know Meryl loves me, even if I am sometimes *so dense*." Karen laughed at Joe's imitation of Meryl's favorite phrase. Having him in her life to share things with made all the difference.

Karen's concerns about Meryl and Jim didn't last very long. That summer they broke up. At first Meryl was hurt and sank into what she described as the deepest state of depression ever experienced. But when she found out Jim was dating Barbie, her hurt turned to anger.

"How could he go out with *her?*" she asked Amy. "Everyone knows her reputation!"

By the end of the summer Jim seemed to have been forgotten. Meryl began dating other boys and going out in mixed-sex groups. She was having more fun than ever and her confidence was growing. The self-consciousness she had shown for the past few years seemed to be gradually fading. Then another blow came. One afternoon when Karen asked Meryl why Amy wasn't coming by so often, Meryl confided in her mother with much bitterness: "She only wants to be with *Bill* these days. Bill this! Bill that! She never wants to be with *me* anymore. Even when she's not with Bill, she just stays home."

"Well maybe something's bothering her, honey," Karen answered sympathetically. "It could be all the trouble her parents have been having. But she's still your best friend, you know. You just have to work on getting her to open up."

"But that's just it, Mom," Meryl persisted. "She doesn't act like a best friend. We used to tell each other *everything.* Now when I ask her what's wrong, she just says she doesn't want to talk about it. It's like she doesn't trust me anymore, and I don't know why. I've never blabbed secrets to anybody—not ever."

"Well, give her time, Meryl. She can't cut herself off from her best friend forever."

In time Meryl did find out what was the matter with Amy. She was pregnant. Her parents were insisting she have an abortion, but Amy wasn't sure. Finally she relented. Afterward she hardly seemed the same person. The girl who had once been so full of energy and self-assurance was now apathetic and depressed. Then in the spring Amy's father was transferred to Los Angeles. Although Meryl and Amy exchanged letters for a while, they gradually grew apart. Meryl was devastated by this loss. It was some time before she had another friend as close as Amy.

"How can you eat that lettuce?" asked 17-year-old Meryl, looking at her mother incredulously. "Don't you know about the terrible conditions of the farm workers?"

"You're right," said Karen, feeling slightly guilty. "But what's summer without salads?"

"Don't you think that's a little hypocritical, Mom?" Meryl asked. "I mean, if you think the farm workers are being exploited, you shouldn't give money to the guys who are doing the exploiting."

Karen felt trapped. On the one hand, she knew her daughter had a point and she was pleased with Meryl's convictions about injustice in the world. On the other hand, Meryl could be so dogmatic. It was frustrating! She vowed to herself not to get dragged into another argument. Last week when Meryl had attacked the "morality" of making big commissions from selling houses, Karen had been totally exasperated. Where was that sweet little girl who used to be so proud her mother was a "real estate lady"? When Karen had tried to explain that real estate agents often work long hours on deals that never pay off, Meryl shook her head self-righteously and walked out of the room, sipping her Diet Coke.

"It's just a stage," Karen would say over and over to Joe. "It's all part of growing up—isn't it?"

"Don't ask me," Joe would answer, throwing up his hands in mock despair. "I'm just that dumb city editor who persists in covering trite local news when the arms race is threatening to blow up the whole world."

Karen laughed and gave him a hug. "But you're lovably dumb," she said.

Despite their occasional frustration over the intensity of some of Meryl's convictions, Karen and Joe had much to be proud of in their daughter. The talent for art she had shown all through childhood began to blossom and mature. Her sketches and watercolors were exhibited in city-wide art shows, and a few pieces had even been sold. This year Meryl was given the job of set director for the senior-class play. She threw herself into the project with great enthusiasm, spending long hours painting scenery and attending to every detail. Opening night, at the end of the performance, when Meryl came out to take a shy bow, Karen felt so proud that it brought tears to her eyes.

Gradually Meryl began to think about the possibility of teaching art someday. "If you want to teach," Joe suggested, "it wouldn't be a bad idea to get a little practice talking in front of a group. When I was your age I used to have a great time on the high-school debating team!"

Meryl looked at him as if he had just told her to walk to San Francisco. "The *debating* team?" she asked in disbelief. "No *way* I'm gonna volunteer to stand up and give a speech—in front of judges no less!"

Pursuing the idea of a possible teaching career, Meryl applied to Fresno State for the following fall. She thought she would major in art, with a minor in education. The day she received her acceptance, the whole family celebrated. Two of Meryl's friends would be going there as well, so the three girls decided to share an apartment near campus.

"You know, honey," Karen said to Meryl a week later, when all the excitement had died down, "I've been doing some thinking about my own future lately. I'd like to take some courses in business this fall, and Fresno State's the perfect place. How would you feel about bumping into your mom once in a while on campus?"

"I think that'd be great, Mom!" Meryl said with genuine pleasure. "With all that business sense of yours, you should really go for it!"

"Thanks," said Karen, smiling and putting an arm affectionately around Meryl's shoulder. "Did I ever tell you how lucky I am to have a daughter like you?"

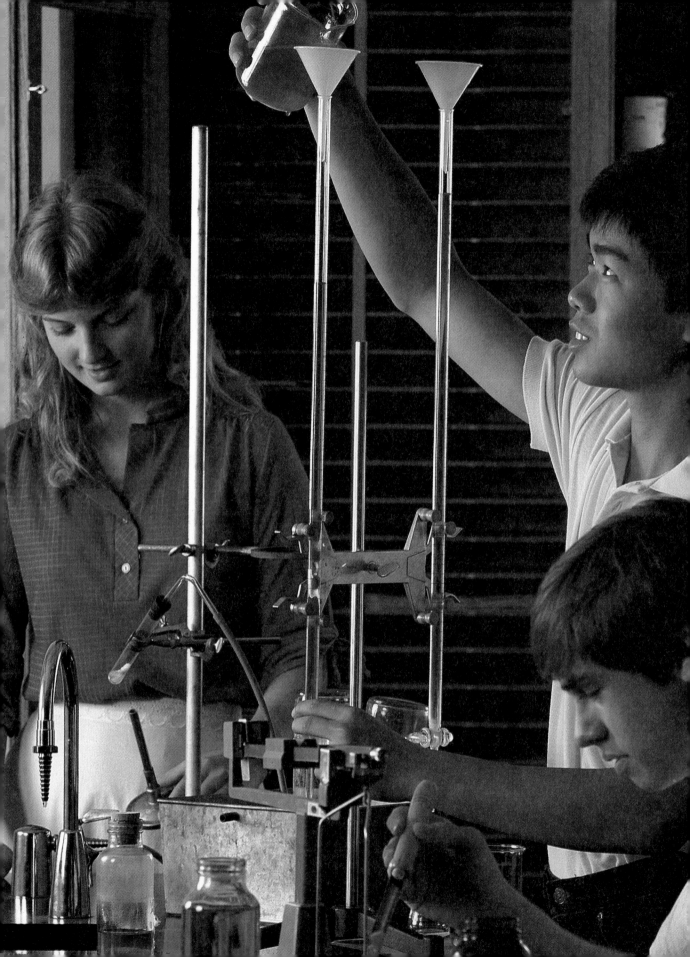

14

Physical and Cognitive Development in Adolescence

Fourteen-year-old Mike Gordon stood before the mirror, combing his hair for the third time. Tonight's party was important to him. He wanted to look good. Finished, he stood back and tried to appraise himself with an impartial eye. He was too short, that was certain. With a father who was over 6 feet tall, how could he still be only 5 feet 7 inches? And those arms! They were so scrawny they looked like a girl's! Mike pulled his shoulders back and tried flexing his muscles. It was no use. He was still skinny. There was no getting around it. He decided to put on a long-sleeved shirt over his favorite blue T-shirt. Of course, everyone would look at him funny for wearing a shirt like that on such a hot night, even if he did roll up the sleeves. All the kids would *know* he was trying to hide those scarecrow arms of his. Would the other guys give him a hard time? Sam and Doug might. As much as he wanted to be accepted by these other boys, he had to admit they weren't like "real" friends. Real friends didn't jump at every chance to put a guy down, and Sam and Doug were always doing that. Well, it was better than still hanging out with wimps like Richie and Jeff. Mike took one last critical look in the mirror, adjusted his collar, and walked out the door.

Adolescence, the period from roughly age 13 until graduation from high school, is a time of dramatic and far-reaching change. It is characterized by an especially close connection between physical development and a young person's psychological world. Notice in the brief episode about Mike the major concerns that arise from the way he views his physical appearance. In his mind he is not maturing fast enough, and this causes him to feel self-conscious. The example of Mike also illustrates adolescent egocentrism—the teen-age tendency to think that other people focus as much attention on you as you yourself do. For instance, because Mike is so conscious of his wiry build, he assumes that everyone else must be too. This kind of egocentrism is partly the product of new cognitive skills that Mike has acquired. So just as in the period of concrete operations, emerging cognitive skills are initially responsible for a new form of egocentrism and then as they mature, are responsible for its decline. Emerging cognitive abilities are also responsible for the new way in which he is able to think about friendship. Compared with elementary school children, he seems to have a much more psychological view of the phenomenon. He sees friends as people who offer each other emotional support and avoid inflicting psychological discomfort. This new, more mature understanding of friendship goes hand in hand with Mike's increased introspection and his greater ability to conceptualize human thoughts and feelings. In this chapter we will discuss these and other changes that come with adolescence.

Adolescence took on the status of a unique developmental period only in the twentieth century (Hamburg, 1974; Konopka, 1973; Sprinthall and Collins, 1984). Before then the passage through puberty was viewed as a time of entry into adulthood. The view of adolescence as a special stage was partly inspired by the work of G. Stanley Hall (1904). Like Freud, Hall argued that adolescence is a period when all earlier developmental issues are reworked. He also saw it as a time of inevitable storm and stress, emanating from the rapid and dramatic physical changes that occur. Many psychologists now question this conflict-ridden view of adolescence. Nevertheless, Hall made an enduring contribution by recognizing the specialness of this developmental period and the key role that biological changes play in it.

Because of the importance of biological changes during adolescence, we will devote the first section of this chapter to them. An understanding of the physical transformations at puberty sets the stage for understanding other aspects of adolescent development, both cognitive and social ones. From our discussion of physical development during the teen-age years, we go on to explore some of the basic changes in thinking that adolescents experience. Here we will compare Piaget's perspective with the views of

Adolescence is a time of rapid change, which occurs at different ages for different individuals. Differences in timing of physical maturation, as illustrated in this picture, pose emotional challenges. *(Renate Hiller/ Monkmeyer Press.)*

other, more recent researchers. Finally, we will look at changes during adolescence that are related to cognitive development. These include changes in young people's thoughts about themselves, in the nature of their values, and in their moral reasoning.

BIOLOGICAL CHANGES DURING ADOLESCENCE

The dramatic biological changes that occur in adolescence are apparent to everyone. The teen-ager experiences an accelerated growth rate, more rapid than at any time since infancy. Accompanying this spurt in growth are changes in body shape and proportions, such as development of broader shoulders in boys and wider hips in girls. These developments are controlled by hormone changes. The same hormone changes also affect adolescents' emotions, often triggering waves of new and sometimes unsettling feelings. Researchers speculate that adolescent hormone changes may even affect the organization of the central nervous system, thus having important implications for cognitive development (Case, 1985; Epstein, 1974, 1980). At the same time, biological changes at **puberty** (the entry into adolescence) have important social implications. Teen-agers begin to think of themselves as no longer children, and parents begin to expect more mature and responsible behavior of them. Increased sexual urges and the capacity for reproduction are issues that both teen-agers and their families must face. The timing of physical changes also has a major impact on peer relations and a young person's self-image. Let's begin our look at the critical factor of biological change in adolescence by exploring the concept of puberty and its timing.

The age at which puberty begins varies widely among adolescents. *(Barbara Rios/ Photo Researchers, Inc.)*

Puberty: Norms and Individual Differences

Some researchers argue that puberty is a single event, the change from a sexually immature person to one who is capable of reproduction (Chumlea, 1982). For girls this event is **menarche,** the onset of menstruation. For boys the critical change is the ability to ejaculate mobile sperm. Other researchers use the term *puberty* more broadly. To them it refers to a more extended period in early adolescence when sexual organs and other sexual characteristics are developing rapidly (Kimmel and Weiner, 1985). In this chapter we will be using the second definition. Although the major developmental changes of puberty usually occur over a period of about four years, the total duration of puberty may actually be longer than this. The very earliest phases can begin as young as age 7 or 8, and the latest phases can continue into the mid-teens. In most cases puberty begins about two years earlier in girls than it does in boys (Petersen and Taylor, 1980).

There are substantial differences in the timing of puberty among youngsters of the same sex. The onset is influenced by heredity, nutrition, level of stress, and amount of exercise, all of which vary from one individual to the next. Defining the "normal" range for beginning and completing puberty is really a statistical task. James Tanner, a highly respected researcher in this field, defines "normal" as the range experienced by 95 percent of the population. According to this definition, it is normal for menstruation to begin as early as age 9 or as late as age 16, and it is normal for sperm production to occur as early as age 10 or as late as age 19. But note that although these ranges are considered normal from statistical and biological perspectives, youngsters who fall at the outermost extremes may encounter special psychological issues with which they must deal. We will discuss these issues in Chapter 15.

Very early puberty may sometimes arise from a physiological problem caused by illness or a tumor. In girls, it is sometimes the result of a medication or the use of cosmetics such as their mother's anti-aging lotions that contain female hormones. It is not usually caused by abnormalities in the girls' own hormone systems, although this may sometimes be the case. Similarly, a late puberty is not generally cause to assume some hormonal deficiency. Instead, it is most often the result of a normal biological clock that differs from those of most other teen-agers.

The average age at which puberty begins has been decreasing at least over the last 100 years and perhaps even longer. Girls now begin menstruating at about age 12 rather than at age 14 as their grandmothers and great-grandmothers did (Bullough, 1981; Tanner, 1962). Boys, too, show signs of an earlier onset of puberty. Improved nutrition and health care may in part account for these facts. In keeping with this explanation, one study conducted in Hong Kong found that menarche came earlier to girls from rich families than it did to girls from poor families (Tanner, 1962). Will the trend toward earlier puberty continue throughout the world? Probably not in countries with already high standards of living. In the United States, for instance, the average age of menarche has been relatively stable over the last few decades, suggesting that we may have reached the limits of accelerating puberty (McAnarney and Greydanus, 1979).

Hormonal Control of Puberty

Puberty, of course, is not a transformation that arises out of thin air. It is the final stage in a much larger process of sexual development. Remember from Chapter 4 that sexual differentiation begins soon after conception. Whether a fertilized egg becomes male or female depends on the presence or absence of a Y chromosome, which in turn governs the amount of male hormones or androgens that the embryo produces. A relative abundance of androgens triggers the development of male sex organs, whereas a relative absence of androgens allows the development of female organs. At puberty, hormones once again govern sexual changes, but this time the relative presence or absence of androgens is not the only factor involved. Whereas in boys an increased secretion of androgens results in the production of live sperm and male secondary sex characteristics (broader shoulders, facial hair, a deeper voice, and so forth), in girls a stepped-up secretion of female hormones called estrogens brings about menstruation and other aspects of sexual maturation. Let's take a closer look at both these hormone changes.

Many glands in the body produce hormones. Often, the hormones from one gland influence the rates at which other glands secrete their hormones. This feedback system maintains a proper balance among interrelated hormones. The gland that plays the biggest role in regulating output from other glands is a small structure, called the **pituitary,** attached to the base of the brain. Secretions of hormones from the pituitary are in turn influenced by other hormones produced by a part of the brain known as the **hypothalamus.** These brain hormones, or releasing factors as they are often called, turn the pituitary hormones "on" and "off." Some of the pituitary hormones are called **gonadotropics** because they travel through the bloodstream and affect output from the sex glands, or **gonads.** The gonads of men are the testes, which produce androgens; the gonads of women are the ovaries, which produce estrogens and progesterone. The levels of sex hormones in the blood provide signals to the brain that the hypothalamus monitors, modifying its activities accordingly. This complex control system functions even prior to birth. Through middle childhood it works to keep sex hormones at low levels (Grumbach et al., 1974).

At the end of middle childhood the brain delivers a message for the gonads to step up production of sex hormones. How the brain "knows" it is time to begin puberty is something we do not yet understand. Some think that declining levels of the hormone melatonin produced by the pineal gland may be involved in initiating puberty. Melatonin levels are high for children under 5, drop gradually during middle childhood, and drop still further by age 13 (Waldhauser, 1984). We know that an abundance of melatonin lowers the secretion of sex hormones (Reichlin, 1981). Thus, this inhibiting factor may be steadily lifted as melatonin levels fall, until finally puberty is reached. Of course, the question remains how the pineal gland "knows" when to reduce its production of melatonin. Here the answer may lie in cyclical exposure to light. The pineal gland does not produce melatonin when light strikes the eyes. Perhaps it keeps track of the number of day-night cycles, which provides the basis for the biological clock of puberty (Kimmel and Weiner, 1985).

An alternative explanation, called the **critical weight hypothesis** (Frisch and Revelle, 1970), is based on data suggesting that menarche occurs at a relatively constant weight in girls and that the adolescent growth spurt in both sexes is also weight related. The underlying mechanism is thought to be a change in metabolic rate caused when the body reaches some critical overall weight. The change in metabolic rate presumably leads to a change in the chemistry of the blood, which then initiates the sequence of events leading to greater output of sex hormones. The critical weight hypothesis has been questioned, however. For instance, it is now known that in females at least 17 percent of the body must be made up of fat in order for menstruation to begin or continue (Petersen, 1979). Thus, weight per se may not control menarche, but factors *related* to weight, such as the proportion of fat to lean tissue, may do so. More generally, some researchers now suspect that weight is merely associated with the biological signals that initiate adolescent hormone changes but is not itself one of those signals (e.g., Petersen and Taylor, 1980).

Regardless of what brings about the increased output of sex hormones at the end of middle childhood, increased output is unmistakably the start of the changes we call puberty. Rising levels of sex hormones circulate in the blood, making themselves available to cells throughout the body. When the concentrations of these hormones reach a critical threshold, cells that are receptive to them change their growth patterns (Root, 1973). Note the importance of a critical threshold in the levels of sex hormones. Androgens and estrogens are present in the blood throughout childhood, but they do not trigger puberty until their concentrations rise to some critical level. Only then do the obvious physical changes of adolescence begin.

A Closer Look at the Physical Changes of Puberty

CHANGES IN APPEARANCE

In addition to the production of mature egg and sperm cells, the physical changes of puberty involve noticeable transformations called **secondary sex characteristics.** These include changes in skeletal size and proportions, new distributions of muscle and fat tissue, the growth of hair on certain parts of the body, and specialized changes such as the lowered pitch of the male voice. Various stages of puberty are often defined by the development of major secondary sex characteristics. For instance, Tanner (1962) has identified five such stages on the basis of the development of pubic hair and genitals in boys, and pubic hair and breasts in girls. Table 14.1 presents the specific criteria used to define each stage.

The development of the various secondary sex characteristics does not always occur at the same rate. In fact, a given adolescent may often develop faster in one area than in another. For instance, a male might be at stage 4 for genital development but only at stage 2 for the development of pubic hair. Nevertheless, there are some broad limits within which most individuals mature. Most girls enter stage 2 of pubic hair development between 10½ and 13, whereas most boys enter this stage between

TABLE 14.1   Stages of Puberty

Stage	Pubic Hair Development	Breast Development	Male Genital Development
1	No pubic hair	Elevation of papilla (nipple) only	Penis, scrotum, and testes stay in the same proportion to body size as in early childhood
2	First pubic hair, which is sparse, long, and slightly pigmented appears; usually grows at base of the penis or along the labia	Breast buds appear. The breast and papilla are elevated slightly in a small mound	Scrotum and testes enlarge and scrotum darkens
3	Hair darkens, becomes coarser and more curled; remains sparse but spreads over the midsection of the pubic region	Breast and areola continue to enlarge but there is no separation of their contours	Penis grows, primarily in length, and scrotum and testes continue to grow
4	Hair development is completed, but area covered is still smaller than in adults	Areola and papilla elevate above the mound of the breast to form a secondary mound	Growth of penis includes width and enlargement of glans; scrotum continues to grow and darken
5	Quantity and area covered reach adult proportions	Papilla continues to project, but areola recesses to the general contour of the breast	Genitals attain adult size and shape

Source: Adapted from Tanner, 1962.

12½ and 14½. Later, most girls enter the fifth stage of pubic hair development between 13½ and 15½, whereas most boys enter this stage between 14 and 16. Thus, at the beginning of puberty, females lead males by about two years in the appearance of pubic hair. By the end of puberty, however, males have caught up substantially regarding this characteristic. Now they lag females in pubic hair development by only about half a year. The other secondary sex characteristics included in Table 14.1 may begin developing a little earlier than pubic hair does. For instance, most girls enter stage 2 for breast development between ages 10 and 12, and most boys enter stage 2 for genital development between 10½ and 13. Most girls enter stage 5 for breast development between 13½ and 17, and most boys enter stage 5 for genital development between 14 and 16.

In addition to breast and genital enlargement and the emergence of pubic hair, most adolescents experience noticeable changes in their skin and sweat glands. The skin becomes rougher and more oily, and the sweat glands develop and become more active, especially in the underarm and genital areas. The increased oiliness leads to acne and other skin eruptions, and the increased sweat gland activity leads to new body odors. In our evolutionary past these body odors may have functioned as pheromones, chemical scents used by members of the same species to communicate a message, such as a readiness to mate. Both body odors and acne can be sources of embarrassment for adolescents. Overall, more males experience these problems than females.

Another sign of adolescence is a marked spurt in growth. Figure 14.1 shows that increases in height slow substantially during the late preschool years and early middle childhood. Across this age range, the average height of girls and boys is virtually identical (Tanner, 1970; Tanner, Whitehouse, and Takaishi, 1966). Then the growth spurt for girls

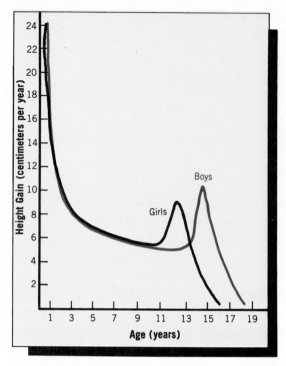

Figure 14.1
Growth Rates for Boys and Girls
The rate of growth, which is at its maximum in infancy, declines through childhood and is followed by a spurt in adolescence. The growth spurt for males is greater, and growth continues over a longer period of time, which is why they are usually taller.

Source: Tanner, Whitehouse, and Takaishi, 1966.

begins, at an average age of 10½. For boys the spurt starts a few years later, on average at age 12½. The adolescent growth spurt reaches its peak about a year and a half after it begins. The peak rate for boys is greater than the peak rate for girls, which partly explains why boys grow to an average height that is 2½ inches taller than that of girls.

Growth occurs at the ends of bones and in rings of cartilage called epiphyseal growing plates. Different patterns of skeletal growth among adolescent boys and girls largely account for the gender-related differences in body shape. The classic male growth pattern leads to broader shoulders, narrower hips, and longer legs relative to torso. The classic female growth pattern leads to narrower shoulders, broader hips, and shorter legs relative to torso (see Figure 14.2). Ultimately, adolescent skeletal growth comes to a halt when increased amounts of sex hormones cause calcification of the cartilage involved in the process.

You may have noticed among both boys and girls that growth occurs in the arms and legs before the torso during the adolescent growth spurt. This can make the limbs seem temporarily out of proportion to the rest of the body and is one source of self-consciousness among teenagers. Meryl expressed this concern to her friend Amy in our earlier story. The torso growth that follows usually brings the whole body back into "normal" proportions. However, individuals differ substantially in the relative size of their torso and limbs. Since Meryl was complaining about having long arms at age 14, we have reason to suspect she may be naturally long limbed.

In addition to increases in size, adolescents also experience increases in weight, strength, and endurance. For instance, people gain about 40 percent of their adult weight after puberty (Chumlea, 1982). Part of this weight gain comes from growth in both the size and number of muscle cells. As a result, adolescents become stronger than they were as children, although males experience a greater increase in strength than females (Malina, 1978). During adolescence the heart and lungs also undergo development. This development contributes to increased endurance and allows for participation in more demanding competitive sports.

The growth patterns we have described are but a sampling of the physical changes that occur during puberty. They are meant to illustrate what a dramatic transformation is going on at this time. In just a few short years youngsters change from looking like children to looking like young adults. In the process, they gain new capacities for strength and endurance and, perhaps most important, for sexual reproduction. All these physical changes taken together help propel adolescents toward a new set of social roles. At the same time, changes in the central nervous system may be related to teenagers' growing ability to think in ways they could not do as children. Before we examine the adolescent's new capacities for thought, let's look at the changes in the brain believed to be tied closely to cognitive development.

CHANGES IN BRAIN STRUCTURE AND FUNCTION

Although some psychologists are still skeptical, mounting evidence suggests that the brain undergoes substantial change during early adolescence. This evidence comes partly from behavioral data, such as studies of how thinking skills develop during puberty. These new thinking skills may in part be the product of altered ways in which the central nervous system is organized. Evidence for brain changes in early adolescence also comes from developmental studies of young animals, as well as from physiological research into how the human brain works. If such brain changes do take place, it is difficult to say what causes them. They may

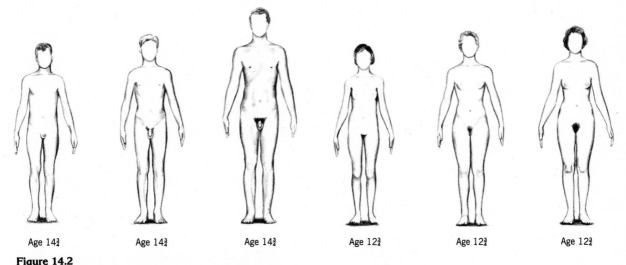

Age 14¾   Age 14¾   Age 14¾   Age 12¾   Age 12¾   Age 12¾

Figure 14.2
Developmental Differences in Same-Age Boys and Girls
The three males in this figure are all the same age (14 3/4 years), as are the three females (12 3/4 years), but they are in different stages of development. These illustrations show the different rates of development within gender and the different patterns of growth for males and females.

Source: Tanner, 1962.

be produced partly by the hormone changes of puberty and partly by experiences during earlier developmental periods. In any case, once adolescence is over, the brain seems to be a somewhat different organ than it was in childhood.

One interesting piece of behavioral data in support of this theory is the ease with which young children are able to learn a new language as compared with the struggle that many adults undergo to accomplish the same task. It is as if the brain of a child is especially designed to soak up certain kinds of information. Interestingly, too, young children recover more readily from brain injuries than adults do. Their brains seem more flexible in the sense that various brain regions can more easily take over functions performed by parts that become damaged. Both these lines of evidence suggest that the brain of a young child has a marked capacity for "reprogramming." By this we mean an ability to make adjustments in understandings of the world and to alter the way in which cognitive activities are carried out. Some of this impressive reprogramming capacity seems to be lost around the time of puberty. However, young adolescents make compensating gains by becoming more effective at advanced reasoning skills.

Another piece of behavioral data in support of the theory that the brain changes at the time of puberty comes from developmental studies of sleep patterns. During sleep the brain emits electrical waves that scientists have measured. These measurements show that brain waves during sleep change between childhood and early adolescence. Children between the ages of 2 and 11 spend about twice as much time in what is called **deep sleep,** a state characterized by extremely slow brain waves, as adults do. Then, between the ages of 11 and 14, the amount of deep, extremely slow brain-wave sleep declines to adult levels (Blakeslee, 1986). We do not know what prompts this nighttime change in brain-wave patterns. One possibility is based on the theory that deep sleep somehow helps the brain recover from its metabolic activities during the day (Kallat, 1985). If the brain becomes more efficient at adolescence, its amount of metabolic activity would decline, as would the need for deep sleep (Blakeslee, 1986; Lund, 1978).

Researchers have also explored developmental changes in the brain more directly by examining brain size and anatomy at different ages. Although the brain grows very little after the beginning of middle childhood, some evidence suggests a brief, spurtlike increase in brain weight around puberty (Epstein, 1977). The cells that support the brain's nerve cells and the **neurons** themselves may grow. At the same time, the number of connections (called **synapses**) among the neurons of the brain may decrease (Huttenlocker, 1979). One researcher has reported a decreased density of synapses in certain parts of an adult's brain compared with the brain of a child (Huttenlocker, 1979). In keeping with this finding PET scans show that between the ages of 10 or 11 and 13 or 14 there is roughly a 50 percent drop in the energy being used within areas of the brain (Blakeslee, 1986; Brown, Holland, and Hopkins, 1981). Since substantial energy is needed to send messages from one neuron to another, this decrease in energy expended could arise partly from a "pruning" of brain synapses. Research on animal brains likewise suggests that interconnections among neurons may at first be overproduced. Some of these synapses are then eliminated. Which ones probably depends on the type of stimulation and demands made of the brain. This system has the advantage of allowing for maximum cognitive flexibility early in life. As Feinberg puts it: "You are born into a situation where you don't know exactly what brain connections you'll need. You have essentially a decade to determine which ones you're going to use." After that the "excess" synapses are pruned away, leaving you with those experience has shown are necessary (quoted in Blakeslee, 1986, p. A20).

How can we summarize all these findings about changes in the brain at puberty? Apparently, during early adolescence the brain becomes more efficient at certain operations, using less energy for them, and some of its parts become more specialized. But these changes come at the price of a decrease in flexibility. After adolescence the brain cannot adapt as readily to new demands, such as recovering from damage or acquiring a whole new way of thinking about the world. This conclusion is consistent with the decline in fluid intelligence that begins in mid-adolescence. Although older teens and adults continue to acquire more and more information (crystallized intelligence), they gradually lose some of their earlier ability to think and reason flexibly. Although we do not know for sure that specific changes in the brain are responsible for this gradual decline, the converging evidence from various sources is interesting and suggestive.

CHANGES IN THINKING DURING ADOLESCENCE

Adolescence is a time when youngsters acquire important new cognitive skills. Some developmentalists, such as Piaget, see these new skills as marking the transition to a qualitatively different period of development. Although these researchers believe the skills of adolescence are built upon those of childhood, they tend to focus on how thinking at this age is *fundamentally* different than it was earlier in life. In contrast, other developmentalists tend to put more stress on continuity with the past. They see the cognitive accomplishments of adolescence more as logical and steady progressions from the skills of middle childhood (e.g., Keating, 1980; Siegler, 1978). Despite these different approaches, however, all

The more complex thinking skills of adolescents are stimulated by more complex problems, such as learning to use a computer as an analytic tool. *(Miriam Reinhart/Photo Researchers, Inc.)*

developmentalists agree that following puberty youngsters become much more mature in their reasoning and problem-solving capabilities.

Although developmentalists disagree about the causes of these new achievements, they do agree on their broad outlines. One major change is that logical thinking is now applied to the possible (what *might* exist), not just to the real (what *does* exist). In one investigation of this change, children were shown poker chips of varying colors, one of which was then hidden in the experimenter's hand (Osherson and Markman, 1975). The experimenter stated: "Either the chip in my hand is green or it is not green." The children were then asked to decide if this statement was true or false. Youngsters in middle childhood had great difficulty answering the question correctly. They kept trying to determine whether or not the chip was green, and upon discovering that they couldn't do so, they said there was no way to answer the researcher's question. These children seemed wedded to a contingent notion of truth: To know if the experimenter's words are true you must *see* what is in his hand. Adolescents, in contrast, are much more apt to break free of this focus on concrete things that the senses can perceive and instead consider the possibilities contained in the statement (the chip may be green or it may be some other color). Using this more abstract perspective, adolescents conclude that the statement necessarily must be true.

A second, related cognitive advance during adolescence is use of what is called **hypothetico-deductive reasoning.** This ability involves thinking up hypothetical solutions to a problem (ideas about what *might* be) and then formulating a logical and systematic plan for deducing which of these possible solutions is the right one. Consider the problem of repairing a car that Mike Gordon faced in our earlier story. He was able to solve this problem not simply because he was knowledgeable about engines but also because he was able to lay out the possible reasons for a malfunction such as his mother describes and then deduce what symptoms would differentiate one possibility from another. Even if a 9-year-old knew a great deal about car engines, he or she could not be this logical and systematic in gathering information about possible causes and isolating the correct one. A knowledgeable 9-year-old would probably simply check the things that had gone wrong in the past or perhaps wiggle the parts that "looked" bad. Note that this approach is the same one generally taken by an adult who lacks the necessary knowledge to repair a car engine. Lacking the appropriate information to make meaningful hypotheses, an adult may end up responding like a young child. Thus, at times adults do not exhibit their highest levels of reasoning (Pitt, 1976). Nevertheless, they do possess the ability to take a hypothetico-deductive approach when they are motivated to do so and have the required knowledge. This ability emerges during adolescence.

A third cognitive advance in adolescence is the ability to think about relationships among mentally constructed concepts, that is, abstract concepts that are built up from the more concrete things we perceive. Number, for instance, is a mentally constructed concept drawn from the more concrete concepts: one, two, three, and so forth. The ability to think about relationships among mentally constructed concepts is evident in a variety of contexts. For instance, it can be seen in teen-agers' introspection and focus on their own thoughts (Elkind, 1974). In general, adolescents have an improved metacognitive capacity—the ability to think about thinking and to know what thinking involves (Flavell, 1985). At the same time, teen-agers acquire a new, more mature grasp of abstract concepts such as identity, justice, religion, society, existence, morality, and friendship. Whereas an elementary school child might define morality as "not stealing" and "telling the truth" (a focus on specific behaviors), an adolescent understands that the term entails interrelations among subordinate concepts such as fairness, honesty, kindness, and so forth.

A fourth cognitive advance of adolescence is a willingness to accept lack of closure, that is, lack of a firm answer to a given question (Collis, 1978; Lunar, 1978). An excellent example can be seen in a study in which youngsters were presented with partial information about the rock formations at Stonehenge in England (Donaldson, 1963). They were then asked to describe what they thought these formations were. In some cases the information was biased so that Stonehenge seemed a religious monument; in other cases the information was biased so that Stonehenge seemed an astronomical observatory. After they had made their initial judgments, the youngsters were given additional information suggesting that Stonehenge served both religious *and* astronomical functions. Once again they were asked what purpose they thought the rock formations served. Elementary school children tended to stick to their original judgments despite the contradictory new information. In contrast, adolescents were willing to modify their initial judgments on the basis of the new facts. Adolescents seemed to take their first conclusions as tentative hypotheses, subject to change as additional information came to light.

What underlies these cognitive changes that occur in adolescence? One interpretation is Piaget's theory of formal operations. **Formal operations** are new kinds of mental transformations that teenagers are able to perform. They allow youngsters to reason more logically about abstract concepts and to think more systematically than ever before. Because Piaget's theory of formal operations has had such an influence on the field, we will describe it in some detail before turning to the views of its critics.

An understanding of the relationships among abstract concepts is one of the cognitive advances that develop during adolescence. *(UPI/Bettman Newsphotos.)*

Exploring Piaget's View of Adolescent Thought

Piaget built his theory of formal operations on extensive research into the capacities that adolescents possess. This research took the form of presenting subjects of different ages with scientific experiments to conduct. The subjects were given an apparatus (such as a pendulum) or a set of materials (such as chemicals capable of producing a certain reaction when combined in a particular way). They were asked to manipulate these items in any way they wished in order to determine how they "worked." Piaget found that adolescents approached and understood these tasks in markedly different ways than elementary school children did. He summarized their higher level of cognitive functioning in terms of two logical models, which we will discuss a little later. But first we want to give you a better idea of Piaget's studies and the findings they produced by describing some of the specific experiments he conducted.

PIAGET'S EXPERIMENTS

As you read about the following experiments, notice the general cognitive abilities that they demonstrate. The first two show the ability to reason about proportions; the second two show the ability to isolate variables that may be having an effect on results; and the last one shows the ability to combine a number of different factors in a systematic way.

The Law of Floating Bodies Study.   In what can be called the law of floating bodies study, youngsters were given objects of different sizes, made of different materials, along with a large container of water. Their first task was to classify the objects according to which they thought would float and which they thought would sink. Then they were asked to explain their classification. Finally, they were given a chance to experiment, see what each object actually did when placed in the water, and describe what they had learned.

At the beginning of middle childhood (ages 6 to 7) youngsters are often wrong in their hypotheses about what will float and what will not. Moreover, when given a chance to experiment and draw more accurate conclusions, their reasoning is often unsystematic, illogical, and incomplete. Consider the remarks of these three young elementary school children (adapted from Inhelder and Piaget, 1955/1958, pp. 26–27):

CHILD 1: (explaining why a large piece of wood floats) "Because this plank is bigger and it came back up." (Interviewer: And why does the ball come up?) "Because it's smaller."

CHILD 2: (explaining why certain items sink) "They are little things." (Interviewer: Why do the little ones go to the bottom?) "Because they aren't heavy; they don't swim on top because it's too light." Later the same child says that a metal key sinks "because it's too heavy to stay on top."

CHILD 3: (explaining why a candle sinks) "Because it's round. (Interviewer: And why does the wooden ball stay on top?) "Because it's round too."

These examples highlight the self-contradictions that young children make in trying to explain why some things float and others do not. Such self-contradictions seem related to a focus on an object's most obvious and directly perceivable features (large, small, round, and so forth) regardless of the question being asked.

Somewhat older children (7 to 10 years of age) try to avoid self-contradictions. They frequently express the idea that light objects float and heavy ones sink. When reminded that some very small objects sink and some very heavy ones float, they grope for an overall explanation that will accommodate these facts. Here is how two older elementary school youngsters tackled the problem (adapted from Inhelder and Piaget, 1955/1958, pp. 29, 35):

CHILD 1: (explaining why the ball floats): "It stays on top. It's wood. It's light." (Interviewer: And this key?) "It goes down. It's iron. It's heavy." (Interviewer: Which is heavier, the key or the ball?) "The ball." (Interviewer: Why does the key sink?) "Because it's heavy." (Interviewer: And the nail?) "It's light but it sinks anyway. It's iron and iron always goes under."

CHILD 2: (explaining why the wooden ball floats while the iron key sinks) "Wood isn't the same as iron. It's lighter; there are holes in between." (Interviewer: And steel?) "It stays under because there aren't any holes in between."

Notice how both these children are quite good at predicting what will float and what will sink. The first one still seems to rely greatly on empirical knowledge ("iron *always* goes under"), while struggling toward an understanding that some things can be "heavy" and still feel relatively light. The second child seems to have moved a step further by developing an implicit notion of an object's density (weight per unit of volume). But this youngster is still unable to articulate the concept maturely.

More mature explanations come in adolescence. Listen to this older adolescent describing the principle in very adultlike terms (adapted from Inhelder and Piaget, 1955/1958, p. 44):

(Explaining why the key sinks despite the fact that it is relatively small and light) "With the same volume the water is lighter than the key." (Interviewer: How would you prove that?) "I would take some modeling clay, then I would make an exact pattern of the key and I would put water inside it. It would have the same volume of water as the key . . . and it would be lighter."

This example illustrates several important characteristics of adolescent thought. First, notice how the cognitive skills of adolescents are built upon those developed in middle childhood. Elementary school children have acquired the concepts of volume and weight, which is why they are able to solve conservation problems. An understanding of density is based on these two earlier concepts. More specifically, density involves an understanding of the ratio or *proportion* of weight to volume. The ability to reason about proportions is one of the new skills that emerge during adolescence. Notice, too, how proportional reasoning involves the ability to think about interrelationships among constructed concepts. During the sensorimotor period infants' concepts are limited to direct perceptual information. Not until they are older do children become able to construct

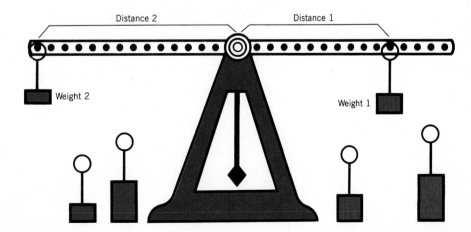

Figure 14.3
Balance Scale Used to Investigate the Development of Proportional Reasoning
Full understanding of the scale involves the knowledge of an inverse proportion; that is, the scale will balance if
$$\frac{\text{Weight 1}}{\text{Weight 2}} = \frac{\text{Distance 2}}{\text{Distance 1}}$$

more abstract concepts such as number, weight, and volume. Finally, during adolescence, they are able to grasp the ways in which two or more constructed concepts can be related to produce a third, even more abstract concept. Thus, they grasp that the proportion of weight to volume yields density. And just as elementary school children understand that weight and volume are conserved despite superficial transformations, so adolescents understand the conservation of density despite superficial changes in the size and shape of an object.

The Balance Scale Study.   Another of Piaget's experiments that shows the emergence of proportional reasoning is the balance scale study. Using a scale like the one shown in Figure 14.3, weights of different sizes can be placed at different distances from the fulcrum. The child is first asked to predict when the scale will balance and when it will tip. Then the youngster is allowed to experiment with actual weights and positions and encouraged to explain the principles involved. To solve the problem correctly a subject must understand that the scale will balance only when the ratio of weights on the two sides is *inversely* proportional to their distances from the fulcrum. In other words, weight 1 divided by weight 2 must equal distance 2 divided by distance 1. Thus, if the weight on side 2 is twice as heavy as the weight on side 1, the side 2 weight must be *half* the distance from the fulcrum that the side 1 weight is.

Piaget discovered that children learn this principle in steps. At about age 5½ they first come to the realization that weight is a relevant factor. Then, at about age 7 or 8, they discover through trial and error that both weight *and* distance from the fulcrum are important. At this stage, however, youngsters do not yet grasp the connection between the two variables. Not until after age 10 can they tell you a heavier weight must be placed closer to the fulcrum in order to balance a lighter weight far out on the scale's opposite side. But their understanding of this relationship is still only qualitative. They simply take a guess at how far to move a weight in order to achieve equilibrium. Finally, after the age of about 14, youngsters come to understand the quantitative nature of the balance principle. Here is how one older adolescent solved the problem (adapted from Inhelder and Piaget, 1955/1958, pp. 174–175):

> The subject discovers immediately that the horizontal distance is inversely related to weight. "How do you explain that?" the interviewer asks. "You need more force to raise [a weight] placed at the extremes than when it's closer to the center . . . because it has to cover a greater distance," the subject explains. "How do you know?" the interviewer questions. The subject answers: "If one weight on the balance is three times the other, you put it a third of the way out because the distance it goes is three times less."

Piaget attributed these changes in children's performance on the balance scale task to changes in underlying cognitive structures that occur as youngsters grow older. In contrast, information-processing theorists attribute these changes in performance to changes in the rules that children use in approaching this problem. Four such rules drawn from the research of Robert Siegler (1981) are shown in Figure 14.4. Children using rule I focus only on weight and predict that if the weights are equal the

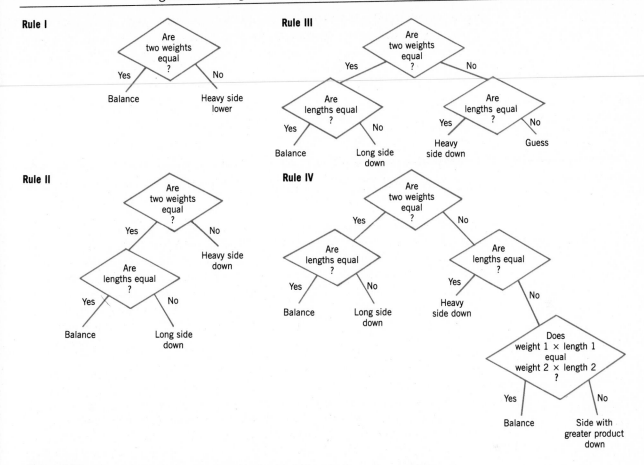

Figure 14.4
Siegler's Rules for Solving the Balance Scale Problem
According to Siegler's information-processing theory, the output of the human
mind depends on the input and the capacity of the brain to store, organize, and
retrieve what it has received.
Source: Adapted from Siegler, 1981.

scale will balance; otherwise, the side with the heavier weight will sink
down. Children using rule II pay attention to weight first, but if the
weights are equal they say that the one farther from the fulcrum will sink
down. Children using rule III consider both weight and distance. However, when the weights and distances are unequal and the heavier weight
is closer to the fulcrum, they are unsure whether the scale will balance.
Finally, children using rule IV make the same proportional calculation
that Piaget described for older adolescents.

How the use of these various rules develops as children grow older
is summarized in Table 14.2. Notice the great similarity between the
changing patterns of behavior that Piaget described and those Siegler
describes. This similarity exists despite great differences in the theoretical
approaches of the two researchers. The greatest discrepancy is at the
oldest levels: Whereas Piaget saw the final stage of reasoning as quite
common among older adolescents and adults, Siegler finds only a minority of subjects over the age of 12 using rule IV. We will return to this
issue later in this chapter.

Source: Adapted from Siegler, 1981.

TABLE 14.2 Number of Children at Each Age Using Different Rules to Solve the Balance Scale Problem

Age	No Rule	Rule I	Rule II	Rule III	Rule IV
5-year-olds	1	17	1	1	
8-year-olds		2	7	9	2
12-year-olds			3	12	3
Adults			1	13	6

The Bending Rods Study. Piaget used the apparatus shown in Figure 14.5 to study the way in which youngsters explore and understand the factors that influence how much a rod will bend when a weight is placed on the end of it. There were five possible variables to manipulate: the rod's material (steel or brass), the rod's cross-sectional area (thick or thin), the rod's cross-sectional shape (square or round), the rod's length (long or short), and the heaviness of the weight placed on the end of the rod. The subjects were to determine which of these five variables were relevant to the amount of bending produced.

Children in early middle childhood noted the variables involved in the task, but they made mistakes in interpreting which of these were important. For instance, 6-year-olds might decide that thinness is what matters. They might insist that a thin rod *always* bends a lot, even though under certain circumstances (when the rod is short and lightly weighted) it hardly bends at all. Here we see very young children contradicting their own observations, just as we saw in the floating bodies study.

By age 8 youngsters make some progress toward understanding that more than one variable is relevant to this problem. But these older elementary school children are not yet able to separate the relevant from the irrelevant. Here is how one child this age discussed what is involved (adapted from Inhelder and Piaget, 1955/1958, p. 50):

"Some of them bend more than others because they are lighter [he points out the thinnest rods] and the others are heavier." The interviewer hands him a short thick rod, a long thin one, and a short thin one and asks him to show how a thin rod can bend more than a thick one. The child places a 200-gram weight on the long thin rod and a 200-gram weight on the short thick one without seeming to notice that the thin rod he has chosen is also the [longer] of the two. "You see," he says. The interviewer then asks whether it is better to make the comparison that the child just made or to compare instead a short thick rod with a short thin one. "These two," the child answers, pointing to the long thin rod and the short thick one. The interviewer asks why. "They are more different," the child says, overlooking the critical idea of holding all other factors equal while the effects of thickness are explored.

With the onset of adolescence children begin to put together the full solution to the problem. But at first they still seem to lack systematic use of the "all-other-things-equal" procedure. Notice the flaws in this young adolescent's efforts to demonstrate the relevant variables (adapted from Inhelder and Piaget, 1955/1958, p. 57):

"There are flat ones, wider ones, and thinner ones, and longer ones. If they are both long and thin, they bend still more." The interviewer asks the youngster to show that a thin rod bends more than a wide one. The subject puts a 100-gram weight on a round, thick steel rod 50 centimeters long, but he then puts a 200-gram weight on a round, thin steel rod of the same length. Repeating the question doesn't help him to isolate the variable of thickness from the variable of weight.

In contrast, older adolescents are quite adept at isolating each variable in order to determine its effect. Here is how one 16-year-old girl confidently approached the task (adapted from Inhelder and Piaget, 1955/1958, p. 60):

The interviewer first asks her what factors are involved here. "Weight, material, length of the rod, perhaps form," she answers. The interviewer then asks if she can prove her hypotheses. The subject compares the 200- and 300-gram weights on the same steel rod. "You see, the role of weight is demonstrated," she explains. She then proceeds to isolate each of the other variables and to discover the relationships among them. Throughout she shows a clear understanding that the effects of any variable can only be demonstrated when all of the other factors are held constant.

The Pendulum Study. The need to hold all other factors constant while investigating the effects of a single variable also played a central role in another of Piaget's experiments, the pendulum study. Here subjects had to figure out which of four factors determines the period of a pendulum, the time it takes to complete a swing from one side to the other and back. The four factors are the length of the pendulum, the size of the weight suspended from it, the height from which the pendulum is first released, and the force with which the pendulum is pushed when set in motion. The solution to this problem is contrary to most adults' intuitions: Only the *length* of the pendulum influences the period of its swing. This is what makes the pendulum problem such a good way of demonstrating the new skills in experimentation and logical deduction that adolescents acquire. Elementary school children do not appropriately isolate each of

Figure 14.5
Piaget's Bending Rods Problem
In this problem the child's task is to predict how much a rod will bend. The rods vary in material (as is shown by whether they are colored or white), cross-sectional size (shown at left), and cross-sectional shape (also shown at the left). The child can adjust the length of the bending part of the rod by moving it in and out in the frame. In addition, the child can vary the amount of weight on the end of the rod.

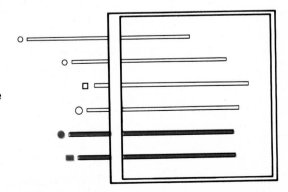

the possible variables, and so they draw the wrong conclusions. Adolescents, in contrast, systematically test each of the factors while holding the other ones constant. This enables them to discover that length is the sole cause.

The All-Possible-Combinations Study. Another experiment that Piaget designed to assess the cognitive skills of adolescents is one in which the subject is required to systematically try all possible combinations of five different liquids in order to determine which combinations cause the color yellow to appear. The five different liquids are all colorless to begin with. Four of them are in large flasks numbered 1 through 4. The fifth is in a smaller bottle with an eye dropper in it (Piaget labels this g). The experimenter shows the subject a flask with an unidentified liquid, which actually contains liquids 1 and 3. To this he adds a few drops of g from the small bottle, and the liquid in the flask turns yellow. The subject is then asked to reproduce the yellow color in as many ways as possible using the five liquids originally provided.

Elementary school children typically take the small bottle labeled g and place a few drops from it in each of flasks 1 through 4. When nothing happens they usually realize that the liquids from more than one flask must first be mixed together, but their approach to finding the right combinations is haphazard. If they happen to stumble on the 1 + 3 + g combination through trial and error, they generally stop their search, not thinking that some other combination might also produce yellow. (As it turns out, 1 + 3 + 2 + g produces yellow too.) In contrast, subjects in mid-adolescence or older adopt a systematic approach and try all possible combinations. After working through the two-liquid combinations (1 + g, 2 + g, and so on), they proceed to the three-, four-, and five-liquid ones, trying to avoid repeats while not missing any. These older subjects readily discover the two combinations that work.

PIAGET'S THEORY OF FORMAL OPERATIONS

Findings from these and similar experiments helped Piaget develop his theory of formal operations. In summarizing this theory it is useful to stress three characteristics (Neimark, 1982). First, Piaget saw the new thinking skills of adolescents as the product of new kinds of mental transformations, which he labeled formal operations. Like concrete operations, formal operations are used to manipulate information, producing a fuller, more mature understanding of things. However, formal operations are applied to mental representations that are more abstract and structured than those to which concrete operations are applied.

A second major characteristic of Piaget's theory is the way he saw formal operations organized. Formal operations are a powerful and flexible thinking system not only because of the value of each operation itself but also because of the interrelations among the parts. Piaget described these interrelations using two logical models. The first is called the **system of 16 binary operations.** Each binary operation is a logical relationship that might occur among the factors involved in a simple experiment. We say the experiment is simple because it entails only two different variables, each with two different possible configurations. Those variables, for example, might be long versus short length and heavy versus light weight, as in Piaget's bending rods study—thus the term *binary*, which means "involving two." Beyond their ability to analyze information in terms of the 16 binary operations when presented with appropriate experiments, adolescents can also perceive broader logical relations among the conclusions they draw. For instance, they can perceive in the bending rods study that length compensates for weight and vice versa. A long rod will bend even with a light weight, while a heavy weight will make even a short rod bend. In other words, adolescents see the relationship between these two factors as a *reciprocal* one. Piaget identified four of these broader logical relationships. All can be used to manipulate conclusions and produce deeper understandings. The four relationships are identity, negation, reciprocity, and correlativity. Using the first letter of each of these terms, Piaget called this the **INRC group.**

A third and final major characteristic of Piaget's theory can be stated very simply. He believed that the cognitive skills that constitute formal operations are new and qualitatively different from anything in the past. Nevertheless, he saw these skills as produced by the same processes of adaptation and equilibration that produced earlier cognitive structures. Thus, cognitive structures and abilities may change, but the underlying processes of development do not.

Adolescents show remarkable improvements in skills for scientific thinking compared to children in middle childhood. Piaget's descriptions of the emergence of some of these skills have proved to be quite accurate, although his explanation of these developments is often disputed. *(Paul Conklin/ Monkmeyer Press.)*

Is Piaget's View Correct?

You have seen that there are two aspects to Piaget's view of adolescent thought. One is simply his description of how the ability to solve certain problems changes during this period. The other is his theory of how these new abilities are made possible by fundamental transformations in a young person's cognitive structures, transformations presumably captured in Piaget's logical models. How have each of these aspects of Piaget's approach fared in the eyes of subsequent researchers?

The descriptive aspect of Piaget's work has fared quite well. Although many refinements to his original descriptions have been made over the years, this part of Piaget's contribution is still evaluated positively. Other researchers have found similar age-related changes in performance on the tasks that Piaget designed. What's more, agreement is widespread that these tasks do a good job in sampling the range of thinking skills that emerge during adolescence (Keating, 1980; Neimark, 1982).

The theory that Piaget offered to explain adolescents' new skills has received much more criticism, however. Referring to the structural models of both concrete and formal operations, John Flavell argues that to varying degrees they are "unclear, incorrect, and incomplete as theoretical descriptions of the thinking capabilities of children and adolescents" (Flavell, 1985, p. 92). Piaget himself recognized weaknesses in the original formulation of his theory, which is why he continued to modify it throughout his lifetime. Unfortunately, he died before he could present comprehensive new models. Piaget's theoretical contributions, then, have undeniable flaws. Nevertheless, his models of adolescent cognitive development still provide the basic organizing framework for research into this topic (Neimark, 1982). Although much current work is directed toward illustrating problems with the theory of formal operations, no comprehensive and integrated alternative to it has yet been formulated.

Although the use of formal operations develops during adolescence, some adolescents and even adults do not use formal operations on a regular basis. *(J. H. Sullivan/Photo Researchers, Inc.)*

Thus, we can present no equally broad competing theory in this chapter. Instead, we focus on narrower criticisms of Piaget's ideas, beginning with the observation that formal operations may not be as pervasive in older adolescents as Piaget suggested.

HOW PERVASIVE ARE FORMAL OPERATIONS?

Research by Robert Siegler (1978), which we mentioned earlier, shows that only a minority of subjects over the age of 12 use the most advanced rule in solving the balance scale problem, the rule that corresponds to Piaget's quantitative proportional reasoning. A number of other studies likewise show that many adolescents and even adults do not normally use formal operations to solve problems (Blasi and Hoeffel, 1974). In one study, for example, only 32 percent of 15-year-olds and 34 percent of 18-year-olds were even beginning to use formal operations, and only 13 and 19 percent, respectively, used them in mature ways (Epstein, 1979). Individual differences are substantial, of course, in the use of formal operations. Generally speaking, the higher the scholastic ability and performance of a teen-ager, the more likely he or she is to employ this kind of thinking (Shayer, 1980). But this fact does not negate the overall finding that adolescents and adults often fail to reason as Piaget described. When tests are given to assess the use of formal operations, only about a third of older subjects pass (Capon and Kuhn, 1979; Keating, 1980).

How much does this finding challenge the validity of Piaget's research and theory? Defenders of Piaget say the criticism must be viewed in light of the typical adolescent's **cognitive competence,** or *optimal* ability, not just his or her **cognitive performance,** or actual behavior in a particular context. People might not always employ their optimal abilities for a number of reasons. For instance, they might fail to recognize that these abilities are appropriate to the situation. Or they might lack the specific knowledge needed to use higher-level reasoning (for example, the person who knows nothing about engines aimlessly fiddling to repair a car). Other explanations include inattention, lack of motivation, and information overload that prompts a mental "tuning out." In view of all these factors, some psychologists question the value of developing models of cognitive competence rather than focusing on everyday cognitive performance. Others dispute this perspective, however, and argue that the distinction between competence and performance is important. According to them, the fact that teen-agers may possess the skills of formal operations but fail to use them in many circumstances captures an important characteristic of adolescent thought. This latter view is currently more dominant.

CAN FORMAL OPERATIONS BE TAUGHT?

As we said in Chapter 12, Piaget did not believe that the cognitive skills of a given developmental period can easily be taught to younger children. As you also learned in Chapter 12, however, this view is not entirely correct. Researchers have had some success teaching the concrete operation of conservation to very young elementary school children, particularly those who are in a transitional phase with regard to this skill. Similar success has been obtained in efforts to teach formal operations (Beilin, 1976, 1980; Inhelder, Sinclair, and Bovet, 1974). Most of this success has been with youngsters in later middle childhood and with adolescents who do not show formal operational reasoning on a pretest. Using the same training procedures with younger children often has no effect, although the findings are mixed with regard to very bright younger children. In one study, for instance, very bright 8-year-olds were taught how to isolate variables in order to determine which factor was causing a certain result (Case, 1974). Improvement occurred both in those who received the training and in control subjects who did not. Apparently, high intelligence may help promote early onset of formal operational skills.

Neimark (1982) has argued that perhaps training in formal operations is effective with older youngsters because often we are not actually seeing the results of teaching a brand new skill. Instead, we may be seeing the results of procedures that encourage existing competencies to be displayed. This view is consistent with the frequent finding that adolescents and adults sometimes fail to exhibit their highest level of reasoning because of limitations on performance rather than lack of skills. You can see this quite clearly in a study in which adults were presented with an experiment similar to Piaget's problem on combinations of liquids. Even chemistry professors performed poorly when they were simply given the equipment and encouraged to plunge ahead and find the solution. Both they and other subjects performed much better when asked to plan their strategy before actually beginning to gather data. Thus, training studies may be better at telling us how to get people to perform at their peak ability than they are at revealing much about the development of new competencies.

ARE FORMAL OPERATIONS RELATED TO ACADEMIC PERFORMANCE?

Another question psychologists have raised about formal operations is how useful these reasoning skills are to academic performance. Since performance on formal operational tasks is related to measures of intelligence and since measures of intelligence, as you know from Chapter 12, predict performance in school, it is not surprising that tests of formal operations can also be used to predict school success. However, assessments of formal operations provide different insights into cognitive skills than IQ tests do. For one thing, tests of formal operations predict performance in science and math better than overall academic performance (Cooper and Robbins, 1981). This finding makes sense when you consider the kinds of experiments used to assess formal operational reasoning.

Researchers have found that explicit training in formal operations can improve a student's grades in science classes (Cooper and Robbins, 1981). In fact, even simple exposure to formal operational tasks, without explicit instruction in the principles involved, can sometimes have a similar effect. In one study, for example, the subjects were students in an introductory college astronomy class. When initially tested, 53 percent of them failed to exhibit formal operations on at least five out of eight tasks. The researchers then designed a set of laboratory exercises which required that data be collected and evaluated but which gave no explicit instruction in formal operational skills. Half the students were allowed to use these exercises as supplemental training for the class. The other half were merely given supplemental audiovisual material. The students who completed the laboratory exercises not only showed greater improvement on a posttest of formal operations, but they also received higher average grades in their astronomy course (Cooper and Robbins, 1981).

GENERAL CONCLUSION

Research since Piaget's original studies of formal operations suggests that these skills are indeed characteristic of some of adolescent thinking. Furthermore, the link between formal operational abilities and academic performance indicates that these skills are important in carrying out some of the daily cognitive tasks that teen-agers encounter. There is a great deal more to learn about adolescent thought, however. According to Daniel Keating (1980), we still know very little about how the thinking of adolescents differs from that of children except for the simple descriptions we have of their performance on various tasks. What is more, in Keating's view, Piaget's theory is not a very accurate account of how cognitive change occurs. We believe that Keating's assessment is probably too negative. Nevertheless, his perspective appropriately points out that the strength of Piaget's contribution lies in his description of adolescent thinking, not in the explanatory models of it that he proposed.

OTHER CHANGES RELATED TO COGNITIVE DEVELOPMENT

The new cognitive skills of adolescence do much more than simply allow teen-agers to think more systematically and with more mature logic when solving certain kinds of problems. These same skills also have an impact on many other aspects of life. For instance, their effects can be seen in a new kind of egocentrism that develops during adolescence, an egocentrism quite unlike that which younger children display. The effects of new cognitive skills can also be seen in the emergence of explicit values during the teen-age years, as well as in new ways that adolescents are able to reason about moral issues. In the rest of this chapter, we will explore each of these three topics.

Adolescent Egocentrism

Egocentrism, as you know, involves a failure to distinguish one's own point of view from a more objective conception of reality. Young infants are egocentric with respect to objects because they believe that objects exist only when they personally perceive them. Later, as children acquire object permanence, this kind of egocentrism disappears, but other kinds of egocentrism linger throughout the preschool years. For instance, you saw in Chapter 10 that when 4-year-olds select a gift for an adult they act as if the adult's desires are the same as their own. The cognitive development that occurs during middle childhood frees youngsters from this and other forms of early egocentrism. Then, during adolescence, dramatic new cognitive abilities develop. Youngsters are now able to think about their own thinking and to consider abstract possibilities. This gives rise to a new kind of egocentrism.

The physical changes of adolescence and adolescent egocentrism lead frequently to a preoccupation with bodily changes. *(Steve Leonard/Black Star.)*

In describing adolescent egocentrism, David Elkind (1967) stresses the concept of an **imaginary audience.** By this he means the teen-ager's unjustified concern that he or she is the focus of other people's attention. Because adolescents can think about the thoughts of others, they are able to consider what others might be thinking *of them.* You saw an example of such self-consciousness in our earlier story of Meryl, who was sure the whole world was staring at her long arms. Notice how Meryl's cognitive ability to dwell on others' opinions was interacting with her awareness of the physical changes of puberty. These physical changes, especially when they seem awkward and ungainly, are a major source of concern for adolescents and are one reason why they turn their thoughts to others' opinions of them. This kind of egocentrism may help explain the adolescent's desire for privacy: Teens who believe that others are viewing them negatively would want privacy in order to escape their imaginary audience. Oddly enough, an imaginary audience may also help explain why teens sometimes act in a loud and boorish manner, thus drawing real attention to themselves. If they think that others are already observing them critically, being loud and boorish will make no difference.

In addition to his concept of the imaginary audience as an aspect of adolescent egocentrism, Elkind also proposes the idea of teen-agers' personal fables. A **personal fable** is a belief in your own uniqueness to the point where you think that no one else has ever had your special thoughts and feelings. Elkind (1978) gives the example of the adolescent girl who says to her mother: "You just don't know how it feels to be in love!" The girl is convinced that her emotions are special, beyond the capacity of anyone else to know or understand, especially adults. Why do adolescents develop this egocentric viewpoint? To some extent, the reason is that their new cognitive skills allow them to think about concepts, such as romantic love, with which they have little experience and which they seldom discuss with others. Lacking a broader perspective for viewing new thoughts and feelings, they come to the conclusion that these thoughts and feelings are unique to them. Because many of the concerns that accompany this kind of egocentrism are private and personal, communication with close friends is particularly important in encouraging the decline of personal fables. By mid-adolescence, when youngsters have a better understanding that many thoughts and feelings are shared by almost everyone, they begin to lose the sense of being so unique and different from others.

In the course of moral development, adolescence provides many opportunities to examine the role of rules and law in our society. *(Ken Karp; Paul Conklin/Monkmeyer Press.)*

Values and Adolescent Thinking

Values are ideas about "good" and "right" behavior. They are beliefs about how we should try to act in a given situation and about the kind of person we should generally strive to be. Values are standards that guide every facet of our lives: from our words and actions to our attitudes, our judgments, our justifications, and our attempts to influence others (Rokeach, 1973). Because values are abstract notions, their development must usually await the cognitive changes of puberty. This is not to say that youngsters in middle childhood have no sense of right and wrong. Certainly, they have implicit notions of "ought" and "ought not." But elementary school children do not explicitly think about the standards that underlie their choices of behavior. Such explicit concern with values—values becoming objects of systematic thought and evaluation—does not occur until adolescence. With puberty, youngsters are able to systematically consider the values they hold as well as alternative values. In their eagerness to use these new abilities, they may seem somewhat overly idealistic, carried away with issues of right and wrong. We see this in Malcolm, with his passionate feelings about fairness in urban redevelopment. Piaget argued that developing cognitive skills inherently "want" to be exercised. This belief certainly seems to be the case with respect to values.

When values initially emerge as an explicit focus of thought, they tend to promote another kind of egocentrism. Adolescents are often convinced that their views are right beyond any question, that people who think differently simply don't see things as clearly and correctly as they do. This kind of egocentrism frequently prompts overblown claims about hypocrisy of others, especially parents and other members of the "older" generation. We see this in Meryl when she attacks her mother's hypocrisy in eating lettuce despite the plight of farm workers. As with other types of adolescent egocentrism, this type gradually declines as teen-agers have the chance to interact with others over value issues. Through these experiences they come to realize that their own set of values is not a logical necessity and also that logic alone is not enough to settle disputes over values.

Given the adolescent's common preoccupation with values, you may wonder what specific values the average young person holds. Table 14.3 presents the results of a survey on values conducted among male college students. It shows what they considered the four most important "instrumental values" (those concerning conduct to achieve some goal) and the four most important "terminal values" (those concerning the kind of person they ultimately wanted to be). Notice how the data show both cross-cultural variation and consistency. It is also interesting that when young people's values are examined over time we do see change, as many expect, but we also see stability (Yankelovich, 1974). Apparently, the reexamination of values that each new generation undertakes usually leads to evolution, not revolution, in standards.

The Development of Moral Reasoning

Closely related to issues of value is the subject of moral judgment, making decisions about the "proper" thing to do in a particular situation. Whereas values are the abstract ideas of good and bad that guide our behavior, moral judgment is the actual process of thinking and reasoning about the right course of action in a given situation. Piaget (1932) included the development of moral reasoning within his broad theory of cognitive development. Later, Lawrence Kohlberg (1958, 1969) expanded on Piaget's approach, producing a six-stage model of how moral reasoning changes. There are, of course, other approaches to moral development. Psychoanalytic theorists usually focus on emotional responses to moral issues, responses such as guilt when breaking a rule. Social learning theorists tend to focus on how specific prosocial behaviors are acquired through observation of others and the expectation of rewards. We will not consider these other approaches here because they are not specifically tied to developing cognitive skills. In contrast, the models of Piaget and Kohlberg are concerned with how the ability to reason about moral issues changes as children's cognitive capacities change.

Piaget's model begins with an amoral stage, characteristic of children until they are about 7. Then, during the cognitive subperiod of concrete operations, the stage of **moral realism** emerges. Children at this age treat morality as absolute and moral constraints as unalterable. Behavior in their view is either totally right or totally wrong. They also believe in "immanent justice," a kind of inherent retribution. If they break a moral precept, they think that God or some other moral authority will make bad things happen to them. Piaget's next stage, called **autonomous morality,** is usually attained during late middle childhood or early adolescence. Now youngsters see morality as more relative to the situation. In judging whether a particular action is right or wrong, they consider intentions as well as consequences. Youngsters at this stage also recognize the possibility of diverse opinions regarding moral standards. They no

TABLE 14.3   Most and Least Important Values for Male College Students in Five Countries (1 = highest; 18 = lowest)

Rank	United States	Canada	Australia	Israel	Papua New Guinea
Terminal Values					
1	Freedom	Freedom	Wisdom	A world at peace	A world at peace
2	Happiness	Happiness	True friendship	National security	Equality
3	Wisdom	Mature love	Freedom	Happiness	Freedom
4	Self-respect	Self-respect	A sense of accomplishment	Freedom	True friendship
15	Pleasure	A world of beauty	A world of beauty	A comfortable life	A sense of accomplishment
16	Salvation	Social recognition	Social recognition	Social recognition	Pleasure
17	National security	National security	National security	A world of beauty	Mature love
18	A world of beauty	Salvation	Salvation	Salvation	A world of beauty
Instrumental Values					
1	Honest	Honest	Honest	Honest	Honest
2	Responsible	Responsible	Broad-minded	Responsible	Helpful
3	Ambitious	Loving	Responsible	Logical	Responsible
4	Broad-minded	Broad-minded	Loving	Capable	Ambitious
15	Cheerful	Imaginative	Imaginative	Clean	Independent
16	Polite	Polite	Polite	Imaginative	Clean
17	Clean	Clean	Clean	Obedient	Logical
18	Obedient	Obedient	Obedient	Forgiving	Imaginative

Source: Feather, 1980, p. 266.

longer consider moral rules as absolute but rather as the result of social agreement. These rules are therefore subject to change if people's values change.

Piaget believed that moral development is a direct consequence of both cognitive development and increased social experience. For instance, with the decline of centration in middle childhood, youngsters become able to consider simultaneously both consequences *and* intentions when judging the morality of an act. Then later, in adolescence, the ability to systematically consider one's own and others' opinions enables recognition of different moral viewpoints and the idea of moral rules as based on social agreement.

Kohlberg's model of moral development is broadly similar to Piaget's, although Kohlberg identifies more stages that people potentially pass through. Kohlberg derived his stages by presenting subjects of different ages with moral dilemmas to solve. Table 14.4 gives an example of one of these dilemmas, as well as the reasoning typical of subjects at each of Kohlberg's six stages.

Kohlberg's first two stages are part of a broader **preconventional period**—preconventional in the sense that the judgments children make are not based on any reasoning adults would call moral. For instance, during stage 1, "good" behavior is defined simply by a desire to avoid punishment imposed by some external authority. Kohlberg calls this the obedience and punishment orientation. In stage 2, "good" is whatever satisfies one's own needs (even if indirectly, as in helping another person so that person will help you). Kohlberg calls this the hedonistic and instrumental orientation.

As children advance into the next major period, the period of **conventional morality,** their moral judgments are based on internalized standards arising from concrete experience in the social world. Kohlberg calls their reasoning conventional in the sense that it focuses either on the opinions of others or on formal laws. In the first stage within this period, stage 3 in Kohlberg's overall model, the child's goal is to act in ways that others will approve of. This stage is referred to as the good-boy, good-girl orientation. In the second stage within this period, stage 4 of Kohlberg's model, the basis of moral judgments shifts to concern over doing one's duty as prescribed by society's laws. Kohlberg calls this the authority or law and order orientation.

The last major period in Kohlberg's model is called **postconventional** or **principled morality.** During this time youngsters transcend conventional reasoning and begin to focus on more abstract principles underlying right and wrong. In the first stage of this period, Kohlberg's stage 5, the goal is to meet one's obligation to keep society running smoothly. Particular laws may even be considered somewhat arbitrary, but they are nevertheless deemed important because they allow people to live together in reasonable harmony. Kohlberg calls this the social contract orientation. In the sixth and final stage of moral reasoning, the goal is to make decisions on the basis of the highest relevant moral principle. At this level of thinking, the rules of society are integrated with the dictates of conscience to produce a hierarchy of moral principles. Kohlberg calls this the hierarchy of principles orientation.

How are Kohlberg's stages of moral reasoning related to cognitive development? You might guess that children at the preoperational level in Piaget's cognitive system would be in Kohlberg's premoral period. Likewise, you might guess that youngsters at the level of concrete operations would be in Kohlberg's conventional period, while those who had acquired formal operations would have reached the period of principled morality. These are very reasonable predictions, but they turn out to be wrong. The development of moral judgment seems to lag behind the cognitive skills needed to engage in a particular level of moral reasoning. Kohlberg (1976) concludes that premoral reasoning (stages 1 and 2) is characteristic of most children until about age 9, and conventional reasoning (stages 3 and 4) is characteristic of most adolescents and adults. One long-term longitudinal study has shown that stage 3 reasoning peaks in mid-adolescence and then declines, whereas stage 4 reasoning increases dramatically in later adolescence and young adulthood (Colby et al., 1980). Probably only a minority of people ever reach the postconventional level of moral reasoning that Kohlberg describes.

TABLE 14.4   Kohlberg's Heinz Dilemma and Representative Responses

Dilemma

In Europe, a woman was near death from a special kind of cancer. There was one drug that the doctors thought might save her. It was a form of radium that a druggist in the same town had recently discovered. The drug was expensive to make, but the druggist was charging ten times what the drug cost him to make. He paid $200.00 for the radium and charged $2000.00 for a small dose of the drug. The sick woman's husband, Heinz, went to everyone he knew to borrow the money, but he could only get together about $1000.00, which is half of what it cost. He told the druggist that his wife was dying and asked him to sell it cheaper or let him pay later. But the druggist said: "No, I discovered the drug and I'm going to make money from it." So Heinz got desperate and broke into the man's store to steal the drug for his wife. Should the husband have done that?

Stage 1

Action is motivated by avoidance of punishment and "conscience" is irrational fear of punishment.

   Pro—If you let your wife die, you will get in trouble. You'll be blamed for not spending the money to save her and there'll be an investigation of you and the druggist for your wife's death.

   Con—You shouldn't steal the drug because you'll be caught and sent to jail if you do. If you do get away, your conscience would bother you thinking how the police would catch up with you at any minute.

Stage 2

Action motivated by desire for reward or benefit. Possible guilt reactions are ignored and punishment viewed in a pragmatic manner. (Differentiates own fear, pleasure, or pain from punishment-consequences.)

   Pro—If you do happen to get caught you could give the drug back and you wouldn't get much of a sentence. It wouldn't bother you much to serve a little jail term, if you have your wife when you get out.

   Con—He may not get much of a jail term if he steals the drug, but his wife will probably die before he gets out so it won't do him much good. If his wife dies, he shouldn't blame himself; it wasn't his fault she has cancer.

Stage 3

Action motivated by anticipation of disapproval of others, actual or imagined hypothetical (e.g., guilt). (Differentiation of disapproval from punishment, fear, and pain.)

   Pro—No one will think you're bad if you steal the drug but your family will think you're an inhuman husband if you don't. If you let your wife die, you'll never be able to look anybody in the face again.

   Con—It isn't just the druggist who will think you're a criminal, everyone else will too. After you steal it, you'll feel bad thinking how you've brought dishonor on your family and yourself, you won't be able to face anyone again.

Stage 4

Action motivated by anticipation of dishonor, i.e., institutionalized blame for failure of duty, and by guilt over concrete harm done to others. (Differentiates formal dishonor from informal disapproval. Differentiates guilt for bad consequences from disapproval.)

   Pro—If you have any sense of honor, you won't let your wife die because you're afraid to do the only thing that will save her. You'll always feel guilty that you caused her death if you don't do your duty to her.

   Con—You're desperate and you may not know you're doing wrong when you steal the drug. But you'll know you did wrong after you're punished and sent to jail. You'll always feel guilt for your dishonesty and lawbreaking.

Stage 5

Concern about maintaining respect of equals and of the community (assuming their respect is based on reason rather than emotions). Concern about own self-respect, i.e., to avoid judging self as irrational, inconsistent, nonpurposive. (Discriminates between institutionalized blame and community disrespect or self-disrespect.)

   Pro—You'd lose other people's respect, not gain it, if you don't steal. If you let your wife die, it would be out of fear, not out of reasoning it out. So you'd just lose self-respect and probably the respect of others too.

   Con—You would lose your standing and respect in the community and violate the law. You'd lose respect for yourself if you're carried away by emotion and forget the long-range point of view.

Stage 6

Concern about self-condemnation for violating one's own principles. (Differentiates between self-respect for general achieving rationality and self-respect for maintaining moral principles.)

   Pro—If you don't steal the drug and let your wife die, you'd always condemn yourself for it afterward. You wouldn't be blamed and you would have lived up to the outside rule of the law but you wouldn't have lived up to your own standards of conscience.

   Con—If you stole the drug, you wouldn't be blamed by other people but you'd condemn yourself because you wouldn't have lived up to your own conscience and standards of honesty.

Sources: Kohlberg, 1969, p. 379; Rest, 1969.

Both Kohlberg's theory of moral development and Piaget's have been criticized for a number of reasons. The most common objection is that measures of moral reasoning are often only weakly related to actual moral behavior, or they are not related at all (Krebs, 1967; Rest, 1983). Thus, a boy may talk about doing his duty and following established rules, but when it comes to a real-life situation, he may ignore these rules. This weak relationship between thought and action concerning moral issues has led many to wonder how meaningful stages of moral reasoning are. Others have objected to the idea that the *form* of moral reasoning can be separated from the *content* of moral judgments (see Rest, 1983). For instance, what matters in Kohlberg's model is not the nature of the solution a person offers to a moral dilemma; Kohlberg does not consider any one choice better than another. Instead, the basis on which the person reasons in making a decision is deemed important. Critics question whether this approach is always valid—whether content can always be ignored in assessing a person's level of moral thinking.

Stage theories of moral reasoning have sometimes also been criticized for the methods used to gather the data on which these theories are based. For instance, Kohlberg's method of evaluating a person's solution to a moral dilemma has been challenged on a number of grounds, including reliability (Kurtines and Grief, 1974). Will a child evaluated one day by a particular researcher be assessed at the same moral level a few days later when scored by someone else? This problem has been exacerbated by frequent revisions in Kohlberg's scoring system as well as in the theoretical framework used to support it (Rest, 1983). In 1986 Kohlberg and his students developed a new scoring system, but it has not yet been released for general use. Some think that a different approach to assessment may be preferable. For instance, James Rest (1983) has developed an objectively scored test of moral reasoning that overcomes many of the limitations inherent in Kohlberg's measure.

One of the most interesting challenges to Kohlberg's approach is that it is biased. For example, Carol Gilligan (1982) has charged that Kohlberg's assessment of moral reasoning is biased against women. Women, Gilligan argues, are more likely to respond to moral dilemmas based on concepts such as caring, personal relationships, and interpersonal obligations—concepts that are apt to be scored at the stage 3 level. Men, in contrast, are more likely to appeal to abstract concepts, such as justice and equity—concepts that are apt to be scored at stage 5 or even 6. These general patterns are believed to result from the different ways that males and females are socialized in our culture. If this is true, is it fair to consider a woman to be at a lower level of moral reasoning simply because she has been taught since childhood to value compassion toward others and social obligations? Recent research with highly educated people found that women averaged higher stage scores than men (Funk, 1986). This finding challenges the generalizibility of Gilligan's study but again emphasizes the role of socialization history. In general, critics charge that Kohlberg's approach fails to take into account a person's socialization history. How much this failure weakens the universality Kohlberg claims for his six stages is still hotly debated. At the very least, such criticisms introduce well-deserved cautions when evaluating the meaning of someone's approach to moral reasoning.

Chapter Review

1. A stepped-up production of sex hormones late in middle childhood brings about the beginning of adolescence, a time known as **puberty.** During puberty, youngsters undergo sexual maturation, which is accompanied by the development of **secondary sex characteristics** and a noticeable spurt in growth. There are substantial individual differences in the onset of puberty and the pace of its many changes. These differences are influenced by environmental factors such as nutrition and exercise, but they are also caused by the different biological clocks that people inherit. How the brain "knows" that it is time to start puberty is not yet understood. Some think that declining levels of a hormone from the pineal gland may serve as an important signal. Others think that critical signals may somehow be related to increases in a youngster's weight. These signals could prompt changes in metabolism and blood chemistry.

2. Although some psychologists are still skeptical, mounting evidence indicates that the brain undergoes substantial change during early adolescence. The evidence comes partly from studies of how thinking skills mature at puberty, partly from developmental studies of young animals, and partly from physiological research into how the human brain works. One change that may take place is a decrease in the number of connections among brain cells. Such a decrease could help explain why the brain functions of a young child are more flexible than those of an adult. During early adolescence pathways in the brain may then become more specialized. This increased specialization could help explain why teen-agers are more efficient than elementary school children at higher-level cognitive tasks.

3. Researchers generally agree on the broad outlines of the new cognitive abilities that emerge in adolescence. First, teen-agers are able to apply logical thinking skills not just to concrete objects, as elementary school children can, but also to ideas about what is *possible*. This ability opens up a whole new realm of thinking. Second, adolescents become able to use **hypothetico-deductive reasoning,** which involves thinking up hypothetical solutions to a problem and then formulating a logical and systematic plan for deducing which of the possible solutions is right. Third, adolescents become able to think about relationships among mentally constructed concepts—that is, about abstract concepts that are built up from more concrete ones. Fourth, adolescents acquire a willingness to accept lack of closure, or firm answers to questions. They are more willing than younger children to consider their first conclusions as merely tentative, subject to change as additional information is learned.

4. Many interpretations have been offered for what underlies the cognitive changes of adolescence. One is Piaget's theory of formal operations. **Formal operations** are new kinds of mental transformations that teen-agers are able to perform. They allow youngsters to reason more logically about abstract concepts and to think more systematically than ever before. Piaget built his theory of formal operations on extensive research into the cognitive capacities of adolescents. This research took the form of presenting subjects of different ages with scientific experiments to conduct. Some of these experiments, such as the law of floating bodies study and the balance scale study, demonstrated adolescents' ability to reason about proportions. Others, such as the bending rods study and the pendulum study, demonstrated the ability to isolate variables that are having an effect on results. And still others, such as the all-possible-combinations study, showed teen-agers' ability to combine a number of different factors in a systematic way. In his theory of formal operations Piaget proposed how the new cognitive abilities of adolescence are tied together—organized in a coherent and logical fashion in the youngster's mind.

5. Although psychologists generally agree that Piaget's experiments did a good job in sampling the range of thinking skills that emerge in adolescence, they are less satisfied with his theoretical model of formal operations. To give one specific criticism, many researchers have found that formal operational thinking is much less pervasive among older adolescents than Piaget thought. This finding may simply mean that people do not always use their highest level of cognitive competence. Still, some critics question whether it wouldn't be more useful to focus on everyday cognitive performance than on optimal thinking abilities used only intermittently. Another criticism of Piaget's theory stems from his suggestion that training in formal operations should not be very effective in fostering early onset of these skills. Later researchers have often found that older elementary school children and very young adolescents *do* benefit from such training efforts. The significance of these findings is still open to question. It may be that training simply helps youngsters to display competencies they have already acquired but as yet seldom show.

6. The new cognitive skills of adolescence have an impact on many other areas of life. For instance, they allow teen-agers to display a new kind of egocentrism. Because adolescents can now think extensively about other people's thoughts, they are able to be self-conscious that others might be viewing them negatively. This feeling often promotes the sense of having an **imaginary audience,** an unjustified concern about being the focus of everyone else's attention. Often, too, young teen-agers develop **per-sonal fables.** This term refers to a belief in their own uniqueness to the point where they think that no one else has ever had their special thoughts and feelings.

7. The cognitive skills of adolescence also give rise to an explicit concern with values. Youngsters are now able to consider systematically the values they hold as well as alternative values. Closely related is the ability to reason more maturely about moral issues. Piaget believed that during adolescence youngsters reach a stage of moral reasoning called **autonomous morality.** Now they see morality as less absolute, more relative to the situation, and they are also able to recognize the possibility of diverse opinions regarding moral standards. Another cognitive theory of how moral reasoning changes is that of Lawrence Kohlberg. The highest level of moral reasoning in Kohlberg's model occurs in his so-called period of principled morality. During this time youngsters transcend conventional notions of right and wrong and begin to focus more on abstract principles underlying moral judgments. Although you might think that youngsters who are able to perform formal operations would have reached Kohlberg's period of principled morality, in fact the development of moral reasoning seems to lag behind the cognitive skills needed for the task.

15

Social Development in Adolescence

I just have all these feelings and things inside. . . . The feelings are so strong, and my parents don't understand. They won't let me do anything. I'm afraid that by the time I'm old enough to do the things I need to do—by the time they'll let me—I won't have the feelings anymore.

The words of this 15-year-old girl, interviewed by one of the authors of this book 20 years ago, illustrate the timelessness of the central social and emotional issues of adolescence. Adolescence is a wonderful time of life, filled with new feelings, a higher level of self-awareness, and a sense of almost unlimited horizons to explore. But adolescence is also a very challenging period of development. The new feelings teen-agers experience are strong and imperative, demanding to be expressed. The emerging inner sense of self is not yet firmly established and at times may seem ephemeral. The statement of the teen-ager above reflects these difficult challenges. She worries that her strong feelings and sense of self will disappear before she has a chance to act on them. While her parents remain an important resource in her life, there is a sense that they are unable to understand her situation, that all her new thoughts and emotions cannot really be shared with them.

To a great extent, the young woman quoted above was in the process of reworking many of the issues she faced in earlier developmental periods. Issues such as developing trust, establishing autonomy, and fashioning an expanded sense of competence and self were all confronting her again. This time, however, she had to work through those issues not only with her parents but also with peers similarly caught up in the challenges of adolescence.

To become free and independent agents, to forge their personal identities, teen-agers must "de-identify" with parents, while still staying connected to them. They must at the same time share their deepest selves with same-age friends and come to grips with the knowledge that no one else can ever completely know them. These are among the tasks of adolescence we'll be exploring in this chapter.

THE SOCIAL WORLD OF ADOLESCENCE: AN OVERVIEW

How Stormy Is Adolescence?

We often hear the view that the challenges of adolescence make it a stressful, stormy period of life. Psychologists G. Stanley Hall, Anna Freud, and Peter Blos (1962) are among those who have claimed that inner turmoil and disruption are necessary to becoming a separate person. They argue that a difficult break with parents is essential in order to forge an identity that is autonomous and unique. But other psychologists believe that the struggle of adolescence has been greatly exaggerated (Adelson, 1979; Hill, in press). They point out that many teen-agers get along fine with their parents, and families that were functioning well before a child reached puberty tend to continue functioning well afterward (Block, Block, and Morrison, 1981). Who is right in this disagreement? As it turns out, neither one side nor the other is right. How stormy or harmonious adolescence is depends on which teen-agers you look at, when you look

In spite of differences in styles of dress and other behaviors, parents and teen-agers can often enjoy a pleasant relationship. (© *Carolyn A. McKeone/FPG International.*)

at them, what aspects of their behavior you consider, and what perspective you take.

For instance, many of the studies that support the storm and stress view of adolescence have investigated younger teens, 13 to 16 years old, while studies that support the more harmonious view of parent-child relations have generally looked at the later teen-age years. It appears that early adolescence is a unique subphase of development during which youngsters experience more turmoil, parents more stress and dissatisfactions, and families more conflict than they have before or will in subsequent years (Hamburg, 1974). Later in this chapter we will discuss specific problems tied to the onset of puberty, problems that generally subside within two or three years (Hill et al., 1985; Steinberg, 1981).

Whether adolescence seems full of conflict or relatively harmonious also depends on what aspects of it you study. As far as parent-child relations are concerned, teens and their parents tend to argue most about everyday activities such as homework or household chores. Teen-agers and their parents are also frequently at odds about mannerisms, hair styles, and clothing. In contrast, there is seldom much of a clash within the family regarding basic values and beliefs. Most adolescents have similar basic values and beliefs to those of their parents (Douvan and Adelson, 1966; Montemayer and Hanson, 1985; Rutter et al., 1976). In addition, very few teen-agers (only 3 percent of females and 5 to 9 percent of males) express outright rejection of their parents. In fact, only about one-third express any criticism of their parents at all in interviews (Rutter et al., 1976). Thus, most teens continue to be influenced by their parents, to get along with them, and to respect the need for the limits they impose. This does not mean, however, that adolescence is largely a stress-free time of life. Nearly half of the subjects interviewed in one study reported feelings of unhappiness (Rutter et al., 1976). But this unhappiness reflects largely *inner* turmoil, not so much overt conflict with others.

There are, of course, substantial individual differences in how conflict-ridden adolescence is. Among boys, for example, three patterns of development seem to occur (Offer and Offer, 1975). About one-quarter experience **tumultuous growth,** filled with conflict and crisis; about one-third experience **surgent growth,** marked by reasonable adjustment interspersed with negative periods (anger, defiance, immaturity); and about one-quarter undergo **continuous growth,** characterized by self-assurance, a sense of purpose, and mutual respect between child and parents. The rest cannot be readily classified. A range of individual variations also occurs in adolescent girls. How stormy or peaceful the teen-age years are depends partly on the person involved.

One individual difference that can influence the quality of adjustment during adolescence is the timing of a youngster's puberty. For instance, early maturing girls often have an unusually prolonged period of conflict with their parents (Hill et al., 1985). Compared with girls who reach puberty late, early maturing girls tend to be more dissatisfied with themselves and their bodies, more negatively evaluated by peers, and more likely to experience depression and negative consequences of divorce (Blyth, Bulcroft, and Simmons, 1981; Hetherington, in press; Petersen, 1986; Petersen and Taylor, 1980; Tobin-Richards, Boxer, and Petersen, 1983). In contrast, it is *late* maturing boys who are apt to experience more problems than early maturing ones, both with parents and peers (Sprin-thall and Collins, 1984; Tobin-Richards, Boxer, and Petersen, 1983). Late maturing boys are often seen by others as bossy, tense, and restless, and when they reach early adulthood they are frequently viewed as impulsive and nonconforming (Jones, 1957; Jones and Bayley, 1950). This is not to say that *early* maturing boys are without special problems. While often viewed as competent, poised, and successful, they may also seem inflex-ible and overcontrolled (Peskin, 1967). Special challenges, then, appear to accompany early and late physical maturation, although these patterns may also have their advantages.

To summarize the findings we have presented, storm and stress may occur during adolescence, but that is far from the only theme of this period. Early adolescence is the time of most conflict with parents, but even then the conflict tends to center on less important matters of behav-ior and style, not fundamental values and beliefs. The typical conflicts of adolescence are best thought of as arising out of normal self-assertion, not rebellion and defiance. Parents for a time may see their child as "impos-sible" or "lost." But this period soon gives way to a realignment, in which the youngster carves out a new place within the family, a new stance toward the world, and a new sense of self-awareness (Steinberg, 1985).

A Cross-Cultural Perspective

The reason why many adolescents in Western nations experience some difficult periods is partly explained by the culture they live in. Complex, industrialized democracies demand skilled and knowledgeable adults. Young people must therefore learn a great deal before they are given the responsibilities and privileges of adulthood, and this makes for a pro-tracted period of adolescence and dependency on parents. Even young adults who attend college and graduate school will probably be well into their twenties before obtaining their first "real" job. No wonder Kurt Lewin (1951) has labeled adolescents "marginal persons": On the one hand, they have matured physically and are clearly no longer children; on the other hand, they have much more to learn and are not yet ready to be launched into the world of adults. This "no man's land" can give rise to a sense of ambiguity, impatience, and frustration.

Not surprisingly, societies that place different demands on their mem-bers often treat adolescents differently than we do. In some, the transition to adult roles begins much earlier. From a very young age, children in these cultures are given much responsibility, such as taking care of younger siblings, making tools and utensils, or helping their parents in the fields (Whiting and Whiting, 1975). One such society is Samoa in the south Pacific. When anthropologist Margaret Mead studied its people in the 1920s, she found that adolescence was not a stressful period, but rather one of gradually maturing interests and activities (Mead, 1925/ 1939). Samoans not only begin the transition to adulthood early, they also let it proceed gradually. In other societies, in contrast, the change comes much more suddenly. Among the Gusii of Kenya, for example, the transition to adulthood is very abrupt, with children being given greatly expanded duties in a short period of time (Levine and Levine, 1966). Such societies often have special ceremonies to mark the entry into new

In some cultures the transition from childhood to adulthood is clearly marked. *(Martin Etter/AnthroPhoto.)*

adult roles. These ceremonies, called **puberty rites** or **rites of passage,** may include genital operations or other arduous physical challenges. Children anticipate these rites for years in advance; there is no question in their minds when they will be considered adults.

Compared with the nonindustrialized cultures of the world, Western cultures present a mixed picture. Not only do we withhold adult responsibilities and authority from young people for a protracted period of time, we also expect them to delay full entry into adult sexual roles. Yet we are fairly abrupt in changing our expectations when young people finally reach a certain stage. Many parents have in mind a certain time at which they expect their children to be "on their own," earning a living and behaving as adults, but our society has no universally agreed-upon markers to tell us when this time has come. For some it is graduation from high school, for others graduation from college, for still others landing a first job. This ambiguity, a product of our culture and the different demands placed on people who pursue different careers, imposes special challenges on both adolescents and their parents.

The Tasks of Adolescence

Regardless of how the transition to adulthood is carried out, important tasks face every adolescent. For one thing, the adolescent must achieve a sense of self-unity, accompanied by a feeling that the self has continuity over time. He or she must also achieve some sense of uniqueness, of being in some ways different from other people. Erik Erikson (1981) calls all these developments regarding the self the process of establishing a personal **identity.** A personal identity not only must be perceived by the individual but also must be recognized and confirmed by others.

These major achievements are made possible by cognitive advances—in particular, by the adolescent's new capacities to reflect on the self and to consider a range of possible alternatives. Thus, the adolescent can examine the self at present, relate that self to past behavior, and project the self into the future with the many different roles it offers. Yet even with essential cognitive skills, the task is difficult. Achieving a sense of unity and consistency when confronted with a rapidly changing body and powerful new sexual drives is no easy matter; nor is the job of obtaining confirmation of the emerging self from parents, while at the same time pulling away from them. This process is particularly hard because youngsters are now becoming aware that parents have weaknesses and inconsistencies. De-identification with parents in light of this new awareness is sometimes marked by tension, anger, and impatience.

It is now possible to summarize what may be considered four critical tasks of adolescence:

1. Adolescents must evolve an identity, a new understanding of the self as cohesive, integrated, continuous, and unique.
2. Adolescents must achieve a new level of closeness and trust with peers. Often this is accomplished first with peers of the same gender before moving on to intimate cross-gender relationships.
3. Adolescents must acquire a new status in the family. Relationships with parents become more equal as the child grows more independent and responsible. Family ties are not severed; connections with parents merely take a different form.
4. Adolescents must move toward a more autonomous stance with respect to the larger world. This includes anticipating future roles, making career choices, and committing themselves to certain values. These changes cannot just involve following parental wishes, plans, and values in an unthinking way. Instead, the process must entail decisions that teen-agers themselves make and then actively translate into practice.

These four tasks represent the major sections in the remainder of this chapter.

DEVELOPMENT OF THE SELF

Progress Toward Identity

During adolescence, youngsters attain a qualitatively new level of self-development. First, the self becomes more cohesive, more unified and integrated than ever before. Second, teen-agers are able to tie together their past behaviors and their anticipated future roles in ways that younger children simply cannot. Third, adolescents acquire the important capacity for self-reflection. They are not simply aware that the self exists, they are also able to examine the content of the self and to ponder what others think of them as people. "While children are aware of themselves," writes David Elkind, "they are not able to put themselves in other people's shoes and to look at themselves from that perspective. Adolescents can do this and engage in such self-watching to a considerable extent. Indeed, the characteristic self-consciousness of adolescents results from the very fact that young people are now very concerned with how others react to them. This is a concern that is largely absent in childhood" (Elkind, 1971, p. 111).

THE CONCEPT OF A PERSONAL IDENTITY

As we said earlier, Erik Erikson (1968) introduced the term identity to describe the new way of thinking about the self that develops in adolescence. The concept of identity includes the quest for personal discovery, the resulting sense of "who I am," and the growing understanding of the "meaning" of one's existence. Identity also involves integrating into a coherent whole one's past experiences, one's ongoing personal changes, and society's demands and expectations for one's future (Sprinthall and Collins, 1984). James Marcia (1980) writes that identity refers to a structure of abilities, beliefs, and past experiences regarding the self. "The better developed this structure is, the more aware individuals appear to be of their own . . . strengths and weaknesses. . . . The less developed this structure is, the more confused individuals seem to be about their own distinctiveness from others and the more they have to rely on external sources to evaluate themselves" (p. 159).

Discovering the answer to the question "Who am I?" is a major issue for adolescents. *(Gabe Palmer/The Stock Market.)*

In Erikson's theory the difficulty that teen-agers encounter when trying to establish their personal identities is referred to as an **identity crisis.** Remember that as they take on this challenging task, adolescents are caught in the middle of two changing systems (Sprinthall and Collins, 1984). One is their own biological system, with its hormone changes and resulting transformations in the body. This system is linked to new sexual urges, as well as to new ways of thinking and reasoning. The other is the social system in which the adolescent lives. Parents and other adults are rapidly making new demands on the youngster, but not always clearly and consistently. Often the teen-ager is expected to behave maturely, almost like an adult; yet many restrictions are still being imposed, as if the youngster were still considered a child. No wonder some adolescents have a difficult time coping. Somehow they are expected to emerge in the end with a stable, well-integrated, and consistent view of who they are.

INDIVIDUAL DIFFERENCES IN IDENTITY FORMATION

Researchers are only now beginning to understand the different routes that teen-agers take in establishing a personal identity. Some are overwhelmed by the task; others retreat from it. Some get there slowly by fits and starts, while for others it is relatively smooth sailing. On the basis of extensive interviews with adolescents, James Marcia (1980) has grouped these different patterns into four categories: foreclosure, identity diffusion, moratorium, and identity achievement. They are summarized in Table 15.1.

Foreclosure involves coping with the task of identity formation by retreating from the challenge of exploring different roles and possibilities. Teen-agers who take this route do not struggle to reconcile incompatible aspects of the self or to evolve their own goals and purposes. Instead, they simply accept the roles that others, most often their parents, pre-

TABLE 15.1   Marcia's Four Patterns of Identity Development

Pattern	Characteristics
Foreclosure	Individuals in a state of foreclosure have never experienced an identity crisis. Rather, they have prematurely established an identity on the basis of their parents' choices rather than on their own. They have made occupational and ideological commitments, but these commitments reflect more an assessment of what one's parents or authority figures could do rather than an autonomous process of self-assessment. This is a kind of "pseudo-identity" that generally is too fixed and rigid to serve as a foundation for meeting life's future crises.
Identity diffusion	Individuals experiencing identity diffusion have found neither an occupational direction nor an ideological commitment of any kind, and they have made little progress toward these ends. They may have experienced an identity crisis, but if so they were unable to resolve it.
Moratorium	This category is reserved for those who have begun to experiment with occupational and ideological choices, but who have not yet made definitive commitments to either. These individuals are directly in the midst of an identity crisis and are currently examining alternate life choices.
Identity achievement	This signifies a state of identity consolidation in which the individual has made his or her own conscious, clear-cut decisions concerning occupation and ideology. The individual is convinced that these decisions were autonomously and freely made, and that they reflect the individual's true nature and deep inner commitments.

Source: Marcia, 1980. Reported in Damon, 1983, pp. 331-332.

scribe for them. These adolescents cannot be said to have a genuine personal identity. Their "identity" is acquired in an unquestioning manner from the dictates of others. As Erikson argues in his biographies of Gandhi (1962) and Martin Luther (1970), true identity cannot be achieved without active searching and struggle.

Identity diffusion is a second response to the challenge of identity formation. Teen-agers who take this route are so overwhelmed by the possibilities of life that they are unable to find direction. They may try out social roles but then abandon them. They have few commitments and no long-range goals. They live for the moment, for immediate pleasures. They seem to have no unified core. Instead they have what David Elkind calls a "patchwork self."

Moratorium is a third pattern seen in adolescents. Teen-agers who follow this path begin to explore alternatives but need "breathing space." They are not yet ready to settle on an identity. Periods of consolidating a sense of self may be followed by periods of retreat, but the goal of some ultimate commitment is always maintained. In our complex society, with its multiplicity of choices, moratorium is one healthy route to identity formation.

Identity achievement is a fourth path that adolescents may take. By exploring alternatives and making conscious choices, young people who follow this route arrive at their own ideology and sense of purpose. They are confident about the consistency and continuity of the self, and equally confident that others see these same qualities in them. Because these youngsters independently make their own choices, they often are firmly committed to who they are and what they plan to do.

In studying young people who fall into each of these four categories, researchers have found some interesting patterns. For instance, those who are identity achievers tend to have the highest levels of self-esteem. The next highest are those in the moratorium group, followed by those who adopt foreclosure, and last those who are floundering in identity diffusion (Bunt, 1968; Damon, 1983). As you might expect from their reliance on parents to make their life decisions for them, those who adopt foreclosure tend to be very obedient to authority (Marcia and Friedman, 1970; Waterman and Waterman, 1971). Are adolescents who adopt foreclosure or identity diffusion forever locked into these two patterns? Fortunately, no. During the college years (ages 18 to 22), young people often abandon foreclosure or identity diffusion and become identity achievers (Waterman, 1982).

You may be wondering what promotes the different responses that adolescents adopt when confronted with the challenge of forming an identity. Why do some young people take this challenge in stride, while others find it more difficult? According to Erikson, two critical sets of ingredients are needed to consolidate an "optimal" sense of personal identity. First, adolescents must carry forward from middle childhood an inner confidence about their competence and ability to master new tasks, along with a sense of basic trust, autonomy, and initiative from earlier developmental periods. Little research has been done to determine if Erikson is right in stressing the importance of these factors. All we have at present are findings which show that a college student's approach to identity formation is often related to feelings of competence, trust, and autonomy, among other things (Bourne, 1978; Damon, 1983). These studies, however, are of older adolescents and young adults. To verify this aspect of Erikson's theory, we need longitudinal studies, beginning in childhood, that explore how the resolution of issues in each developmental period is related to later identity achievement. This kind of study is only now being done (e.g., Block, 1987).

The second set of ingredients that Erikson sees as critical to optimal identity formation has to do with the adolescent's environment. Teenagers must have ample opportunity to experiment with new roles, both in fantasy and practice, and they must get support in this effort from parents and other adults. We will explore this second set of factors when we discuss family influences later in this chapter.

Changes in Self-Concept Across the Teen-Age Years

Forming a personal identity—the sense of an integrated, coherent, goal-directed self—is a major task of adolescence. As you have just seen, this task is tackled differently by different teen-agers, and some are more successful at it than others. But regardless of individual differences in how identities are formed, all adolescents experience substantial changes in their self-concepts across the teen-age years. Just as younger and older teen-agers differ in how they think and reason, so do they differ in how they view themselves. In this section we will examine these developmental changes in self-concept.

THE DECLINING FRAGILITY OF THE SELF

As a youngster's sense of self emerges, at first it is very fragile. Like scientists who have just formulated a new theory, teen-agers are unsure about the new self's validity (Okun and Sasfy, 1977). Others can easily challenge a young adolescent's view of the self. The feeling that the self is fragile is linked to a concern that the self is also very transparent, readily scrutinized by others. This gives rise to David Elkind's concept of an imaginary audience, the belief that others are watching you and evaluating your performance (see Chapter 14). No wonder young adolescents appear to their parents to be much less open than they were as children. Teen-agers feel they must be careful not to disclose too much, or else their new and fragile sense of self might somehow be lost. This attitude helps account for the strict conformity of young teen-agers in dress and hair style, which hides yet expresses their uniqueness. The fragile sense of self characteristic of young adolescents also provides insight into their frequent expressions of invulnerability. The claim that no harm can befall me is a good example of a *personal fable* (Elkind, 1967), a distorted belief that I am fundamentally different from other people. Psychoanalysts, of course, would see this as a defense against feelings of remarkable uncertainty and vulnerability. The fragility of the self also underlies the adolescent's tendency to fantasize many different roles. Just as play provided a safe haven for the preschooler to work through conflicts, so fantasies allow the adolescent to experiment with possible new dimensions of the self before actually committing to them.

In time the uncertain, fragile sense of self that emerges in early adolescence becomes more firmly established. Through interactions with others, through performance at school and achievements in the larger world, teen-agers' beliefs about the self are increasingly confirmed (Okun and Sasty, 1977). They become more sure of themselves and less self-conscious. Gradually they are able to formulate more realistic self-appraisals, which include evaluations of both strengths and weaknesses. This may be why ratings of self-worth actually drop by the end of high school (Dusek and Flaherty, 1981). Twelfth graders are able realistically to size up both their good and bad features, integrating them into a coherent and stable sense of self.

OTHER CHANGES IN SELF-CONCEPT

Studies in which adolescents are encouraged to talk about themselves or write self-descriptions reveal other ways in which self-concepts change during adolescence (Damon, 1983; McCandless and Evans, 1973). First, self-concepts become more *differentiated*. Rather than seeing themselves as always having certain characteristics, teen-agers evolve a more complex picture that takes situational factors into account. For instance, an adolescent might say, "I generally follow the rules, *except* when my dad is being unfair to me." Second, the self-concepts of teens become more *individuated*, more distinct from others'. Whereas younger children describe themselves in terms of similarities with peers, adolescents describe themselves more in terms of their special characteristics. Third, self-conceptions become more *psychological*, less physical in nature. We saw the beginnings of this change in middle childhood, but it is much more marked in adolescence. Fourth, teen-agers increasingly view themselves as *self-reflective* and able to make free choices about values and behaviors. Fifth, adolescents increasingly think of the self as a *coherent system* made up of diverse but integrated parts. The young person now strives to reconcile disparate aspects of the self. The following comparison between the self-description of a 9-year-old boy and that of a 17-year-old girl clearly illustrates many of these important changes (Montemayor and Eisen, 1977, pp. 317–318):

Commitment to ideology is often a hallmark of adolescence. *(Barbara Gundle/Archive Pictures Inc.)*

9-year-old: My name is Bruce C. I have brown eyes. I have brown hair. I have brown eyebrows. I'm nine years old. I love! sports. I have seven people in my family. I have great! eye site. I have lots! of friends. I live on 1923 Pinecrest Drive. I'm going on ten in September. I'm a boy. I have an uncle that is almost seven feet tall. My school is Pinecrest. My teacher is Mrs. V. I play hockey! I'm almost the smartest boy in the class. I love food! I love fresh air. I love school.

17-year-old: I am a human being. I am a girl. I am an individual. I don't know who I am. I am Pisces. I am a moody person. I am an indecisive person. I am an ambitious person. I am a big curious person. I am not an individual. I am an American (God help me). I am a Democrat. I am a liberal person. I am a radical. I am conservative. I am a pseudoliberal. I am an atheist. I am not a classifiable person (i.e., I don't want to be).

Notice how physical and concrete the traits are that the 9-year-old chooses to mention. He seems to be characterized by what has been called "unreflective self acceptance" (Santrock, 1984). In contrast, the 17-year-old takes a much more psychological view of the self. She focuses on her feelings, her values and beliefs, and on her characteristic behaviors when interacting with others. She is also very introspective, in the sense that she seems to be searching for a deeper understanding of her own identity. Whereas the boy simply lists unquestioned "truths" about the self, the girl sees aspects of the self as problematic self-hypotheses (Am I liberal? Conservative? Pseudoliberal? Am I classifiable at all?). Notice, too, how this young woman is reaching toward a coherent and integrated view of the self. She seems to be trying to reconcile disparate parts of the self into a meaningful whole. The need to do this does not seem even to have occurred to the 9-year-old.

EVIDENCE FOR TWO ADOLESCENT SUBPHASES

Much of the research on changing self-concepts during the teen-age years supports the view that there are two subphases of adolescent social development. Young adolescents (ages 13 to 15) have an understanding of the self that is well advanced over that of elementary-school children. However, by later adolescence (ages 17 to 18) there are further qualitative advances in how the self is viewed.

Older adolescents have a more integrated sense of self than younger adolescents, and a much greater understanding of the uniqueness and separateness of people. *(Louis Fernandez © 1983/ Black Star.)*

Evidence that older adolescents have a more complex, sophisticated self-understanding than younger adolescents do comes partly from the research of Robert Selman (1980) that we mentioned in Chapter 13. You may remember that Selman told subjects of different ages a story about a boy named Mike who had lost his dog, Pepper. Two of Mike's friends were contemplating buying him a new dog for his birthday and were trying to decide if this was a good idea. Selman probed each subject's conception of the self by asking questions about what he or she believed the thoughts and feelings of someone in Mike's position would be. He found that young adolescents possess an understanding that the self can sometimes manipulate inner experiences. "I can fool myself into thinking I don't want another puppy," one young teen-ager explained. However, it was only in older adolescence that subjects started to grasp the notion of conscious and unconscious *levels* of experience. Here is how one such youngster described these levels in Mike:

> He might feel at some level that it would be unloyal to Pepper to just go out and replace the dog. He may feel guilty about it. He doesn't want to face these feelings, so he says no dog. (Interviewer: Is he aware of this?) Probably not. (p. 106)

Additional support for a more complex, sophisticated self-understanding in later adolescence comes from the research of John Broughton (1978), who asked subjects of different ages questions about the self, the mind, and the body. Broughton found that young adolescents make a distinction between mental and physical reality. They see the mind as a decision-making, governing entity separate from the self's physical activities. One of Broughton's young teen-age subjects explained the mind's role: "With our minds we can make our own judgments and do what we think is right." Young adolescents also know that the self is aware of the mind's processes in a special way: "I know what I feel about things," one young teen-ager put it, "but I don't know someone else." These are clear advances over the elementary-school child's grasp of the mind and the self. However, it is not until later adolescence that youngsters come to know the full complexity of the mental system we call the self. For instance, they understand the difference between a "real" and a "phony" self and they can explain how these two are related.

Another aspect of self-understanding that differentiates late from early adolescence is an increased knowledge of how different aspects of the self are tied together into an integrated whole. Young teen-agers make a start in this direction in their ability to link together their past and future selves when giving self-descriptions (Secord and Peevers, 1974). But it is only in later adolescence that youngsters are able to unify contradictory aspects of the self (Bernstein, 1980). For instance, a 15-year-old might say that he is talkative with his friends, but quiet with his family, and have no reason for this. In contrast, an older teen-ager might offer an explanation based on different situational factors: "I am really talkative with my friends because they are treating me like a person. . . . My family doesn't listen to what I say, so I just don't like talking to hear myself speak" (Damon, 1983, p. 318).

As self-understanding becomes more complex from early to late adolescence, so the teen-ager's self-consciousness steadily tends to wane. In one study, for instance, researchers demonstrated a declining belief that others are scrutinizing the self by asking subjects of different ages to complete the Imaginary Audience Scale shown in Table 15.2. Self-conscious answers peaked at age 12 and then dropped off (Simmons, Rosenberg, and Rosenberg, 1973). In a later study other researchers had much the same results. The answers given by eighth graders on the Imaginary Audience Scale were more self-conscious than those given by fourth, sixth, and twelfth graders (Elkind and Bowen, 1979). These findings are similar to those in which youngsters are tested for self-consciousness about their bodies. Concerns about body image are high among eighth graders compared with fourth graders, but decline by the time adolescents reach grade 12 (McCartney and Weiss, 1985).

PEER RELATIONS IN ADOLESCENCE

Peer relations continue to gain in importance during the adolescent years. For one thing, they become more important in the sense that they grow deeper, as teen-agers acquire the potential for mutual exploration and discovery. This increased depth of peer relations is made possible by cognitive advances we talked about in Chapter 14. At the same time, peer relations during adolescence become increasingly important in the sense that they have new implications for other aspects of development. For instance, involvement with peers is critical to progress in self-understanding and identity achievement. You discover your inner feelings, your deeper level of consciousness, largely through close relationships. Peer-group membership is also a part of identity, for the group of friends to which you belong helps define who you are. And peer groups offer chances for trying out various roles, a vital part of identity formation. Finally, involvement with peers of the same gender helps to pave the way for close heterosexual relationships. Let's take a look at the many ways that peer relations change during the adolescent years.

Advances in Understanding Others

Understanding the self and understanding others go hand-in-hand, so it is not surprising that an adolescent's advances in self-awareness are accompanied by a growing sense of what others are like. Teen-agers know that they have inner motives, so they deduce that others do too. They know that they have coherent selves, so others must also. These new understandings can be seen in adolescents' efforts to explain the behavior of others. Even younger teens infer that others must have certain traits that prompt them to act as they do: "He's a jock. She's sensitive" (Lively and Bromly, 1973). By age 16 they try to reconcile inconsistent behavior in others by pointing to interrelated motives: "He's dying to be on the basketball team, but he's also worried about his grades" (Gollin, 1958).

TABLE 15.2   The Imaginary Audience Scale (IAS)

Instructions: Please read the following stories carefully and assume that the events actually happened to you. Place a check next to the answer that best describes what you would do or feel in the real situation.

---

1. You have looked forward to the most exciting dress-up party of the year. You arrive after an hour's drive from home. Just as the party is beginning, you notice a grease spot on your trousers or skirt. (There is no way to borrow clothes from anyone.) Would you stay or go home?
   _____ Go home.
   _____ Stay, even though I'd feel uncomfortable.
   _____ Stay, because the grease spot wouldn't bother me.

2. Let's say some adult visitors came to your school and you were asked to tell them a little bit about yourself.
   _____ I would like that.
   _____ I would not like that.
   _____ I wouldn't care.

3. It is Friday afternoon and you have just had your hair cut in preparation for the wedding of a relative that weekend. The barber or hairdresser did a terrible job and your hair looks awful. To make it worse, that night is the most important basketball game of the season and you really want to see it, but there is no way you can keep your head covered without people asking questions. Would you stay home or go to the game anyway?
   _____ Go to the game and not worry about my hair.
   _____ Go to the game and sit where people won't notice me very much.
   _____ Stay home.

4. If you went to a party where you did not know most of the kids, would you wonder what they were thinking about you?
   _____ I wouldn't think about it.
   _____ I would wonder about that a lot.
   _____ I would wonder about that a little.

5. You are sitting in class and have discovered that your jeans have a small but noticeable split along the side seam. Your teacher has offered extra credit toward his/her course grade to anyone who can write the correct answer to a question on the blackboard. Would you get up in front of the class and go to the blackboard, or would you remain seated?
   _____ Go to the blackboard as though nothing had happened.
   _____ Go to the blackboard and try to hide the split.
   _____ Remain seated.

6. When someone watches me work . . .
   _____ I get very nervous.
   _____ I don't mind at all.
   _____ I get a little nervous.

By this age they also give more psychological reasons for others' behavior, just as they do for their own (Selman, 1980).

Robert Selman's research that we mentioned earlier shows how understandings of others are generally at the same level as self-understandings. Recall that Selman's studies involved asking youngsters of different ages questions about the feelings of people in stories, such as the story of Mike's losing his dog and his friend Tom's wanting to buy him another. Adolescents in their mid-teens consider the feelings of both Mike and Tom in this situation, and they know that each boy will make inferences about the *intentions* of the other. As one 15-year-old explained it: "Mike will understand what Tom was trying to do, and even if he doesn't like the dog, he'll appreciate that Tom thought he would" (Selman, 1980, p. 106). Here we see a grasp of other people's thoughts and feelings that

TABLE 15.2—Continued

7. Your class is supposed to have their picture taken, but you fell the day before and scraped your face. You would like to be in the picture but your cheek is red and swollen. Would you have your picture taken anyway or stay out of the picture?
_____ Get your picture taken even though you'd be embarrassed.
_____ Stay out of the picture.
_____ Get your picture taken and not worry about it.

8. One young person said, "When I'm with people I get nervous because I worry about how much they like me."
_____ I feel like this often.
_____ I never feel like this.
_____ I feel like this sometimes.

9. You have been looking forward to your friend's party for weeks, but just before you leave for the party your mother tells you that she accidentally washed all your good clothes with a red shirt. Now all your jeans are pink in spots. The only thing left to wear are your jeans that are too big and too baggy. Would you go to the party or would you stay home?
_____ Go to the party, but buy a new pair of jeans to wear.
_____ Stay home.
_____ Go to the party in either the pink or baggy jeans.

10. Suppose you went to a party that you thought was a costume party but when you got there you were the only person wearing a costume. You'd like to stay and have fun with your friends but your costume is very noticeable. Would you stay or go home?
_____ Go home.
_____ Stay and have fun joking about your costume.
_____ Stay, but try to borrow some clothes to wear.

11. Let's say you wrote a story for an assignment your teacher gave you, and she asked you to read it aloud to the rest of the class.
_____ I would not like that at all.
_____ I would like that but I would be nervous.
_____ I would like that.

12. If you were asked to get up in front of the class and talk a little bit about your hobby . . .
_____ I wouldn't be nervous at all.
_____ I would be a little nervous.
_____ I would be very nervous.

Source: Elkind and Bowen, 1979, pp. 40-41.

closely matches the youngster's depth of understanding about the self. Table 15.3 summarizes Selman's ideas about the close coordination between these two areas of social understanding.

Changes in the Nature of Friendship

Developmental changes in understanding the self and others underlie changes in the nature of friendship during adolescence. Compared with younger children, teen-agers have a much greater capacity for true *mutual understanding* (Youniss, 1980). Elementary-school children grasp the importance of give and take between friends, but they do not fully understand one another *as persons*. Adolescents, in contrast, are increasingly aware of their own unique feelings, and this goes hand in hand with a recognition that others have unique feelings too (Damon, 1983). Partly because of this growing capacity for true mutual understanding, teen-age

TABLE 15.3   Stages in Understanding Self and Others

Level	Concept of Persons	Concept of Relations
0: Egocentric perspective taking (under 6 years)	Undifferentiated: confuses internal (feelings, intentions) with external (appearance, actions) characteristics of others	Egocentric: fails to recognize that self and others have different feelings and thoughts as well as external physical characteristics
1: Subjective perspective taking (ages 5–9)	Differentiated: distinguishes feelings and intentions from actions and appearances	Subjective: recognizes that others may feel and think differently than self—that everyone is subjective but has limited conceptions of how these different persons may affect each other (e.g., gifts make people happy, regardless of how appropriate they are)
2: Self-reflective or reciprocal perspective taking (ages 7–12)	Second-person: can reflect on own thoughts and realizes that others can do so as well (cf. recursive thought); realizes appearances may be deceptive about true feelings	Reciprocal: puts self in others' shoes *and* realizes others may do same; thus thoughts and feelings, not merely actions, become basis for interactions; however, the two subjective perspectives are not assumed to be influencing each other
3: Mutual perspective taking (ages 10–15)	Third-person: knows that self and others act *and* reflect on effects of their action on themselves; recognizes own immediate subjective perspective and also realizes that it fits into own more general attitudes and values	Mutual: can imagine another person's perspective on oneself and one's actions, coordinates other's inferred view with own view (i.e., sees self as others see one); thus comes to view relationships as ongoing mutual sharing of social satisfaction or understanding
4: In-depth and societal-symbolic perspective taking (ages 12–adult)	In-depth: recognizes that persons are unique, complex combinations of their own histories; furthermore, realizes that persons may not *always* understand their own motivations (i.e., that there may be unconscious psychological processes)	Societal-symbolic: individuals may form perspectives on each other at different levels, from shared superficial information or interests to common values or appreciation of very abstract moral, legal, or social notions

Source: Selman, 1980. Reported in Sprinthall and Collins, 1984.

friends want to share their inner experiences and life histories. This desire for *self-disclosure* accounts for the many hours they spend talking with each other, either on the phone or face to face. As one teen-ager described this aspect of friendship:

> A friend is a person you can talk to, and know your feelings. And he'll talk to you. . . . Someone you can tell your problems and she'll tell you her problems. . . . You can tell a friend everything. (Youniss, 1980, p. 181)

When important inner feelings are shared in the process of mutual understanding, the relationship between the friends cannot be taken lightly. This is clear in the distress we portrayed in Meryl when Amy no longer confides in her.

Closely related to the growth of mutual understanding is the increased capacity and desire for *intimacy* among teen-age friends (Youniss, 1980). Intimacy refers to the emotional aspects of a friendship. Understanding that friends share experiences and extend themselves for each other, teen-agers have a deeper sense of commitment to their relationships. This increased commitment has been described as a new *loyalty* and *fidelity* among friends (Berndt, 1981; Bigelow, 1977; Damon, 1983; Douvan and Adelson, 1966; Sprinthall and Collins, 1984). One teen-ager explained commitment this way:

> I think [a friend is] somebody that is loyal. Somebody that would stay on your side no matter what anybody—well, if somebody started a rumor and everyone believed it, somebody that wouldn't believe it. Or somebody that, if they knew you did it, they wouldn't say, 'ah, you did it' just to be like everybody else. (Konopka, 1976, p. 84)

Another aspect of commitment is the ability to *keep confidences*, to refrain from telling something that a friend told you in private. The ability to keep confidences is very important to teens, as this adolescent reveals:

> Friends can keep secrets together. They can trust that you won't tell anybody else. . . . If you tell somebody something, they won't use it to get revenge on you when you get in a fight. You talk about things you wouldn't tell other people. (Youniss, 1980, p. 181)

Throughout adolescents' descriptions of friendship, words like "trust," "faith," and "believe in" are mentioned again and again. The preciousness of inner feelings for an adolescent, who is so newly aware of them, demands absolute loyalty from friends. The highly sensitive nature of these feelings makes the teen-ager very vulnerable to betrayal. Mutual understanding and intimacy lead to the trust that is needed to make teen-age friendships work. But without some degree of trust to begin with, teens cannot have the confidence to share their inner experiences and thus build mutual understanding and closeness with a peer.

All the changes in friendships we have just described appear in early to mid-adolescence. Then, during the later adolescent years, another qualitative advance occurs. In keeping with the older teen-ager's ability to integrate diverse aspects of the self, older teens are also able to coordinate a broader range of friends. Friendships no longer need to be so exclusive, as pairs of friends accept each other's need to establish relationships with other people and to grow through these experiences (Selman, 1980). Here is how William Damon explains this broadening of friendships: "Friends are still seen as mutually supportive in a psychological way. Only now this support is seen on a broader scale, extending to a variety of friendship relations of differing significance and intensity" (Damon, 1983, p. 256). This broadening process is accompanied by an increased stability in friendships among older teens. Before age 15 there is only moderate stability across a two-week period in the peers whom adolescents identify as their "best friends." By 16 to 19, however, best friends are highly stable (Hartup and Sancilio, 1986). Here we see patterns of friendship and stability coming closer to those found among adults.

In Erik Erikson's theory, identity is considered a prerequisite for true intimacy among peers. People must have a sense of who they are before they can join another in a close, emotionally sharing relationship. They must also be able simultaneously to process their own thoughts and feelings as well as those of others in order to be capable of genuine mutual understanding. This demands a great deal of self-development. But at the same time identity achievement is strongly dependent on peer interactions. Not only do peers offer many opportunities to experiment with social roles and styles of behavior, they also offer vital confirmation that one's ideas about the self are valid. It is only through self-disclosure with close friends that we come to know that others see us as we ourselves do. Harry Stack Sullivan (1953) goes even further by arguing that personal identity is an *outgrowth* of intimate relations, first with friends of the same gender and later with opposite-gender peers. Whatever the cause-and-effect connection between intimacy and identity is, correlational research shows that the two do go hand in hand. For instance, college students with a stable sense of personal identity have been found more likely to have attained emotional intimacy with someone else (Kacerguis and Adams, 1978). How these two factors are related cannot be said with certainty. Perhaps they are mutually influencing in a cyclical way, with advances in identity promoting deeper intimacy, and deeper intimacy further consolidating identity.

Peer Groups in Adolescence

Not only does the nature of friendship change in adolescence, the nature of peer groups changes as well. Two new structures that emerge are the **clique** and the **crowd.** A clique is a close-knit group of a few friends who are "related to one another in an intimate fellowship that involves going places and doing things together, a mutual exchange of ideas, and the acceptance of each personality by the others" (Hollingshead, 1949). Cliques, especially those of girls, are relatively closed to newcomers (Sones and Feshbach, 1971). The crowd is larger, less exclusive, and more loosely organized than the clique. In one study of 300 high-school students, there were 44 cliques (made up of three to nine members) and only 12 crowds (Dunphy, 1963). These crowds were made up of cliques, but not every clique was part of a crowd. Cliques are apparently the dominant peer-group structure during adolescence. The crowd, in contrast, offers a broader range of informal contacts, usually on weekends.

How do cliques and crowds develop across the teen-age years and what functions do they serve for adolescents? Table 15.4 summarizes the major developments. In stage 1, the precrowd stage, which occurs in early adolescence, teen-agers participate only in unisex cliques. Their small size and close-knit nature allow for mutual understanding and sharing. Then, in stage 2, both male and female unisex cliques begin to interact within a loosely formed crowd. These early crowd activities allow young adolescents to have casual, nonthreatening heterosexual contacts. Stage 3 represents a transition during which some upper status members of the crowd form a heterosexual clique. The crowd is fully developed in stage 4, with several heterosexual cliques in close association. Finally, in late adolescence, the crowd begins to disintegrate into loosely linked groups

TABLE 15.4   The Progression of Peer Group Relations in Adolescence

Early Adolescence

Stage 1: Precrowd stage. Isolated uni-sexual cliques. *(Left: Paul Conklin/ Monkmeyer Press. Right: Charles Har-butt/Archive Pictures Inc.)*

Stage 2: The beginning of the crowd. Unisexual cliques in group-to-group in-teraction. *(Renate Hiller/Monkmeyer Press.)*

Stage 3: The crowd in structural tran-sition. Unisexual cliques with upper status members forming a heterosexual clique. *(Paul Conklin/Monkmeyer Press.)*

Late Adolescence

Stage 4: The fully developed crowd. Heterosexual cliques in close associa-tion. *(Peter Vandermark/Stock, Bos-ton.)*

Stage 5: Beginning of crowd disinte-gration. Loosely associated groups of couples. *(Jerry Cooke/Photo Research-ers, Inc.)*

Source: Adapted from Dunphy, 1963, p. 236.

of couples (Dunphy, 1963). This progression, as you can see, has a certain logic. It would allow the teen-ager to move "from intimate single-sex friendships through a series of casual heterosexual contacts to a final phase of heterosexual intimacy" (Damon, 1983, p. 259).

Dating and Sexual Activity

Dating and sexual activity are often the offspring of crowd activities. Few adolescents begin dating before they participate in crowds. Whereas before age 12 less than 10 percent of youngsters date, by age 16, 90 percent are dating (Dickinson, 1975). Similarly, sexual experimentation usually does not begin until mid-adolescence (Offer, 1969). And even then, mutually satisfying sexual intimacy is still a long way off. Couples in mid-adolescence tend to operate in a "parallel" manner—together, but not mutually involved on an emotional level (Damon, 1983). It is only in later adolescence, in the eleventh grade and beyond, that intimacy with an opposite-sex friend becomes comparable to that occurring between same-sex friends (Sharabany, Gershoni, and Hofman, 1981).

Patterns of dating and sexual activity have changed more slowly over the years than many people think (Rutter, 1980). If there ever was a sexual "revolution" it was shortly after World War I, not during the 1960s which received so much publicity as a time of new sexual freedom. There is also little evidence that teen-agers today are rejecting the value of stable sexual relationships. Exclusivity and fidelity among sexual partners have remained desired qualities (Yankelovitch, 1974). There is a trend toward valuing premarital intercourse with one's future spouse, but this trend had been occurring over several decades and does not imply promiscuity (Reiss, 1976). Most adolescents, particularly younger ones, remain hesitant with regard to heterosexual expression. Many seem to perceive it as threatening (Gilligan et al., 1971). Thus, masturbation remains the primary sexual outlet, especially for boys (Santrock, 1984). Only toward the end of adolescence do girls accept their full sexual capacity and do boys accept that sexuality is a part of mutual understanding (Haeberle, 1978).

The Relative Influence of Peers

A topic of great interest to parents and researchers alike is the influence of peers on the behavior and development of adolescents. Teen-agers, especially in early adolescence, adopt a manner of dress and style that sets them apart from other age groups. Developmentalists interpret this as identification with the peer group, a way of both affirming and concealing uniqueness while de-identifying with parents. Recent surveys tend to confirm this interpretation. They find that while young teens are becoming more autonomous from parents, they are also becoming more dependent on peers (Steinberg and Silverberg, 1986). Thus, involvement with peers may help youngsters carve out a more mature relationship with their parents. Peer-group identification also allows teens to maintain a distance from adult roles and commitments while still gaining the interpersonal experience needed to perform these tasks.

Just how much conformity is there to the peer group during adolescence? The answer depends upon what phase of adolescence you con-

Figure 15.1
Changes in Conformity to Peers with Age
Youngsters of different ages were asked to decide which lines in a set matched as to length.
Source: Costanzo, 1970, p. 368.

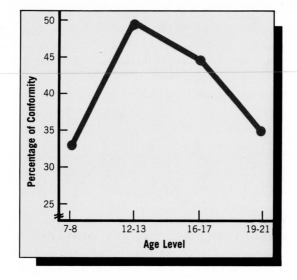

sider (Brown, Clasen, and Eicher, 1985). In one study, whose results are shown in Figure 15.1, 12- to 13-year-olds went along with the incorrect opinions of others much more than 7- to 8-year-olds did. By age 16 to 17 such conformity had declined, and by age 19 to 21 it was no greater than it had been in middle childhood (Costanzo, 1970). Similar findings emerged from another study in which youngsters were given hypothetical situations that involved opposing pressures from parents and peers (Berndt, 1979). It was young adolescents who experienced the most conflict, finding it hard to decide which side to go along with. These findings show that the peak period of conformity to peer group beliefs and behavior seems to be during the early teen-age years. This makes sense when you consider that young adolescents have well-developed social-comparison skills but are still very self-conscious about what others think of them. Older adolescents, in contrast, have largely overcome the imaginary-audience phase. Thus, when youngsters appear very conforming during the early teen-age years, it does not mean that they will always adhere so closely to the views of others.

Even during early adolescence, youngsters are not all alike in their degree of conformity. For instance, middle status peers are more likely to conform than are high or low status ones (Lansbaum and Willis, 1971). Perhaps they perceive they have more to gain in terms of group acceptance by going along with what others do (Sprinthall and Collins, 1984). Teens are also more influenced by their friends, especially long-term ones, than they are by mere acquaintances. For example, friends are more likely to behave similarly with regard to using marijuana. Even recent friends exert a noticeable influence on one another. Teen-agers who become friends during the current school year are more similar at the end of that year than they were at the beginning (Kandel, 1978). All this suggests that Christine in our earlier story had good reason to be concerned when 14-year-old Mike was hanging out with the "wrong" crowd.

Parents often view their teen-ager's conformity to the peer group as a sign that their own influence is waning, and that the youngster may be abandoning basic values taught in the home in favor of those adopted by peers. What truth is there to this concern? The answer is quite reassuring. Peer influence does not remove parental influence, which remains high even while peer influence increases (Chassin and Sherman, 1985).

The *kinds* of influences that parents and peers exert are often different, however. Peers tend to have the greatest effect on more superficial behaviors such as dress and mannerisms. Parents, in contrast, tend to retain a substantial influence on a youngster's basic values and philosophy of life. This was shown in a classic study in which ninth to eleventh graders were presented with hypothetical situations in which a teen-ager faced a dilemma (Brittain, 1963). Sometimes the subjects were informed as to what the parents thought the teen-ager should do; other times they were told what peers advised doing. Each subject was then asked how the dilemma should be resolved. Many responded with their own judgments, although often the views of parents and peers exerted an influence. Peer opinions were most influential in matters dealing with status in the peer group, whereas parental judgments were most influential in matters of important life decisions, education, and ethics. Other studies agree with this general split in influence during the teen-age years (Douvan and Adelson, 1966; Lesser and Kandel, 1969).

This is not to say that peers never exert an influence on important matters. Sometimes they do. One study found that, by the age of 14, the influence of peers regarding the decision to smoke surpassed that of parents (Krosnick and Judd, 1982). Peers also influence decisions about the use of drugs and other problem behaviors. But these peer influences tend to diminish by late adolescence (Berndt, 1979). In contrast, the influence of parents often continues into adulthood, as you will see in our next section.

FAMILY RELATIONS IN ADOLESCENCE

The family is a critical context in which adolescents work on the major task of identity formation. Personal identity represents a sense of continuity with the past, a pulling together of all past identifications into a new synthesis. This synthesis should not be merely a thoughtless copy of parental beliefs and values (foreclosure). But neither should it be totally at odds with the goals and standards set in the family (identity diffusion). A history of experiences within the family is the foundation upon which a coherent new identity is built. In addition, parents may actively support identity seeking by allowing their adolescent to explore new roles and values, by tolerating self-expression and discussing different views, while still providing guidelines and limits when needed. Parents are also a vital source of recognition, of confirming the adolescent's emerging sense of direction and purpose. This is an essential part of achieving a stable identity.

James Youniss (1983) has outlined what he calls a **social construction view** of identity formation. He stresses that achieving an identity involves more than merely coming up with a set of beliefs to adopt. Identity involves understanding one's own unique perspective and how it relates to the perspectives of others. This can be accomplished only through social interaction. More specifically, identity formation requires a supportive relationship in which mutual criticisms can be aired and both sides can receive clarification and confirmation of their newly evolving roles. Cognitive development may underlie identity formation, but the process of shared exploration and mutual understanding is also critical.

This view of the transition from childhood to adulthood is analogous to the view we took in describing the transition from infancy to childhood during the toddler period. We argued that the toddler was not just separating from the parents, but rather was becoming connected to them in a new way. The toddler's assertiveness and the parents' setting of limits led the child to a new understanding of the boundaries between self and others. Gradually the toddler came to see the self not as an extension of the parent, but rather as a separate person who is linked to the parent through strong psychological ties. In a similar fashion, the adolescent's new level of self-assertion and the parents' mix of accepting and challenging this new status promote a new level of mutual understanding. By late adolescence or early adulthood sons and daughters have usually gained renewed respect for their parents (White, Speisman, and Costos, 1983). It is not the adoration of the young child, but a powerful connection nonetheless.

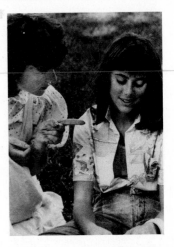

The adolescent, like the toddler, must evolve a new way of relating to parents that involves more separateness, but not a loss of closeness. *(Erika Stone © 1984/Peter Arnold, Inc.)*

The Changing Family Structure

To say that family relations remain important during adolescence is not to say that they remain static. Roles and patterns of interaction within the family change dramatically at this time, and necessarily so. The child is undergoing enormous change, physically, cognitively, and socially; far-reaching changes in family structure are needed to accommodate this development. Thus, it is not only the adolescent who is developing but also the family.

One reason why family relationships are pressed toward change in this period has to do with the child's changing level of understanding. The same formal operational skills that permit hypothetical thinking and exploration of inconsistencies allow teen-agers to anticipate how parents will counter their arguments, to note imperfections in the parents' behavior, and to conceive of other ways in which the family might function (Clark and Delia, 1976). Adolescents can now resent an unsatisfactory family situation because they can see what *might* be (Elkind, 1967). Teen-agers also have a new understanding of parent-child relationships and parental authority (see Table 15.5). By late adolescence they see mutual tolerance and respect as the basis of interactions between themselves and their parents. No longer can the adolescent simply accept parental dictates without reasons and chance for input. Increased size, competence, and understanding all press the youngster to seek greater autonomy in behavior and decision making. In one study, 80 percent of several thousand 14- to 16-year-olds said they wanted their parents to be less restrictive and to allow them more independence (Douvan and Adelson, 1966).

During this same period, parents themselves are changing. Often they are dealing with what has been called a midlife crisis (Aldous, 1978; Sprinthall and Collins, 1984). A midlife crisis is similar to a second

TABLE 15.5   Levels of Understanding Parent-Child Relations

Level 0: Pragmatic Parenting and Reactive-Punitive Responses	

View of Punishment: emphasis on effects rather than parent's motives

Interviewer:	What does punishment do for children? How does it work?
Child:	It makes us upset.

Age 5 1/2

Interviewer:	Why do parents want their children to be upset?
Child:	Because the child was bad.

Level 1: Authoritarian Parenting and Punishment as a Lesson from Above	

View of Punishment: to teach children what is good or bad, to protect the child from danger

Interviewer:	Why do you think parents sometimes punish their children?
Child:	Because they do bad things and they want to teach them a lesson.

Age 9

Interviewer:	Why do children get punished?
Child:	Well, they done something wrong, and then they should get paid back for it.

Age 8

Level 2: The Parent-Child Relation as a Source of Reciprocal Emotional Ties and Punishment as a Form of Communication	

View of Punishment: to help children reflect on their actions, beginnings of a questioning of the effectiveness of punishment

Interviewer:	Why do you think parents punish sometimes?
Child:	I guess to make you feel . . . make you think about it . . . or something like that.

Age 12

Interviewer:	Should children be punished if they disobey?
Child:	Yeah. 'Cause then when you tell them not to do something, they won't do it. And if she don't punish them, they're just gonna go back and do it again, and they have command of their parents.

Age 13

Level 3: Parents and Children as Separate Personalities and Punishment as a Need for Control	

View of Punishment: coordination of the child's and parent's perspectives

Interviewer:	
Child:	Parents have their lives too. If a kid is always screwing up, it's not just the kid who needs to see the light.

Age 16

Interviewer:	Why do parents sometimes punish their children?
Child:	Punishment is not necessary; there are other techniques to achieve obedience. It depends on the capabilities and needs of the child . . . It depends on the parents, what they are like as well as the children.

Age 17

Level 4: Punishment and Power, Some Speculations	

View of Punishment: involves subtle, unconscious motives

Interviewer:	Should children be punished when they disobey?
Child:	Not when they are older. The mother cannot keep the child, or the father, if that child is eighteen years old or so. Parents often think that they still run their child, but they can't because they are old enough to decide that they want something.

Age 18

Interviewer:	Why do parents sometimes punish their children?
Child:	Some kids will do something wrong just to get punished, to see if the parents really care.

Age 18

Source: Adapted from R. Selman, 1980, pp. 124–130.

adolescence in that the adult renews the search for purpose, meaning, and commitment. Conflicts within the family, including those involving young teen-agers, may exacerbate the parents' own struggles. The parents may resent the teen-ager's idealism and extreme stances on questions of values. The parents' view is more pragmatic, more constrained by a sense of limited time. To them cutting loose from long-followed patterns no longer seems a viable option. Moreover, the teen-ager's strivings toward identity and purpose often reawaken the parents' own turmoil and unresolved issues of adolescence (Boxer et al., 1984). All this can make the onset of an offspring's puberty as difficult for the parents as it is for the child.

How much conflict typically results from this confrontation between individuals with different needs, outlooks, and developmental tasks? In early adolescence there is often a great deal of conflict (Douvan and Adelson, 1966; Montemayer and Hanson, 1985; Rutter, 1980). This conflict is usually over mundane matters such as chores, personal hygiene, friends, and "disturbing" behaviors (leaving lights on, playing the radio too loudly, tying up the phone). Nevertheless, it seems ubiquitous from the parents' viewpoint. Not surprisingly, parental stress is generally low when children are between the ages of 10 and 12, peaks at ages 14 to 15, and then declines in late adolescence (Hakim-Larson, Livingston, and Tron, 1985; Small, Cornelius, and Eastman, 1983). Parental satisfaction shows the opposite pattern: high in their offspring's late middle childhood, low in early adolescence, and rising again at the end of the teenage years (Montemayer and Brownlee, 1986). It is interesting that the amount of family conflict during early adolescence does not distinguish healthy from unhealthy families (Prinz et al., 1979). Conflict at this time is part of the normal realignment process that must take place. Total avoidance of conflict between parents and young adolescents would be the more worrisome sign (Sprey, 1971; Strauss, 1979).

Partly as a result of increased argumentativeness and conflict within the families of adolescents, a new, more symmetrical power structure evolves. This evolution has been shown in research. In one study, parents and sons discussed solutions to hypothetical problems, such as what to do when the son comes home late. Across the ages of 11 to 16, the sons had a growing influence on these discussions as measured by the amount of time they spent talking, the number of times they interrupted their parents, and the increased tendency on the parents' part to adopt the youngster's point of view (Jacob, 1974). In another study, parents and sons again engaged in problem-solving tasks, such as planning a vacation together (Steinberg, 1981). This time, however, the same boys were followed from late middle childhood until past the peak of puberty. It was found that as the youngsters entered adolescence they began deferring less to their mothers. Mother and son interrupted each other more, responded less to each other's opinions, interacted in a more contentious and rigid manner, and offered fewer explanations for their own views. During this period the fathers typically stepped in, asserted their opinions more strongly, and the boys continued to defer to them. After the peak of puberty had passed, family interactions became more flexible again. Mothers interrupted less often and sons became more willing to justify their thinking. At this older age the sons' relative influence in these laboratory discussions remained greater than that of the mothers, but still less than the fathers'. This finding does not imply that mothers have less power within the family than their older adolescent sons do. Instead, it could be interpreted to mean that because of the security of the mother-

Some behaviors of adolescents are difficult for others to tolerate. (*Ed Lettau/Photo Researchers, Inc.*)

son relationship, mothers are increasingly willing to be open to their teen-ager's point of view. In any case, the data from such studies reveal a changing pattern of family interaction and a recognition by all that there is now greater symmetry in relationships.

Parenting Patterns and Adolescent Development

As power relations become more symmetrical within the family, the tasks of parenting change. Parents of adolescents must respond to their children's new ways of thinking, new striving for autonomy, self-expression, and influence. They have to switch from monitoring the child to monitoring the child's own monitoring of the self (Maccoby, 1980). In other words, the parents must gradually turn over more and more responsibility to the newly emerging adult. Parents, of course, still need to impose some limits, but guidance and feedback generally replace demands and directives. Nonetheless, researchers agree that adolescent development goes best when parents stay involved with their teens (Hetherington, in press; Patterson and Dishion, in press).

Research on successful parenting of adolescents shows that many of the same factors important in earlier periods continue to be important now. Warmth, support, and authoritativeness are commonly found to have positive influences (Bell and Bell, 1983; Enright et al., 1980; Sprinthall and Collins, 1984). For instance, in one study of 7000 high-school students, those who lived in "democratic" families (where the adolescents had influence over decisions, although final authority rested with the parents) were more self-confident and independent than those in nondemocratic families (Elder, 1963). This democratic style of parenting should promote identity achievement by modeling responsible attitudes, providing opportunities for decision making, exploring and clarifying points of disagreement, and fostering sharing and mutual respect. One cross-cultural study supported these generalizations (Kandel and Lesser,

1972). In it researchers compared parenting practices and adolescent development in Denmark and the United States. Danish families are generally more democratic and discussion-oriented than American families are. As expected, Danish adolescents seem to display a greater sense of independence, to have more internalized standards of behavior, and to be less rebellious than their American counterparts. Such correlational studies based on interviews cannot pinpoint causes, of course. Danish adolescents may be more independent for reasons other than patterns of decision making within the family. There may also be a difference between what parents and teen-agers report to psychologists and what they do. Such studies suggest interesting leads for future research.

Some more recent studies have relied on direct observation to explore the links between parenting practices and adolescent development (Bell and Bell, 1983; Cooper, Grotevant, and Condon, 1983; Fleeson, 1987; Powers et al., 1983). In these studies the researchers observed parents and their teen-age children interacting with one another while they discussed dilemmas, solved problems, or planned activities together. Sometimes the researchers rated the subjects along several broad dimensions, such as conflict resolution, mutual acceptance, and support for autonomy. Other times the investigators categorized hundreds of specific statements and actions. For instance, if in planning a joint vacation one family member said, "I'd like to go to Italy," this would be categorized as showing self-assertion. If instead the same person asked, "Would either of you like to go back to Italy?" this would be coded as showing respect for others' views (Cooper, Grotevant, and Condon, 1983). No single statement or action was considered revealing in and of itself. It was the *pattern* of behavior from which the researchers drew their inferences. In addition to observing patterns of family interaction, the researchers who conducted these studies also made independent assessments of the degree of maturity, identity formation, and positive adjustment in the teen-agers involved.

A study of this type conducted by Stephen Powers and his colleagues (1983) made several valuable findings. First, it showed that an atmosphere of warmth, support, and positive emotion in the family is extremely important. The degree to which these qualities existed in the home was enough to predict a youngster's level of ego maturity as assessed by a sentence-completion test (Loevinger, 1976). Apparently, genuine acceptance of a teen-ager by the parents strongly promotes development. Second, this same study suggested that it is not enough for parents simply to prod a teen-ager into exploring alternatives and questioning opinions. In order for this kind of "cognitive challenge" to encourage identity achievement, it must take place within a warm and supportive family context. Under these conditions such challenge comes across as a sign of the parents' interest and respect, not their criticism.

The importance of support and responsiveness on the part of parents was also suggested in a study conducted by Catherine Cooper and her colleagues (1983). They explored adolescents' success at two key tasks involved in identity achievement: (1) exploring alternatives regarding the self, and (2) role-taking (the ability to perceive and coordinate different points of view). Success at these tasks was related to the parents' behavior during a joint vacation-planning discussion. When the parents responded to the adolescent's feelings, accepted disagreements, and initiated com-

Roles and patterns of inter-action within the family must change as a result of divorce and remarriage. Parenting styles may need to accommodate the needs of more than one emerging adult when two single-parent families are joined. (© *Sybil Shelton/Peter Arnold, Inc.*)

promises, the youngster was more likely to be at a relatively high level regarding the two key tasks studied. Since this was a correlational study one cannot draw conclusions about cause and effect. It is possible that the teen-ager's ability to explore alternatives and coordinate different roles helped promote the parents' supportive and responsive style as much as the other way around. Nevertheless, these findings are in keeping with the social construction view of identity formation—a view that stresses the importance of supportive relationships.

Bi-Directional Influences

Although parents clearly affect their children and the quality of their development, children also have an impact on their parents and the patterns of interaction that occur in the family. Different children seem to "bring out" different parenting responses, just as different parenting styles seem to foster different reactions in children. One of the clearest examples of these bidirectional influences can be seen in studying developmental differences among boys and girls.

During the teen-age years not only do girls suffer from greater self-consciousness and generally lower self-esteem, they also tend to seek autonomy in different ways than boys do (Peterson, 1986; Simmons and Blyth, in press). One study conducted in England found that adolescent girls primarily seek recognition of their emerging uniqueness and independent thought *within* the family, whereas adolescent boys often struggle to escape the confines of the family (Coleman, 1974). In a complementary way, suggesting bidirectional lines of influence, parents allow their sons greater freedom to be away from home, and have more concerns about their daughters' sexual behavior (Block, 1979; Hoffman and Manis, 1977). By the first year of college, girls continue to have conflicts at home, more than boys do, and these conflicts frequently concern emotional issues that don't affect boys as often (Kinloch, 1970). Apparently an interaction of the parents, the child, and the child's gender gives rise to significant differences in patterns of development.

The Impact of Divorce on Adolescents

We discussed the impact of divorce in our middle childhood chapter, but some very important findings concern the adolescent age-group. First, it appears that divorce can prompt a "sleeper" effect—a result that is not apparent at the actual time of the separation but shows up some years later, in this case during adolescence. Second, during adolescence we see continuing differences in the effects of divorce on males and females. For girls whose parents divorced during the youngster's middle childhood, the consequences usually appear more slowly and take different forms than they do for boys. Finally, studies of teen-agers in single-parent homes show that it is not just the absence of a father that can cause negative effects. Disruption caused by divorce often has different consequences than disruption caused by the death of a father, for instance.

These three conclusions were clearly illustrated in a study by Mavis Hetherington (1972). She studied girls ages 13 to 17, none of whom had brothers. Some of the girls came from intact families, with both a mother and a father at home; others came from divorced families where the mother had child custody and had never remarried; and still others came from mother-headed families in which the father had died. Hetherington found that girls from father-absent homes were just as sex-typed in their behavior as girls from intact homes. However, the girls with absent fathers tended to show impairments in their opposite-sex relations, the form of which varied greatly depending upon whether the father's absence was due to death or divorce.

In general, girls whose fathers had died were shy and hesitant with males, whereas girls of divorced fathers tended to be sexually forward. Consider the way the two groups behaved at a recreation-center dance. The daughters of widows tended to stay at the "girls' end" of the hall, surrounding themselves with other females. Two even retreated for the entire evening to the security of the restroom. In contrast, the daughters of divorcees often were found at the "stag line," initiating contact with boys. Equally revealing was their behavior later when interviewed by a male psychologist. While the daughters of widows tended to sit far away from the interviewer, avoid eye contact with him, and constrict their body posture, the daughters of divorcees tended to choose a seat near the interviewer, look at him often, and position their bodies in open, even provocative ways. These tendencies, which were especially pronounced in girls who had lost their fathers early, did not go unnoticed by the mothers. While the widows often described their daughters as "almost too good," the divorcees often used words such as "promiscuous" and "tramp." There were, of course, exceptions to these patterns.

Hetherington speculates that the attitudes and behaviors of the mothers involved may largely account for these frequent differences. Many of the divorced mothers were still hostile toward their ex-husbands, recalled their marriages with bitterness, and were generally dissatisfied with life. Some of their daughters may have therefore concluded that happiness greatly depends on being "successful" with men. However, because they lacked experience with males in the family, their approach to this goal was often inappropriate. In sharp contrast, the widows tended to cling to happy memories of marriage. As a result, the image that they painted of their husbands may have been so perfect that the daughters tended to view all males as unapproachable. These are only hypotheses, of course. But whatever the explanation it is clear that the *meaning* a girl attaches to the loss of her father can be a very important factor.

ADOLESCENTS IN THE BROADER WORLD

During adolescence developmental contexts beyond the home and peer group become increasingly important. These include not just the school but often the workplace as well. The school and workplace, of course, are often intimately tied to both family and friends. Family life and peer relations greatly influence how well an adolescent performs in these contexts (Coleman, 1961). These contexts, in turn, provide opportunities for interactions with peers, as well as for shared pride and conflict within the family. Perhaps most important, the school and the workplace are vital proving grounds for the adolescent's developing sense of identity. Not only can accomplishments in the classroom and on the job give teenagers a feeling of competence, they also allow young people to explore and anticipate future roles. Projecting the self into the future and forming goals in life are central to Erikson's theory of identity achievement.

Adolescents at School

In some ways middle schools and high schools support adolescent development. Students are given more responsibility for mastering course material, such as completing homework assignments and doing special projects. Occasionally there are courses in which youngsters can explore diverse opinions on social issues through class discussion. Being exposed to peers from diverse backgrounds, as occurs especially in public schools, can also encourage adolescents to perceive different points of view. These are some of the positive aspects of the school environment. All too often, however, there are many negative factors with which to contend. For one thing, schools are often highly regimented. They demand conformity and uphold a very narrow definition of traditional values. In addition, the peer culture at school rewards popularity and athletic performance far more than it does scholastic achievement (Coleman, 1961).

Generally speaking, youngsters' grades decline during adolescence. This may be due in part to harder classes and harder grading, but it is also tied to the process of changing from one school to another (Petersen, 1986). In one study, for example, young adolescents who remained in the

Adjusting to a new school can be difficult for the teenager. *(Ed Lettau/Photo Researchers, Inc.)*

same school from kindergarten through eighth grade received better marks than those who switched to a middle school at the age of 12 (Simmons and Blyth, 1986). The critical variable underlying this difference is the amount of change experienced—in this case, the change of having to adjust to a new school setting. Other kinds of changes can also prompt a decline in academic performance. Youngsters who are in the throes of puberty or who are being affected by other sudden turns in their lives are most likely to suffer a drop in school grades.

Researchers have wanted to discover the factors that encourage adolescents to strive for achievement in school. Their interest arises partly from the great importance our society attaches to academic performance, and partly from the fact that school achievement is to some extent a marker of good adjustment. Some psychologists have argued that if parents are achievement-oriented and model this behavior for their children, the children will follow that example and strive for achievement too (Bandura, 1977a).

It is easy to be too simplistic in adopting this view, however. Adolescents are not the same people as their parents. They may have a different level of self-confidence, different beliefs about their abilities, and different outlooks about their capacity to influence success or failure. Some teen-agers are convinced that success in school is under their own control, while others think that grades are largely a matter of outside factors such as luck (Weiner, Kun, and Benesh-Wiener, 1983). The first of these outlooks represents an internal locus of control, while the second represents an external locus (see Chapter 13). Research shows that youngsters with an external locus of control believe that nothing they do will make a difference, because events are not within their power to influence. Such youngsters actually prefer tasks with built-in reasons for failure. They are worried about failing, but they have difficulty accepting that what happens to them is largely their responsibility. As a result, they give up in the face of setbacks, avoid challenging courses, and don't bother to develop more efficient study habits (Bryant, 1974; Phares and Lamiell, 1975).

Psychologists have been disturbed to discover that girls, in general, face more obstacles to school achievement than boys do. For one thing, girls are often socialized away from feelings of instrumental competence (thinking they have the ability to accomplish things) and toward feelings of helplessness when confronted with a challenge (Block, 1979; Dweck, 1975; Hoffman and Manis, 1977). For instance, parents tend to believe that adolescent boys have more natural talent for math, and they convey this belief to their children (Parsons, Adler, and Kaezala, 1982). As a result, girls usually have lower expectations for success at math and a variety of other tasks, despite the fact that, overall, they earn better grades than boys do (Petersen, 1986; Stein and Bailey, 1973). When girls fail they are also more likely than boys to attribute that failure to something they cannot change, such as innate lack of ability (Dweck and Repucci, 1973). This prompts them to give up trying more readily than boys. And even when girls achieve at academic tasks, that success doesn't always give them as much pride as it does boys. For girls, high achievement in certain areas, such as mathematics, is often related to a more negative self-image (Petersen, 1986).

In summary, many of today's teen-agers, both female and male, seem to be caught in a bind (Elkind, 1978; Santrock, 1984). On the one hand, they are experiencing strong pressure to succeed in what is portrayed as an increasingly competitive world. On the other hand, parents, teachers, and peers sometimes give them insufficient support for academic achievement, and they may lack the personal outlooks needed to promote success. As they forge an identity, teen-agers need to feel that by their own efforts they can master the tools needed to equip them for adult life.

Adolescents at Work

Another area in which teen-agers can develop a sense of pride and accomplishment is in the workplace. About 75 percent of high-school seniors have a part-time job, averaging 16 to 20 hours a week, and about one-third of sophomores and juniors also do some kind of paid work outside the home (Bachman, 1982; Cole, 1981). A job can contribute to self-esteem and a sense of personal identity, by allowing adolescents to feel they are doing something useful. They often show pride in their place of work as well as in themselves as workers. Not only are they expressing the sense of industry and competence they worked on developing in middle childhood, they are also anticipating their future role as economically self-sufficient individuals. At the same time, by taking responsibility for showing up on time and doing the tasks they are given, they confirm their emerging status as adults. The self-earned pay, of course, helps to make them more independent from their parents, and it also gives them experience with managing money. By forcing teens to budget their time, balance demands, and make choices, a part-time job can foster maturity (Greenberger and Steinberg, 1980).

But jobs for adolescents may also have drawbacks. For one thing, the work that is available to teens is often routine and impersonal, with the youngsters seldom feeling close to the adults around them (Greenberger and Steinberg, 1980). As a result, teen-agers may not really enjoy their jobs and may develop the sense that they are working only for the money (Cole, 1980). Even more important, a part-time job may cause them to neglect other areas, such as time spent with friends or on schoolwork. One extensive survey found that high-school students with jobs were generally less involved in school activities, enjoyed school less, and received lower grades than their nonworking peers (Greenberger and Steinberg, 1980). However, it was not work per se that affected grades, but rather the number of hours spent working. Tenth graders who worked more than 14 hours a week and eleventh graders who worked more than 20 were the ones whose grades suffered.

Adolescents and Career Development

Anticipating a future career is part of forming an identity during adolescence. This is not to say that many teens firmly settle on their life's work. In our complex society, with so many jobs to choose from, making a career decision often takes place in early adulthood. Nevertheless, assessing one's own abilities and starting to explore the options is an important foundation of career development that takes place during ad-

Jobs can be not only a source of income, but also a source of self-esteem for the teenager. *(Audrey Gottlieb/ Monkmeyer Press.)*

olescence (Ginzberg, 1972). The teen-age years are a time in which young people acquire a vocational self-concept—the sense of being a hard and competent worker, capable of someday taking one's place in the career world of adults (Super, 1976).

Although examining career options during adolescence is important, this exploration process is seldom either systematic or thorough. Most high-school students know relatively little about how to obtain vocational information. On average, they spend less than three hours a year with high-school guidance counselors (Super and Hall, 1978). For some this lack of specific career information poses little problem, since they have parents who are involved in satisfying work and who instill in them a sense of open opportunities. For others, however, circumstances converge to make the possibilities look far more negative and restricted. Such youngsters have parents who are unhappy in their work or who cannot find jobs at all, and they also receive little support in their search for a vocation from their schools and communities.

COMMON PROBLEMS OF ADOLESCENCE

We will be discussing some serious psychological problems of adolescence in Chapter 16. Here we want to mention briefly some of the more common difficulties that teens encounter as they struggle with the new options, demands, and relationships associated with moving toward adulthood. These problems include excessive use of alcohol or other drugs, becoming pregnant as a teen-ager, and running away from home. It is difficult to say when the behaviors related to these problems become signs of impending trouble. Some experimentation with drugs and sexuality is part of normal adolescent exploration, just as some resistance to parental authority is sometimes part of normal individuation. Nevertheless, drug addiction, teen-age pregnancy, and runaway youth are nationwide problems that seem to be on the rise. And because early sexual intercourse, heavy drinking, and frequent use of drugs tend to predict later difficulties in adulthood, it is all the more important that we understand their causes and work toward possible prevention (Donovan and Jesser, 1985; Jesser, 1983, 1984).

Alcohol and Drug Use

Figure 15.2 shows the results of one survey in a Midwestern city compared with the results of a nationwide survey on drug and alcohol use among adolescents. The results coincide with those of other studies, which show that more than 90 percent of high-school students have some contact with drinking and that at least 500,000 of these youths have a serious drinking problem (Jesser, 1984). Marijuana follows alcohol as the most popular mind-altering drug among adolescents. Slightly more than 50 percent of American high-school students have tried marijuana (Johnston and Bachman, 1981). The most common reason for using it is that friends do (Santrock, 1984). Marijuana and alcohol use are strongly re-

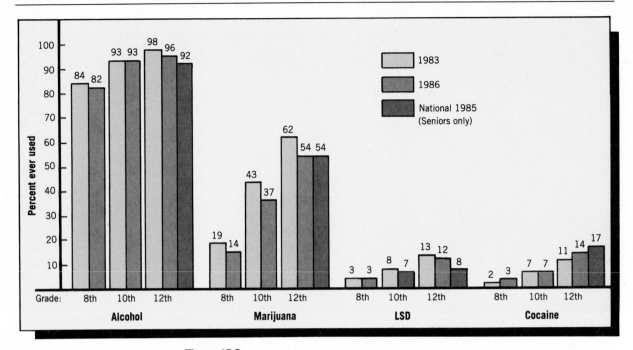

Figure 15.2
Trends in Adolescent Drug Usage
For some drugs, such as alcohol and LSD, use has been high but has declined slightly. For other drugs, such as cocaine, use has increased.
Source: Minneapolis Star and Tribune survey, 1986; Search Institute, 1983; Institute for Social Research, University of Michigan, 1985.

lated, although probably not because one causes the other. Instead, the same psychological factors underlie attraction to both drugs. Some alcohol and marijuana use is fostered by adolescents' normal tendency to try new experiences. Some represents an effort to move away from parents and identify with peers. Drug use also can help adolescents to feel as if they are no longer children, and thus becomes a sign that they have come of age. In addition, teen-agers drink and use marijuana for the same reasons adults do: to have fun, to reduce self-consciousness, and to ease tensions in social situations.

But the reduced anxiety and increased self-esteem that drug use can provide are very temporary. They cannot substitute for the pride and self-confidence that come from actual achievement. When drug use dominates peer encounters, it constricts the mutual exploration and genuine self-disclosure that are so important to identity achievement. Drug abusing teens may also curtail the development of effective coping skills by believing that problems have simple solutions or can be easily avoided. Mind-altering drugs can make it even more difficult than normal for adolescents to discern the lines between fantasy and reality.

Teen-Age Pregnancy

As Figure 15.3 shows, teen-age pregnancy dramatically increased from 1950 to the 1980s (Phipps-Yonas, 1980). Each year there are over a million teen-age pregnancies in this country, 400,000 of which end in

Figure 15.3
Births to Unmarried Women
15 to 19 Years Old
The graph shows the increase in teen pregnancy for the years 1950 to 1983.

Source: Adapted from Hindelang, Gottfredson, and Flanagan, 1981; and Monthly Vital Statistics Report, September 1984 and September 1985.

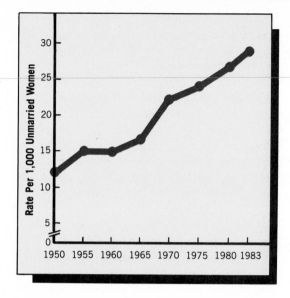

abortion and more than 500,000 in live births (Alan Guttmacher Institute, 1981). It is estimated that 50 percent of black infants are now born to unwed teen-age mothers (Sprinthall and Collins, 1984). Teen-age pregnancy is a problem not only because it can curtail the mother's education and career but also because so many of these adolescents are ill-prepared for motherhood. With good social support they can provide adequate care for their babies, but unfortunately very few of these young women have supportive networks available to them. As a result a cycle of poverty and insufficient care is often perpetuated.

Why do girls who become pregnant take the risk of unprotected intercourse? Part of the answer lies in simple ignorance. Despite sex education programs, most adolescents remain unaware of the high risk period for conception (Alan Guttmacher Institute, 1981). What's more, few teenagers use contraception during their first sexual experiences. Many young people feel that it is somehow wrong to plan to have sex, and many are convinced that they are protected by their uniqueness (an unwanted pregnancy could never happen *to them*).

Another important question is why so many girls decide to give birth to the baby and try to raise the child alone. Studies suggest that many see pregnancy as a way out of an unhappy home life and a chance finally to have "someone to love me." Thus, a search for emotional closeness (first from the man, then from the baby) may be more of a reason for teenage pregnancies than simple sexual exploration. Parental conflict and parental failure to monitor the child's dating behavior are also associated with teen-age pregnancy (Hogan, 1982).

Running Away

One way in which teen-agers break away from parents is by literally leaving the family and striking out on their own. This typically occurs in early adolescence. Each year hundreds of thousands of young teenagers run away from home. This behavior is associated with unresolved conflict in the family, physical or sexual abuse of the child, and totally inadequate communication (D'Angelo, 1974). If teens cannot find some degree of freedom and support at home, they may express their autonomy by the extreme action of running away. Many cities now have safe places for runaways to go to (Santrock, 1984). The fact that young teens often seek out these facilities suggests that they do not want to escape all structure, just an unsatisfactory home situation.

Another form of running away is seen in later adolescence. Currently it takes the form of joining religious cults. Hundreds of thousands of young people are at some time members of cults (Swope, 1980). Cults demand total commitment from their members and impose complete control over their lives. As such, they tap the feelings of loneliness and alienation that many young people experience, as well as the formal idealism of late adolescence (Levine, 1978; Swope, 1980). If older teens cannot find meaning within the family or inside traditional institutions, they will be vulnerable to becoming absorbed by authoritarian ideologies. This was a lesson of Nazi Germany and is a lesson of cults today. Idealism and commitment are healthy aspects of adolescence, but they can be directed toward negative as well as positive causes.

Chapter Review

1. In Erik Erikson's theory adolescence is a critical developmental stage. Not only does it involve major qualitative advances in every domain, it is also a time when previous developmental issues are reworked. The teen-age years are a turning point, a second chance so to speak, and the challenges of it may cause disruptions of various kinds. But adolescence should not be seen as an inevitably stormy time. How much turmoil teen-agers undergo depends upon who they are, when you view them, and what aspects of their behavior you consider. Age is particularly important to the experiences teens are having. Early and late adolescence seem to be distinct subphases.

2. One of the major tasks of adolescence is forming a personal **identity,** a new understanding of the self as different from other people, while at the same time integrated and coherent across time. Different teen-agers take different routes to establishing an identity. Some simply retreat from the challenge and accept the self that parents prescribe (identity **foreclosure**). Others are so overwhelmed by the task that they are unable to find direction **(identity diffusion).** Still others ultimately progress toward a consolidated sense of self, but experience hesitations and setbacks along the way **(moratorium).** And some proceed quite smoothly toward a sense of purpose and commitment **(identity achievement).**

3. The steps involved in forming an identity illustrate some of the psychological differences between early and late adolescence. Young adolescents become aware that they have inner thoughts and feelings different from those of other people. But they have trouble integrating different aspects of the self, as well as truly understanding the perspectives that others hold. They are also egocentric, self-conscious, and vulnerable to criticism to a degree that older adolescents are not. Older adolescents have a more integrated sense of self, and a much greater understanding of the uniqueness and separateness of people. They no longer think, as younger adolescents do, that others are scrutinizing their inner feelings. They may be more susceptible to feelings of loneliness because of their new awareness that no one can ever really know them. But they are also more at peace with themselves, more comfortable with who they are.

4. Many developmentalists believe that the sense of self is forged not in isolation, but within social relationships. Who we are is a product of our past and current dealings with others. This is the **social construction view** of identity formation. During adolescence relationships with peers become increasingly important to self-exploration and identity achievement. Compared with younger children, teen-agers have a much greater capacity for true mutual understanding. This increased capacity is linked to a new desire for self-disclosure in close and intimate friendships. Friends are now expected to be loyal and trustworthy, particularly with regard to shared confidences. In later adolescence friendships become less exclusive, as teens grow less vulnerable to feelings of betrayal. Adolescents now understand that people can form many friendships, of different depths and significance, and grow because of these experiences. Different friendships allow them to try out new roles and confirm their consolidating sense of self.

5. During adolescence peer influences do not replace those of parents. Instead, parental influences remain high, even while peer influences increase. A history of experiences within the family is the foundation upon which adolescents build their new identities. But roles and patterns of interaction within the family must change to accommodate the emerging new adult. The adolescent, like the toddler, must evolve a new way of relating to parents, one that involves more separateness but not a loss of closeness. Both the young adolescent and the toddler assert themselves and take a new "contrary" position as a way of exploring and bringing about this new relationship. The toddler is breaking away from the physical connection of infancy, the adolescent from the psychological identification of childhood. The adolescent, in short, is "de-identifying" with parents. In the end, a much more equal relationship develops between the parents and the teen-ager. The parents can be particularly helpful in fostering identity achievement by offering a warm and supportive atmosphere in the family, while still providing guidelines and limits when needed.

6. In addition to moving toward greater autonomy with respect to parents, adolescents must also take a more autonomous stance toward the larger world. This includes taking on more responsibility for schoolwork and school-related activities. Learned attitudes about the self and one's capacity to influence outcomes are especially important to academic achievement. Becoming more autonomous may also involve taking a part-time job. A job can boost a teen-ager's self-esteem, sense of identity, and feelings of financial independence from parents. However, working a large number of hours each week can detract from essential time spent on schoolwork and interactions with friends. A final aspect of seeking autonomy in the larger world involves the adolescent's exploration of careers. Few teen-agers firmly settle on their life's work, but examining the options is an important foundation for future career commitment.

7. Given the tremendous challenges that adolescents face, we can expect some will encounter problems as they develop. Among the most common problems of adolescence are excessive drug use, teen-age pregnancy, and running away. Many hundreds of thousands of teens in this country have serious problems with drugs. Drug dependence impairs the ability to move toward identity achievement and to develop effective coping skills. The incidence of teen-age pregnancy has also become a major problem. Teen-age pregnancy not only curtails the mother's education and career but also is a hardship for the baby when the mother is unprepared for child care. A search for emotional closeness and escape from an unhappy home life are often major factors underlying this problem. Running away is a problem that can take two forms. In early adolescence it typically involves leaving home and often going to a shelter where other runaways live. In later adolescence it may take the form of committing oneself to an authoritarian ideology, such as a religious cult. Both types of running away are closely related to the adolescent's search for identity.

Adolescence

Adolescence can be thought of as a second revolution in development, the first occurring during the toddler period, when a child emerges from an infant. During adolescence the child is transformed into a young adult. Qualitative advances can be seen in all developmental areas during the teen-age years. Among the most obvious are the physical changes. Just as toddlers lose their former babyish shape, so adolescents lose the look of children. Not only do they grow taller, heavier, and stronger, but their body proportions change and secondary sex characteristics develop. For males this includes a broadening of the shoulders, enlargement of the genitals, and production of hair on various parts of the body. For females it includes a widening of the hips, development of breasts, and the growth of pubic hair. Both sexes, of course, acquire the capacity for reproduction.

Equally important are the cognitive changes occurring in adolescence. Teen-agers are able to consider hypotheticals, to engage in "what-if" thinking about possibilities. (What if all the lakes in this country became polluted? What if I were put in charge of planning the first community to settle on a space station?) They can form generalizations from known facts and discern implications. These capacities allow them to make inferences in the absence of direct experience. Adolescents can also reason in more systematic ways than younger children can. They are able to proceed step by step to logical conclusions. As a result, they can understand abstractions such as $A = 2X$ with as much certainty as they know that the sun is shining.

Finally, adolescents can embrace multiple viewpoints. They can take one perspective and then consider several others, examining the differences among them. Taken together, these new abilities represent a qualitative advancement that sets the adolescent's thinking apart from the elementary-school child's. Essentially, the older adolescent has the cognitive capacities of an adult, even though these skills are still unseasoned by adult experience. Twenty years from now you will think about many things differently because of all you have learned in life. But the basic tools you use to solve problems and think about the world will be much the same as those you acquired by late adolescence.

Along with the cognitive changes of adolescence come dramatic changes in self-understanding. Even toddlers know that they exist as separate people with continuity over time. Adolescents, however, have a much fuller self-awareness. They can reflect upon the nature of the self—its history, its uniqueness, its complexity. At the same time, teen-agers develop much greater feelings of autonomy, which is why psychoanalytic theorists refer to adolescence as a second individuation. The first period of individuation occurs in toddlerhood, when children come to understand their basic separateness from parents. In adolescence the individuation process is carried much further. Now young people come to understand that they have inner feelings which even parents can't know. They acquire the sense that, ultimately, they are "alone" in the world. Accompanying this important individuation is a de-identification with parents. Teen-agers are moving toward their own ideals, goals, and values, their own unique characters. In Erikson's terms, they are establishing a sense of personal identity, a knowledge of who they are as separate from their parents and of what their place in the world is. Adolescence is especially critical in Erikson's theory because teen-agers must rework all previous developmental issues—trust, autonomy, initiative, industry—in light of their newly emerging identity.

A growing sense of identity and self-awareness inevitably brings changes in an adolescent's relationships with others. Consider friendships, for example. While sharing and loyalty are often seen in childhood friendships, the intimacy and self-disclosure among pairs of adolescent friends put their relationships in a different league. At first these close relationships are with friends of the same gender, but gradually heterosexual contact develops. By the second phase of adolescence, most teens are not only dating but also forming intimate relationships with members of the opposite sex. This is a marked change from the strict segregation by gender that occurred during the elementary-school years.

As relationships with peers change and mature, so do relations with parents. Early adolescence is often a period of new assertiveness on the youngster's part, which typically produces increased conflict with parents and distancing from them. This new assertiveness is in some ways analogous to the contrariness of toddlers as they try to establish themselves as separate people. Both the toddler's behavior and that of the young teen-ager seem to be an important part of individuation in our culture. Then, following each of these phases, there comes a period of realignment with parents. The 3-year-old become more cooperative and more self-confident; the older adolescent accepts the parents on a new level, and the relationships among them become more symmetrical. The parents are now advisers, counselors, and "sounding boards," more than controllers and disciplinarians. This new, more mature relationship is carried forward to young adulthood.

Three Teen-Agers, Four Themes

All the dramatic developmental changes mentioned above are apparent in our three teenagers: Malcolm, Mike, and Meryl. Each shows advances in thinking and self-reflection. This can be seen in Meryl's discussions of her relationship with Amy and in her concerns for migrant workers, in Mike's new concern about the environment, especially the marine environment, and in Malcolm's growing political idealism and thoughts about social justice. At the same time, each shows a new self-assertiveness with parents, especially during early adolescence. Meryl tells her parents that they just don't understand, that "things are different now." Mike insists that his mother stop calling him Mikey, a name that to him is embarrassingly babyish. And Malcolm flatly refuses to go on the church retreat, no matter how hard his parents and grandmother try to persuade him. The peer relations of these young people also show the typical adolescent changes, although Mike seems to be getting involved in dating more slowly than the others. In basic ways these three youngsters are typical adolescents. But Malcolm, Mike, and Meryl also have distinctive personalities, arising from their different temperaments, life histories, and genders. Let's take a closer look at each of them to see how they are typical, yet at the same time distinct. In doing so we return to one of the themes of this book—that of normative development versus individual differences. These three teenagers, in fact, offer an excellent way to summarize several major themes of this text.

Normative and Individual Development

Mike illustrates many of the characteristic features of adolescent development. His desire for privacy early in adolescence, his broadening interest in the world, and the great pride he takes in his first summer job are all common among teen-agers. Academic problems early in adolescence, like those Mike experienced, are also fairly frequent, although his were probably compounded by his parents' divorce and his father's remarriage. Mike, however, pulls himself through these difficult years. His solid early care, the continued involvement of his parents, and the special interest of his uncle and that of a gifted teacher all help him to turn out fine. You can think of these factors as reinforcing one another. The biology teacher is able to ignite a spark because Mike already has a positive image of his own intellectual abilities, an image fostered by years of being told by his family that he is smart and capable. The biology teacher is partly reacting to positive characteristics he sees in Mike, characteristics that Mike's parents helped encourage by their love and interest in him.

Malcolm's movement toward independence and his growing concern for questions about right and wrong are also fairly typical of his age group. But Malcolm clearly places his own distinctive stamp on how he handles these changes of adolescence. His flamboyant nature and boundless enthusiasm are fully predictable from his history. We would have a hard time believing that Malcolm would ever become a socially isolated, hesitant, pessimistic teenager. For him, life is full speed ahead—getting a job, dating, spending time with friends, becoming involved in political activities. Asserting himself and embracing the future seem to pose little problem. Malcolm still retains the tendency toward impulsiveness he showed throughout childhood. But because he cares about himself and others, this impulsiveness will probably not get out of hand. He may make mistakes, as he has in the past, but we can expect that he will learn from them and work to make things right.

Meryl, too, has become a fine young person. To be sure, she still has vestiges of shyness and hesitancy in new situations. When her body first started maturing, she felt awkward and self-conscious. Even in later adolescence she steers away from certain kinds of self-exposure, such as joining the debating team. Still, she handles relationships with peers well, both with other girls and with boys. Her relationship with Amy beautifully illustrates the loyalty, commitment, and self-disclosure typical of adolescent friendships. When allowed to select extra-curricular activities of special interest to her (doing art work, being set director for the senior-class play), she shows much persistence and competence. She is growing in self-confidence day by day. She also has a plan for her future and looks forward to college. It is particularly noteworthy that Meryl broke a two generation cycle by not becoming pregnant as a teen-ager. We see the contributions of grandmother, mother, and daughter to this accomplishment: Mrs. Polonius for facing her own guilt and building a strong relationship with Karen, Karen for building a close and open relationship with Meryl, and Meryl for carving out her own identity, developing good relations with peers, and making wise choices.

Our three teen-agers, then, have much in common by virtue of the fact that they are facing similar issues. All reflect the general or normative trends in adolescent development. Yet each has a different style of tackling developmental tasks. For instance, they all assert their independence from their parents, but in distinctive ways. Mike does it with a "PRIVATE" sign on his bedroom door, Malcolm by loudly announcing his plans and opinions, and Meryl by informing her mother that they are *not* the same people, even though she stays close to Karen through frequent conversations. Thus, both general trends and individual adaptations characterize development.

The Interaction of Experience and Cognitive Change

Another theme we have mentioned throughout this book and which appears again in the stories of our three adolescents is the idea that a person's experiences and cognitive advances are mutually influencing. For instance, Malcolm's ability to coordinate multiple perspectives, to think in terms of abstract concepts, such as fairness and justice, and to contemplate the future and his place within it allow him to participate in political events in a new way. At the same time, participation in the political process will stimulate Malcolm's cognitive development, encouraging him to think more deeply about social issues. This give and take between the social and cognitive realms of development can be seen over and over. A person's social relationships and other life experiences both influence and are influenced by cognitive advances.

Continuity and Discontinuity

A third theme of this book concerns continuity and discontinuity. Are our three teen-agers the same people they were in early childhood? Were their developmental outcomes inevitable, or could they have become quite different given other circumstances? Complex issues are involved in answering these questions. We constructed each of our three adolescents to show some degree of continuity, but Meryl and Mike especially show discontinuity as well. Meryl has done better than we might have predicted early in her life, and Mike has had more problems. How can we reconcile these two seemingly contradictory aspects of development?

We can reconcile them by saying that some degree of discontinuity is very likely when life circumstances change, but even if a large number of reversals occur we can still see threads from the past in virtually any child. For instance, the hesitancy Meryl showed in early childhood can still be glimpsed, even though she has learned to cope well with her initial shyness in new situations. We can easily picture Malcolm standing to make a speech at his first political meeting, but this is something we cannot imagine Meryl doing. For Mike, too, the past has never been completely discarded, not even during his most difficult developmental periods. His fundamental belief in himself as a competent, valuable person, a belief forged in infancy and early childhood, has served him well in disruptive and challenging situations. Thus, Meryl and Mike's early life experiences have remained with them, transformed to be sure by later experiences, but never completely erased.

Malcolm, as we said, shows less discontinuity than Meryl and Mike. But his more steady development should not be viewed as somehow inevitable. Throughout his life Malcolm has experienced notable continuity in care. There was no divorce, no new father, no other major stress; hence his development has made continuous progress.

But even with the obvious continuity in Malcolm's development, we *cannot* say he is the "same" person he was years ago. Every individual is continually evolving, based on an interaction of his or her biology and experiences. Malcolm is no exception. If we started Malcolm's life over in the same family, he would probably not turn out exactly as he is today. Every life has twists and turns, and complex multiple influences. We would expect that if Malcolm started over in the same family he would still end up exuberant and self-confident. These characteristics can be expressed in many different ways, however. Recall the model of branching developmental pathways we talked about in Chapter 2, a model that looks much like a tree lying on its side. A proliferation of smaller branches lies at the end of each major branch. Even essentially the same pathway can lead to a diversity of possible outcomes.

The Contexts of Development

A final theme of this book has been the importance of developmental contexts in shaping how children's lives unfold. One critical context is the family, which time and again has affected the fates of our three children. Without Joe's coming along and marrying Karen, without Christine and Frank's conflict and eventual divorce, and without ongoing social support in Malcolm's household, adolescence would have been quite different for these three young people.

Broader contexts beyond the family also exert powerful influences during adolescence. Relationships with peers, teachers, and others take on new significance as teen-agers come to better understand themselves and establish their places in the world. Societal, cultural, and economic contexts continue to be important too. For instance, Meryl's artistic expression is influenced in part by cultural ideas about "appropriate" areas of achievement for females. Similarly, Mike's interest in marine biology is influenced by current ecological concerns in American society, and Malcolm's interest in minority politics is in part a product of the economic and social realities of his community.

The difference between the broader social context in which Malcolm is developing, and the broader social contexts of Meryl and Mike, can be seen in one of the arguments Malcolm gives in favor of a part-time job. Of our three teenagers, only he would mention avoidance of gang involvement as a reason for working after school.

Beyond these direct influences of context, there are indirect influences as well. Contextual factors often influence children through their impact on parents. The beneficial counseling experiences we described for Karen ultimately would be seen to benefit Meryl. Frank Gordon's employment problems were viewed as contributing to his drinking and lowered self-esteem, to the marital tension between him and Christine, and indirectly to Mike's experience. Finally, at the broadest level, Christine's assertiveness concerning a career outside the home would have been unlikely 100 years ago. Such changing cultural patterns not only have a dramatic influence on mothers' and marital relationships but on children as well, because of both changing role models and changes in parent-child interaction.

Moving Toward Adulthood

All three of our adolescents are reasonably well-adjusted. Because the contexts of their lives have been sufficiently supportive, they have managed to handle developmental issues favorably. Each is now on the threshold of young adulthood. All have the aptitude, the means, and the motivation for higher education, and a college degree will serve them well as they make their way in today's complex world. We can be optimistic that they will face no more than the normal struggles in coping with future challenges. None is seriously disturbed, and serious psychiatric problems do not seem likely in their futures. Could it have been otherwise if life had gone differently for them? We turn to this question in our final chapter.

Part Seven

Psychopathology and Individual Lives

16

Developmental Psychopathology

The three children we have been following—Mike, Malcolm, and Meryl—represent basically healthy patterns of development. To be sure, we have portrayed each as facing difficulties, having problems, and showing vulnerabilities, as all of us do. Mike has a tendency to feel more responsibility than is sometimes appropriate, especially when things go wrong in important relationships. Malcolm at times can be impulsive and others do not always appreciate his exuberant style. He also faces the issue of being male in a tough, urban environment. Meryl is still somewhat shy and hesitant, and she has special difficulty adapting to new situations. Friends sometimes view her as unduly sensitive and lacking in self-confidence. Still, all three, now in late adolescence, are purposeful and well-directed in their goals, successful in dealing with other people, and sufficiently competent at managing their own lives.

But what if they had received poorer quality nurturance and less guidance from their families? Would it have made sense then to have

Mike be a candidate for adolescent depression? Would this have set the stage for Malcolm becoming a problem child, labeled "hyperactive" or suffering from an "attention deficit disorder"? Would the expected outcome for Meryl have been a severe anxiety disorder or some psychosomatic problem?

While it is difficult to answer such hypothetical questions, studies of people who have developed emotional problems indicate that teen-agers like Mike, Malcolm, and Meryl might have turned out differently in less supportive circumstances. Such studies suggest that the people who succumb to emotional problems often are not different in qualitative ways from others. Instead, what they have in common are life histories that are more demanding in critical ways, histories that provided poor support for important aspects of development.

It is also interesting to ask whether other youngsters, provided with the same experiences as our three children, would have nevertheless developed emotional or behavioral problems. This question emphasizes a child's genetic or biological vulnerability. For instance, perhaps a child with a biological predisposition to depression would have suffered depression during adolescence if confronted with the same life history as Mike Gordon. Most researchers who study emotional and behavioral problems believe that such genetic factors always interact with environment. Thus, where a person falls on the continuum from emotionally healthy to unhealthy is seen as a product of heredity and experience.

The study of developmental challenges and vulnerabilities, of contrasting patterns of psychological adaptation over time, belongs to a special subfield of developmental psychology called **developmental psychopathology.** (The term *pathology* refers to any marked deviation from a normal, healthy state.) Developmental psychopathology includes the study of disturbed children, the developmental roots of adult disorders, the patterns those disorders follow, and even the reasons why some people turn out to be emotionally healthy despite profiles predictive of psychological problems (Cicchetti, 1984; Sroufe and Rutter, 1984). Researchers in this field are particularly interested in locating causes. Believing there is a logic and predictability to human behavior, they search for factors that contribute to behavioral and emotional problems, as well as those that aid people in coping with and recovering from disorders. They hope that their findings will enable others to help sufferers, to bring about cures in some cases, and to take steps toward prevention.

In this chapter we will explore some basic concepts and findings in the emerging field of developmental psychopathology. As we describe major childhood disorders, we will be emphasizing a developmental viewpoint.

MODELS OF PSYCHOPATHOLOGY

A model is a framework for explaining why things happen. It is a set of ideas and assumptions about the causes—the **etiology**—of some event or condition. Researchers have proposed a number of models for understanding psychopathology (Lazare, 1973; Zubin, 1972). Some focus mainly on the biological underpinnings of emotional and behavioral problems, while others focus mainly on environmental factors. As you know, these two approaches are not incompatible. Most researchers believe that psychological disorders often involve a complex interplay of biology and environment. The various models of psychopathology differ in where the stress is placed, in which factors are considered the primary determinants of a disorder and which secondary. Thus we classify models of psychopathology according to whether they stress biological or environmental causes (see Figure 16.1).

Biological Perspectives

THE TRADITIONAL MEDICAL MODEL

The traditional medical model draws a clear-cut analogy between psychological disorders and physical diseases. It holds that psychological disorders should be considered "mental illnesses," to be diagnosed by doctors in an effort to effect a cure. According to this model, some structural or physiological malfunction of the body, typically affecting the brain, gives rise to a set of emotional or behavioral symptoms. The medical model assumes that whenever a psychological disturbance arises it has an underlying biological cause, even though that cause may not yet have been identified.

Certain mental disorders do indeed fit the medical model. For instance, *general paresis*, an irreversible deterioration of all mental and physical processes, has been traced to an attack on the body's organs by the bacteria that cause syphilis. Similarly, *Huntington's chorea*, which is a severe mental and physical disorder, is known to stem from a defective gene passed on from parent to child. Early childhood *autism*, another severe condition, in which the youngster shows almost no responsiveness to other people, also appears to be the result of biological abnormality. However, for most of the behavioral and emotional problems that children suffer, as well as for many serious adult disorders such as depression and schizophrenia, biological factors are better viewed as contributors rather than sole causes.

To say without evidence that Meryl's early irritability was due to an inborn "difficult temperament" or that Malcolm's high activity level was caused by "minimal brain dysfunction" would not enhance our understanding of either child. Moreover, such assumptions might cause us to overlook environmental factors that were having important impacts on these youngsters' lives. Assuming that there *must* be a biological cause whenever a child shows a psychological problem is totally unwarranted. Yet the medical model has been so influential that this often happens.

MODERN NEUROLOGICAL AND PHYSIOLOGICAL MODELS

An explosion of knowledge in the neurosciences has given rise to complex theories about how malfunctions of the brain and nervous system contribute to psychological disorders. Rather than blaming structural brain damage for such conditions as hyperactivity and depression, scientists now suggest that chemical imbalances in the brain are the cause. These imbalances involve either neurotransmitters (chemicals that govern

Models of Psychopathology

Biological Perspectives
Traditional Medical Models
Neurological Models
Physiological Models
Genetic Models

Environmental Perspectives
Behavioral Models
Psychodynamic Models
Family Models

Figure 16.1
Classification of Models
The models used by researchers studying the development of psychopathology are divided into two categories, depending on the kind of primary cause they focus on: biological or environmental.

the transfer of signals from one nerve cell to another) or other chemicals that control the activities of neurotransmitters (Iverson, 1980; Mendels and Frazer, 1974; Wender and Klein, 1986). The findings surrounding these theories are sometimes quite persuasive. For example, we know that certain drugs used to alleviate depression have the effect of raising the level of particular neurotransmitters in the brain. Could not depression, therefore, be due in part to a deficiency of these neurotransmitters?

Such hypotheses turn out to be very difficult to test because we cannot yet directly measure the chemical workings of the brain. However, there is some evidence for a genetic contribution to one form of adult depression, and perhaps the genes involved affect neurotransmitter levels (Gershon et al., 1983). But to date there is no consistent evidence linking any childhood disorder to a specific neurotransmitter imbalance. And even if such a link is found, cause and effect would not be established (Connors, 1977). Could not depression, for example, cause a change in brain chemistry just as plausibly as the other way around?

GENETIC MODELS

Genetic models of psychopathology are closely related to neurological and physiological models. Researchers who take a genetic perspective assume that some people inherit the predisposition to develop emotional and behavioral problems. Of course, the genes we inherit express themselves through activities within the cells of our bodies, which is why genetic models can be thought of as a subclass of neurological and physiological ones.

Like neurological and physiological models, genetic models have become quite sophisticated. Virtually no behavior geneticist believes, for instance, that there is a gene directly causing schizophrenia (Gottesman, 1979). A theory of a single defective gene could not account for the distribution of schizophrenia found in human families. If one dominant gene caused this disorder, the children of two schizophrenic parents would inherit the condition at least 75 percent of the time; if one recessive gene was the root of the problem, we would *always* find schizophrenia in youngsters who have two schizophrenic parents. The actual statistics concerning the offspring of schizophrenic couples are very different: When both the mother and father have the disorder, only 25 to 35 percent of their children develop it, and one must consider strong environmental influences even in these cases (Kringlen, 1978). Virtually all geneticists believe that the inherited component of schizophrenia must be polygenic—that is, it must arise from many genes acting together.

How do scientists know that there is *any* genetic component involved in schizophrenia? Couldn't the greater incidence of schizophrenia in children born and raised by schizophrenic parents be caused as easily by environment as by biological make-up? To get around this problem, researchers often study children born of schizophrenic mothers but raised in adoptive, nonschizophrenic families. Such studies show that these adopted children have a greater chance of developing schizophrenia than do children born to mothers who do not have the disorder (Kety et al., 1978). Of course, it could be that these two groups of children experienced different intrauterine environments. Perhaps the schizophrenic mothers were more anxious during their pregnancies and received poorer nutrition. Also, these mothers more often give up the infant for adoption when it is not healthy, when the course of pregnancy was difficult, and when they were more economically and socially disadvantaged (Sameroff and Zax, in press). This might partly account for their children's higher susceptibility to schizophrenia. However, the preponderance of evidence from twin studies, adoption studies, and other genetic research makes a good case for a hereditary factor in at least some schizophrenia.

There is also evidence for a substantial contribution of environment to schizophrenia. Even identical twins, with their identical genetic make-ups, are only 20 to 60 percent *concordant* (or matched) for schizophrenia, depending upon the study (Gottesman and Shields, 1972). This means that when one twin develops the disorder there exists a good chance that the other twin will *not* (Achenbach, 1982).

An interactionist view of the contributions made by both heredity and environment is found in the **diathesis/stress model** of schizophrenia (see Figure 16.2). It holds that everyone has some degree of biological vulnerability to this disorder (diathesis), as well as a number of difficult life experiences (stress). For people with a high biological predisposition, relatively little stress is enough to cause the disorder to develop. Conversely, people with a low biological predisposition would need a great deal of cumulative stress in order to succumb. According to this view, the likelihood of any individual developing schizophrenia is not fixed at birth. Instead, it depends on whether that person exceeds the amount of stress he or she can tolerate. This idea is similar to the concept of a reaction range, which we introduced in Chapter 12 when discussing intelligence. One does not inherit a specific IQ, but rather a range of intellectual potential. Likewise, one does not inherit a specific probability of developing schizophrenia, but rather a range of probabilities, with the outcome depending on environment. Clearly, environmental factors are of great importance, even in genetic models of psychopathology.

The Amish Gene. Early in 1987, a flurry of media attention was focused on the discovery of "the gene for depression," a particular gene found to be defective in each of 14 depressed Amish people in Lancaster County, Pennsylvania. However, the importance of this finding is not that it proves that all, or even most, cases of depressive disorder are caused by a genetic anomaly. In fact, it provides no such proof. Two other studies in the same issue of *Nature* failed to detect this defect in other samples of depressed

Figure 16.2
The Diathesis/Stress Model
Individuals vary both in the extent of their biological vulnerability and the degree of stress or challenge they face. According to the diathesis/stress model, one may develop a disorder (be above the curve) either by having a high vulnerability and experiencing moderate stress or by having low vulnerability and experiencing a great deal of stress.
Source: From Zubin and Spring, 1977.

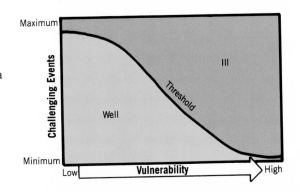

people (e.g., Hodgkinson et al., 1987). Nor does it prove that a genetic anomaly is a *sufficient* cause for the disorder. People could have this anomaly and because of other factors still not develop the disorder. Both environmental factors and other genes likely would modify the expression of this gene, as is generally the case. Rather, the importance of this discovery is that it provides a clue that may be useful for understanding the course and nature of this disorder. Psychopathologists speak of a *final common pathway*—that is, even where there are multiple causes that may be influential in varying combinations, in the end they lead to common difficulties. Locating individuals who are at different points along this pathway, especially at early points, is critical for understanding the course of the disorder. The importance, then, of locating the so-called Amish gene is that it gives researchers one access to the final common pathway and perhaps to following a sizeable group of subjects likely to enter this pathway.

Environmental Perspectives

SOCIOLOGICAL MODELS

Sociological models of psychopathology stress the social context surrounding disturbed individuals. Suppose a researcher who adopts this framework is interested in the causes of depression. He or she would look to the victims' social situations. Have they lost a loved one recently? Are they new in a community? Are they cut off from important sources of social support? Assistance might take the form of helping depressed people become more involved with others (Lazare, 1973).

Many other kinds of emotional and behavioral problems have been approached from a sociological viewpoint. For instance, critics of our educational system have argued that the sedentary and regimented environment of most schools inhibits the normal development of many children, perhaps especially of boys (Holt, 1964; Kohl, 1967). When a child has a problem in the school context, according to these critics, we should look to the nature of the school situation, or to the particular classroom. Notice how this view contrasts sharply with that of the biological perspective. Proponents of neurological and physiological models would look for some kind of brain dysfunction in a child who is persistently disruptive at school, assuming that the child has a physical deficit giving rise to hyperactivity. From the sociological perspective, in contrast, that youngster is presumed to be suffering from a poorly conceived learning situation. Which view is right is, of course, a matter of debate and perhaps depends on the particular child.

BEHAVIORAL MODELS

Behavioral models also focus on environmental factors. Here, however, the emphasis is specifically on the rewards, punishments, and modeled behaviors available to the child (Bandura, 1977a). Suppose a boy is hyperactive and disruptive in the classroom. Those who adopt a behavioral model would not emphasize neurological problems or concern themselves with the general nature of the school regime. Instead, they would

The behavioral model focuses on changing the child's expressed behavior, regardless of whether the child is seriously disturbed or just misbehaving. *(Mimi Forsyth/Monkmeyer Press.)*

look to see how people in the immediate environment (teachers, classmates) are responding to the boy's behavior.

It would be assumed that the hyperactive and disruptive responses persist because they are being reinforced by the outcomes they produce. For example, the boy is probably getting attention whenever he "acts up," and even negative attention can be rewarding to some children. The recommended treatment would involve changing environmental contingencies—that is, changing the connections between the child's behaviors and their consequences. The environment must be restructured so that the boy is rewarded for appropriate responses, not for disruptive ones.

This form of treatment has been found to be quite effective. When hyperactive youngsters are rewarded for staying in their chairs, paying attention, and working on assignments, their behavior within that setting improves dramatically (O'Leary and O'Leary, 1977). Usually the rewards involved in such efforts are points or tokens that the child can later exchange for desirable items such as candy. This procedure can even be applied successfully to an entire special classroom of disruptive children. Likewise, training parents to be consistent and firm in discipline leads to significant reductions in aggressive behavior (Patterson and Dishion, in press).

The earliest behavioral models assumed that the symptoms *are* the disorder. In other words, when a child is hyperactive and disruptive in the classroom, those negative behaviors themselves are the problem. There is no need to dig any deeper in a search for "hidden" causes within the child. According to this classic behavioral view, all the factors maintaining unwanted behavior are plainly visible in the environment, as long as we take the time to observe contingencies carefully.

More recently, however, this classic perspective has been altered to take into account internal cognitive processes, including a person's expectations, beliefs, and ways of viewing the world (Mischel, 1973). This responded to the difficulty in getting the results of behavioral therapy to carry over, or **generalize,** to settings other than the one in which treatment took place. For instance, a hyperactive boy who was rewarded for appropriate behavior in the classroom might remain disruptive in the cafeteria or on the playground. **Cognitive behavioral therapists** would try to teach such a youngster some basic cognitive skills to help him or her behave appropriately in a variety of situations (Kendall, 1981; Meichenbaum, 1977). For example, the child might be taught things he could routinely say to himself in order to encourage deliberation before acting.

PSYCHODYNAMIC MODELS

Psychodynamic models have evolved over the years from Sigmund Freud's psychoanalytic theory. Like medical models they assume that disturbed behavior is often the manifestation of underlying causes. Those causes, however, are not thought to be physical in nature. Instead, the underlying causes are mental thoughts and feelings—fears, anxieties, conflicts, irrational beliefs and outlooks—produced by life experiences. This is why those who adopt a psychodynamic perspective believe that it is not enough simply to treat the behavioral symptoms of a problem. In their view if you treated a hyperactive boy only by rewarding him for acceptable behavior, you would be ignoring the core of his problem. You would be leaving untouched the fear of abandonment, tension between parents, or other underlying factors that are producing the child's negative actions. Thus, psychodynamic therapists might address the youngster's anxieties in individual treatment sessions, or they might broach the problem of parental conflict in sessions with the family. Advocates of this approach make a clear distinction between primary and secondary causes. A child may be disruptive in the classroom because of the attention this gets him (secondary cause), but he may be seeking the attention because of conflict in the home (primary cause).

To understand further how psychodynamic models compare with other models, consider a woman who is deeply depressed after her husband dies (Lazare, 1973). Within a medical model, psychologists would be concerned with diagnosis, presence of depression among genetic relatives, previous episodes, and the person's response to medication or electric shock therapy. Within a sociological model, the focus would be support systems, current living arrangements, and so forth. Behavior therapists might conclude that the woman has lost a major source of positive reinforcement now that her husband is gone. Consequently, they might help her to seek other sources of reward and satisfaction and would encourage others she knows not to support her complaints of helplessness. Psychodynamic therapists, in contrast, would probe for deeper solutions. What was the nature of this woman's relationship with her husband? Did it mirror any earlier relationships, such as the one she had with her father, who had died when she was a teen-ager? Was the woman ambivalent about her father? Did she adequately mourn this earlier loss? If not, might she somehow feel responsible for the death of her father and now her husband because of the link between her father and him? Is she unable to express her anger toward the husband for "leaving her"? There is some support for this viewpoint of depression (Bowlby, 1980; Brown, Harris, and Bifulco, 1985). We will discuss the relevance of psychodynamic models to other disorders in later sections of this chapter.

FAMILY MODELS

Family models take yet another perspective in the effort to search the environment for the causes of psychopathology. This view holds that, while one person in a family is usually identified as the member who is "disturbed," in fact that person's symptoms are a reflection of disturbance in the larger family system. It is the system, not the individual, that is disturbed (Minuchin, 1974; Sroufe and Fleeson, in press; Watzlawick and Weakland, 1977). In one family, for example, the hyperactive son was labeled "the problem," but a look at the entire family revealed that the real problem was much broader (Andolphi et al., 1983). The husband and wife were estranged, and the husband devoted all of his energies to caring for his dependent parents. He felt burdened by the further responsibility of a wife and three children and was totally unable to express his own needs for care. The wife, who felt neglected and uncared for, got what little satisfaction she could from the antics of her so-called hyperactive 6-year-old. The two other children were models of deportment, mature beyond their years. Clearly, problems in this interconnected system can be seen by looking at *any* of the members. It might seem arbitrary that the son was labeled the problem, but this too served a family function. In its stress on finding the deeper meanings behind people's behaviors, the family perspective on psychopathology has something in common with psychodynamic models.

Findings from a recent longitudinal study illustrate the family systems viewpoint. Researchers identified a set of mothers who behaved seductively toward their young sons (Sroufe and Ward, 1980). These mothers were found to have had fathers who sexually or emotionally exploited them and mothers who were distant from or rejected their daughters. How would such women now behave toward *their* daughters? A family systems viewpoint, which expects patterns of relationships to be reproduced generation after generation, would predict that they would treat their daughters in a hostile, derisive manner. This prediction was confirmed (Sroufe et al., 1985). Thus, one relationship in the family predicts the quality of other relationships, with the network forming a coherent whole (Sroufe and Fleeson, in press).

Disturbed systems often are rooted in the "family of origin"—that is, the family in which the husband or wife grew up (Boszormenyi-Nagy and Spark, 1973; Minuchin, 1974). For instance, in families where father-daughter incest occurs, it is common for both the father and mother to have experienced abuse and incest when they were children, even though they may never have admitted their pasts to one another until the current incest is discovered. In addition to the present father-daughter incest, the

Family theorists focus on the entire family, including the husband's and wife's families of origin. (*George S. Zimbel/Monkmeyer Press.*)

mother may have a seductive or "special" relationship with a son. How two such adults find each other and re-create their own histories are topics of active interest to researchers (Sroufe and Fleeson, 1986; Sroufe et al., 1985). Such cases show the inadequacy of labeling one member of a family "the problem" and ignoring the rest of the family system.

A Developmental Perspective

In trying to understand the behavioral and emotional problems of children, we may draw upon any or all of the models just described. The developmental perspective does this by pulling together the numerous factors that have influenced a child's behavior (Eisenberg, 1977; Rutter, 1980). In the case of a child like Meryl, is hesitancy in new situations caused by her biological make-up? By our cultural stereotypes about "appropriate" female behavior? By her mother's inconsistency in reinforcing positive responses? Or is it due to insecurity stemming from ambivalent care during infancy? To early conflict between her mother and grandmother? To unrealistic expectations that Karen developed for Meryl?

The developmental perspective considers all these possibilities. It also explores how this basic style of behavior in Meryl adapts over time: As Karen worked out problems with her mother and developed a supportive relationship with Joe, she became more consistent in handling Meryl, and Meryl responded by growing more confident and capable. In a developmental perspective the features of a person's life are brought together.

Serious emotional problems can also be approached from a developmental perspective. Consider juvenile depression, for example. Developmental psychopathologists have identified a whole range of factors that seem to contribute to this disorder (Sroufe and Rutter, 1984). For instance, they have observed a marked rise in juvenile depression following puberty, which suggests that biological factors may be involved. At the same time, they have noted that more girls than boys are depressed during adolescence. Perhaps this is partly due to the fact that girls in our culture are socialized toward greater helplessness. The point is that the developmental perspective encourages a broad search for explanations.

In addition to disorders that arise in childhood, developmental psychopathologists are concerned with identifying patterns of childhood behavior that lead to disorders in later life. Even if a person is not seriously disturbed as a child, we want to know if that person is showing responses typically associated with some serious future problem.

Connections between childhood functioning and later disorder turn out to be quite complex. Some of the most dependable signs in childhood, for example, predict several different disorders. Poor peer relations are a good example. While not necessarily meaning that a child currently suffers from an emotional disturbance, they are an indication that a youngster has an increased chance of developing one of various adult disorders (Cowen, Zax, and Zax, 1973; Kohlberg et al., 1984; Roff et al., 1972). There are two probable reasons for this fact. First, poor peer relations in childhood represent a major adaptational failure with broad, far-reaching implications. Second, strong, supportive peer relationships in both childhood and adulthood undoubtedly provide a buffer against numerous life stresses that can promote emotional problems (Sroufe and Rutter, 1984).

Even childhood disorders are related to adult disorders in complex ways. Researcher Lee Robins (1966; 1978; 1979) obtained adult outcome data on many children who were seen at a clinic in St. Louis. She asked questions such as: What were adult schizophrenics like as children? What are aggressive children like when they grow up? What is the outcome for shy, withdrawn youngsters? Psychiatric problems in childhood were related to problems in adulthood. Thirty-four percent of the clinic cases had serious adult disorders, whereas only 8 percent of a control group from the same neighborhood did. Moreover, only 20 percent of the clinic cases were free of problems, compared with 57 percent of the controls.

More specific links between childhood and adult problems varied greatly depending on the particular disorders involved. Some links were strong. For example, among the clinic cases who in childhood were classified as "sociopaths" (behaving irresponsibly with no concern for others and no signs of remorse), 94 percent had been arrested by adulthood (17 percent of controls) and 70 percent had major adult problems such as alcoholism, imprisonment, and psychosis. Similarly, virtually all the diagnosed adult sociopaths had shown sociopathic behavior as children. Other childhood problems were not so strongly linked to adult disorders. For example, children who were anxious, shy, and withdrawn—so-called internalizing children (Achenbach, 1982)—were no more likely to have adult problems than control children. (Thus, we might be optimistic about a child like Meryl.) Finally, some links were strong but complex. For instance, adult schizophrenia, a disorder marked by severe withdrawal and social isolation, is not generally associated with the same symptoms in childhood. Instead, schizophrenics often show conduct disorders in childhood, behaviors such as overaggressiveness or antisocial tendencies. Depression in adulthood also has been found to be linked to conduct disorders in childhood (Zeitlin, 1982), again making it clear that conduct disorders are a serious sign of risk for later problems.

Other researchers have followed not children who already are disordered but children who are for some reason "at risk" for later disorder. A group of individuals is considered at risk when some factor they have in common makes it more likely that they will develop some disorder. Peer problems and conduct problems in childhood are risk factors. So too are poverty, unemployment, low parental education, overcrowded living, parental criminality, marital instability, psychiatric disorder, and social isolation. There also are specific risks for specific disorders—for example, for depression, a biological parent who was depressed or early death of a parent (Brown et al., 1985). When many risk factors exist together, risk may be quite high. When only one or two exist or when, despite multiple risks, a loving parent is present, risk is greatly reduced (Rutter, 1979b). One can see that at an early point Meryl might have fit a high risk categorization; yet in the end she is doing fine. Psychologists are quite interested in these "resilient" children, those at risk who do not develop disorder (Masten and Garmezy, 1985).

Much attention has been given to the longitudinal study of groups of children genetically at risk for schizophrenia. When one biological parent is schizophrenic, the probability of a child's developing schizophrenia is

6–10 percent, compared with about 1 percent in the general population. Researchers have compared the development of risk and non-risk groups, and within the risk group those who did and did not develop the disorder. Increases in both schizophrenia and antisocial behavior were found in risk samples, and within the risk group those later ill showed differences in physiological functioning in late childhood (Kety et al., 1978; Mednick, 1970). Investigators continue to actively pursue these leads, with special interest in factors that seem to protect vulnerable children (Erlenmeyer-Kimling, Cornblatt, and Golden, 1983; Watt et al., 1984).

Others have been concerned with family factors, either as mediators of genetic risk or as risk factors themselves. For instance, researchers have observed that families with a schizophrenic member often have trouble maintaining a shared focus of attention when they talk to each other (Singer et al., 1979). One person may broach a topic, and rather than responding to the remark, the listener simply talks about a different topic. Such failure to share a focus happens to everyone at times. But in many families of schizophrenics members routinely talk past one another, make irrelevant comments, and fail to respond directly. In an important risk project at UCLA, researchers assessed the degree of this **Communication Deviance,** as well as that of hostility, in families where an adolescent had been referred for treatment (Goldstein, 1985). These assessments predicted well which teen-agers later became schizophrenic.

Developmental psychopathologists are interested in the variety of signs, singly and in combination, that indicate risk for later disorder. At the same time, they are interested in factors that protect or buffer vulnerable children against disorder. In these are clues for intervention. In the same way, researchers are interested in the development of various childhood disorders, the topic we turn to now.

SOME CHILDHOOD DISORDERS

Space does not permit us to discuss all the emotional and behavioral disorders that can arise during childhood and adolescence. We have limited our coverage to just six of those most widely studied. These six vary both in the severity of their symptoms and in the likelihood that biological causes are involved. Autism, for example, is a highly disabling disorder that seems to have biological origins in the vast majority of cases. Anxiety disorders, in contrast, are less severe and appear to be caused more by situational stresses than by physical problems. Cause does not necessarily limit treatment, however. The behavioral manifestations of an organic disorder may respond to psychological treatment just as the physical manifestations of a psychological disorder may sometimes be helped by medications.

Early Childhood Autism

You are touring a locked ward of a state-run psychiatric hospital. On a couch across from you, an 8-year-old boy sits rhythmically rocking forward and back. Occasionally he starts to perform a strange, ritualistic flicking of his fingers in front of his face. All the while he seems oblivious of you. As you approach him, however, his rocking intensifies. When you sit on the couch a short distance from him, he hurriedly rises and goes to a corner of the room, where he again starts to rock and flick his fingers, this time furiously.

This child has received a diagnosis of **early childhood autism,** a rare disorder affecting only four children in 10,000 (DeMyer, Hingten, and Jackson, 1981). According to Leo Kanner (1943), who first identified this extreme disturbance, the core features of autism are (1) a powerful insistence on preserving sameness in the environment, (2) extreme social isolation or autistic aloneness, and (3) severe speech deficits. The first of these symptoms could account for the autistic child's strange, ritualistic behaviors, such as the repetitive body rocking and finger-flicking in the example above. These youngsters seem to need to maintain complete control over their environment. Any new stimulus intruding on their perceptions causes them great distress. Even a small change of routine that most people would hardly notice (putting a chair in a different place, offering milk in a different cup) can provoke a tantrum.

The second symptom, autistic aloneness, is equally extreme. Autistic children recoil from personal contact. As babies they do not cuddle when held by their parents. Nor do they babble, make eye contact, or engage in social smiling, imitation, or other forms of social play (Rutter, 1978). Their attachment relationships are grossly abnormal. Often they seem to form "attachments" to objects.

A third symptom of early childhood autism is severe speech deficits. These youngsters do not use language in spontaneous communication. Many are mute, and most of those who do speak are **echolalic**—that is, they lifelessly repeat a word or phrase they have heard, with no concern for its meaning (Wenar, 1982). Autistic children also have great trouble learning even simple abstract concepts, such as "larger than," even though they appear to have normal memories for routinized information, such as where particular toys are kept (Hermelin and O'Connor, 1970). At the same time, autistic youngsters seem to have difficulty modulating input from their senses (Schwartz and Johnson, 1981). As a result, they

Autistic children often seem lost in their own worlds. *(Mimi Forsyth/Monkmeyer Press.)*

have trouble making sense of their experiences and are easily over-whelmed by complex stimulation. This helps to explain why they find social interaction so difficult and try to avoid it. How confusing interacting with others must be for a child who can't even make sense out of simple stimuli.

What could account for such seriously disturbed behavior? Autistic children have physically normal appearance, and their memories seem normal too. Usually they do not have any obvious brain damage. Still, most researchers agree that some form of organic disorder must be involved. There are several reasons for this widespread conclusion. First, the behavior of these children is so atypical. Large-scale studies, including dozens of abused and neglected youngsters, are unlikely to turn up a single autistic child. Second, the siblings of autistic children are usually normal, and the parents are typically no different from other parents in fundamental ways. Third, the profound language and cognitive deficits of autistic youngsters often remain even following years of treatment. And fourth, autism is statistically related to certain biological problems such as rubella during pregnancy (see Chapter 4), and many autistic children do develop signs of brain pathology (seizures, for instance) as they get older (Chess, 1977; Knobloch and Pasamanick, 1975).

Despite all the signs that there must be some organic basis to autism, there is little agreement as to the specific nature of the problem (Wenar, 1982). Dozens of theories have been proposed with no resolution. Drugs have not proved effective in treating the disorder; structured, one-to-one therapy programs are more successful. Sometimes these can improve the child's functioning markedly, though certain autistic features tend to remain (Wing, 1976).

It is hard to be optimistic about the long-term adjustment of most autistic children. Among those who are totally unable to communicate with language and have IQ scores under 50, only a very small percentage can live outside of institutions by the time they reach adulthood (DeMyer et al., 1981). For those who have some language skills, the outlook is better: Given the necessary extensive therapy, approximately half of these attain marginally adequate adjustment (Lotter, 1974). But even among those who hold down jobs and function with relative independence, social behavior generally remains impaired. Few marry, for example (Wing, 1976).

Hyperactivity or Attention Deficit Disorder

> Brad was always in trouble. His neighbors were mad at him, both because he trampled their flowers as he ran home from school and because he poured milk down the pockets of their new pool table "just to see what would happen." Brad's teachers were also upset because he was constantly whistling and generally disrupting the classroom. Other children steered clear of Brad because he and trouble naturally went together. Brad's parents were at their wits' end. They had tried everything from bargaining to belts, but they couldn't make him "shape up."
>
> Yet Brad was a bright child with an IQ of 125. He was not malicious and he had a good sense of humor, along with an infectious grin. One day the

lifeguard pulled him off the bottom of the community pool. It turned out he wasn't drowning; he was just trying to pull out the plug because he thought it would be funny to see all those kids in the pool with no water!

Brad's problem has been given many labels over the last three decades: hyperkinetic impulse disorder, special learning and behavioral problem, minimal brain damage or minimal brain dysfunction, and **attention deficit disorder,** which is believed often to be accompanied by **hyperactivity** (now called **attention deficit/hyperactivity disorder**). We prefer the simple terms *hyperactive* and *attention problem*. The other, fancier titles imply more knowledge of cause than we have, and they frequently suggest an organic basis that is not at all established.

Hyperactive children are heterogeneous; they do not represent a single type (Paternite and Loney, 1980; Ross and Ross, 1982; Werry, 1968). Some are impulsive; others are not. Some are more easily distracted than others and have a harder time concentrating. All, however, seem to have attention-related difficulties (Douglas and Peters, 1980; Sroufe, 1975). Hyperactive children have trouble maintaining attention when given routine tasks (Sroufe et al., 1973). They appear careless and hurried. Their schoolwork is often sloppy, incomplete, or superficial. Many also seem restless and fidgety (Barkley and Cunningham, 1978). This restlessness prompts them to do things that get them in trouble, such as whistling in class. Most notably, they are usually on the move, "born without brakes" so to speak (Laufer and Denhoff, 1957). By definition the term hyperactivity is restricted to children of at least normal intelligence with no neurological handicaps. Unlike autism, hyperactivity is common. Estimates range as high as 10 percent for boys and 1 to 2 percent for girls. Hyperactivity is also more frequent in first-borns.

Parents can often help hyperactive children through a variety of special techniques, including teaching the child how to divide work into small manageable segments. (© *Suzanne Szasz/Photo Researchers, Inc.*)

CAUSES OF HYPERACTIVITY

Over the years organic theories of hyperactivity have predominated, yet all the evidence offered in support of a general biological cause is open to question. First, although brain damage does sometimes lead to hyperactivity, most brain-damaged people are not hyperactive and most hyperactive children show no clear signs of brain damage (Ross and Ross, 1982; Sroufe and Stewart, 1973; Werner and Smith, 1977). Second, although mothers of hyperactive children often report that the pregnancy or delivery was difficult and that the child has "always been like that," studies that follow youngsters from birth through childhood fail to substantiate these claims (Graham et al., 1962; Jacobvitz and Sroufe, in press; Werner and Smith, 1977). Third, when comparing hyperactive and nonhyperactive youngsters, researchers sometimes report differences in the brain's electrical activity or in levels of neurotransmitters (Ross and Ross, 1982; Wender, 1971). But the results from such studies are inconsistent; to date there is no biological marker that can reliably distinguish hyperactive children from their normal peers (Dubey, 1976; Ross and Ross, 1982; Sroufe, 1975). And even if such a marker is found, we will still not know cause from effect. An unusual brain-wave pattern, for instance, might be the *result* of a hyperactive state, not the cause. Finally, just because medication often reduces the symptoms of hyperactivity, this does not necessarily mean that we are dealing with an organic problem.

Tranquilizers, for example, can reduce symptoms of anxiety that are totally environmental in origin.

At this point organic theories are neither proven nor disproven. For a few hyperactive children biological factors may be a large part of the problem. For instance, some hyperactive children have minor physical anomalies, such as a large head circumference and low-set ears (Rapoport, Quinn, and Lamprecht, 1974). It could be that these children are also different in other ways—ways that contribute to hyperactivity. But most hyperactive children do not show such physical differences, and many children with such anomalies are not hyperactive. There is no justification for presuming that hyperactive children suffer from brain dysfunction just because they are distractible, fidgety, and inattentive.

An alternative approach to the causes of hyperactivity was reflected in a recent study (Jacobvitz and Sroufe, in press). The researchers looked at potential influences of parenting styles, specifically at parents who are intrusive, seductive, and/or overstimulating toward their youngsters. The investigators reasoned that if parents provoke and stimulate when their young children are in need of calming, the youngsters might later be unable to regulate their own arousal and so be prone to attention problems and hyperactivity. This hypothesis was borne out, with predictions being made from patterns of care as early as age 6 months. The researchers found little evidence that children who became hyperactive were innately different from others. The youngsters who developed the disorder had not been overactive or distractible as infants. While one study is certainly not enough to prove that hyperactivity is usually caused by parenting problems, such factors should receive increased attention in the future.

Whatever the origins of hyperactivity, this problem poses real challenges for parents. We can easily imagine a cycle in which the reactions of the parents and of the child feed each other, prompting the child to become more difficult and the parents more exasperated. Even if the parents do play a role in the onset of this disorder, they need support and assistance, not blame. Troubled children pose difficulties and these are no exceptions. For parents who want to know more about the subject, some thoughtful books are available (e.g., Steward and Olds, 1973).

TREATMENT AND PROGNOSIS

A common treatment for hyperactivity is use of a stimulant drug, most often Ritalin. It may strike you as strange that *stimulants* are given to hyperactive children. Why would we want to speed up their physiological processes? Some people have argued that this is a **paradoxical drug effect**—that the stimulants are actually slowing these children down instead of speeding them up. They suggest that hyperactive children need Ritalin to offset a biochemical deficiency in the brain. If there was no biochemical need for the drug, they reason, why would it have any positive effects? On the basis of this argument, hundreds of thousands of hyperactive children have been given stimulants.

A thorough review of the evidence, however, reveals that this argument has at least three flaws (Ross and Ross, 1982; Sroufe, 1975). First, there is nothing paradoxical about the effects of stimulants on hyperactive children. Such drugs do not slow these youngsters down. Instead, their activity levels increase in unconstrained situations, their heart rates and blood pressures rise, and their general energy levels are boosted. The drugs work because stimulants also enhance the abilities to concentrate, sustain attention, and persist at routine tasks. These are the same effects that stimulants have on normal children and adults (Peloquin and Klorman, 1986; Rapoport et al., 1978; Shetty, 1971; Sroufe, 1975). Second, just because stimulants can improve the performance of hyperactive children does not indicate a biochemical need for them. There are no dependable predictors as to which hyperactive children will respond best to Ritalin and similar drugs. Third, there is reason to doubt the long-term effectiveness of stimulants. Most studies that show favorable results are of short duration—4 to 6 weeks. Long-term studies show no lasting improvement for children taking these medications (Barkley and Cunningham, 1978). This is not surprising when you consider that the negative side effects of stimulants (sleeplessness, loss of appetite, irritability, crying without provocation) disappear within a few weeks. There is no reason to expect that any positive effects would last much longer. If a child's behavior worsens when Ritalin is withdrawn, this could merely be because dependency has developed, not because the drug is still working (Sroufe, 1975).

Behavioral therapies, which reinforce the child for appropriate behavior, offer one alternative to medication—an alternative that has been quite successful at reducing symptoms in particular settings, such as the classroom (O'Leary and O'Leary, 1977). Behavioral treatment with medication has been shown to be more effective than medication alone (Cantwell, 1987). You may also have heard that cutting down on sugar and food additives in the diet can be beneficial to hyperactive youngsters, but this view is without scientific support (Connors et al., 1976). There is some evidence that red dye in foods may contribute to hyperactivity in some children (Garfinkel, 1987). Other approaches to treatment, such as family therapy, have not been sufficiently evaluated.

It is only partly true that most hyperactive children grow out of this disorder. Recent studies show that many of them continue to have problems through adolescence, although the problems may take different forms (underachievement, immaturity, and antisocial behavior rather than hyperactivity per se). Such problems are no less common in adolescents who have been treated over the years with stimulant drugs (Barkley and Cunningham, 1978; Charles and Schain, 1981; Weiss and Hechtman, 1986). To us this raises more doubts about the wisdom of medication, although others might say it suggests a need to continue drug treatment throughout the teen-age years. Before this is done, however, it is critical to evaluate the long-term consequences stimulants have on the body. It is now known that the weight and growth suppression (about 1 inch) associated with stimulant drug treatment is due to influences on growth hormone (Garfinkel, 1987). Such a fact also raises concerns about sexual development in children treated during adolescence and about long-term health consequences for kidneys and the cardiovascular system. We must also consider the damaging psychological effects on youngsters who come to think they *need* a drug in order to function normally and control themselves. As one child put it: "I can't do it. I didn't have my human pill today."

Conduct Disorders

Mark is a bright, capable 11-year-old, but he also is a daredevil and a loner. A favorite activity is racing his motor bike through the woods. Younger boys are at times attracted to Mark's daring antics (such as sneaking into adult bookstores), but friendships between Mark and others are always short-lived. Mark was referred for treatment because for two years he had been ransacking and robbing houses. He is a "master of the sincere lie" and is viewed by professionals as unreachable. A routine of his, which ultimately got him caught, was to show up back at the scene of his latest robbery and offer to help put the house back in order. "His manner was one of sincere concern, and he asked for no favors in return." (adapted from Wenar, 1982, pp. 216–217)

In the system of classification accepted by the American Psychiatric Association and described in the revised third edition of the *Diagnostic and Statistical Manual* (called *DSM-III-R* for short), Mark's behavior would be diagnosed as a conduct disorder. A **conduct disorder** is defined as a persistent pattern of behavior in which the child repeatedly violates either the basic rights of others or age-appropriate social norms. Youngsters who engage in drug abuse and violent acts, as well as those who chronically lie, cheat, and show no regard for others, fall into this category. Juvenile delinquency, a legal concept, is also subsumed under this diagnosis. Children who engage in chronic truancy, vandalism, stealing, or who otherwise break the law, and those who repeatedly run away from home would all be classified as having a conduct disorder. Characteristics associated with this broad category are listed in Table 16.1. It is important to know whether children who display conduct disorders are actually conforming to the aberrant peer-group norms of an adolescent gang. The problems of these gang-socialized children may stem more from larger societal problems than they do from individual psychological disturbance.

Distinctions are often made among children with conduct disorders depending on whether they are aggressive or not and on whether they are able to form normal bonds of friendship and affection. For instance, we would view Mark's behavior with even more alarm if it included acts of deliberate interpersonal violence (such as setting fire to houses in which people were sleeping) or if his lack of concern for others extended to members of his own family. Such a child would be said to be displaying an aggressive, "undersocialized" type of conduct disorder. This pattern corresponds to the classic sociopath we described a little earlier. A sociopath seems to have no conscience and therefore no guilt over any act of disregard or aggression toward others, no matter how callous it may be (Hare, 1970).

Conduct disorder is one of the most frequent diagnoses given to children referred to mental-health centers, especially boys (Atkeson and Forehand, 1981). These problems are also among the most persistent (Robins, 1966, 1979; Rutter et al., 1976). Aggression and antisocial behavior are not only stable across the childhood years but also very strong predictors of similar problems in adulthood.

Some researchers have proposed biological theories about the origins

TABLE 16.1   Conduct Disorder Classification in *DSM-III-R*[1]

The essential feature of this disorder is a repetitive and persistent pattern of misconduct such as delinquent acts, destructiveness, or other violations of the rights of others beyond the ordinary mischief and pranks of children and adolescents. It includes three types:

Group type
Solitary aggressive type
Undifferentiated type

Group Type
Misconduct occurring mainly as a group activity with peers
Persistent pattern of actions that conflict with norms
Violation of important rules at home and school
Truancy, substance abuse, lying, vandalism
Stealing, but without confronting victim
Aggressive physical behavior possibly present

Solitary Aggressive Type
Aggressive physical behavior toward both adults and peers, initiated by the individual (not as a group activity)
Failure to form affectionate bonds with others
Absence of meaningful peer relations
Orientation toward immediate benefit
Manipulative and callous behavior; lack of concern for others
Absence of guilt

Undifferentiated Type
Mixture of clinical features that cannot be classified as either solitary aggressive type or group type

[1] Based on diagnostic criteria described in the *Diagnostic and Statistical Manual of Mental Disorders*, 3rd edition–revised, pages 53–60.

of conduct disorders. One that received a great deal of publicity was the idea that men with an extra Y (or male) chromosome are more likely to be aggressive and to commit crimes. This hypothesis arose from the curious finding that the double Y chromosome pattern was more prevalent among men in prisons than among men in the general population. Further study revealed a flaw in this reasoning, however. Investigation of a large number of men with this genetic pattern showed that, on average, they were no more aggressive or less socialized than other males (Witkin et al., 1976). But these men did have lower than average intelligence, which may have some relation to their increased likelihood of being imprisoned.

Although the extra Y chromosome theory of conduct disorders has been abandoned, some maintain that there still may be a genetic component to this problem. Evidence comes from the fact that identical twins, who share the same genetic make-up, are more likely to be concordant for conduct disorders than fraternal twins are (Garfinkel, in press). There is no agreement as to what physical traits might be inherited. One possibility has to do with how easily the brain and nervous system become aroused. According to this view, sociopaths have a high threshold of arousal and a high threshold of fear (Hare and Cox, 1978). Thus, the sociopath may engage in aggression and antisocial behavior simply to feel adequately stimulated.

Low intelligence is another partly inherited factor that might contribute to conduct disorders. If a child is not bright enough to grasp social norms or to understand the link between offenses and penalties, that youngster might be very cavalier about violating rules. Still other biological factors that could be involved in conduct disorders are inherited size, strength, and gender, all of which tend to influence how successful a person is at aggression. Finally, there is the idea that inherited differences in the levels of certain hormones might also encourage aggression.

But certainly these biological factors could not be the whole story explaining conduct disorders. If a child has a greater than normal need for aggression or stimulation, there are more socially acceptable outlets than conduct disorders. As the ultimate explanations for why a child becomes delinquent or shows no concern for others, environmental factors seem more plausible. A large number of studies have found a link between conduct disorders and parental marital discord, hostility, unavailability, rejection, or abuse of children (Caspi and Elder, in press; Hetherington and Martin, 1979; Patterson and Dishion, in press; Rutter, 1979). Mark's history, for instance, fits this pattern, in that his father was extremely cold and distant (Wenar, 1982). Of course, correlational studies cannot tell us for certain whether negative parenting patterns and family conflict *cause* the conduct disorders. However, the fact that these same findings consistently appear is very suggestive. Therapists working with hard-core offenders attest to their histories of early mistreatment, and large-scale interview studies further support this frequent relationship (Kruttschnitt, Heath, and Ward, 1986). Morever, Gerry Patterson's work shows that the link between child aggression and parental mistreatment is greater than the correlation between child aggression and parental general levels of aggresiveness (the expectation based on genetic cause).

The Minnesota Preschool Project has offered some insights into how the negative environmental factors in a child's family could trigger early manifestations of conduct disorders. While few of the preschoolers in this study had received psychiatric diagnoses, they had all been observed extensively over long periods of time. Some of the children persistently showed antisocial behavior and/or hostile aggression. Significantly, more of these youngsters had a history of anxious-avoidant attachment during infancy than did non-aggressive youngsters (Sroufe, 1983). Here is a case where a baby's having an emotionally rejecting parent predicts the emergence of conduct disorders years later (probably because it predicts ongoing inadequate care as well).

More such prospective studies are needed to clarify the causes of these serious developmental problems and to offer early avenues of intervention. Once conduct disorders have been allowed to progress to the point where the child is clearly disturbed, especially by the teen-age years, these problems are usually very hard to treat. Family, behavioral, cognitive-behavioral, and psychodynamic therapies have all been tried, but none has proved highly successful (e.g., Andolphi et al., 1983; Minuchin, 1974; Staats and Butterfield, 1965). The treatments with the best success records are usually very intensive, requiring that the youngster live for a substantial amount of time in a special therapeutic residence.

It is normal for young children to cling to parents in times of threat. But will this child continue to be so preoccupied with contact later? If so, this may be one sign of anxiety disorder. *(Index Stock International, Inc.)*

Anxiety Disorders

Donny was an impeccably dressed, well-mannered 8-year-old who tested in the gifted range on the Stanford-Binet IQ test. His behavior mimicked his dress. He avoided dirt and messiness of any kind. He would even turn down chocolate milk because it might spill on his tie; playing with finger paint was out of the question. The play he did engage in was excessively precise and orderly. He would lay out the buildings for an airport in exact alignment. He also had an array of irrational fears. He was frightened, for example, that spiders might come out of the toilet and bite him, even though he realized that this was impossible. Not surprisingly, Donny was overtly anxious. At times he talked rapidly with pursed lips; other times he wrung his hands. Yet he showed no evidence of thought disorder or loss of contact with reality. Despite his great anxiety, he was clearly not psychotic.

Janice also showed anxiety, although in different ways. She was always upset when her mother dropped her off at kindergarten. Much of the day she spent hovering near the teacher, hoping for attention. When the teacher tried to encourage her to play with the other children, she remained on the sidelines, never joining the activities. Her face constantly bore a worried expression and her eyes seemed perpetually filled with tears. She had chronic stomach aches, and when it came time for first grade, she refused to go to school at all.

According to the *DSM-III-R* classification system, both these children have **anxiety disorders.** Donny would be said to have an **overanxious disorder,** characterized by very general and pervasive worries and fears. Janice's problem, in contrast, would probably be labeled a **separation anxiety disorder**—excessive anxiety caused by separation from someone to whom the child is emotionally attached. One could easily imagine a child like Meryl showing either of these patterns had her life not stabilized in early childhood.

Anxiety disorders are less frequent than conduct disorders. School refusal like Janice's occurs in an estimated 1 percent of children, and some form of overanxious pattern affects some 2 to 3 percent of youngsters (Kennedy, 1965; Yule, 1981). Compared with conduct disorders, anxiety disorders are more likely to show **spontaneous remission**—that is, they are apt to recede without professional help. Finally, as you learned earlier in this chapter, these internalizing behaviors are generally not predictive of serious problems in adulthood (Robins, 1979).

What would prompt a child to be chronically worried and fearful the way Donny is, or overly anxious about leaving her mother as Janice is? Unfortunately, the causes of these problems have not been extensively studied, perhaps because they are considered less serious than other childhood disorders. Based on the evidence that we do have, there is no reason to believe that anxiety disorders in children are caused largely by biological factors (Knopf, 1984). Instead, factors in the family environment seem to be the principal cause. For example, nonnurturant fathers and anxiously overinvolved mothers have been linked to anxiety disorders in boys (Hetherington and Martin, 1979). Somehow these children seemed to have formed an *inner working model,* or view, of the world as unpredictable or threatening and of themselves as impotent, unable to influence events. The most frequent fear of the school-refusing child is that harm will befall the mother while the child is away (Wenar, 1982). Such children have apparently learned to be worried about the care giver's continued availability. These concerns might derive from anxious patterns of attachment.

Anxiety disorders are generally quite responsive to treatment, using a variety of approaches. In one study, both behavioral and psychodynamic therapies were found to be equally successful and, with children ages 6 to 10, more successful than simply waiting for the problem to go away by itself (Miller et al., 1972). All effective treatments of school refusal involve getting the youngsters back into their classroom as soon as possible if they have been allowed temporarily to remain at home. Focusing on the parents' anxiety also seems useful in such cases, for this seems to be a key to the problem.

Anorexia Nervosa

> When Alma came in for consultation, she looked like a walking skeleton, scantily dressed in shorts and halter, with her legs sticking out like broomsticks, every rib showing, and her shoulder blades standing up like little wings . . . . Alma's arms and legs were covered with soft hair, her complexion had a yellowish tint, and her dry hair hung down in strings. Most striking was the face—hollow like that of a shriveled-up old woman with a wasting disease . . . . Alma insisted that she looked fine and there was nothing wrong with her being so skinny. (Bruch, 1979, pp. 2–3)

Alma suffers from a condition called **anorexia nervosa,** a serious eating disorder characterized by extreme reduction in food intake and loss of at least 25 percent of original body weight. There is no physical illness to account for this dramatic weight loss. Anorectics deliberately starve themselves to thinness. This intentional weight loss is accompanied by a highly distorted body image. No matter how emaciated they become, anorectics are convinced that they are still overweight and need to continue drastically restricting their diets. They also have an intense fear of being fat, which does not decrease as weight loss progresses. Reassurances, admonitions, even threats from concerned friends or relatives in no way weaken their resolve. Anorectics firmly and flatly *refuse* to maintain normal weight. Many eat almost nothing and exercise excessively. Others occasionally go on eating binges, but then induce vomiting to keep their weight down—a practice known as **bulimia.** This self-abuse can produce very serious side effects, including physical ailments and in some cases death (AMA, 1980; Bemis, 1978; Sours, 1969).

Many researchers feel that our culture's preoccupation with thinness is a factor contributing to the increase of anorexia nervosa. (*Jay Nadelson/The Stock Market.*)

Anorexia nervosa is primarily a disorder of adolescent girls and young adult women. It is much more common in the middle class than in the lower economic strata. These girls are often bright, academically successful, and viewed as perfect children—neatly dressed, well-mannered, and compliant (Wenar, 1982). In fact, a perfectionist tendency is one clue to the cause of this disorder. Another clue lies in some of the side effects that anorexia produces: It both drastically curtails development of the adult female figure and often causes cessation of the menstrual cycle.

Why would an intelligent, academically successful, economically well-off girl deliberately starve herself? Biological theories have included the possibility of a dysfunctional hypothalamus (the brain region that regulates hunger and affects the production of hormones throughout the body). There is little evidence to support such theories, however. Although anorectics often suffer abnormal hormone secretions (which is why their menstrual cycles cease), these abnormalities seem to be more effect than cause. This is suggested by the fact that prisoners of war who are starved for long periods show many of the same symptoms. Moreover, if an anorectic is finally persuaded to gain appropriate weight, her hormone and menstrual functioning will return to normal (Crisp, 1970; Sherman, Halmi, and Zamedia, 1975). Also arguing against biological causes of this disorder is the lack of evidence that anorexia can be transmitted through heredity (Halmi and Brodland, 1973).

More promising are psychological theories of anorexia nervosa, especially ones that focus on the family. The families of these young women are repeatedly described as overinvolved or overentangled (Minuchin, Rosman, and Baker, 1978). The parents expect the child to be perfect. Questioning the system or expressing anger are not permitted. The parents demand absolute compliance in return for nurturance, and they repeatedly suggest that the child could be "just a little bit better." The youngster comes to feel that her life, her self, even her body are not her own (Bruch, 1973). "The child is living out a parental image of proper behavior which permeates every facet of her life—her physical appearance, . . . the food she eats, the clothes she wears, her friends, her activities" (Wenar, 1982, p. 178). In short, the child has been exquisitely overcontrolled and is left without a sense of autonomy. Since she has been made to feel that she has been given love in return for her loyalty, any rebellion on her part produces guilt and shame. Finally, with the crisis of adolescence, she manages to "confront" her parents indirectly by asserting control over how much she eats. This confrontation, however, is a pitiful caricature of autonomy. "It is control without self-confidence, nagging doubts leading to increasingly restricted food intake in pursuit of an unattainable ideal of thinness" (Wenar, 1982, p. 80). She does, of course, gain some control over her parents by causing them to worry and feel helpless to change her. But for this small, sad victory she pays an enormous price.

You may wonder why it is food on which the adolescent girl focuses in trying to assert some autonomy over her life. Part of the answer undoubtedly lies in cultural contributions to this problem (Litt, 1985). Anorexia is a disorder of modern industrialized society, and its incidence has increased greatly over the past 20 years. Girls today are barraged with images of extreme thinness on television, in fashion magazines, and in the world of popular music. Extreme thinness is associated with beauty, affluence, and success. It is therefore not surprising that this is the image to which a troubled girl aspires.

Anorexia nervosa is quite difficult to treat because of the person's entrenched beliefs that she *must* remain thin or even become thinner. However, there is some evidence that behavioral therapies may be effective in the short run and that family therapy may have longer-term success (Geller et al., 1978; Ollendrick, 1979; Minuchin, Rosman, and Baker, 1978; Selvini, 1971). A direct comparison between behavioral and family therapy favored the latter (Erwin, 1977). A first goal of any treatment is to get the adolescent eating, but the long-term aim must be to help her believe that she has a right to self-expression, including the expression of anger, and that as a person she has worth. The obsessive need to be thin often recedes as the child is set free from overcontrol. Family approaches seem to work not only because the family is subtly supporting the anorectic's self-starvation but also because the family holds the key to the adolescent's freedom.

Depression

> The patient, an adolescent male, was profoundly depressed. He sat slouched in his chair, avoiding eye contact with the therapist and appearing withdrawn and glum. As the therapist proceeded to draw him into conversation, he began to talk about his sense of inferiority, inadequacy, and self-hate. He dwelled on his physical appearance, describing himself as funny-looking, ugly, weird, skinny, awkward—in sum, a "jerk." Adding to the vividness of his negative self-image, he related an incident in which a girl he had asked for a date had laughed at him. (adapted from Strupp and Binder, 1984, p. 150)

There are some interesting similarities between depression and anorexia nervosa, which both increase during adolescence and are more prevalent in females than males (Rutter, 1983). Like anxiety disorders, they are considered *internalizing* problems. Hopelessness, helplessness, and feelings of low self-worth are cardinal features of **depression,** as they are of anorexia. However, rather than being "keyed up" and intent on vigorous exercise, as many anorectics are, depressed teen-agers are typically lethargic and unmotivated (APA, 1980). They may refuse food due

Depression in children is now recognized with greater frequency. *(Ulrike Welsch/ Photo Researchers, Inc.)*

to a loss of appetite, but their more immediate physical danger arises from frequent thoughts of suicide. Social isolation and poor school performance also characterize adolescent depression.

Controversy exists over the prevalence of depression earlier in childhood. Many investigators believe it is quite common, perhaps affecting 2 percent of the general child population and 15 to 20 percent of youngsters referred to clinics (Kasahni et al., 1981; Pearce, 1977). Recorded statistics, however, may be lower than this because childhood depression can be obscured by other complaints (conduct disorders, psychosomatic ailments) and because young children have trouble talking about feelings of despair. Despite these problems in identifying depressed children, there is no doubt that the condition can exist before adolescence and that depressed children, like depressed teens and adults, show tendencies to blame themselves and feel powerless (Garber et al., 1985; Leon, Kendall, and Garber, 1980).

Biological theories appear to be helpful in explaining some cases of adult depression, and the same may be true of certain instances of depression in teen-agers (Gershon et al., 1983). Some researchers have therefore tried to demonstrate biological causes of childhood depression. For instance, it has been found that many depressed adults respond with suppression of the hormone cortisol when the drug dexamethosone is given, and this same reaction has been reported in depressed children (Garfinkel, in press; Puig-Antich, 1982). Investigators speculate that this response may be a ''biological marker'' of depression, a reaction unique to depressed individuals and showing that they are physiologically different from other people. The problem is that we have very little data on the frequency of this reaction in emotionally normal children, especially those undergoing the stress of a hospital test. And even if this reaction was found to be specific to depressed children, we would not know whether it was cause or effect. Depression could be promoting the changes in body chemistry rather than vice versa; indeed, monkeys separated from their mothers show such biochemical changes (McKinney,

1977). In short, there is little clear evidence at present that biological factors are major explanations of childhood depression (Schulterbrandt and Raskin, 1977).

Psychological theories of adult depression often center on the early loss of a parent through death, desertion, or divorce (Brown, Harris, and Bifulco, 1985). Since many children experience losses without developing depression, it is clear that a complex set of factors must be involved. Bowlby (1980) has suggested that depression can be triggered by a series of early losses, or by a major loss in the context of inadequate care, which leads to inadequate mourning. An alternative view is that loss of a parent, negative cognitions, and "learned helplessness" are the common factors underlying a depressed response (Wenar, 1982). This view also stresses the child's relationship with the remaining parent, and whether that parent grows to be emotionally dependent on the child. (This is why we portrayed at some length the relationship between Mike and Christine after her divorce from Frank.) Evidence that these various factors are important comes from the finding that young adults who have lost a parent before the age of 16 have more suicidal thoughts and attempted suicides than peers from intact families; however, consistent nurturance from another adult can lessen these negative reactions (Adam, 1973).

Other psychological theories of childhood depression focus on severe emotional neglect by parents (Kaufman and Cicchetti, 1986). In the Minnesota Preschool Project, for example, young children whose parents were very emotionally distant and unavailable to them were later more likely to show symptoms of depression (Sroufe, 1986). It may be that having an early environment that is highly unresponsive prompts children to see the world as ungiving and themselves as unable to achieve care. Thus, the children who ultimately become depressed may have given up on the possibility of ever receiving nurturance.

Chapter Review

1. The study of developmental challenges and vulnerabilities, evolving patterns of psychological adaptation and the reasons for them, is part of a subfield of developmental psychology called **developmental psychopathology.** Researchers in this area want to understand the causes of emotional and behavioral problems in both children and adults. In their search for causes, some focus largely on biological factors, while others emphasize environmental ones.

2. The classic biological perspective on mental disorders is known as the medical model. It draws an analogy between psychological problems and physical diseases. Most modern neurological and physiological perspectives look to chemical imbalances in the brain as important causes of psychological disorders. Genetic

models add to this understanding by focusing on the hereditary aspects of emotional and behavioral problems—that is, on physical predispositions toward developing them. In general, biological perspectives make their biggest contributions in helping to explain certain severe psychological disorders such as early childhood autism, schizophrenia, and some forms of depression.

3. Sociological models focus on the overall social and cultural context surrounding the disturbed individual. Behavioral models, in contrast, focus specifically on the rewards, punishments, and modeled behaviors in the person's environment. Recommended treatment involves changing the contingencies between the disturbed behavior and its consequences. Modern cognitive behavioral approaches in addition seek to change the disturbed person's negative thoughts and expectations. Psychodynamic models of psychopathology all have in common a focus on the troubled individual's fears, anxieties, and conflicts. A final type of environmental approach is the family or systems model. It assumes that a disturbed person's symptoms are often a reflection of troubled relationships throughout the entire family unit.

4. Environmental perspectives on psychological disorders are not incompatible with biological ones. Most researchers believe that many disorders involve a complex interplay of both kinds of factors. For instance, it seems likely that a high genetic predisposition toward schizophrenia interacts with the amount of environmental stress a person experiences to determine whether or not the disorder ultimately develops. Those who take a developmental perspective on disorders draw upon any or all of the models outlined above.

5. *The Diagnostic and Statistical Manual of Mental Disorders* of the American Psychiatric Association includes a large number of disorders first evident in infancy, childhood, or adolescence. Among the most severe is **early childhood autism,** characterized by a powerful insistence on preserving sameness in the environment, extreme social isolation, and extreme speech deficits. Most psychologists believe that autism is usually caused by some as yet unidentified biological factor. In contrast, there is currently much debate as to whether **hyperactivity** and attention problems, often called **attention deficit disorders,** are biological in origin. Some investigators think they may often stem instead from such environmental factors as persistent overstimulation early in life. Those who take this view do not generally endorse the regular use of stimulant drugs to treat hyperactivity. **Conduct disorders** constitute a broad classification in which the child repeatedly violates either the basic rights of others or age-appropriate social norms. Children who display an aggressive, undersocialized type of conduct disorder (where the youngster both deliberately seeks to harm others and is unable to form normal bonds of affection) are particularly hard to treat. **Anxiety disorders,** too, involve several different subtypes, including **overanxious disorder** and **separation anxiety disorder.** The first involves very general and pervasive worries and fears; the second is characterized by excessive anxiety over separation from a parent. Both respond quite well to treatment. **Anorexia nervosa** is an increasingly common eating disorder in which the person deliberately reduces food intake to the point of losing at least 25 percent of original body weight. Anorexia is primarily a disorder of bright, middle-class, academically successful adolescent girls and young women. There are many indications that it is associated with parents who seek perfection and stifle their child's autonomy. **Depression** is a disorder that often first develops during adolescence, although it is also found in childhood. Key features are low self-esteem and feelings of hopelessness. Biological theories of depression focus on inherited biochemical deficits; psychological theories focus on early losses as well as emotional neglect.

Psychopathology and Individual Lives

As a way of summarizing the material we've discussed on developmental psychopathology, let's return again to the three children we have followed throughout this book and assess their degree of vulnerability to various disorders.

Malcolm Williams

Malcolm represents an interesting case because of all the things that might have gone wrong in his development. Conduct disorders, especially the gang-socialized type, are very common among boys raised in inner cities, yet for solid reasons we portrayed Malcolm as making a positive social adaptation. He did occasionally show bad judgment, as when he brought a knife to elementary school, but he seemed to learn from these experiences and he matured well. The nurturance and firm guidance from his caring family appear to be the critical factors leading him to such a good adjustment (Maston and Garmezy, 1985).

With his active, exuberant nature Malcolm was also ripe for being judged to have an attention deficit disorder, or hyperactivity. In fact, as we constructed it, his kindergarten teacher at one point tried to apply that label to him, as often happens with black, inner-city, male children. Malcolm was fortunate in that his family would not accept the label. They were convinced that he was a lively, but perfectly normal child who simply had to work a little harder at controlling his impulses.

But wait, you may be saying to yourself. Isn't attention deficit disorder or hyperactivity something that a child either has or doesn't have? How can we say that Malcolm avoided this diagnosis simply because his parents so strongly supported him? We can say this precisely because such disorders are *not* givens; they aren't something that children either are or are not born with. Instead these are developmental problems that depend on the interaction of internal and external factors. It makes sense that in the case of Malcolm firm guidance and limits provided by his family would allow him to acquire an adequate degree of self-management. Even academic failure at school is not something we should think of as always stemming from innate characteristics. In the Minnesota Preschool Project, being required to repeat kindergarten was not predicted by IQ or early language comprehension tests. Instead, it was predicted by social and emotional factors, such as a child's attachment history.

One could imagine that Malcolm might have shown school refusal when he was having difficulty with gang members on the streets. But note that, if this had occurred, the school refusal would have stemmed from a serious external conflict, not from anxiety over leaving home. In fact, any form of internalizing disorder would be out of character for Malcolm as we have described him—a boy filled with a sense of personal ability and confidence. The overcontrol and perfectionism of the anorectic or the hopelessness and self-contempt of the depressed adolescent would not make sense in his case. Likewise, adult schizophrenia would be unlikely to develop in Malcolm. He shows none of the precursors of it. He is successful socially and academically; there is no history of family psychopathology and no disturbed pattern of family interaction. While our present state of knowledge doesn't allow us to rule out the possibility of later disorders, Malcolm seems well on his way to good adult adjustment, with just the normal ups and downs we all have.

Meryl Polonius Turner

Meryl was constructed to be in many ways the opposite of Malcolm. As is common for females in our culture, she is portrayed as being socialized toward internalizing problems. School refusal and other forms of anxiety disorder were possibilities for her. Indeed, during the early preschool years she showed signs of such problems: She had great difficulty adapting to new situations and she tended to fall to pieces under stress. As a female, especially with her tendency to internalize stress, she might also have been at risk for anorexia nervosa and depression.

However, as we constructed Meryl's history, many factors in her life worked against her actually developing those disorders. When Karen met Joe and her life stabilized, Meryl's development underwent a critical turnaround. Increasingly her parents helped her to become a self-sufficient and autonomous person. Especially in Meryl's adolescence, Karen and Joe tolerated her normal pushing away from them—her criticisms, argumentativeness, and other forms of de-identification. At the same time, they provided Meryl with a great deal of nurturance, supporting her and helping her learn to seek support when she needed it. Karen and Joe's own relationship modeled the vital role that social support can play in alleviating stress. While they had their periods of marital tension, they were able to talk about and resolve their conflicts, and Meryl was not made to feel responsible when things went wrong. All this would have served a child like Meryl well. We therefore described her as becoming more competent and confident in herself, thereby moving away from the path toward adult depression.

It is noteworthy, too, that as a teen-ager Meryl did not become pregnant, as her mother and grandmother both had done. A two-generation cycle was broken. Again, this vulnerability was overcome in the context of positive family relationships.

With the history we described for Meryl, the possibility of any form of adult conduct disorder would be very remote. It would be inconceivable, for example, to see Meryl headed for a career of violent crime. Lee Robin's (1978) research substantiates this. Aggressive, antisocial behavior is simply not congruent with the early personality or style of coping illustrated by Meryl.

Neither would adult schizophrenia be likely for someone like Meryl. Granted, for girls there may be a link between adult schizophrenia and certain internalizing symptoms, primarily withdrawal (Watt et al., 1984). But Meryl's family history was too benign to make this disorder probable. Most important, she shows social competence and academic success, which together indicate the unlikelihood of serious adult disorders.

For a person like Meryl, however, we would predict that new situations would probably continue to be challenging. If confronted with a crisis, she might respond at first by becoming disorganized; but then, with effort, she likely would cope effectively. Meryl, on the one hand, might be quite demanding of the men with whom she forms close relationships; on the other hand, with her keen sensitivity to others and eagerness to please, she would also give a great deal.

Mike Gordon

Mike was the only one of our three children described as experiencing prolonged parental conflict and eventually divorce. He was also the only one showing significant problems as late as adolescence. His parents burdened him with their relationship, and he felt he had to keep the family together. His mother at times leaned on him, and for a while he feared that his father might be turning most of his attention to his new wife and son. Such factors may be associated with conduct disorders, hyperactivity, and depression.

At one time or another Mike did show behavior congruent with some of those disorders. Still, we never intended to portray him as seriously disturbed, nor would we anticipate in him any serious adult disorders. His history of support and solid early adaptation would serve as "protective factors" during stressful periods (Masten and Garmezy, 1985).

Mike at first showed more of a tendency toward internalizing symptoms than Malcolm would have done in his situation. Remember our description of the guilt he felt over his parents' separation and how in the year following the breakup of the marriage he became less outgoing. But with the divorce and his father's remarriage, we presented him as expressing his pain in acting-out behaviors. This is in keeping with cultural patterns of socialization for boys. Frank Gordon's son was not going to sit around moping and having stomach aches for long. It is hard to say how likely it would have been for a teen-ager like Mike to continue down the path toward conduct disorders, perhaps eventually abusing drugs or alcohol. Without our inclusion of the excellent support from his mother, his uncle, and his high-school biology teacher, and the continuing interest shown by his father, it would have been more difficult to have things work out so well for him in our story.

Some would argue that alcoholism, conduct disorders, and schizophrenia are genetically related to one another (Garfinkel, in press). If so, Frank's lapse into alcoholism during the rockiest time of his first marriage, coupled with Mike's brief bouts of misconduct during early adolescence, might provide reasons for putting Mike at higher than normal risk for schizophrenia. But there were many factors counteracting these negative warning signs: Mike's solid developmental beginnings, his good adjustment, and his ongoing social support all worked in his favor. The problems in his family were clear and overt. In time we could expect him to understand fully that he was not the cause of them.

But how would a person like Mike later face the roles of husband and father? We might expect him to have doubts about his ability to provide for a partner. After all, in the story his father was unable to meet his mother's emotional needs, and Mike himself experienced a sense of failure in his efforts to fill the gap. Emotionally caring for a parent is too big a task for a child. Doubts about his own care-taking abilities might also arise when Mike eventually becomes a parent. But he appears to have overall positive self-esteem; doubts and lack of confidence do not predominate in his general image of himself. A basic commitment to family life will probably help Mike be successful as both husband and father. He will certainly have some vulnerabilities as he faces these adult tasks, as we all do, but he also has particular strengths that he can bring to these challenges.

Conclusion: Psychopathology and Normal Development

As summarized here, the three children portrayed in this book have all been at risk for various disorders, but the adjustments and accomplishments that we have seen them achieve through adolescence are an indication of their successful growth and development. Developmental psychopathology, as presented in Chapter 16, is the study of deviations from normal development, deviations which at times seriously impair the person's functioning and result in patterns of behavior referred to as **psychiatric syndromes**. Developmental psychopathologists seek to understand the origins and course of such deviations and factors which promote the return to normal developmental pathways.

It turns out that the same principles and influences found to be important in the study of normal development are critical for understanding pathological development. These include the interplay of biological and environmental factors, the surrounding rings of contextual influence (social support, poverty, cultural expectations, etc.) and the person's previous developmental history.

Glossary

The boldface number after each entry refers to the chapter in which the term is discussed.

accelerated longitudinal design A study of several age-groups simultaneously for a designated period of time. **1**

accommodation The tendency to alter schemes or structures to conform with aspects of the environment. **2, 6**

Acquired Immune Deficiency Syndrome (AIDS) An incurable virus that affects babies born to mothers with the disease by retarding growth and impeding overall development and that often leads to death. **4**

acuity The degree of detail one can see. **5**

adaptation The process by which one's behavior is adjusted to meet environmental demands. **2, 6**

adaptational theory A Bowlbian theory of human development that integrates many psychological theories, including the evolutionary focus on adaptation with Freud's emphasis on the importance of early social relations. **2**

affective sharing The sharing of emotional experiences. **9**

agency The tendency to take initiative, to rise to challenges, and to try to influence events. **13**

algorithm A set of rules arranged in a logical order that will solve all instances of a certain type of problem. **2**

allele Any of several forms of a gene for the same trait. **4**

alpha-fetoprotein A fetal serum protein that may serve as an indicator for the presence of neural tube defects or Down syndrome. **4**

altruism Unselfish concern for or devotion to the welfare of others. **11**

amniocentesis A technique whereby a needle is inserted through the mother's abdomen at approximately the fifteenth week of pregnancy to withdraw a sample of the fluid that surrounds the developing fetus, for the purpose of detecting chromosomal abnormalities. **4**

amniotic sac A fluid-filled covering that forms around the embryo and serves as protection against foreign substances, jostling, temperature change, etc. **4**

androgen A male sex hormone secreted by the testes. **4**

anorexia nervosa An eating disorder characterized by extreme reduction in food intake and loss of at least 25 percent of original body weight. **16**

anoxia A lengthy disruption of a steady supply of oxygen to the infant during delivery. **4**

anxiety disorder A condition in which severe and persistent anxiety interferes with daily functioning. **16**

anxious avoidant A term that refers to a child who, following the stress of a brief separation, avoids interaction with the care giver to such a degree that the child's exploration of the environment is inhibited. **7**

anxious resistant A term that refers to a child who, following separation from the care giver, is unable to be settled by the care giver, often even angrily rejecting her. **7**

anxiously attached A child who is not confident about the availability and responsiveness of the care giver. **7**

appearance-reality problem The tendency to define reality by surface appearance. **10**

artificial insemination The impregnation of a female by artificial introduction of semen taken from a male. **4**

assimilation The tendency to try to act on or interpret the world through existing schemes or structures. **2, 6**

associative learning Learning that certain events go together or are associated to one another. **5**

attachment An emotional bond between two people, especially infant and care giver, that endures over time and space. **7**

attention deficit disorder A disorder in which excessive activity and attention-related difficulties are displayed. **16**

attention span The limit on the number of mental elements that can be considered at any one time. **6**

authoritarian A style of child rearing in which the parents' word is law and misconduct is punished. **13**

authoritative A style of child rearing in which parents set limits and provide guidance, and at the same time are willing to listen to the child's ideas and make compromises. **11**

autonomous morality The view of morality as relative to a situation and subjective. **14**

babbling Playful, repetitive sounds made by the infant prior to the development of speech. **8**

base rate A length of time to be used as a standard in measurement. **5**

behavioral reorganization A new way of organizing one's thoughts and actions, resulting in increasingly complex behavior. **1**

behaviorism The study of observable behavior learned through associations. **2**

behaviorist view A perspective of psychology that maintains that the development and functioning of personality is a learned response, rather than a result of unconscious conflicts and urges. **8**

bidirectional effect The view that the way one individual acts toward another is determined, in part, by the way the second individual acts toward the first. **3**

binocular depth cue A cue about depth and distance that results from visual information reaching the brain from two eyes rather than one. **5**

birth order effects Systematic differences in children's behavior depending on whether they are first-born, second-born, and so on. **3**

blastocyst A hollow, ball-like structure consisting of over a hundred cells. **4**

breech birth A delivery of an infant in a feet-first position. **4**

bulimia An eating disorder characterized by binges and induced vomiting. **16**

caesarean section A surgical method of delivery that involves surgical incision into the abdomen and uterus. **4**

centration The tendency to consider only one piece of information when multiple pieces are relevant. **10**

cephalocaudal development The tendency for control over motor movements to progress from head to toe. **5**

cephalocaudal pattern The concept that development of the embryo proceeds from the head downward. **4**

child directed speech (CDS) A form of speech characterized by redundancy, a higher than normal pitch, exaggerated intonations, very few lapses in fluency, extremely simplistic grammar and content that tends to focus on objects and events discussed in the present tense, using concrete nouns. This speech is used most often by parents when speaking to young children. **8**

chorionic villus sampling A technique performed in weeks 8 to 12 of pregnancy whereby cells are suctioned from a developing placenta via a small tube which is passed through the vagina and cervix, to be analyzed later to determine the fetus's genetic makeup. **4**

chromosome In the structure of every cell, beadlike strings of genes consisting primarily of protein and DNA that perpetuate traits from one generation to another. **4**

circular reaction A behavior producing an event that leads to the behavior being repeated. **6**

class inclusion The concept that a particular class can be a subset of another class. **12**

classical conditioning A process whereby a normally neutral stimulus comes to evoke a response when paired with a stimulus that ordinarily evokes the response. **2**

classification The act of sorting or organizing things into a category or system of categories. **10**

clique A close-knit group of a few friends who do things together, exchange ideas, and accept each other's personalities. **15**

co-dominant genes A pair of alternative alleles in which each allele's effect is equally dominant as the other. **4**

cognitive ability A thinking skill that is common to all normal humans. **6**

cognitive behavioral therapist A therapist who teaches individuals new cognitions—adaptive beliefs, expectations, and ways of thinking—to eliminate abnormal emotions and behavior. **16**

cognitive competence The optimal cognitive ability of an individual. **14**

cognitive developmental theory The study of how people think about the world and how they mentally represent and organize reality. **2**

cognitive performance The actual behavior of an individual that reflects cognitive understanding. **14**

cognitive view A perspective of psychology that maintains that in almost any learned association, important thought processes intervene between the stimulus and the response. **8**

collection Any entity composed of subparts that, because of their proximity to one another, seem to be automatically related. **10**

collective monologue A type of speech characteristic of pairs of young children in which the form imitates adult conversation, but the conversations are independent of each other. **10**

communication deviance A pattern of behavior whereby individuals routinely talk past one another, make irrelevant comments, and fail to respond directly. **16**

compensation The awareness that change in one dimension is affected by change in another. **12**

conception When development within the fertilized egg begins. **4**

concrete operational subperiod The latter part of the concrete period during which skills are organized into a system of logical thinking that expands the child's cognitive capabilities. **2**

concrete period Two subperiods of child development extending from 2-6 years old during which children acquire most of their thinking and reasoning skills. **2**

conditional response (CR) A response aroused by some stimulus other than the one that automatically produces it. **5**

conditioned stimulus (CS) An initially neutral stimulus which, after repeated pairing with an unconditioned stimulus, comes to elicit a conditioned response. **5**

conduct disorder A persistent pattern of behavior in which a child repeatedly violates either the basic rights of others or age-appropriate social norms. **16**

conservation In Piagetian theory, the concept that certain properties of a given quantity of matter (volume, weight, etc.) remain constant despite changes in shape, length, or position. **10**

constant identity The realization that a substance is the same even though it has been altered. **12**

constraint seeking A method of inquiry whereby, with each consecutive question, one attempts to narrow down the range of possible alternatives. **12**

constructive memory New information consisting of data just processed as well as inferences made on data previously stored in one's memory. **12**

contingency The connection between an action and its consequences. **5**

contingent truth A conclusion contingent on information gathered through one's senses. **12**

continuous growth A type of adolescent development characterized by self-assurance, a sense of purpose, and mutual respect between child and parents. **15**

conventional morality The second stage of Kohlberg's model of moral development during which children make moral judgments based on internalized standards arising from concrete experience in the social world. **14**

convergence A binocular depth cue whereby the eyes turn inward to focus on a near object. **5**

cooing Soft vowel-like sounds made by the very young infant. **8**

critical period A limited time during which some part of a developing organism is susceptible to influences that can bring about specific and permanent change. **4**

critical weight hypothesis A theory that suggests that menarche occurs at a relatively constant weight in girls and that the adolescent growth spurt in both sexes is also weight related. **14**

cross-sectional study A study that compares different groups of people at different ages. **1**

crossing over The fusion of genetic material. **4**

crowd A group of friends, larger, less exclusive, and more loosely organized than a clique. **15**

crystallized intelligence Processes of thinking assessed by measuring what a person knows, such as vocabulary size, reading comprehension, etc. **12**

cultural context The beliefs, values, and guidelines for behavior (in the Bronfenbrenner model) shared by a particular society. **3**

culture-fair IQ test An intelligence test that is not culturally biased. **12**

culture-free IQ test An intelligence test that is not culturally biased. **12**

cycle of poverty The concept that children born into lower socioeconomic classes are more likely to have developmental problems, do poorly in schools, and have difficulty finding jobs, which will lead to their raising their own children in the same impoverished conditions. **4**

deep sleep A state characterized by extremely slow brain waves. **14**

deferred imitation The ability to recreate an action or mimic a person one has witnessed in the past. **6**

delay of gratification To forgo something attractive at present in order to receive something better at a later date. **11**

depression A pattern of sadness, anxiety, fatigue, insomnia, underactivity, and reduced ability to function and to work with others. **16**

DNA (deoxyribonucleic acid) A chemical in the nucleus of cells that contains the genetic code that guides development. **4**

development Age-related change that is orderly, cumulative, and directional. **1**

developmental psychopathology The branch of psychology that seeks to comprehend the nature and development of mental and emotional disorders that occur in human beings throughout the life cycle, from conception to death. **16**

diathesis stress model A theory that maintains that every person has some degree of biological vulnerability, as well as a number of different life experiences that may combine to lead to schizophrenia. **16**

discourse analysis The study of the various understandings people have and conventions they follow when they talk to one another. **8**

disequilibrium A state of encountering a task that one is unable to master efficiently. **2**

dizygotic twins The result of the fertilization of two ova by two different sperm. **4**

dominant gene One of a pair of alternative alleles that masks the effect of the other when both are present in the same cell or organism. **4**

Down syndrome A form of mental retardation caused by an extra chromosome. Characteristics of children born with this disease include a broad face, flat facial features, and heart defects. **4**

early childhood autism A rare disorder characterized by a powerful insistence on preserving sameness in the environment, extreme social isolation, and severe speech deficits. **16**

echolalic One who lifelessly repeats a word or phrase he or she has overheard, with no concern for its meaning. **16**

ecological validity The concept that findings inside the laboratory may not generalize to the outside world. **1**

ego The psychic structure in Freudian theory that mediates between impulses and environmental demands. **2**

ego resiliency The ability to modify self-restraint as circumstances require. **11**

egocentric One who sees the world from his or her own viewpoint and is unable to take the perspective of another person. **10**

embryo A blastocyst that is firmly implanted in the uterine wall. **4**

embryonic induction Interaction among tissues to eventually shape various parts of the body of the embryo, caused by chemicals that pass from one tissue to another. **4**

embryonic period The length of time between the end of the second week to the end of the eighth when the rapid differentiation of cells begins. **4**

emotion A state of feeling that arises when a person psychologically processes certain kinds of external stimuli. **7**

emotional dependency A need for continual reassurance and attention from others in order to function. **11**

empathy The ability to experience the thoughts and emotions of another person. **11**

enactive mode In Bruner's theory, the first mode of representing objects and events, in which infants associate them with motor acts. **6**

equilibration The process of evolving new and more serviceable schemes or structures when encountering new experiences that are not readily assimilated. **2**

error of overextension The inappropriate use of a word due to an insufficiently restricted definition. **8**

error of underextension When a word is used correctly but in too restricted a way. **8**

estrogen The female hormone that controls sexual maturation. **4**

ethology The study of observing species in their natural habitats to understand their behavior. **1**

etiology The study of causation. **16**

evaluation An appraisal. **7**

executive competence A children's realization of his or her own autonomy and ability to act, as well as react. **9**

executive processing space Case's term for working memory. **6**

experiment A study in which researchers manipulate conditions so as to exclude all influences except the one being investigated. **1**

external locus of control The belief that successes are beyond one's personal control, and they are governed by external factors. **13**

externalizing behavior A problem that tends to be expressed outwardly, such as aggression, hyperactivity, and sociopathic behaviors. **16**

extinction A gradual decline in a conditioned response. **5**

extra-utero fertilization Fertilization outside the uterus, which is then planted in a woman's uterus. **4**

family day care A type of child care in which several children are cared for in someone else's home. **3**

fetal alcohol syndrome Symptoms caused by heavy alcohol consumption during pregnancy such as retardation in growth and intellectual development, defects in facial features, limbs, the brain, etc. **4**

fetal period The period of time from the ninth week until birth when body parts grow rapidly and become refined in structure. **4**

fetus The organism from the ninth week of development until the thirty-eighth or when birth occurs. **4**

fixation The state in which an individual becomes locked in a psychological mode of conflict, expressing it in symbolic ways. **2**

fluid intelligence Processes of thinking and reasoning that are measured by analogy problems, series completion tasks, problems in classification, etc. **12**

follow-back study A method of research whereby early records of selected individuals are studied to determine the source of a particular characteristic or behavior common to the group. **16**

foreclosure Erikson's term for premature identity formation, in which the young person does not explore all the identities that are available. **15**

formal operations In Piaget's theory, mental transformations that youngsters are able to perform that allow them to reason more logically about abstract concepts and hypothetical statements and ideas. **14**

formal operational period The period of development from age 12 and older during which the ability to reason systematically about hypothetical problems and abstract issues emerges. **2**

gender concept The sense of being male or female. **11**

gender constancy An understanding that gender is permanent despite changes in age or behavior. **11**

gene A microscopic particle, carried by the chromosomes, that contains instructions that guide the development of physical traits and behavioral dispositions. **4**

generalize To respond to a similar way to stimuli that have some property in common. **16**

genetic engineering A process whereby scientists induce mutations by inserting new genes into simple organisms. **4**

genotype The specific genes that one possesses. **4**

germinal period The period of time when the zygote implants itself in the lining of the uterus and begins to form the life-support system that allows it to feed off the mother. **4**

goal-directed chain A series of actions performed not for their own sake, but as a means of accomplishing something else. **6**

gonad A sex gland. Testes in males; ovaries in females. **14**

gonadotropic A pituitary hormone that travels through the bloodstream to affect output from the sex glands. **14**

grammatical morpheme A unit of language such as a prefix, suffix, or auxiliary verb that changes the meaning of a root word. **8**

grasping reflex The action elicited by stimulating a newborn's palm, whereby the child curls the fingers inward. **5**

growth error A mistake caused by the emergence of a more advanced way of thinking. **8**

habituation A decrease in attention that occurs when the same stimulus is presented repeatedly. **5**

heterozygous Having different alleles at a given chromosome in genes inherited by both parents. **4**

heuristics A basic strategy that provides a general approach to solving a problem. **2**

hierarchical classification A method of organization whereby items are ranked successively with each level subordinate to the one above. **12**

holophrase A word that is used to convey a broader meaning. **8**

homologous Affecting the same aspects of development. **4**

homozygous Having the same alleles at a given chromosome site in genes inherited by both parents. **4**

hormone A glandular secretion that influences gender development, metabolism, etc. **4**

hostile aggression Aggression aimed purely at hurting someone else. **11**

hyperactivity A state of excessive activity, usually accompanied by an inability to concentrate and impulsive behavior. **16**

hypothalamus The part of the forebrain involved with motives, emotions, and the functions of heart rate, respiration, etc. **14**

hypothesis A testable proposition that is derived from a theory. **1**

hypothesis scanning A method of inquiry whereby each question asked is a single, self-controlled hypothesis, unrelated to previous questions. **11**

hypothetico-deductive reasoning The ability to think up hypothetical solutions to a problem and then formulate a logical and systematic plan for deducing which of these possible solutions is the right one. **14**

id That part of the human psyche that consists only of primitive drives and instincts. **2**

identification Taking on the behaviors and qualities of a respected person that one would like to emulate. **2**

identity The sense of who one is and who one wants to be, given one's social environment. **15**

identity achievement Erikson's term for a person's achievement of a sense of who he or she is as a unique individual. **15**

identity crisis A period of instability usually experienced by adolescents whereby personal biological changes conflict with social and parental demands. **15**

identity diffusion Erikson's term for the experience of a young person who is uncertain what path to take toward identity formation, and therefore becomes apathetic and disoriented. **15**

imaginary audience The constant scrutiny that many adolescents typically imagine themselves to be under. **14**

imitative learning A mode of learning whereby one mimics the behavior of others. **5**

individual development Variations around the normative course of development of a particular ability; the uniqueness of an individual. **1**

information-processing A process whereby one takes in information and processes that information by making comparisons and adjustments. **2**

inner working model An attitude or representation, developed during childhood and carried forward, that is subject to change. **7**

INRC group (Identity, Negation, Reciprocity, Correlativity) In Piaget's theory, the four types of logical relationships between operations that can be used to manipulate conclusions and produce deeper understandings. **14**

insensitive care When the care giver's behavior is not appropriately adapted to fulfill the infant's wishes or needs. **7**

instrumental aggression Aggression aimed at possessing objects. **11**

instrumental conditioning A process whereby a response is strengthened or changed as a result of rewards or punishments. **2**

instrumental dependency A need for help from others in order to solve complex problems or perform difficult tasks. **11**

intelligence quotient (IQ) Mental age divided by chronological age and multiplied by 100. **12**

interactionist view A concept of human development that attributes behavior to both inborn factors and environment. **2**

internal locus of control The belief in one's own personal effectiveness. **13**

internal working model A set of generalized expectations of the care giver as available and responsive (or unresponsive), which determines a view of the self as worthy or unworthy of care. **2**

internalizing behavior A problem that tends to be expressed inwardly, such as anxiety, shyness, nail biting, or psychosomatic ailments. **16**

interposition The partial overlap of objects that makes a partially covered object appear farther away. **5**

invariant That which remains constant. **2**

Lamaze method A technique of delivery that stresses the importance of natural childbirth. Characteristics of this method include prior knowledge of the birth process, participation of both parents in the pregnancy and delivery, breathing techniques practiced by the mother during labor, and a decreased reliance on medication during delivery. **4**

language acquisition device (LAD) Postulated innate capacities of the brain that allow individuals to perceive and understand the world in specific ways. **8**

latency period In Freudian theory, the period from age five or six until puberty, during which sexual impulses are repressed while the child learns social and cognitive skills. **13**

learning/mediational view A perspective on language acquisition that maintains that language serves to connect a stimulus to an ultimate overt response by setting up a chain of internal, covert responses. **8**

Leboyer method A technique of delivery that emphasizes the baby's experience of birth and making the transition from the uterus to the outside world as gradual as possible. **4**

lexical contrast theory A model that explains the order in which children learn a word's defining characteristics, which maintains that a child's communication needs and current state of knowledge are what promote attention to particular features, encourage new words to be acquired, and cause further restrictions of still overextended meanings. **8**

linear perspective The seeming convergence of parallel lines as they extend away from the viewer, thus giving the impression of increasing distance. **5**

longitudinal prospective study A method of research whereby subjects who demonstrate no abnormal behavior are studied over a period of time to determine what circumstances may lead to a particular behavior. **16**

longitudinal study A study of one group over a period of weeks, months, or years. **1**

mastery play Any form of play that leads to a mastering of new skills. **6**

matrix classification A multiplication of classes whereby one classification dimension is multiplied by another. **12**

maturation The physical development of an organism as it grows toward fulfilling its genetic potential. **2**

meiosis Cell division in which four cells, each containing 23 chromosomes, are produced. **4**

menarche The onset of menstruation. **14**

mental age (MA) A term used in intelligence testing that indicates the average age of people correctly answering the same number of items as the tested person. **12**

mental power An information-processing capacity used for storing the memory of objects and behavior on a short-term basis. **6**

metacognition The capacity to think about thinking. **12**

metamemory Knowledge about memory and memory processes. **12**

mitosis Cell division that results in two new cells identical in number of chromosomes to the original. **4**

mnemonic strategy A cognitive method of facilitating memory. **12**

modifier gene A gene that does not influence traits directly, but rather the way other genes operate. **4**

monocular depth cues A cue about depth and distance that results from visual information reaching the brain through each eye independently. **5**

monozygotic twins The result of a single fertilized egg splitting into two separate units during its early cell division. **4**

moral realism The view of moral constraints as unalterable and morality as absolute. **14**

moratorium Erikson's term for the informal pause in the process of identity formation that allows young people to explore alternatives without making final choices. **15**

Moro reflex The action in response to a newborn's head or body being dropped backward, whereby the infant flings out his or her arms and then brings them back toward the body's midline, with the hands curling in as if to grasp something. **5**

morpheme The smallest unit of meaning in a language. **8**

morphology The study of morphemes, or the smallest meaningful units in a language. **8**

motherese A form of speech characterized by redundancy, a higher than normal pitch, exaggerated intonations, very few lapses in fluency, extremely simplistic grammar, and content that tends to focus on objects and events discussed in the present tense, using concrete nouns. This speech is used most often by mothers when speaking to young children. **8**

mutation A naturally occurring change in genes that alters the instructions they give. **4**

nativist view The perspective that perceptual processes are accounted for partly by learning and partly by the ways in which sensory systems work. **8**

natural experiment A study that uses groups found naturally in the population instead of creating experimental groups. **1**

natural selection The process by which individuals who are best adapted for survival are more likely to pass on their traits to the next generation. **1**

naturalistic observations A method of collecting data in which researchers carefully observe and record behavior in natural settings. **1**

necessary truth A logical necessity. **12**

negative reinforcement The withdrawal of a painful stimulus following a response so as to increase the strength of that response. **2**

neonate A newborn child. **5**

neural tube defect Any abnormality such as absence of part of the brain or skull or failure of the spine to close. **4**

neuron A nerve cell from the brain. **14**

nonorganic failure to thrive syndrome When a baby experiences a lack of, or decline in, normal growth that has no physical cause. **7**

norm A rule of conduct. **13**

normative development Patterns of behavioral change over time shown by most children. **1**

nothing added or subtracted criterion The idea that when there is lack of a relevant change, an overall situation will remain unchanged. **12**

object permanence The understanding that objects and people continue to exist even when they cannot be seen. **6**

organogenesis The origin and development of an organ. **4**

orienting response A strong response to a new stimulus. **5**

outcome study A method of research whereby an individual's early records are studied or the individuals themselves are studied over a long period of time to determine what elicited a particular behavior. **16**

overanxious disorder An anxiety disorder characterized by very general and pervasive worries and fears. **16**

overcontrolling A care giver whose actions reflect his or her own personal needs for interaction rather than the child's needs. **7**

overregularization An error in speech in which regular plural forms are imposed on irregular nouns and verbs. **8**

ovum The egg cell. **4**

paradoxical drug effect An effect elicited by a drug that is opposite to its usual effect. **16**

parity The number of previous pregnancies a woman has had. **4**

pattern of adaptation One's individual style of responding to the environment. **9**

patterned speech A type of speech producing a range of sounds like the phonemes of a language. **8**

peer group A group of one's age-mates. **13**

perception The process whereby the brain interprets information from the senses, giving it order and meaning. **5**

personal fable An individual's belief in his or her own uniqueness in which that person thinks that no one else has ever had his or her special thoughts and feelings. **14**

phenotype The observable physical traits of an individual. **4**

phoneme The smallest unit of sound in a language. **8**

phonology The study of the sounds of a language. **8**

pituitary A small gland at the base of the brain that regulates other endocrine glands and secretes several hormones. **14**

placenta A mass of tissue formed from cells of the uterine lining and cells that make up the trophoblast, which supplies oxygen and nutrients to the embryo and carries away waste products. **4**

pleasure principle The desire to satisfy biological needs and thereby reduce tension. **2**

polygenic A characteristic that is influenced by several gene pairs on different chromosomes. **4**

polymorphism The phenomenon of different members within a particular species having variations on the basic species pattern. **4**

positive reinforcement The presentation of a pleasurable reward following an action or response. **2**

postconventional morality The third stage of Kohlberg's model of moral development during which children transcend conventional reasoning and begin to focus on more abstract principles underlying right and wrong. **14**

postterm A baby born later than the 38th week of gestation. **4**

pragmatics The study of rules governing how language is used in different social contexts. **8**

preadapt A genetic bias or inclination. **5**

preconventional period The first stage of Kohlberg's model of moral development during which the judgments children make are not based on moral reasoning, but rather by a desire to avoid punishment by an external authority. **14**

prenatal period The period of time prior to birth. **4**

preoperational subperiod The first part of the concrete period during which skills are acquired relatively independently of one another. **2**

preparedness The genetic predisposition to learn certain things. **5**

primary circular reaction A circular reaction in which one's body is the source of the response. **6**

primitive rule A judgment rendered regardless of any qualitative or quantitative differences between the initial groups. **12**

principled morality The third stage of Kohlberg's model of moral development during which child transcend conventional reasoning and begin to focus on more abstract principles underlying right and wrong. **14**

productive skill The mental skill that allows one to put ideas into words. **8**

protolanguage Prelingual sound patterns that are uttered in conjunction with speechlike intonation contours. **8**

proximodistal development The tendency for control over motor movements to progress from the center of the body out to the extremities.

proximodistal pattern The concept that parts at the center of the body develop earlier than those at the extremities. **4**

psychoanalysis A Freudian method of therapy that attempts to bring unconscious material into patients' awareness so that they can gain control over their behavior. **2**

puberty The period or age at which a person is first capable of sexual reproduction of offspring. **14**

puberty rite A special ceremony to mark the adolescent's entry into new adult roles. **15**

punctuate To interrupt periods of gradual change in a species with rapid changes in its genetic makeup. **1**

pursuit eye movement A smooth, continuous movement of the eye. **5**

qualitative change A transformation in ability that emerges through development. **1, 2**

qualitative rule A judgment based on the fact that there is a difference between two groups, but ignoring the degree of that difference. **12**

quantitative rule A judgment based on the degree of difference between groups. **12**

reaction range The limits within which the effects of genes can vary depending on environment. **12**

recall The ability to remember something in the absence of an obvious cue. **10**

receptive skill The mental skill that allows one to understand what other people say. **8**

recessive gene One of a pair of alternative alleles whose effect is masked by the activity of the second when both are present in the same cell or organism. **4**

reciprocal determinism The view that the way one individual acts toward another is determined, in part, by the way the second individual acts toward the first. **3**

recognition tests A measure of memory whereby an infant is shown some previously seen stimulus and evaluated for signs that he or she recognizes it. **6**

recognitory assimilation The process whereby an infant assimilates an event to an established scheme, leading to recognition. **7**

reflective abstraction The process whereby one, by reflecting on behaviors, can see the similarity between two problems or apply the solution of one problem to new problems. **2, 6**

reflex An automatic reaction elicited by a particular stimulus. **5, 6**

rehearsal The repetition of something one wants to remember. **12**

reinforcement The presentation or withdrawal of an event following a response so as to increase the likelihood of that response occurring again. **2**

representation Having ideas or images that stand in place of objects and events. **8**

representational thought The ability to make one thing stand for something else. **6**

repress To push a traumatic memory or idea into the unconscious. **2**

retinal disparity A binocular depth cue that results from the eyes being set apart and viewing the world from different angles. **5**

reversibility The awareness that an operation can be reversed to bring back the original situation. **12**

risk research A method of research whereby subjects with backgrounds putting them "at risk" for a behavior or characteristic are studied over a period of time for later evidence of the particular behavior or trait. **16**

rite of passage A special ceremony to mark the adolescent's entry into new adult roles. **15**

rooting reflex The action elicited by stroking a newborn's cheek or touching a corner of his or her mouth, whereby the child turns the head toward the side that was touched.

rubella A disease commonly known as German measles that may cause severe fetal defects such as blindness, deafness, mental retardation, and heart defects when contracted by a woman early in pregnancy. **4**

rule of conservation A maxim that states that certain characteristics of physical objects remain unchanged despite transformations carried out on them. **10**

saccade Discontinuous or sporadic movement.

saccadic eye movement A rapid, jerky movement of the eye. **5**

scaffolding The support system that others can contribute to the learning process by observing the learner's behavior, providing guidance, hints, or advice. **12**

scheme Piaget's term for a pattern of action or mental structures that is involved in the acquisition and structuring of knowledge. **2**

script An abstract representation of a sequence of actions needed to accomplish some goal. **10**

secondary circular reaction A circular reaction that one continues in order to elicit a response from an object or another person. **6**

secondary sex characteristic A sexual feature, other than the actual sex organs, that distinguishes male from female.

securely attached An infant who is comfortable when in contact with the parent, uses the parent as a secure base, and is readily comforted by the parent when frightened or distressed. This reflects confidence in parental availability and responsiveness. **7**

security The sense that care givers will be available and responsive to one's needs. **2**

self-constancy The perception of one's self as stable and enduring despite varied behaviors and varied responses from others. **11**

self-esteem One's thoughts and feelings about the self. **11**

semantic features hypothesis A model that views words in terms of their semantic features, or defining characteristics. **8**

semantics The study of the meaning that language conveys. **8**

sense of industry A belief in one's own competence and ability to master the world. **13**

sensitive care When the care giver adapts his or her behavior to fulfill the infant's wishes and needs. **3**

sensorimotor period Piaget's term for the first stage of cognitive development whereby children use the senses and motor skills to explore and manipulate the environment. **2, 6**

separation anxiety A state of distress experienced by children when separated from their primary care giver. **7, 16**

separation-individuation The psychological separation of the child from the care giver as well as the child's growing awareness of his or her autonomy. **9**

seriation The ability to arrange things in a logical progression. **10**

shape To reinforce successive approximations of a desired behavior. **2**

shape constancy The perceptual process of seeing the shape of an object as constant, even though the retina image is changing. **5**

size constancy The perceptual process of seeing the size of an object as constant, even though the size of the retina image is changing. **5**

social and economic context The outside influences (in the Bronfenbrenner model) that act upon our immediate environment. **3**

social construction view A concept of identity formation, developed by James Youniss, that expresses identity as involving understanding of one's own unique perspective and how it relates to the perspectives of others. **15**

social learning theory A theory that maintains that learning is not solely one's reaction to a stimuli but also how one applies cognitive processes to that stimuli. **2**

social referencing A learning process whereby one watches the emotional reactions of others to some new event or object and uses that reaction to determine their own. **9**

social self An awareness that one's identity is affected by other people and groups. **13**

socialization The process of acquiring the rules, standards, and values of a society. **9**

socially competent The ability to interact with peers, to be highly regarded by them, and to be able to sustain the give-and-take of peer interaction. **11**

sociolinguistics The study of differences in people's use of language as a result of belonging to different social groups or social categories. **8**

sociometrics The measurement of attitudes of social acceptance or rejection through expressed preferences among members of a social grouping. **11**

spontaneous remission A sudden and unprompted cessation of a symptom. **16**

state A term used to refer to the degree of physiological arousal (from deep sleep to active wakefulness and crying) in the young infant. **5**

stepping reflex The movement of an infant's feet in a rhythmic stepping motion when the child is held upright and lowered to a surface. **5**

stranger distress A baby's negative reaction to strangers. **7**

subculture A particular group whose members adhere to norms and values that differ in some ways from those of the dominant culture. **3**

sublimation Blocking and redirecting biological drives into acceptable activities. **9**

sucking reflex The action elicited when the mouth captures something. **5**

superego That part of the human psyche that internalizes social rules and values to make them part of the self. **2**

surgent growth A type of adolescent development characterized by reasonable adjustment interspersed with conflict. **15**

surrogate mother A woman who agrees to be artificially inseminated and who also agrees to carry the resulting fetus through to birth. **4**

symbiotic period When the child begins to distinguish the care giver from other people and coordinate his or her behavior with that of the care giver. **9**

synapse The small space between neurons, across which chemical messages travel. **14**

syndrome A group of symptoms that together are characteristic of a specific condition or disease. **16**

syntax The study of the rules that govern how words are organized into sentences. **8**

system of 16 binary operations A model depicting formal operations as a logical relationship that might occur among the factors involved in a simple experiment. **14**

telegraphic speech A speech pattern in which all words are eliminated with the exception of those that are essential to conveying the central meaning of the idea. **8**

temperament The general style of responding to the world that an individual displays. **7**

teratogen An environmental agent that can cause fetal abnormalities. **4**

tertiary circular reaction A circular reaction whereby each repetition of the response is a slight variation of that basic response. **6**

theory An organized set of assumptions about how things operate. **2**

thought All the concepts, representations, and active manipulations of information that go on within a person's mind. **8**

transactional model A developmental model emphasizing the ongoing mutual influence of person and environment. **3**

transitive inference The ability to infer the relationship between two objects from their respective relationships to a third. **10**

trimester A three-month period of pregnancy.

trophoblast The part of the blastocyst that becomes the life-support system. **4**

tumultuous growth A type of adolescent development characterized by emotional and social problems. **15**

ultrasound A technique to detect fetal disorders early in pregnancy that produces a computer image of the fetus by bouncing sound waves off it. **4**

umbilical cord The cord that connects the embryo to the placenta. **4**

unconditioned response (UCR) An unlearned response to a stimulus. **5**

unconditioned stimulus (UCS) A stimulus that evokes a response that has not been learned. **5**

undercontrolling A care giver who does not initiate interactions with the child and whose behavior fails to elicit much social responsiveness from the child. **7**

validity The degree to which a test measures that which it was designed to measure. **1**

verbal mediator A word or series of words used to connect a stimulus to an ultimate covert response by setting up a chain of internal, covert responses. **8**

wh question A sentence that begins with an interrogative word (what, where, when, why, who, how). **8**

working memory The part of the mind comprising human perceptions, images, and concepts one actively considers at any given moment in consciousness. **2, 6**

X chromosome The chromosome that, when paired with an X, determines the female sex. **4**

Y chromosome The chromosome that, when paired with an X, determines the male sex. **4**

yes/no question An interrogatory sentence that can always be answered with a simple yes or no. **8**

zone of proximal development The gap between a child's current performance and that child's potential performance if given guidance by someone more skilled. **10**

zygote The cell that results from the union of an ovum and a sperm cell. **4**

References

The number in brackets at the end of each entry refers to the chapter of the text in which that work is cited.

Abernathy, R. (1987). Report on NBC Nightly News, March 11, 1987. [3]

Abramovitch, R., and Grusec, J. (1978). Peer imitation in a natural setting. *Child Development, 49,* 60–65. [5]

Abramovitch, R., Pepler, D., and Corter, C. (1982). Patterns of sibling interaction among preschool children. In M. Lamb and B. Sutton-Smith (Eds.), *Sibling relationships: Their nature and significance across the lifespan* (pp. 61–86). Hillsdale, N.J.: Erlbaum. [13]

Abravanel, E., and Gingold, H. (1985). Learning via observation during the second year of life. *Developmental Psychology, 21,* 614–623. [5]

Achenbach, T. (1982). *Developmental psychopathology* (2nd ed.). New York: Wiley. [16]

Adam, K. (1973). Childhood parental loss, suicidal ideation, and suicidal behavior. In E. J. Anthony and C. Koupernik (Eds.), *The child and his family: The impact of disease and death* (Vol. 2). New York: Wiley. [16]

Adelson, J. (1979, January). Adolescence and the generalization gap. *Psychology Today,* pp. 33–37. [15]

Ainsworth, M. (1967). *Infancy in Uganda.* Baltimore: Johns Hopkins University Press. [7]

Ainsworth, M. (1973). The development of infant-mother attachment. In B. Caldwell and H. Ricciuti (Eds.), *Review of child development research, 3.* Chicago: University of Chicago Press. [7]

Ainsworth, M., and Bell, S. (1974). Mother-infant interaction and the development of competence. In K. Connolly and J. Bruner (Eds.), *The growth of competence.* New York: Academic Press. [7, 13]

Ainsworth, M., Bell, S., and Stayton, D. (1974). Infant-mother attachment and social development: Socialization as a product of reciprocal responsiveness to signals. In M. Richards (Ed.), *The integration of the child into the social world.* Cambridge, Eng.: Cambridge University Press. [3, 9, 11]

Ainsworth, M., Blehar, M., Waters, E., and Wall, S. (1978). *Patterns of attachment.* Hillsdale, N.J.: Erlbaum. [7]

Akiyami, M. M. (1984). Are language acquisition strategies universal? *Developmental Psychology, 20,* 219–228. [8]

Alan Guttmacher Institute. (1981). *Teenage pregnancy: The problem that hasn't gone away.* New York: Author. [15]

Alberts, J. R. (1981). Ontogeny of olfaction: Reciprocal roles of sensation and behavior in the development of perception. In R. N. Aslin, J. R. Alberts, and M. R. Petersen (Eds.), *Development of perception* (Vol. 1). New York: Academic Press. [5]

Aldous, J. (1978). *Family careers: Developmental changes in families.* New York: Wiley. [15]

Allen, J. (1978). *Visual acuity development in human infants up to 6 months of age.* Unpublished doctoral dissertation, University of Washington. [5]

Allen, V. L. (1976). *Children as teachers.* New York: Academic Press. [12]

Allen, V., and Newtson, D. (1972). Development of conformity and independence. *Journal of Personality and Social Psychology, 22,* 18–30. [12]

Alvy, K. T. (1968). Relation of age to children's egocentric and cooperative communication. *Journal of Genetic Psychology, 112,* 275–286. [13]

American Humane Association. (1987). *Highlights of official child neglect and abuse reporting.* Denver, Col.: Author. [9]

American Psychiatric Association. (1987). *Diagnostic and statistical manual of mental disorders* (3rd ed., rev.). Washington, D.C.: Author. [16]

Ames, A. (1951). Visual perception and the rotating trapezoidal window. *Psychological Monographs,* Series No. 324. [5]

Amsterdam, R. (1972). Mirror self-image reactions before age two. *Developmental Psychobiology, 5,* 297–305. [9, 11]

Anderson, D. R., and Levin, S. (1976). Young children's attention to *Sesame Street. Child Development, 47,* 806–811. [10]

Anderson, D., and Smith, R. (1984). Young children's TV viewing: The problem of cognitive continuity. In F. Morrison, C. Lord, and D. Keating (Eds.), *Advances in applied developmental psychology.* New York: Academic Press. [3]

Andolphi, M., Angelo, C., Menghi, P., and Nicolo-Corigliano, A. (1983). *Behind the family mask: Therapeutic change in rigid family systems.* New York: Brunner/Mazel. [16]

André-Thomas and Dargassies, Saint-Anne, S. (1952). *Études neurologiques sur le nouveau-né et le jeune nourrisson.* (Neurological studies of the newborn and the toddler). Paris: Mason. [5]

Antell, S. E., and Keating, D. P. (1983). Perception of numerical invariance in neonates. *Child Development, 54,* 695–706. [6]

Apgar, V., and Beck, J. (1974). *Is my baby all right?* New York: Pocket Books. [4]

Apgar, V., Holaday, D. A., James, L. S., Weisbrot, I. M., and Berrien, C. (1958). Evaluation of the newborn infant—second report. *Journal of the American Medical Association, 168,* 1985–1988. [4]

Appel, L. F., Cooper, R. G., McCarrell, N., Sims-Knight, J., Yussen, S. R., and Flavell, J. H. (1972). The development of the distinction between perceiving and memorizing. *Child Development, 43,* 1365–1381. [10]

Arend, R. (1983). *Infant attachment and patterns of adaptation in a barrier situation at age 3 1/2 years.* Unpublished doctoral dissertation, University of Minnesota. [11]

Arend, R., Gove, F., and Sroufe, L. A. (1979). Continuity of individual adaptation from infancy to kindergarten: A predictive study of ego-resiliency and curiosity in preschoolers. *Child Development, 50,* 950–959. [1, 11]

Arling, G., and Harlow, H. (1967). Effects of social deprivation on maternal behavior of rhesus monkeys. *Journal of Comparative and Physiological Psychology, 64,* 371–377. [7]

Arms, K., and Camp, P. (1987). *Biology* (3rd ed.). Philadelphia: Saunders. [1, 4]

Asher, J., and Garcia, R. (1969). The optimal age to learn a foreign language. *Modern Language Journal, 53,* 334–341. [8]

Asher, S., Singleton, L., Tinsley, R., and Hymel, S. (1979). A reliable sociometric measure for preschool children. *Developmental Psychology, 15,* 443–444. [11]

Asher, S., and Wheeler, V. A. (1985). Children's loneliness: A comparison of rejected and neglected peer states. *Journal of Consulting and Clinical Psychology, 53,* 500–505. [13]

Aslin, R. N. (1977). Development of binocular fixation in human infants. *Journal of Experimental Child Psychology, 23,* 133–150. [5]

Aslin, R. N. (1981). Development of smooth pursuit in human infants. In D. F. Fisher, R. A. Monty, and J. W. Senders (Eds.), *Eye movements: Cognition and visual perception.* Hillsdale, N.J.: Erlbaum. [5]

Aslin, R. N., and Banks, M. S. (1978). Early visual experience in humans: Evidence for a critical period in the development of binocular vision. In H. L. Pick, Jr., H. W. Leibowitz, J. E. Singer, A. Steinschneider, and H. W. Stevenson (Eds.), *Psychology: From research to practice.* New York: Plenum. [5]

Aslin, R. N., Pisoni, D. B., and Jusscyk, P. W. (1983). Auditory development and speech in infancy. In P. H. Mussen (Ed.), *Handbook of child psychology* (Vol. 2., 4th ed.): M. M. Haith and J. J. Campos (Eds.), *Infancy and developmental psychobiology.* New York: Wiley. [5]

Aslin, R. N., and Salapatek, P. (1975). Saccadic localization of peripheral targets by the very young human infant. *Perception and Psychophysics, 17,* 293–302. [5]

Atkeson, B., and Forehand, R. (1981). Conduct disorders. In E. Mash and L. Terdal (Eds.), *Behavioral assessment of childhood disorders.* New York: Guilford Press. [16]

Atkinson, R. C., and Shiffrin, R. M. (1968). Human memory: A proposed system and its control processes. In K. W. Spence and J. T. Spence (Eds.), *The psychology of learning and motivation: Advances in research and theory* (Vol. 2). New York: Academic Press. [10]

Bachman, J. (1982, June). *The American high school: A profile based on national survey data.* Paper presented at the Conference on the American High School Student Today and Tomorrow, Berkeley, Calif. [15]

Baillargeon, R. (1986). *Young infants' representation of the physical and spatial characteristics of a hidden object.* Unpublished manuscript. [6]

Baillargeon, R. (in press). Representing the existence and the location of hidden objects: Object permanence in six- and eight-month-old infants. *Cognition.* [6]

Baillargeon, R., Spelke, E. S., and Wasserman, S. (1985). Object permanence in five-month-old infants. *Cognition, 20,* 191–208. [6]

Baldwin, A., Cole, R., and Baldwin, C. (1982). Parental pathology, family interaction, and the competence of the child in school. *Monographs of the Society for Research in Child Development, 47* (No. 5). [12, 13]

Baldwin, J. M. (1897). *Social and ethical interpretations in mental development.* New York: Macmillan. [9]

Bandura, A. (1965). Influence of model's reinforcement contingencies on the acquisition of imitative processes. *Journal of Personality and Social Psychology, 1,* 589–595. [3]

Bandura, A. (1977a). *Social learning theory.* Englewood Cliffs, N.J.: Prentice-Hall. [2, 3, 5, 9, 15, 16]

Bandura, A. (1977b). Self-efficacy: Toward a unifying theory of behavioral change. *Psychological Review, 84,* 191–215. [11]

Bandura, A. (1985). A model of causality in social learning theory. In M. Mahoney and A. Freedman (Eds.), *Cognition and therapy.* New York: Plenum. [2, 3]

Bandura, A., Ross, D., and Ross, S. A. (1963). Imitation of film-mediated aggressive models. *Journal of Abnormal and Social Psychology, 66,* 3–11. [2]

Banks, M. S. (1980). The development of visual accommodation. *International Ophthalmology Clinics, 20,* 205–232. [5]

Banks, M. S. (1987). Visual recalibration and the development of contrast and optic flow perception. In A. Yonas (Ed.), *Minnesota Symposia on Child Psychology.* Hillsdale, N.J.: Erlbaum. [5]

Banks, M. S., and Salapatek, P. (1983). Infant and visual perception. In P. H. Mussen (Ed.), *Handbook of child psychology* (Vol. 2, 4th ed.): M. M. Haith and J. J. Campos (Eds.), *Infancy and developmental psychobiology.* New York: Wiley. [5]

Banta, T. (1970). Tests for the evaluation of early childhood education: The Cincinnati Autonomy Test Battery (CATB). In J. Helmuth (Ed.), *Cognitive studies.* New York: Brunner/Mazel. [11]

Barbero, G., and Shaheen, E. (1967). Environmental failure to thrive: A clinical view. *Journal of Pediatrics, 71,* 639–644. [7, 9]

Barglow, P., Vaughn, B., and Molitor, N. (in press). Effects of maternal absence due to employment on the quality of infant-mother attachment in a low-risk sample. *Child Development.* [7]

Barker, R., and Wright, H. (1955). *Midwest and its children: The psychological ecology of an American town.* Evanston, Ill.: Row, Peterson. [3]

Barkley, R., and Cunningham, C. (1978). Do stimulant drugs improve the academic performance of hyperkinetic children? A review of outcome research. *Clinical Pediatrics, 17,* 85–93. [16]

Barrera, M. E., and Maurer, D. (1981). Recognition of mother's photographed face by the three-month-old. *Child Development, 52,* 558–563. [5]

Barry, H., Bacon, M. K., and Child, I. (1957). A cross-cultural survey of some sex differences in socialization. *Journal of Abnormal and Social Psychology, 55,* 327–332. [9]

Baruch, G. K. (1972). Maternal influences upon college women's attitudes toward women and work. *Developmental Psychology, 6,* 32–37. [3]

Bates, E., and MacWhinney, B. (1982). A functionalist approach to grammatical development. In L. Gleitman and H. E. Wanner (Eds.), *Language acquisition: The state of the art.* Cambridge, Eng.: Cambridge University Press. [8]

Bates, J. (1980). The concept of difficult temperament. *Merrill-Palmer Quarterly, 26,* 299–319. [5, 7]

Bates, J., Masling, C., and Frankel, K. (1985). Attachment security, mother-child interaction, and temperament as predictors of behavior problem ratings at age three years. In I. Bretherton and E. Waters (Eds.), *Growing points in attachment theory and research. Monographs of the Society for Research in Child Development, 50* (Whole No. 209), 167–193. [7]

Bateson, W. (1909). *Mendel's principles of heredity.* Cambridge, Eng.: Cambridge University Press. [4]

Baumrind, D. (1967). Child care practices anteceding three patterns of preschool behavior. *Genetic Psychology Monographs, 75,* 43–88. [11, 13]

Baumrind, D. (1977). *Socialization determinants of personal agency.* Paper presented at the biennial meetings of the Society for Research in Child Development, New Orleans. [13]

Bayley, N. (1933). *The California first-year mental scale.* Berkeley: University of California Press. [12]

Bayley, N. (1949). Consistency and variability in the growth of intelligence from birth to eighteen years. *Journal of Genetic Psychology, 75,* 165–169. [12]

Bayley, N. (1969). *Bayley Scales of Infant Development.* New York: Psychological Corporation. [12]

Beck, F., Moffat, D., and Lloyd, J. (1973). *Human embryology and genetics.* Oxford, Eng.: Blackwell Scientific Publications. [4]

Becker, W. (1964). Consequences of different kinds of parental discipline. In M. Hoffman and L. Hoffman (Eds.), *Review of child development research, 1.* New York: Russell Sage. [13]

Beckman, D. A., and Brent, R. L. (1986). Mechanisms of known environmental teratogens: Drugs and chemicals. *Clinics in Perinatology, 13,* 649–687. [4]

Beckwith, L., and Parmelee, A. (1983). *Preterm infants from birth to five years: Social factors and cognitive development.* Paper presented at the International Society for Behavioral Development, Munich. [4]

Beeghly, M., and Cicchetti, D. (in press). An organizational approach to symbolic development in children with Down syndrome. In D. Cicchetti and M. Beeghly (Eds.), *Atypical symbolic development.* San Francisco: Jossey-Bass. [4]

Beilin, H. (1976). Constructing cognitive operators linguistically. In H. Reese (Ed.), *Advances in child development and behavior.* New York: Academic Press. [14]

Beilin, H. (1980). Piaget's theory: Refinement, revision, or rejection? In R. Kluwe and H. Spada (Eds.), *Developmental models of thinking.* New York: Academic Press. [14]

Bell, D., and Bell, L. (1983). Parental validation and support in the development of adolescent daughters. In H. Grotevant and C. Cooper (Eds.), *Adolescent development in the family: New directions in children development.* San Francisco: Jossey-Bass. [15]

Bell, R. (1968). A reinterpretation of the direction of effects in studies of socialization. *Psychological Review, 75,* 81–95. [2, 3, 9, 11]

Bell, R., and Harper, L. (1977). *Child effects on adults.* Hillsdale, N.J.: Erlbaum. [7]

Bell, S. (1970). The development of the concept of the object as related to infant-mother attachment. *Child Development, 41,* 291–311. [7]

Bell, S., and Ainsworth, M. (1972). Infant crying and maternal responsiveness. *Child Development, 43,* 1171–1190. [7]

Beller, E. (1955). Dependency and independence in young children. *Journal of Genetic Psychology, 87,* 25–35. [11]

Belsky, J. (1980a). Child maltreatment: An ecological integration. *American Psychologist, 35,* 320–335. [3, 9]

Belsky, J. (1980b). A family analysis of parental influence on infant exploratory competence. In F. Pederson (Ed.), *The father-infant relationship: Observational studies in a family context.* New York: Praeger. [12]

Belsky, J. (1981). Early human experience: A family perspective. *Developmental Psychology, 17,* 3–23. [9, 11]

Belsky, J. (1984). The determinants of parenting: A process model. *Child Development, 55,* 83–96. [3, 7]

Belsky, J. (1986). Infant day care: A cause for concern. *Zero to Three, 6* (5), 1–9. [3]

Belsky, J., and Isabella, R. A. (1987a). Individual, familial, and extrafamilial determinants of attachment security: A process analysis. In J. Belskey and T. Nezworski (Eds.), *Clinical implications of attachment.* Hillsdale, N.J.: Erlbaum. [3]

Belsky, J., and Isabella, R. A. (1987b). Maternal, infant, and social-contextual determinants of attachment security: A process analysis. In J. Belsky and T. Nezworski (Eds.), *Clinical implications of attachment.* Hillsdale, N.J.: Erlbaum. [7, 9]

Belsky, J., and Most, R. K. (1981). From exploration to play: A cross-sectional study of infant free play behavior. *Developmental Psychology, 17,* 630–639. [8]

Belsky, J., and Pinsky, E. (in press). Developmental histories, personality, and family relationships: Toward an emergent family system. In R. Hinde and J. Stevenson-Hinde (Eds.), *Relations between relationship within families.* Oxford, Eng.: Oxford University Press. [7]

Belsky, J., and Rovine, M. (in press a). Temperament and attachment in the strange situation: An empirical rapproachment. *Child Development.* [7]

Belsky, J., and Rovine, M. (in press b). Nonmaternal care in the first year of life and the security of infant-caregiver attachment. *Child Development.* [7]

Belsky, J., and Steinberg, L. D. (1978). The effects of day care: A critical review. *Child Development, 49,* 929–949. [7]

Belsky, J., Steinberg, L., and Walker, A. (1982). The ecology of day care. In M. Lamb (Ed.), *Childrearing in nontraditional families* (pp. 71–115). Hillsdale, N.J.: Erlbaum. [7]

Bem, D., and Funder, D. (1978). Predicting more of the people more of the time: Assessing the personality of situations. *Psychological Review, 85,* 485–501. [1]

Bemis, K. (1978). Current approaches to the etiology and treatment of anorexia nervosa. *Psychological Bulletin, 85,* 593–617. [16]

Benedict, R. (1938). Continuities and discontinuities in cultural conditioning. *Psychiatry, 1,* 161–167. [15]

Benenson, J., and Dweck, C. (1986). The development of trait explanations and self-evaluations in the academic and social domains. *Child Development, 57,* 1179–1187. [13]

Benn, R. (1986). Factors promoting secure attachment relationships between employed mothers and their sons. *Child Development, 57,* 1124–1231. [3]

Bennett, T. L. (1982). *Introduction to physiological psychology.* Monterey, Calif.: Brooks/Cole. [4]

Benton, A. (1971). Productivity, distributive justice, and bargaining among children. *Journal of Personality and Social Psychology, 18,* 68–78. [12]

Berg, W. K., and Berg, K. M. (1979). Psychophysiological development in infancy: State, sensory function, and attention. In J. D. Osofsky (Ed.), *Handbook of infant development.* New York: Wiley. [5]

Berko, J. (1958). The child's learning of English morphology. *Word, 14,* 150–177. [8, 10]

Berlyne, D. (1966). Curiosity and exploration. *Science, 153,*

25–33. [7, 9, 11]

Bernal, M. (1968). Behavior modification and the brat syndrome. *Journal of Consulting and Clinical Psychology, 32,* 447–455. [13]

Berndt, T. (1979). Developmental changes in conformity to peers and parents. *Developmental Psychology, 15,* 608–616. [15]

Berndt, T. (1981a). Effects of friendship on prosocial intentions and behavior. *Child Development, 52,* 636–643. [13, 15]

Berndt, T. (1981b). Relations between social cognition, nonsocial cognition, and social behavior: The case of friendship. In J. H. Flavell and L. Ross (Eds.), *Social cognitive development: Frontiers and possible future.* Cambridge, Eng.: Cambridge University Press. [15]

Berndt, T., Hawkins, J., and Hoyle, S. (1986). Changes in friendship during a school year: Effects on children's and adolescents' impressions of friendship and sharing with friends. *Child Development, 57,* 1284–1297. [13]

Bernstein, R. (1980). The development of the self system during adolescence. *Journal of Genetic Psychology, 136,* 231–245. [15]

Berzonsky, M. (1971). The role of familiarity in children's explanations of physical causality. *Child Development, 42,* 705–715. [10]

Bettes, B. (1986). *Motherese of depressed and nondepressed mothers.* Unpublished doctoral dissertation, Cornell University. [8]

Bever, T. (1970). The cognitive basis for linguistic structures. In J. R. Hayes (Ed.), *Cognition and the development of language.* New York: Wiley. [8, 10]

Bickhard, M. H. (1978). The nature of developmental stages. *Human Development, 21,* 217–233. [12]

Bigelow, B. (1977). Children's friendship expectations: A cognitive development study. *Child Development, 48,* 246–253. [13, 15]

Bigner, J. J. (1974). Second borns' discrimination of sibling role concepts. *Developmental Psychology, 10,* 564–573. [13]

Biller, H. B. (1971). *Father, child, and sex role.* Lexington, Mass.: Heath. [13]

Biller, H., and Solomon, R. (1986). *Child maltreatment and paternal deprivation.* Lexington, Mass.: Heath. [3, 9]

Bingol, N., Fuchs, M., Diaz, V., Stone, R., and Gromisch, D. (1987). Teratogenicity of cocaine in humans. *Journal of Pediatrics, 110,* 93–96. [4]

Birch, H. G., and Gussow, J. D. (1970). *Disadvantaged children: Health, nutrition and school failure.* New York: Grune & Stratton. [4]

Bisanz, G. L., Vesonder, G. T., and Voss, J. F. (1978). Knowledge of one's own responding and the relation of such knowledge to learning: A developmental study. *Journal of Experimental Child Psychology, 25,* 116–128. [12]

Bischof, N. (1975). A systems approach toward the functional connections of attachment and fear. *Child Development, 46,* 801–817. [7, 9]

Blasi, A., and Hoeffel, E. C. (1974). Adolescence and formal operations. *Human Development, 17,* 344–363. [14]

Blehar, M., Lieberman, A., and Ainsworth, M. (1977). Early face-to-face interaction and its relation to later infant-mother attachment. *Child Development, 48,* 182–194. [2, 7]

Blevins, B., and Cooper, R. G. (1986). The development of transitivity of length in young children. *Journal of Genetic Psychology, 147,* 395–405. [10]

Block, J. (1971). *Lives through time.* Berkeley, Calif.: Bancroft Books. [13]

Block, J. (1977). Recognizing the coherence of personality. In D. Magnusson and N. Endler (Eds.), *Personality at the crossroads: Current issues in interactional psychology.* Hillsdale, N.J.: Erlbaum. [1]

Block, J. (1987, April). *Longitudinal antecedents of ego-control and ego-resiliency in late adolescence.* Paper presented at the biennial meeting of the Society for Research in Child Development, Baltimore. [11, 15]

Block, J., von der Lippe, A., and Block, J. H. (1973). Sex-role and socialization patterns: Some personality concomitants and environmental antecedents. *Journal of Consulting and Clinical Psychology, 41,* 321–341. [13]

Block, J. H. (1979). *Personality development in males and females: The influence of different socialization.* Master Lecture Series of the American Psychological Association, New York. [3, 12, 13, 15]

Block, J. H., and Block, J. (1980). The role of ego-control and ego-resiliency in the organization of behavior. In W. A. Collins (Ed.), *Minnesota Symposia on Child Psychology, 13.* Hillsdale, N.J.: Erlbaum. [11, 12]

Block, J. H., Block, J., and Gjerde, P. (1986). The personality of children prior to divorce: A prospective study. *Child Development, 57,* 827–840. [3, 13]

Block, J. H., Block, J., and Morrison, A. (1981). Parental agreement-disagreement on childrearing orientations and gender-related personality correlates in children. *Child Development, 52,* 965–974. [13]

Bloom, K., and Esposito, A. (1975). Social conditioning and its proper control procedures. *Journal of Experimental Child Psychology, 19,* 209–222. [7]

Bloom, L. M. (1973). *One word at a time: The use of single word utterances before syntax.* The Hague: Mouton. [8]

Blos, P. (1962). *On adolescence.* New York: Free Press. [15]

Blos, P. (1970). *The young adolescent.* New York: Free Press. [13]

Blyth, D., Bulcroft, R., and Simmons, R. (1981). *The impact of puberty on adolescents.* Paper presented at the Annual Meeting of the American Psychological Association, Los Angeles. [15]

Bonney, M., and Powell, J. (1953). Differences in social behavior between sociometrically high and sociometrically low children. *Journal of Educational Research, 46,* 481–495. [12]

Borke, H. (1971). Interpersonal perception of young children: Egocentrism or empathy? *Developmental Psychology, 5,* 263–269. [11]

Bornstein, M. H. (1978). Chromatic vision in infancy. In H. W. Reese and L. P. Lipsitt (Eds.), *Advances in child development and behavior* (Vol. 12). New York: Academic Press. [5]

Bornstein, M. H. (1981). "Human infant color and color perception" reviewed and reassessed: A critique of Werner and Wooten (1979). *Infant Behavior and Development, 4,* 119–150. [5]

Bornstein, M. H., and Sigman, M. D. (1986). Continuity in mental development from infancy. *Child Development, 57,* 251–274. [12]

Boszormenyi-Nagy, I., and Spark, G. (1973). *Invisible loyalties: Reciprocity in intergenerational family therapy.* New York: Harper & Row. [16]

Bourne, E. (1978). The state of research on ego identity: A review and appraisal. *Journal of Youth and Adolescence, 7,* 223–251 (Part 1) and 371–392 (Part 2). [15]

Bowen, M. (1978). *Family therapy in clinical practice.* New York: Aronson. [12]

Bower, T. G. R. (1966). Slant perception and shape constancy in infants. *Science, 151,* 832–834. [6]

Bower, T. G. R. (1967). The development of object-permanence: Some studies of existence constancy. *Perception and Psychophysics, 2*, 411–418. [6]

Bower, T. G. R. (1974). *Development in infancy.* San Francisco: Freeman. [5]

Bower, T. G. R. (1977). *A primer of infant development.* San Francisco: Freeman. [5, 6, 7]

Bowerman, M. (1981). Keynote address, Child Language Research Forum, Stanford University, Stanford, Calif. [8]

Bowlby, J. (1969). *Attachment and loss: Vol. 1. Attachment.* New York: Basic Books. [2, 7]

Bowlby, J. (1973). *Separation.* New York: Basic Books. [4, 7, 11]

Bowlby, J. (1980). *Attachment and loss: Vol. 3. Loss.* New York: Basic Books. [16]

Bowlby, J. (1982). *Attachment and loss* (2nd ed.). New York: Basic Books. [2, 7]

Boxer, A., Solomon, B., Offer, D., Petersen, A., and Halprin, F. (1984). Parents' perceptions of young adolescents. In R. Cohen, B. Cohler, and S. Weissman (Eds.), *Parenthood: A psychodynamic perspective.* New York: Guilford Press. [15]

Brackbill, Y. (1958). Extinction of the smiling response in infants as a function of reinforcement schedule. *Child Development, 29*, 115–124. [7]

Brackbill, Y. (1979). Obstetrical medication and infant behavior. In J. D. Osofsky (Ed.), *Handbook of infant development* (pp. 76–125). New York: Wiley. [4, 7]

Brazelton, T. B. (1969). *Infants and mothers: Differences in development.* New York: Dell. [6, 7]

Brazelton, T. B. (1973). Neonatal behavioral assessment scale. *Clinics in Developmental Medicine, 50.* Philadelphia: Lippincott. [5]

Brazelton, T. B. (1976a). Early parent-infancy reciprocity. In V. C. Vaughan and T. B. Brazelton (Eds.), *The family: Can it be saved?* Chicago: Yearbook Medical Publishers. [7]

Brazelton, T. B. (1976b). *Toddlers and parents.* New York: Dell. [9]

Brazelton, T. B., Koslowski, B., and Main, M. (1974). The origins of reciprocity: The early mother-input interaction. In M. Lewis and L. Rosenblum (Eds.), *The effect of the infant on its caregiver.* New York: Wiley. [7]

Breger, L. (1974). *From instinct to identity: The development of personality.* Englewood Cliffs, N.J.: Prentice-Hall. [2, 3, 9, 11]

Breslow, L. (1981). Reevaluation of the literature on the development of transitive inferences. *Psychological Bulletin, 89*, 325–351. [10]

Bretherton, I. (1985). Attachment theory: Retrospect and prospect. In I. Bretherton and E. Waters (Eds.), *Growing points in attachment theory and research. Monographs of the Society for Research in Child Development, 50* (Serial No. 209). [9]

Bretherton, I., and Ainsworth, M. (1974). Response of one-year-olds to a stranger in a strange situation. In M. Lewis and L. Rosenblum (Eds.), *The origins of fear.* New York: Wiley. [9]

Brittain, C. (1963). Adolescent choice and parent-peer cross pressures. *American Sociological Review, 28*, 385–391. [3, 15]

Brody, S., and Axelrod, S. (1970). *Anxiety and ego formation in infancy.* New York: International Universities Press. [7]

Bromwich, R. (1976). Focus on maternal behavior in infant intervention. *American Journal of Orthopsychiatry, 46*, 439–446. [9]

Bronfenbrenner, U. (1970a). *Two worlds of childhood: U.S. and U.S.S.R.* New York: Russell Sage. [7]

Bronfenbrenner, U. (1970b). Reaction to social pressure from adults versus peers among Soviet day school and boarding school pupils in the perspective of an American sample. *Journal of Personality and Social Psychology, 15*, 179–189. [12]

Bronfenbrenner, U. (1977). Toward an experimental ecology of human development. *American Psychologist, 32*, 513–531. [3]

Bronfenbrenner, U. (1979). *The ecology of human development.* Cambridge, Mass.: Harvard University Press. [3]

Bronfenbrenner, U. (1986). Ecology of the family as a context for human development: Research perspectives. *Developmental Psychology, 22*, 723–742.

Bronson, G., and Pankey, W. (1977). On the distinction between fear and wariness. *Child Development, 48*, 1167–1183. [7]

Bronson, W. (1981). *Toddlers' behavior with agemates: Issues of interaction, cognitive and affect.* Norwood, N.J.: Ablex. [9, 11]

Brookman, K. E. (1980). *Ocular accommodation in human infants.* Unpublished doctoral dissertation, Indiana University. [5]

Broughton, J. (1978). Development of concepts of self, mind, reality, and knowledge. *New Directions for Child Development, 1*, 75–100. [13, 15]

Brown, A. L., Bransford, J. D., Ferrara, R. A., and Campione, J. C. (1983). Learning, remembering, and understanding. In P. H. Mussen (Ed.), *Handbook of child psychology* (Vol. 3, 4th ed.): J. H. Flavell and E. M. Markman (Eds.), *Cognitive development.* New York: Wiley. [12]

Brown, B., Clasen, D., and Eicher, S. (1985). *Peer pressure, peer conformity, and self-reported behavior among adolescents.* Paper presented at the biennial meeting of the Society for Research in Child Development, Toronto. [15]

Brown, G., and Harris, T. (1978). *Social origins of depression.* London, Eng.: Tavistock Publications. [12]

Brown, G., Harris, T., and Bifulco, A. (1986). Long-term effects of early loss of parent. In M. Rutter, C. Izard, and P. Read (Eds.), *Depression in young people.* New York: Guilford Press. [16]

Brown, R. (1973). *A first language: The early stages.* Cambridge, Mass.: Harvard University Press. [8, 10]

Brown, R., Cazden, C., and Bellugi, U. (1969). The child's grammar from I to III. In J. P. Hill (Ed.), *Minnesota symposia on child psychology* (Vol. 2). Minneapolis: University of Minnesota Press. [8, 10]

Brown, R., and Hanlon, C. (1970). Derivational complexity and order of acquisition. In J. R. Hayes (Ed.), *Cognition and the development of language.* New York: Wiley. [8]

Brown, S. W. (1970). A comparative study of maternal employment and nonemployment. *Dissertation Abstracts International, 30*, 4708A. (University Microfilms No. 70-8610.)

Brownell, C., and Brown, E. (1985). *Age differences in possession negotiations during the second year.* Paper presented at the biennial meeting of the Society for Research in Child Development, Toronto. [1, 9]

Bruch, H. (1973). *Eating disorders: Obesity, anorexia nervosa, and the person within.* New York: Basic Books. [16]

Bruch, H. (1979). *The golden cage: The enigma of anorexia nervosa.* New York: Vintage Books. [16]

Bruner, J. S. (1964). The course of cognitive growth. *American Psychologist, 19*, 1–15. [8]

Bruner, J. S. (1970). The growth and structure of skill. In K. Connolly (Ed.), *Mechanisms of motor skill development.* New York: Academic Press. [5, 6]

Bruner, J. S. (1973). Organization of early skilled action.

Child Development, 44, 1–11. [6]

Bruner, J. S. (1975). The ontogenesis of speech acts. *Journal of Child Language, 2,* 1–19. [12]

Bruner, J. S. (1981). Intention in the structure of action and interaction. *Advances in Infancy Research, 1,* 41–56. [5]

Bruner, J. S. (1983). The acquisition of pragmatic commitments. In R. Golinkoff (Ed.), *The transition from prelinguistic to linguistic communication.* Hillsdale, N.J.: Erlbaum. [6]

Bruner, J. S., Olver, R. R., and Greenfield, P. M. (1966). *Studies in cognitive growth.* New York: Wiley. [6, 12]

Brunnquell, D., Crichton, L., and Egeland, B. (1981). Maternal personality and attitude in disturbances of child rearing. *American Journal of Orthopsychiatry, 51,* 680–691. [9]

Bryant, B. (1974). Locus of control related to teacher-child interperceptual experiences. *Child Development, 45,* 157–174. [15]

Bryant, B. (1979, September). *Siblings as caretakers.* Paper presented at the annual meeting of the American Psychological Association, New York. [13]

Bryant, B. (1982). Sibling relationships in middle childhood. In M. Lamb and B. Sutton-Smith (Eds.), *Sibling relationships: Their nature and significance across the lifespan* (pp. 87–122). Hillsdale, N.J.: Erlbaum. [13]

Bryant, B. (1985). The neighborhood walk: Sources of support in middle childhood. *Monographs of the Society for Research in Child Development, 50* (3, Serial No. 210). [3]

Bryant, B., and Crockenberg, S. B. (1980). Correlates and dimensions of prosocial behavior: A study of female siblings with their mothers. *Child Development, 51,* 529–544. [13]

Bryant, P. E., and Trabasso, T. R. (1971). Transitive inferences and memory in young children. *Nature, 232,* 456–458. [10]

Bugental, D., and Shennum, W. (1984). Difficult children as elicitors and targets of adult communication patterns: An attributional-behavioral analysis. *Monographs of the Society for Research in Child Development, 49* (Serial No. 205). [3]

Buhler, C. (1930). *The first year of life* (P. Greenberg and R. Ribin, Trans.). New York: John Day. [5]

Bullough, V. L. (1981). Age at menarche: A misunderstanding. *Science, 213,* 365–366. [14]

Bunt, M. (1968). Ego identity: Its relationships to the discrepancy between how an adolescent views himself and how he perceives that others view him. *Psychology, 5,* 14–25. [15]

Bushnell, I. W. R. (1979). Modification of the externality effect in young infants. *Journal of Experimental Child Psychology, 28,* 211–229. [5]

Butler, N. R., and Goldstein, H. (1973). Smoking in pregnancy and subsequent child development. *British Medical Journal, 4,* 573–575. [4]

Butler, R. (1953). Discrimination learning by rhesus monkeys to visual exploration motivation. *Journal of Comparative and Physiological Psychology, 46,* 95–98. [3]

Butterworth, G. (1974). *The development of the object concept in human infants.* Unpublished doctoral dissertation, University of Oxford, Eng. [6]

Butterworth, G. (1975). Object identity in infancy: The interaction of spatial location codes in determining search errors. *Child Development, 46,* 866–870. [6]

Butterworth, G. (1977). Object disappearance and error in Piaget's stage IV task. *Journal of Experimental Child Psychology, 23,* 391–401. [6]

Campbell, R. L., and Bickhard, M. H. (1986). *Knowing levels and developmental stages.* New York: Karger. [12]

Campos, J. J., Bertenthal, B. I., and Caplovitz, K. (1982). The interrelationship of affect and cognition in the visual cliff situation. In C. Izard, J. Kagan, and R. Zajonc (Eds.), *Emotion and cognition.* New York: Plenum. [5]

Campos, J. J., Hiatt, S., Ramsay, D., Henderson, C., and Svejda, M. (1978). The emergence of fear on the visual cliff. In M. Lewis and L. Rosenblum (Eds.), *The origins of affect.* New York: Wiley. [5]

Caplow, T. (1968). *Two against one: Coalition in triads.* Englewood Cliffs, N.J.: Prentice-Hall. [13]

Capon, N., and Kuhn, D. (1979). Logical reasoning in the supermarket: Adult females' use of a proportional reasoning strategy in an everyday context. *Developmental Psychology, 15,* 450–452. [14]

Carey, S. (1978). The child as word learner. In M. Halle, J. Bresnan, and G. A. Miller (Eds.), *Linguistic theory and psychological reality.* Cambridge, Mass.: MIT Press. [8]

Carey, S. (1985). Are children fundamentally different thinkers and learners from adults? In S. G. Chipman, J. W. Segal, and R. Glaser (Eds.), *Thinking and learning skills* (Vol. 2, pp. 485–517). Hillsdale, N.J.: Erlbaum. [2]

Caron, A. J., Caron, R. F., and Carlson, V. R. (1979). Infant perception of the invariant shape of objects varying in slant. *Child Development, 50,* 716–721. [5]

Carr, S., Dabbs, J., and Carr, T. (1975). Mother-infant attachment: The importance of the mother's visual field. *Child Development, 46,* 331–338. [9, 11]

Case, R. (1974). Structure and strictures: Some functional limitations on the course of cognitive growth. *Cognitive Psychology, 6,* 544–573. [14]

Case, R. (1978). Intellectual development from birth to adulthood: A neo-Piagetian interpretation. In R. Siegler (Ed.), *Children's thinking: What develops?* Hillsdale, N.J.: Erlbaum. [14]

Case, R. (1985). *Intellectual development: Birth to adulthood.* New York: Academic Press. [2, 6, 14, V-4, V Summary]

Casler, L. (1967). Perceptual deprivation in institutional settings. In G. Newton and S. Levine (Eds.), *Early experience and behavior.* New York: Springer. [7]

Caspi, A., and Elder, G. H. (in press). Emergent family patterns: The intergenerational construction of problem behavior and relationships. In R. Hinde and J. Stevenson-Hinde (Eds.), *Relations between relationships within families.* Oxford, Eng.: Oxford University Press. [3, 13, 16]

Cattell, R. B. (1971). *Abilities: Their structure, growth, and action.* Boston: Houghton Mifflin. [12]

Caudill, W., and Weinstein, H. (1966). Maternal care and infant behavior in Japanese and American urban middle class families. In R. Konig and R. Hill (Eds.), *Yearbook of the International Sociological Association.* Madrid: International Sociological Association. [7]

Caudill, W., and Weinstein, H. (1969). Maternal care and infant behavior in Japan and America. *Psychiatry, 32,* 12–43. [3]

Cazden, B. (1983). Peekaboo as an instructional model: Discourse development at school and at home. In B. Brain (Ed.), *The sociogenesis of language and human conduct: A multidisciplinary book of readings.* New York: Plenum. [12]

Cazden, C. (1968). The acquisition of noun and verb inflections. *Child Development, 39,* 438–443, [8, 10]

Centers for Disease Control. (1984). Fetal alcohol syndrome: Public awareness week. *Morbidity and Mortality Weekly Report, 33,* 1–2. Atlanta: Author. [4]

Centers for Disease Control. (1986). Rubella and congenital rubella syndrome—New York City. *Morbidity and Mortality Weekly Report, 35,* 770–774, 779. Atlanta: Author. [4]

Charles, L., and Schain, R. (1981). A four year follow-up study of the effect of methylphenidate on the behavior and academic achievement of hyperactive children. *Journal of Abnormal Child Psychology, 9,* 495–505. [16]

Charlesworth, W. R. (1966, September). *The development of the object concept: A methodological concept.* Paper presented at the meeting of the American Psychological Association, New York. [6]

Charlesworth, W. R. (1969). The role of surprise in cognitive development. In D. Elkind and J. H. Flavell (Eds.), *Studies in cognitive development.* Oxford, Eng.: Oxford University Press. [3]

Charlesworth, W. R. (1982). An ethological approach to research on facial expressions. In C. Izard (Ed.), *Measuring emotions in infants and children* (317–334). Cambridge, Eng.: Cambridge University Press. [7]

Chase, W. G., and Simon, H. A. (1973). Perception in chess. *Cognitive Psychology, 4,* 55–81. [12]

Chassin, L., and Sherman, S. (1985). *Adolescents' changing relationships with parents and peers: A cohort-sequential study.* Paper presented at the biennial meeting of the Society for Research in Child Development, Toronto. [15]

Chervenak, F. A., Isaacson, C., and Mahoney, M. J. (1986). Advances in the diagnosis of fetal defects. *New England Journal of Medicine, 315,* 305–307. [4]

Chess, S. (1977). Follow-up report on autism and congenital rubella. *Journal of Autism and Childhood Schizophrenia, 7,* 69–81. [16]

Chi, M. T. H. (1978). Knowledge structure and memory development. In R. S. Siegler (Ed.), *Children's thinking: What develops?* Hillsdale, N.J.: Erlbaum. [10, 12]

Chi, M. T. H., and Ceci, S. J. (1986). The restructuring of knowledge in memory development. In H. W. Reese and L. P. Lipsitt (Eds.), *Advances in child development and behavior* (Vol. 22, pp. 1–42). New York: Academic Press. [2]

Chi, M. T. H., and Ceci, S. J. (1987). Content knowledge: Its role, representation, and restructuring in memory development. In H. W. Reese and L. Lipsett (Eds.), *Advances in child development and behavior.* New York: Academic Press. [10]

Chomsky, N. (1957). *Syntactic structures.* The Hague: Mouton. [8]

Chukovsky, K. (1941/1971). *From two to five.* (M. Morton, Trans. and Ed.). Berkeley, Calif.: University of California Press. [10]

Chumlea, W. C. (1982). Physical growth in adolescence. In B. B. Wolman (Ed.), *Handbook of developmental psychology.* Englewood Cliffs, N.J.: Prentice-Hall. [14]

Cicchetti, D. (1984). The emergence of developmental psychopathology. *Child Development, 55,* 1–7. [16]

Cicchetti, D., and Beeghly, M. (in press). *Down syndrome: A developmental perspective.* Cambridge, Eng.: Cambridge University Press. [4]

Cicchetti, D., and Sroufe, L. A. (1978). An organizational view of affect: Illustration from the study of Down syndrome infants. In M. Lewis and L. Rosenblum (Eds.), *The development of affect.* New York: Plenum. [4, 7]

Clark, E. V. (1973). What is in a word? On the child's acquisition of semantics in his first language. In T. E. Moore (Ed.), *Cognitive development and the acquisition of language.* New York: Academic Press. [8]

Clark, E. V. (1983). Meanings and concepts. In P. H. Mussen (Ed.), *Handbook of child psychology* (Vol. 3, 4th ed.): J. H.

Flavell and E. M. Markman (Eds.), *Cognitive development.* New York: Wiley. [8]

Clark, E. V. (1987). The principle of contrast: A constraint on language acquisition. In B. MacWhinney (Ed.), *Mechanisms of language acquisition.* Hillsdale, N.J.: Erlbaum. [8]

Clark, R., and Delia, J. (1976). The development of functional persuasive skills in childhood and early adolescence. *Child Development, 47,* 1008–1014. [15]

Clarke, A. M., and Clarke, A. D. B. (1976). *Early experience: Myth and evidence.* New York: Free Press. [7]

Clarke-Stewart, K. A. (1973). Interactions between mothers and their young children. *Monographs of the Society for Research in Child Development, 38* (No. 153). [7, 8, 9]

Clarke-Stewart, K. A. (1977). *Child care in the family: A review of research and some propositions for policy.* New York: Academic Press. [3]

Clarke-Stewart, K. A. (1978a). And daddy makes three: The father's impact on mother and young child. *Child Development, 49,* 466–478. [3]

Clarke-Stewart, K. A. (1978b). Recasting the lone stranger. In J. Glick and K. A. Clarke-Stewart (Eds.), *The development of social understanding* (pp. 109–176). New York: Gardner Press. [9]

Clarke-Stewart, K. A. (1980). The father's contribution to child development. In F. A. Pedersen (Ed.), *The father-infant relationship: Observational studies in a family context.* New York: Praeger. [9]

Clarke-Stewart, K. A., Friedman, S., and Koch, J. (1985). *Child development: A topical approach.* New York: Wiley. [5]

Clausen, J. (1968). Perspectives on childhood socialization. In J. Clausen (Ed.), *Socialization and society.* Boston: Little, Brown. [11]

Clifford, E. (1959). Discipline in the home: A controlled observational study of parental practices. *Journal of Genetic Psychology, 95,* 45–82. [13]

Cohen, L. B., and Campos, J. (1974). Father, mother, and stranger as elicitors of attachment behaviors in infancy. *Developmental Psychology, 10,* 146–154. [3, 7]

Cohen, L. B., DeLoache, J., and Strauss, M. S. (1979). Infant visual perception. In J. Osofsky (Ed.), *Handbook of infant development.* New York: Wiley. [7]

Cohen, L. B., and Strauss, M. S. (1979). Concept acquisition in the human infant. *Child Development, 50,* 419–424. [6]

Cohen, L. B., and Younger, B. A. (1984). Infant perception of angular relations. *Infant Behavior and Development, 7,* 37–47. [6]

Cohen, S., and Beckwith, L. (1979). Preterm infant interaction with the caregiver in the first year of life and competence at age two. *Child Development, 50,* 767–776. [3]

Colby, A., Kohlberg, L., Gibbs, J., and Lieberman, M. (1980). A longitudinal study of moral judgment. *Monographs of the Society for Research in Child Development, 48* (1, Serial No. 200). [14]

Cole, J. (1974). An evaluation of the cross-situational stability of children's curiosity. *Journal of Personality, 42,* 93–116. [11]

Cole, S. (1980). *Working kids on working.* New York: Lothrop, Lee, & Shephard. [15]

Coleman, J. (1961). *The adolescent society.* New York: Free Press. [15]

Coleman, J. (1974). *Relationships in adolescents.* London, Eng.: Routledge & Kegan Paul. [15]

Coleman, J. (1980). Friendship and the peer group in adolescence. In J. Adelson (Ed.), *Handbook of adolescent psychology.* New York: Wiley. [15]

Collis, K. F. (1978). Operational thinking in elementary mathematics. In J. A. Keats, K. F. Collis, and G. S. Halford (Eds.), *Cognitive development research based on a neo-Piagetian approach*. New York: Wiley. [14]

Condon, W., and Sander, L. (1974). Neonate movement is synchronized with adult speech: Interactional participation and language acquisition. *Science, 183,* 99–101. [7]

Congressional Budget Office. (1985). Reducing poverty among children. Washington, D.C.: Author. [3]

Connell, D. B. (1976). *Individual differences in attachment: An investigation into stability, implications, and relationships to structure of early language development*. Unpublished doctoral dissertation, Syracuse University. [7]

Conners, C. K. (1977). Discussion of Rapoport's chapter. In J. Schulterbrandt and A. Raskin (Eds.), *Depression in childhood*. New York: Raven Press. [16]

Conners, C. K., Goyette, C., Southwick, D., Lees, J., and Andrulonis, P. (1976). Food additives and hyperkinesis: A controlled double-blind experiment. *Pediatrics, 58,* 154–166. [16]

Connolly, J., and Doyle, A. (in press). Relations of social fantasy play to social competence. *Developmental Psychology*. [11]

Connor, J. M., and Serbin, L. A. (1977). Behaviorally-based masculine and feminine activity-preference scales for preschoolers: Correlates with other classroom behaviors and cognitive tests. *Child Development, 48,* 1411–1416. [11]

Cooper, C., Grotevant, H., and Condon, J. (1983). Individuality and connectedness in the family as a context for adolescent identity formation and role-taking skill. In H. Grotevant and C. Cooper (Eds.), *Adolescent development in the family: New Directions in Child Development*. San Francisco: Jossey-Bass. [15]

Cooper, C. R. (1980). Development of collaborative problem solving among preschool children. *Developmental Psychology, 16,* 433–440. [10]

Cooper, C. R., and Cooper, R. G. (1985). Peer learning discourse: What develops? In S. Kuczaj (Ed.), *Children's discourse*. New York: Springer-Verlag. [10, 12]

Cooper, C. R., Marquis, A., and Edwards, D. (1986). Four perspectives on peer learning among elementary school children. In E. C. Mueller and C. R. Cooper (Eds.), *Process and outcome in peer relationships*. New York: Academic Press. [12]

Cooper, R. G. (1973). *A developmental study of conceptual ability as assessed by two rule-learning tasks*. Unpublished Ph.D. dissertation, University of Minnesota, Minneapolis. [10]

Cooper, R. G. (1976, April). *The role of estimators and operators in number conservation*. Paper presented at the Southwestern Psychological Association, Albuquerque. [10]

Cooper, R. G. (1984). Early number development: Discovering number space with addition and subtraction. In C. Sophian (Ed.), *Origins of cognitive skills*. Hillsdale, N.J.: Erlbaum. [6, 10, 12]

Cooper, R. G., Leitner, E., and Moore, N. V. (1977, March). *The development of skills underlying perception, representation, and construction of series*. Paper presented at the biennial meeting of the Society for Research in Child Development, New Orleans. (ERIC Document Reproduction Service No. ED 136-952.) [10]

Cooper, R. G., and Robbins, R. R. (1981). The effect of cognitive skills on learning astronomy. *Proceedings of the 1980 Frontiers in Education Conference*. Houston, Tex.: Southwest Astronomy and Astrophysics Society. [14]

Coopersmith, S. (1967). *The antecedents of self-esteem*. San Francisco: Freeman. [11, 13]

Corman, H. H., and Escalona, S. K. (1969). Stages of sensorimotor development: A replication study. *Merrill-Palmer Quarterly, 15,* 351–361. [6]

Corsaro, E. (1977). The clarification request as a feature of adult interactive styles with young children. *Language in Society, 8,* 315–337. [8]

Costanzo, P. (1970). Conformity development as a function of self-blame. *Journal of Personality and Social Psychology, 14,* 366–374. [3, 15]

Cottrell, L. (1969). Interpersonal interaction and the development of the self. In D. Goslin (Ed.), *Handbook of socialization, theory, and research* (pp. 543–570). Chicago: Rand-McNally. [13]

Cowan, P., Cowan, C., and Heming, G. (1986). *Risks to marriage when partners become parents: Implications for family development*. Paper presented at the annual meeting of the American Psychiatric Association, Washington, D.C. [3]

Cowan, W. N. (1979). Development of the brain. *Scientific American, 241,* 112–114. [4]

Cowen, E., Pederson, A., Babijian, H., Izzo, L., and Trost, M. (1973). Long-term follow-up of early detected vulnerable children. *Journal of Consulting and Clinical Psychology, 41,* 438–446. [13, 16]

Cox, M., Owen, M., Lewis, J., Riedel, C., Scalf-McIver, L., and Suster, A. (in press). Intergenerational influences on the parent-infant relationship in the transition to parenthood. *Journal of Family Issues*. [9]

Cox, S. (1966). *Family background effects on personality development and social acceptance*. Unpublished doctoral dissertation, Texas Christian University. [13]

Crandall, R. (1973). The measurement of self-esteem and related constructs. In J. Robinson and P. Shaver (Eds.), *Measures of social psychological attitudes*. Ann Arbor: Institute for Social Research. [12]

Crisp, A. (1970). Premorbid factors in adult disorders of weight, with particular reference to primary anorexia nervosa (weight phobia): A literature review. *Journal of Psychosomatic Research, 14,* 1–22. [16]

Crockenberg, S. (1981). Infant irritability, mother responsiveness and social support influences on the security of infant-mother attachment. *Child Development, 52,* 857–865. [3, 7]

Crockenberg, S. (1984). Social support and the maternal behavior of adolescent mothers. ICIS. [7, 9]

Crockenberg, S. (1986, April). *Maternal anger and the behavior of two-year-old children*. Paper presented at the International Conference on Infant Studies, Beverly Hills, Calif. [9]

Crook, C. K. (1978). Taste perception in the newborn infant. *Infant Behavior and Development, 1,* 52–69. [5]

Cross, T. G. (1977). Mother's speech adjustments: The contribution of selected child-listener variables. In C. E. Snow and C. A. Ferguson (Eds.), *Talking to children: Input and acquisition*. Cambridge, Eng.: Cambridge University Press. [8]

Cummings, E., Zahn-Waxler, C., and Radke-Yarrow, M. (1981). Young children's responses to expressions of anger and affection by others in the family. *Child Development, 52,* 1274–1282. [9]

Cupoli, J. M., Hallock, J. A., and Barness, L. A. (1980). Failure to thrive. *Current Problems in Pediatrics, 10,* 3–42. [7]

Curtiss, S. (1977). *Genie: Psycholinguistic study of a modern-day wild child*. New York: Academic Press. [3]

Cytryn, L., and McKnew, D. H. (1979). Affective disorders. In J. Noshpitz (Ed.), *Basic handbook of child psychiatry* (Vol. 2). New York: Basic Books. [2, 16]

Dale, P. (1976). *Language development* (2nd ed.). New York: Holt, Rinehart & Winston. [8, 10]

Damon, W. (1977). *The social world of the child.* San Francisco: Jossey-Bass. [13]

Damon, W. (1983). *Social and personality development.* New York: Norton. [12, 13, 15]

Damon, W., and Hart, D. (1982). The development of self-understanding from infancy through adolescence. *Child Development, 53,* 841–864. [13]

D'Angelo, R. (1974). *Families of Sand: A report concerning the flight of adolescents from their families.* Columbus, Ohio: State University School of Social Work. [15]

Daniels, D., and Plomin, R. (1985). Origins of individual differences in infant shyness. *Developmental Psychology, 21,* 118–121. [11]

Davids, A., Holden, R., and Gray, G. (1963). Maternal anxiety during pregnancy and adequacy of mother and child adjustment eight months following childbirth. *Child Development, 34,* 993–1002. [4, 7, 9]

Day, M. C. (1975). Developmental trends in visual scanning. In H. W. Reese (Ed.), *Advances in child development and behavior* (Vol. 10). New York: Academic Press. [10]

Day, R. H., and McKenzie, B. E. (1981). Infant perception of the invariant size of approaching and receding objects. *Developmental Psychology, 17,* 670–677. [5]

Dayton, G. O., Jr., and Jones, M. H. (1964). Analysis of characteristics of fixation reflexes in infants by use of direct current electrooculography. *Neurology, 14,* 1152–1156. [5]

DeCasper, A., and Fifer, W. (1980). Of human bonding: Newborns prefer their mothers' voices. *Science, 208,* 1174–1176. [5]

DeMyer, M., Hingten, J., and Jackson, R. (1981). Infantile autism reviewed: A decade of research. *Schizophrenia Bulletin, 7,* 388–451. [16]

Denney, N. W. (1972). Free classification in preschool children. *Child Development, 43,* 1161–1170. [10]

Dennis, W., and Dennis, M. C. (1940). The effect of cradling practices upon the onset of walking in Hopi children. *Journal of Genetic Psychology, 56,* 77–86. [5]

Detera-Wadleigh, S., Berrettini, W., Goldin, L., Borman, D., Anderson, S., and Gershon, E. (1987). Close linkage of C-Harvey-ras-1 and the insulin gene to affective disorder is ruled out in three North American pedigrees. *Nature, 325,* 806–808. [16]

deVilliers, J. G., and deVilliers, P. A. (1978). *Language acquisition.* Cambridge, Mass.: Harvard University Press. [8, 10]

Dickinson, G. (1975). Dating behavior of black and white adolescents before and after desegregation. *Journal of Marriage and the Family, 37,* 602–608. [15]

Dietrich, K. N., Starr, R. H., Jr., and Weisfeld, G. E. (1983). Infant maltreatment: Caretaker-infant interaction and developmental consequences at different levels of parenting failures. *Pediatrics, 72,* 532–540. [7]

DiPietro, J. A. (1981). Rough and tumble play: A function of gender. *Developmental Psychology, 17,* 50–59. [11]

Dittman, A. T. (1972). Developmental factors in conversational behavior. *Journal of Communication, 22,* 404–423. [13]

Dix, T., Ruble, D., Grusec, J., and Nixon, S. (1987). Social cognition in parents: Inferential and affective reactions to children of three age levels. *Child Development, 57,* 879–894. [2]

Dodge, K. A., and Frame, C. L. (1982). Social cognitive biases and deficits in aggressive boys. *Child Development, 53,* 620–635. [13]

Dodge, K. A., Petit, G. S., McClaskey, C. L., and Brown, M. M. (1986). Social competence in children. *Monographs of the Society for Research in Child Development, 51* (2, Serial No. 213). [13]

Donaldson, M. (1963). *A study of children's thinking.* London, Eng.: Tavistock. [14]

Donovan, J., and Jesser, R. (1985). Structure of problem behavior in adolescence and young adulthood. *Journal of Consulting and Clinical Psychology, 53,* 890–904. [15]

Douglas, V., and Peters, K. (1980). Toward a clearer definition of the attentional deficit of hyperactive children. In G. Hale and M. Lewis (Eds.), *Attention and the development of cognitive skills* (pp. 173–247). New York: Plenum. [16]

Douvan, E. (1963). Employment and the adolescent. In F. Nye and L. Hoffman (Eds.), *The employed mother in America.* Chicago, Ill.: Rand-McNally. [3]

Douvan, E., and Adelson, J. (1966). *The adolescent experience.* New York: Wiley. [15]

Dove, A. (1968, July 15). Taking the chittling test. *Newsweek,* 51–52. [12]

Dubey, D. (1976). Organic factors in hyperkinesis: A critical evaluation. *American Journal of Orthopsychiatry, 46,* 353–366. [16]

Dunn, J. (1985). *The transition from infancy to childhood.* Address presented to the Society for Research in Child Development, Toronto. [11]

Dunn, J. (in press). Mothers and siblings: Connections between three family relationships. In R. Hinde and J. Stevenson-Hinde (Eds.), *Towards understanding families.* Cambridge, Eng.: Cambridge University Press. [3]

Dunn, J., and Kendrick, C. (1982a). Interaction between young siblings: Association with the interaction between mother and firstborn child. *Developmental Psychology, 17,* 336–343. [3, 13]

Dunn, J., and Kendrick, C. (1982b). *Siblings.* Cambridge, Mass.: Harvard University Press. [11]

Dunn, J., Plomin, R., and Daniels, D. (1986). Consistency and change in mothers' behavior toward young siblings. *Child Development, 57,* 348–356. [13]

Dunphy, D. (1963). The social structure of urban adolescent peer groups. *Sociometry, 26,* 230–246. [15]

Dusek, J., and Flaherty, J. (1981). The development of the self-concept during the adolescent years. *Monographs of the Society for Research in Child Development, 46,* (No. 4). [15]

Dweck, C. (1975). The role of expectations and attributions in the alleviation of learned helplessness. *Journal of Personality and Social Psychology, 31,* 674–685. [15]

Dweck, C. S., Davidson, W., Nelson, S., and Erra, B. (1978). Sex differences in learned helplessness: II. The contingencies of evaluation feedback in the classroom: III. An experimental analysis. *Developmental Psychology, 14,* 268–276. [13]

Dweck, C. S., and Reppucci, N. D. (1973). Learned helplessness and reinforcement responsibility in children. *Journal of Personality and Social Psychology, 25,* 109–116. [15]

Easterbrooks, M. A., and Emde, R. N. (in press). Marital and parent-child relationships: The role of affect in the family system. In R. Hinde and J. Stevenson-Hinde (Eds.), *Towards understanding families.* Cambridge, Eng.: Cambridge University Press. [3, 7, 9]

Eckerman, C. O., Whatley, J., and Kutz, S. L. (1975). The growth of social play with peers during the second year of life. *Developmental Psychology, 11,* 42–49. [9, 11]

Edwards, C. P., and Whiting, B. (1977). *Sex differences in children's social interaction.* Unpublished report to the Ford Foundation.

Edwards, C. P., and Whiting, B. (1980). Differential socialization of girls and boys in light of cross-cultural research. In C. M. Super and S. Harkness (Eds.), *New directions in child development: Anthropological perspectives.* San Francisco: Jossey-Bass. [13]

Egeland, B., Breitenbucher, M., and Rosenberg, D. (1980). Prospective study of the significance of life stress in the etiology of child abuse. *Journal of Consulting and Clinical Psychology, 48,* 195–205. [3, 7, 9]

Egeland, B., and Brunnquell, D. (1979). An at-risk approach to the study of child abuse: Some preliminary findings. *Journal of the American Academy of Child Psychiatry, 18,* 219–225. [3, 9, 12]

Egeland, B., and Farber, E. (1984). Infant-mother attachment: Factors related to its development and changes over time. *Child Development, 55,* 753–771. [2, 3, 7]

Egeland, B., Jacobvitz, D., and Papatola, K. (in press). Intergenerational continuity of parental abuse. In J. Lancaster and R. Gelles (Eds.), *Biosocial aspects of child abuse.* New York: Jossey-Bass. [9]

Egeland, B., Jacobvitz, D., and Sroufe, L. A. (in press). Breaking the cycle of abuse: Relationship predictions. *Child Development.* [9]

Egeland, B., and Sroufe, L. A. (1981). Developmental sequelae of maltreatment in infancy. In D. Cicchetti and R. Rizley (Eds.), *New directions in child development: Developmental approaches to child maltreatment.* San Francisco: Jossey-Bass. [3, 7, 9, 13]

Egeland, J., Gerhard, D., Pauls, D., Sussex, J., Kidd, K., Allen, C., Hostetter, A., and Housman, D. (1987). Bipolar affective disorders linked to DNA markers on chromosome 11. *Nature, 325,* 783–787. [16]

Eimas, P. D., Siqueland, E. R., and Jusczyk, P. W. (1971). Speech perception in infants. *Science, 171,* 303–306. [5]

Eisenberg, A. R., and Garvey, C. (1981). Children's use of verbal strategies in resolving conflicts. *Discourse Processes, 4,* 149–170. [10]

Eisenberg, L. (1977). Development as a unifying concept in psychiatry. *British Journal of Psychiatry, 131,* 225–237. [16]

Eisenberg, R., Corsin, D., Griffin, E., and Hunter, M. (1964). Auditory behavior in the human neonate: A preliminary report. *Journal of Speech and Hearing Research, 7,* 245–269. [7]

Elardo, R., Bradley, R., and Caldwell, B. (1975). The relationship of infants' home environments to mental test performance from 6 to 36 months: A longitudinal analysis. *Child Development, 46,* 71–76. [3]

Elardo, R., Bradley, R., and Caldwell, B. (1977). A longitudinal study of the relation of infants' home environments to language development at age three. *Child Development, 48,* 595–603. [3]

Elder, G. (1963). Parental power legitimation and its effect on the adolescent. *Sociometry, 26,* 50–65. [15]

Elder, G. H., Jr., Caspi, A., and Burton, L. M. (1987). Adolescent transitions in developmental perspective: Historical and sociological insights. In M. Gunnar (Ed.), *Minnesota Symposia on Child Psychiatry* (Vol. 21). Hillsdale, N.J.: Erlbaum. [3]

Elder, G. H., Jr., Caspi, A., and Downey, G. (1986). Problem

behavior and family relationships: Life-course and intergenerational themes. In A. B. Sorensen, F. E. Weinert, and L. R. Sherrod (Eds.), *Human development and the life course: Multidisciplinary perspectives.* Hillsdale, N.J.: Erlbaum. [2, 3]

Elkind, D. (1967). Egocentrism in adolescence. *Child Development, 38,* 1025–1034. [10, 14, 15]

Elkind, D. (1971). *Sympathetic understanding of the child 6 to 16.* Boston: Allyn & Bacon. [15]

Elkind, D. (1974). *Children and adolescents* (2nd ed.). New York: Oxford University Press. [14]

Elkind, D. (1978). Understanding the young adolescent. *Adolescence, 13,* 127–134. [10, 15]

Elkind, D., and Bowen, R. (1979). Imaginary audience behavior in children and adolescents. *Developmental Psychology, 15,* 38–44. [15]

Ellingson, R. (1967). The study of brain electrical activity in infants. In L. Lipsitt and C. Spiker (Eds.), *Advances in child development and behavior* (Vol. 3). New York: Academic Press. [7]

Ellis, S., and Rogoff, B. (1982). The strategies and efficacy of child versus adult teachers. *Child Development, 53,* 730–735. [10, 12]

Ellis, S., and Rogoff, B. (1986). Problem solving in children's management of instruction. In E. C. Mueller and C. R. Cooper (Eds.), *Process and outcome in peer relationships.* New York: Academic Press. [10]

Emde, R. (1985). The affective self: Continuities and transformations from infancy. In J. Call, E. Galenson, and R. Tyson (Eds.), *Frontiers in infant psychiatry—II.* New York: Basic Books. [7, 9]

Emde, R., Gaensbauer, T., and Harmon, R. (1976). Emotional expression in infancy: A biobehavioral study. *Psychological Issues Monograph Series, 10* (Serial No. 37). [7, 9]

Emde, R. N., Johnson, W. F., and Easterbrooks, M. A. (1985). *The do's and don'ts of early moral development: Psychoanalytic tradition and current research.* Unpublished manuscript. [9]

Emde, R. N., and Koenig, K. L. (1969). Neonatal smiling and rapid eye movement states. *Journal of the American Academy of Child Psychiatry, 8,* 57–67. [7]

Emde, R. N., and Robinson, J. (1979). The first two months: Recent research in developmental psychology and the changing view of the newborn. In J. Noshpitz and J. Call (Eds.), *Basic handbook of child psychiatry.* New York: Basic Books. [7]

Emery, R. (1982). Marital turmoil: Interparental conflict and the children of discord and divorce. *Psychological Bulletin, 92,* 310–330. [3, 12, 13]

Emmerich, W. (1964). Continuity and stability in early social development. *Child Development, 35,* 311–332. [12]

Emmerich, W. (1977). Structure and development of personal-social behaviors in economically disadvantaged preschool children. *Genetic Psychology Monographs, 95,* 191–245. [13]

Emmerich, W., Goldman, K. S., Kirsh, B., and Sharabany, R. (1976). *Development of gender constancy in economically disadvantaged children.* Report of the Educational Testing Service, Princeton, N.J. [11]

Engen, T. L., Lipsitt, L., and Peck, M. B. (1974). Ability of newborn infants to discriminate sapid substances. *Developmental Psychology, 10,* 741–744. [5]

Engfer, A. (in press). The interrelatedness of marriage and the mother-child relationship. In R. Hinde and J. Stevenson-Hinde (Eds.), *Relations between relationships in families.* Oxford, Eng.: Oxford University Press. [7]

English, P. C. (1978). Failure to thrive without organic reason. *Pediatric Annals, 7,* 774–781. [7]

Enright, R., Lapsley, D., Drivas, A., and Fehr, L. (1980). Parental influences on the development of adolescent autonomy and identity. *Journal of Youth and Adolescence, 9,* 529–545. [15]

Epps, E., and Smith, S. (1984). School and children: The middle childhood years. In W. A. Collins (Ed.), *Development during middle childhood.* Washington, D.C.: National Academy Press. [13]

Epstein, H. (1977). A neuroscience framework for restructuring middle school curricula. *Transescence: The Journal on Emerging Adolescent Education, 5,* 6–11. [14]

Epstein, H. T. (1974). Phrenoblysis: Special brain and mind growth periods. *Developmental Psychobiology, 7,* 217–224. [14]

Epstein, H. T. (1979). Correlated brain and intelligence development in humans. In M. E. Hahn, C. Jensen, and B. C. Dudek (Eds.), *Development and evolution of brain size: Behavioral implications.* New York: Academic Press. [14]

Epstein, H. T. (1980). EEG developmental stages. *Developmental Psychobiology, 13,* 629–631. [14]

Epstein, S. (1983). The stability of behavior across time and situations. In R. Zucker, J. Aronoff, and A. I. Rabin (Eds.), *Personality and the prediction of behavior.* New York: Academic Press. [11]

Erickson, M., Egeland, B., and Sroufe, L. A. (1985). The relationship between quality of attachment and behavior problems in preschool in a high risk sample. In I. Bretherton and E. Waters (Eds.), *Growing points in attachment theory and research. Monographs of the Society for Research in Child Development, 50* (1-2, Series No. 209), 147–186. [2, 3, 7, 9, 11, 16]

Erikson, E. H. (1958). *Young man Luther.* New York: Norton. [15]

Erikson, E. H. (1959). Identity and the life cycle. *Psychological Issues, 1,* 89. [15]

Erikson, E. H. (1963). *Childhood and society* (2nd ed.). New York: Norton. [2, 9, 11, 13]

Erikson, E. H. (1968). *Identity, youth, and crisis.* New York: Norton. [15]

Erikson, E. H. (1969). *Gandhi's truth.* New York: Norton. [15]

Erikson, E. H. (1981). *Youth, change, and challenge.* New York: Basic Books. [15]

Erlenmeyer-Kimling, L., Cornblatt, H., and Golden, R. (1983). Early indicators of vulnerability to schizophrenia in children at high genetic risk. In S. Guze, F. Earls, and J. Barrett (Eds.), *Childhood psychopathology and development* (pp. 247–264). New York: Raven Press. [16]

Erwin, W. (1977). A 16-year follow-up of a case of severe anorexia nervosa. *Journal of Behavior Therapy and Experimental Psychiatry, 8,* 157–160. [16]

Evans, S., Reinhart, J., and Succop, R. (1972). Failure to thrive: A study of 45 children and their families. *Journal of the American Academy of Child Psychiatry, 79,* 209–215. [7, 9]

Fagan, J. F., III. (1973). Infants' delayed recognition memory and forgetting. *Journal of Experimental Child Psychology, 16,* 424–450. [6]

Fagan, J. F., III. (1979). The origins of facial pattern recognition. In M. H. Bornstein and W. Kessen (Eds.), *Psychological development from infancy: Image to intention.* Hillsdale, N.J.: Erlbaum. [6]

Fagan, J. F., III., and McGrath, S. K. (1981). Infant recognition memory as a measure of intelligence. *Intelligence, 5,* 121–130. [12]

Fagot, B. I. (1978). The influence of sex of child on parental reactions to toddler children. *Child Development, 49,* 459–465. [11]

Fantz, R. L., Ordy, J. M., and Udelf, M. S. (1962). Maturation of pattern vision in infants during the first six months. *Journal of Comparative Physiological Psychology, 55,* 907–917. [5]

Farber, E., and Egeland, B. (1982). Developmental consequences of out-of-home care for infants in a low-income population. In E. Zigler and E. Gordon (Eds.), *Day care: Scientific and social policy issues.* Boston: Auburn House. [7]

Fawl, C. L. (1963). Disturbances experienced by children in the natural habitats. In R. G. Barker (Ed.), *The stream of behavior.* New York: Appleton-Century-Crofts. [11]

Fein, G. (1978). *Child development.* Englewood Cliffs, N.J.: Prentice-Hall. [11]

Feinman, S., and Lewis, M. (1983). Is there a social life beyond the dyad? A social psychological view of social connections in infancy. In M. Lewis (Ed.), *Beyond the dyad.* New York: Plenum. [9]

Feiring, C., Lewis, M., and Starr, M. (1984). Indirect effects and infants' reaction to strangers. *Developmental Psychology, 20,* 485–491. [9]

Ferguson, C. A. (1964). Baby talk in six languages. *American Anthropologist, 66,* 103–114. [8]

Ferreira, C. B. (1969). *Prenatal environment.* Springfield, Ill.: Thomas. [4]

Field, T. M., and Goldson, E. (1984). Pacifying effects of nonnutritive sucking on term and preterm neonates during heelstick procedures. *Pediatrics, 74,* 1012–1015. [5]

Finkelstein, N., and Ramey, C. (1977). Learning to control the environment in infancy. *Child Development, 48,* 806–819. [7]

Fischer, K. (1980). A theory of cognitive development: The control and construction of hierarchies of skills. *Psychological Review, 87,* 477–531. [2, 6]

Fischer, K., and Bullock, D. (1984). Cognitive development in school-age children. In W. A. Collins (Ed.), *Development during middle childhood.* Washington, D.C.: National Academy Press. [11, 12, 13]

Fischer, K., and Lazerson, A. (1984). *Human development: From conception through adolescence.* New York: Freeman. [4, 6]

Flavell, J. H. (1963). *The developmental psychology of Jean Piaget.* New York: Van Nostrand. [12]

Flavell, J. H. (1970). Concept development. In P. H. Mussen (Ed.), *Carmichael's manual of child psychology* (Vol. 1). New York: Wiley. [10]

Flavell, J. H. (1977). *Cognitive development.* Englewood Cliffs, N.J.: Prentice-Hall. [11]

Flavell, J. H. (1985). *Cognitive development* (2nd ed.). Englewood Cliffs, N.J.: Prentice-Hall. [6, 8, 10, 12, 14]

Flavell, J. H., Beach, D. H., and Chinsky, J. M. (1966). Spontaneous verbal rehearsal in a memory task as a function of age. *Child Development, 37,* 283–299. [12]

Flavell, J. H., Botkin, P. T., Fry, C. L., Wright, J. W., and Jarvis, P. E. (1968). *The development of role-taking and communication skills in children.* New York: Wiley. [10]

Flavell, J. H., Friedrichs, A. G., and Hoyt, J. D. (1970). Developmental changes in memorization processes. *Cognitive Psychology, 1,* 324–340. [12]

Flavell, J. H., and Wellman, H. M. (1977). Metamemory. In R. B. Kail and J. E. Hagen (Eds.), *Perspectives on the development of memory and cognition.* Hillsdale, N.J.: Erlbaum. [12]

Fleeson, J. (1987). *Assessment of parent-adolescent relationships: Implications for adolescent development.* Unpublished doctoral dissertation, University of Minnesota. [15]

Forbes, H. S., and Forbes, H. B. (1927). Fetal sense reaction: Hearing. *Journal of Comparative Psychology, 7,* 353–355. [5]

Forman, E. A. (1982). *Understanding the role of peer interaction in development: The contribution of Piaget and Vygotsky.* Paper presented at the meetings of the Jean Piaget Society, Philadelphia. [12]

Fox, N. (1977). Attachment of kibbutz infants to mother and metapelet. *Child Development, 48,* 1228–1239. [7]

Fraiberg, S., Adelson, E., and Shapiro, V. (1975). Ghosts in the nursery. *Journal of the American Academy of Child Psychiatry, 14,* 387–421. [7, 9]

Frazier, T. M., Davis, G. H., Goldstein, H., and Goldberg, I. D. (1961). Cigarette smoking and prematurity: A prospective study. *American Journal of Obstetrics and Gynecology, 81,* 988–996. [4]

Freedman, D. (1974). *Human infancy: An evolutionary perspective.* Hillsdale, N.J.: Erlbaum. [7]

Freedman, J. (1984). Effects of television violence on aggressiveness. *Psychological Bulletin, 96,* 227–246. [11]

Freedman, J. (1986). Television violence and aggression: A rejoinder. *Psychological Bulletin, 100,* 372–378. [11]

French, J. W. (1951). *The description of aptitude and achievement tests in terms of rotated factors.* Chicago: University of Chicago Press. [12]

Freud, A., and Dann, S. (1951). An experiment in group upbringing. *Psychoanalytic Study of the Child, 6,* 127–168. [7, 11]

Frey, K. (1979, March). *Differential teaching methods used with girls and boys of moderate and high achievement.* Paper presented at the biennial meeting of the Society for Research in Child Development, San Francisco. [3, 12]

Frey, K., and Ruble, D. (1985). What children say when the teacher is not around: Conflicting goals in social comparison and performance assessment in the classroom. *Journal of Personality and Social Psychology, 48,* 550–562. [3]

Friedrich, L., and Stein, A. H. (1973). Aggressive and prosocial television programs and the natural behavior of preschool children. *Monographs of the Society for Research in Child Development, 38* (Serial No. 151). [11]

Friedrich-Cofer, L., and Huston, A. (1986). Television violence and aggression: The debate continues. *Psychological Bulletin, 100,* 364–371. [11]

Fries, M. (1954). Some hypotheses on the role of the congenital activity type in personality development. *International Journal of Psychoanalysis, 35,* 206–207. [7]

Frisch, R. E., and Revelle, R. (1970). Height and weight at menarche and a hypothesis of critical body weights and adolescent events. *Science, 169,* 397–399. [14]

Frodi, A. (1984). When empathy fails: Aversive infant crying and child abuse. In B. Lester and Z. Boukydis (Eds.), *Infant crying: Theoretical and research perspectives.* New York: Plenum. [9]

Funk, J. L. (1986). *Gender differences in the moral reasoning of conventional and post-conventional adults.* Unpublished doctoral dissertation, University of Texas. [14]

Furman, W., and Buhrmester, D. (1985). Children's perceptions of the qualities of sibling relationships. *Child Development, 56,* 448–461. [13]

Furman, W., Rahe, D., and Hartup, W. (1979). Rehabilitation of socially withdrawn preschool children through mixed age and same age socialization. *Child Development, 50,* 915–922. [11]

Furstenberg, F. (1980). *Teenage parenthood and family support.* Paper presented at the National Research Forum on Family Issues, Washington, D.C. [7, 15]

Furstenberg, F., and Crawford, A. (1978). Family support: Helping teenage mothers to cope. *Family Planning Perspectives, 10,* 322–333. [7, 9]

Furth, H. G. (1966). *Thinking without language: Psychological implications of deafness.* Englewood Cliffs, N.J.: Prentice-Hall. [8]

Fuson, K. (1979). The development of self-regulating aspects of speech: A review. In G. Ziven (Ed.), *The development of self-regulation through private speech.* New York: Wiley. [11]

Gaensbauer, T., Harmon, R., Cytryn, L., and McKnew, D. (1984). Social and affective development in infants with a manic-depressive parent. *American Journal of Psychiatry, 141,* 223–229. [7, 9]

Gamble, T., and Zigler, E. (1986). Effects of infant day care. *American Journal of Orthopsychiatry, 56,* 26–42. [3, 7]

Garbarino, J. (1981). An ecological approach to child maltreatment. In L. Pelton (Ed.), *The social context of child abuse and neglect.* New York: Human Sciences Press. [3]

Garbarino, J., and Gilliam, G. (1980). *Understanding abusive families.* Lexington, Mass.: Lexington Press. [9]

Garbarino, J., Guttmann, E., and Seeley, J. W. (1986). *The psychologically battered child.* San Francisco: Jossey-Bass. [9]

Garbarino, J., and Sherman, D. (1980). High-risk neighborhoods and high-risk families: The human ecology of child maltreatment. *Child Development, 51,* 188–198. [9]

Garber, H., and Heber, R. (1973, March). *The Milwaukee project: Early intervention as a technique to prevent mental retardation.* University of Connecticut Technical Paper. [12]

Garber, J., Cohen, E., Bacon, P., Egeland, B., and Sroufe, L. A. (1985). *Depression in preschoolers: Reliability and validity of a behavioral observation measure.* Paper presented at the Society for Research in Child Development, Toronto. [16]

Garcia, J., and Koelling, R. (1966). Relation of cue to consequences in avoidance learning. *Psychonometric Science, 4,* 123–124. [5]

Garfinkel, B. (1987, June). *Treatment strategies for AD-HD.* Paper presented at the Conference on Attention-Deficit Hyperactivity Disorders in Children and Adolescence, Minneapolis. [16]

Garfinkel, B. (in press). The genetic investigation of behavioral disorders in childhood. In D. N. Abuelo and B. Garfinkel (Eds.), *Hereditary aspects of neurologic and psychiatric disorders.* Cambridge, Mass.: Academic Guild. [16]

Garmezy, N. (1978). DSM-III: Never mind the psychologists—Is it good for the children? *Clinical Psychologist, 31,* 3–6. [16]

Garmezy, N., and Streitman, S. (1974). Children at risk: The search for antecedents of schizophrenia. Part I: Conceptual models and research methods. *Schizophrenia Bulletin, 8,* 14–90. [16]

Garnica, O. (1974). *Some characteristics of prosodic input to young children.* Unpublished doctoral dissertation, Stanford University. [8]

Garvey, C. (1977). *Play.* Cambridge, Mass.: Harvard University Press. [9, 11]

Geller, M., Kelley, J., Traxler, W., and Marone, F. (1978). Behavioral treatment of an adolescent female's bulimic anorexia. *Journal of Clinical Child Psychology, 7,* 138–142. [16]

Gelles, R. (1976). Abused wives: Why do they stay? *Journal of Marriage and the Family, 38,* 659–668. [9]

Gelman, R. (1972). The nature and development of early

number concepts. In H. W. Reese (Ed.), *Advances in child development and behavior* (Vol. 7). New York: Academic Press. [10]

Gelman, R. (1978). Cognitive development. *Annual Review of Psychology, 29,* 297–332. [2]

Gelman, R. (1982). Accessing one-to-one correspondence: Still another paper on conservation. *British Journal of Psychology, 73,* 209–220. [12]

Gelman, R., and Baillargeon, R. (1983). A review of some Piagetian concepts. In P. H. Mussen (Ed.), *Handbook of child psychology* (Vol. 3, 4th ed.): J. H. Flavell and E. M. Markman (Eds.), *Cognitive development.* New York: Wiley. [6, 12]

Gelman, R., Meck, E., and Merkin, S. (1986). Young children's numerical competence. *Cognitive Development, 1,* 1–29. [12]

Genishi, C., and Di Paolo, M. (1982). Learning through argument in a preschool. In L. C. Wilkinson (Ed.), *Communicating in the classroom.* New York: Academic Press. [10]

Genishi, C., and Dyson, A. H. (1984). *Language assessment in the early years.* Norwood, N.J.: Ablex. [8]

George, C., and Main, M. (1979). Social interactions of young abused children: Approach, avoidance, and aggression. *Child Development, 50,* 306–318. [7, 9]

Gershon, E., Nurnberger, J., Nadi, N., Berrettini, W., and Goldin, L. (1983). *The origins of depression: Current concepts and approaches.* New York: Springer-Verlag. [16]

Gewirtz, J. (1965). The course of infant smiling in four child-rearing environments in Israel. In B. M. Foss (Ed.), *Determinants of infant behavior III.* London, Eng.: Methuen. [7]

Gewirtz, J., and Boyd, E. (1977). Experiments on mother-infant interaction underlying mutual attachment acquisition: The infant conditions the mother. In T. Alloway, P. Pliner, and L. Krames (Eds.), *Attachment behavior.* New York: Plenum. [7]

Gibson, E. J., and Walk, R. D. (1960). The "visual cliff." *Scientific American, 202,* 64–71. [5]

Gibson, H. (1969). Early delinquency in relation to broken homes. *Journal of Child Psychology and Psychiatry, 10,* 195–204. [13]

Gilligan, C. (1982). *In a different voice: Psychological theory and women's development.* Cambridge, Mass.: Harvard University Press. [14]

Gilligan, C., Kohlberg, L., Lerner, M., and Belsky, M. (1971). *Moral reasoning about sexual dilemmas. Technical report of the U. S. Commission on Obscenity and Pornography, VI.* Washington, D.C.: U. S. Government Printing Office. [15]

Ginzberg, E. (1972). Toward a theory of occupational choice: A restatement. *Vocational Guidance Quarterly, 20,* 169–176. [15]

Gittelman, R., Abikoff, H., Pollack, E., Klein, D., Katz, S., and Mattes, J. (1980). A controlled trial of behavior modification and methylphenidate in hyperactive children. In C. Whalen and B. Henker (Eds.), *Hyperactive children.* New York: Academic Press. [16]

Gleason, J. B. (1975). Fathers and other strangers: Men's speech to young children. In D. Dato (Ed.), *Georgetown University roundtable on language and linguistics.* Washington, D.C.: Georgetown University Press. [8]

Gleitman, L. R., Newport, E. L., and Gleitman, H. (1984). The current status of the motherese hypothesis. *Journal of Child Language, 11,* 43–79. [8]

Glucksberg, S., and Krauss, R. M. (1967). What do people say after they have learned to talk? Studies of the development of referential communication. *Merrill-Palmer Quarterly, 13,* 309–316. [10]

Gold, D., and Andres, D. (1978). Developmental comparisons between ten-year-old children with employed and unemployed mothers. *Child Development, 49,* 75–84. [3]

Goldfarb, W. (1955). Emotional and intellectual consequences of psychological deprivation in infancy: A reevaluation. In P. Hock and J. Rubin (Eds.), *Psychopathology of childhood.* New York: Grune & Stratton. [7]

Goldsmith, H. (1983). Genetic influences on personality from infancy to adulthood. *Child Development, 54,* 331–355. [3]

Goldstein, M. (1985). *The U.C.L.A. family project.* Paper presented at the High Risk Consortium, San Francisco. [16]

Gollin, E. (1958). Organizational characteristics of social judgment: A developmental investigation. *Journal of Personality, 26,* 139–154. [15]

Goodenough, F. L. (1931). *Anger in young children.* Minneapolis: University of Minnesota Press. [11]

Goodnow, H., Cashmore, J., Cotton, S., and Knight, R. (1984). Mothers' developmental timetables in two cultural groups. *International Journal of Psychology, 19,* 1–13. [3, 13]

Goodnow, J. J. (1973). Compensation arguments on conservation tasks. *Developmental Psychology, 8,* 140. [12]

Gordon, A., and Jameson, J. (1979). Infant-mother attachment in patients with nonorganic failure to thrive syndrome. *Journal of the American Academy of Child Psychiatry, 18,* 251–259. [7, 9]

Gordon, F. R., and Yonas, A. (1976). Sensitivity to binocular depth information in infants. *Journal of Experimental Child Psychology, 22,* 413–422. [5]

Gottesman, I. (1979). Schizophrenia and genetics: Toward understanding uncertainty. *Psychiatric Annals, 9,* 1–12. [16]

Gottesman, I., and Shields, J. (1972). *Schizophrenia and genetics: A twin study vantage point.* New York: Academic Press. [16]

Gottlieb, B. H. (1980). Social networks, social support, and child maltreatment. In J. Garbarino and S. H. Stocking (Eds.), *Supporting families and protecting children.* San Francisco: Jossey-Bass. [3]

Gottlieb, G. (1976). Conceptions of prenatal development: Behavioral embryology. *Psychological Review, 83,* 215–234. [4]

Gottman, J. (1983). How children become friends. *Monographs of the Society for Research in Child Development, 48* (3, Serial No. 201). [13]

Gottman, J., Gonzo, J., and Rasmussen, B. (1975). Social interaction, social competence, and friendship in children. *Child Development, 46,* 709–718. [13]

Gould, S. (1977). *Ontogeny and phylogeny.* Cambridge, Mass.: Harvard University Press. [1, 3]

Gove, F. (1983). *Patterns and organizations of behavior and affective expression during the second year of life.* Unpublished doctoral dissertation, University of Minnesota. [9]

Graham, F., Ernhart, C., Thurston, D., and Craft, M. (1962). Development three years after perinatal anoxia and other potentially damaging newborn experiences. *Psychological Monographs, 76,* 1–53. [16]

Granrud, C. E., and Yonas, A. (1984). Infants' perception of pictorially specified interposition. *Journal of Experimental Child Psychology, 37,* 500–511. [5]

Gratch, G. (1975). Recent studies based on Piaget's view of object concept development. In L. B. Cohen and P. Salapatek (Eds.), *Infant perception: From sensation to cognition.* New York: Academic Press. [6]

Gratch, G., Appel, K. J., Evans, W. F., LeCompte, G. K., and Wright, N. A. (1974). Piaget's Stage IV object concept error: Evidence of forgetting or object conception? *Child Devel-*

opment, 45, 71–77. [6]

Gray, S. W., Ramsey, B. K., and Klaus, R. A. (1982). *From 3 to 20: The early training project.* Baltimore: University Park Press. [12]

Graziano, W. (1984). The development of social exchange processes. In J. C. Masters and K. Yarkin-Levin (Eds.), *Boundary areas in psychology: Social and developmental.* New York: Academic Press. [13]

Greenberger, E., and Steinberg, L. (1980). Part-time employment of in-school youth: A preliminary assessment of costs and benefits. In B. Linder and R. Taggart (Eds.), *A review of youth employment problems, programs, and policies: Vol. 1. The youth employment problem: Causes and dimensions.* Washington, D.C.: Vice-President's Task Force on Youth Employment. [15]

Greenfield, P. (1984). *Mind and media.* Cambridge, Mass.: Harvard University Press. [3]

Greenman, G. (1963). Visual behavior of newborn infants. In A. Solnit and S. Provenci (Eds.), *Modern perspective in child development.* New York: Hallmark. [7]

Gregory, I. (1965). Anterospective data following childhood loss of a parent: Pathology, performance, and potential among college students. *Archives of General Psychiatry, 13,* 110–120. [13]

Gross, T. F. (1985). *Cognitive development.* Monterey, Calif.: Brooks/Cole. [7, 12]

Grossman, K., and Grossman, K. E. (1982). *Maternal sensitivity to infants' signals during the first year as related to the year olds' behavior in Ainsworth's strange situation in a sample of Northern German families.* Paper presented at the International Conference on Infant Studies, Austin, Tex. [7]

Grossman, K., Grossman, K. E., Spangler, G., Suess, G., and Unzer, L. (1985). Maternal sensitivity and newborn orienting responses as related to quality of attachment in Northern Germany. In I. Bretherton and E. Waters (Eds.), *Growing points of attachment theory and research. Monographs of the Society for Research in Child Development, 50,* 233–256. [7]

Grumbach, M. M., Roth, J. C., Kaplan, S. L., and Kelch, R. P. (1974). Hypothalamic-pituitary regulation of puberty in man: Evidence and concepts derived from clinical research. In M. M. Grumbach, G. D. Grave, and F. E. Mayer (Eds.), *Control of the onset of puberty.* New York: Wiley. [14]

Guardo, C., and Bohan, J. (1971). Development of a sense of self-identity in children. *Child Development, 42,* 1909–1921. [13]

Guilford, J. P. (1967). *The nature of human intelligence.* New York: McGraw-Hill. [12]

Gunnar, M. (1980). Contingent stimulation: A review of its role in early development. In S. Levine and H. Ursin (Eds.), *Coping and health.* New York: Plenum. [7]

Gunnar, M., and Stone, C. (1984). The effects of positive maternal affect on infant responses to pleasant, ambiguous, and fear-provoking toys. *Child Development, 55,* 1231–1236. [9]

Guttentag, M., and Bray, H. (1977). Teachers as mediators of sex-role standards. In A. Sargent (Ed.), *Beyond sex roles.* St. Paul: West. [13]

Haeberle, E. (1978). *The sex atlas.* New York: Seabury. [15]

Haith, M. M. (1966). The response of the human newborn to visual movement. *Journal of Experimental Child Psychology, 3,* 235–243. [7]

Haith, M. M. (1980). *Rules newborns look by.* Hillsdale, N.J.: Erlbaum. [5]

Haith, M. M., Bergman, T., and Moore, M. J. (1977). Eye contact and face scanning in early infancy. *Science, 198,* 853–855. [5]

Hakim-Larson, J., Livington, J., and Tron, R. (1985). *Mothers and adolescent daughters: Personal issues.* Paper presented at the biennial meeting of the Society for Research in Child Development, Toronto. [15]

Hall, E., Perlmutter, M., and Lamb, M. E. (1982). *Child psychology today.* New York: Random House. [4]

Hall, G. S. (1904a). *Adolescence.* New York: Appleton. [14]

Hall, G. S. (1904b). *Adolescence: Its psychology and its relation to physiology, anthropology, sociology, sex, crime, religion, and education* (Vol. 1). Englewood Cliffs, N.J.: Prentice-Hall. [15]

Halliday, M. (1979). One child's protolanguage. In M. Bullowa (Ed.), *Before speech: The beginning of interpersonal communication.* Cambridge, Eng.: Cambridge University Press. [8]

Halmi, K., and Brodland, G. (1973). Monozygotic twins concordant and discordant for anorexia nervosa. *Psychological Medicine, 3,* 521–524. [16]

Halverson, H. M. (1931). An experimental study of prehension in infants by means of systematic cinema records. *Genetic Psychology Monographs, 10,* 1413–1430. [5]

Hamburg, B. (1974). Early adolescence: A specific and stressful stage of the life cycle. In G. Coelho, D. Hamburg, and J. Adams (Eds.), *Coping and adaptation* (pp. 101–124). New York: Basic Books. [15]

Handlon, B. J., and Gross, P. (1959). The development of sharing behavior. *Journal of Abnormal and Social Psychology, 59,* 425–428. [13]

Hare, R. (1970). *Psychopathy: Theory and research.* New York: Wiley. [16]

Hare, R., and Cox, D. (1978). Psychological research on psychopathy. In W. Reid (Ed.), *The psychopath.* New York: Brunner/Mazel. [16]

Harlow, H. (1953). Mice, monkeys, men, and motives. *Psychological Review, 60,* 23–32. [11]

Harlow, H., and Harlow, M. (1962). Social deprivation in monkeys. *Scientific American, 207,* 137–146. [7]

Harlow, H. F., and Harlow, M. K. (1966). Learning to love. *American Scientist, 54,* 244–272. [1, 7]

Harris, P. L. (1974). Perseverative errors in search by young infants. *Journal of Experimental Child Psychology, 18,* 535–542. [6]

Harris, P. L. (1983). Infant cognition. In P. H. Mussen (Ed.), *Handbook of child psychology* (Vol. 2, 4th ed.): M. M. Haith and J. J. Campos (Eds.), *Infancy and developmental psychobiology.* New York: Wiley. [2, 5, 6]

Harter, S. (1980). A model of intrinsic mastery motivation in children: Individual differences and developmental change. In W. A. Collins (Ed.), *Minnesota Symposia on Child Psychology* (Vol. 13). Hillsdale, N.J.: Erlbaum. [3, 12, 13]

Harter, S. (1983). Developmental perspectives on the self system. In P. H. Mussen (Ed.) *Handbook of child psychology* (Vol. 4, 4th ed.): E. M. Hetherington (Ed.), *Socialization, personality, and social development* (pp. 275–385). New York: Wiley. [13]

Hartup, W. W. (1966). Dependence and independence. In H. W. Stevenson (Ed.), *Child psychology: The 62nd yearbook of the National Society for the Study of Education.* Chicago: University of Chicago Press. [11]

Hartup, W. W. (1974). Aggression in childhood: Developmental perspectives. *American Psychologist, 29,* 336–341. [11]

Hartup, W. W. (1980). Peer relations and family relations: Two social worlds. In M. Rutter (Ed.), *Scientific founda-*

tions of developmental psychiatry. London, Eng.: Heinnemann. [13]

Hartup, W. W. (1983). Peer relations. In P. Mussen and E. M. Hetherington (Eds.), *Manual of child psychology* (4th ed.). New York: Wiley. [3, 12, 13]

Hartup, W. W., and Sancilio, M. (1986). Children's friendships. In E. Schopler and G. Mesibov (Eds.), *Social behavior in autism*. New York: Plenum. [13, 15]

Harvey, P., Winters, K., Weintraub, S., and Neale, J. (1981). Distractibility in children vulnerable to psychopathology. *Journal of Abnormal Psychology, 90,* 298–304. [16]

Hayes, A. (1984). Interaction, engagement, and the origins of communication: Some constructive concerns. In L. Feagans, C. Garvey, and R. Golinkoff (Eds.), *The origins and growth of communication*. Norwood, N.J.: Ablex. [7]

Haynes, H., White, B. L., and Held, R. (1965). Visual accommodation in human infants. *Science, 148,* 528–530. [7]

Haywood, H., and Burke, W. (1977). Development of individual differences in intrinsic motivation. In I. Uzgivis and F. Weizmann (Eds.), *The structuring of experience*. New York: Plenum. [11]

Hecox, K. (1975). Electro-physiological correlates of human auditory development. In L. B. Cohen and P. Salapatek (Eds.), *Infant perception: From sensation to cognition* (Vol. 2). New York: Academic Press. [5]

Heinicke, C., Diskin, S., Ramsey-Klee, D., and Given, K. (1983). Pre-birth parent characteristics and family development in the first year of life. *Child Development, 54,* 194–208. [7, 9]

Heinicke, C., and Westheimer, I. (1966). *Brief separations*. New York: International Universities Press. [7, 9]

Heinonen, O. P., Slone, D., and Shapiron, S. (1977). *Birth defects and drugs in pregnancy*. Littleton, Mass.: Publishing Sciences Group. [4]

Henderson, B., and Moore, S. (1979). Measuring exploratory behavior in young children: A factor analytic study. *Developmental Psychology, 15,* 113–119. [11]

Henderson, B., and Moore, S. (1980). Children's responses to objects differing in novelty in relation to level of curiosity and adult behavior. *Child Development, 51,* 457–465. [11]

Hermelin, B., and O'Connor, N. (1970). *Psychological experiments with autistic children*. New York: Pergamon. [16]

Hess, R., and Camara, K. (1979). Post-divorce family relations as mediating factors in the consequences of divorce for children. *Journal of Social Issues, 35,* 79–86. [13]

Hess, R., Kashiwagi, K., Azuma, H., Price, G., and Dickson, W. (1980). Maternal expectations for early mastery of developmental tasks and cognitive and social competence of preschool children in Japan and the United States. *International Journal of Psychology, 15,* 259–272. [3]

Hetherington, E. M. (1965). A developmental study of the effects of sex of the dominant parent on sex-role preferences, identification, and imitation in children. *Journal of Personality and Social Psychology, 2,* 188–194. [3, 11]

Hetherington, E. M. (1966). Effects of paternal absence on sex-typed behaviors in Negro and white preadolescent males. *Journal of Personality and Social Psychology, 4,* 87–91. [3, 13]

Hetherington, E. M. (1972). Effects of father absence on personality development in adolescent daughters. *Developmental Psychology, 7,* 313–326. [12, 15]

Hetherington, E. M. (in press). Parents, children, and siblings six years after divorce. In R. Hinde and J. Stevenson-Hinde (Eds.), *Relations between relationships within families*. Oxford, Eng.: Oxford University Press. [3, 13, 15]

Hetherington, E. M., and Brackbill, Y. (1963). Etiology and covariation of obstinacy, orderliness, and parsimony in young children. *Child Development, 34,* 919–943. [9]

Hetherington, E. M., Cox, M., and Cox, R. (1977). Beyond father absence: Conceptualization of the effects of divorce. In E. M. Hetherington and R. Parlee (Eds.), *Contemporary readings in child psychology*. New York: McGraw-Hill. [3]

Hetherington, E. M., Cox, M., and Cox, R. (1978). *Family interaction and the social, emotional, and cognitive development of children following divorce*. Paper presented at the Symposium on the Family Sponsored by Johnson & Johnson, Washington, D.C. [3, 13]

Hetherington, E. M., and Frankie, G. (1967). Effects of parental dominance, warmth, and conflict on imitation in children. *Journal of Personality and Social Psychology, 6,* 119–125. [11]

Hetherington, E. M., and Martin, B. (1979). Family interaction. In H. Quay and J. Werry (Eds.), *Psychopathological disorders of childhood* (2nd ed.). New York: Wiley. [16]

Hetherington, E. M., and Parke, R. (1979). *Child psychology*. New York: McGraw-Hill. [3, 7]

Hiatt, S., Campos, J., and Emde, R. (1979). Facial patterning and infant emotional expression: Happiness, surprise, and fear. *Child Development, 50,* 1020–1035. [7]

Hill, J. (in press). The role of conflict in familial adaptation to biological change. In M. Gunnar (Ed.), *Minnesota Symposia on Child Psychology*. [15]

Hill, J., Holmbeck, G., Marlow, L., Green, T., and Lynch, M. (1985). Menarcheal status and parent-child relations in families of seventh-grade girls. *Journal of Youth and Adolescence, 14,* 301–316. [15]

Hill, J., and Lynch, M. (1983). The intensification of gender-related role expectations during early adolescence. In J. Brooks-Gunn and A. Peterson (Eds.), *Girls at puberty: Biological and psychosocial perspectives* (pp. 201–228). New York: Plenum. [15]

Hill, R. (1970). *Family development in three generations*. Cambridge, Mass.: Schenkman. [3]

Hindelang, M. J., Gottfredson, M. R., and Flanagan, T. J. (Eds.). (1981). *Sourcebook of criminal justice statistics—1980*. U. S. Department of Justice, Washington, D.C.: U. S. Government Printing Office. [15]

Hirschhorn, K. (1973). Chromosomal abnormalities I: Autosomal defects. In V. A. McKusick and R. Claiborne (Eds.), *Medical genetics*. New York: H. P. Publishing. [4]

Hirsh-Patek, K., Treiman, R., and Schneiderman, M. (1984). Brown and Hanlon revised: Mothers' sensitivity to ungrammatical forms. *Journal of Child Language, 11,* 81–88. [8]

Hodgkinson, S., Sherrington, R., Gurling, H., Marchbanks, R., Reeders, S., Mallet, J., McInnis, M., Petursson, H., and Brynjolfsson, J. (1987). Molecular genetic evidence for heterogeneity in manic depression. *Nature, 325,* 805. [16]

Hoffman, L. (1972). Early childhood experiences and women's achievement motive. *Journal of Social Issues, 28,* 129–155. [13]

Hoffman, L. (1977). Changes in family roles, socialization, and sex differences. *American Psychologist, 84,* 712–722. [13]

Hoffman, L. (1979). Maternal employment. *American Psychologist, 34,* 859–865. [3]

Hoffman, L. (1984). Work, family, and the socialization of the child. In R. D. Rarke (Ed.), *Review of child development research: Vol. 7. The family*. Chicago: University of Chicago Press. [3]

Hoffman, L., and Manis, J. (1977, April). *Influences of children on marital interaction and parental satisfactions and dissatisfactions*. Paper presented at the Conference on Human and Family Development, Pennsylvania State University. [15]

Hoffman, M. (1960). Power assertion by the parent and its impact on the child. *Child Development, 31,* 129–143. [3]

Hoffman, M. (1963). Child rearing practices and moral development: Generalizations from empirical research. *Child Development, 34,* 295–318. [3]

Hoffman, M. (1975). Altruistic behavior and the parent-child relationship. *Journal of Personality and Social Psychology, 31,* 937–943. [13]

Hoffman, M. (1979). Development of moral thought, feeling, and behavior. *American Psychologist, 34,* 958–966. [3, 11]

Hogan, D. (1982). Family structure affects risk of teen pregnancy. *University of Chicago Chronicle, 2,* 4. [15]

Hogarth, P. (1978). *Biology of reproduction.* New York: Wiley. [4]

Hollingshead, A. (1949). *Elmtown's youth.* New York: McGraw-Hill. [15]

Holt, J. (1964). *How children fail.* New York: Dell. [16]

Honzik, M. P. (1983). Measuring mental abilities in infancy: The value and limitations. In M. Lewis (Ed.), *Origins of intelligence in infancy and early childhood.* New York: Plenum. [12]

Horn, J. L. (1968). Organization of abilities and the development of intelligence. *Psychological Review, 75,* 242–259. [12]

Horn, J. L. (1982). The aging of human abilities. In B. B. Wolman (Ed.), *Handbook of developmental psychology.* Englewood Cliffs, N.J.: Prentice-Hall. [12]

Householder, J., Hatcher, R., Burns, W. J., and Chasnoff, I. (1982). Infants born to narcotic-addicted mothers. *Psychological Bulletin, 92,* 453–468. [4]

Hoving, K., Hamm, N., and Calvin, P. (1969). Social influence as a function of stimulus ambiguity at three age levels. *Developmental Psychology, 1,* 631–636. [13]

Hoy, E. A. (1975). Measurement of egocentrism in children's communication. *Developmental Psychology, 11,* 392. [10]

Hrncir, E. (1985). *Antecedents and correlates of stress and coping in school age children.* William T. Grant Foundation Fifth Annual Faculty Scholars Program in Mental Health of Children. [13]

Hruska, K., and Yonas, A. (1971). *Developmental changes in cardiac responses to the optical stimulus of impending collision.* Paper presented at the Meetings for Psychophysiological Research, St. Louis. [7]

Hubel, D. H., and Wiesel, T. N. (1965). Binocular interaction in striate cortex of kittens reared with artificial squint. *Journal of Neurophysiology, 28,* 1041–1059. [7]

Huesman, L., and Eron, L. (1986). *Television and the aggressive child: A cross-national comparison.* Hillsdale, N.J.: Erlbaum. [11]

Humphrey, T. (1969). Postnatal repetition of human prenatal activity sequences with some suggestions of their neuroanatomical basis. In R. J. Robinson (Ed.), *Brain and early behavior.* New York: Academic Press. [5]

Husain, J. S., and Cohen, L. B. (1982). Infant learning of ill-defined categories. *Merrill-Palmer Quarterly, 27,* 443–456. [6]

Huston, A. C., Carpenter, C. J., and Atwater, J. B. (1986). Gender, adult structuring of activities, and social behavior in middle childhood. *Child Development, 57,* 1200–1209. [13]

Hutt, C. (1966). Exploration and play in children. *Symposia of the Zoological Society of London, 18,* 61–81. [9]

Huttenlocker, J. (1974). The origins of language comprehension. In R. L. Solso (Ed.), *Theories in cognitive psychology.* New York: Wiley. [8]

Huttenlocker, P. (1979, July). Press release. University of Chicago. [14]

Iannotti, R. (1985). Naturalistic and structured assessments of prosocial behavior in preschool children. The influence of empathy and perspective taking. *Developmental Psychology, 21,* 46–55. [11]

Inhelder, B., and Piaget, J. (1955/1958). *The growth of logical thinking from childhood to adolescence.* New York: Basic Books. [14]

Inhelder, B., and Piaget, J. (1964). *The early growth of logic in the child.* London, Eng.: Routledge & Kegan Paul. [10, 12]

Inhelder, B., Sinclair, H., and Bovet, B. (1974). *Learning and development of cognition.* Cambridge, Mass.: Harvard University Press. [14]

Institute of Medicine. (1985). *Preventing low birthweight.* Washington, D.C.: National Academy Press. [4]

Iverson, S. (1980). Brain chemistry and behavior. *Psychological Medicine, 10,* 427–539. [16]

Jackson, D. (1977). The study of the family. In P. Watzlawick and J. H. Weakland (Eds.), *The interactional view.* New York: Norton. [12]

Jacob, T. (1974). Patterns of family conflict and dominance as a function of child age and social class. *Developmental Psychology, 10,* 1–12. [15]

Jacobs, P. I., and Vandeventer, M. (1968). Progressive matrices: An experimental, developmental, nonfactorial analysis. *Perceptual and Motor Skills, 27,* 759–766. [12]

Jacobs, P. I., and Vandeventer, M. (1971). The learning and transfer of double classification skills by first graders. *Child Development, 42,* 149–159. [12]

Jacobson, S. W. (1979). Matching behavior in the young infant. *Child Development, 50,* 425–430. [5]

Jacobvitz, D., and Sroufe, L. A. (in press). The early caregiver—child relationship and attention deficit disorder with hyperactivity in kindergarten: A prospective study. *Child Development, 58.* [2]

Jahoda, M. (1958). *Current concepts of positive mental health.* New York: Basic Books. [12]

Jarvik, L. F., and Erlenmeyer, K. L. (1967). Survey of familial correlations in measured intellectual functions. In J. Zubin and G. A. Jervis (Eds.), *Psychopathology of mental development.* New York: Grune & Stratton. [12]

Jessor, R. (1983). The stability of change: Psychosocial development from adolescence to young adulthood. In D. Magnusson and V. Allen (Eds.), *Human development: An interactional perspective.* New York: Academic Press. [15]

Jessor, R. (1984). Adolescent development and behavioral health. In J. Matarazzo, S. Weiss, J. Herd, N. Miller, and S. Weiss (Eds.), *Behavioral health.* New York: Wiley. [15]

Johnston, L., and Bachman, J. (1981). *Highlights from student drug use in America, 1975–1980.* National Institute on Drug Abuse, Washington, D.C.: U. S. Government Printing Office. [15]

Jones, K. L., Smith, D. W., Ulleland, C. N., and Streissguth, A. P. (1973). Patterns of malformation in offspring of chronic alcoholic mothers. *Lancet, 1,* 1267–1271. [4]

Jones, M. (1957). The later careers of boys who were early or late maturing. *Child Development, 28,* 113–128. [15]

Jones, M., and Bayley, N. (1950). Physical maturing among boys as related to behavior. *Journal of Educational Psychology, 41,* 129–148. [15]

Kacerguis, M., and Adams, G. (1980). Erikson stage resolution: The relationship between identity and intimacy. *Journal of Youth and Adolescence, 9,* 117–126. [15]

Kagan, J. (1971). *Change and continuity in infancy.* New York: Wiley. [7]

Kagan, J. (1984). *The nature of the child.* New York: Basic Books. [7]

Kagan, J., Kearsley, R. B., and Zelazo, P. (1978). *Infancy: Its place in human development.* Cambridge, Mass.: Harvard University Press. [7]

Kagan, S., and Madsen, M. (1972). Experimental analyses of cooperation and competition of Anglo-American and Mexican children. *Developmental Psychology, 6,* 49–59. [3]

Kail, R. (1979). *The development of memory in children.* San Francisco: Freeman. [12]

Kail, R., and Hagan, J. (1982). Memory in childhood. In B. B. Wolman (Ed.), *Handbook of developmental psychology.* Englewood Cliffs, N.J.: Prentice-Hall. [12]

Kalat, J. W. (1984). *Biological psychology* (2nd ed.). Belmont, Calif.: Wadsworth. [5, 14]

Kalnins, I. V., and Bruner, J. S. (1973). The coordination of visual observation and instrumental behavior in early infancy. *Perception, 2,* 307–314. [5]

Kamerman, S. B., and Hayes, C. D. (Eds.). (1982). *Families that work: Children in a changing world.* Washington, D. C.: National Academy Press. [3]

Kandel, D. (1973). Adolescent marijuana use: Role of parents and peers. *Science, 181,* 1067–1070. [15]

Kandel, D. (1978). Similarity in real life adolescent friendship pairs. *Journal of Personality and Social Psychology, 36,* 306–312. [15]

Kandel, D., and Lesser, G. (1972). *Youth in two worlds: U. S. and Denmark.* San Francisco: Jossey-Bass. [15]

Kanner, L. (1943). Autistic disturbances of affective contact. *Nervous Child, 2,* 217–250. [16]

Kaplan, B. H., and Pokorny, A. (1959). Self-derogation and psychosocial adjustment. *Journal of Nervous and Mental Disease, 149,* 421–434. [12]

Kasahni, J., Husain, A., Shekim, W., Hodges, K., Cytryn, L., and McKrew, D. (1981). Current perspectives on childhood depression. *American Journal of Psychiatry, 138,* 143–153. [16]

Kaufman, J., and Cicchetti, D. (1986). *The effects of maltreatment on school-aged children. Assessments in a day camp setting.* Unpublished manuscript, University of Rochester. [16]

Kavale, K. A., and Karge, B. D. (1986). Fetal alcohol syndrome: A behavioral teratology. *The Exceptional Child, 33,* 4–16. [4]

Kaye, K. (1982). *The mental and social life of babies.* Chicago: University of Chicago Press. [7]

Kaye, K., and Marcus, J. (1981). Infant imitation: The sensory-motor agenda. *Developmental Psychology, 17,* 258–265. [7]

Kaye, K., and Wells, A. J. (1980). Mothers jiggling and the burst-pause pattern in neonatal feeding. *Infant Behavior and Development, 3,* 29–46. [7]

Keating, D. P. (1980). Thinking processes in adolescence. In J. Adelson (Ed.), *Handbook of adolescent psychology.* New York: Wiley. [14]

Keeney, T. J., Cannizzo, S. R., and Flavell, J. H. (1967). Spontaneous and induced verbal rehearsal in a recall task. *Child Development, 38,* 953–966. [12]

Keller, A., Ford, L., and Meachum, J. (1978). Dimensions of self-concept in preschool children. *Developmental Psychology, 14,* 483–489. [11, 13]

Kempe, R. S., and Kempe, H. C. (1978). *Child abuse.* Cambridge, Mass.: Harvard University Press. [9]

Kendall, P. (1981). Cognitive-behavioral interventions with children. In B. Laheg and A. Kazdin (Eds.), *Advances in clinical child psychology* (Vol. 4). New York: Plenum. [16]

Kendler, T. S., and Kendler, H. H. (1962). Inferential behavior in children as a function of age and subgoal constancy. *Journal of Experimental Psychology, 61,* 442–448. [6]

Kennedy, W. (1965). School phobia: Rapid treatment of 50 cases. *Journal of Abnormal Psychology, 70,* 285–289. [16]

Kermoian, R., and Liederman, H. (1982). *Infant attachment to mother and child caretaker in an East African community.* Paper presented at the International Conference on Infant Studies, Austin, Tex. [7, 9]

Kessen, W. (1965). *The child.* New York: Wiley. [3]

Kessen, W. (1975). *Childhood in China.* New Haven, Conn.: Yale University Press. [3]

Kessler, J. (1966). *Psychopathology of childhood.* Englewood Cliffs, N.J.: Prentice-Hall. [16]

Kety, S., Rosenthal, D., Wender, P., Schultzinger, F., and Jacobson, B. (1978). The biologic and adopted individuals who became schizophrenic. Prevalence of mental illness and other characteristics. In L. Wynne, R. Cromwell, and S. Matthysse (Eds.), *The nature of schizophrenia.* New York: Wiley. [16]

Kierkegaard, Sören. (1938). *Purity of heart is to will one thing.* New York: Harper & Row. [9]

Kimmel, D. C., and Weiner, I. B. (1985). *Adolescence: A developmental transition.* Hillsdale, N.J.: Erlbaum. [14]

Kinloch, G. (1970). Parent-youth conflict at home: An investigation among university freshmen. *American Journal of Orthopsychiatry, 40,* 658–664. [15]

Kiselevsky, B. S., and Muir, D. W. (1984). Neonatal habituation and dishabituation to tactile stimulation during sleep. *Developmental Psychology, 20,* 367–373. [6]

Kitchener, R. F. (1983). Developmental explanations. *Review of Metaphysics, 36,* 791–817. [1]

Klahr, D., and Wallace, J. G. (1976). *Cognitive development: An information processing view.* Hillsdale, N.J.: Erlbaum. [2, 12]

Klaus, M., and Kennell, J. (1976). *Maternal infant bonding.* St. Louis: Mosby. [7]

Knobloch, H., and Pasamanick, B. (1975). Some etiological and prognostic factors in early infantile autism. *Pediatrics, 55,* 182–191. [16]

Knopf, I. (1984). *Childhood psychopathology* (2nd ed.). Englewood Cliffs, N.J.: Prentice-Hall. [16]

Kohl, H. (1967). *36 children.* New York: Knopf. [16]

Kohlberg, L. (1958). *The development of modes of moral thinking and choice in the years 10 to 16.* Unpublished doctoral dissertation, University of Chicago. [14]

Kohlberg, L. (1966). A cognitive-developmental analysis of children's sex-role concepts and attitudes. In E. Maccoby (Ed.), *The development of sex differences.* Stanford, Calif.: Stanford University Press. [11]

Kohlberg, L. (1969). Stage and sequence: The cognitive-developmental approach to socialization. In D. A. Goslin (Ed.), *Handbook of socialization theory and research.* Chicago: Rand McNally. [14]

Kohlberg, L. (1976). Moral stages and moralization: Cognitive-developmental approach. In R. Lickona (Ed.), *Moral development and behavior: Theory, research, and social issues.* Chicago: Rand McNally. [14]

Kohlberg, L., Ricks, D., and Snarey, J. (1984). Childhood development as a predictor of adaptation in adulthood. *Genetic Psychology Monographs, 110,* 91–172. [16]

Kohn, M. (1963). Social class and parent-child relationship: An interpretation. *American Journal of Sociology, 68,* 471–480. [3]

Kohn, M. (1979). The effects of social class on parental values and practices. In D. Reiss and H. A. Hoffman (Eds.),

The American family: Dying or developing. New York: Plenum. [3]

Konopka, G. (1973). Requirements for healthy development of adolescent youth. *Adolescence, 31,* 291–316. [14]

Konopka, G. (1976). *Young girls: A portrait of adolescence.* Englewood Cliffs, N.J.: Prentice-Hall. [14, 15]

Kopp, C. (1982). Antecedents of self-regulation: A developmental perspective. *Developmental Psychology, 18,* 199–214. [11]

Kopp, C. B., Krakow, J. B., and Vaughn, B. E. (1983). The antecedents of self-regulation in young handicapped children. In M. Perlmutter (Ed.), *Minnesota Symposia on Child Psychology* (Vol. 17). Hillsdale, N.J.: Erlbaum. [11]

Kopp, C. B., and Parmelee, A. H. (1979). Prenatal and perinatal influences on infant behavior. In J. Osofsky (Ed.), *Handbook of infant development.* New York: Wiley. [4]

Korner, A. (1972). State as a variable, as obstacle, and as mediator of stimulation in infant research. *Merrill-Palmer Quarterly, 18,* 77–94. [7]

Kotelchuck, M. (1976). The infant's relationship to the father: Experimental evidence. In M. E. Lamb (Ed.), *The role of the father in child development.* New York: Wiley. [9]

Kramer, J., Hill, K., and Cohen, L. (1975). Infants' development of object permanence: A refined methodology and new evidence of Piaget's hypothesized ordinality. *Child Development, 46,* 149–155. [6]

Krauss, R., and Glucksberg, S. (1969). The development of communication: Competence as a function of age. *Child Development, 40,* 255–266. [13]

Krebs, R. L. (1967). *Some relations between moral judgment, attention, and resistance to temptation.* Unpublished doctoral dissertation, University of Chicago. [14]

Kreppner, K., Paulse, S., and Schuetze, Y. (1982). Infant and family development: From triads to tetrads. *Human Development, 25,* 373–391. [3, 13]

Kreutzer, M. A., Leonard, C., and Flavell, J. H. (1975). An interview study of children's knowledge about memory. *Monographs of the Society for Research in Child Development, 40,* (1, Serial No. 159). [12]

Kringlen, E. (1978). Adult offspring of two psychotic parents with special reference to schizophrenia. In L. Wynne, R. Cromwell, and S. Matthysse (Eds.), *The nature of schizophrenia.* New York: Wiley. [16]

Kron, R. E., Kaplan, S. L., Phoenix, M. D., and Finnegan, L. P. (1977). Behavior of infants born to narcotic-dependent mothers: Effects of prenatal and postnatal drugs. In J. L. Renentaria (Ed.), *Drug abuse in pregnancy and neonatal effects.* New York: Wiley. [4]

Krosnick, J., and Judd, C. (1982). Traditions in social influence at adolescence: Who induces cigarette smoking? *Developmental Psychology, 18,* 359–368. [15]

Kruttschnitt, C., Heath, L., and Ward, D. (1986). Family violence, television viewing habits, and other violent criminal behavior. *Criminology, 24,* 201–233. [16]

Kuczynski, L. (1984). Socialization goals and mother-child interactions: Strategies for long-term and short-term compliance. *Developmental Psychology, 20,* 1061–1073. [11]

Kurtines, W., and Grief, E. G. (1974). The development of moral thought: Review and evaluation of Kohlberg's approach. *Psychological Bulletin, 81,* 453–470. [14]

Labov, W. (1970). The logic of nonstandard English. In F. Williams (Ed.), *Language and poverty: Perspectives on a theme.* Chicago: Markham. [8]

Ladd, G. W. (1983). Social networks of popular, average, and rejected children in school settings. *Merrill-Palmer Quarterly, 29,* 283–308. [13]

LaFrenier, P. (1983). *From attachment to peer relations: An analysis of individual patterns of social adaptation during the formation of a preschool peer group.* Unpublished doctoral dissertation, University of Minnesota. [11]

LaFrenier, P., and Sroufe, L. A. (1985). Profiles of peer competence in the preschool: Interrelations between measures, influence of social ecology, and relation to attachment history. *Developmental Psychology, 21,* 56–69. [11]

Lamb, M. (1975). Fathers: Forgotten contributors to child development. *Human Development, 18,* 245–266. [3]

Lamb, M. E. (1976). Twelve-month-olds and their parents: Interaction in a laboratory playroom. *Developmental Psychology, 12,* 237–244. [7]

Lamb, M. E. (1981). The development of father-infant relationships. In M. E. Lamb (Ed.), *The role of the father in child development* (2nd ed.). New York: Wiley. [3, 9, 11]

Lamb, M. E., and Campos, J. (1982). *Development in infancy.* New York: Random House. [9, 11]

Lamb, M., Frodi, A., Hwang, C., and Steinberg, J. (1982). Mother- and father-infant interactions involving play and holding in traditional and nontraditional Swedish families. *Developmental Psychology, 18,* 215–221. [9]

Landesman-Dwyer, S., Ragozin, A. S., and Little, R. E. (1981). Behavioral correlates of prenatal alcohol exposure: A four-year follow-up study. *Neurobehavioral Toxicology and Teratology, 3,* 187–193. [4]

Langlois, J., and Downs, A. (1980). Mothers, fathers, and peers as socialization agents of sex-typed play behaviors in young children. *Child Development, 51,* 1217–1247. [3, 11, 13]

Lansbaum, J., and Willis, R. (1971). Conformity in early and late adolescence. *Developmental Psychology, 4,* 334–337. [15]

Larsson, G., Bohlin, A. B., and Tunell, R. (1985). Prospective study of children exposed to variable amounts of alcohol in utero. *Archives of Disease in Childhood, 60,* 316–321. [4]

Laufer, M., and Denhoff, E. (1957). Hyperkinetic behavior syndrome in children. *Journal of Pediatrics, 50,* 463–474. [16]

Lazare, A. (1973). Hidden conceptual models in clinical psychiatry. *New England Journal of Medicine, 288,* 345–350. [16]

Lazer, I., Darlington, R. B., Murray, H., Royce, J., and Snipper, A. (1982). Lasting effects of early education. *Monographs of the Society for Research in Child Development, 47* (2–3, Serial No. 195). [12]

Lee, C. L., and Bates, J. E. (1985). Mother-child interaction at age two years and perceived difficult temperament. *Child Development, 56,* 1314–1325. [9, 13]

Lefkowitz, M. M. (1981). Smoking during pregnancy: Long-term effects on offspring. *Developmental Psychology, 17,* 192–194. [4]

Leiman, B. (1978). *Affective empathy and subsequent altruism in kindergartners and first graders.* Paper presented at the annual meeting of the American Psychological Association, Toronto.

Leimbach, M., and Hartup, W. (1981). Forming cooperative coalitions during a competitive game in same-sex and mixed-sex triads. *Journal of Genetic Psychology, 139,* 165–171. [12]

Leiter, M. P. (1977). A study of reciprocity in preschool play groups. *Child Development, 48,* 1288–1295. [11]

Lenneberg, E. (1967). *Biological foundations of language.* New York: Wiley. [3, 8]

Leon, G., Kendall, P., and Garber, J. (1980). Depression in children: Parent, teacher, and child perspectives. *Journal of Abnormal Child Psychology, 8,* 221–235. [16]

Leonard, M., Rhymes, J., and Solnit, A. (1966). Failure to thrive in infants: A family problem. *American Journal of Diseases in Children, 3,* 600–612. [7]

Lesser, G. (1974). *Children and television.* New York: Random House. [3]

Lesser, G., and Kandel, D. (1969). Parental and peer influence on educational plans of adolescents. *American Sociological Review, 34,* 213–223. [15]

Lester, R. M., Kotechuck, M., Spelke, E., Sellers, U. J., and R. E. Klein. (1974). Separation protest in Guatemalan infants: Cross-cultural and cognitive findings. *Developmental Psychology, 10,* 79–84. [7]

Lever, J. (1976). Sex differences in the games children play. *Social Problems, 23,* 479–487. [13]

Levine, M., and Sutton-Smith, B. (1973). Effects of age, sex, and task on visual behavior during dyadic interaction. *Developmental Psychology, 9,* 400–405. [12]

Levine, R., and Levine, B. (1966). *Nyansongo: A Guisii community in Kenya.* New York: Wiley. [15]

Levine, S. (1978). Youth and religious cults: A societal and clinical dilemma. In S. Feinstein and P. Giovacchini (Eds.), *Adolescent psychiatry.* Chicago: University of Chicago Press. [15]

Lewin, K. (1951). *Field theory in social science.* New York: Harper & Row. [15]

Lewis, M., and Brooks, J. (1978). Self-knowledge and emotional development. In M. Lewis and L. Rosenblum (Eds.), *The development of affect.* New York: Plenum. [9, 11]

Lewis, M., and Feiring, C. (1981). Direct and indirect interactions in social relationships. In L. Lipsitt (Ed.), *Advances in infancy research.* Norwood, N.J.: Ablex. [9]

Lewis, M., Feiring, C., McGuffog, C., and Jaskir, J. (1984). Predicting psychopathology in six-year-olds from early social relations. *Child Development, 55,* 123–136. [16]

Lewis, M., and Goldberg, S. (1969). Perceptual-cognitive development in infancy: A generalized expectancy model as a function of mother-infant interaction. *Merrill-Palmer Quarterly, 15,* 81–100. [7]

Liben, L. S., and Posnansky, C. J. (1977). Inferences on inferences: The effects of age, transitive ability, memory load, and lexical factors. *Child Development, 48,* 1490–1497. [12]

Liberman, A. M., Harris, K. S., Hoffman, H. S., and Griffith, B. C. (1957). The discrimination of speech sounds within and across phoneme boundaries. *Journal of Experimental Psychology, 54,* 358–368. [5]

Lieberman, A. F. (1977). Preschoolers' competence with a peer: Relations with attachment and peer experience. *Child Development, 48,* 1277–1287. [3]

Lipsitt, L. P., Kaye, H., and Bosack, T. N. (1966). Enhancement of neonatal sucking through reinforcement. *Journal of Experimental Child Psychology, 4,* 163–168. [5]

Li-Repac, D. (1982). *The impact of acculturation on the child-rearing attitudes and practices of Chinese-American families.* Unpublished doctoral dissertation, University of California at Berkeley. [3]

Litt, I. (1985, March). Anorexia nervosa. Paper presented at the Center for Advanced Study in the Behavioral Sciences, Stanford, Calif. [16]

Livesly, W. J., and Bromley, O. B. (1973). *Person perception in childhood and adolescence.* London, Eng.: Wiley. [13, 15]

Loehlin, J., Willerman, L., and Horn, J. (1982). Personality resemblances between unwed mothers and their adopted-away offspring. *Journal of Personality and Social Psychology, 42,* 1089–1099. [7]

Loevinger, J. (1976). *Ego development.* San Francisco: Jossey-Bass. [2, 15]

Loevinger, J., and Wessler, R. (1970). *Measuring ego development* (Vol. 1). San Francisco: Jossey-Bass. [12]

Londerville, S., and Main, M. (1981). Security of attachment, compliance, and maternal training methods in the second year of life. *Developmental Psychology, 17,* 289–299. [3, 9, 11]

Lotter, V. (1974). Factors related to outcome in autistic children. *Journal of Autism and Childhood Schizophrenia, 4,* 262–277. [16]

Lowry, L. (1982). *Developmental effects of teenage childbearing on children.* Unpublished doctoral dissertation, University of Minnesota. [7]

Lunzar, E. A. (1978). Normal reasoning: A reappraisal. In B. Z. Presseisen, D. Goldstein, and M. H. Appel (Eds.), *Topics in cognitive development* (Vol. 2). New York: Plenum. [14]

Luria, A. R. (1961). *The role of speech in the regulation of normal and abnormal behavior.* New York: Pergamon Press. [11]

Luster, T. (1985). *Influences on maternal behavior: Child rearing beliefs, social support, and infant temperament.* Unpublished doctoral dissertation, Cornell University. [2]

Maccoby, E. E. (1967). Selective auditory attention in children. In L. P. Lipsitt and C. C. Spiker (Eds.), *Advances in child development and behavior.* New York: Academic Press. [5]

Maccoby, E. E. (1980). *Social development.* New York: Harcourt Brace Jovanovich. [3, 11, 12, 13, 15]

Maccoby, E. E., and Martin, J. A. (1983). Socialization in the context of the family. In E. M. Hetherington (Ed.), *Handbook of child psychology: Socialization personality and social development* (Vol. 4). New York: Wiley. [11, 13]

MacFarlane, A. (1975). Olfaction in the development of social preferences in the human neonate. *Parent-infant interaction.* Amsterdam: CIBA Foundation Symposium 33, ASP. [5]

MacFarlane, J., Allen, L., and Honzik, M. (1954). *A developmental study of the behavior problems of normal children.* Berkeley: University of California Press. [16]

Madsen, M. (1971). Development and cross-cultural differences in cooperative and competitive behavior of young children. *Journal of Cross-Cultural Psychology, 2,* 365–371. [3]

Mahler, M., Pine, R., and Bergman, A. (1975). *The psychological birth of human infants.* New York: Basic Books. [9, 11]

Main, M., Kaplan, N., and Cassidy, J. (1985). Security in infancy, childhood, and adulthood: A move to the level of representation. In I. Bretherton and E. Waters (Eds.), *Growing points in attachment theory and research. Monographs of the Society for Research in Child Development, 50* (Whole No. 209), 66–104. [9]

Main, M., and Weston, D. (1981). The quality of the toddler's relationship to mother and to father as related to conflict behavior and readiness to establish new relationships. *Child Development, 52,* 932–940. [7]

Malina, R. M. (1978). Growth of muscle tissue and muscle mass. In F. Falkner and J. M. Tanner (Eds.), *Human growth: Vol. 2. Postnatal growth.* New York: Plenum. [14]

Mans, L., Cicchetti, D., and Sroufe, L. A. (1978). Mirror reactions of Down syndrome infants and toddlers: Cognitive underpinnings of self-recognition. *Child Development, 49,* 1247–1250. [1, 9]

Maratsos, M. (1983). Some current issues in the study of the acquisition of grammar. In P. H. Mussen (Ed.), *Handbook of child psychology* (Vol. 3, 4th ed.): J. H. Flavell and E. M. Markman (Eds.), *Cognitive development.* New York: Wiley. [8]

Marcia, J. (1980). Identity in adolescence. In J. Adelson (Ed.), *Handbook of adolescent psychology* (pp. 159–187). New York: Wiley. [15]

Marcia, J., and Friedman, M. (1970). Ego identity status in college women. *Journal of Personality, 38,* 249–263. [15]

Margolis, L. (1982). Help wanted. *Pediatrics, 69,* 816–818. [3]

Markman, E. M. (1978). Empirical versus logical solutions to part-whole comparison problems concerning classes and collections. *Child Development, 49,* 168–177. [12]

Markman, E. M. (1979). Classes and collections: Conceptual organization and numerical abilities. *Cognitive Psychology, 11,* 395–411. [10]

Markman, E. M., and Siebert, J. (1976). Classes and collections: Principles of organization in the learning of hierarchical relations. *Cognitions, 8,* 227–241. [12]

Markus, H., and Nurius, P. (1984). Self-understanding and self-regulation in middle childhood. In W. A. Collins (Ed.), *Development in middle childhood.* Washington, D. C.: National Academy Press. [Part V Summary]

Marvin, R. (1977). An ethological-cognitive model of the attenuation of mother-child attachment behavior. In T. Alloway, P. Pliner, and L. Krames (Eds.), *Attachment behavior.* New York: Plenum. [9]

Masangkay, Z. S., McCluskey, K. A., McIntyre, C. W., Sims-Knight, J., Vaughn, B. E., and Flavell, J. H. (1974). The early development of inferences about the visual percepts of others. *Child Development, 45,* 357–366. [10]

Mason, W., and Kenney, M. (1974). Redirection of filial attachments in rhesus monkeys: Dogs as mother surrogates. *Science, 183,* 1209–1211. [7]

Masten, A., and Garmezy, N. (1985). Risk, vulnerability, and protective factors in developmental psychopathology. In B. Lahey and A. Kazdin (Eds.), *Advances in clinical child psychology* (Vol. 8, pp. 1–52). New York: Plenum. [16]

Masters, J. (1971). Social comparison by young children. *Young Children, 27,* 37–60. [13]

Masur, E., and Gleason, J. B. (1980). Parent-child interaction and the acquisition of lexical information during play. *Developmental Psychology, 16,* 404–409. [8]

Matas, L., Arend, R., and Sroufe, L. A. (1978). Continuity of adaptation in the second year: The relationship between quality of attachment and later competence. *Child Development, 49,* 547–556. [3, 9, 11]

Matheny, A., Wilson, R., and Nuss, S. (1984). Toddler temperament: Stability across settings and over ages. *Child Development, 55,* 1200–1211. [9]

Maurer, D., and Salapatek, P. (1976). Developmental changes in the scanning of faces by young infants. *Child Development, 47,* 523–527. [1, 5, 7]

Maww, M., and Maww, E. (1970). Self-concept of high and low curious boys. *Child Development, 41,* 123–129. [11]

McAnarney, D., and Greydanus, D. (1979). Adolescent pregnancy: A multifaceted problem. *Pediatrics in Review, 1,* 123–126. [14]

McCall, R. (1981). Nature-nurture and the two realms of development: A proposed integration with respect to mental development. *Child Development, 52,* 1–12. [3]

McCall, R. B. (1977). Childhood IQs as predictors of adult educational and occupational status. *Science, 197,* 482–483. [12]

McCall, R. B. (1979). Qualitative transitions of behavioral development in the first years of life. In M. H. Bornstein and W. Kessen (Eds.), *Psychological development from infancy.* Hillsdale, N.J.: Erlbaum. [6]

McCall, R. B., Eichorn, D. H., and Hogarty, P. S. (1977). Transitions in early mental development. *Monographs of the Society for Research in Child Development, 42.* [6]

McCandless, B., and Evans, E. (1973). *Children and youth: Psychosocial development.* Evanston, Ill.: Dryden Press. [15]

McCartney, K., Scarr, S., Phillips, D., and Grajek, S. (1985). Day care as intervention: Comparisons of varying quality programs. *Journal of Applied Developmental Psychology, 6,* 247–260. [7]

McCartney, K., and Weiss, E. (1985). *The development of personal and social concerns in adolescence.* Paper presented at the biennial meeting of the Society for Research in Child Development, Toronto. [15]

McClelland, D. C. (1973). Testing for competence rather than for intelligence. *American Psychologist, 28,* 1–14. [12]

McCord, J. (in press). Parental behavior in the cycle of aggression. *Psychiatry.* [13]

McGhee, P. E. (1976). Children's appreciation of humor: A test of the cognitive congruency principle. *Child Development, 47,* 420–426. [12]

McGraw, M. B. (1935). *Growth: A study of Johnny and Jimmy.* New York: Appleton-Century-Croft. [5]

McGraw, M. B. (1940). Suspension grasp behavior of the human infant. *American Journal of Disabilities in Children, 60,* 799–811. [5]

McGraw, M. B. (1940). Neural maturation as exemplified by the achievement of bladder control. *Journal of Pediatrics, 6,* 580–590. [15]

McKinney, W. (1977). Animal behavioral/biological models relevant to depression and affective disorders in humans. In J. Schulterbrandt and A. Raskin (Eds.), *Depression in childhood.* New York: Raven Press. [2, 16]

Mead, G. H. (1934). *Mind, self, and society.* Chicago: University of Chicago Press. [9]

Mead, M. (1925/1939). *Coming of age in Samoa.* New York: William Morrow. [12, 15]

Mead, M. (1935). *Sex and temperament in three primitive societies.* New York: William Morrow. [11]

Mednick, S. (1970). Breakdown in individuals at high-risk for schizophrenia: Possible predispositional factors. *Mental Hygiene, 54,* 50–63. [16]

Meichenbaum, D. (1977). *Cognitive-behavior modification: An integrative approach.* New York: Plenum. [16]

Meltzoff, A., and Moore, M. (1977). Imitation of facial and manual gestures by human neonates. *Science, 198,* 75–78. [5, 7]

Mendels, J., and Frazer, A. (1974). Brain biogenic amine depletion and mood. *Archives of General Psychiatry, 30,* 447–451. [16]

Mendelson, W., Johnson, N., and Stewart, M. (1971). Hyperactive children as teenagers: A follow-up study. *Journal of Nervous and Mental Disease, 153,* 273–279. [12]

Menig-Peterson, C. L. (1975). The modification of communicative behavior in preschool-aged children as a function of the listener's perspective. *Child Development, 46,* 1015–1018. [10]

Menning, B. (1977). *Infertility: A guide for childless couples.* Englewood Cliffs, N.J.: Prentice-Hall. [4]

Michaels, R. H., and Mellin, G. W. (1960). Prospective experience with maternal rubella and the associated congenital malformations. *Pediatrics, 26,* 200–209. [4]

Milavsky, J., Stipp, H., Kessler, K., and Rubbens, W. (1982). *Television and aggression.* New York: Academic Press. [11]

Milewski, A. E. (1978). Young infants' visual processing of internal and adjacent shapes. *Infant Behavior and Development, 1,* 359–371. [5]

Miller, G. A. (1981). *Language and speech.* San Francisco: Freeman. [8]

Miller, L., Barrett, C., Hampe, E., and Noble, H. (1972). Comparison of reciprocal inhibition, psychotherapy, and waiting list control for phobic children. *Journal of Abnormal Psychology, 79,* 269–279. [16]

Miller, N., and Maruyama, G. (1976). Ordinal position and peer popularity. *Journal of Personality and Social Psychology, 33,* 123–131. [13]

Miller, S. A., Shelton, J., and Flavell, J. H. (1970). A test of Luria's hypothesis concerning the development of self-regulation. *Child Development, 41,* 651–665. [11]

Minnett, A. M., Vandell, D. L., and Santrock, J. W. (1983). The effects of sibling status on sibling interaction: Influence of birth order, age, spacing, sex of child, and sex of sibling. *Child Development, 54,* 1064–1072. [13]

Minuchin, P. (1971). Correlates of curiosity and exploratory behavior in disadvantaged preschool children. *Child Development, 42,* 939–950. [11]

Minuchin, P. (1985). Families and individual development: Provocations from the field of family therapy. *Child Development, 56,* 289–302. [3]

Minuchin, P., and Shapiro, E. (1983). The school as a context for social development. In P. H. Mussen (Ed.), *Handbook of child psychology* (Vol. 4, 4th ed.): E. M. Hetherington (Ed.), *Socialization, personality, and social development.* New York: Wiley. [3]

Minuchin, S. (1974). *Families and family therapy.* Cambridge, Mass.: Harvard University Press. [12, 16]

Minuchin, S., Rosman, B., and Baker, L. (1978). *Psychosomatic anorexia nervosa in context.* Cambridge, Eng.: Harvard University Press. [16]

Mira, M., and Cairns, G. (1981). Intervention in the interaction of a mother and child with nonorganic failure to thrive. *Pediatric Nursing, 7,* 41–45. [9]

Mischel, H., and Mischel, W. (1983). The development of children's knowledge of self-control strategies. *Child Development, 54,* 603–619. [7, 13]

Mischel, W. (1968). *Personality and assessment.* New York: Wiley. [11]

Mischel, W. (1973). Toward a cognitive social learning reconceptualization of personality. *Psychological Review, 80,* 252–283. [16]

Mischel, W. (1974). Processes in delay of gratification. In L. Berkowitz (Ed.), *Advances in experimental psychology* (Vol. 7). New York: Academic Press. [2]

Mischel, W., and Metzner, R. (1962). Preference for delayed reward as a function of age, intelligence, and length of delay interval. *Journal of Abnormal Psychology, 64,* 425–431. [13]

Mischel, W., and Patterson, C. (1978). Effective plans for self-control in children. In W. A. Collins (Ed.), *Minnesota Symposia on Child Psychology* (Vol. 11). Hillsdale, N.J.: Erlbaum. [12]

Mischel, W., and Underwood, B. (1974). Instrumental ideation in delay of gratification. *Child Development, 45,* 1083–1088. [11]

Mischel, W., Zeiss, R., and Zeiss, A. (1974). Internal-external control and persistence: Validation and implications of the Stanford Preschool Internal-External Scale. *Journal of Personality and Social Psychology, 29,* 265–278. [13]

Moely, B. E., Olson, F. A., Halwes, T. G., and Flavell, J. H. (1969). Production deficiency in young children's clustered recall. *Developmental Psychology, 1,* 26–34. [12]

Moffitt, A. (1971). Consonant cue perception by twenty- to twenty-four-week-old infants. *Child Development, 42,* 717–782. [7]

Moffitt, A. R. (1973). Intensity discrimination and cardiac reaction in young infants. *Developmental Psychology, 8,* 357–359. [5]

Molfese, D. L., and Molfese, V. J. (1979). Hemisphere and stimulus differences as reflected in the cortical responses of newborn infants to speech stimuli. *Developmental Psychology, 15,* 505–511. [8]

Molfese, D. L., Molfese, V. J., and Carrell, P. L. (1982). Early language development. In B. B. Wolman (Ed.), *Handbook of developmental psychology.* Englewood Cliffs, N.J.: Prentice-Hall. [8]

Moliter, N., Joffe, L., Barglow, P., Benveniste, R., and Vaughn, B. (1984, April). *Biochemical and psychological antecedents of newborn performance on the Neonatal Behavioral Assessment Scale.* Paper presented at the International Conference on Infant Studies, New York. [4, 7, 9]

Money, J. (1975). Alblatiopenis: Normal male infant sex-reassigned as a girl. *Archives of Sexual Behavior, 4,* 65–72. [11]

Money, J., and Ehrhardt, A. A. (1972). *Man and woman, boy and girl.* Baltimore: Johns Hopkins Press. [4]

Montemayer, R. (1983). Parents and adolescents in conflict: All families some of the time and some families most of the time. *Journal of Early Adolescence, 3,* 83–103. [15]

Montemayer, R., and Brownlee, J. (1986). *The mother-adolescent relationship in early and middle adolescence: Differences in maternal satisfaction.* Paper presented at the Society for Research on Adolescence, Madison, Wisc. [15]

Montemayer, R., and Eisen, M. (1977). The development of self-conceptions from childhood to adolescence. *Developmental Psychology, 13,* 314–319. [15]

Montemayer, R., and Hanson, E. (1985). A naturalistic view of conflict between adolescents and their parents and siblings. *Journal of Early Adolescence, 5,* 23–30. [15]

Moore, K. L. (1974). *Before we are born.* Philadelphia: Saunders. [4]

Moore, M. K., Borton, R., and Darby, B. L. (1978). Visual tracking in young infants: Evidence for object identity or object permanence? *Journal of Experimental Child Psychology, 25,* 183–198. [6]

Morris, D. (1981, April). *Infant attachment and problem solving in the toddler: Relations to mother's family history.* Paper presented at a meeting of the Society for Research in Child Development, Boston. [7]

Morris, D. (1983). Attachment and intimacy. In G. Stricker and M. Fisher (Eds.), *Intimacy.* New York: Plenum. [9]

Mosher, F. A., and Hornsby, J. R. (1966). On asking questions. In J. S. Bruner, R. Olver, and P. M. Greenfield (Eds.), *Studies in cognitive growth.* New York: Wiley. [12]

Moshman, D., and Timmons, M. (1982). The construction of logical necessity. *Human Development, 25,* 309–323. [12]

Moss, H., and Robson, K. (1968). *The role of protest behavior in the development of mother-infant attachment.* Paper presented at the American Psychological Association, San Francisco. [7]

Motti, E. (1986). *Patterns of behaviors of preschool teachers with children of varying developmental history.* Unpublished predoctoral dissertation, University of Minnesota. [9, 11]

Motti, F., Cicchetti, D., and Sroufe, L. A. (1983). From infant affect expression to symbolic play: The coherence of development in Down syndrome children. *Child Development, 54,* 1168–1175. [8]

Mueller, E., and Lucas, T. (1975). A developmental analysis

of peer interaction among toddlers. In M. Lewis and L. A. Rosenblum (Eds.), *Friendship and peer relations*. New York: Wiley. [9, 11]

Mueller, E., and Vandell, D. (1979). Infant-infant interaction. In J. Osofsky (Ed.), *Handbook of infant development*. New York: Wiley. [11]

Mugny, G., Perret-Clermont, A. N., and Doise, W. (1981). Interpersonal coordinations and sociological differences in the construction of the intellect. In G. M. Stephenson and J. M. Davis (Eds.), *Progress in applied social psychology* (Vol. 1). New York: Wiley. [12]

Munroe, R. L., and Munroe, R. H. (1975). *Cross-cultural human development*. Monterey, Calif.: Brooks/Cole. [3]

Murray, A. D., Dolby, R. M., Natson, R. L., and Thomas, D. P. (1981). The effects of epidural anesthesia on newborns and their mothers. *Child Development, 52,* 71–82. [7]

Murray, F. B. (1972). The acquisition of conservation through social interaction. *Developmental Psychology, 6,* 1–6. [12]

Murray, F. B. (1981). The conservation paradigm. In D. Brodzinsky, I. Sigel, and R. Golinkoff (Eds.), *New direction in Piagetian research and theory*. Hillsdale, N.J.: Erlbaum. [12]

Myles-Worsley, M., Cromer, C. C., and Dodd, D. H. (1986). Children's preschool script construction: Reliance on general knowledge as memory fades. *Developmental Psychology, 22,* 22–30. [10]

Nash, J. (1978). *Developmental psychology: A psychobiological approach*. Englewood Cliffs, N.J.: Prentice-Hall. [4]

National Center for Health Statistics. (1984). *Monthly Vital Statistics Report* (DHHS Publication No. PHS 84–1120). Washington, D.C.: U. S. Government Printing Office. [15]

National Center for Health Statistics. (1985). *Monthly Vital Statistics Report* (DHHS Publication No. PHS 85–1120). Washington, D.C.: U. S. Government Printing Office. [15]

National Council of Organizations for Children and Youth. (1976). *America's children 1976: A bicentennial assessment*. Washington, D.C.: Author. [3]

National Institutes of Health. (1981). Caesarian childbirth. In *Consensus development conference summary* (Vol. 3, No. 6). Washington, D.C.: U. S. Government Printing Office. [4]

Naus, M. J., and Ornstein, P. A. (1983). Development of memory strategies: Analysis, questions, and issues. In M. T. C. Chi (Ed.), *Trends in memory development research*. Basel, Switzerland: Karger. [12]

Neimark, E. D. (1982). Adolescent thought: Transition to formal operations. In B. B. Wolman and G. Strickler (Eds.), *Handbook of developmental psychology*. Englewood Cliffs, N.J.: Prentice-Hall. [14]

Nelson, K. (1973). Structure and strategy in learning to talk. *Monographs of the Society for Research in Child Development, 38.* [8]

Nelson, K. (1974). Concept, word, and sentence: Interrelations in acquisition and development. *Psychological Review, 81,* 267–285. [8]

Nelson, K. (1981a). Experimental gambits in the service of language acquisition theory. In S. Kuczaj (Ed.), *Language development: Syntax and semantics*. Hillsdale, N.J.: Erlbaum. [8]

Nelson, K. (1981b). Social cognition in a script framework. In J. H. Flavell and L. Ross (Eds.), *Social cognition*. Cambridge, Eng.: Cambridge University Press. [10]

Nelson, K., and Gruendel, J. (1979). At morning it's lunchtime: A scriptal view of children's dialogues. *Discourse Processes, 2,* 73–94. [10]

Nelson, N., Enkin, M., Saigal, S., Bennett, K., Milner, R., and Sackett, D. (1980). A randomized clinical trial of the Leboyer approach to childbirth. *New England Journal of Medicine, 302,* 655–660. [4]

Newberger, C., Melnicoe, L., and Newberger, E. (1986). The American family in crisis: Implications for children. *Current Problems in Pediatrics, 16,* 674–721. [3, 4, 13]

Newcomb, A., Brady, J., and Hartup, W. (1979). Friendship and incentive condition as determinants of children's task-oriented social behavior. *Child Development, 50,* 878–881. [13]

Newman, C. G. H. (1986). The thalidomide syndrome: Risks of exposure and spectrum of malformations. *Clinics in Perinatology, 13,* 555–573. [4]

Newport, E. H., Gleitman, H., and Gleitman, L. R. (1977). Mother, I'd rather do it myself: Some effects and noneffects of maternal speech style. In C. E. Snow and C. A. Furguson (Eds.), *Talking to children: Language input and acquisition*. Cambridge, Eng.: Cambridge University Press. [8]

Newson, J. (1974). Towards a theory of infant understanding. *Bulletin of the British Psychological Society, 27,* 251–257. [7]

Newson, J., and Newson, E. (1974). *Cultural aspects of child-rearing in the English-speaking world*. Cambridge, Eng.: Cambridge University Press. [3]

Nezworski, M. T. (1983). *Continuity in adaptation into the fourth year: Individual differences in curiosity and exploratory behavior of preschool children*. Unpublished doctoral dissertation, University of Minnesota. [11]

Nicholls, J. G., Patashnick, M., and Mettetal, G. (1986). Conceptions of ability and intelligence. *Child Development, 57,* 636–645. [12]

Nicolich, L. (1977). Beyond sensorimotor intelligence: Assessment of symbolic maturity through analysis of pretend play. *Merrill-Palmer Quarterly, 23,* 89–99. [8, 9, 11]

Niswander, K. R., and Gordon, M. (Eds.). (1972). *The collaborative perinatal study of the National Institute of Neurological Diseases and Stroke: The women and their pregnancies*. Washington, D.C.: U.S. Government Printing Office. [4]

Norton, A. J., and Glick, P. C. (1986). One parent families: A social and economic profile. *Family Relations, 35,* 9–18. [3]

Novak, M. (1979). Social recovery of monkeys isolated for the first year of life: Long-term assessment. *Developmental Psychology, 15,* 51–61. [11]

Novak, M., and Harlow, H. (1975). Social recovery of monkeys isolated for the first year of life. *Developmental Psychology, 11,* 453–465. [7]

Nuckolls, K. B., Cassel, J. C., and Kaplan, B. H. (1972). Psychosocial assets, life crisis, and prognosis of pregnancy. *American Journal of Epidemiology, 95,* 431–441. [4]

Nuechterlein, K. (1983). Signal detection in vigilance tasks and behavioral attributes among offspring of schizophrenic mothers and among hyperactive children. *Journal of Abnormal Psychology, 92,* 4–28. [16]

Oates, R., and Yu, J. (1971). Children with nonorganic failure to thrive: A community problem. *Medical Journal of Australia, 2,* 199–203. [7, 9]

Offer, D. (1969). *The psychological world of the teenager: A study of normal adolescent boys*. New York: Basic Books. [15]

Offer, D., and Offer, J. (1975). *From teenage to young manhood*. New York: Basic Books. [15]

Okun, M., and Sasty, J. (1977). Adolescence, the self-concept, and formal operations. *Adolescence, 12,* 373–379. [15]

O'Leary, K. D., and Becker, W. (1967). Behavior modification of an adjustment class: A token reinforcement program. *Exceptional Children, 33,* 637–642. [12]

O'Leary, K. D., and O'Leary, S. (1977). *Classroom management: *The successful use of behavior modification* (2nd ed.). New York: Pergamon Press. [16]

Ollendrick, T. (1979). Fear reduction techniques with children. In M. Hersen, R. Eisler, and P. Miller (Eds.), *Progress in behavior modification* (Vol. 8). New York: Academic Press. [16]

Olsho, L. W., Schoon, C., Sakai, R., Turpin, R., and Sperduto, V. (1982). Preliminary data on frequency discrimination in infancy. *Journal of the Acoustical Society of America, 71,* 509–511. [5]

Olson, G. (1981). The recognition of specific persons. In M. Lamb and L. Sherrod (Eds.), *Infant social cognition.* Hillsdale, N.J.: Erlbaum. [6]

Olson, G., and Sherman, T. (1983). Attention, learning, and memory in infants. In P. H. Mussen (Ed.), *Handbook of child psychology* (Vol. 3, 4th ed.): M. M. Haith and J. J. Campos (Eds.), *Infancy and developmental psychobiology.* New York: Wiley. [5, 6]

Olweus, D. (1980). Bullying among school boys. In R. Barnen (Ed.), *Children and violence.* Stockholm: Akademic Litteratur. [12]

Osherson, D. N., and Markman, E. M. (1975). Language and the ability to evaluate contradictions and tautologies. *Cognition, 2,* 213–226. [14]

Osofsky, J. (1979). *Handbook of infant development.* New York: Wiley. [2]

Osofsky, J. D., and Connors, K. (1979). Mother-infant interaction: An integrative view of a complex system. In J. D. Osofsky (Ed.), *Handbook of infant development* (pp. 519–548). New York: Wiley. [7]

Oster, H. (1975, April). *Color perception in ten-week-old infants.* Paper presented at the meeting of the Society for Research in Child Development, Denver, Colorado. [5]

Ostrea, E. M., and Chavez, C. J. (1979). Perinatal problems (excluding neonatal withdrawal) in maternal drug addiction: A study of 830 cases. *Journal of Pediatrics, 94,* 292–295. [4]

Overton, W. F., and Brodzenskey, D. (1972). Perceptual and logical factors in the development of multiplicative classification. *Developmental Psychology, 6,* 104–109. [12]

Oyama, S. (1973). *A sensitive period for the acquisition of a second language.* Unpublished doctoral dissertation, Harvard University. [8]

Papoušek, H. (1959). A method of studying conditioned food reflexes in young children up to the age of six months. *Pavlov Journal of Higher Nervous Activities, 9,* 136–140. [6]

Papoušek, H. (1967a). Conditioning during early postnatal development. In Y. Brackbill and G. G. Thompson (Eds.), *Behavior in infancy and early childhood.* New York: Free Press. [5, 6]

Papoušek, H. (1967b). Experimental studies of appetitional behavior in human newborns and infants. In H. W. Stevenson, E. H. Hess, and H. L. Rheingold (Eds.), *Early behavior.* New York: Wiley. [5, 7]

Papoušek, H. (1969). Individual variability in learned responses in human infants. In R. J. Robinson (Ed.), *Brain and early behavior.* New York: Academic Press. [3, 7]

Papoušek, H., and Papoušek, M. (1978). Interdisciplinary parallels in studies of early human behavior: From physical to cognitive needs, from attachment to dyadic education. *International Journal of Behavioral Development, 1,* 37–49. [7]

Paris, S. G. (1975). Integration and inference in children's comprehension and memory. In F. Restle, R. Shiffrin, J. Castellan, H. Lindman, and D. Pisoni (Eds.), *Cognitive theory* (Vol. 1). Hillsdale, N.J.: Erlbaum. [12]

Paris, S. G., Lindauer, B. K., and Cox, G. L. (1977). The development of inferential comprehension. *Child Development, 48,* 1728–1733. [12]

Paris, S. G., and Upton, L. (1976). Children's memory for inferential comprehension. *Child Development, 47,* 660–668. [12]

Parke, R. (1979). Perspectives on father-infant interaction. In J. Osofsky (Ed.), *Handbook of infant development.* New York: Wiley. [3]

Parke, R. (1981). *Fathers.* Cambridge, Mass.: Harvard University Press. [3]

Parke, R., Berkowitz, L., Leyens, J., West, S., and Sebastian, R. (1977). Some effects of violent and nonviolent movies on the behavior of juvenile delinquents. In L. Berkowitz (Ed.), *Advances in experimental social psychology* (Vol. 10). New York: Academic Press. [11]

Parke, R. D., and Collmer, C. W. (1975). Child abuse: An interdisciplinary analysis. In E. M. Hetherington (Ed.), *Review of child development research* (Vol. 5, pp. 509–590). Chicago: University of Chicago Press. [9]

Parke, R. D., and O'Leary, S. (1976). Family interaction in the newborn period: Some findings, some observations, and some unresolved issues. In K. F. Riegel and J. Meacham (Eds.), *The developing individual in a changing world: Vol. 2. Social and environmental issues.* The Hague: Mouton. [3, 9]

Parker, S., and Bavosi, J. (1979). *Life before birth: The story of the first 9 months.* Cambridge, Eng.: Cambridge University Press. [4]

Parson, J., Adler, T., and Kaezala, C. (1982). Socialization of achievement attitudes and beliefs: Parental influences. *Child Development, 53,* 310–321. [15]

Parsons, T., and Bales, R. (1955). *Family socialization and interaction process.* London, Eng.: Free Press. [3]

Parten, M., and Newhall, S. W. (1943). Social behavior of preschool children. In R. G. Barker, J. S. Kownin, and H. F. Wright (Eds.), *Child behavior and development.* New York: McGraw-Hill. [11]

Pascual-Leone, J. (1970). A mathematical model for the transition rule in Piaget's developmental stages. *Acta Psychologica, 32,* 301–345. [6]

Pascual-Leone, J. (1976). A view of cognition from a formalist's perspective. In K. F. Riegel and J. Meacham (Eds.), *The developing individual in a changing world.* The Hague: Mouton. [6]

Pastor, D., Vaughn, B., and Dodds, M. (1981, April). *The effects of different family patterns on the quality of the mother-infant attachment.* Paper presented at the meeting of the Society for Research in Child Development, Boston. [7]

Paternite, C., and Loney, J. (1980). Childhood hyperkinesis: Relationships between symptomology and home environment. In C. Whalen and B. Hensler (Eds.), *Hyperactive children: The social ecology of identification and treatment* (pp. 195–241). New York: Academic Press. [16]

Patterson, G. (1976). The aggressive child: Victim and architect of a coercive system. In E. Mash, L. Hamerlynck, and L. Handy (Eds.), *Behavior modification and families.* New York: Brunner/Mazel. [13]

Patterson, G., Littman, R., and Bricker, W. (1967). Assertive behavior in young children: A step toward a theory of aggression. *Monographs of the Society for Research in Child Development, 35* (No. 5). [11, 12]

Patterson, G. R., and Dishion, T. J. (in press). A mechanism for transmitting the antisocial trait across generations. In R. Hinde and J. Stevenson-Hinde (Eds.), *Relations between relationships within families.* Oxford, Eng.: Oxford University Press. [3, 11, 13, 15, 16]

Pavlov, I. (1927). *Conditioned reflexes*. Oxford, Eng.: Oxford University Press. [2]

Pearce, J. (1977). Depressive disorders in childhood. *Journal of Child Psychology and Psychiatry, 18,* 79–83. [16]

Pederson, F., Anderson, B., and Cain, R. (1977). *An approach to understanding linkages between the parent, infant, and spouse relationships*. Paper presented at the Society for Research in Child Development, New Orleans. [2, 12]

Peill, E. J. (1975). *Invention and the discovery of reality.* New York: Wiley. [12]

Peloquin, L., and Klorman, R. (1986). Effects and methylphenidate on normal children's mood, event-related potentials, and performance in memory scanning and vigilance. *Journal of Abnormal Psychology, 95,* 88–98. [16]

Perlmutter, M., and Myers, N. A. (1979). Development of recall in 2- to 4-year-old children. *Developmental Psychology, 15,* 73–83. [11]

Peskin, H. (1967). Pubertal onset and ego functioning. *Journal of Abnormal Psychology, 72,* 1–15. [15]

Petersen, A. (1979, May). Can puberty come any earlier? *Psychology Today,* 45–47. [14]

Petersen, A. (1986, April). *Early adolescence: A critical developmental transition?* Paper presented at the annual meeting of the American Educational Research Association, San Francisco. [15]

Petersen, A., and Taylor, B. (1980). The biological approach to adolescence: Biological change and psychological adaptation. In J. Adelson (Ed.), *Handbook of adolescent psychology.* New York: Wiley. [14, 15]

Pfouts, J. H. (1976). The sibling relationship: A forgotten dimension. *Social Work,* 200–204. [13]

Phares, E., and Lamiell, J. (1975). Internal-external control, interpersonal judgments of others in need, and attribution of responsibility. *Journal of Personality, 43,* 23–28. [15]

Philips, S. (1973). Syntax and vocabulary of mothers' speech to young children: Age and sex comparisons. *Child Development, 44,* 182–185. [8]

Phipps-Yonas, S. (1980). Teenage pregnancy and motherhood: A review of the literature. *American Journal of Orthopsychiatry, 50,* 403–431. [15]

Piaget, J. (1930/1969a). *The child's conception of physical causality.* Totowa, N.J.: Littlefield, Adams & Co. [10]

Piaget, J. (1930/1969b). *The mechanisms of perception.* New York: Basic Books. [10]

Piaget, J. (1932/1965). *The moral judgment of the child.* New York: Free Press. [12, 14]

Piaget, J. (1952a). *The child's conception of number.* New York: Humanities Press. [7]

Piaget, J. (1952b). *Play, dreams, and imitation in childhood.* New York: Norton. [5, 8]

Piaget, J. (1952/1963). *The origins of intelligence in children.* New York: Norton. [6, 7, 10]

Piaget, J. (1959). *The language and thought of the child* (3rd ed.). London, Eng.: Routledge & Kegan Paul. [10]

Piaget, J. (1970). Piaget's theory. In P. H. Mussen (Ed.), *Carmichael's manual of child psychology.* New York: Wiley. [10]

Piaget, J., and Inhelder, B. (1973). *Memory and intelligence.* New York: Basic Books. [12]

Pianta, R., Egeland, B., and Sroufe, L. A. (in press). Continuity and discontinuity in maternal caregiving at 6, 24, and 42 months in a high-risk sample. *Child Development.* [9, 11]

Pick, H. L., Jr., and Pick, A. D. (1970). Sensory and perceptual development. In P. H. Mussen (Ed.), *Carmichael's manual of child psychology* (Vol. 1). New York: Wiley. [5]

Piers, M. (1978). *Infanticide.* New York: Norton. [3]

Pitt, R. B. (1976). *Toward a comprehensive model of problem-solving: Application to solutions of chemistry problems in high school and college students.* Unpublished Ph.D. dissertation, University of California, San Diego. [14]

Plomin, R. (1983). Developmental behavior genetics. *Child Development, 54,* 253–259. [2]

Plomin, R., and DeFries, J. (1983). The Colorado adoption study. *Child Development, 54,* 276–289. [3]

Plomin, R., and Rowe, D. (1979). Genetic and environmental etiology of social behavior in infancy. *Developmental Psychology, 15,* 62–72. [7]

Plunkett, J., Meisels, S., Stiefel, G., Pasicke, P., and Roloff, D. (1986). Patterns of attachment among preterm infants of varying biological risk. *Journal of the American Academy of Child Psychiatry, 25,* 794–800. [7]

Pollitt, E., Eichler, A., and Chan, C. (1975). Psychosocial development and behavior of mothers of failure to thrive children. *American Journal of Orthopsychiatry, 45,* 523–537. [7]

Powers, S., Hauser, S., Schwartz, J., Noam, G., and Jacobson, A. (1983). Adolescent ego development and family interaction. In H. Gotivant and C. Cooper (Eds.), *Adolescent development in the family.* San Francisco: Jossey-Bass. [15]

Prechtl, H., and Beintema, D. (1964). *Clinics in developmental medicine: No. 12. The neurological examination of the full-term newborn infant.* London, Eng.: Heinemann. [5]

Prinz, R., Foster, S., Kent, R., and O'Leary, K. D. (1979). Multivariate assessment of conflict in distressed and non-distressed mother-adolescent dyads. *Journal of Applied Behavioral Analysis, 12,* 691–700. [15]

Provence, S., and Lipton, R. (1976). *Infants in institutions.* New York: International Universities Press. [9]

Puig-Antich, J. (1982). Major depression and conduct disorder in pre-puberty. *Journal of the American Academy of Child Psychiatry, 21,* 118–128. [16]

Quigley, M. E., Sheehan, K. L., Wilkes, M. M., and Yen, S. S. C. (1979). Effects of maternal smoking on circulating catecholamine levels and fetal heart rates. *American Journal of Obstetrics and Gynecology, 133,* 685–690. [4]

Quinton, D., Rutter, M., and Liddle, C. (1984). Institutional rearing, parenting difficulties, and marital support. *Psychological Medicine, 14,* 107–124. [3, 7]

Radke-Yarrow, M., Richters, J., and Wilson, W. E. (in press). Child development in a network of relationships. In R. Hinde and J. Stevenson-Hinde (Eds.), *Relations between relationships within families.* Oxford, Eng.: Oxford University Press. [3]

Radke-Yarrow, M., and Zahn-Waxler, C. (1984). Roots, motives, and patterns in children's pro-social behavior. In E. Staub, D. Bartal, J. Karylowski, and J. Reykowski (Eds.), *The development and maintenance of pro-social behaviors.* New York: Plenum. [2, 11, 13]

Radke-Yarrow, M., Zahn-Waxler, C., and Chapman, M. (1983). Children's pro-social dispositions and behavior. In P. Mussen (Ed.), *Carmichael's manual of child psychology* (Vol. 4, 4th ed.). New York: Wiley. [11]

Ramey, C. T., and Campbell, F. A. (1979). Compensatory education for disadvantaged children. *School Review, 87,* 171–289. [12]

Ramey, C. T., and Haskins, R. (1981). The modification of intelligence through early experience. *Intelligence, 5,* 5–19. [12]

Ramey, C. T., Starr, R., Pallas, J., Whitten, C., and Reed, V. (1979). Nutrition, response-contingent stimulation, and the maternal-deprivation syndrome: Results of an early intervention program. *Merrill-Palmer Quarterly, 21,* 45–53. [12]

Rapoport, J., Quinn, P., and Lamprecht, F. (1974). Minor physical anomalies and plasma dopamine-beta hydroxylase in hyperactive boys. *American Journal of Psychiatry, 181,* 386–390. [16]

Rapoport, J., Zahn, T., Ludlow, C., and Mikkelson, E. (1978). Dextroamphetamine: Cognitive and behavioral effects in normal prepubertal boys. *Science, 199,* 560–563. [16]

Rebelsky, F., and Hanks, C. (1971). Fathers' verbal interaction with infants in the first three months of life. *Child Development, 42,* 63–68. [9]

Reich, P. A. (1976). The early acquisition of word meaning. *Journal of Child Language, 3,* 117–123. [8]

Reichlin, S. (1981). Neuroendocrinology. In R. H. Williams (Ed.), *Textbook of endocrinology* (6th ed.). Philadelphia: Saunders. [14]

Reiss, I. (1976). *Family systems in America.* Hillsdale, Ill.: Dorsey Press. [15]

Resnick, L. B., Siegel, S. W., and Kresh, E. (1971). Transfer and sequence in learning double-classification skills. *Journal of Experimental Child Psychology, 11,* 139–149. [12]

Rest, J. (1983). Morality. In P. H. Mussen (Ed.), *Handbook of child psychology* (Vol. 3, 4th ed.): J. H. Flavell and E. M. Markman (Eds.), *Cognitive development.* New York: Wiley. [14]

Reznick, J. S., Kagan, J., Snidman, N., Gersten, M., Baak, K., and Rosenberg, A. (1986). Inhibited and uninhibited children: A follow-up study. *Child Development, 57,* 660–680. [9, 11]

Rheingold, H. (1956). The modification of social responsiveness in institutional babies. *Monographs of the Society for Research in Child Development, 21* (No. 63). [7]

Rheingold, H. (1983, May). *Two-year-olds chart an optimistic future.* Paper presented at the Harvard Medical School Conference on Affective Development in Infancy, Boston. [9]

Rheingold, H. L., and Cook, K. U. (1975). The contents of boys' and girls' rooms as an index of parents' behavior. *Child Development, 46,* 459–463. [11]

Rheingold, H. L., and Eckerman, C. O. (1970). The infant separates himself from his mother. *Science, 768,* 78–83. [7]

Rheingold, H. L., and Eckerman, C. O. (1971). Departures from the mother. In H. R. Schaffer (Ed.), *The origins of human social relations.* New York: Academic Press. [9]

Rheingold, H. L., and Eckerman, C. O. (1974). Fear of the stranger: A critical examination. In H. Reese (Ed.), *Advances in child development and behavior.* New York: Academic Press. [7]

Rheingold, H. L., Gewirtz, J., and Ross, B. (1959). Social conditioning of vocalizations in the infant. *Journal of Comparative and Physiological Psychology, 52,* 68–73. [7]

Rheingold, H. L., Hay, D. F., and West, M. J. (1976). Sharing in the second year of life. *Child Development, 47,* 1148–1158. [9]

Richards, M. (1975). Early separation. In R. Lewin (Ed.), *Child alive!* Garden City, N.Y.: Anchor Press. [7]

Ricks, M. (1985). The social transmission of parental behavior: Attachment across generations. In I. Bretherton and E. Waters (Eds.), Growing points in attachment theory and research. *Monographs of the Society for Research in Child Development, 50* (Serial No. 209), 211–227. [9]

Riegel, K. (1976). The dialectics of human development. *American Psychologist, 31,* 689–700. [15]

Riessman, F. (1962). *The culturally deprived child.* New York: Harper & Row. [3]

Riley, C. A., and Trabasso, T. (1974). Comparatives, logical structures, and encoding in a transitive inference task. *Journal of Experimental Child Psychology, 45,* 972–977. [10]

Rimm, D. C., and Masters, J. C. (1974). *Behavior therapy: Techniques and empirical findings.* New York: Academic Press. [7]

Robb, M., and Mangelsdorf, S. (1987). *Sibling relationships in school-age children. Differences in play as a function of sex composition and maternal behavior.* Paper presented at the biennial meeting of the Society for Research in Child Development, Baltimore. [3]

Roberts, C. J., and Lowe, C. R. (1975). Where have all the conceptions gone? *Lancet, 1,* 498–499. [4]

Roberts, M., and Maddux, J. (1982). A psycho-social conceptualization of nonorganic failure to thrive. *Journal of Clinical Child Psychology, 11,* 216–226. [7]

Roberts, W. L. (1983). *Family interactions and child competence in a preschool setting. Part 1: Overview.* Paper presented at the biennial meeting of the Society for Research in Child Development, Detroit. [11]

Robins, L. (1966). *Deviant children grown up.* Baltimore: Williams and Wilkins. [13, 16]

Robins, L. (1978). Sturdy childhood predictors of adult antisocial behavior: Replications from longitudinal studies. *Psychological Medicine, 8,* 611–622. [16]

Robins, L. (1979). Follow-up studies. In H. Quay and J. Werry (Eds.), *Psychopathological disorders of childhood* (2nd ed.). New York: Wiley. [16]

Rode, S., Chang, P., Fisch, R., and Sroufe, L. A. (1981). Attachment patterns of infants separated at birth. *Developmental Psychology, 17,* 188–191. [7]

Roff, M., and Ricks, D. (Eds.). (1970). *Life history research in psychopathology* (Vol. 1). Minneapolis: University of Minnesota Press. [13]

Roff, M., Sells, S., and Golden, M. (1972). *Social adjustment and personality development in children.* Minneapolis: University of Minnesota Press. [16]

Roffwarg, H. P., Muzio, J. N., and Dement, W. C. (1966). Ontogenetic development of the human sleep-dream cycle. *Science, 152,* 604–619. [5]

Rohwer, W. D., Jr. (1973). Elaboration and learning in childhood and adolescence. In H. W. Reese (Ed.), *Advances in child development and behavior* (Vol. 8). New York: Academic Press. [12]

Rokeach, M. (1973). *The nature of human values.* New York: Free Press. [14]

Romaine, S. (1985). *The language of children and adolescents: The acquisition of communicative competence.* New York: Blackwell. [8]

Root, A. W. (1973). Endocrinology of puberty: Normal sexual maturation. *Journal of Pediatrics, 83,* 187–200. [14]

Rosenberg, D. M. (1984). *The quality and content of preschool fantasy play: Correlates in concurrent social-personality function and early mother-child attachment relationships.* Unpublished doctoral dissertation, University of Minnesota. [11]

Rosenberg, M. (1979). *Conceiving the self.* New York: Basic Books. [12, 13, 15]

Rosenblith, J., and Sims-Knight, J. (1985). *In the beginning: Development in the first two years.* Belmont, Calif.: Brooks/Cole. [4, 6, 14]

Rosenhan, D. (1969). Some origins of concern for others. In P. Mussen, J. Langer, and M. Covington (Eds.), *Trends and issues in developmental psychology.* New York: Holt, Rinehart & Winston. [13]

Rosenn, D. W., Loeb, L. S., and Jura, M. B. (1980). Differentiation of organic from nonorganic failure to thrive syndrome in infancy. *Pediatrics, 66,* 698–704. [7]

Rosenweig, M. (1966). Environmental complexity. *Psychologist, 21,* 321–332. [7]

Ross, D., and Ross, S. (1982). *Hyperactivity* (2nd ed.). New York: Wiley. [16]

Ross, H. S., and Goldman, B. D. (1977). Establishing new social relations in infancy. In T. Alloway, P. Pliner, and L. Krames (Eds.), *Attachment behavior.* New York: Plenum. [9]

Rotenberg, K., and Mann, L. (1986). The development of the norm of reciprocity of self-disclosure and its function in children's attraction to peers. *Child Development, 57,* 1349–1357. [13]

Rothbaum, F. (in press). Patterns of parental acceptance. *Child Development.* [13]

Rotter, J. (1966). Generalized expectancies for internal versus external locus of control of reinforcement. *Psychological Monographs: General and Applied, 80,* 1–28. [12]

Rovee-Collier, C. K. (1979). *Reactivation of infant memory.* Paper presented at the biennial meeting of the Society for Research in Child Development, San Francisco. [6]

Rovee-Collier, C. K., and Gekoski, M. J. (1979). The economics of infancy: A review of conjugate reinforcement. In H. W. Reese and L. P. Lipsitt (Eds.), *Advances in child development and behavior* (Vol. 13). New York: Academic Press. [5]

Rovee-Collier, C. K., and Rovee, D. (1969). Conjugate reinforcement of infant exploratory behavior. *Journal of Experimental Child Psychology, 8,* 33–39. [7]

Rovee-Collier, C. K., Sullivan, M. W., Enright, M., Lucas, D., and Fagan, J. W. (1980). Reactivation of infant memory. *Science, 208,* 1159–1161. [6]

Rowe, D., and Plomin, R. (1978). The Burt controversy: A comparison of Burt's data on IQ with data from other studies. *Behavior Genetics, 8,* 81–84. [2]

Rubin, K. H., and Daniels-Beirness, T. (1983). Concurrent and predictive correlates of sociometric status in kindergarten and grade one children. *Merrill-Palmer Quarterly, 29,* 337–352. [13]

Rubin, K., and Krasnor, L. (1985). Social-cognitive and social-behavioral perspectives on problem solving. In M. Perlmutter (Ed.), *Minnesota Symposia on Child Psychology* (Vol. 18). Hillsdale, N.J.: Erlbaum. [13]

Rubin, K., LeMare, L., and Lollis, S. (in press). Social withdrawal in childhood: Developmental pathways to peer rejection. In Asher and Coie (Eds.), *Children's status in the peer group.* Cambridge, Eng.: Cambridge University Press. [11]

Rubin, L. B. (1979). *Women of a certain age: The mid-life search for self.* New York: Harper & Row. [3]

Rubin, Z. (1980). *Children's friendships.* Cambridge, Mass.: Harvard University Press. [3]

Ruble, D., Boggiano, A., Feldman, N., and Loebl, J. (1980). A developmental analysis of the role of social comparison in self-evaluation. *Developmental Psychology, 16,* 105–115. [13]

Ruch, J., and Shirley, J. (1985, March). "Genie" as an adult. Presentation at the Center for Advanced Study in the Behavioral Sciences, Stanford, Calif. [3, 7]

Russell, J. (1981). Children's memory for the premises in a transitive measurement task assessed by elicited and spontaneous justification. *Journal of Experimental Child Psychology, 31,* 300–309. [11]

Rutter, M. (1968). Concepts of autism: A review of research. *Journal of Child Psychology and Psychiatry, 9,* 1–25. [16]

Rutter, M. (1971). Parent-child separation: Psychological effects on the children. *Journal of Child Psychology and Psychiatry, 12,* 233–260. [13]

Rutter, M. (1979a). Maternal deprivation 1972–1978: New findings, new concepts, new approaches. *Child Development, 50,* 283–305. [12, 16]

Rutter, M. (1979b). Protective factors in children's responses to stress and disadvantage. In M. Kent and J. Rolf (Eds.), *Primary prevention of psychopathology: Vol. III. Social competence in children.* Hanover, N.H.: University Press of New England. [16]

Rutter, M. (1980a). *Scientific foundations of developmental psychiatry.* London, Eng.: Heinemann. [16]

Rutter, M. (1980b). *Changing youth in a changing society: Patterns of adolescent development and disorder.* Cambridge, Mass.: Harvard University Press. [15]

Rutter, M. (1981). Epidemiological-longitudinal approaches to the study of development. In W. A. Collins (Ed.), *Minnesota Symposia on Child Psychology* (Vol. 15). Hillsdale, N.J.: Erlbaum. [13]

Rutter, M. (1982). Social-emotional consequences of day care for preschool children. *American Journal of Orthopsychiatry, 51,* 4–28. [7]

Rutter, M. (1983). The developmental psychopathology of depression: Issues and perspectives. In M. Rutter, C. Izard, and P. Read (Eds.), *Depression in childhood.* New York: Guilford Press. [16]

Rutter, M. (in press). Functions and consequences of relationships: Some psychopathological considerations. In R. Hinde and J. Stevenson-Hinde (Eds.), *Towards understanding families.* Oxford, Eng.: Oxford University Press. [3, 7]

Rutter, M., Grahan, P., Chadwick, O., and Yule, W. (1976). Adolescent turmoil: Fact or fiction? *Journal of Child Psychology and Psychiatry, 17,* 35–56. [16]

Rutter, M., Maughan, B., Mortimore, P., and Ouston, J. (1979). *Fifteen thousand hours: Secondary schools and their effects on children.* Cambridge, Mass.: Harvard University Press. [3, 13]

Rutter, M., and Schopler, E. (1978). *Autism: A reappraisal of concepts and treatment.* New York: Plenum. [16]

Rutter, M., and Shaffer, D. (1980). DSM-III: A step forward or back in terms of the classification of child psychiatric disorders? *Journal of the American Academy of Child Psychiatry, 19,* 371–394. [16]

Rutter, M., Tizard, J., Yule, W., Graham, P., and Whitmore, K. (1976). Research report: Isle of Wight studies, 1964–74. *Psychological Medicine, 6,* 313–332. [16]

Sackett, G. P. (1968). Abnormal behavior in laboratory research rhesus monkeys. In M. Fox (Ed.), *Abnormal behavior in animals.* Philadelphia: Saunders. [7]

Sackett, G. P. (1978). Measurement in observational research. In G. P. Sackett (Ed.), *Data collection and analysis methods: Vol. 2. Observing behavior.* Baltimore: University Park Press. [1]

Salapatek, P., and Banks, M. (1967). Infant sensory assessment: Vision. In F. Minifie and L. Lloyd (Eds.), *Communicative and cognitive abilities—Early behavioral assessment.* Baltimore: University Park Press. [7]

Salapatek, P., and Kessen, W. (1966). Visual scannings of triangles by the human newborn. *Journal of Experimental Child Psychology, 3,* 155–167. [5]

Salapatek, P., and Kessen, W. (1973). Prolonged investigation of a plane geometric triangle by the human newborn. *Journal of Experimental Child Psychology, 15,* 22–29. [5]

Salzinger, S., Kaplan, S., and Artemyeff, C. (1983). Mothers' personal social networks and child maltreatment. *Journal of Abnormal Psychology, 92,* 68–76. [3]

Sameroff, A. J. (1968). The components of sucking in the human newborn. *Journal of Experimental Child Psychology*, 6, 607–623. [3, 5, 7]

Sameroff, A. J. (1978). Organization and stability of newborn behavior: A commentary on the Brazelton Neonatal Behavior Assessment Scale. *Monographs of the Society for Research in Child Development*, 43 (Serial No. 177). [7]

Sameroff, A. J. (1986). The social context of development. In N. Eisenberg (Ed.), *Contemporary topics in developmental psychology* (pp. 273–291). New York: Wiley. [3]

Sameroff, A. J., and Chandler, M. (1975). Reproductive risk and the continuum of caretaking casualty. In F. D. Horowitz (Ed.), *Child development research* (Vol. 4). Chicago: University of Chicago Press. [3, 9]

Sameroff, A. J., Seifer, R., and Elias, P. (1982). Sociocultural variability in infant-temperament ratings. *Child Development*, 53, 164–173. [7]

Sameroff, A. J., and Zax, M. (in press). The child of psychotic parents. In S. Wolkind (Ed.), *Medical aspects of adoption and foster care*. New York: Spastics International Medical Publications. [16]

Sander, L. W. (1975). Infant and caretaking environment. In E. J. Anthony (Ed.), *Explorations in child psychiatry*. New York: Plenum. [7, 9, 11]

Santrock, J. (1984). *Adolescence*. Dubuque, Iowa: William C. Brown. [15]

Satir, V. (1967). *Conjoint family therapy*. Palo Alto, Calif.: Science & Behavior Books. [3]

Scarlett, H., Press, A., and Crockett, W. (1971). Children's descriptions of peers: A Wernerian developmental analysis. *Child Development*, 42, 439–453. [12]

Scarr, S. (1982). Similarities and differences among siblings. In M. Lamb and B. Sutton-Smith (Eds.), *Sibling relationships*. Hillsdale, N.J.: Erlbaum. [2, 3]

Scarr, S., and McCartney, K. (1983). How people make their own environments: A theory of genotype—environment effects. *Child Development*, 54, 425–435. [2, 3]

Scarr, S., and Salapatek, P. (1970). Patterns of fear development during infancy. *Merrill-Palmer Quarterly*, 16, 53–90. [7]

Scarr, S., and Weinberg, R. A. (1983). The Minnesota adoption studies: Malleability and genetic differences. *Child Development*, 34, 260–267. [12]

Schaefer, E. (1959). A circumflex model for maternal behavior. *Journal of Abnormal and Social Psychology*, 59, 226–235. [13]

Schaffer, H. R. (1977). *Mothering*. Cambridge, Mass.: Harvard University Press. [7]

Schaffer, H. R., and Callender, M. (1959). Psychological effects of hospitalization in infancy. *Pediatrics*, 24, 528–539. [7, 9]

Schaffer, H. R., and Emerson, P. E. (1964a). Patterns of response to physical contact in early human development. *Journal of Child Psychology*, 5, 1–13. [11]

Schaffer, H. R., and Emerson, P. E. (1964b). The development of social attachments in infancy. *Monographs of the Society for Research in Child Development*, 29 (No. 94). [7]

Schaller, M. J. (1975). Chromatic vision in human infants: Conditioned operant fixation to "hues" of varying intensity. *Bulletin of the Psychonomic Society*, 6, 39–42. [5]

Schank. R. C., and Abelson, R. (1977). *Scripts, plans, goals, and understanding*. Hillsdale, N.J.: Erlbaum. [10]

Schiefflin, B., and Ochs, E. (1983). A cultural perspective on the transition from prelinguistic to linguistic communication. In R. Golinkoff (Ed.), *The transition from prelinguistic to linguistic communication*. Hillsdale, N.J.: Erlbaum. [8]

Schneider-Rosen, K., and Cicchetti, D. (1984). The relationship between affect and cognition in maltreated infants: Quality of attachment and the development of visual self-recognition. *Child Development*, 55, 648–658. [9]

Schulman-Galambos, C., and Galambos, R. (1979). Brainstem-evoked response audiometry in newborn hearing screening. *Archives of Otolaryngology*, 105, 86–90. [5]

Schulterbrandt, J., and Raskin, A. (Eds.) (1977). *Depression in children*. New York: Raven Press. [16]

Schutze, Y., Kreppner, K., and Paulsen, S. (1982). *The social construction of the sibling relationship*. Paper presented at the 10th World Congress of Sociology, Mexico City. [12]

Schwartz, A., Campos, J., and Baisel, E. (1973). The visual cliff: Cardiac and behavioral correlates on the deep and shallow sides at 5 and 9 months of age. *Journal of Experimental Child Psychology*, 15, 85–99. [7]

Schwartz, M., and Day, R. H. (1979). Visual shape perception in infancy. *Monographs of the Society for Research in Child Development*, 44 (7, Serial No. 182). [6]

Schwartz, P. (1983). Length of day-care attendance and attachment behavior in eighteen-month-old infants. *Child Development*, 54, 1073–1078. [7]

Schwartz, S., and Johnson, J. (1981). *Psychopathology of childhood*. New York: Pergamon. [16]

Sears, P., and Feldman, D. H. (1966). Teachers' interactions with boys and girls. *National Elementary Principal*, 46, 30–35. [13]

Sears, R. R., Maccoby, E. E., and Levin, H. (1957). *Patterns of child rearing*. Evanston, Ill.: Row, Peterson. [9, 11]

Secord, P., and Peevers, B. (1974). The development and attribution of person concepts. In T. Mischel (Ed.), *Understanding other persons*. Totowa, N.J.: Rowman & Littlefield. [12, 13, 15]

Segal, J., and Yahres, H. (1978, November). Bringing up mother. *Psychology Today*, pp. 92–96. [9]

Select Committee on Children, Youth, and Families. (1984). *Demographic and social trends: Implications for federal support of dependent care services for child and the elderly*. Washington, D.C.: U. S. Government Printing Office. [3, 13]

Seligman, M. E. P. (1970). On the generality of the laws of learning. *Psychological Review*, 77, 406–418. [5]

Selman, R. (1971). Taking another's perspective: Role-taking development in early childhood. *Child Development*, 42, 1721–1734. [11]

Selman, R. (1980). *The growth of interpersonal understanding*. New York: Academic Press. [13, 15]

Selvini, M. (1971). Anorexia nervosa. In S. Arieti (Ed.), *World biennial of psychiatry and psychotherapy* (Vol. 1). New York: Basic Books. [16]

Serbin, L. A., O'Leary, K. D., Kent, R. N., and Tonick, I. J. (1973). A comparison of teacher response to the pre-academic and problem behavior of boys and girls. *Child Development*, 44, 796–804. [13]

Shaffer, D. R. (1985). *Developmental psychology: Theory, research, and applications*. Monterey, Calif.: Brooks/Cole. [4]

Shantz, C. U. (1975). The development of social cognition. In E. M. Hetherington (Ed.), *Review of child development research* (Vol. 3). Chicago: University of Chicago Press. [10]

Sharabany, R., Gershoni, R., and Hofman, J. (1981). Girlfriend, boyfriend: Age and sex differences in intimate friendship. *Developmental Psychology*, 17, 800–808. [15]

Shatz, M. (1978). The relation between cognitive processes and the development of communication skills. In C. B. Keasy (Ed.), *Nebraska Symposium on Motivation, 1977*.

Lincoln: University of Nebraska Press. [6, 10]

Shatz, M. (1983). Communication. In P. H. Mussen (Ed.), *Handbook of child psychology* (Vol 3, 4th ed.): J. H. Flavell and E. M. Markman (Eds.), *Cognitive development*. New York: Wiley. [10]

Shatz, M., and Gelman, R. (1973). The development of communication skills: Modifications in the speech of young children as a function of listening. *Monographs of the Society for Research in Child Development, 38* (5, Serial No. 152). [8, 10]

Shayer, M. (1980). Piaget and science education. In S. Modgil and C. Modgil (Eds.), *Towards a theory of psychological development*. Windsor, Can.: NFER Publishing Co. [14]

Sherif, M., Harvey, O., White, B., Hood, W., and Sherif, C. (1961). *Intergroup conflict and cooperation: The Robbers Cave experiment*. Norman: University of Oklahoma Press. [13]

Sherif, M., and Sherif, C. (1953). *Groups in harmony and tension*. New York: Harper & Row. [13]

Sherman, B., Halmi, K., and Zamedia, R. (1975). LH and FSH response to gonadotrophin releasing hormone in anorexia nervosa: Effect of nutritional rehabilitation. *Journal of Clinical Endocrinology and Metabolism, 41*, 135–142. [16]

Shetty, T. (1971). Photic responses in hyperkinesis of childhood. *Science, 174*, 1356–1357. [16]

Shirley, M. M. (1933). *The first two years*. Minneapolis: University of Minneapolis Press. [5]

Shore, C. (1986). Combinatorial play, conceptual development, and early multi-word speech. *Developmental Psychology, 22*, 184–190. [8]

Shrauger, J., and Patterson, M. (1974). Self-evaluation and the selection of dimensions for evaluating others. *Journal of Personality, 42*, 569–582. [12]

Shultz, T. R., and Zigler, E. (1970). Emotional concomitants of visual mastery in infants: The effects of stimulus movement on smiling and vocalizing. *Journal of Experimental Child Psychology, 10*, 390–402. [7]

Siegler, R. S. (1978). The origins of scientific reasoning. In R. S. Siegler (Ed.), *Children's thinking: What develops?* Hillsdale, N.J.: Erlbaum. [14]

Siegler, R. S. (1981). Developmental sequences within and between concepts. *Monographs of the Society for Research in Child Development, 46* (2, Serial No. 189). [14]

Siegler, R. S. (1983). Information-processing approaches to development. In P. H. Mussen (Ed.), *Handbook of child psychology* (Vol. 1, 4th ed.): W. Kessen (Ed.), *History, theory, and methods*. New York: Wiley. [2, 12]

Siegler, R. S. (1986). *Children's thinking* (2nd ed.). Englewood Cliffs, N.J.: Prentice-Hall. [6]

Siegler, R. S., and Richards, D. D. (1982). The development of intelligence. In R. J. Sternberg (Ed.), *Handbook of human intelligence*. New York: Cambridge University Press. [12]

Siegler, R. S., and Robinson, M. (1982). The development of numerical understandings. In H. W. Reese and L. P. Lipsett (Eds.), *Advances in child development and behavior* (Vol. 16). New York: Academic Press. [12]

Sigman, M., Cohen, S., Beckwith, L., and Parmelee, A. (1981). Social and familial influences on the development of preterm infants. *Journal of Pediatric Psychology, 6*, 1–13. [7]

Simmons, R., and Blyth, D. (in press). *Moving into adolescence: The impact of pubertal change and school context*. New York: Aldine/Hawthorne. [15]

Simmons, R., Rosenberg, F., and Rosenberg, M. (1973). Disturbance in the self-image at adolescence. *American Sociological Review, 38*, 553–568. [15]

Singer, M., Wynne, L., and Toohey, B. (1979). Communication disorders and the families of schizophrenics. In S. Matthyse (Ed.), *Attention and information processing in schizophrenia: Proceedings of the Scottish Rite Schizophrenia Research Program Conference*. Oxford, Eng.: Pergamon Press. [16]

Sinnet, J. M., Pisoni, D. B., and Aslin, R. N. (1984). A comparison of pure tone auditory thresholds in human infants and adults. *Infant Behavior and Development, 6*, 3–17. [5]

Skarin, K. (1977). Cognitive and contextual determinants of stranger fear in six- and eleven-month-old infants. *Child Development, 48*, 537–544. [7]

Skeels, H. (1966). Adult status of children with contrasting early life experiences. *Monographs of the Society for Research in Child Development, 31* (No. 3). [7]

Skinner, B. F. (1957). *Verbal behavior*. New York: Appleton-Century-Crofts. [8]

Skinner, E. (1985). Determinants of mother-sensitive and contingency-responsive behavior: The role of child rearing and socioeconomic status. In I. Sigel (Ed.), *Parental belief systems*. Hillsdale, N.J.: Erlbaum. [2]

Skodak, M., and Skeels, H. M. (1949). A final follow-up study of one-hundred adopted children. *Journal of Genetic Psychology, 75*, 85–125. [12]

Skolnick, A. (1981). *The ties that bind: Attachment theory and the social psychology of close relationships*. Paper presented at the 1975 NCFR Pre-conference: Theory construction and research methodology workshop, Berkeley, Calif. [3]

Skuse, D. (1985). Nonorganic failure to thrive: A reappraisal. *Archives of Disease in Childhood, 60*, 173–178. [7]

Slaby, R. G., and Frey, K. S. (1975). Development of gender constancy and selective attention to same-sex models. *Child Development, 46*, 849–856. [11]

Slatter, A., Morrison, V., and Rose, D. (1984). Habituation in the newborn. *Infant Behavior and Development, 7*, 183–200. [6]

Slobin, D. I. (1972, July). Children and language: They learn the same way all around the world. *Psychology Today*, pp. 71–74, 82. [8]

Slobin, D. I. (1973). Cognitive prerequisites for the development of grammar. In C. A. Ferguson and D. I. Slobin (Eds.), *Studies of child language development*. New York: Holt, Rinehart & Winston. [8]

Slobin, D. I. (1975). On the nature of talk to children. In E. H. Lenneberg and E. Lenneberg (Eds.), *Foundations of language development* (Vol. 1). New York: Academic Press. [8]

Small, S., Cornelius, S., and Eastman, G. (1983). *Parenting adolescent children: A period of storm and stress?* Paper presented at the annual meeting of the American Psychological Association, Anaheim, Calif. [15]

Smetana, J. G., and Letourneau, K. J. (in press). Development of gender constancy and children's sex-typed free-play behavior. *Developmental Psychology*. [11]

Smith, D. W., and Wilson, A. A. (1973). *The child with Down syndrome (mongolism)*. Philadelphia: Saunders. [4]

Smith, G. (1950). Sociometric study of best-liked and least-liked children. *Elementary School Journal, 51*, 77–85. [12]

Smith, J. M. (1978). The evolution of behavior. *Scientific American, 239*, 176–192. [11]

Smith, M. E. (1926). An investigation of the development of the sentence and the extent of vocabulary in young children. *University of Iowa Studies in Child Welfare, 3*, No. 5. [8]

Smith, P. K., and Daglish, L. (1977). Sex differences in parent and infant behavior in the home. *Child Development, 48,* 1250–1254. [11]

Smolak, L. (1986). *Infancy.* Englewood Cliffs, N.J.: Prentice-Hall. [8]

Snow, C. E. (1972). Mother's speech to children learning language. *Child Development, 43,* 549–565. [8]

Snow, C. E. (1977). The development of conversation between mothers and babies. *Journal of Child Language, 4,* 1–22. [8]

Sones, G., and Feshbach, N. (1971). Sex differences in adolescent reactions toward newcomers. *Developmental Psychology, 4,* 381–386. [15]

Sontag, L. W., and Wallace, R. F. (1935). The movement response of the human fetus to sound stimuli. *Child Development, 6,* 253–258. [5]

Sorce, J., and Emde, R. (1981). Mother's presence is not enough: The effect of emotional availability on infant exploration and play. *Developmental Psychology, 17,* 737–745. [9, 11]

Sorce, J., Emde, R., and Klinnert, M. (1981). *Maternal emotional signaling: Its effect on the visual cliff behavior of one-year-olds.* Paper read at the meeting of the Society for Research in Child Development, Boston. [9, 11]

Sostek, A. M., and Anders, T. F. (1977). Relationships among the Brazelton neonatal scale, Bayley infant scale, and early temperament. *Child Development, 48,* 320–328. [7]

Sostek, A. M., and Anders, T. F. (1981). The biosocial importance and environmental sensitivity of infant sleep-wake behaviors. In K. Bloom (Ed.), *Prospective issues in infancy research.* Hillsdale, N.J.: Erlbaum. [5]

Sostek, A. M., Sameroff, A., and Sostek, A. (1972). Failure of newborns to demonstrate classically conditioned Babkin responses. *Child Development, 43,* 509–519. [5]

Sours, J. (1969). Anorexia nervosa. In G. Caplan and S. Lebovici (Eds.), *Adolescence: Psychosocial perspectives.* New York: Basic Books. [16]

Spearman, C. (1927). *The abilities of man.* New York: Macmillan. [12]

Spitz, R. A. (1945). Hospitalism: An inquiry into the genesis of psychiatric conditions in early childhood. *Psychoanalytic Study of the Child, 1,* 53–74. [3]

Spitz, R., Emde, R., and Metcalf, D. (1970). Further prototypes of ego formation. *Psychoanalytic Study of the Child, 25,* 417–444. [5, 7]

Spivack, G., Marcus, J., and Swift, M. (1986). Early classroom behaviors and later misconduct. *Developmental Psychology, 22,* 123–131. [16]

Sprafkin, J., and Rubinstein, E. (1979). Children's television viewing habits and prosocial behavior: A field correlational study. *Journal of Broadcasting, 23,* 265–275. [11]

Sprey, J. (1971). On the management of conflict in families. *Journal of Marriage and the Family, 33,* 26–39. [15]

Sprinthall, N., and Collins, W. A. (1984). *Adolescent psychology.* New York: Addison-Wesley. [15]

Sroufe, L. A. (1975). Drug treatment of children. In F. Horowitz (Ed.), *Review of child development research* (Vol. 4). Chicago: University of Chicago Press. [16]

Sroufe, L. A. (1977a). *Knowing and enjoying your baby.* New York: Spectrum. [7]

Sroufe, L. A. (1977b). Wariness of strangers and the study of infant development. *Child Development, 48,* 731–746. [7]

Sroufe, L. A. (1978). Attachment and the roots of competence. *Human Nature, 1,* 50–57. [7]

Sroufe, L. A. (1979a). Socioemotional development. In J. Osofsky (Ed.), *Handbook of infant development.* New York: Wiley. [7]

Sroufe, L. A. (1979b). The coherence of individual development. *American Psychologist, 34,* 834–841. [7]

Sroufe, L. A. (1983). Infant-caregiving attachment and patterns of adaptation and competence. In M. Perlmutter (Ed.), *Minnesota Symposia in Child Psychology* (Vol. 16). Hillsdale, N.J.: Erlbaum. [9, 11, 16]

Sroufe, L. A. (1985). Attachment classification from the perspective of infant-caregiver relationships and infant temperament. *Child Development, 56,* 1–14. [7, 16]

Sroufe, L. A. (in press). An organizational perspective on the self. In D. Cicchetti and M. Beeghly (Eds.), *Transitions from infancy to childhood: The self.* Chicago: Univeristy of Chicago Press. [11]

Sroufe, L. A., and Fleeson, J. (1986). Attachment and the construction of relationships. In W. Hartup and Z. Rubin (Eds.), *Relationships and development.* Hillsdale, N.J.: Erlbaum. [2, 3, 16]

Sroufe, L. A., and Fleeson, J. (in press). The coherence of family relationships. In R. Hinde and J. Stevenson-Hinde (Eds.), *Towards understanding families.* Oxford, Eng.: Oxford University Press. [2, 16]

Sroufe, L. A., Fox, N., and Pancake, V. (1983). Attachment and dependency in developmental perspective. *Child Development, 54,* 1615–1627. [9, 11]

Sroufe, L. A., Jacobvitz, D., Mangelsdorf, S., DeAngelo, E., and Ward, M. J. (1985). Generational boundary dissolution between mothers and their preschool children: A relationship systems approach. *Child Development, 56,* 317–325. [16]

Sroufe, L. A., and Rutter, M. (1984). The domain of developmental psychology. *Child Development, 55,* 17–29. [16]

Sroufe, L. A., Schork, E., Motti, F., Lawroski, N., and LaFrenier, P. (1984). The role of affect in social competence. In C. Izard, J. Kagan, and R. Zajonc (Eds.), *Emotions, cognition, and behavior.* Oxford, Eng.: Oxford University Press. [11, 13]

Sroufe, L. A., Sonies, B., West, W., and Wright, F. (1973). Anticipatory heart-rate deceleration and reaction time in children with and without referral for learning disability. *Child Development, 44,* 267–273. [16]

Sroufe, L. A., and Stewart, M. (1973). Treating problem children with stimulant drugs. *New England Journal of Medicine, 289,* 407–413. [12, 16]

Sroufe, L. A., and Ward, M. J. (1980). Seductive behavior of mothers and toddlers: Occurrence, correlates, and family origins. *Child Development, 51,* 1222–1229. [9, 12, 16]

Sroufe, L. A., and Ward, M. J. (1984). The importance of early care. In D. Quarm, K. Borman, and S. Gideonse (Eds.), *Women in the workplace: The effects on families.* Norwood, N.J.: Ablex. [7]

Sroufe, L. A., and Waters, E. (1971). Attachment as an organizational construct. *Child Development, 48,* 1184–1199. [7, 9]

Sroufe, L. A., and Waters, E. (1976). The ontogenesis of smiling and laughter: A perspective on the organization of development in infancy. *Psychological Review, 83,* 173–189. [7]

Sroufe, L. A., Waters, E., and Matas, L. (1974). Contextual determinants of infant affective response. In M. Lewis and L. Rosenblum (Eds.), *The origins of fear.* New York: Wiley. [7]

Sroufe, L. A., and Wunsek, J. P. (1972). The development of laughter in the first year of life. *Child Development, 43,* 1326–1344. [7]

Staats, A., and Butterfield, W. (1965). Treatment of nonreading in a culturally deprived juvenile delinquent: An application of reinforcement principles. *Child Development, 36*, 925–942. [16]

Starkey, P., and Cooper, R. G. (1980). Perception of number by human infants. *Science, 210*, 1033–1035. [6]

Starkey, P., and Gelman, R. (1982). The development of addition and subtraction abilities prior to formal schooling in arithmetic. In T. Carpenter, J. J. Noser, and T. Romberg (Eds.), *Addition and subtraction: A cognitive perspective.* Hillsdale, N.J.: Erlbaum. [10]

Starkey, P., Spelke, E. S., and Gelman, R. (1983). Detection of one-to-one correspondence by human infants. *Science, 222*, 179–181. [6]

Stedman, D. J., and Eichorn, D. H. (1964). A comparison of the growth and development of infants and young children with Down syndrome (mongolism). *American Journal of Mental Deficiency, 69*, 391–401. [4]

Steele, S. (1986). Nonorganic failure to thrive: A pediatric social illness. *Issues of Comprehensive Pediatric Nursing, 9*, 47–58. [7]

Stein, A. H., and Bailey, M. (1973). The socialization of achievement orientation in females. *Psychological Bulletin, 80*, 345–365. [15]

Stein, A. H., and Friedrich, L. (1975). Impact of television on children and youth. In E. M. Hetherington (Ed.), *Review of child development research* (Vol. 5). Chicago: University of Chicago Press. [3, 13]

Stein, A. H., Susser, M., Saenger, G., and Marolla, F. (1975). *Famine and human development: The Dutch hunger winter of 1944/45.* New York: Oxford University Press. [4]

Steinberg, L. (1981). Transformations in family relations at puberty. *Developmental Psychology, 17*, 883–850. [15]

Steinberg, L. (1985). *The ABCs of transformations in the family at adolescence: Changes in affect, behavior, and cognition.* Paper presented at the Conference of Adolescent Research, Tucson, Ariz. [15]

Steinberg, L., and Silverberg, S. (1986). The vicissitudes of autonomy in early adolescence. *Child Development, 57*, 841–851. [15]

Steiner, J. E. (1977). Facial expressions of the neonate infant indicating the hedonics of food-related chemical stimuli. In J. M. Weiffenbach (Ed.), *Taste and development: The genesis of sweet preference.* Washington, D.C.: U. S. Government Printing Office. [5]

Stenberg, C., Campos, J., and Emde, R. (1983). The facial expression of anger in seven-month-old infants. *Child Development, 54*, 178–184. [7, 9]

Stern, D. N. (1974). The goal of structure of mother and infant play. *Journal of the American Academy of Child Psychiatry, 13*, 402–421. [7]

Stern, D. N. (1977). *The first relationship: Infant and mother.* Cambridge, Mass.: Harvard University Press. [7]

Stern, M., and Hildebrandt, K. (1984). Prematurity stereotype: Effects of labeling on adults' perceptions of infants. *Developmental Psychology, 20*, 360–362. [2]

Stevenson, H. W. (1972). *Childrens' learning.* New York: Appleton-Century-Crofts. [5]

Stewart, M., and Olds, S. (1973). *Raising a hyperactive child.* New York: Harper & Row. [12, 16]

Stewart, R. B. (1983). Sibling attachment relationships: Child-infant interactions in the strange situation. *Developmental Psychology, 19*, 192–199. [13]

Stillwell, R., and Dunn, J. (1985). Continuities in sibling relationships: Patterns of aggression and friendliness. *Journal of Child Psychology and Psychiatry, 26*, 627–637. [13]

Stolnick, A. (1981). Married lives: Longitudinal perspectives on marriage. In D. Eichorn, J. Clausen, N. Haan, M. Honzik, and P. Mussen (Eds.), *Present and past in middle life* (pp. 243–265). New York: Academic Press. [3]

Stone, L. J., Smith, H., and Murphy, L. (1973). *The competent infant.* New York: Basic Books. [2]

Strauss, M. (1979). Measuring intra-family conflict and violence: The conflict tactics scale. *Journal of Marriage and the Family, 41*, 75–95. [15]

Strauss, M. S., and Curtis, L. E. (1984). Development of numerical concepts in infancy. In C. Sophian (Ed.), *Origins of cognitive skills.* Hillsdale, N.J.: Erlbaum. [6]

Strayer, F. F. (1977, April). Peer attachment and affiliative subgroups. In F. F. Strayer (Ed.), *Ethological perspectives on preschool social organization.* Remonde Recherche [Research Paper] No. 5, University of Quebec at Montreal, Department of Psychology. [11]

Strayer, J., and Strayer, F. F. (1978). Social aggression and power relations among preschool children. *Aggressive Behavior, 4*, 173–182. [11]

Streater, A., and Chertkoff, J. (1976). Distribution of rewards in a triad: A developmental test of equity theory. *Child Development, 47*, 800–805. [13]

Streissguth, A. P. (1977). Maternal alcoholism and the outcome of pregnancy. In M. Greenwealth (Ed.), *Alcohol problems in women and children.* New York: Grune & Stratton. [4]

Streissguth, A. P., Martin, D. C., Barr, H. M., Sandman, B. M., Kirchner, G. L., and Darby, B. L. (1984). Intrauterine alcohol and nicotine exposure: Attention and reaction time in four-year-old children. *Developmental Psychology, 20*. [4]

Strodtbeck, F. (1955). Husband-wife interaction over revealed differences. In A. Hare, E. Borgatta, and R. Bales (Eds.), *Small groups* (pp. 464–472). New York: Knopf. [12]

Strupp, H., and Binder, J. (1984). *Psychotherapy in a new key: A guide to time limited psychotherapy.* New York: Basic Books. [16]

Sullivan, H. S. (1953). *The interpersonal theory of psychiatry.* New York: Norton. [13, 15]

Sullivan, M. W., Rovee-Collier, C. K., and Tynes, D. M. (1979). A conditioning analysis of infant long-term memory. *Child Development, 50*, 152–162. [6]

Suomi, S. J. (1977a). Development of attachment and other social behaviors in rhesus monkeys. In T. Alloway, P. Pliner, and L. Krames (Eds.), *Advances in the study of communication and affect: Vol. 3. Attachment behavior.* New York: Plenum. [3, 7, 9]

Suomi, S. J. (1977b). Adult male-infant interaction among monkeys living in nuclear families. *Child Development, 48*, 1255–1271. [7, 11, 13]

Suomi, S. J. (1979). Differential development of various social relationships by rhesus monkey infants. In M. Lewis and L. A. Rosenblum (Eds.), *The child in its family.* New York: Plenum. [9]

Suomi, S. J., and Harlow, H. F. (1971). Abnormal social behavior in young monkeys. In J. Helmuth (Ed.), *Exceptional infant* (Vol. 2). New York: Brunner/Mazel. [7]

Suomi, S. J., and Harlow, H. F. (1972). Social rehabilitation of isolate-reared monkeys. *Developmental Psychology, 6*, 487–496. [11]

Suomi, S. J., Harlow, H., and McKinney, W. (1972). Monkey psychiatrists. *American Journal of Psychiatry, 128*, 41–46. [7]

Super, D. (1976). *Career education and the meanings of work.* Washington, D.C.: U. S. Office of Education. [15]

Super, D., and Hall, D. (1978). Career development: Exploration and planning. *Annual Review of Psychology, 29*, 333–372. [15]

Sutton, E. H. (1975). *An introduction to human genetics.* New York: Holt, Rinehart & Winston. [4]

Sutton-Smith, B. (1971). A reply to Piaget: A play theory of copy. In R. E. Herron and B. Sutton-Smith (Eds.), *Child's play.* New York: Wiley. [11]

Swadesh, M. (1971). *The origin of diversification of language.* Chicago: Aldine-Atherton. [8]

Swope, G. (1980). Kids and cults: Who joins and why? *Media and Methods, 16,* 18–21. [15]

Symonds, P. (1939). *The psychology of parent-child relationships.* New York: Appleton-Century-Crofts. [13]

Takahashi, K. (1986). Examining the strange situation procedure with Japanese mothers and 12-month-old infants. *Developmental Psychology, 22,* 265–270. [3]

Tanner, J. M. (1961a). *Education and physical growth.* London, Eng.: University of London Press. [1]

Tanner, J. M. (1961b). *Growth at adolescence.* Springfield, Ill.: Thomas. [14]

Tanner, J. M. (1962). *Growth of adolescence.* Springfield, Ill.: Thomas. [14]

Tanner, J. M. (1970). Physical growth. In P. H. Mussen (Ed.), *Carmichael's manual of child psychology* (3rd. ed.). New York: Wiley. [14]

Tanner, J. M., Whitehouse, R. H., and Tadaishi, M. (1966). Standards from birth to maturity for height, weight, height velocity, and weight velocity: British children, 1965. *Archives of Disease in Childhood, 41,* 613–635. [14]

Taussig, H. B. (1962). A study of the German outbreak of phocomelia: The thalidomide syndrome. *Journal of the American Medical Association, 180,* 1106–1114. [4]

Tennes, K., Emde, R., Kisley, A., and Metcalf, D. (1972). The stimulus barrier in early infancy: An exploration of some formulations of John Benjamin. In R. Holt and E. Peterfreund (Eds.), *Psychoanalysis and contemporary sciences.* New York: Macmillan. [7]

Terman, L. M., and Oden, M. H. (1959). *Genetic studies of genius: Vol. 4. Mental and physical traits of a thousand gifted children.* Stanford, Calif.: Stanford University Press. [12]

Thelen, E. (1981). Rhythmical behavior in infancy: An ethological perspective. *Developmental Psychology, 17,* 237–257. [5]

Thelen, E. (1986). Treadmill-elicited stepping in seven-month-old infants. *Child Development, 57,* 1498–1506. [5]

Thomas, A., and Chess, S. (1982). Infant bonding: Mystique and reality. *American Journal of Orthopsychiatry, 52,* 213–222. [3]

Thomas, A., and Chess, S. (1977). *Temperament and development.* New York: Brunner/Mazel. [3, 7]

Thompson, S. K. (1975). Gender labels and early sex-role development. *Child Development, 46,* 339–347. [11]

Thorne, B. (1986). Girls and boys together . . . but mostly apart: Gender arrangements in elementary schools. In W. Hartup and Z. Rubin (Eds.), *Relationships and development.* Hillsdale, N.J.: Erlbaum. [13]

Thurstone, L. L. (1938). *Primary mental abilities.* Chicago: University of Chicago Press. [12]

Tinsley, R., and Parke, R. (1984). Grandparents as support and socialization agents. In M. Lewis (Ed.), *Beyond the dyad.* New York: Plenum. [3, 7]

Tobin-Richards, M., Boxer, A., and Petersen, A. (1983). The psychological significance of pubertal change: Sex differences in perceptions of self during early adolescence. In J. Brooks-Gunn and A. Petersen (Eds.), *Girls at puberty: Biological and psychological perspectives* (pp. 127–154). New York: Plenum. [15]

Tomasello, M., and Mannle, S. (1985). Pragmatics of sibling speech to one-year-olds. *Child Development, 56,* 911–917. [8]

Tomasello, M., Mannle, S., and Kruger, C. (1986). Linguistic environment of 1- to 2-year-old twins. *Developmental Psychology, 22,* 169–176. [8]

Tracy, R. L., Lamb, M. E., and Ainsworth, M. D. (1976). Infant approach behavior as related to attachment. *Child Development, 47,* 571–578. [7]

Trevarthen, C. (1977). Descriptive analyses of infant communicative behavior. In H. R. Schaffer (Ed.), *Studies in mother-infant interaction.* New York: Academic Press. [7]

Tronick, E., Als, H., Adamsen, L., Wise, S., and Brazelton, T. (1978). The infant's response to entrapment between contradictory messages in face to face interaction. *Journal of the American Academy of Child Psychiatry, 17,* 1–11. [7]

Troy, M., and Sroufe, L. A. (1987). Victimization among preschoolers: Role of attachment relationship history. *Journal of the American Academy of Child and Adolescent Psychiatry, 26,* 166–172. [11]

Truby-King, F. (1937). *Feeding and care of baby* (rev. ed.). Oxford, Eng.: Oxford University Press. [3]

Tweddell, F. (1916). *A young mother's guide.* Toronto: Mother's Guide Association. [3]

U. S. Department of Health, Education, and Welfare. (1979). *Smoking and health: A report to the Surgeon General.* (DHEW Pub. No. PHS 79-50066.) Washington, D.C.: U. S. Government Printing Office. [4]

Ungerer, J., Brody, L. R., and Zelazo, P. R. (1978). Long-term memory for speech in 2- to 4-week-old infants. *Infant Behavior and Development, 1,* 127–140. [6]

Ungerer, J., Zelazo, P., Kearsley, R., and O'Leary, K. (1981). Developmental changes in the representation of objects in symbolic play from 18 to 34 months of age. *Child Development, 52,* 186–195. [9, 11]

Uzgiris, I. C. (1972). Patterns of vocal and gestural imitation in infants. In F. Monks, W. Hartup, and J. de Wit (Eds.), *Determinants of behavioral development.* New York: Academic Press. [5]

Uzgiris, I. C., and Hunt, J. M. (1975). *Assessment in infancy: Ordinal scales of psychological development.* Champaign: University of Illinois Press. [5, 6]

Van Leishout, C. F. M. (1975). Young children's reactions to barriers placed by their mothers. *Child Development, 46,* 879–886. [11]

Vaughn, B. (1978). *The development of greeting behavior in infants from six-to-twelve months of age.* Unpublished doctoral dissertation, University of Minnesota. [7]

Vaughn, B. (1980, April). *Coherence in caregiving during the first two years: A context for understanding continuity of infant adaptation.* Symposium, International Conference of Infant Studies, New Haven, Conn. [7]

Vaughn, B., Deinard, A., and Egeland, B. (1980). Measuring temperament in pediatric practice. *Journal of Pediatrics, 96,* 510–518. [7]

Vaughn, B., Egeland, B., Waters, E., and Sroufe, L. A. (1979). Individual differences in infant-mother attachment at 12 and 18 months: Stability and change in families under stress. *Child Development, 50,* 971–975. [3, 7, 9]

Vaughn, B., Gove, F., and Egeland, B. (1980). The relationship between out-of-home care and the quality of infant-mother attachment in an economically deprived population. *Child Development, 51,* 1203–1214. [3, 7]

Vaughn, B., and Sroufe, L. A. (1979). The temporal relationship between infant heart-rate acceleration and crying in an aversive situation. *Child Development, 50,* 558–567. [7]

Vaughn, B., and Waters, E. (1980). Social organization among preschool peers: Dominance, attention, and sociometric correlates. In D. Omark, F. Strayer, and D. Freedman (Eds.), *Dominance relations: An ethological view of human conflict and social interaction.* New York: Garland. [11]

Veroff, J., Douvan, E., and Kulka, R. (1981). *The inner Americans: A self-portrait from 1957 to 1976.* New York: Basic Books. [3]

Von Hofsten, C. (1977). Binocular convergence as a determinant of reaching behavior in infancy. *Perception, 6,* 139–144. [5]

Vouenw, W. (1978). The state of research on ego identity: A review and appraisal. *Journal of Youth and Adolescence, 7,* 223–251, 371–392. [15]

Vurpillot, E. (1968). The development of scanning strategies and their relation to visual differentiation. *Journal of Experimental Child Psychology, 6,* 632–650. [10]

Vygotsky, L. S. (1934/1962). *Thought and language.* Cambridge, Mass.: MIT Press. [8]

Vygotsky, L. S. (1978). *Mind and society.* Cambridge, Mass.: Harvard University Press. [10, 12]

Wachs, T. (1976). Utilization of a Piagetian approach in the investigation of early experience effects. *Merrill-Palmer Quarterly, 22,* 11–30. [3]

Waddington, C. H. (1957). *The strategy of the genes.* London, Eng.: Allen and Unwin. [2, 3]

Waddington, C. H. (1966). *Principles of development and differentiation.* New York: Macmillan. [3]

Waldhauser, F., Frisch, H., Waldhauser, M., Weiszenbacher, G., Zeithuber, U., and Wurtman, R. (1984). Fall in nocturnal serum melatonin during prepuberty and pubescence. *The Lancet, 1,* 362–365. [14]

Waldrop, M. F., and Halverson, C. F. (1975). Intensive and extensive peer behavior: Longitudinal and cross-sectional analyses. *Child Development, 46,* 19–26. [13]

Walk, R. D., and Gibson, E. J. (1961). A comparative and analytical study of visual depth perception. *Psychological Monographs, 75* (Whole No. 519). [5]

Walker, E., Hoppes, E., Emory, E., Mednick, S., and Schulsinger, F. (1981). Environmental factors related to schizophrenia in psychophysiologically labile high-risk males. *Journal of Abnormal Psychology, 90,* 313–320. [16]

Wallerstein, J. S., and Kelly, J. B. (1982). *Surviving the breakup: How children and parents cope with divorce.* New York: Basic Books. [11]

Ward, M. (1983). *Patterns of maternal behavior with first- and second-born children: Evidence for consistency in family relations.* Unpublished doctoral dissertation. University of Minnesota. [9, 13]

Ward, M. J., and Robb, M. D. (1986). *Social-emotional behavior in siblings: Investigating consistency and role of the mother.* Paper presented at the biennial meeting of the Society for Research in Child Development, Toronto. [11]

Ward, M. J., Vaughn, B. E., and Robb, M. D. (1987). *Attachment and adaptation in siblings: The role of the mother in cross-sibling consistency.* Unpublished manuscript. [11]

Wasz-Hockert, O., Lind, J., Vuorenkoski, V., Partanen, T., and Valanne, E. (1968). *A spectrographic and auditory analysis.* Suffolk: Lavenham Press. [5]

Waterman, A. (1982). Identity development from adolescence to adulthood: An extension of theory and a review of research. *Developmental Psychology, 18,* 341–358. [15]

Waterman, A., and Waterman, C. (1971). A longitudinal study of changes in ego identity status during the freshman year of college. *Developmental Psychology, 5,* 167–173. [15]

Waters, E. (1978). The stability of individual differences in infant-mother attachment. *Child Development, 49,* 483–494. [7]

Waters, E., Matas, L., and Sroufe, L. A. (1975). Infants' reactions to an approaching stranger: Description, validation, and functional significance of wariness. *Child Development, 46,* 348–356. [7]

Waters, E., and Sroufe, L. A. (1983a). A developmental perspective on competence. *Developmental Review, 3,* 79–97. [11]

Waters, E., and Sroufe, L. A. (1983b). A road careened into the woods: Comments on Dr. Morrison's commentary. *Developmental Review, 3,* 108–114. [1]

Waters, E., Vaughn, B., and Egeland, B. (1980). Individual differences in infant-mother attachment relationships at age one: Antecedents in neonatal behavior in an urban, economically disadvantaged sample. *Child Development, 51,* 203–216. [7]

Waters, E., Wippman, J., and Sroufe, L. A. (1979). Attachment, positive affect, and competence in the peer group: Two studies in construct validation. *Child Development, 50,* 821–829. [7, 9, 11]

Waters, H. S., and Andreassen, C. (1983). Children's use of memory strategies under instructions. In M. Pressley and J. R. Levin (Eds.), *Cognitive strategies: Developmental, educational, and treatment-related issues.* New York: Springer-Verlag. [10, 12]

Watson, J. B. (1928). *Psychological care of infant and child.* New York: Norton. [1, 2, 3]

Watson, J. S. (1972). Smiling, cooing, and "the game." *Merrill-Palmer Quarterly, 18,* 323–340. [3, 7].

Watson, J. S., Hayes, L. A., and Vietze, P. (1979). Bi-dimensional sorting in preschoolers with an instrumental learning task. *Child Development, 50,* 1178–1183. [10]

Watson, J. S., and Ramey, C. T. (1972). Reactions to response-contingent stimulation in early infancy. *Merrill-Palmer Quarterly, 18,* 219–227. [5, 7]

Watson, M. (1981). Development of social roles: A sequence of social-cognitive development. In K. Fischer (Ed.), *New directions for child development: No. 12. Cognitive development.* San Francisco: Jossey-Bass. [Part V Summary]

Watson, M., and Fischer, K. (1977). A developmental sequence of agent use in late infancy. *Child Development, 48,* 828–836. [9, 11]

Watt, N., Anthony, E. J., Wynne, L., and Rolf, J. (1984). *Children at risk for schizophrenia: A longitudinal perspective.* Cambridge, Eng.: Cambridge University Press. [16, Part VII Summary]

Watzlawick, P., and Weakland, J. (1977). *The interactional view.* New York: Norton. [16]

Weiner, B., Kun, A., and Benesh-Wiener, M. (1983). The development of mastery, emotion, and morality from an attributional perspective. In W. A. Collins (Ed.), *Minnesota Symposia on Child Psychology* (Vol. 13), Hillsdale, N.J.: Erlbaum. [15]

Weisner, T. (in press). The social ecology in childhood: A cross-cultural view. In M. Lewis and L. Rosenblum (Eds.), *Social connections beyond the dyad.* New York: Academic Press. [12]

Weiss, G., and Hechtman, L. (1979). The hyperactive child syndrome. *Science, 205,* 1348–1354. [16]

Weiss, G., and Hechtman, L. (1986). *Hyperactive children grown up.* New York: Guilford. [16]

Wellman, H. M. (1983). Metamemory revisited. In M. T. H. Chi (Ed.), *Trends in memory development.* Basel, Switzerland: Karger. [12]

Wellman, H. M. (1986). A child's theory of mind: The development of conceptions of cognition. In S. R. Yussen

(Ed.), *The growth of reflection*. New York: Academic Press. [12]

Wellman, H. M., Ritter, K., and Flavell, J. H. (1975). Deliberate memory behavior in the delayed reactions of very young children. *Developmental Psychology, 11,* 780–787. [10]

Wellman, H. M., Sommerville, S. C., and Haake, R. J. (1979). Development of search procedures in real-life spatial environments. *Developmental Psychology, 15,* 530–542. [10]

Wenar, C. (1976). Executive competence in toddlers: A prospective, observational study. *Genetic Psychology Monographs, 93,* 189–285. [9]

Wenar, C. (1982). *Psychopathology from infancy through adolescence.* New York: Random House. [16]

Wender, P. (1971). *Minimal brain dysfunction in children.* New York: Wiley. [16]

Wender, P., and Klein, D. (1986). *Mind, mood, and medicine: A guide to the new psychobiology.* New York: Farrar, Straus & Giroux. [11, 16]

Werner, E., and Smith, R. (1977). *Kauai's children come of age.* Honolulu: University of Hawaii Press. [16]

Werry, J. (1968). Studies of the hyperactive child: IV. An empirical analysis of the minimal brain dysfunction syndrome. *Archives of General Psychiatry, 19,* 9–16. [16]

White, B. L., and Watts, J. C. (1973). *Experience and environment: Major influences on the development of the young child.* Englewood Cliffs, N.J.: Prentice-Hall. [9]

White, K., Spiesman, J., and Costa, D. (1983). Young adults and their parents. In H. Gotevant and C. Cooper (Eds.), *New directions in child development: Adolescent development in the family.* San Francisco: Jossey-Bass. [15]

White, R. (1959). Motivation reconsidered: The concept of competence. *Psychological Review, 66,* 297–333. [2, 3, 11]

White, S. (1965). Evidence for a hierarchical arrangement of learning processes. In L. Lipsitt and C. Spiker (Eds.), *Advances in child development and behavior.* New York: Academic Press. [3]

Whitehead, L. (1979). Sex differences in children's responses to family stress: A reevaluation. *Journal of Child Psychology and Psychiatry, 20,* 247–254. [13]

Whitehurst, G. J. (1982). Language development. In B. B. Wolman (Ed.), *Handbook of developmental psychology.* Englewood Cliffs, N.J.: Prentice-Hall. [8]

Whiting, B., and Whiting, J. (1975). *Children of six cultures: A psycho-cultural analysis.* Cambridge, Mass.: Harvard University Press. [3, 9, 13, 15]

Wickens, D. D., and Wickens, C. A. (1940). A study of conditioning in the neonate. *Journal of Experimental Psychology, 26,* 94–102. [5]

Wiegman, O., Kuttschreuter, M., and Baarda, B. (1986). Television viewing related to aggression and prosocial behavior. The Hague: Foundation for Educational Research in the Netherlands. [11]

Wiesenfeld, A., Malatesta, C., and DeLoach, L. (1981). Differential parental response to familiar and unfamiliar infant distress signals. *Infant Behavior and Development, 4,* 281–295. [5]

Wijting, J., Arnold, C., and Conrad, K. (1978). Generational differences in work values between parents and children and between boys and girls across grade levels 6, 9, 10, and 12. *Journal of Vocational Behavior, 12,* 245–260. [15]

Williams, T. (1986). *The impact of television.* New York: Academic Press. [11]

Wilson, R., and Matheny, A. (1983). Asssessment of temperament in infant twins. *Developmental Psychology, 19,* 172–183. [9]

Wing, L. (1976). *Early childhood autism.* Oxford, Eng.: Pergamon Press. [16]

Winick, M. (1975). Effects of malnutrition on the maturing central nervous system. In W. J. Friedlander (Ed.), *Advances in neurology* (Vol. 13). New York: Raven Press. [4]

Witkin, H., Mednick, S., Schulsinger, F., Bakkestrom, E., Christiansen, K., Goodenough, D., Hirschhorn, K., Lundsteen, C., Owen, D., Philip, J., Rubin, D., and Stocking, M. (1976). Criminality in XYY and XXY men. *Science, 193,* 547–555. [16]

Wolf, D. (1982). Understanding others: A longitudinal case study of the concept of independent agency. In G. Furman (Ed.), *Action and thought.* New York: Academic Press. [9]

Wolf, T. (1973). Effects of live-modeled sex-inappropriate play behavior in a naturalistic setting. *Developmental Psychology, 9,* 120–123. [13]

Wolff, P. H. (1963). Observations on the early development of smiling. In B. M. Foss (Ed.), *Determinants of infant behavior II.* London, Eng.: Methuen. [7]

Wolff, P. H. (1969). The natural history of crying and other vocalization in early infancy. In B. M. Foss (Ed.), *Determinants of infant behavior, IV.* London, Eng.: Methuen. [5]

Wolkind, S., and Rutter, M. (1985). Sociocultural factors. In M. Rutter and L. Hersov (Eds.), *Child and adolescent psychiatry.* Oxford, Eng.: Blackwell. [3]

Woolacott, M. H. (in press). Children's development of posture and balance control: Changes in motor coordination and sensory integration. In D. Gould and M. Weiss (Eds.), *Advances in pediatric sport sciences: Behavioral issues.* Champaign, Ill.: Human Kinetics Publishers. [5]

Wortman, C., and Loftus, E. (in press). *Psychology* (3rd ed.). New York: Random House. [8]

Wright, H. F. (1967). *Recording and analyzing child behavior.* New York: Harper & Row. [3, 12, 13]

Yankelovich, D. (1974). *The new morality: A profile of American youth in the '70s.* New York: McGraw-Hill. [14, 15]

Yarrow, L. (1964). Separation from parents during early childhood. In M. Hoffman and L. Hoffman (Eds.), *Review of child development research* (Vol. 1). New York: Russell Sage. [7]

Yarrow, L. (1972). Attachment and dependency: A developmental perspective. In J. Gewirtz (Ed.), *Attachment and dependency.* New York: Wiley. [9]

Yarrow, L., Rubenstein, J., and Pederson, F. (1975). *Infant and environment.* New York: Halsted. [3, 7]

Yarrow, M. R., Scott, P., de Leeuw, L., and Heinig, C. (1962). Childrearing in families of working and nonworking mothers. *Sociometry, 25,* 122–140. [3]

Yerushalmy, J. (1972). Infants with low birth weight born before their mothers started to smoke cigarettes. *American Journal of Obstetrics and Gynecology, 112,* 277–284. [4]

Yonas, A., Cleaves, W., and Pettersen, L. (1978). Development of sensitivity to pictorial depth. *Science, 200,* 77–79. [5]

Yonas, A., Oberg, C., and Norcia, A. (1978). Development of sensitivity to binocular information for the approach of an object. *Developmental Psychology, 14,* 147–152. [5]

Younger, B. A., and Cohen, L. B. (1985). How infants form categories. In G. Bower (Ed.), *The psychology of learning and motivations: Advances in research and theory.* New York: Academic Press. [6]

Younger, B. A., and Cohen, L. B. (1986). Developmental change in infants' perception of correlations among attributes. *Child Development, 57,* 803–815. [6]

Youniss, J. (1980). *Parents and peers in social development: A Sullivan-Piaget perspective.* Chicago: University of Chicago Press. [13, 15]

Youniss, J. (1983). Social construction of adolescence by adolescents and parents. In H. Gotevant and C. Cooper (Eds.), *New directions for child development: Adolescent development in the family.* San Francisco: Jossey-Bass. [15]

Yule, W. (1981). The epidemiology of child psychopathology. In B. Lahey and A. Kazdin (Eds.), *Advances in clinical child psychology* (Vol. 4). New York: Plenum. [16]

Yussen, S. R., and Kane, P. T. (1983). Children's ideas about intellectual ability. In R. L. Leahy (Ed.), *The child's construction of social inequality.* New York: Academic Press. [12]

Zahn-Waxler, C., Radke-Yarrow, M., and King, R. (1979). Childrearing and children's prosocial initiations toward victims of distress. *Child Development, 50,* 319–330. [11]

Zajonc, R., and Markus, G. (1975). Birth order and intellectual development. *Psychological Review, 82,* 74–88. [3]

Zaporozhets, A. V. (1965). The development of perception in the preschool child. *Monographs of the Society for Research in Child Development, 30* (Serial No. 100). [5]

Zeanah, C. H., Keener, M. A., and Anders, T. F. (in press). Adolescent mothers' prenatal fantasies and working models of their infants. *Psychiatry.* [7]

Zeitlin, H. (1982). *The natural history of psychiatric disorder in children.* Unpublished M.D. thesis, University of London, Eng. [16]

Zelazo, P. R. (1972). Smiling and vocalizing: A cognitive emphasis. *Merrill-Palmer Quarterly, 18,* 349–365. [7]

Zigler, E., and Gordon, E. (1982). *Day care: Scientific and social policy issues.* Boston: Auburn House. [7]

Zubin, J. (1972). Scientific models for psychotherapy in the 1970s. *Seminars in Psychiatry, 4,* 287–291, 293, 295. [16]

Name Index

Subject Index